D1071934

SOUTHWESTERN POTTERY:

An Annotated Bibliography and List of Types and Wares

second edition, revised and expanded

by

Norman T. Oppelt

The Scarecrow Press, Inc.
Metuchen, N.J., & London
1988

Ref.
E
78
.S7
O77
1988

Previous edition published as Southwestern Pottery: An Annotated
Bibliography and List of Types and Wares. Occasional Publications
In Anthropology, Archaeological Series, No. 7. Museum of Anthro-
pology, University of Northern Colorado, Greeley, Colorado, 1976.

TITLE PAGE ILLUSTRATION: Design from McElmo Black-on-White
bowl. Yellowjacket (A.D. 1050-1250)
Drawing by Pat Oppelt

Library of Congress Cataloging-in-Publication Data

Oppelt, Norman T.
    Southwestern pottery.

    Includes index.
    1. Indians of North America--Southwest, New--
Pottery--Bibliography. 2. Indians of North America--
Southwest, New--Pottery--Indexes. 3. Southwest,
New--Antiquities--Bibliography. 4. Indians of North
America--Southwest, New--Antiquities--Bibliography.
I. Title.
Z1208.S68066 1988 [E78.S7] 016.7383'0897079 88-6424
ISBN 0-8108-2119-2

Copyright © 1988 by Norman T. Oppelt
Manufactured in the United States of America

CONTENTS

iii

Hohokam Santa Cruz Red-on-Buff (n.d.)
Drawing by Pat Oppelt

INTRODUCTION TO THE SECOND EDITION

The first edition of <u>Southwestern Pottery: An Annotated Biblio-graphy and List of Types and Wares</u>, published in 1976, has become a standard reference for Southwesternists doing research in prehistoric or historic pottery or related topics. In the past decade the first edition has become outdated. Soon after the first edition gained general use, the writer began to solicit suggestions from users concerning changes to incorporate in the revision. Most feasible changes have been made in this revision.

The update has resulted in the addition of 300 annotated citations and 180 pottery types and variety names. The annotated citations in this edition total 965, and there are approximately 1,240 type, ware, and variety names in the list. Most of these additions have been published since 1975; a few are omissions from the first edition.

In addition to adding citations and type names to bring this edition up to date, other changes have been made to make it more valuable for the user. Dates are given in the revised list for all dated types, varieties, and wares. The major single source for these dates is Breternitz, 1966. Other dates were obtained from a variety of publications with priority given to the most recently published dates. These dates vary from firm dates based on tree-rings, Carbon 14, and other precise techniques to some questionable dates based on tenuous associations and speculations. The reader is referred to Breternitz (1963, 1966) and the other descriptions cited in the bibliography to judge the validity of the dates given.

Synonyms are included for all types known to have two or more names. All published names, except a few local "field types," are listed, including a few that have been dropped by consensus of researchers. The reader is directed to the most recent descriptions for discussion of the commonly accepted names.

The new annotations are broader than those in the first edition which emphasized descriptions and illustrations of pottery. This change reflects users' recommendations and changes in research on Southwestern ceramics during the past decade. There has been a move away from describing and naming new pottery types to analysis of characteristics of pottery and the study of the relationship of these characteristics to culture of prehistoric peoples of the South-west. Synthesis of knowledge concerning prehistoric ceramics has also become a more common topic of study as exemplified by Volume 15 of the <u>Arizona Archaeologist</u> edited by Al Schroeder in 1982. The increased use of quotations in the annotations is necessitated by the more comprehensive conclusions and the technical content of some articles that make adequate paraphrasing more difficult.

The index to the revision has been expanded to include more detailed topics and cross references to assist the researcher in reviewing the literature. Examination of the lists of references in the publications cited will give the user a comprehensive list of relevant research.

For this revision the literature on Southwestern prehistoric and historic pottery through 1986 has been searched. The reader should not rely on this volume for research published after 1986. A few relevant citations from regions of the United States other than the Southwest are presented, but other related research from outside this region is not included. Some pertinent studies from the portion of the greater Southwest in Northern Mexico are cited.

Geographical areas and topics that have received special attention in ceramic studies since the first edition are: Mogollon ceramics, particularly the Mimbres Branch; Chaco Canyon and its outliers; Casas Grandes (Di Peso et al., 1974); Black Mesa, Arizona (Gumerman et al.); Fremont ceramics (Madsen, 1977); Rio Grande glazes (i.e., Warren's petrographic studies); analysis of pottery designs; and the use of computers in analyzing ceramic data.

This bibliography and list can be used in three ways: specific pottery types and wares can be studied through the use of the alphabetic list of names and references; topics may be reviewed through the use of the index and the annotations cited; and the work of a specific researcher can be found by examining all citations under his or her name.

Norman T. Oppelt
University of Northern Colorado
Greeley, Colorado

ACKNOWLEDGMENTS

The following persons provided valuable assistance and/or encouragement in the preparation of this revision: Stew Peckham, Santa Fe, New Mexico; Priscilla Ellwood, Boulder, Colorado; Ted Frisbie, Carbondale, Illinois; Sharon Urban, Tucson, Arizona; Watson Smith, Tucson, Arizona; Regge Wiseman, Santa Fe, New Mexico; Jack Mills, Elfrida, Arizona; John Wilson, Las Cruces, New Mexico; Francis Harlow, Los Alamos; Richard Fischer, Quemado, New Mexico; Walter Duering, Arizona; Jack Ross, Roswell, New Mexico; Marion Smith, Columbia, South Carolina; Dave Breternitz, Dove Creek, Colorado; Bill Creutz, Mesa Verde National Park; Gerald X. Fitzgerald, El Paso, Texas; and Bill Sundt, Albuquerque, New Mexico.

Library personnel who have been of special help in searches for obscure publications are Laura Holt, Laboratory of Anthropology, Santa Fe, New Mexico; Katherine Bartlett, Museum of Northern Arizona, Flagstaff, Arizona; Lucy Schweers, University of Northern Colorado, Greeley, Colorado; and Bev Cunningham, Mesa Verde Museum.

Finally, I would like to thank Ms. Cathy Baird, who typed the final manuscript with great care and good humor.

Red Mesa Black-on-White.   Red Mesa Valley (A.D. 870-950)
Drawing by Pat Oppelt

ANNOTATED BIBLIOGRAPHY ON SOUTHWESTERN POTTERY

1. Abel, Leland J. 1955 "San Juan Red Ware, Mesa Verde Gray
Ware, Mesa Verde White Ware, and San Juan White Ware. Pottery
Types of the Southwest 5A, 10A, 10B, and 12A." Museum of
Northern Arizona Ceramic Series No. 3B, Flagstaff, Arizona.
   General introduction to the four wares included and good
descriptions of these wares and the 28 types listed below. Types
are illustrated, but better illustrations are available in later pub-
lications. Wares and types described are San Juan Red Ware,
5A: Abajo Red-on-orange, 5A-1; Abajo Black-on-gray, 5A-2;
Abajo Polychrome, 5A-3; Bluff Black-on-red, 5A-4; La Plata
Black-on-red, 5A-5; Deadmans Black-on-red, 5A-6; Middleton
Black-on-red, 5A-7; Middleton Red, 5A-8; Nankoweap Polychrome,
5A-9; Amusovi Polychrome, 5A-10; and Machonpi Polychrome, 5A-
11. Mesa Verde Gray Ware, 10A: Chapin Gray, 10A-1; Twin
Trees Plain, 10A-2; Moccasin Gray, 10A-3; Mancos Gray, 10A-4;
Mancos Corrugated, 10A-5; Mesa Verde Corrugated, 10A-6;
Hovenweep Gray, 10A-7; and Hovenweep Corrugated, 10A-8.
Mesa Verde White Ware, 10B: McElmo Black-on-white, 10B-1;
Mesa Verde Black-on-white, 10B-2; Mesa Verde Polychrome, 10B-
3; and Galisteo Black-on-white, 10B-4. San Juan White Ware,
12A: Chapin Black-on-white, 12A-1; Twin Trees Black-on-white,
12A-2; Cortez Black-on-white, 12A-4; and Mancos Black-on-
white, 12A-5.

2. Adams, E. Charles. 1979 "Native Ceramics from Walpi." Walpi
Archaeological Project, Phase II, Vol. 3 (unpublished). Museum
of Northern Arizona, Flagstaff, Arizona.
   Type and ware descriptions based on pottery from the Hopi
First Mesa pueblo of Walpi. The writer notes that this typology
pertains only to the ceramics of First Mesa. The pottery upon
which these descriptions are based is housed at the Museum of
Northern Arizona. Further data on tempering material are presented in an unpublished manuscript titled Petrographic Analysis
of Historic Ceramics by Peter S. Winn on file at MNA. Wares
and types described are Walpi Orange Ware, Walpi Plain, Wepo
Plain, Wepo Black-on-plain, Polacca Yellow Ware, Payupki Polychrome (three varieties), Polacca Polychrome (four varieties),
and Hano Polychrome (three varieties).

3. Adams, Jenny L. 1985 "Test Excavation of a Pit Structure at

the Snow Site (5 MT 3880, Cortez, Colorado." Southwestern
Lore, Vol. 51, No. 4, pp. 1-31.
    Excavation of a Pueblo I hamlet at Totten Lake, northeast of
Cortez, Colorado. More than 2,000 sherds and four partially
restorable vessels were found. The vessel types were Moccasin
Gray, Chapin Gray, Mancos Black-on-white, and Piedra Black-
on-white. In addition to these four types, sherds were found
of: Chapin Black-on-white, Bluff Black-on-red, Deadmans Black-
on-red, San Juan Red, Mancos Gray, and corrugated. Two
ceramic pendants and two worked pendant blanks were uncovered.
Based on sherds, the site was dated AD 875-925. A typology
for pithouse structures is proposed from data accumulated from
numerous excavations.

4. Adams, Richard N. 1949 "Halfhouse: A Pithouse in Chaco Can-
    yon, New Mexico." Papers of the Michigan Academy of Science,
    Arts and Letters, No. 35, Ann Arbor, Michigan.
        A very short section on pottery recovered at this site, pages
    278-280. Pottery at all levels was primarily gray. The most
    significant thing about the pottery complexes of the various
    levels of the Halfhouse site are the comparisons they make pos-
    sible with the pottery of Shabik'eschee and Judd's Chaco Can-
    yon Pithouse #2. Illustrations: La Plata Black-on-white sherds,
    Pl. 7; Kiatuthlanna and White Mound Black-on-white, P.,8; and
    Orange ware sherds, Pl. 9.

5. Adams, William Y. and Adams, Nettie K. 1959 "Inventory of
    Prehistoric Sites on the Lower San Juan River, Utah." Museum
    of Northern Arizona Bulletin 31 (Glen Canyon Series No. 1),
    Museum of Northern Arizona, Flagstaff, Arizona.
        Survey of sites along the San Juan River between its con-
    fluence with the Colorado River and a point 70 miles upstream
    near the mouth of Grand Gulch. Potsherds were collected from
    the surface of 81 of the 83 sites recorded. A total of 6,643 pot-
    sherds were collected from all sites. Wares found were Tusayan
    White, Tusayan Gray, Tsegi Orange, Mesa Verde Gray, and
    Mesa Verde White. Also minute quantities of San Juan White.
    Small quantities of Jeddito Yellow Ware and Awatovi Yellow Ware
    indicate Hopi visits to this area after abandonment during the
    Pueblo IV Period. Dating by pottery types indicates occupation
    of this area from AD 1100 to at least 1250.

6. Aikens, C. Melvin. 1966 "Fremont-Promontory-Plains Relation-
    ships in Northern Utah." University of Utah Anthropological
    Papers No. 82, University of Utah, Salt Lake City, Utah.
        Pottery, pages 16-33. Descriptions of Great Salt Lake Gray,
    p. 26, ill. Fig. 10; Sevier Gray, p. 30, ill. Fig. 21; and Promon-
    tory Ware, pp. 32-33, ill. Fig. 20. Illustration of Great Salt
    Lake Black-on-gray, Fig. 20.

7. Aikens, C. Melvin. 166a "Virgin-Kayenta Cultural Relationships."

University of Utah Anthropological Papers, No. 79, University
of Utah Press, Salt Lake City, Utah.
   Discusses relationships between Fremont pottery and Anasazi
pottery of the Kayenta region.   ~

8.   Aikens, C. Melvin. 1967 "Excavations at Snake Rock Village
     and the Bear River Site, No. 2." University of Utah Anthro-
     pological Papers, No. 87, Salt Lake City, Utah.
        Snake Rock Village, located in Sevier County Utah, one
     mile upstream from the mouth of Ivie Creek Canyon, east of
     Richfield, Utah. Pottery, pp. 16-23. The indigenous pottery
     types found were Turner Gray: Emery Variety, 53%; Sevier
     Gray, 33%; Ivie Creek Black-on-white, 13.3%; and Snake Valley
     Black-on-gray, .5%. Illustrations of Turner Gray: Emery
     Variety, Figs. 18 and 19; Sevier Gray, Figs. 18 and 19; Ivie
     Creek Black-on-white, Figs. 20 and 21; Ceramic pipes and
     figurines, Fig. 11; worked sherds, Fig. 23. Bear River No.
     2 site--in north-central Utah, 5 miles west of Brigham City.
     Pottery, pp. 44-48. Types found were Great Salt Lake Gray,
     60%; Turner Gray: Cisco Variety, 12%; Sevier Gray, 2%; Pro-
     montory Ware, 23%; Snake Valley Black-on-gray, .2%; and Ivie
     Creek Black-on-white, .1%. Illustrations of: Snake Valley
     Black-on-gray, Ivie Creek Black-on-white, and Turner Gray,
     Fig. 36; and Great Salt Lake Gray and Promontory Ware with
     punched and applique surfaces, Fig. 37.

9.   Alexander, Wayne and Ruby, Jack W. 1962 "1962 Excavations at
     Summit, Utah: A Progress Report." Nevada State Museum An-
     thropological Papers, No. 9, pp. 17-32.
        Describes Fremont and Virgin Branch Anasazi Pottery from
     the Evans Mound in Southwestern Utah.

10. Allen, Laura Graves. 1984 Contemporary Hopi Pottery. Museum
     of Northern Arizona, Flagstaff, Arizona.
        An introduction to contemporary Hopi pottery with descrip-
     tions and photos of many vessels from the collections of the
     Museum of Northern Arizona. Many of these ceramics were ob-
     tained at the Hopi Craftsman Exhibitions held annually at MNA
     since 1930. An excellent book for everyone from the beginning
     collector to the advanced connoisseur.

11. Allen, Norton. 1953 "A Hohokam Pottery Bell." El Palacio,
     Vol. 60, No. 1, pp. 16-19.
        The bell described in this report was found in the western
     Hohokam area at the Twelve Mile Site near the Gila River some
     14 miles north from Gila Bend, Arizona. "In color this bell
     is light brown common to Gila Plain Ware of the region. Super-
     ficially the clay appears the same. Its walls are extremely thin,
     in places hardly 1/16 of an inch. The exterior surface is
     smooth and unslipped and shows small flakes of mica. There
     is no indication that a polishing stone was used. Over the

interior surface are clear impressions which suggest the manner
by which it was made," p. 16. There is a drawing of the bell
on page 18 and drawings of similarly shaped copper bells from
the Gila Bend area on page 19.

12.   Allen, J.W. and McNutt, C.H. 1955 "A Pithouse Site Near
      Santa Ana Pueblo, New Mexico." American Antiquity, Vol. 20,
      No. 3, pp. 241-256.
         Description of Tamaya Red, a subtype of Lino Gray, p. 249.
      Tamaya Red is indicated as a "sherd type" not a pottery type.
      (See Frisbie, 1975a)

13.   Alves, Eileen E. 1931 "Pottery of the El Paso Region." Bul-
      letin of the Texas Archaeological and Paleontological Society,
      Vol. 3, pp. 57-59, Abilene, Texas.
         Named El Paso Polychrome, p. 57.

14.   Ambler, J. Richard. 1977 The Anasazi. Museum of Northern
      Arizona, Flagstaff, Arizona.
         A good general introduction to the Anasazi culture and
      archaeology of the area for the layman. Pottery is covered on
      pages 31-44. Section includes a brief history of pottery, its
      manufacture, and its importance to archaeology. The following
      types are illustrated by excellent photographs: Awatovi Poly-
      chrome, p. 30; Lino Black-on-gray, p. 31; Chapin Black-on-
      gray, p. 31; Lino Gray, p. 32; Kana-a Gray, p. 32; San Mar-
      cial Black-on-gray, p. 32; Sosi Black-on-white, p. 33; McElmo
      Black-on-white, pp. 33 and 38; Chaco Black-on-white, p. 33;
      Dogoszhi Black-on-white, p. 34; Black Mesa Black-on-white,
      p. 34; Medicine Black-on-red, p. 35; Tusayan Black-on-red,
      p. 35; Kiet Siel Polychrome, p. 35; Tusayan Polychrome, p. 35;
      Kayenta Black-on-white, p. 36; Tusayan Black-on-white, p. 36;
      Chaco Black-on-white, p. 36; inside front cover; Mesa Verde
      Black-on-white, pp. 37, 38, 47; Corrugated types, p. 39;
      Jeddito Black-on-yellow, p. 39; Wiyo Black-on-white, p. 40;
      Potsuwi'i Incised, p. 40; Biscuit A and Biscuit B, p. 40; Jemez
      Black-on-gray, p. 41; Sankawi Black-on-cream, pp. 41, 42;
      Kuaua Glaze Polychrome, p. 42; Agua Fria Glaze-on-red, p. 43;
      Espinosa Glaze Polychrome, p. 43; Walnut Balck-on-white, p. 47;
      and Flagstaff Black-on-white, p. 47.

15.   Ambler, J. Richard; Lindsay, Alexander J.; and Stein, M.A.
      1964 "Survey and Excavations on Cummings Mesa, Arizona and
      Utah 1960-61." Glen Canyon Series, No. 5. Museum of Northern
      Arizona, Bulletin 39, Flagstaff, Arizona.
         "Potsherds were found at 160 of the 180 sites recorded by
      the survey," p. 17. "Tusayan White Ware is the dominant white
      ware for the area. Sosi, Dogoszhi, Flagstaff, and Tusayan
      Black-on-white types occurred with great frequency ... Kayenta
      and Black Mesa Black-on-white types occurred in much less
      frequency," p. 17. "Tusayan Gray Ware was found at nearly

all sites where sherd collections were made. Tusayan Corrugated, Moenkopi Corrugated, and Kiet Siel Gray were the
principal types collected," p. 17. "Tsegi Orange Ware is widely
distributed on the Cummings Mesa and was recovered in con-
sistently substantial quantities," p. 17. "Tusayan Black-on-red,
Tusayan Polychrome and Tsegi Orange occurred most frequently,"
pp. 17-18. Four partially restorable vessels were found: Mc-
Elmo Black-on-white bowl, Fig. 6a; Flagstaff Black-on-white
bowl, Fig 6b; miniature Moenkopi Corrugated jar, Fig. 6c.
Excavations produced the following vessels: Kiet Siel Black-on-
red dipper, Fig. 16; Tusayan Polychrome bowl, Kiet Siel Polychrome jar, Tsegi Orange bowl and dipper, Moenkopi Corrugated jar, Fig. 40. Sherds illustrated: Sosi Black-on-white,
Dogoszhi Black-on-white, Flagstaff Black-on-white, Tusayan Black-
on-white, Fig. 62. Sherds illustrated: Tsegi Orange Ware,
Medicine Black-on-red, Tusayan Black-on-red, Cameron Polychrome, Citadel Polychrome, and Tusayan Polychrome, Fig. 63.
Vessels: Flagstaff Black-on-white, Tusayan Black-on-red,
Tusayan Polychrome, Kiet Siel Black-on-red, Fig. 64. Gray
ware vessels: Kiet Siel Gray, Tusayan Corrugated and Moenkopi
Corrugated, Fig. 65. Worked sherds of various types, Fig. 66.

16.   Ambler, J. Richard and Olson, Alan P. 1977 "Salvage Arch-
       aeology in the Cow Springs Area." Museum of Northern Arizona
       Technical Series, No. 15. Flagstaff, Arizona.
          Sites found in this study of the Klethia Valley of northeastern
       Arizona were from the Basketmaker III and Pueblo II and III
       periods. Pithouses typical of Basketmaker III times continued
       to be used during the Pueblo II and III periods indicating these
       subterranean structures continued to be used throughout the
       occupation of this area. The types of pottery recovered pri-
       marily Kayenta wares, are illustrated.

17.   Amsden, Charles A. 1928 "Archaeologic Reconnaissance in
       Sonora." Southwest Museum Papers, No. 1, Los Angeles, Cali-
       fornia.
          Descriptions of the following types of Chihuahua Red Ware:
       Babicora Polychrome and Huerigos Polychrome.

18.   Amsden, Charles A. 1931 "Pottery of Pecos; Dull Paint Wares."
       Papers of the Southwestern Expedition, Vol, 1. No. 5, New
       Haven, Connecticut. (See Kidder, A. V., Pottery of the Pecos,
       Vol. 1, New Haven, 1931).

19.   Amsden, Charles A. 1936 "An Analysis of Hohokam Pottery
       Design." Medallion Paper 23. Gila Pueblo, Globe, Arizona.
          Good summary of Hohokam design elements and combinations
       with an analysis of their relationships.

20.   Amsden, Charles A. 1949 Prehistoric Southwesterners from
       Basketmaker to Pueblo. Southwest Museum, Los Angeles,
       California.

Short section on Basketmaker III pottery and a few illustrations, pp. 116-126. Illustrations of mud vessels and Basketmaker III vessels and figurines. Good bibliography on prehistoric southwesterners, pp. 142-163.

21. Anderson, Bruce A. 1976 "Kokopelli: The Humpbacked Flute
     Player." American Indian Art Magazine, Vol. 1, No. 2, pp. 36-
     40.
         A popular article on this interesting deity of the prehistoric
     Southwest includes descriptions and photos of several pottery
     vessels. These are a humpbacked effigy figure of black-on-
     white found in the Black Mesa area of Arizona, a Hohokam red-
     on-buff bowl with painted figures on Kokopelli, and a Cochiti
     Polychrome spouted vessel with a figure of Kokopelli painted
     on it.

22. Anderson, Keith M. 1960 "Utah Virgin Branch Plain Utility
     Pottery." Masters thesis, University of Utah, Salt Lake City,
     Utah.
         Description of Shinarump Brown, p. 33; Paria Gray, p. 33;
     Johnson Gray-tan, p. 33; North Creek Gray, pp. 7, 33; and
     Hurricane Black-on-gray.

23. Anderson, Keith M. 1963 "Ceramic Clues to Pueblo-Puebloid
     Relationships." American Antiquity, Vol. 28, No. 3, pp. 303-
     307.
         The problem of relationships between the Sevier and Fre-
     mont Cultures and the Virgin branch of the Kayenta Anasazi
     culture is approached by comparison of the representative plain
     pottery types. Statistical comparison of the representative
     plain pottery types. Statistical comparison of modes of techni-
     que shows markedly more similarity between Snake Valley Gray
     (Sevier) and North Creek Gray (Virgin Branch) than between
     Turner Gray; Emery Variety (Fremont) and North Creek Gray.
     Distribution map of Sevier, Fremont, and Virgin Branch plain
     pottery types. Drawings of rim forms of plain gray vessels.

24. Anderson, Keith M. 1969 "Archaeology on the Shonto Plateau,
     Northeast Arizona." Southwestern Monuments Association Tech-
     nical Series, Vol. 7, Globe, Arizona.
         Discussion of gray, white, and red wares from sites along
     entrance road to Navajo National Monument, pp. 39-49. All
     pottery found was indigenous Kayenta types. Illustrations of
     Tusayan Black-on-red, p. 41; Medicine Black-on-red, Flagstaff
     Black-on-white, Black-Mesa Black-on-white, p. 42; Citadel Poly-
     chrome, p. 43; Cameron Polychrome, p. 44; and Tusayan Poly-
     chrome. Short section on worked sherds of various types,
     pp. 48-50.

25. Andrews, Michael J. 1980 "St. Michaels Pueblo: Pueblo III
     Subsistence and Adaptation in Black Creek Valley, Arizona."
     Arizona Archaeologist, No. 13, Phoenix, Arizona.

The most common ware found was indented corrugated. Wares
of decorated types were Cibola White Wares, 42.8%; White Mountain Red Wares, 39.8%; Tsegi Orange Ware, 5.8%; Little Colorado
White Ware, 4.4%; and Mesa Verde White Ware, 2.1%; 39.1% of
the sherds were decorated.

Types illustrated are Kiatuthlanna Black-on-white, Red Mesa
Black-on-white, Puerco Black-on-white, Puerco Black-on-white:
Escavada Variety, Puerco Black-on-white: Gallup Variety, and
Reserve-Tularosa Black-on-white, Fig. 13; Klageto Black-on-
white, Fig. 14; White Mountain Redward sherds, Fig. 15; Tsegi
Orange Ware sherds, Fig. 16; and corrugated sherds, Fig. 18.
Also a list of worked sherds.

26. Angleman, Frances B. 1967 "Abstract Geometric Design in the
     White Mountain Red Wares: AD 1000-1450." Masters thesis,
     University of Arizona, Tucson, Arizona.
        Abstract: "There has been devised for use by student and
     archaeologist, a system for analysis and classification of ab-
     stract geometric design in pottery decoration. The system
     presented in Chapter 1 has been applied to the analysis of six
     styles of design. These six styles represent a developmental
     continuum in the White Mountain area of east central Arizona
     and west central New Mexico from the period AD 1000-1450.
     The analysis has served to test the method, and the results
     obtained are presented where possible, in tabular from in Chap-
     ter 3. Those qualitative attributes of decoration which did not
     land themselves to quantification are discussed in the same
     chapter.
        "The results indicate that the method of analysis can serve
     as a useful tool in the systematic ordering of archaeological
     data and that its use in future comparative studies may yield
     information pertaining to cultural factors," p.xi.

27. Annand, Richard E. 1967 "A Description and Analysis of Sur-
     face Collections, Colbran Region, Colorado." Southwestern
     Lore, Vol. 33, No. 2, pp. 47-60.
        Pottery groups: Group I Uncompahgre Brown Ware, Group
     II and Group III Ute Culture, possible Southern Paiute. These
     groups were comprised of sherds collected by youths near Col-
     bran, Colorado, and were grouped on physical characteristics.
     These groupings are tentative until more material can be
     gathered and analyzed.

28. Anonymous. 1914 "Prehistoric Remains in New Mexico." In
     Explorations and Field-work of the Smithsonian Institution in
     1915. Smithsonian Miscellaneous Collection, Vol. 65, No. 6,
     pp. 62-72.
        Fewke's investigations of Mimbres sites near Deming, New
     Mexico. Main site is called Old Town ruin, 22 miles north of
     Deming. The pottery found was primarily Mimbres Black-on-
     white and some Chihuahua polychrome. Eleven Mimbres bowls
     are shown.

29. Antieau, John M.   1981   "The Palo Verde Archaeological Investi-
     gations."   Museum of Northern Arizona Research Paper,   No. 20.
     Museum of Northern Arizona, Flagstaff, Arizona.
          A report of the study of several Hohokam sites along the
     route of the wastewater conveyance system between the Phoenix
     Sewage Treatment Plant and the Palo Verde Nuclear Generating
     Station, near Wintersburg, Arizona.   The study includes des-
     cription and analysis of pottery found at the Cashion and Van
     Liere sites and a lesser quantity from other sites.   Also pre-
     sented are illustrations and descriptions of ceramics in the
     early Simmons and Parker Collections from this area.
          Presented are type definitions and illustrations of Gila Plain,
     Wingfield Plain, Vahki Red, Sacaton Red, Gila Red, Salt Red,
     Sweetwater Red-on-gray, Snaketown Red-on-buff, Gila Butte
     Red-on-buff, Santa Cruz Red-on-buff, Sacaton Red-on-buff,
     Sacaton Buff, and Casa Grande Red-on-buff, pp. 31-36.

30. Appleton, Leroy H.   1970   American Indian Design and Decora-
     tion.   Dover Publications, New York (originally published in
     1950 by Charles Scribners and Sons).
          Drawings of historic and prehistoric pottery designs from
     the Southwest, Pls, 34-40.

31. Arizona Highways.   Vol. 50, No. 2, February, Phoenix, Arizona.
     1974   This issue is almost entirely devoted to prehistoric pottery
     of Arizona.   A good general text of types from various regions
     of the state and excellent color photos of many vessels by Jerry
     D. Jacka.   "Prehistoric Pottery of Arizona: by Peter Pilles, Jr.,
     and Edward B. Danson, pp. 2-5, 10-15, 43-45.   "Effigy Vessels
     in the Prehistoric Southwest" by Laurens C. Hammack, pp. 33-
     35, illustrated.   Color illustrations of the following types:
     Estrella Red-on-gray, p. 3; Sweetwater Red-on-gray, effigy
     vessel, p. 3; Snaketown Red-on-buff, plate, p. 3; Gila Poly-
     chrome, inside front cover, pp. 14, 17, 35; Salado Red Ware,
     inside front cover, p. 17; Tonto Polychrome, inside front cover,
     pp. 17, 18, 19, 31; Sacaton Red-on-buff, p. 17; Reserve Black-
     on- white, pp. 17, 26; Kayenta Black-on-white, pp. 17, 20,
     27; Santa Cruz Red-on-buff, pp. 17, 18; Roosevelt Black-on-
     white, pp. 19, 20, 32, 35; Tusayan Black-on-white, p. 20;
     Homolovi Polychrome, p. 20; Fourmile Polychrome, pp. 21, 31;
     Bidahochi Polychrome, p. 21; Jeddito Black-on-yellow, pp. 22,
     26, 35; Kinishba Polychrome, pp. 22, 35; Chaco Black-on-
     white, p. 23; Mimbres Black-on-white, p. 23; Wingate Poly-
     chrome, p. 26; Tusayan Corrugated, p. 28; Little Colorado
     White Ware, p. 29; Walnut Black-on-white, p. 29; Tularosa Black-
     on white, pp. 30, 31; Showlow Polychrome, pp. 31, 32; Pine-
     dale Polychrome, p. 31; St. Johns Black-on-red, p. 31; Mogollon
     Incised and Corrugated, p. 31; Red Mesa Black-on-white, pp.
     32, 35; Casa Grande Red-on-buff, inside back cover; and
     "Making a Pot" photos, pp. 4-5.

32. Arizona Highways, Vol. 50, No. 5, May, Phoenix, Arizona.
    1974 Entire issue devoted to pictorial articles on contemporary
    Southwestern pottery. Good collection of color photographs of
    contemporary pottery. Articles include "Southwestern Pottery
    Today" by Patrick T. Houlihan, "The Beauty Collectors" by
    Barbara Cartwright, "Blue Corn" by Mike Tharp, "The Beauty
    Makers" by Maggie Wilson, "The Quality Market" by Anita Da.
    Color illustrations of pottery from the following pueblos and
    tribes: Hopi, Zuni, San Ildefonso, Maricopa, Yuma, Acoma,
    Santa Clara, Taos, Jemez, Cochiti, Isleta, Santo Domingo, La-
    guna, Tesuque, Papago, Navajo, Zia, and Mohave. Pictures of
    Feather Woman firing pottery. Pictures of the following potters:
    Frog Woman, Maria, Popvi Da, Tony Da, Nampeyo, Dextra, Blue
    Corn, Joseph Lonewolf, Teresita Naranjo, Grace Medicine Flower,
    Margaret Tafoya, Marie Z. Chino, Christina Naranjo, and Tse-
    Pe and Dora Gonzales.

33. The Arizona State Museum. 1959 The University of Arizona
    Press, Tucson, Arizona.
        Illustrations of Yuma Ware dolls, p. 17 (cover); Maricopa
    ware, p. 17; Mimbres Black-on-white, p. 9; Tularosa Black-on-
    white, p. 2; and Cochiti Polychrome, p. 1.

34. Asch, C. M. 1960 "Post Pueblo Occupation at the Willow Creek
    Ruin, Point of Pines." Kiva, Vol. 26, No. 2, pp. 31-42.
        The description of the excavation of one room and a study
    of post-Pueblo stone rings. The investigators found a variety
    of pottery types including four whole or restorable vessels.
    One of Kinishba White-on-red and a Point of Pines Polychrome
    bowl are illustrated in Fig. 14.

35. Ashton, Robert J. 1976 "Nampeyo and Lesou." American
    Indian Art Magazine, Vol. 1, No. 3, May, pp. 24-33.
        An article explaining the development of the pottery style
    Nampeyo and her husband Lesou, devised from the designs on
    prehistoric and historic sherds from excavations in the Hopi
    area. It is stated that Nampeyo and Lesou began making pottery
    in 1880-85 rather than 1895 as usually believed. Lesou should
    be given more credit for his contributions in finding the sherds
    used as bases for the designs and decorating some of the ves-
    sels. Nampeyo and Lesou ceased making pottery in about 1915.
    He died in 1932 and she in 1942.

36. Atwood, W. 1974 "Appendix B. Ceramic Descriptions." In
    W. J. Judge, The Excavation of Tijeras Pueblo, 1971-1973, Pre-
    liminary Report, Cibola National Forest, New Mexico, Archaeolo-
    gical Report 43, U.S.D.A. Forest Service, Southwest Region,
    Albuquerque, New Mexico.
        Description of the excavations at Tijeras Pueblo east of Al-
    buquerque, New Mexico. The pottery types found and briefly
    described are Agua Fria Glaze-on-red, Arenal Glaze Polychrome,

Biscuit A, Biscuit B, Casa Grande Black-on-white, Chupadero
Black-on-white, Cienguilla Glaze-on-yellow, Galisteo Black-on-
white, Los Lunas Smudged, Los Padillos Glaze Polychrome, Pindi
Black-on-white, Poge Black-on-white, San Clemente Glaze Polychrome, Santa Fe Black-on-white, Socorro Black-on-white, St.
Johns Polychrome, Wingate Black-on-red, and Wiyo Black-on-
white.

37. Bahti, Tom. 1964 Southwestern Indian Arts and Crafts. KC
     Publications, Flagstaff, Arizona.
        Illustrations of Laguna Polychrome, p. 28; Papago Black-on-
     white, p. 28; Papago Black-on-red, p. 28; Papago Red, p. 28;
     Santo Domingo Polychrome, p. 29; Maricopa Ware, p. 29; Mo-
     have Ware, p. 28; Pima Ware, p. 29; Navajo Ware (utility),
     p. 29; Zuni Polychrome, p. 29; Zia Polychrome, p. 29; and
     Acoma Polychrome, p. 29.

38. Baker, Bayla. 1971 "The Riverside Site, Grant County, New
     Mexico." Southwestern New Mexico Research Reports No. 5
     Case Western Reserve University, Cleveland, Ohio.
        This site excavated by Stanley D. Bussey for the Museum
     of New Mexico in 1965 is located west of Riverside, Grant County,
     New Mexico. No complete vessels were found during the exca-
     vations but one Gila Polychrome vessel, one indented corrugated
     jar, and one small brownware bowl were partially restorable.
     These bowls are illustrated in Fig. 6. There were 1,599 sherds
     found which were typed, counted, weighed, and catalogued in
     the field. Predominant types at this site were Three Circle Red-
     on-white, Mogollon Red-on-brown, Mimbres Boldface Black-on-
     white, and undifferentiated Mimbres sherds. Eighteen sherds
     of Gila Polychrome were present and one sherd each of Chu-
     padero Black-on-white, El Paso Polychrome and Tularosa Black-
     on-white. The brown wares were grouped into these four cate-
     gories based on surface treatment: clapboard corrugated, 447
     sherds; indented corrugated, 241 sherds; plain scored, 11
     sherds; and plain undercorated, 590 sherds.

39. Baldwin, Gordon C. 1937 "Pottery of Kinishba." Kiva. Vol.
     3, No. 1, pp. 1-4.
        Brief article on pottery found during excavations by Cum-
     mings in 1930s. Types briefly described include Black-on-white
     types, Black-on-red (White Mountain), St. Johns Polychrome,
     Gila Polychrome, and Pinedale Polychrome Fourmile Polychrome
     is also described. Many types of pottery were found at Kinishba
     representing the Little Colorado and Gila cultural areas. Illus-
     trations of two Gila Polychrome bowls, p. 3.

40. Baldwin, Gordon C. 1938 "A New Pottery Type from Eastern
     Arizona." Southwestern Lore, Vol. 4, No. 2, pp. 22-26.
        Description of Kinishba Polychrome, p. 21.

41. Baldwin, Gordon C. 1939 "The Material Culture of Kinishba."
    American Antiquity, Vol. 4, No. 4, pp. 314-327.
       Brief description of pottery found, pp. 314-317. Photos of
    Tonto Polychrome and Fourmile Polychrome bowls, Pl. 15.

42. Baldwin, Gordon C. 1950 "The Pottery of the Southern Paiute."
    American Antiquity, Vol. 16, No. 1, pp. 50-56.
       Description and photos of Southern Paiute Utility Ware from
    Utah, Arizona, Nevada, and California.

43. Baldwin, Stuart, J. 1976 "Trade Pottery from Mesa Verde
    and Adjacent Areas." Pottery Southwest, Vol. 3, No. 1, pp.
    2-3.
       Description of a study to gather and collate data from pub-
    lished sources concerning the evidence for prehistoric trade in
    the Mesa Verde area.

44. Baldwin, Stuart J. 1976a "Why Trade Pottery?" Pottery South-
    West, Vol. 3, No. 4, pp. 7-9.
       Explores the question of why pottery was traded in prehis-
    toric times. Presents and discusses the following hypotheses:
    (1) the aesthetic hypothesis, (2) the local manufacture hypothe-
    sis, (3) the specialization hypothesis, (4) the special use hy-
    pothesis, and (5) the container hypothesis.

45. Baldwin, Stuart J. 1978 "Notes on the Origin and Spread of
    Potsherd Tempering in the Southwest, Up to AD 1300." Pottery
    Southwest, Vol. 5, No. 4, October, pp. 1-8.
       Examines the temporal and spatial distribution of potsherd
    tempering within the Southwest.
       General conclusions are: "(a) The tempering of southwestern
    pottery with crushed and/or ground sherds seems to occur first
    at about AD 825-850; (b) The area(s) of first occurrence are
    the region of the Petrified Forest and/or the Chaco Canyon and
    Acoma regions; (c) Tempering with potsherds is at first re-
    stricted to Black-on-white pottery with an apparent lag of more
    than a century before application of the technique to other kinds
    of pottery; (d) Up to AD 1300, use of potsherd tempering
    spread to and was usually restricted to peoples classified as
    being Anasazi, with most--but not all--Anasazi regional popula-
    tions adopting the technique; (e) Potsherd tempering may be
    an independent invention in the Southwest, rather than a
    borrowed (diffused) technique," p. 2.
       Potsherds may have been used rather than sand for temper
    because it produces a stronger paste. It may also have been
    used to produce exceptionally fine ceramic vessels, p. 6.

46. Baldwin, Stuart J. 1984 "Hendron's Stratigraphic Test at Ala-
    meda Pueblo and Its Implications for the Rio Grande Glaze Se-
    quence." Pottery Southwest, Vol. 11, No. 2, April, pp. 3-6.
       The results of a master's thesis by J. W. Hendron in 1935

question Mera's Rio Grande Glaze sequence. Other old lost
tests by Hendron at Puaray and Kuaua, if found, may cast
more light on this topic.

47. Barber, Edwin A. 1876 "The Ancient Pottery of Colorado,
Utah, Arizona and New Mexico." American Naturalist, Vol. 10
No. 8, pp. 449-464, Cambridge, Massachusetts.
Description of pottery found by the U.S.G.S. led by F. V.
Hayden in 1875. Drawings of vessels reconstructed from large
sherds, primarily black-on-white types. One of the earliest
papers on prehistoric pottery of the Southwest. It mentions
five classes of pottery: (I) Plain burned clay; (II) the lami-
nated or indented; (III) the embossed or molded; (IV) the
glazed ware (a. plain white; b. ornamental in colors; c. red or
brick) and (V) glazed and corrugated. Some of the conclusions
included are now known to be incorrect but this is quite ac-
curate considering the lack of research at the time it was
written.

48. Barnett, Franklin. 1968 Birds on Rio Grande Pottery. Yuma,
Arizona.
Discussion of the evolution of the bird as a design factor on
Rio Grande pottery. Illustrations of designs.

49. Barnett, Franklin. 1969 Tongue Pueblo: A Report of Partial
Excavation of an Ancient Pueblo IV Indian Ruin in New Mexico.
Albuquerque Archaeological Society, New Mexico.
Chapter VI, pp. 138-197, on pottery. Design elements are
described and illustrated. Illustrations of Rio Grande Glaze
Polychrome, Sankawi Black-on-cream, Sankawi Polychrome, Rio
Grande Culinary Ware, and Tewa Polychrome.

50. Barnett, Franklin. 1970 "Matli Ranch Ruins: A Report of Five
Small Prehistoric Ruins of the Prescott Culture in Arizona."
Museum of Northern Arizona Technical Series No. 10, Flagstaff,
Arizona.
Ceramic Wares, pp. 66-89. Illustrations of Verde Black-on-
gray, pp. 70-73, and Flagstaff Black-on-white, p. 73. A
scheme is given for classifying the variations of Prescott Gray
Ware, p. 88.

51. Barnett, Franklin. 1973 "Lonesome Valley Ruin in Yavapai
Country." University of Northern Arizona Technical Series No.
13, Flagstaff, Arizona.
The pottery found in this two room Prescott Culture site
was primarily Prescott Gray Ware and Verde Brown. Photographs of Verde Black-on-gray sherds, Fig. 11. Photographs
of vessels of the following types from a nearby burial: p. 24,
Tuzigoot Plain Jars, Nos. 4-5; Verde Black-on-gray bowl, No.
6; and Verde Black-on-gray jar, No. 3. Site was occupied AD
1125-1250, based on analysis of dated pottery types.

52. Barnett, Franklin 1973a Dictionary of Prehistoric Indian Arti-
     facts of the American Southwest. Northland Press, Flagstaff,
     Arizona.
         Most of the artifacts included are non-ceramic but the follow-
     ing clay objects are illustrated and described: bird call made
     of sherds, p. 34; jar fingerhold containers, p. 44; discs made
     from sherds, p. 47; fetish made from a sherd, p. 52; human
     figurines made from sherds, p. 53; gaming pieces made from
     sherds, p. 58; sherd gorgets, p. 59; sherd jar covers, p. 64;
     sherd pendants, p. 86; clay pipes, p. 91; potsherd pottery
     smoothing inplements, p. 94; and sherd spindle whorls, p. 106.

53. Barnett, Franklin 1973b San Ysidro Pueblos: Two Prehistoric
     Pueblo IV Ruins in New Mexico. Albuquerque Archaeological
     Society, Albuquerque, New Mexico.
         Section IV, pp. 38-62. William M. Sundt. A description of
     the vessels found and those in other collections from the two
     sites excavated. Most common type found in both sites was
     Aqua Fria Glaze-on-red. Other types found in both Site 115
     and Site 142 were San Clemente Glaze Polychrome, Cienguilla
     Glaze-on-yellow, Espinosa Glaze-on-yellow, Abiquiu and Bandelier
     Black-on-white, and culinary wares. In addition to those above,
     types illustrated are: Pottery Mound Polychrome, Jemez Black-
     on-white, an "unnamed white-on-red," culinary "duck pots,"
     and objects made of sherds.

54. Barnett, Franklin 1974 Sandstone Hill Pueblo: Cibola Culture
     in Catron County, New Mexico. Albuquerque Archaeological
     Society, Albuquerque, New Mexico.
         Description of the excavation of a small pueblo ruin 10.9km
     north of Quemado, New Mexico. Only six whole or restorable
     vessels were found. A total of 5,236 sherds were sorted and
     analyzed by E. D. Danson and Kathleen James. Tularosa Black-
     on-white was the most common painted ware found. Miscellan-
     eous brown corrugated was the predominant undecorated ware.
     Types illustrated are Kiatuthlanna Black-on-white, Pinedale Black-
     on-red, Pinedale Polychrome, Puerco Black-on-red, Red Mesa
     Black-on-white, Reserve Black-on-white, St. Johns Black-on-
     red, St. Johns Polychrome, Tularosa Black-on-white, Wingate
     Black-on-red, Wingate Polychrome, Reserve Corrugated, Smudged,
     p. 23, and Reserve Patterned Corrugated, p. 23.

55. Barnett, Franklin. 1974a Excavation of Main Pueblo at Fitz-
     maurice Ruin. Museum of Northern Arizona Special Publication,
     Flagstaff, Arizona.
         Ceramic Wares, Chapter V, pp. 96-129. Discussion and
     analysis of sherds and vessels found at Fitzmaurice Ruin. Types
     found were primarily Verde Brown, Verde Gray, and Tuzigoot
     Plain. Analysis of potsherds and ceramic wares by Kathleen G.
     James, pp. 106-129. Designs and forms are described in rela-
     tion to the Tuzigoot, Verde and Prescott traditions, and the

vessel shapes and designs are well illustrated. Gila Plain:
Perry Mesa Variety is described and illustrated. Design motifs
for Tuzigoot Black-on-brown, Verde Black-on-brown, Verde
Red-on-buff, Verde Black-on-gray, and Verde Red-on-gray
are included.

56. Barry, John W. 1981 American Indian Pottery: An Identification and Value Guide. Books Americana, Florence, Alabama.
     This book is directed primarily to the layman. It attempts
to give a broad overview of Indian pottery, prehistoric to contemporary, throughout North America. It includes a brief
history, methods of production, value of contemporary pottery,
selection of pottery, care and handling of pottery, and classification. There are sections on prehistoric pottery of New Eng-
land and Canada, the midwest, and the Southwestern United
States. The longest section is on contemporary and historic
pottery, primarily of the Southwest.
     This book contains many photos of pottery, most of which
are clear but a few are dark and indistinct. There are a number of spelling and other typographical errors in this book
which detract from an overall good effort.
     Types of prehistoric pottery illustrated are Bidahochi Poly-
chrome, Jeddito Polychrome, Jeddito Black-on-yellow, Awatovi
Black-on-yellow, Fourmile Polychrome, Homolovi Polychrome,
Bidahochi Black-on-white, and Jeddito Black-on-white, all from
Nuvaqueotaka Pueblo at Chavez Pass, Arizona.
     Other types of prehistoric Southwestern pottery illustrated
are North Creek Fugitive Red, Mesa Verde Corrugated, Mancos
Black-on-white, Deadmans Black-on-red?, Tusayan Black-on-
white, Santa Fe Black-on-white, Mesa Verde Black-on-white,
Tonto Polychrome, Fourmile Polychrome, Tularosa Black-on-
white, Salado Red, Roosevelt Black-on-white, Pinedale Polychrome, Mimbres Black-on-white, Reserve Black-on-white, Kayenta Black-on-white?, Casas Grandes Polychrome, Jemez Black-
on-gray, and Kuaua Glaze Polychrome.
     Historic and contemporary types illustrated are Sikyatki Poly-
chrome, Walpi Polychrome, and pottery by the following Hopi
and Tewa potters: Frogwoman, Dextra Nampeyo, Garnet Paveta
[sic], Fannie Nampeyo, Sadie Adams, Myrtle Young, Verla
Dewakuku, Helen Poolheco, Vina Harvey, Ada Yayetewa, Elva
Nampeyo, Rodina Huma, Marsha Ricky, and Marcia Fritz. There
is also a vessel of Sichomori [sic] Polychrome shown.
     Contemporary pottery from the following pueblos and non-
pueblo tribes are presented:
Acoma--Many polychrome and black-on-white vessels by the
Lewis family and other well known Acoma potters and a white
corrugated jar by Stella Shutiva.
Laguna--Photos of a few pots by Evelyn Cheromiah and unknown
potters.
Zia--Illustrations of several contemporary and historic pieces.
Santa Ana--Pots by Eudora Montoya and unnamed potters.

Santo Domingo--Photos of pottery made by Robert Tenorio, Santana Melcher, and others.

Cochiti--Pots by a number of potters and a Helen Cordera storyteller figure.

Jemez--Many illustrations of historic and contemporary figurines and vessels by a variety of artists.

Pecos--Photos of prehistoric pots from this ruin and reproductions of Pecos Glaze V types made by Persingula M. Casiquito, Evelyn Vigil, Juanita Toledo, and Rachel Lovetto of Jemez.

Tesuque--A few vessels and figurines from this pueblo.

Nambe and Pojoaque--Pottery by Virginia Guitierrez and Joe and Thelma Talachy.

Santa Clara--Photos of many ceramics from this prolific pottery making pueblo.

San Ildefonso--Photos of pottery by Maria Martinez and other noted potters from this pueblo.

San Juan--A few pots are shown from this pueblo.

Taos and Picuris--Micaceous and polychrome pots.

Isleta--Stella Teller's polychrome pieces.

Isleta-Tigua--Pottery by Lucy F. Rodella from this pueblo village near El Paso, Texas.

A few Navajo jars by unknown Navajo potters are shown. Zuni polychrome jars of the historic and contemporary periods and one by Jennie Laate are illustrated. A few pots from the non-pueblo groups of Papago, Pima, Yuma, Mohave, Maricopa, and a few from eastern tribes are also shown.

This book also contains a glossary and a price guide which, like all such guides, will soon become out-of-date.

57. Bartlett, Katherine. 1977 "A History of Hopi Pottery." Plateau, Vol. 49, No. 3, Winter, pp. 2-13.

An excellent brief history of pottery of the Hopi. It covers: beginnings, great drought, yellow wares, mission period, Sikyatki revival, the museums' influence, and modern trends.

Illustrations of modern polychrome and black-on-yellow, p. 3; Jeddito Black-on-yellow, p. 4; Citadel Polychrome and Yellow Jeddito Corrugated, p. 5; Kiet Siel Polychrome, p. 6; Sikyatki Polychrome and Medicine Black-on-red, p. 7; Sikyatki revival jar, p. 8; modern Black-on-white, p. 9; Polacca Polychrome, p. 10; Walpi Polychrome, p. 11; and Sikyatki revival Black-on-yellow, p. 12.

58. Baumhof, Martin A. and Heizer, Robert F. 1959 "Some Unexploited Possibilities of Ceramic Analysis." Southwestern Journal of Anthropology, Vol. 15, No. 3, pp. 308-316.

Suggestions are given for a technique of matching sherds to estimate the numbers of vessels used at a site. It is also stated that they estimated the number of vessels from the weight of the sherds of different types.

59. Beal, John D. 1982 "Archaeological Investigations in the Eastern

Red Mesa Valley: The Plains/Escalante Generating Station."
Report 005, Archaeological Division, School of American Research, Santa Fe, New Mexico.
Chapter 2--Ceramics and site Chronology in the Eastern Red Mesa Valley: A Reevaluation of the Local Uses of Pueblo I-III Pottery for Phase Sequencing, Kiatuthlanna Through Wingate.
"Working at the 14 Prewitt sites which produced ceramics provided a collection of 9,291 pottery sherds and five whole or restorable vessels.... The primary goal in the study of this collection was to determine the relative positions in time of the 14 sites, using the pottery as a chronological indicator" (Pottery Southwest).

60. Beals, Ralph L.; Brainerd, George W.; and Smith, Watson.
     1945 "Archaeological Studies in Northeast Arizona." University of California Publications in American Archaeology and Ethnology, Vol. 44, No. 1, Berkeley, California, University of California Press, pp. 1-237. (Reprint, 1971, University of California Press.)
     Painted pottery designs of the Kayenta area, pp. 87-150. Description of work of Rainbow Bridge--Monument Valley Expedition, 1933-1938, mainly in the Tsegi drainage. Section on pottery designs of the Kayenta area is good. Descriptions and illustrations of Kayenta Black-on-white; Black-on-white Ware, Pueblo, I, II, III; Tsegi Orange Ware; Tusayan Black-on-red, pp. 116, 118, 120, 122; Tsegi Black-on-orange, pp. 112, 122, 130; Tusayan Polychrome, pp. 122, 124, 126, 128, 130; Kiet Siel Polychrome, pp. 120-122; Tsegi Red-on-orange, p. 128. Pottery illustrations, Pls. 23-30; and illustrations of Kana-a Black-on-white, Figs. 18-24; Flagstaff Black-on-white, Figs. 35e and f, 46; Black Mesa Black-on-white, Figs. 24-33; Sosi Black-on-white, Fig. 34a-I; Dogoszhi Black-on-white, Figs. 31, 32; Tusayan Black-on-white, Figs. 56, 57a, b, d, e, f, h, i, j, 39, 41, 42, 43, 44, 45, Pl. 26.

61. Beaver, William T. 1952 "Navajo Pottery and Basketry." Masterkey, Vol. 26, No. 3, p. 109.
     Brief one page description of Navajo ware, p. 109.

62. Beckett, Patrick H. 1985 "Distribution of Chupadero Black-on-white: Or the Black and White of Jug Use." In Charles H. Lang (Ed.), Southwestern Culture History: Collected Papers in Honor of Albert H. Schroeder, pp. 27-30. Papers of the Archaeological Society of New Mexico, No. 10, Ancient City Press, Santa Fe, New Mexico.
     Suggests working hypotheses pertaining to the people responsible for the wide distribution of this type and its uses. Possible uses of Chupadero Black-on-white jugs are the transportation of water or the storage of food.

63. Bennett, Ann. 1974 "Basic Ceramic Analysis." Eastern New

Mexico University Contributions in Anthropology, Vol. 6, No.
1, Portales, New Mexico.
    Description of the method of ceramic data recording used at
Salmon Ruins by the San Juan Valley Archaeological Project.
Includes sections on sherd analysis record, record of reconstructed artifacts, provenience data record, and painted decoration analysis. Recording forms are included for each section.
These analyses are designed for computer processing by SEL-
GEM system of storage and analysis. Persons must have a
knowledge of Southwestern pottery characteristics and methods
of construction to use this manual without instructions.

64. Berman, Mary Jane. 1978 "The Mesa Top Site: An Early
     Mogollon Village in Southeastern Arizona." Cultural Resources
     Management Division Report No. 280. New Mexico State Univer-
     sity, Las Cruces.
         Ceramics analyzed by Tony M. Preslar in Chapter VII.
         "Ceramics removed from the Mesa Top Site were neither
     numerous or diverse but were sufficient to provide a general
     cultural and temporal placement of the site. The ceramic popu-
     lation totaled 1,362 sherds distributed disproportionately be-
     tween two known types of pottery, Alma Plain and San Francisco
     Red, both associated with the Mogollon Culture," p. 103.
         The ceramics from the Mesa Top Site are systematically de-
     scribed and intersite and intrasite analyses are reported. Of
     the sherds recovered, 93.2% were identified as Alma Plain or
     San Francisco Red. Of the total identified, 92.1% were Alma
     Plain and the remaining 7.9% were San Francisco Red. Based
     on sherd analysis, 42.1% of the vessels were bowls and 57.9%
     were jars.

65. Berry, Michael S. 1972 "The Evans Site." Special Report,
     University of Utah Department of Anthropology. Salt Lake City,
     Utah.
         Describes and discusses Fremont and Virgin Branch Anasazi
     pottery recovered from the Evans Site.

66. Bice, Richard A. 1975 Prehispanic Pueblo Pottery. Museum
     of Albuquerque and Albuquerque Archaeological Society, Al-
     buquerque, New Mexico.
         A 20-page booklet based on an exhibit of pottery at the Mu-
     seum of Albuquerque. A discussion of the development of the
     major pottery types in seven river basins. The following types
     are mentioned and illustrated. (Some photos are poor.) San
     Juan Basin: Kiatuthlanna Black-on-white, SJ5; Piedra Black-
     on-white, SJ4; Cortez Black-on-white, SJ7; Mancos Black-on-
     white and Escavada Black-on-white, SJ1 and SJ19; Gallup Black-
     on-white, SJ13; Mesa Verde Black-on-white, SJ12, 16, and 18;
     Chaco Black-on-white, SJ2, 3, 9, and 10; McElmo Black-on-
     white, SJ6 and 8; Tusayan Polychrome, SJ11. Little Colorado
     Basin: Black Mesa Black-on-white, LC2; Acoma Poly, SJ14;

Kayenta Black-on-white, LC4; Jeddito Black-on-white and Black-
on-orange, LC5, 7, and 8; Bidihachi [sic] Black-on-white, LC6;
Sikyatki Polychrome, LC9 and 10; Hopi Jar, LC11; Kiatuthlanna
Black-on-white, LC19; Red Mesa Black-on-white, LC15 and 17;
Gallup Black-on-white, LC12; Puerco Black-on-white, LC12;
Puerco Black-on-red, LC1; Cebolleta Black-on-white, LC3;
Wingate Polychrome, LC21; St. Johns Polychrome and Springer-
ville Polychrome, LC18, 20, and 22. Upper Gila Basin: Re-
serve Smudged, UG 13-14; Reserve Black-on-white, UG12, 16-
17; Zuni Polychrome, UG3; Snowflake Black-on-white, UG1;
Tularosa Black-on-white, UG2, 5-11, 15, 18-20. Mimbres Basin:
Mimbres Black-on-white, M1-10, 12-14; Mimbres Polychrome, M11.
Lower Gila Basin: Babicomari Black-on-red, LG1; Tonto Poly-
chrome, LG2; Sacaton Red-on-buff, LG3-4; Pinto Polychrome,
LG5; Gila Red, LG6; San Carlos Red-on-buff, LG7. Chihuahua
Basin: Ramos Polychrome, C1, 3, 5, 7, 9-12, 14-15, 17, 19;
Babicora Polychrome, C2; Madera Black-on-red, C4, 8, 13, 18;
Playas Red, C6, 16. Rio Grande Basin: Vallecitos Black-on-
white, RG1, 15; Rio Grande Glaze IV, RG2, 9, 11, 13, 21;
Santo Dominto Polychrome, RG3; Galisteo Black-on-white, RG4,
10; Gallina Black-on-white, RG5, 8, 12, 16; Cienguilla Yellow,
Glaze I, RG6; Socorro Black-on-white, RG7; Tsankawi Black-on-
white, RG18; and Rio Grande Plain Yellow, RG19.

67.   Bice, Richard A. 1979 "Basketmaker III-Pueblo I Manifesta-
      tions in the Rio Puerco of the East." Technical Note No. 1
      Albuquerque Archaeological Society, Albuquerque, New Mexico,
      February.
         Surface survey of a "control site," in the bottom of the
      Puerco Valley west of Albuquerque. Pottery found and illus-
      trated is Lino Gray, abundant, Figs. 2 and 3; Lino Black-on-
      gray, scarce, Fig. 1; Lino Red, occasional; La Plata Black-on-
      white, occasional, Fig. 4; Kana-a Gray, occasional, Fig. 2;
      San Francisco Redware, scarce, Fig. 4; Brownware, scarce, Fig.
      4; and White Mesa, Kiatuthlanna, and Red Mesa Black-on-white,
      Fig. 4.

68.   Bice, Richard A. and Sundt, William M. 1972 Prieta Vista:
      A Small Pueblo III Ruin in North Central New Mexico. Albu-
      querque Archaeological Society, Albuquerque, New Mexico.
         A good section on ceramics by Sundt, pp. 98-176. The
      pottery found is well analyzed and compared to other Pueblo
      III sites in the region. Sherds were carefully examined and
      classified into varieties based on temper and other physical
      characteristics. Several new varieties and types are described.
      The analysis of the often ignored culinary ware is very useful
      and hopefully will set an example for further investigations.
      Types described and illustrated are McElmo Black-on-white,
      Chaco jar from Prieta Vista, p. 104, Figs. 59-63; Santa Fe
      Black-on-white, p. 122, Figs. 66-68; Vallecitos Black-on-white,
      p. 132, Figs. 70-71; Prieta Smeared Indented, p. 154, Fig. 79;
      and Pajarito Smeared Indented, p. 162, Fig. 82. Illustrations

of Galisteo Black-on-white, Fig. 65; St. Johns Polychrome, Fig.
73; Wingate Polychrome, Fig. 73; Kwahe'e Black-on-white and
Puerco Black-on-white, Fig. 74; Corrugated culinary ware,
Figs. 80, 81, 83; and utilized and worked sherds, Fig. 88.
Ceramic studies set a period of occupation of AD 1220-1240 for
Prieta Vista.

69. Bilbo, Michael J. 1969 "An El Paso Polychrome Olla from Hueco
    Bolson." Artifact, Vol. 7, No. 2, El Paso Archaeological Society,
    El Paso, Texas.
    The description and illustration of an El Paso Polychrome
    olla.

70. Blair, Mary Ellen and Blair, Lawrence R. 1986 Margaret Ta-
    foya: A Tewa Potter's Heritage and Legacy. Schiffer Publish-
    ing Co., West Chester, Pennsylvania.
    A biography of the noted Santa Clara potter, Margaret Ta-
    foya.
    Chapter 1 is a history of Santa Clara and other pueblos from
    prehistory to Margaret Tafoya's birth in 1904. Her life is de-
    scribed in Chapter 2. Chapter 3 is a detailed description of
    pottery making at Santa Clara Pueblo. In Chapter 4 Margaret's
    descendents are listed and discussed.
    Appendices include evolution of Santa Clara pottery, slip
    casting, and genealogy of Santa Clara Pueblo inhabitants. There
    are excessive errors in spelling and grammar in this book which
    detract from an otherwise valuable contribution to the under-
    standing of Margaret Tafoya's major contributions to pueblo
    pottery. Illustrations of many Santa Clara ceramics are included.

71. Blinman, Eric. 1984 "Dating with Neckbands: Calibration of
    Temporal Variations in Moccasin Gray and Mancos Gray Ceramic
    Types." In Dolores Archaeological Program Synthetic Report,
    1978-81, pp. 128-138, Bureau of Reclamation, Engineering and
    Research Center, Denver, Colorado.
    Conclusion: "Variation in neckband style within the Dolores
    River valley provides high resolution dating technique for sites
    occupied between AD 775 and 950.... The rate of stylistic
    change was not constant through time and was accelerated be-
    tween AD 850 and 900. This improves the dating resolution in
    this time (coinciding with the population maximum in the Dolores
    River valley), and it also may be an independent measure of
    relative cultural stability," p. 136.

72. Blinman, Eric and Wilson, C. Dean. 1986 "Ceramic Data and
    Interpretations: The Middle Canyon Sites." In Allen E. Kane
    and Christine K. Robinson (compilers) Dolores Archaeological
    Program; Anasazi Communities at Dolores; Middle Canyon Area,
    Book 2, Bureau of Reclamation, Denver, Colorado.
    Chapter 7, pp. 1091-1119: "This chapter provides back-
    ground information that will help the reader understand ceramic
    data presentations in the descriptive reports and the basis for

ceramic dating inferences. In addition, this report explores
selected aspects of temporal and intersite variability in ceramic
data for the Middle Canyon area during the AD 800-920 time
period. Also comparisons are made of Middle Canyon site assemblages with McPhee Community Cluster assemblages," p. 1091.
Describes: Dolores Brown, Dolores Corrugated, Dolores
Red, and Bluff Black-on-red: McPhee Variety.

73. Bluhm, Elaine. 1957 "The Sawmill Site: A Reserve Phase Village, Pine Lawn Valley, Western New Mexico." Fieldiana: Anthropology, Vol. 47, No. 1, Chicago Natural History Museum,
Chicago, Illinois.
    Pottery chapter III, pp. 28-45. Predominant types found
were Alma Plain, 54%; Alma Rough, 20.5%; Reserve Plain Corrugated, 14.5%, and Reserve Smudged, 3.88%. Illustrations of
sherds: Alma Pinched, Alma Punched, Reserve Plain, Alma Incised, Fig. 9; Reserve Black-on-white, Fig. 10; Reserve Black-
on-white effigy pitcher, Fig. 11; Alma Plain and punched miniature vessels, Fig. 12; and worked sherds, Fig. 16.

74. Boggs, Stanley. 1936 "A Survey of the Papago People." M.A.
thesis, Department of Anthropology, University of Arizona,
Tucson, Arizona.
    Description and illustrations of papago pottery manufacture
and vessels.

75. Bohn, Dave and Jeff, Stephen. 1977 House of the Three Tur-
keys: Anasazi Redoubt. Capra Press, Santa Barbara, Cali-
fornia.
    Short book with many good black and white photos and quo-
tations from other publications. A brief history and archaeolo-
gical precis of this interesting and well preserved Anasazi site.
    Unpainted types found and their percentages were: Little
Colorado Corrugated, 43.4%; Undescribed rough type, 29.0%;
Tusayan Corrugated, 17.6%. Decorated types: Mesa Verde
Black-on-white, 66.7%; Undescribed black-on-white, 6.7%; Tsegi
Orange Ware, 13.3% Tusayan Black-on-red, 3.3%; St. Johns
Polychrome, 6.7%; and Klageto Black-on-yellow, 3.3%.

76. Bond, Mark C. 1983 "White Mesa Ceramics, 1981." In 1981 Excavations on White Mesa, San Juan County Utah. William Davis,
pp. 165-240. Plano Archaeological Consultants, Longmont, Colorado, and Abajo Archaeologists, Bluff, Utah.
    Description of Tin Cup Polychrome.

77. Bower, Nathan; Faciszewski, Steve; Renwick, Stephen; and
Peckham, Stewart. 1986 "A Preliminary Analysis of Rio Grande
Glazes of the Classic Period Using Scanning Electronic Micro-
scopy with X-ray Fluorescence." Journal of Field Archaeology,
Vol. 13, No. 3, pp. 307-315.
    Analysis of 15 sherds shows that intrusive wares can be

identified, that trading patterns can be described, and that a
source of glaze components appears to have been located near
the Cerrillos Mining District of New Mexico.

78. Bradfield, Wesley. 1931 Cameron Creek Village, A Site in the
     Mimbres Area in Grant County, New Mexico. Monograph School
     of American Research, No. 1, Santa Fe, New Mexico.
         Many good illustrations of Classic Mimbres pottery and as-
     sociated types. Good description of each vessel. Location:
     Near Cameron Creek, Grant County, New Mexico. Wares dis-
     cussed are early red paste, early gray paste, and early white.

79. Bradford, Kathleen C. 1975 "The Tesuque Rain God." Pottery
     Southwest, Vol. 2, No. 4, January, pp. 2-4.
         Brief description and history of these figures. Asks the
     following questions of the readers: (1) When was the poster-
     paint Tesuque Rain God first introduced? (2) Did everyone at
     Tesuque make the Rain God or was only a certain segment of
     the population involved? (3) Does evidence exist for a pre-
     1890 figure similar to the Tesuque Rain God? (4) Was the figu-
     rine concept borrowed or of an indigenous nature? (5) Were the
     first Rain Gods sold to sources other than the Gunther Candy
     Co.?
         Illustrations of three Rain God figurines and one Tesuque
     clay pipe.

80. Bradley, Bruce. 1974 "Preliminary Report of Excavations at
     Wallace Ruin, 1969-1974." Southwestern Lore, Vol. 40, Nos.
     3 and 4, December, pp. 63-76.
         Description of excavations done at this Pueblo II-III ruin.
     Local ceramics were La Plata Black-on-white, Mancos Black-on-
     white, Cortez Black-on-white, McElmo Black-on-white, Mesa
     Verde Black-on-white, and gray and corrugated wares. A
     wide variety of intrusive types were found and drawings of a
     Tusayan Polychrome bowl and a Chaco Black-on-white pitcher
     are included.

81. Bradley, Zorro A. 1971 Site Bc 236, Chaco Canyon National
     Monument, New Mexico. National Park Service, U.S. Depart-
     ment of the Interior, pp. 43-50.
         Types found were Kiatuthlanna Black-on-white, Red Mesa
     Black-on-white, Escavada Black-on-white, Gallup-Chaco Black-
     on-white, McElmo Black-on-white, and Mesa Verde Black-on-
     white. Sherds of the above types are illustrated in Pls. 15-20.

82. Brainerd, George. 1942 "Symmetry in Prehistoric Conventional
     Design." American Antiquity, Vol. 8, No. 2, pp. 164-166.
         "The general purpose of this paper is to present a general
     applicable, objective terminology for a classification of conven-
     tional design. The terminology is based on symmetry of ar-
     rangement, which we have found more useful than any other
     scheme in elucidating complex designs," p. 164.

83. Brand, Donald D. 1935 "The Distribution of Pottery in North-
     west Mexico." American Anthropology, Vol. 37, No. 2, pp.
     287-305.
         Good discussion of pottery of Northwest Mexico. Two maps,
     no illustrations. Types discussed are Babicora Polychrome,
     Huerigos Polychrome, Carretas Polychrome, Villa Ahumada Poly-
     chrome, Carmen Red-on-gray, and Madera Black-on-red.

84. Brand, Donald D.; Hawley, F. M.; and Hibben, F. C. 1937
     "Tseh So, A Small House Ruin, Chaco Canyon, New Mexico."
     University of New Mexico Bulletin, Anthropological Series,
     Vol. 2, No. 2, Albuquerque, New Mexico.
         Summary of pottery from Tseh So by Florence M. Hawley.
     "Basketmaker III pit houses and sections of the dump are rep-
     resented by Lino Gray and by La Plata Black-on-white. The
     pottery complex from Pueblo I rooms, from Pueblo I burials,
     and from Pieblo I levels of the dump for Tseh So is consistent,
     Red Mesa and Escavada Black-on-white, Lino Gray and Kana-a
     Gray, and Exuberant Corrugated being the prevalent types.
     In the Pueblo II rooms, burials and levels of the dump, the com-
     plex was made up of small amounts of the preceding types plus
     larger portions of Gallup and Chaco Black-on-white," p. 85.
         Illustrations: Plate 15, McElmo Black-on-white bowl, Red Mesa
     Black-on-white pitcher, corrugated pots; Plate 16, Gallup Black-
     on-white jug, McElmo Black-on-white bowl, two large corrugated
     jars; and Plate 17, three McElmo Black-on-white bowls and
     Gallup Black-on-white bowl.

85. Breed, William J. 1927 "Hopi Bowls Collected by John Wesley
     Powell." Plateau, Vol. 45, No. 1, pp. 44-46.
         Two Hopi bowls collected by Major Powell and obtained by
     MNA by trade from Canterbury Museum, New Zealand. The
     bowls illustrated on pp. 45-46 are a Hopi Polychrome, possibly
     Polacca Polychrome, and a polychrome bowl with a figure of a
     human face.

86. Breternitz, David A. 1957 "1956 Excavations Near Flagstaff."
     Plateau, Vol. 30, No. 1, pp. 22-30.
         The Matson Site, NA 4375. Two miniature Rio de Flag ves-
     sels were found, one double bowl and a hand molded jar. Draw-
     ing of these vessels on p. 85. The sherd count included pri-
     marily Alameda Brown Ware indicating ceramic dates of AD 900-
     1050.

87. Breternitz, David A. 1959 "Excavations at Nantack Village,
     Point of Pines, Arizona." University of Arizona Anthropological
     Papers, No. 1, Tucson, Arizona.
         Pottery, pp. 24-38. Short chapter on the pottery found
     and some pottery illustrations.
         Illustrations: Three Circle Neck Corrugated: Point of Pines
     Variety, P. 21; Nantack Red-on-brown and Encinas Red-on-
     brown, p. 29.

Intrusives: Mangus Black-on-white, p. 30; Wingate Black-
on red, p. 31.
Miniature vessels, p. 32; worked sherds, pp. 33-34. Descriptions of two new types: Pine Flat Corrugated, pp. 25-27,
ills, pp. 27-28; Nantack Red-on-brown, pp. 29-30. Twenty
whole or restorable vessels were found.

88. Breternitz, David A. 1960 "Excavations at Three Sites in the
Verde Valley, Arizona." Museum of Northern Arizona Bulletin,
No. 34, Flagstaff, Arizona.
Pottery section, pp. 10-13. Verde Brown was the dominant
plain ware, also Tuzigoot Red and Red Smudged were found.
Drawings of vessels and rim shapes.

89. Breternitz, David A. 1960a "Orme Ranch Cave, NA6656."
Plateau, Vol. 33, No. 2, pp. 25-39.
Descriptions of Orme Ranch Plain, pp. 28-29, and Ash
Creek Brown, pp. 29-30. illus., Fig. 3

90. Breternitz, David A. 1963 Archaeological Interpretation of
Tree Ring Specimens for Dating Southwestern Ceramic Styles.
Ph.D. dissertation, University of Arizona, Tucson, Arizona.
"The interpretation of approximately 5,715 dated tree-ring
specimens from about 342 archaeological sites in the American
Southwest is the basis for 'dating' the pottery found in association. The provenience and site situation interpretation for both
the dated tree-ring specimens and the associated pottery is
tabulated for each site and site area which has tree-ring dates,
except when these data are accessible in the literature. Approximately 325 pottery types, varieties, and ceramic categories
are dated on the basis of archaeological associations with tree-
ring specimens. A progressive increase in the amount and
range of traded pottery is noted through time. The increase
in the distribution of various pottery types after about AD 1250
is also accompanied by an increase in attempts to make local
copies of certain pottery types obtained by trade," Abstract.
"Decorated pottery types which occur as trade products tend
to persist in the later archaeological contexts. Southwestern
pottery is distributed in prehistoric times on the basis of hand-
to-hand or person-to-person contact and although the amount of
trade and spatial dispersal increased in time, particularly after
AD 1250, this trade never reaches the same degree of institu-
tionalization that is seen in Mesoamerica. An associated feature
is an emphasis on the trading of small, decorated vessels as
opposed to large, utility or undecorated, ceramic containers,"
Abstract.

91. Breternitz, David A. 1966 "An Appraisal of Tree-Ring Dated
Pottery in the Southwest." Anthropological Papers of the Uni-
versity of Arizona, No. 10, Tucson, Arizona.
The best source for dates of southwest pottery. Lists sites

and indigenous pottery types. Good map of major sites. No
illustrations or descriptions. A revised and shortened version
of the author's doctoral dissertation (Breternitz, 1963).

92. Breternitz, David A. 1982 "The Four Corners Anasazi Ceramic
    Tradition." Arizona Archaeologist, No. 15, pp. 129-148, Ari-
    zona Archaeological Society, Phoenix, Arizona.
       An excellent overview of ceramics in the Four Corners area
    including initial appearance of pottery in this area, transmis-
    sion of pottery techniques, and a summary statement. The
    author concludes that Anasazi ceramics owe their original source
    and subsequent technological developments to a southern source.
    Anasazi potters adapted and adopted rather than innovated.
    Production of redware by oxidation during the final phase of
    firing appears to be the single Anasazi innovation. The basic
    characteristics of ceramics in the Anasazi area are: basic gray
    utility pottery, reduction firing with some oxidation, manufac-
    ture by coil and scrape process, black-on-gray as the first
    decorated type followed by black-on-white, and general shape
    and design similarities are over board areas. Future studies of
    Anasazi ceramics should be based upon tempering material oc-
    curences and distributions.

93. Breternitz, David A.; Gifford, J. C.; and Olson, A. P. 1957
    "Point of Pines Phase Sequence and Utility Pottery Type Re-
    visions." American Antiquity, Vol. 22, No. 4, pp. 412-416.
       As a result of new information, revisions are suggested in
    the sequence of utility pottery found at Point of Pines. Photo-
    graphs of sherds are presented in one plate. Types illustrated
    are all textured pottery types of the Point of Pines region.
    These are Point of Pines Indented Corrugated, Point of Pines
    Plain Corrugated, Prieto Indented Corrugated, Point of Pines
    Patterned Corrugated, Point of Pines Obliterated Corrugated,
    McDonald Grooved Corrugated, McDonald Painted Corrugated,
    McDonald Patterned Corrugated, Reserve Indented Corrugated,
    Reserve Incised Corrugated, Reserve Punched Corrugated, Re-
    serve Plain Corrugated, Tularosa Patterned Corrugated, Three
    Circle Neck Corrugated, and Pine Flat Neck Corrugated.

94. Breternitz, David A.; Rohn, Arthur H.; and Morris, Elizabeth
    A. 1974 "Prehistoric Ceramics of the Mesa Verde Region."
    Museum of Northern Arizona Ceramic Series No. 5, Flagstaff,
    Arizona.
       Good introductory statement, descriptions, and illustrations
    of Mesa Verde pottery. Types described and illustrated are
    Chapin Gray, p. 1; Moccasin Gray, p. 5; Mancos Gray, p. 9;
    Mummy Lake Gray, p. 13; Mancos Corrugated, p. 17; Mesa
    Verde Corrugated, p. 21; Chapin Black-on-white, p. 25; Piedra
    Black-on-white, p. 29; Cortez Black-on-white, p. 33; Mancos
    Black-on-white, p. 37; McElmo Black-on-white, p. 41; Mesa
    Verde Black-on-white, p. 45; Abajo Red-on-orange, p. 49; Abajo

Polychrome, p. 53; Buff Black-on-red, p. 59; and Deadmans
Black-on-red, p. 61.

95. Breternitz, David A.; Rohn, Arthur H.; and Morris, Elizabeth
     A. 1984 "Prehistoric Ceramics of the Mesa Verde Region,"
     2nd edition. Museum of Northern Arizona Ceramic Series, No.
     5, Flagstaff, Arizona. (Published by Interpark, Cortez, Colo-
     rado)
          In addition to the descriptions and illustrations in the first
     edition (1974), this edition includes a brief discussion and
     references to Dolores Corrugated, Dolores Red, and Tin Cup
     Polychrome. An illustration of Dolores Corrugated is included.

96. Brew, John O. 1941 "Preliminary Report of the Peabody Mu-
     seum Awatovi Expedition of 1939." Plateau, Vol. 13, No. 3,
     pp. 37-48, Flagstaff, Arizona.
          General discussion of the work done during this season and
     a description of a reconnaissance of sites in the Jeddito Valley.
     A preliminary sherd analysis and survey of 296 sites indicates
     the following chronological distribution: pure sites, 141; mixed,
     70; occupied and abandoned sites, 61. This was only a pre-
     liminary analysis of sherds on the surface. It appears that
     White Mound Black-on-white may have existed well into the 18th
     century. Final dating of sites must await tree-ring data. No
     descriptions or illustrations of pottery are presented in this re-
     port. (Pottery of Western Mound described in Smith, 1971).

97. Brew, John O. 1946 "Archaeology of Alkali Ridge, Southwest-
     ern Utah." Papers of the Peabody Museum of American Ar-
     chaeology and Ethnology, Harvard University, Vol. 21, Cam-
     bridge, Massachusetts.
          Excellent review of the prehistory of Mesa Verde region of
     the San Juan. Sites include pottery from Basketmaker I to
     Pueblo III. Description and illustrations of Abajo Red-on-
     orange, pp. 261, 263, 265, 268, Figs. 99, 102, 104-109; Mancos
     Black-on-white, pp. 273, 277, Figs. 111-142; Mesa Verde Black-
     on-white, pp. 273, 277, 286, Figs. 151, 153, 166-169; Lino
     Gray, Figs. 99-100; Kana-a Gray, Fig. 99; Abajo Polychrome,
     Fig. 101; Lino and La Plata Black-on-white, Fig. 103; and Cor-
     rugated, Figs. 148-161. Good list of references, pp. 303-314.

98. Briggs, Walter. 1973 "The Cities That Died of Fear." New
     Mexico, Vols. 7-8, pp. 13-24.
          Illustration of Tabira' Polychrome, p. 19.

99. Broder, Patricia J. 1978 Hopi Painting: The World of the
     Hopis. Brandywine Press, New York.
          Chapter 10, Hopi Pottery Motifs. Description and discussion
     of the continuity of motifs on Hopi pottery. Illustrations of
     designs and pottery vessels.

100. Brody, J. J.   1977 <u>Mimbres Painted Pottery</u>. School of Ameri-
      can Research, University of New Mexico Press, Albuquerque,
      New Mexico.
          An excellent study of Mimbres pottery and those who made
      it from the points of view of art and archaeology.
          Good photos of these types of pottery: Mimbres Black-on-
      white, Figs. 2-23, 31, 51, 54, 60, 61, 63, 64, 66, 67, 69-96,
      98-122, 124-178, Plates 6, 7, 10, 11-15; Mangus Black-on-
      white, Figs. 27-30, 32, 33, 40, 68, 97, 123; Dos Cabezas Red-
      on-brown, Fig. 24; Mogollon Red-on-brown, Fig. 25; Sweetwater
      Red-on-gray, Fig. 34; Santa Cruz Red-on-buff, Figs. 35, 39;
      Gila Butte Red-on-buff, Fig. 36; Sacaton Red-on-buff, Fig. 38;
      Kana-a Black-on-white, Fig. 41; Kiatuthlanna Black-on-white,
      Fig. 42; Tunicha Black-on-white, Fig. 43; Rosa Black-on-white,
      Fig. 44; Mesa Verde Black-on-white, Fig. 45; Tularosa Black-
      on-white, Fig. 47; Reserve Black-on-white, Fig. 48; Chuska
      Black-on-white, Fig. 49;Gila Polychrome, Fig. 50; Socorro
      Black-on-white, Fig. 52; Sikyatki Polychrome, Fig. 55, Pl. 5;
      Ramos Polychrome, Fig. 56; Red Mesa Black-on-white, Fig.
      47; Tabira' Black-on-white, Fig. 58; Chupadero Black-on-white,
      Fig. 59; Mimbres Corrugated, Fig. 62; San Ildefonso Black-on-
      black (Maria and Popovida), Fig. 179; Acoma Black-on-white,
      Figs. 181-182; Three Circle Red-on-white, Mimbres Polychrome,
      Pls. 4, 8, 16; and San Clemente Glaze-on-yellow, Pl. 9.
          Also includes a description of the Swarts Site, a typical
      Mimbres village. Maps of village dwelling cultures and Mimbres
      sites. Very good descriptions of Mimbres Black-on-white,
      Mangus Black-on-white, and Mimbres Polychrome.

101. Brody, J. J.   1977a "Mimbres Art: Sidetracked on the Trail
      of a Mexican Connection." <u>American Indian Art Magazine</u>,
      Vol. 2, No. 4, August, pp. 26-31.
          Short article concerning possible relationships between the
      figures on Mimbres Black-on-white pottery and Mexican legends.
      Photos of eight Mimbres Black-on-white bowls.

102. Brody, J. J., et al.   1983 <u>Mimbres Pottery: Ancient Art of</u>
      <u>the American Southwest</u>. American Federation of Arts, Hudson
      Hills Press, New York.
          Tony Berlant presents a good discussion of Mimbres pottery
      from the viewpoint of an artist in the introduction. The Mim-
      bres culture is discussed by Steven A. LeBlanc, and Catherine
      J. Scott presents the evolution of Mimbres Pottery. J. J.
      Brody gives an excellent introduction to Mimbres painting.
      The many excellent black and white and color photos include
      Three Circle Red-on-white, San Francisco Red, Mimbres Cor-
      rugated, Boldface Black-on-white, Mimbres Classic Black-on-
      white, and Mimbres Polychrome. This book was published in
      conjunction with an exhibition of Mimbres pottery which cir-
      culated in January 1984 to October 1985.

103. Bronitsky, Gordon.   1984 "Ceramics and Temper: An Experi-

mental Assessment of the Role of Temper in Durability of
Ceramics." Pottery Southwest, Vol. 11, No. 1, pp. 1-13.
    A grant proposal submitted to the National Science Founda-
tion for funding. This research design is designed to investi-
gate the relationship between ceramic temper and the potential
vessel performance in prehistoric Hohokam vessels.

104. Bronitsky, Gordon. 1986 "Compressive Testing of Ceramics:
     A Southwest Example." Kiva, Vol. 51, No. 2, pp. 85-98.
         Abstract: "Recent research has begun to evaluate the
     utility of selected analytical approaches from the discipline of
     materials science in the characterization of ceramics for the
     archaeological study of social and economic change. Characteri-
     zation describes those features of composition and structure
     of a material that are important for the preparation of a pro-
     duct, the study of its properties, or its ultimate use. Com-
     parative analyses of compressive strength values of samples of
     St. Johns Polychrome and Alameda Plain are presented and the
     ramifications of such characterization for archaeology are dis-
     cussed," p. 85.

105. Brook, Vernon R. 1975 "Some Aberrant Forms of the Jornada
     Branch." Pottery Southwest, Vol. 2, No. 4, pp. 2-5.
         "Two sherds having a rim rest at the base of an El Paso
     Polychrome vessel and an El Paso Brown ware effigy are be-
     lieved to be the first such forms reported for the Jornada
     Branch. Also reported is an El Paso Polychrome effigy," p. 2.

106. Brook, Vernon R. 1977 "Two Unique El Paso Polychrome
     Bowls." Pottery Southwest, Vol. 4, No. 4, October, pp. 3-8.
         "A recent excavation resulted in the recovery of two El
     Paso Polychrome bowls that have unique painted designs on
     both sides of the vessels while one has an oblong shape. The
     exterior painted surfaces and the aberrant shape are the first
     known examples for the ware. One example may be the transi-
     tional form between Jornada Polychrome and El Paso Polychrome,"
     pp. 3-4.
         Both bowls were excavated at the Hot Well Site in 1976 and
     are illustrated and described in detail.

107. Brown, James A. and Freeman, Leslie G. 1962 "A Univac
     Analysis of Sherd Frequencies from the Carter Ranch Pueblo,
     Eastern Arizona." American Antiquity, Vol. 22, Pt. 1, pp.
     162-167.
         The first use of a Univac computer to analyze potsherd
     frequencies in the Southwest.

108. Brown, Jeffrey L. 1974 "Pueblo Viejo Salado Sites and Their
     Relationship to Western Pueblo Culture." Artifact, Vol. 12,
     No. 2, pp. 1-53.
         A report of several sites in the area of the Safford Valley,

Arizona. Discusses pottery from the following sites: Buena
Vista, Whitmer, Mirijilda, Earven Flat, and Yuma Wash. Notes
resemblances between the Pueblo Viejo sites and the Salado
complexes of the Tonto Basin, Gila Basin, and the Reeve Ruin.
The following pottery types are illustrated: Tonto Polychrome,
Fig. 4; Maverick Mountain Black-on-red, Fig. 5; Maverick
Mountain Polychrome, Fig. 5; Salado Polychrome, Figs. 6, 9;
and Gila Polychrome, Figs. 7, 8.

109. Brown, Jeffrey L. and Grebinger, Paul. 1969 "A Lower Ter-
      race Compound at San Cayentano Del Tumacacori." Kiva,
      Vol. 34, Nos. 2-3, pp. 185-198.
          Illustrations of a Peck Red bowl, Ramanote Red-on-brown
      bowls, and a Tanque Verde Red-on-brown bowl, Fig. 2.

110. Brugge, David. 1963 "Navajo Pottery and Ethnology." Nava-
      jo Publications, Series 2, Navajo Tribal Museum, Window Rock,
      Arizona.
          Descriptions of Dinetah Utility, pp. 5-6; Navajo Utility,
      pp. 8-9; Pinyon Utility, pp. 11-12; Gobernador Polychrome,
      pp. 13-14; and Navajo Painted, pp. 16-17; and drawings of
      vessel shapes, p. 29.

111. Brugge, David. 1964 "Navajo Ceramic Practices." South-
      western Lore, Vol. 30, No. 3, pp. 37-46.
          Description of the manufacture of Navajo pottery taken from
      the study of two Navajo potters in 1961.

112. Brugge, David. 1981 "Navajo Pottery and Ethnohistory."
      Navajo Nation Papers in Anthropology, Number 5, Navajo Na-
      tion Cultural Resource Program, Window Rock, Arizona.
          A reprint and update of Brugge, 1963. Contains updated
      descriptions and illustrations of Dinetah Gray, Navajo Gray,
      Pinyon Gray, Gobernador Polychrome, and Navajo Painted.
      New names are proposed as Dinetah Gray, Navajo Gray and Pin-
      yon Gray for Dinetah Utility, Navajo Utility and Pinyon Utility,
      respectively.

113. Brugge, David. 1982 "Apache and Navajo Ceramics." Ari-
      zona Archaeologist, No. 16, pp. 279-298, Arizona Archaeologi-
      cal Society, Phoenix, Arizona.
          This discussion includes origins, typology, early variations,
      later history and conclusions concerning the Navajo and Apache
      series in the Southwest and areas to the east. The Apache
      series and types discussed are Cuartelejo Series: Scott Plain
      and Scott Micaceous; Jicarilla Series: Ocate Micaceous and
      Cimarron Micaceous; Lovitt Series: Lovitt Plain, Lovitt Simple
      Stamped, and Lovitt Mica Tempered; Lipan Series: Lipan
      Gray ("Dark Gray Plainware"); Faraon Series: Perdido Plain;
      and Western Apache Series: a thin-walled gray and a thick-
      walled gray. The Navajo series includes Dinetah Gray, Navajo

Gray, and Pinyon Gray. Navajo painted types briefly discussed are Frances Polychrome, Gobernador Polychrome, and Navajo Painted.

114. Brunson, Judy L. 1985 "Corrugated Ceramics as Indicators of Interaction Spheres." In Ben Nelson (Ed.), Decoding Prehistoric Ceramics, pp. 102-127, Southern Illinois University Press, Carbondale, Illinois.
    "The analysis found at least five corrugated types that are of analytical value: Banded Corrugated, Patterned Corrugated, Obliterated Corrugated, Nonobliterated Indented Corrugated, and Paritally Obliterated Indented Corrugated. Whether one is willing to explain the distribution of corrugated ceramics by using the theory of networks, provinces, and MES units, the fact remains that each corrugated type showed a patterned distribution over the Apache-Sitgreaves Forest. Integration was occurring within definable areas, and areas could be discerned on the basis of corrugated types," p. 127.

115. Bryan, Bruce. 1961 "Initial Report on Galaz Sherds." Masterkey, Vol. 35, pp. 13-18.
    Discussion and illustrations of some of the sherds found during the 1927 excavations at Galaz Ruin in the Mimbres Valley. Table of types found shows 10% were intrusive types indicating Galaz may have been a trade center.

116. Bryan, Bruce. 1962 "An Unusual Mimbres Bowl." Masterkey, No. 36, pp. 29-32.
    The central figure in the interior of this bowl is a jackrabbit; the tip of one ear passes through the broad interior framing line indicating the figure was painted prior to the painting of the framing lines.

117. Bullard, William R. 1962 "The Cerro Colorado Site and Pithouse Architecture in the Southwestern United States Prior to AD 900." Papers of the Peabody Museum of Archaeology and Ethnology, Vol. 44, No. 2, Harvard University, Cambridge, Massachusetts.
    This pithouse village is located eight miles north of Quemado, New Mexico. Two types of pottery, Cerro Colorado Plain and Cerro Colorado Red, were found here and named for this site. Their complete descriptions are found in Wasley, 1959.

118. Bullen, A. K., and Bullen, R. P. 1942 "A Pueblo Cave Site at Tres Piedras, New Mexico." American Antiquity, Vol. 8, No. 1, pp. 57-64.
    Tesuque Smeared-indented and a dark gray plain type were found at this site. Possible relationships to plains pottery types are discussed.

119. Bunzel, Ruth. 1929 The Pueblo Potter. Columbia University

Contributions to Anthropology, No. 3, New York.
Very good general discussion and illustrations of pueblo
pottery, primarily of the historic period. Descriptions and
illustrations of Zuni Polychrome, p. 13; Acoma Polychrome, p.
29; Hopi Polychrome, p. 39; San Ildefonso Polychrome, p. 42;
and San Bernardo Polychrome, p. 79. An excellent discussion
of designs and illustrations of the designs on the above types.

120. Burgh, Robert F. 1959 "Ceramic Profiles in the Western
     Mound at Awatovi." American Antiquity, Vol. 25, No. 2, pp.
     184-202.
         Brief explanation of time sequences in the Western Mound.
     Most of the material appears in Smith, 1971. No illustrations
     of pottery or descriptions.

121. Burgh, Robert F. 1960 "Potsherds and Forest Fires in the
     Pueblo Country." Plateau, Vol. 33, No. 2, pp. 54-56.
         "These observations suggest the possibility of a broader
     application of technical knowledge to general archaeological
     studies of particular relevance for two inquiries already under-
     way in the Southwest. One of these is the problem of pottery
     classification and interpretation of ceramic evidence. The other
     relates to the prehistoric occurrence of forest fires. The
     problem of pottery classification in relation to the technological
     data is so obvious it can be stated in a single sentence. Black-
     on-white sherds that have been oxidized on the surface of
     the ground by exposure to forest fires may in all innocence be
     wrongly classified as to type or in cases of extreme color
     change, classified as trade wares from other districts. The
     application of technological data to establish the location and
     age of prehistoric forest fires in the pueblo country might be
     made by archaeologists now working in the field. If an at-
     tempt were made to collect from the surface oxidized sherds
     of normally Black-on-white types, the feasibility of undertak-
     ing a systematic study might readily be tested," p. 55.

122. Bushnell, George H. and Digby, Adrian. 1955 Ancient Ameri-
     can Pottery. Pitman Publishing Corp., New York.
         Good color illustrations of primarily middle and South Ameri-
     can pottery. Illustrations of Matsaki Polychrome, Pl. 8A;
     Hawikuh Polychrome Pl. 8B; Corrugated jar, Zuni Creek, NM,
     Pl. 1; Black-on-white bird jar, Zuni Creek, NM, Pl. 2A; De-
     velopmental Pueblo Black-on-white seed jar, Mesa Redonda, AZ,
     Pl. 2B; Black-on-white pitcher, Mesa Redonda, AZ, Pl. 3A;
     Black-on-white ladle, Developmental Pueblo, Zuni Creek, NM,
     Pl. 3B; Black-on-white pitcher, Pl. 4A; Two Tularosa Black-
     on-white pitchers, Pl. 4B; White Mountain Redware bowl, Pl.
     5A; Mesa Verde Black-on-white bowl, Pl. 5B; Homolovi Poly-
     chrome bowl, Pl. 6A Polychrome bowl, Kechipawan, NM, Pl.
     6B; Plain duck pot, Kechipawan, NM, Pl. 7; Red-on-yellow
     olla, Kechipawan, NM, Pl. 7A; Sacaton Red-on-buff, Snaketown,

Pl. 9; Casas Grandes Polychrome bowl, Chihuahua, Mexico,
Pl. 10A; and Mimbres Black-on-white geometric bowl, Pl. 10B.

123. Bussey, Stanley D.; Kelly, Richard; and Southward, Judith.
      1976 "LA 4821, Three Rivers, Otero County, New Mexico: A
      Project of Excavation, Stabilization, and Interpretation of a
      Prehistoric Village." Cultural Resources Management Division
      Report No. 69, New Mexico State University, Las Cruces, New
      Mexico.
           "The local ceramics from this site include both oxidized
      (brownwares and terra cottas) and reduced pottery (Chupadero
      Black-on-white), as well as 13 intrusive types," p. 58.
           Description by Southward of Three Rivers Red-on-terra
      cotta, San Andres Red-on-terra cotta, Jornada Red, and
      Brownware. Illustrations of Three Rivers Red-on-terra cotta,
      Chupadero Black-on-white, and worked sherds. This site is
      dated to AD 900-1400.

124. Butcher, Russell D. 1968 "Winged Messengers." El Palacio,
      Vol. 75, No. 1, pp. 39-43, Santa Fe, New Mexico.
           Discussion of bird motifs on pueblo pottery, primarily from
      the 19th century. A few illustrations of bird motifs from Zuni,
      Zia, Acoma, Cochiti, San Ildefonso, and Santo Domingo Pottery.

125. Byers, Douglas S. and Morss, Noel. 1957 "Unfired Clay Ob-
      jects from Waterfall Ruin, Northeastern Arizona." American
      Antiquity, Vol. 23, pp. 81-83.
           A cave ruin in Chinle Wash, about 12 miles above Poncho
      House. Byers excavated Waterfall Ruin in 1933. The pottery
      found was predominantly Deadmans Black-on-red, Kana-a Gray,
      Kana-a Black-on-white and some Black Mesa Black-on-white
      and corrugated ware. Small unfired clay figurines excavated
      may be babes in cradles.

126. Callahan, Martha M. and Fairley, Helen C. 1983 "Rainbow
      Gray: A Distinctive Utility Ware in the Northern Kayenta
      Region." Pottery Southwest, Vol. 10, No. 2, pp. 1-6.
           Description and illustration of Rainbow Gray.

127. Carey, Henry A. 1931 "An Analysis of the Northwestern Chi-
      huahua Culture." American Anthropologist, Vol. 33, No. 3,
      pp. 325-374.
           A good discussion of sites and pottery of Northwestern Chi-
      huahua. Illustrations of Casas Grandes pottery. Descriptions
      of Babicora Polychrome and Huerigos Polychrome.

128. Carlson, Roy L. 1961 White Mountain Redware: A Stylistic
      Tradition in the Prehistoric Pottery of East Central Arizona.
      Ph.D. dissertation, University of Arizona, Tucson, Arizona.
           A thorough study of White Mountain Redware. See. R. L.
      Carlson, 1970, for more readily available source of the results
      and conclusions.

129. Carlson, Roy L. 1963 "Basketmaker III Sites Near Durango,
      Colorado." Colorado Studies in Anthropology, No. 8, Univer-
      sity of Colorado, Boulder, Colorado.
         Pottery and clay discussed, pp. 30-38. Descriptions and
      illustrations of the Basketmaker types of Lino Gray: Durango
      Variety, p. 31, Pls. 10-22; Lino Black-on-gray: Durango
      Variety, pp. 33, Pls. 12-13; and layout and motifs on Lino
      Black-on-gray, Fig. 10. Mudware described, p. 38, Pls. 17-
      18.

130. Carlson, Roy L. 1964 "Two Rosa Phase Pithouses." South-
      Western Lore, Vol. 29, No. 4, March, pp. 69-76.
         Report of excavations made by Earl Morris in 1915. Types
      found at these sites were Rosa Black-on-white, Rosa Brown,
      Rosa Gray, Rosa Neckbanded, Rosa-Gallina Transitional, Piedra
      Black-on-white, Kana-a Black-on-white, and Cortez Black-on-
      white. Illustrations of sherds of all the types listed above.
      Illustration of a Rosa Gray jar and a Rosa-Gallina Transitional
      bowl.

131. Carlson, Roy L. 1965 "Eighteenth Century Navajo Fortresses
      of the Gobernador District." Colorado Series in Anthropology,
      No. 10, University of Colorado, Boulder, Colorado.
         Pottery described and illustrated, pp. 51-90: Gobernador
      Polychrome, p. 51; Gobernador Red-on-yellow, p. 57; Goberna-
      dor Black-on-yellow, p. 64; Dinetah Scored, pp. 64-65; Go-
      bernador Filleted, p. 65; Zuni-Acoma Types: Ashiwi Poly-
      chrome, pp. 68-71; Ashiwi White-on-red, p. 71; Santa Fe
      Types: Puname Polychrome, pp. 75-80; Rio Grande Tewa
      Types: pp. 80-83; and Hopi Types: Payupki Polychrome, pp.
      83-84. Illustrations of Tewa Polychrome, Pl. 34; Ogapoge Poly-
      chrome, Pl. 34; Gobernador Indented, Pl. 36; Pojoaque Poly-
      chrome, Pl. 33; Jemez Black-on-white, Pl. 32; Kotyiti Poly-
      chrome, Pl. 32; Biscuit Black, Pl. 32; and Matsaki Brown-on-
      buff, Pl. 27.

132. Carlson, Roy L. 1970 "White Mountain Redware: A Pottery
      Tradition of East-Central Arizona and Western New Mexico."
      Anthropological Papers of the University of Arizona, No. 19,
      Tucson, Arizona.
         Excellent descriptions and illustrations of 12 types of White
      Mountain Redware. Types described and illustrated are Puerco
      Black-on-red, p. 7; Wingate Black-on-red, p. 11; Wingate
      Polychrome, p. 17; St. Johns Black-on-red, p. 29; St. Johns
      Polychrome, p. 31; Springerville Polychrome, p. 41; Pinedale
      Polychrome, p. 47; Pinedale Black-on-red, p. 53; Cedar Creek
      Polychrome, p. 57; Fourmile Polychrome, p. 65; Showlow Poly-
      chrome, p. 73; Point of Pines Polychrome, p. 77; Heshota
      Polychrome, Heshota Black-on-red, and Kwakina Polychrome,
      p. 82. Chapters on design, styles, and change and continuity
      of White Mountain Redware. Maps of geographical distribution
      of the types covered.

133. Carlson, Roy L. 1977 "Eighteenth Century Painted Pottery from Gobernador District of New Mexico." American Indian Art Magazine, Vol. 2, No. 4, Autumn, pp. 38-43.
    Brief descriptions of all and illustrations of some of the following types of pottery: Gobernador Polychrome, Fig. 3; Ashiwi Polychrome, Fig. 4; Puname Polychrome; and Tewa Polychrome. Color illustrations of Pojoaque Polychrome, Oga-poge Polychrome, and Tewa Black-on-white.

134. Carlson, Roy L. 1982 "The Polychrome Complexes." Arizona Archaeologist, Vol. 15, pp. 201-229, Arizona Archaeological Society, Phoenix, Arizona.
    A very good discussion of the development and historical relationships among the styles of prehistoric polychrome pottery in the Southwest. Includes all the major areas except the Rio Grande glazes. Each area is discussed in relation to the early development and changes that took place in the production of polychrome types. Relationships of the polychromes from one area to another are presented. Carlson suggests that the major role of polychromes may have been ritual. A number of styles of polychromes are illustrated and dates of polychrome types are listed.

135. Carr, Pat. 1979 "Mimbres Mythology." Southwestern Studies, Monograph No. 56, University of Texas, El Paso, Texas Western Press.
    A study of the possible relationships between the figures painted on Mimbres Black-on-white bowls and the myths of the Pueblo people of the Southwest. Figures on one or more bowls are related to the following myths: Creating and Emergence, Kokopelli (the humpbacked flute player), the wandering of the People, Masau'u (skelton man), the Little War Twins, Spider Woman, the flood, Baholikonga (the horned water serpent), Parrot Girl, the Corn Maidens, and the priest's son who lost everything gambling. The writer expresses the hope that further study will provide better understanding of Mimbres and ancient Pueblo mythology. Drawings of the designs on 27 Mimbres bowls are presented in this book.

136. Catanach, George S. 1980 "Long House." National Park Service Publications in Archaeology 7H, Wetherill Mesa Series, Government Printing Office, Washington, D.C.
    Ceramics covered on pages 151-241. The types of pottery found in the excavations of this Pueblo III site are described and illustrated. The most common decorated type is the classic Mesa Verde Black-on-white. It is illustrated by many photos of sherds and restored vessels. Other decorated types illustrated are McElmo Black-on-white, Mancos Black-on-white, Cortez Black-on-white, Piedra Black-on-white, and Chapin Black-on-white. The three undecorated types shown are Mesa Verde Corrugated, Mancos Corrugated, Hovenweep Corrugated,

and a few pieces of early unfired pottery. Worked sherds
and other clay artifacts are described and illustrated.

137.   Cate, Caroline S.   1972   "Pottery Vocabulary for the Amateur
        Archaeologist."   Artifact, Vol. 10, No. 3, pp. 53-58.
        A list of basic archaeological terms and definitions.

138.   Caywood, Louis R.   1966   Excavations at Rainbow House,
        Bandelier National Monument, New Mexico.   National Park
        Service, Southwest Archaeology Center, Globe, Arizona.
        Illustrations: Plate IV, Espinozo Glaze bowls; P. V, Sank-
        awi Black-on-cream bowl; Pl. VI, worked sherds Glaze-on-red,
        Glaze-on-yellow, Plain red ware, and Biscuit ware.

139.   Caywood Louis R., and Spicer, Edward H.   1935   Tuzigoot,
        the Excavation and Repair of a Ruin on the Verde River Near
        Clarkdale, Arizona.   Field Division of Education, National Park
        Service, Berkeley, California.
        Description of Verde-Black-on-gray, p. 50; Bidahochi Black-
        on-white, pp. 52-53; Tuzigood Red, p. 44, illustrations Pls.
        IX, X; Tuzigood White-on-red, p. 50; and Verde Brown, p.
        42, illustrations Pl. VIII.

140.   Chapman, Kenneth, M.   1916   "The Evolution of the Bird in
        Decorative Art."   Art and Archaeology, Vol. 6, pp. 307-316,
        Washington, D.C.
        Discussion of bird motifs in pottery of primitives throughout
        the world. Includes drawings of Southwest pottery.

141.   Chapman, Kenneth, M.   1921   "What the Potsherds Tell."   Art
        and Archaeology, Vol. 11, Nos. 1-2, pp. 39-44, Washington,
        D.C.
        Brief general discussion of how potsherds indicate designs,
        techniques of construction, and painting. Chettro Kettle is
        the primary source of pottery.

142.   Chapman, Kenneth, M.   1922   "Life Forms in Pueblo Pottery
        Decoration."   Art and Archaeology, Vol. 13, pp. 120-122,
        Washington, D.C.
        Brief discussion and a few illustrations of life forms.

143.   Chapman, Kenneth, M.   1923   "Casas Grandes Pottery."   Art
        and Archaeology, Vol. 16, pp. 25-34, Washington, D.C.
        Good illustrations of Casa Grandes plain, black, red, poly-
        chrome. Descriptions of designs.

144.   Chapman, Kenneth, M.   1926   "An Archaeological Site in the
        Jornada Del Muerto, New Mexico."   El Palacio, Vol. 20, No.
        6, pp. 118-122, Santa Fe, New Mexico.
        Potsherds of the following 11 "types" were present at this
        site: Brown without slip, Brown with red slip on one side,

Black-on-red, Mimbres Black-on-white, lower Gila Polychrome,
Casas Grandes Polychrome, Cases Grandes incised or indented,
and Casas Grandes Coiled. A small amount of Rio Grande
Glaze was also found.

145. Chapman, Kenneth, M. 1931 "Indian Pottery." Introduction
to American Indian Art, Pt. II, pp. 3-11, Exposition of Indian
Tribal Arts, Inc., New York.
    A brief introduction to the whole range of American Indian
pottery, emphasizing Southwest prehistoric and historic
ceramics. Illustrated.

146. Chapman, Kenneth, M. 1933 Pueblo Indian Pottery. Vols.
I and II, Editions d'Art C. Nice, France, Szwedzicki.
    Descriptions and illustrations of Cochiti Black-on-cream,
Cochiti Polychrome, Santo Domingo Black-on-cream, Santo
Domingo Polychrome, San Ildefonso Black-on-cream, San Ilde-
fonso Polychrome, San Ildefonso Black-on-red, San Ildefonso
White-on-polished red, San Ildefonso White and Pink-on-
polished red, Tesuque Black-on-cream, and Tesuque Polychrome.
Vessels illustrated are from the Indian Arts Fund Collection.

147. Chapman, Kenneth, M. 1938 The Pueblo Indian Pottery of
the Post Spanish Period. General Series Bulletin, No. 4,
Laboratory of Anthropology, Santa Fe, New Mexico.
    Fourteen page booklet including illustrations of Santa Clara
Black, San Ildefonso Polychrome, Tesuque Polychrome, Santo
Domingo, Santa Ana Polychrome, Zia, Acoma, Zuni, and Hopi
Polychromes.

148. Chapman, Kenneth, M. 1953 The Pottery of Santo Domingo
Pueblo. Memoirs of the Laboratory of Anthropology, Vol. 1,
Santa Fe (first published in 1938), University of New Mexico,
Albuquerque, New Mexico.
    Good discussion and illustrations of designs on Santo Domin-
go pottery, 79 plates. Descriptions of Cochiti Black-on-cream,
p. 6; Cochiti Polychrome, p. 6; Cochiti Black-on-red, p. 6;
Santo Domingo Black-on-cream, and Santo Domingo Polychrome.

149. Chapman, Kenneth, M. 1961 "New Light Upon a Rare South-
western Pottery Type: Starkweather Smudged Decorated."
El Palacio, Vol. 68, No. 4.
    Good descriptions and illustrations of two Starkweather
Smudged Decorated bowls found in the collection of the Art
Institute of Chicago.

150. Chapman, Kenneth, M. 1970 The Pottery of San Ildefonso
Pueblo. School of American Research Monograph, No. 28,
University of New Mexico Press, Albuquerque, New Mexico.
    A definitive study of San Ildefonso pottery, its origins,
forms, decoration, firing, and styles. Illustrations of vessels.

A history of painted Tewa pottery; 174 plates of San Ildefonso
designs. Descriptions of San Ildefonso Black-on-cream, pp.
17-20; San Ildefonso Black-on-red, pp. 21-22; San Ildefonso
Polychrome, pp. 23-27; and Polished Black and Red wares, pp.
33-36. Illustrations of designs of Black-on-cream ware, Pls.
1-59; Black-on-red ware, Pls. 60-90; Polychrome ware, Pls.
91-170; and Matte-on-polished Blackware, Pls. 171-174.

151.   Chapman, Kenneth, M. and Ellis, Bruce. 1951 "The Line-
       Break Problem Child of Pueblo Pottery." El Palacio, Vol. 58,
       No. 9, pp. 251-289, Santa Fe, New Mexico.
           The best article on the puzzling line-break in prehistoric
       and historic Southwest pottery. Prehistoric pottery from four
       museum collections and references to line-breaks in these ves-
       sels. Drawings of line-breaks in pottery designs on historic
       and prehistoric vessels, pp. 258-259. "Summary with no con-
       clusions.... The time and place of origin of the line-break
       are unknown. Its usage may have started in the San Juan
       area near which its first authentic evidences have been found
       on Late Basketmaker III basketry and early Pueblo II pottery.
       In both basketry and pottery the first seven centuries of its
       history were confined to the Southwest and to Anasazi peoples.
       The archaeological record is not complete; however, the pos-
       sibility exists that the idea of the line-break may have been a
       northern trait grafted into the nascent pueblo culture at the
       time of the earliest contact between the Anasazi resident in
       the San Juan or Gobernador and southward moving nomads.
       On pottery its spread during Pueblo II and Pueblo III seems to
       have followed the radiating lines of Chaco influence southwest
       and southeast. In Arizona it was resisted by the Mogollon
       born red and brown wares and the Kayenta Black-on-white
       but later welcomed whole-heartedly by the colorful Middle Gila,
       Little Colorado and Hopi descendents of these austere parents.
       In northern and central New Mexico for the most part it had a
       clear field from the beginning. Nonpueblo peoples, the Apache,
       Navajo, Ute and Paiute in the Southwest and the Pomo and the
       Yuki in California, employed the break in historic times on
       either basketry or pottery or both. Whether or not evidence
       of such usage by any of these groups or their ancestors can
       be pushed back into prehistory is a question which can be
       solved only by archaeology. At present, the prehistoric cul-
       ture of none of them can be more than sketchily pictured.
       The original meaning of the break can only be conjectured,
       concerning recent interpretations perhaps the main conclusion
       deducible from the review of them as given above is that the
       Fourth Annual Report of B.A.E. concerning Cushing's treatise
       has had a wider circulation among the pueblos than is generally
       recognized. The majority of these interpretations however do
       hold with a fair amount of consistency to the theme of the
       women artisan's personal health or rather her avoidance by her
       inclusion of the line-break in her work of ill health and

incapacity which in the long run would endanger the group of
which she is the perpetuating factor. Linking this persistent
and directly stated theme to such facts as (1) the pueblo fer-
tility cult, (2) the general primitive menstrual and pregnancy
taboos, and (3) the widespread primitive beliefs concerning
the circle as a trap or confining element. All as outlined
above, a trail may have come into view which might lead well
back to the break's primal significance. This possibility is
further bolstered by the trait's known history. During the
first two centuries of its proved use on pottery, it seems to
have been a specialized practice employed only upon occasion
for a presumably specific and temporary purpose. Later its
significance evidently changed and became a general craft mark
with many groups. A mark so extensively used that it must
have been important to all of the potters of these groups and
thus to the groups as entities at all times. In such a state
it passed recent eras. It still survives weakly but with the
change pottery has undergone as a factor in Indian life, the
loss of its old household importance and its adaption to a completely new field of white stimulated commercialism. The line-
break no longer has any real reason for existence beyond
identification of the potter's work with the ceramic style of her
tribe. Today if a tourist wants an exit trail of life or being
on a new piece of Indian pottery he may have a hard time finding it outside of Zia, Santo Domingo, or Cochiti, but even at
Cochiti where he will get it whether he wants it or not he will
have to apply his own explanation for the particular freak,"
p. 289.

152. Chenall, Robert G. 1967 "The Silo Site." Arizona Archaeologist, No. 2, December.
      Types at this site were mainly from the Hohokam Colonial
phase. Hohokam decorated types recovered were Estrella Red-
on-gray, Sweetwater Red-on-gray, Snaketown Red-on-buff,
Gila Butte Red-on-buff, Santa Cruz Red-on-buff, and Sacaton
Red-on-buff.
      Hohokam red types: Gila Red, Gila Smudged, Salt Red,
Salt Smudged, Sacaton Red, and Vahki Red. Sosi or Flagstaff
Black-on-white and Trincheras Purple-on-red were the intrusive types at this site. Mentions Civano Plain and Civano
Smudged as described by Schroeder at Gila Pueblo.
      Illustrations of Sacaton Red-on-buff, Santa Cruz Red-on-
buff, Gila Butte Red-on-buff, and Snaketown Red-on-buff,
Fig. 12; Sosi or Flagstaff Black-on-white, Trincheras Purple-
on-red, and "Onionskin" plain, Fig. 12. Worked sherds found
are shown in Fig. 13.

153. Christensen, E. O. 1955 Primitive Art. Thomas Y. Crowell
and Co., New York.
      A general survey with fine illustrations including some of
pueblo pottery.

154. Cibola White Ware Conference. 1958 "Concordances and Pro-
      ceedings." Mimeo, 14 pages, Museum of Northern Arizona,
      Flagstaff, Arizona.
          "The Cibola White Ware, including the majority of mineral
      painted pottery types in the Southwest, has long presented a
      number of problems in ceramic taxonomy. The lack of adequate
      communication and concurrence of opinion between the various
      students who have worked in this ceramic area has hampered
      the formulation of type descriptions of usable status," p. 1.
      At the suggestion of Dr. Paul Martin, Dr. Harold S. Colton
      called a conference at the Museum of Arizona in September
      1958 to discuss the above mentioned problem. "While it is
      obvious that the complete reorganization and adequate descrip-
      tion of the types composing this ware were not affected, cer-
      tain agreements were reached which will simplify future tax-
      onomic effort," p. 1. Types described are White Mound Black-
      on-white, p. 4; Kiatuthlanna Black-on-white, p. 5; Red Mesa
      Black-on-white, p. 6; Puerco Black-on-white, pp. 7-8; Reserve
      Black-on-white, p. 9; and Tularosa Black-on-white, pp. 10-11.
      Piedra Black-on-white was removed from Cibola White Ware
      and placed in San Juan White Ware. Dead River Black-on-
      white is a variety of Kiatuthlanna Black-on-white and should
      be so described. These types need further description: Snow-
      flake Black-on-white, and Kokop Black-on-white. These types
      need further definition: Cebolleta Black-on-white, Wide Ruin
      Black-on-white, Klageto Black-on-white, and Roosevelt Black-
      on-white. Gordon Black-on-white is a Red Mesa Derivative;
      this type also needs better description.

155. Clarke, Elanor P. 1935 "Designs on the Prehistoric Pottery
      of Arizona." Arizona University Social Science Bulletin, No.
      9, Tucson, Arizona, 77 pp.
          Many good colored and black and white illustrations. Some
      are also in Cumming's 1953 book. One of the earliest books
      with color plates. Pottery from the following areas: Kayenta
      pottery, pp. 30-39; Little Colorado pottery, pp. 40-45; Upper
      Gila pottery, pp. 46-47; and Middle Gila pottery, pp. 48-57.

156. Collins, John E. (Introduction) 1974 Nampeyo, Hopi Potter:
      Her Artistry and Legacy. Muckenthaler Cultural Center, Fuller-
      ton, California.
          An illustrated catalog of the Hopi pottery of Nampeyo and
      her descendants. Good introduction covering a brief history
      of Hopi pottery and the history of Nampeyo and her family.
      Photographs of 38 Hopi vessels made by the Nampeyo family
      from various private collections and museums. Types illus-
      trated in addition to modern Hopi are Sikyatki Polychrome and
      Polacca Polychrome.

157. Collins, John E. 1977 Hopi Traditions in Pottery and Painting
      Honoring Grace Chapella. NU Masters Gallery, Alhambra,
      California.

Booklet for an exhibit of 12 Hopi potters and 5 painters,
February-April 1977.

Brief biographies and photos of these Hopi potters: Grace
Chapella, Sadie Adams, Juanita Healing, Patricia Honie, Lorna
Lomakema, Patty Maho, Beth Sakeva, Alma Tahbo, Caroline
Talayumptewa, and Ethel Youvella.   Photo of a bowl by Grace
Chapella.

158.   Collins, Michael B.   1969   "What is the Significance of the
Southwestern Ceramics Found in the Llano Estacado?"   Tran-
actions of the Fifth Regional Archaeological Symposium for
Southwestern New Mexico and Western Texas, pp. 45-49.

"In general, it appears that several explanations account
for the presence of Southwestern ceramics on the Llano Estacado.   Relatively permanent (possibly Puebloan) hunting-
gathering communities seem to have existed; an indigenous
peoples may have received Puebloan ceramics in trade.   It is
even possible, but unlikely, that hunting groups operating out
of the Eastern Puebloan settlements transported some pottery
into the region," p. 46.

159.   Colton, Harold S.   1932   "A Survey of Prehistoric Sites in the
Region of Flagstaff, Arizona."   Bureau of American Ethnology,
Bulletin 104, Washington, D.C.

Potsherds described, pp. 9-13.   List of 23 types of pottery
found.   Illustrations of black-on-white sherds of various types,
Pl. 1; and corrugated potsherds of several types, Pl. 2.   Good
maps of sites.

160.   Colton, Harold S.   1933   "Pueblo III in the San Francisco
Mountains, Arizona."   Museum of Northern Arizona Bulletin,
No. 4, pp. 3-14, Flagstaff, Arizona.

Illustrations of six bowls of Deadmans Black-on-white from
sites in San Francisco Mountains.   The stage called Pueblo III
is determined by a pottery type called Deadmans Black-on-
white.

161.   Colton, Harold S.   1939   "An Archaeological Survey of North-
western Arizona, including the Description of Fifteen New
Pottery Types."   Bulletin 10, Museum of Northern Arizona,
Flagstaff, Arizona.

Descriptions of Boulder Gray, p. 19; Cerbat Brown, p. 8;
Cerbat Red-on-brown, p. 9; Cerbat Black-on-brown, p. 9;
Sandy Brown, p. 11; Aquarius Brown, p. 10; Aquarius Black-
on-gray, p. 16 (synonym Prescott Black-on-brown); Aquarius
Orange, p. 17; Aquarius Black-on-orange, p. 18; Needles Red-
on-buff, p. 12; Topoc Red-on-buff, p. 14; Topoc Buff, p. 13;
and Pyramid Gray, p. 15.

162.   Colton, Harold S.   1939a   "Primitive Pottery Firing Methods."
Museum Notes, Vol. 11, No. 1, Museum of Northern Arizona,
Flagstaff, Arizona.

Discussion of Indian methods of firing pottery in the Southwest.

163. Colton, Harold S. 1939b "The Reducing Atmosphere and Oxidizing Atmosphere in Prehistoric Southwestern Ceramics." American Antiquity, Vol. 4, No. 3, pp. 224-231, Menasha, Wisconsin.
Brief discussion of this subject.

164. Colton, Harold S. 1941 "Black Mesa Black-on-white." American Antiquity, Vol. 7, No. 2, pp. 164-165, Menasha, Wisconsin.
Recommends the name Black Mesa Black-on-white be used rather than Deadmans Black-on-white because of prior publications, wider use, and being more descriptive of the area in which this type is found.

165. Colton, Harold S. 1941a "Winona and Ridge Ruin, Part II, Notes on the Technology and Taxonomy of the Pottery." Museum of Northern Arizona Bulletin, No. 19, Flagstaff, Arizona.
Chapter II, pp. 7-18, general discussion of ceramic technology in the prehistoric Southwest. Chapter III, pp. 18-25, special pottery techniques used at Winona. Taxonomy of pottery types from Winona. Many wares and types were present. The wares and types described are: Angell Brown, pp. 36-38, ill., p. 87; Young's Brown, pp. 38-39, ill., p. 38; Sunset White-on-red, pp. 39-40, ill., p. 40; Sunset Tooled, p. 40; Turkey Hill White-on-red, p. 41, ill., p. 42; Tonto Smudged, pp. 42-43; Chavez Brown, p. 44; Kinnikinnick Brown, pp. 44-45; Hohokam Plain Ware, p. 45; Wingfield Plain, p. 46; Hohokam Buff Ware, pp. 46-47; Shato Black-on-white, pp. 49-50; Chevelon Black-on-white, p. 54; Cibola White Ware, pp. 55-56; Chambers Black-on-white, pp. 56-57, ill., p. 57; Puerco Black-on-white, pp. 58-59, ill., p. 59; Gordon Black-on-white, pp. 60-62, ill., p. 61; Snowflake Black-on-white, pp. 62-63, ill., p. 62; and Cheta Black-on-white, pp. 63-64, ill., p. 64.

166. Colton, Harold S. 1943 "The Principle of Analogous Pottery Types." American Anthropologist, Vol. 45, No. 2, pp. 316-320.
Indicates how the principle of analogous types may be applied to Southwestern pottery and used to distinguish the relationship of prehistoric tribes known as branches.

167. Colton, Harold S. 1946 "The Sinagua: A Summary of the Archaeology of the Region of Flagstaff, Arizona." Musuem of Northern Arizona, Bulletin 22, Flagstaff, Arizona.
Analysis of Pottery Complexes, pp. 18-32. Illustrations of vessels: Lino Black-on-gray bowl, p. 19; Kana-a Black-on-white pitcher and bowl, p. 19; Black Mesa Black-on-white vessels, p. 19; Sosi Black-on-white pitcher and bowl, p. 21; Dogoszhi Black-on-white jar, Flagstaff Black-on-white bowl,

p. 21; Wupatki Black-on-white jars, p. 21; Kayenta Black-on-
white bowl, p. 21; Rio de Flag Brown, eight vessels, p. 24;
Lino Gray bowl, p. 29; Kana-a Gray jar, p. 29; Tusayan Corrugated jars, pp. 29, 31; Deadmans Fugitive Red, p. 30; and
Deadmans Gray pitchers, p. 30. Descriptions of the following
sites with a ceramic analysis for each: Old Caves Pueblo,
NA 72, NA 74; Turkey Tank Fort, NA 113; Turkey Tank
Caves, NA 117; Elden Pueblo, NA 113; Antelope Valley, NA
152, 153; NA 192, NA 194; Wukoki or Tower House, NA 203;
NA 236; 238; Rio de Flag Arroyo, NA 283; The Citadel, NA
355; Nalakihu, NA 358, NA 379; Lomaki Ruin J; Wupatki, NA
405; Sites NA 72-886, pp. 37-87; Sites NA 1121-1975, pp. 88-
167; and Sites NA 2000-3996, pp. 168-247. Methods used in
dating pottery types, p. 248. Pottery wares as indicators of
branches, pp. 255-257. Additional pottery correlations between
sites in the Sinaqua branch and the Chaco and Cibola branches,
Appendix 4, p. 318.

168.   Colton Harold S.   1952 "Pottery Types of the Arizona Strip
       and Adjacent Areas in Utah." Museum of Northern Arizona,
       Ceramic Series, No. 1, Flagstaff, Arizona.
          Description of types. Some illustrations. Descriptions of
       Washington Black-on-gray, p. 39; St. George Black-on-gray,
       p. 41; St. George Fugitive Red, p. 43, North Creek Black-on-
       gray, p. 45; Hurricane Black-on-gray, p. 49; Shinarump gray
       ware, p. 55; Shinarump Corrugated, p. 59; Shinarump White,
       p. 61; Virgin Black-on-white, p. 63; Toquerville Black-on-
       white, p. 65; Moapa Gray ware (Olivine temper), p. 67;
       Boulder Gray, p. 69; Boulder Black-on-gray, p. 71; Moapa
       Gray, p. 73; Moapa Fugitive Red, p. 73; Moapa Corrugated,
       p. 75; Trumbull Black-on-gray, p. 77. Moapa Black-on-gray,
       p. 79; Toroweap Black-on-gray, p. 81; Logandale Gray Ware
       (calcite temper), p. 83; Logandale Gray, p. 85; and Fredonia
       Black-on-gray, p. 53.

169.   Colton, Harold S.   1953 "Potsherds: An Introduction to the
       Study of Prehistoric Southwestern Ceramics and Their Use in
       Historic Reconstruction." Museum of Northern Arizona, Bul-
       letin 25, Flagstaff, Arizona.
          Good general introductory source on the study of South-
       west ceramics. Illustrations of Hopi pottery making, pp. 10-
       11; illustrations of surface treatments, p. 37; illustrations of
       rim forms, p. 44; and illustrations of vessel forms, p. 45.
       Illustrations of sherds of the following design styles: Lino,
       Kana-a, Black Mesa, Sosi, Dogoszhi, Flagstaff, Kayenta, and
       Tularosa. Rules for naming pottery types, pp. 52-53; pottery
       sequences of the Southwest, pp. 75 and 78. Illustrations of
       the following types: Lino Black-on-gray, Kana-a Black-on-
       white, Black Mesa Black-on-white, Sosi Black-on-white, Dogo-
       szhi Black-on-white, Flagstaff Black-on-white, Wupatki Black-
       on-white, and Kayenta Black-on-white.

170. Colton, Harold S. 1955 "Pottery Types of the Southwest."
      Museum of Northern Arizona, Series 3, A., Flagstaff, Arizona.
      Good descriptions and illustrations of the following wares
      and types: Tusayan Gray Ware, 8A; Obelisk Gray, 8A-1;
      Lino Gray, 8A-2; Lino Fugitive Red (variation of Lino Gray),
      8A-3; Lino Black-on-gray, 8A-4; Kana-a Gray, 8A-5; Coconino
      Gray, 8A-9; Tusayan Applique, 8A-10; Tusayan Corrugated,
      8A-11; Moenkopi Corrugated, 8A-12; Kiet Siel Gray, 8A-13.
      Tusayan White Ware, 8B; Kayenta Series--Northeastern Ari-
      zona, Kana-a Black-on-white, 8B-1; Black Mesa Black-on-
      white, 8B-2; Sosi Black-on-white, 8B-3; Dogoszhi Black-on-
      white, 8B-6; Wupatki Black-on-white, 8B-7; Betatakin Black-
      on-white, 8B-8; Tusayan Black-on-white, 8B-9; Kayenta Black-
      on-white, 8B-10. Polacca Series--Southern end of Black Mesa,
      Kia-ko Black-on-white, 8B-11; Bidahochi Black-on-white, 8B-14.
      Virgin Series--Arizona Strip and Southern Utah, Washington
      Black-on-gray, 8B-15; St. George Black-on-gray, 8B-16; St.
      George Fugitive Red, 8B-17; North Creek Black-on-gray, 8B-
      18; Hurricane Black-on-gray, 8B-19. Little Colorado Ware--9A
      (types 1, 2, 3, 4 anticipated when further excavation is done),
      Little Colorado Corrugated 9A-5. Little Colorado White ware,
      9B; St. Joseph Black-on-white, 9B-1; Holbrook Black-on-white,
      9B-2; Padre Black-on-white, 9B-3; Chevelon Black-on-white,
      9B-4; Walnut Black-on-white, 9B-5; and Leupp Black-on-white,
      9B-6.

171. Colton, Harold S. 1955a "Ceramic Depository of the South-
      west." Plateau, Vol. 28, No. 2, pp. 46-47.
      The first portion of this article describes the formation of
      the ceramic depository and indicates the collection now includes
      a large percentage of the known pottery types of Arizona, New
      Mexico, Colorado, Utah, Southern Nevada, and Southeastern
      California. Rules for the Depository:
      "1. As a scientific and public service, the Northern Arizona
      Society of Science and Art, Inc., invites each archaeologist
      who describes a pottery type or ware to place specimens in
      the Ceramic Depository of the Southwest as examples of his
      descriptions.
      2. Each sample should include 8-12 sherds, none to be
      over 4-5 inches in diameter or 1 1/2 inches high. Some sherds
      should show rims, special features, and range of variation.
      3. Sherds deposited in the collection will not be removed
      from the depository for comparison. However, should com-
      parisons be required, and the archaeologist be unable to come
      to Flagstaff, a comparison and report will be made by a staff
      member.
      4. Sherds sent in for comparison must be washed, cal-
      careous deposits removed by acid, and each sherd should
      carry a designative symbol. Sufficient sherds should be in-
      cluded so that the depository can retain an example for future
      reference if it is deemed advisable," p. 47.

172. Colton, Harold S. 1956 "Pottery Types of the Southwest:
      San Juan Red, Tsegi Orange, Homolovi Orange, Winslow
      Orange, Awatovi Yellow, Jeddito Yellow and Sichomovi Red
      Wares." Wares 5A, 5B, 6A, 6B, 7A, 7B, 7C, Museum of
      Northern Arizona Ceramic Series No. 3C, Flagstaff, Arizona.
      Good descriptions and illustrations of the following wares
      and types: San Juan Red Ware, 5A; Abajo Red-on-orange,
      5A-1; Abajo Polychrome, 5A-2; Abajo Black-on-gray, 5A-3;
      Bluff Black-on-red, 5A-4; La Plata Black-on-red, 5A-5; Dead-
      mans Black-on-red, 5A-6; Middleton Black-on-red, 5A-7; Mid-
      dleton Red, 5A-8; Nankoweap Polychrome, 5A-9; Amusovi Poly-
      chrome 5A-10; Machonpi Polychrome 5A-11. Tsegi Orange
      Ware, 5B: Medicine Black-on-red, 5B-1; Tusayan Black-on-
      red, 5B-2; Cameron Polychrome, 5B-3; Citadel Polychrome 5B-
      4; Tsegi Orange, 5B-5; Tsegi Red-on-orange, 5B-6; Tsegi
      Black-on-orange, 5B-7; Tsegi Polychrome, 5B-8; Tusayan
      Polychrome, 5B-9; Dogoszhi Polychrome, 5B-10; Kayenta Poly-
      chrome, 5B-11; Kiet Siel Polychrome, 5B-12; Kiet Siel Black-
      on-red, 5B-13; Jeddito Black-on-orange, 5B-14; Jeddito Poly-
      chrome 5B-15; Klageto Black-on-yellow, 5B-16; Klageto Poly-
      chrome 5B-17; Kintiel Black-on-orange, 5B-18; Kintiel Poly-
      chrome, 5B-19. Homolovi Orange Ware, 6A: Homolovi Cor-
      rugated, 6A-1; Homolovi Plain 6A-2. Winslow Orange Ware, 6B:
      Winslow Series--paste tan, buff, yellow orange, Tuwiuca Orange
      6B-1; Tuwiuca Black-on-orange, 6B-2; Homolovi Polychrome,
      6B-3; Chavez Pass Black-on-red, 6B-4; Chavez Pass Poly-
      chrome, 6B-5, Homolovi Series--dark paste, Black Ax Plain,
      6B-6; Homolovi Black-on-red, 6B-7; Black Ax Polychrome,
      6B-8. Awatovi Yellow Ware, 7A: Jeddito Corrugated, 7A-1;
      Jeddito Plain, 7A-2; Jeddito Tooled, 7A-3. Jeddito Yellow
      Ware, 7B: Huckovi Polychrome, 7B-1; Huckovi Black-on-
      orange, 7B-2; Kokop Polychrome, 7B-3; Kokop Black-on-
      orange, 7B-4; Bidahochi Polychrome, 7B-5; Jeddito Black-on-
      yellow, 7B-6; Jeddito Stippled, 7B-7; Jeddito Engraved, 7B-8;
      Sikyatki Polychrome, 7B-9; Awatovi Polychrome, 7B-10; Kawaioku
      Polychrome, 7B-11; San Bernardo Polychrome, 7B-12; Payupki
      Polychrome, 7B-15; Payupki Black-on-yellow, 7B-16; Polacca
      Polychrome, 7B-17; Walpi Polychrome, 7B-18; Walpi Black-on-
      yellow, 7B-19a; Walpi Yellow, 7B-19b; Hano Polychrome, 7B-
      20; Hano Black-on-yellow, 7B-21. Sichomovi Red Ware, 7C:
      Sichomovi Polychrome, 7C-1; Sichomovi Black-on-red, 7C-3,
      Sichomovi Red.

173. Colton, Harold S. 1958 "Pottery Types of the Southwest:
      Revised Descriptions of Alameda Brown, Prescott Gray, San
      Francisco Mountain Gray Wares." Wares 14, 15, 16, 17, 18,
      Museum of Northern Arizona Ceramic Series No. 3D, Flagstaff,
      Arizona.
           Good descriptions and illustrations of the following wares
      and types: Alameda Brown Ware, 14, Rio de Flag Series: Rio
      de Flag Brown, 14-1; Rio de Flag Smudged, 14-2; Rio de Flag

Tooled, 14-3; Winona Brown, 14-4; Angell Brown, 14-5; Youngs
Brown, 14-6; Turkey Hill Red, 14-7; Turkey Hill Smudged 14-
8; Turkey Hill White-on-red, 14-9. Sunset Series: Sunset
Red, 14-10; Sunset Plain, 14-11; Sunset White-on-red, 14-12;
Sunset Applique, 14-13. Anderson Mesa Series: Kinnikinnick
Brown, 14-14; Kinnikinnick Red, 14-15; Chavez Brown, 14-16;
Grapevine Brown, 14-17; Grapevine Red, 14-18. Verde Valley--
Tonto Series: Tuzigoot Plain, 14-19; Tuzigoot Red, 14-20;
Tuzigoot White-on-red, 14-21; Clear Creek Brown, 14-22;
Hartley Plain, 14-23; Hartley Black-on-brown, 14-24; Verde
Brown 14-25; Verde Red, 14-26; Verde Smudged, 14-27; Hard-
scrabble Brown, 14-28; Polles Brown, 14-29; Pine Brown, 14-
30; Tonto Red, 14-31. Prescott Gray Ware, 17: Verde Black-
on-gray, 17-1; Aquarius Orange, 17-2; Aquarius Black-on-
orange, 17-3; Aquarius Applique, 17-4. San Francisco Mountain Gray Ware, 18: Floyd Gray, 18-1; Floyd Black-on-gray,
18-2; Deadmans Gray, 18-3; Deadmans Fugitive Red, 18-4;
Deadmans Black-on-gray, 18-5; and Kirkland Gray, 18-6.

174. Colton, Harold S. 1965 "Checklist of Southwestern Pottery
      Types." Museum of Northern Arizona Ceramic Series No. 2
      (revised), Flagstaff, Arizona.
          Useful list of pottery types and an excellent bibliography.
      No descriptions or illustrations. Most complete list of types
      and wares and references to sources of descriptions prior to
      present publication. Maps showing geographical distribution
      of pottery wares, p. 4. Appendix 2 gives rules for naming
      and priority, pp. 35-36. Some of these type names are now
      out of date.

175. Colton, Harold S. and Hargrave, Lyndon L. 1937 "Handbook
      of Northern Arizona Pottery Wares." Museum of Northern Ari-
      zona Bulletin 11, Flagstaff, Arizona.
          A valuable early compilation of Anasazi prehistoric pottery
      types and wares. Good descriptions of 189 types and wares.
      Some of these types and ware descriptions have been revised
      since 1937, but this is still a useful volume. Introductory
      chapters have information of use to beginning students and
      avocational archaeologists. Some of this material is also pre-
      sented in Colton's 1953 book, Potsherds. Illustrations of
      sherds or vessels of Linden Corrugated, McDonald Corrugated,
      Bluff Black-on-red, Tusayan Black-on-red, Medicine Black-
      on-red, Citadel Polychrome, Showlow Black-on-red, Homolovi
      Black-on-red, Silver Creek Corrugated, Elden Corrugated,
      Tsegi Red-on-orange, Tusayan Polychrome, Kayenta Polychrome,
      Kiet Siel Polychrome, Wingate Black-on-red, Puerco Black-on-
      red, Winslow Polychrome, Jeddito Black-on-yellow, Bidahochi
      Polychrome, Jeddito Stippled, Lino Black-on-gray, Tusayan
      Corrugated, Deadmans Black-on-white, Walnut Black-on-white,
      Chavez Pass Polychrome, Tsegi Orange, Tsegi Black-on-orange,
      St. Johns Polychrome, Pinedale Polychrome, Fourmile Polychrome,

Showlow Polychrome, Rio de Flag Brown, Walnut Wiped, Coconino Red-on-buff, Lino Gray, Kana-a Gray, Moenkopi Corrugated, Medicine Gray, Coconino Gray, Kana-a Black-on-white, Dogoszhi Black-on-white, Sosi Black-on-white, Betatakin Black-on-white, Kayenta Black-on-white, Flagstaff Black-on-white, Wupatki Black-on-white, Klageto Black-on-white, and Deadmans Black-on-gray. Many of these are the first identified illustrations of these types.

176. Colton, Harold S.; Hargrave, L. L.; and Hubert, V. 1940 "Handbook of Northern Arizona Pottery Wares, Supplement No. 1, Colorado Plates of San Juan Red Ware and Tsegi Orange Ware." Museum of Northern Arizona Bulletin No. 11, Flagstaff, Arizona.
    Color illustrations of Bluff Black-on-red, Pl. 1; Deadmans Black-on-red, Pl. 2; Medicine Black-on-red, Pl. 3; Tusayan Black-on-red, Pls. 4 and 5: Citadel Polychrome, Pls. 4 and 6; Tsegi Orange, Pl. 7; Tsegi Coiled, Pl. 7; Tsegi Black-on-orange, Pl. 7; Tsegi Red-on-orange, Pl. 8; Tsegi Polychrome, Pl. 9; Tusayan Polychrome, Pl. 9; Dogoszhi Polychrome, Pl. 10; Kayenta Polychrome, Pl. 11; and Kiet Siel Polychrome, Pls. 11 and 12.

177. Compton, Carl B. 1956 "An Introductory Survey of Bird-Form Vessels." Bulletin of the Texas Archaeological Society, 27, Austin, Texas.
    Drawings and descriptions of many bird-form vessels from the ancient world and from the Southwestern United States. Sections contain brief discussions of chronology and distribution of bird-form vessels and a bibliography of sources of illustrations.

178. Connolly, Florence 1940 "The Origin and Development of Smudged Pottery in the Southwest." Masters thesis, University of Arizona, Tucson, Arizona.
    The writer concluded that smudged pottery had been made continuously from AD 700 to the present. Smudged pottery was most common in the mountains of east-central Arizona and west-central New Mexico. Smudged pottery developed in the Mogollon Rim area of the Mogollon culture. Woodruff Smudged was the earliest named type of smudged pottery in the Southwest. (As of the date of this publication, smudged pottery was still being made at several of the Pueblos of the Rio Grande.)

179. Connolly, Florence 1940a "Two Pottery Types from East-Central Arizona: A Revised and a New Description." Southwestern Lore, Vol. 5, No. 4, Boulder, Colorado.
    Types described are Silver Creek Corrugated, p. 77, and Silver Creek Plain, pp. 77-78.

180. Cosgrove, Hattie S. and Cosgrove, C. B. 1932 "The Swarts
      Ruin." Papers of the Peabody Museum of American Archaeology
      and Ethnology, Vol. 15, No. 1, Cambridge, Massachusetts.
      Report of excavation during the seasons of 1924-1927. Very
      good study of Mimbres pottery at a rich site in southwestern
      New Mexico. Good illustrations of many Mimbres vessels. Col-
      lection included 963 specimens mostly mortuary vessels. De-
      scriptions and illustrations of Mimbres Classic Black-on-white,
      p. 72, Pls. 81-85, 121-190, and 194-232; Mimbres Boldface
      Black-on-white (synonym for Mangus Black-on-white), p. 76,
      Pls. 86, 108-120; Polychrome Ware, Pls. 192-193; Red or
      Brown Wares, p. 79, Pls. 89-92; Corrugated Wares, p. 83,
      Pls. 94-95; and Mimbres Incised, p. 80. Maps of the Mimbres
      area, the Swarts Ruin, and burials.

181. Cowgill, George L. 1964 "The Selection of Samples from Large
      Sherd Collections." American Antiquity, Vol. 29, No. 4, pp.
      467-473.
      It is suggested that when enormous sherd collections are
      made from a site, it is not necessary or desirable to use the
      total collection for analysis. Lots from each provenience cate-
      gory relevant for each problem and a random sample of each
      lot can be used for analysis. "A relative small number of lots
      from each provenience category will provide an adequate sam-
      ple of common ceramic categories while a larger number of lots
      are needed for rare categories. This procedure ensures that
      certain lots will be preserved in their entirety, while common
      sherd categories may be discarded from other lots if they do
      not add much to any sample of interest," p. 467.

182. Cronin, Constance 1962 An Analysis of Pottery Design Ele-
      ments, Indicating Possible Relationships Between Three Deco-
      rated Types. In "Chapters in the Prehistory of Eastern Ari-
      zona I." Paul S. Martin et al., Chicago Natural History Mu-
      seum, Fieldiana: Anthropology, Vol. 53, pp. 105-114, Chicago,
      Illinois.
      Excavation of seven sites in the Little Colorado drainage in
      1960. Pottery was classified into these five types: Kiatuth-
      lanna Black-on-white, Red Mesa Black-on-white, Reserve Black-
      on-white, Tularosa Black-on-white, and Snowflake Black-on-
      white. The relationships in design among the five types are
      analyzed and discussed.

183. Crotty, Helen K. 1983 Honoring the Dead: Anasazi Ceramics
      from the Rainbow Bridge-Monument Valley Expedition. Mono-
      graph Series No. 22, Museum of Cultural History, University
      of California, Los Angeles, California.
      Published in conjunction with an exhibition of pottery from
      the Rainbow Bridge-Monument Valley Expedition exhibited Oc-
      tober 12 to November 27, 1983. Pottery from a burial ground
      at RB 568, a Pueblo III site near Kayenta, Arizona, is studied

in regard to the social dimensions of mortuary practices. Although the excavations were done in 1937, this is only the second publication concerning the ceramics of this very rich site. Distribution of ceramics and other grave goods by age and sex of the deceased is reported. Two burials of senior women contained 23 ceramic vessels each. A total of over 200 whole or restorable vessels were recovered at RB 568. It was concluded that the assumption that grave goods are articles used by the deceased is not tenable. Also, the differential distribution of grave goods by age and sex indicates some type of social organization. Preferential treatment of senior women indicates high status of women and possibly a matrilineal kinship system. The overall wealth of ceramic grave goods implies a prosperous village and the presence of potters' tools in the very rich burial of a senior woman indicates a possible high status for this craft.

Types illustrated in photographs are Tusayan Corrugated, Sosi Black-on-white, Tusayan Black-on-red, Moenkopi Corrugated, Kayenta Black-on-white, Tusayan Black-on-white, Tsegi Black-on-orange, Tusayan Polychrome, Kiet Siel Polychrome, and Flagstaff Black-on-white. A petrographic analysis of RB 568 ceramics by Beverly M. Larson is presented on pp. 70-75.

184. Crown, Patricia L. 1981 Variability in Ceramic Manufacture at the Chodistaas Site, East-Central Arizona. Ph.D. dissertation, University of Arizona, Tucson, Arizona.

Describes the 197 whole or restorable ceramic vessels found in the excavation of 11 rooms at the Chodistaas Site in east-central Arizona. This site was occupied between AD 1100 and 1250. Study points out the complex nature of ceramic vessel manufacture at this site. The importance of an adequate understanding of technological and formal variability and knowledge of the contexts of manufacture and use are emphasized. The analysis of the ceramics at this site proves the existence of a style of form and formal classes of vessels at one site. Author stresses the questions which can be answered by whole vessels but not by sherds.

185. Cummings, Byron. 1936 "Prehistoric Pottery of the Southwest." Kiva, Vol. 1, No. 2, pp. 1-8, Tucson, Arizona.

A short article with a map showing Southwest cultural areas. A list of types of pottery found in the various drainages. A brief discussion of the changes in manufacture techniques of Southwest pottery such as the introduction of the coiled method of construction. Illustration of Kayenta Black-on-white bowl, p. 8.

186. Cummings, Byron. 1940 Kinishba. Hohokam Museums Association and the University of Arizona, Tucson, Arizona.

Pottery, pp. 77-90. Good illustrations in color drawings of a number of vessels. Most of these are also in Cummings,

1953. Other types illustrated are Kinishba Polychrome, Pl.
26; Fourmile Polychrome, Pl. 32; Kinishba Modified Gila Polychrome, Pl. 11, Late Gila Polychrome, Pls. 3-4, 8, and 9;
Kinishba derivative of St. Johns type, Pls. 17, 18; and Pinedale Black-on-red, Pl. 19.

187. Cummings, Byron. 1953 First Inhabitants of Arizona and the
Southwest. Cummings Publications Council, Tucson, Arizona.
    Chapter on pottery with photos and color illustrations
similar to Clarke, 1935. Pottery, pp. 138-206. Illustrations
of Verde Black-on-gray, p. 145; Kayenta Black-on-white, pp.
147, 164; Kayenta Polychrome, Color Pl. V; Black-on-red, Pl.
VI; Polychrome, Pl. VII, VIII; Variety of Black-on-white, p.
173; Chaco Black-on-white, p. 178; Little Colorado Polychrome,
Pl. IX; St. Johns Polychrome, Pl. X; Pinedale Polychrome,
Pl. XI; Fourmile Polychrome, Pl. XIII; Tularosa Black-on-
white, pp. 184-186; Hopi Brown-on-buff, Pl. XIII; Upper Salt
and Gila Polychrome, Pls. XIV-XX; Gila Polychrome and Chihuahua Ware, p. 196; Hohokam Red-buff, Pls. XXI-XXII;
Gila Polychrome, Pls. XXIII-XXIV; Tucson Polychrome and
Middle Gila, Pl. XIV; and Nogales Polychrome, Pl. XXVIII.

188. Cushing, Frank H. 1886 "A Study of Pueblo Pottery as Illus-
trative of Zuni Culture Growth." Fourth Annual Report of the
Bureau of American Ethnology, pp. 473-521, Washington, D.C.
    Pottery was anticipated by basketry. Discussion of how
basketry influenced the form and designs on early pottery.
Drawings of basketry and pottery. Drawings and discussion
of designs and their symbolism on early Zuni pottery indicates
how early pottery canteens resemble a human breast in form.

189. Dalley, Gardiner F. and McFadden, Douglas A. 1985 "The
Archaeology of the Red Cliffs Site." Cultural Resource Series,
No. 17, Bureau of Land Management, Salt Lake City, Utah.
Ceramics, pp. 142-155.
    Most of the 5,521 sherds recovered from the Red Cliffs
sits in southwestern Utah were local plain gray or local painted
types. No Fremont ceramics were recovered. The local Anasazi ceramics ranged temporally from Basketmaker III to early
Pueblo II.
    Richard Thompson's analysis of the Red Cliff ceramics intro-
duces two new types names: Mesquite Gray and Mesquite
Black-on-gray which are western Anasazi analogs of Lino Gray
and Lino Black-on-gray in the Kayenta Series. The types illustrated are: St. George Black-on-gray, Mesquite Black-on-
gray, Mesquite Gray, and North Creek Gray.

190. Daifuku, Hiroshi. 1961 "Jeddito 264: A Report on the Excavations of a Basketmaker III-Pueblo I Site in Northeastern
Arizona." Papers of the Peabody Museum of Archaeology and
Ethnology, Vol. 33, No. 1, Awatovi Expedition Reports, No.
7, Cambridge, Massachusetts.

Chapter IV pottery, pp. 46-52. Three types of Basketmaker III-Pueblo I Black-on-white sherds were found at this
site: Lino Black-on-gray, La Plata Black-on-white, and White
Mound Black-on-white. Illustrations of Lino Black-on-gray
sherds, Fig. 27; and description of Tallahogan Red, p. 49.
A number of Lino sherds had fugitive red decoration. Later
period types found were Kana-a Black-on-white, Kana-a Gray,
Tusayan Corrugated, Kia-ko Black-on-white, and Sikyatki
Polychrome.

191. Danson, Edward B. 1946 An Archaeological Survey of the
Santa Cruz Valley from the Headwaters to the Town of Tubac,
Arizona. Manuscript, Arizona State Museum, University of
Arizona, Tucson, Arizona.
      A description of Canelo Brown-on-yellow, pp. 29-30. This
type was found only in the San Raphael portion of the Santa
Cruz Valley.

192. Danson, Edward B. 1957 "Archaeological Survey of West
Central New Mexico and East Central Arizona." Papers of the
Peabody Museum of American Archaeology and Ethnology, Vol.
44, No. 1, Cambridge, Massachusetts.
      Pottery, pp. 87-93. Illustrations of sherds of Reserve
Black-on-white and Klageto Black-on-white, Fig. 17. A long
list of types found in the survey is presented on pp. 87-88.
These types range in time from Pre-Pueblo to Pueblo IV. The
relationships of the San Juan Anasazi to Mogollon types in the
southern plateau is mentioned.

193. Danson, Edward B. and Wallace, Roberts M. 1956 "Petrographic Study of Gila Polychrome." American Antiquity, Vol.
22, No. 2, pp. 180-183.
      Conclusions: (1) All Gila Polychrome did not originate from
one site or area but was widely made. (2) Mineral constituents
indicate Gila Polychrome could have been made in the five
valleys studied. (3) Gila Polychrome may have been made at
or near University Indian Ruin, Casa Grande, Gila Pueblo,
Point of Pines, and in the Mimbres areas.

194. Davis, E. Mott. 1963 "A Guide to Pottery Sorting and the
Meaning of Pottery Types and Attributes." Bulletin of the
Texas Archaeological Society, Vol. 34, pp. 189-201.
      Abstract: "This paper reviews basic procedures in the
classification of pottery. Initially specimens are sorted into
descriptive groups made up of similar pieces, the similarities
being based on common attributes--paste, design elements,
and so forth. The next step is the setting up of types which
are, basically, groups of attributes which appear repeatedly
in a given area and time span. The types are established by
tabulating the distribution of descriptive groups. Once established, types can be used in tracing historical relationships

between prehistoric cultures. Attributes can also be used in
this way, independently of types," p. 189.

195. Davis, Emma Lou. 1962 The Magdalena Problem: A Study
      Which Integrates a New Pottery Variety Within the Mesa Verde
      Design Tradition. Manuscript on file at the Mesa Verde Mu-
      seum, Mesa Verde National Park, Colorado.
          A study of sherds from LA1178, Gallinas Valley, New Mexico,
      resulted in the description of Mesa Verde Black-on-white:
      Magdalena Variety, pp. 111-112. Photos of this variety and
      also Cortez Black-on-white, Mancos Black-on-white, McElmo
      Black-on-white, Black Mesa Black-on-white, Sosi Black-on-
      white, Wupatki Black-on-white, Kayenta Black-on-white, Flag-
      staff Black-on-white, St. Johns Polychrome, Tularosa Black-
      on-white, Reserve Black-on-white, Wingate Black-on-red,
      Padre Black-on-white, Walnut Black-on-white, and Mimbres
      Black-on-white.
          The writer concludes that Mesa Verde Black-on-white: Mag-
      dalena Variety was the local production of Mesa Verde potters
      who migrated south to the Gallinas Valley.

196. Davis, Emma Lou. 1964 Anasazi Mobility and Mesa Verde Mi-
      grations. Ph.D. dissertation, University of California, Los
      Angeles, California.
          Description of Magdalena Black-on-white, AD 1250-1350.
          Abstract: "The disturbances previously mentioned had
      initiated stylistic changes in the diagnostic potteries (the sur-
      vey archaeologist's best clues). Intrusions of western peoples
      on the move had introduced carbon pigment and western styl-
      ing in what had previously been a Chacoan style and mineral
      pigment ceramic province. 'Mesa Verde' potteries were a ubi-
      quitous style, like short skirts or compact automobiles. They
      were also an example of cultural drift which, once started,
      became invisible and swept an entire area of subcultures.
      Therefore, when 'Mesa Verde' pottery is discovered in massive
      quantities with no local antecedents on some distant site it is
      probably an indication of migration, but the migrants could
      have been any group from the San Juan area who left home
      after the termination of the Chacoan Ceramic Period and the
      onset of the Mesa Verde Ceramic Period. The trail is lost
      until excavations disclose clusters of specifically Mesa Verde
      traits in some faraway village," p. xvii.

197. Davis, Gordon. 1975a "Cleaning of Pueblo Pottery." Pottery
      Southwest, Vol. 2, No. 2, pp. 7-8.
          Describes a method for removing dust and industrial pol-
      lutants accumulated by pottery during storage.

198. Davis, Gordon. 1975 "Museum Pottery: Patching and Pre-
      paration for Storage." Pottery Southwest, Vol. 2, No. 4, pp.
      5-7.

Presents a 13 step procedure for patching and preparing pottery for storage.

199. Davis, Gordon. 1975b "Mending Pottery." Pottery Southwest, Vol. 2, No. 3, July, pp. 5-6.
     A step-by-step process for mending pottery is described. This process is reversible in case mistakes are made. Supplies needed are listed.

200. Davis, Gordon. 1976 "Pottery Restoration: Mending with Colored Plaster of Paris." Pottery Southwest, Albuquerque Archaeological Society, Vol. 3, No. 2, pp. 8-9.
     Reports results of experiments conducted in the coloring of plaster of Paris for the restoration of pottery.

201. Dean, Jeffrey. 1969 "Chronological Analysis of Tsegi Phase Sites in Northeastern Arizona." Papers of the Laboratory of Tree Ring Research, No. 3, University of Arizona Press, Tucson, Arizona.
     Emphasis is on tree-ring dates of sites in Tsegi Phase. Good map and description of site locations. Lists of ceramic types from the following sites: Betatakin, Kiet Siel, Scaffold House, Swallow's Nest, Lolomaki, Batwoman House, Twin Caves Pueblo, Nagashi Bikin, Calamity Cave, and Long House.

202. De Atley, Susan P. 1973 "A Preliminary Analysis of Patterns of Raw Materials Used in Plainware Ceramics from Chevelon, Arizona." Masters thesis, Department of Anthropology, University of California, Los Angeles, California.
     "Apparent diversity in the use of raw materials in ceramic manufacture is treated in many ways by the archaeologist. It is suggested that the selection of raw materials by primitive potters was not random but was subject to constraints. These constraints tended to standardize the utilization of resources in terms of functional categories and according to economy of labor. A preliminary petrographic analysis was performed on a small sample of plainware sherds from sites in the Chevelon Drainage, east central Arizona. The object was to isolate paste types which would correspond to pottery used for the functional categories of cooking and storage tasks. Two paste types were isolated which conform to the expectations put forth for cooking versus storage wares. These types were used to lay the groundwork for understanding the exploitive strategy employed in the area with regard to those resources which are available and those that are technologically equivalent. At this point, the principle of economy of labor appears to be important in explaining selection of resources among technologically equivalent materials. Consequently, it is possible to utilize constituent analysis of ceramics to gain insight into a population's interaction with its habitat," pp. vi-vii.

203. De Borer, Warren. 1980 "Vessel Shape from Rim Sherds:
      An Experiment on the Effect of the Individual Illustrator."
      Journal of Field Archaeology, Vol. 7, pp. 133-135.
         "Results of an experiment are presented which suggest that
      individual analysts vary systematically in their estimation of
      the diameters and orientations of rim sherds. Implications for
      recording and illustration of ceramic data are discussed," p.
      133.

204. Dedera, Don. 1973 "In Praise of Pueblo Potters." Exxon
      USA, Vol. 12, No. 2, Second Quarter, pp. 1-9.
         General article on contemporary Pueblo pottery and the
      potters. Brief history, description of pottery making, types
      made at various pueblos, and encouragement of this art at
      some pueblos. Illustrations of pottery made by skilled potters
      at a number of the pueblos.

205. Dedrick, Philip. 1958 "An Analysis of the Human Figure Mo-
      tif in North American Prehistoric Painted Pottery." Masters
      thesis, University of New Mexico, Albuquerque, New Mexico.
         A good general study of the types and frequency of human
      figures as they are related to time periods and geographical
      distribution of prehistoric Southwestern pottery. Includes
      illustrations of many vessels with human figures in prehistoric
      types and a modern kiva bowl and ceremonial bowl by Maria
      Martinez.

206. Dedera, Don. 1985 Artists in Clay: Contemporary Pottery
      of the Southwest. Northland Press, Flagstaff, Arizona.
         Presentation on Indian pottery and potters of Arizona and
      New Mexico. Includes Pueblo villages and Navajo, Papago,
      Pima, Maricopa, and Yuma Tribes. Describes prehistoric
      methods of pottery making as they are preserved in today's
      Southwest. A brief description of Mogollon, Hohokam, and
      Anasazi pottery. Illustrations of Lino Black-on-gray, Reserve
      Black-on-white, Mimbres Black-on-white, Santa Cruz Red-on-
      buff, Sikyatki Polychrome, and Fourmile Polychrome. Chapter
      on Arizona potters describes and illustrates pottery of all
      pottery making groups. More lengthy New Mexico chapter
      includes 18 pueblos where at least some pottery is still made
      today. Final section on finding and keeping a worthwhile pot.
      This book is a good introduction to the collecting of pottery
      with excellent photos by Jerry Jacka.

207. Dennis, David M. 1977 "Potters of the Mimbres." Western
      New Mexico Contributions No. 345, in Indian Trader, Vol. 8,
      No. 1, Yuma, Arizona.
         General article with illustrations of 13 Mimbres Black-on-
      white and Mimbres Boldface Black-on-white bowls. Also a re-
      view of studies done on a few bowls.

208. Deutchman, Haree L. 1979 Intra-Regional Interaction on
Black-Mesa and Among the Kayenta Anasazi: The Chemical
Evidence for Prehistoric Ceramic Exchange. Ph.D. dissertation, Southern Illinois University, Carbondale, Illinois.
Abstract: "The identification of intra-regional ceramic exchange among the prehistoric Pueblo II (AD 1050-1200) communities on Black Mesa, Arizona, and among neighboring Kayenta Anasazi groups in the Four Corners Area is the subject
of this investigation."
"The chemical groupings strongly indicate that Sosi and
Dogoszhi were manufactured from different clays. The intra-
regional paste similarity of Dogoszhi tentatively suggests the
exchange of this ceramic."
"The application of chemical analysis to this set of pottery
has proven to be quite valuable in identifying paste composi-
tional differences that would not have been observed by traditional methods of ceramic analysis. The variation of element
abundance and the association of particular archaeological attributes (vessel shape and design style) with ceramic pastes,
offers tentative but compelling evidence for trade. The chemical heterogeneity may be attributable to the exploitation of different raw source procurement zones and locales of manufacture. These small but significant differences between the clays
enable the postulation of intra-regional exchange of pottery
and interaction among the Pueblo II Kayenta Anasazi," abstract.

209. Dillingham, Rick. 1977 "The Pottery of Acoma Pueblo."
American Indian Art Magazine, Vol. 2, No. 4, Autumn, pp.
44-51.
Short description of the historical development of Acoma
pottery from Ako Polychrome to the present.
Color photographs of the following vessels from the collection of the School of American Research: Acomita Polychrome,
Figs. 1, 2, 4; Ako Polychrome, Fig. 3; McCartys Polychrome,
Figs. 5, 7; Trios Polychrome, Fig. 6; Acoma Polychrome, Figs.
8, 10, 11; Zuni Polychrome, Fig. 9; and modern vessels by
Lolita Concho, polychrome, Fig. 12; Marie Z. Chino, black-
on-white, Fig. 13; and Lucy M. Lewis, black-on-white, Fig.
14.

210. Dick, Herbert W. 1965 Picuris Pueblo Excavations. Clearing
House, Springfield, Virginia.
Pottery, pp. 127-147. "As has been mentioned, Picuris
Pueblo is one of the most deeply stratified and longest occupied
sites in the Southwest. In such a site it is only natural that
the ceramic sequence should be of extreme importance. In
addition to isolating three new carbon paint black-on-white
wares that are found in stratigraphic and evolutionary sequence from 1300 to 1696, evidence that local pottery has been
manufactured from 1150 to the present was found," p. 127.

New types described are Talpa Black-on-white, pp. 129-131;
Vadito Black-on-white, pp. 131-134; Trampas Black-on-white,
pp. 134-135; Apodaca Gray, pp. 138-140; Vadito Micaceous,
pp. 142-143; and Penasco Micaceous, p. 144.

211. Dick, Herbert W. 1968 Chapter in: Collected Papers in
Honor of Lynn Lane Hargrave. Albert Schroeder, Ed., Papers
of the Archaeological Society of New Mexico, No. I, Museum of
New Mexico, Santa Fe, New Mexico. (See Schroeder, 1968,
for annotation.)

212. Dickey, Roland. 1957 "The Potters of the Mimbres Valley."
New Mexico Quarterly, Vol. 27, Nos. 1 and 2, Spring and
Summer, pp. 45-51.
   Brief description of Mimbres pottery and statements from
various authorities concerning its uniqueness and excellence.

213. Di Peso, Charles C. 1951 The Babicomari Village Site on the
Babicomari River, Southeastern Arizona. Amerind Foundation,
No. 5, Dragoon, Arizona.
   Descriptions and illustrations of Babicomari Plain, pp. 109-
123, Pls. 46, 47; and Babicomari Polychrome, pp. 123-129,
Pl. 48.

214. Di Peso, Charles C. 1953 The Sobaipuri Indians of the Upper
San Pedro River Valley, Southeastern Arizona. Amerind Founda-
tion, No. 6, Dragoon, Arizona.
   Types described are Sobaipuri Plain, pp. 147-154, Pls. 48-
52; Sobaipuri Red, pp. 157-159; Whetstone Plain, pp. 154-156,
Pl. 53; and Fairbank Plain, pp. 156-157.

215. Di Peso, Charles C. 1956 Upper Pima of San Cayetano del
Tumacacori. Amerind Foundation, No. 7, Dragoon, Arizona.
   Upper Pima and Hohokam Pottery, pp. 271-384. Descriptions
and illustrations of the following types: Ramanote Plain, pp.
298-301; Palopardo Plain, pp. 303-305; Sells Red, pp. 307-309;
Peck Red, pp. 310-313; Tanque Verde Red-on-brown, pp. 321-
323; and San Carlos Brown Smudged, pp. 343-344. Illustrations: Canada del Oro Red-on-brown, p. 355; Rillito Red-on-
brown, p. 355; Rincon Red-on-brown, p. 354; Gila Red and
Salt Red, Pl. 95; Pantano Red-on-brown, Pl. 96; Gila Plain,
Pl. 97; Vahki Plain, Pl. 97; Wingfield Plain, Pl. 97; Sacaton
Red-on-buff, Pl. 97; Santa Cruz Red-on-buff, Pl. 97; Trincheras Purple-on-red, Pl. 99; Nogales Purple-on-red, Pl. 99;
Nogales (Trincheras) Polychrome, Pl. 99; Trincheras Red, Pl.
99; and Dragoon Red, pl. 100. In addition to the above types,
distributions of the following types are given in maps, Figs.
52-53: Tanque Verde Polychrome, Babicomari Polychrome,
Tucson Polychrome, Papago Red, San Carlos Red-on-brown,
Sobaipuri Plain, San Carlos Brown Smudged, Whetstone Plain,
and Trincheras (Altar) Polychrome.

216. Di Peso, Charles C. 1958 C. C. Reeve Ruin of Southwest Arizona: A Study of a Prehistoric Western Pueblo Migration into Middle San Pedro Valley. Amerind Foundation, No. 8, Dragoon, Arizona.
Types described and illustrated are: Gila Black-on-red, pp. 98-99, Fig. 12; Gila Polychrome, pp. 97-98, Pl. 63; Belford Red, p. 104, Pl. 65; Pinto Polychrome, p. 99, Fig. 12; Tonto Polychrome, p. 99, Pl. 63; Gila Red-on-brown, p. 101; Belford Plain, pp. 90-91, Pls. 57-62; Belford Burnished, p. 92, Pl. 58; Belford Perforated Rim, pp. 92-94, Pl. 59; Belford Corrugated, pp. 94-95, Pl. 60; Belford Sobaipuri Plain, pp. 95-96, Pl. 61; Belford Whetstone Plain, p. 96, Pl. 62; Tucson Polychrome, pp. 102-103, Pl. 64; and Tucson Black-on-red, p. 103, Pl. 64.

217. Di Peso, Charles C. 1958a "Western Pueblo Intrusion in the San Pedro Valley." Kiva, Vol. 23, No. 4, pp. 12-16, Tucson, Arizona.
Excavation of the Reeve Ruin located on the summit of a mesa situated on San Pedro River five miles south of Redington, Arizona. Gila and Tucson Polychrome are the principal ceramics at this site. The Ootam Red-on-brown types were conspicuously absent. The Gila Polychrome and Tucson Polychrome pottery styles are believed to have originated in the Pueblo area north of Pimeria Alta in the region between the Mogollon Rim and the Little Colorado River (Haury, 1945).

218. Di Peso, Charles C. 1967 The Amerind Foundation. Amerind Foundation, Dragoon, Arizona.
This booklet describes the Amerind Foundation and its work and includes illustrations of Dragoon Red-on-brown, Trincheras Purple-on-red, Mesa Verde Black-on-white, Pueblo Bonito Black-on-white?, Mimbres Classic Black-on-white, Pecos Glaze bowl, Chupadero Black-on-white, Ramos Polychrome, Upper Pima bowl, Hohokam Red-on-buff, Roosevelt Black-on-white, Tanque Verde Red-on-brown, Sacaton Red-on-buff, Alma Plain, and Kana-a Gray.

219. Di Peso, Charles C. 1969 "The Eleventh Southwestern Ceramic Seminar on Casas Grandes Pottery." Unpublished, Amerind Foundation, Dragoon, Arizona.
Descriptions of the following types: Convento Plainware, p. 1; Convento Scored, p. 1; Convento Corrugated, p. 1; Convento Incised, p. 2; Convento Tool Punched, p. 2; Convento Broad Coil, p. 3; Convento Red, p. 3; Anchondo Red-on-brown, p. 3; Fernando Red-on-brown, p. 3; Victoria Red-on-brown, p. 4; Mata Red-on-brown, p. 5; Leal Red-on-brown, p. 5; Pilon Red-on-brown, p. 5; Pilon Red Rim, p. 5; Mata Polychrome, p. 6; Playas Red, p. 11; Ramos Black, pp. 12-13; Madera Black-on-red, p. 13; Babicora Polychrome, p. 14; Carretas Polychrome, pp. 15-16; Corralitos Polychrome, pp. 16-17; Dublan Polychrome, p. 17; Escondida Polychrome, pp.

18-19; Huerigos Polychrome, pp. 19-20; Ramos Polychrome, pp.
20-21; and Villa Ahumada Polychrome, pp. 22-23.

220. Di Peso, Charles C. 1977 "Casas Grandes Effigy Vessels."
American Indian Art Magazine, Vol. 2, No. 4, Autumn, pp. 32-
37.
Article describing various figures on pottery vessels and
their possible relationships to Meso-American religious figures.
Color illustrations of effigy vessels of Ramos Polychrome, Villa
Ahumanda Polychrome, Carretas Polychrome, Playas Red, and
Ramos Black-on-white.

221. Di Peso, Charles C.; Rinaldo, John B.; and Fenner, Gloria J.
1974 Casas Grandes a Fallen Trade Center of the Gran Chichi-
meca, Volume 6 Ceramics and Shell. Amerind Foundation,
Northland Press, Flagstaff, Arizona.
Detailed descriptions of pottery types found during the extensive excavations at the huge Casas Grandes ruins in Chihuahua, Mexico.
Types described and illustrated: Convento Plainware, pp.
39-40; Convento Scored, pp. 41-42; Convento Scored Rubbed,
pp. 42-43; Convento Patterned Scored, pp. 43-45; Convento
Corrugated, pp. 45-46; Convento Rubbed Corrugated, pp. 47-
48; Convento Vertical Corrugated, pp. 48-49; Convento Pattern
Incised Corrugated, pp. 49-52; Convento Incised, pp. 52-53;
Convento Rubbed Incised, p. 53; Convento Tooled Punched,
pp. 53-54; Convento Cord Marked (not described); Convento
Broad Coiled, p. 55; Convento Red, pp. 55-57; Anchondo Red-
on-brown, pp. 57-59; Fernando Red-on-brown, pp. 59-62;
Victoria Red-on-brown textured, pp. 62-63; Mata Red-on-brown,
pp. 65-68; Leal Red-on-brown, pp. 68-71; Pilon Red-on-brown,
pp. 71-74; Pilon Red Rim, pp. 74-75; Mata Polychrome, pp.
75-76; Casas Grandes Plainware, pp. 108-118; Ramos Plainware,
p. 119; Casas Grandes Scored, pp. 119-122; Casas Grandes
Rubbed Scored, pp. 122-125; Casas Grandes Patterned Scored,
pp. 125-127; Casas Grandes Corrugated, pp. 128-130; Casas
Grandes Rubbed Corrugated, pp. 130-132; Casas Grandes Patterned Incised Corrugated, pp. 132-134; Casas Grandes Incised, pp. 135-138; Casas Grandes Rubbed Incised, pp. 138-
140; Casas Grandes Tooled Punched, pp. 140-143; Casas
Grandes Broad Coil, pp. 143-145; Casas Grandes Armadillo,
pp. 145-146; Playas Red, pp. 147-160; Ramos Black, pp. 160-
168; Madera Black-on-red, pp. 168-182; Ramos Black-on-red,
pp. 182-183; Babicora Polychrome, pp. 183-198; Carretas Polychrome, pp. 198-207; Corralitos Polychrome, pp. 207-220;
Dublan Polychrome, pp. 220-226; Escondida Polychrome, pp.
226-242; Huerigos Polychrome, pp. 242-250; Ramos Polychrome,
pp. 250-299; Villa Ahumada Polychrome, pp. 299-316; San Antonio Plainware, pp. 327-328; San Antonio Red, pp. 328-329;
and San Antonio Red-on-brown (no description), p. 329.

222. Dittert, Alfred E.   1959   "Culture Change in the Cebolleta Mesa
     Region, Central-Western New Mexico."   Doctoral dissertation.
     University of Arizona, Tucson, Arizona.
         Descriptions and illustrations of Northern Gray Corrugated,
     p. 406; Kowina Banded, Kowina Black-on-red, Kowina Black-
     on-white, Kowina Indented, Kowina Polychrome, North Plains
     Black-on-red, and North Plains Polychrome.

223. Dittert, Alfred E. and Eddy, Frank W.   1963   "Pueblo Period
     Sites in the Piedra River Section Navajo Reservoir District."
     Museum of New Mexico Papers in Anthropology, No. 10, Mu-
     seum of New Mexico Press, Santa Fe, New Mexico.
         Description of Payan Corrugated, pp. 95-96 (Mancos Cor-
     rugated, in part).   Illustrations of Arboles Black-on-white,
     Figs. 8, 43; Piedra Black-on-white, Figs. 8, 28, 43; Bluff
     Black-on-red, Fig. 8; Rosa Black-on-white, Figs. 8, 28, 43;
     Rosa Neckbanded, Figs. 8, 28; Rosa Gray, Figs. 8, 9, 28, 29;
     Rosa Brown, Fig. 9; Kana-a Gray, Fig. 28; Arboles Neckbanded,
     Fig. 43; Cortez Black-on-white, Fig. 43; Moccasin Gray, Fig.
     43; Bancos Black-on-white, Fig. 43; Shato Black-on-white, Fig.
     43; Piedra Gray, Fig. 44; Piedra Brown, Fig. 44; Arboles
     Gray, Figs. 46, 59; Payan Corrugated, Fig. 46; and Mancos
     Corrugated, Figs. 47-49.

224. Dittert, Alfred E. and Ruppe, R. J.   1951   "The Archaeology
     of Cebolleta Mesa Region: A Preliminary Report."   El Palacio,
     Vol. 58, No. 4, pp. 116-129.
         During the summers of 1947, 1948, 1949, and 1950, investi-
     gations were carried on in a little known area of west-central
     New Mexico.   This has been designated as the Cebolleta Mesa
     area centering some 20 miles south of Grants, New Mexico,
     and taking its name from the most prominent physical feature.
         Summary and conclusions: "Investigations have revealed a
     predominantly Anasazi population in the area from at least 800
     AD to 1400 AD.   An outstanding characteristic of this area is
     the temper variability.   Of outside influences, the most notice-
     able is the appearance of a substantial amount of brownware
     during the Pueblo II period.   There is reason to believe that
     some of these brownwares are of local manufacture as they ap-
     pear to be direct copies of the numerous gray wares.   This
     could mean that an active exchange of ideas was taking place
     with regions to the south or it may indicate some actual move-
     ment of people.   Cultural similarities with the Pueblo I horizon
     to the north and northwest and later similarities are of those
     to the west especially in the Pueblo III period," p. 129.
         Illustrations from a Pueblo I burial, p. 124; Pottery vessels:
     Kana-a Gray, Forestdale Smudged, Early Cebolleta Black-on-
     white, and a form of Red Mesa Black-on-white (photo is in-
     distinct).   Description of Cebolleta Black-on-white, p. 120.

225. Dittert, Alfred E.; Dickey, F. W.; and Eddy, F. W.   1963a

"Evidences of Early Ceramic Phases in the Navajo Reservoir
District." El Palacio, Vol. 70, Nos. 1-2, pp. 5-12, Santa Fe,
New Mexico.
   Pottery found in Los Pinos Phase sites AD 1-400:   (1) An
unfired vegetal tempered gray ware.   (2) A fired polished
brown ware with sand temper; Sambrito Phase--AD 400-700.
(3) Fired brownware, frequent and locally manufactured,
shapes primarily are small jars, a spouted vessel, and small
narrow canteens. Illustrated in Fig. 3.
   The ceramic information obtained led Dittert to propose at
the Third Ceramic Conference in Flagstaff that: Brownwares
may underlie the total ceramic development in the Four Corners
area.

226.   Dittert, Alfred E.; Dickey, F. W.; and Eddy, F. W. 1963b
       "Excavations at Sambrito Village, Navajo Reservoir District."
       Museum of New Mexico Papers in Anthropology, Museum of New
       Mexico Press, Santa Fe, New Mexico.
          Descriptions and illustrations of Arboles Neckbanded, Ar-
       boles Gray, Piedra Gray, and Piedra Brown.

227.   Dittert, Alfred E. and Plog, Fred. 1980 Generations in Clay:
       Pueblo Pottery of the American Southwest. Northland Press,
       Flagstaff, Arizona.
          A very good presentation of the development of Pueblo
       pottery from Basketmaker to contemporary wares. Good photo-
       graphs and short descriptions of many types. Descriptions
       are not complete but major distinguishing characteristics be-
       tween similar types are listed, making this a very useful book
       for both the layman and the professional archaeologist. One
       of the best overviews of prehistoric pottery of the Anasazi.
          Descriptions of all and photos of most of the following pottery
       types:
          Upper San Juan Brown Ware: Los Pinos Brown, p. 74;
       Sambrito Brown, p. 74; and Rosa Brown, p. 74.
          Tusayan Gray Ware: Lino Gray, p. 74; Obelisk Gray, p.
       74; and Lino Black-on-gray, p. 74.
          Tusayan White Ware: Kana-a Black-on-white, p. 77; Black
       Mesa Black-on-white, p. 78; Sosi Black-on-white, p. 78; Dogo-
       szhi Black-on-white, p. 79; Polacca Black-on-white, p. 79;
       Flagstaff Black-on-white, p. 79; Wupatki Black-on-white, p.
       81; Kayenta Black-on-white, p. 81; Betatakin Black-on-white,
       p. 81; Tusayan Black-on-white, p. 81; Hovapi [sic] Black-on-
       white, p. 81; and Bidahochi Black-on-white, pp. 81 and 136.
          Cibola White Ware: La Plata Black-on-white, p. 85; White
       Mound Black-on-white, p. 136; Kiatuthlanna Black-on-white,
       pp. 136-137; Red Mesa Black-on-white, p. 137; Puerco Black-
       on-white, p. 85; Escavada Black-on-white, p. 85; Gallup Black-
       on-white, p. 85; Chaco Black-on-white, p. 86; Cebolleta Black-
       on-white, p. 137; Reserve Black-on-white, p. 86; Tularosa
       Black-on-white, p. 87; Snowflake Black-on-white, p. 87; and
       Wide Ruins Black-on-white, p. 137.

Little Colorado White Ware: St. Joseph Black-on-white, p.
89; Holbrook A Black-on-white, p. 90; Holbrook B Black-on-
white, p. 90; Padre Black-on-white, p. 90; Walnut Black-on-
white, p. 90; and Leupp Black-on-white, p. 137.
   Mesa Verde White Ware: Chapin Black-on-white, p. 90;
Piedra Black-on-white, p. 90; Cortez Black-on-white, p. 91;
Mancos Black-on-white, p. 91; McElmo Black-on-white, p. 91;
Mesa Verde Black-on-white, p. 92; and Mesa Verde Polychrome,
p. 93.
   Upper San Juan White Ware: Rosa Black-on-white, p. 81;
Piedra Black-on-white, p. 83; Arboles Black-on-white, p. 83;
Bancos Black-on-white, pp. 83, 137; Gallina Black-on-white,
p. 138; Vallecitos Black-on-white, p. 128; and Jemez Black-on-
white, p. 128.
   Early Rio Grande White Ware: San Marcial Black-on-white,
p. 88; Red Mesa Black-on-white: Rio Grande Variety, p. 88;
Kwahe-e Black-on-white, p. 88; Taos Black-on-white, p. 88;
Socorro Black-on-white, p. 88; Chupadero Black-on-white, p.
89; Casa Colorado Black-on-white, p. 89; and Wiyo Black-on-
white, p. 129.
   Biscuit Ware: Abiquiu Black-on-gray, p. 130; Bandelier
Black-on-gray, p. 129; Cuyamungue Black-on-tan, p. 129;
and Sankawi Black-on-cream, p. 129.
   San Juan Red Ware: Abajo Red-on-orange, p. 95; Abajo
Polychrome, p. 95; Bluff Black-on-red, p. 95; Deadmans Black-
on-red, p. 95; Middleton Black-on-red, p. 138; Nankoweap
Polychrome, p. 138; Amusovi Polychrome, p. 138; and Machonpi Polychrome, p. 138.
   Tsegi Orange Ware: Medicine Black-on-red, p. 138; Tusayan Black-on-red, p. 98; Tusayan Polychrome, p. 98; Cameron Polychrome, p. 138; Citadel Polychrome, p. 98; Tsegi
Orange, p. 138; Tsegi Red-on-orange, p. 139; Tsegi Black-on-
orange, p. 139; Tsegi Polychrome, p. 139; Dogoszhi Polychrome,
p. 139; Kayenta Polychrome, p. 139; Kiet Siel Polychrome, p.
139; Kiet Siel Black-on-red, p. 139; Jeddito Black-on-orange,
p. 139; Jeddito Polychrome, p. 139; Klageto Polychrome, p.
139; Klageto Black-on-yellow, p. 139; Kintiel Black-on-orange,
p. 139; and Kintiel Polychrome, p. 139.
   Winslow Orange Ware: Tuwiuca Orange, p. 139; Tuwiuca
Black-on-orange, p. 139; Homolovi Polychrome, p. 139; Chavez
Black-on-red, p. 139; Chavez Polychrome, p. 139; Black Axe
Plain, p. 139; Homolovi Black-on-red, p. 139; and Black Axe
Polychrome, p. 139.
   Jeddito Yellow Ware: Huckovi Polychrome, p. 139; Huckovi
Black-on-orange, p. 139; Jeddito Black-on-yellow, p. 109;
Jeddito Stippled, p. 139; Jeddito Engraved, p. 139; Sikyatki
Polychrome, p. 109; Awatovi Polychrome, p. 139; Kawaioku
Polychrome, p. 139; San Bernardo Black-on-yellow, p. 140;
San Bernardo Polychrome, illus., p. 112; Payupki Polychrome,
p. 131; Polacca Polychrome, p. 140; Walpi Polychrome, p. 140;
Hano Black-on-yellow, illus., p. 33; and Hano Polychrome, p.
31.

White Mountain Red Ware: Puerco Black-on-red, p. 91;
Wingate Black-on-red, p. 102; St. Johns Polychrome, p. 102;
Springerville Polychrome, p. 140; Pinedale Polychrome, p. 102;
Pinedale Black-on-red, p. 102; Cedar Creek Polychrome, p.
102; Fourmile Polychrome, p. 102; Showlow Polychrome, p.
102; Kinishba Polychrome, p. 102; and Point of Pines Poly-
chrome, p. 102.
Rio Grande Glaze A: Los Padillos Glaze Polychrome, p.
124; Agua Fria Glaze-on-red, p. 124; Arenal Glaze Polychrome,
p. 140; Cienguilla Glaze-on-yellow, p. 140; Cieneguilla Glaze
Polychrome, p. 140; Sanchez Glaze-on-red, p. 140; Sanchez
Glaze-on-yellow, p. 140; Sanchez Glaze Polychrome, p. 140;
San Clemente Glaze Polychrome, p. 140; San Clemente Glaze
Polychrome, p. 140; and Pottery Mount Glaze Polychrome, p.
126.
Rio Grande Glaze B: Largo Glaze Polychrome, p. 126;
Largo Glaze-on-red, p. 140; and Medio Glaze Polychrome, p.
140.
Rio Grande Glaze C: Espinozo Glaze Polychrome, p. 125.
Rio Grande Glaze D: San Lazaro Glaze Polychrome, p. 141.
Rio Grande Glaze E: Encierro Glaze Polychrome, p. 141;
Kotyiti Glaze-on-yellow, p. 141; Kotyiti Glaze-on-red, p. 141;
and Cicuye Glaze Polychrome, p. 141.
Later Rio Grande Bichrome Ware: Galisteo Black-on-white,
p. 129; Poge Black-on-white, p. 141; Sakona Black-on-tan,
p. 141; and Powhoge Black-on-red, p. 133.
Later Rio Grande Plain Ware: Potsuwi'i Incised, p. 70;
Potsuwi'i Gray, p. 141; Kapo Gray, p. 141; and Kapo Black,
p. 141.
Later Rio Grande Polychrome Ware: Gobernador Polychrome,
p. 130; Kiua Polychrome, p. 54; Sakona Polychrome, p. 141;
Tewa Polychrome, p. 131; Pojoaque Polychrome, p. 141; Tatungue Polychrome, illus., p. 67; Puname Polychrome, pp.
131, 142; San Pablo Polychrome, illus., p. 131; Trios Polychrome, p. 131; Zia Polychrome, p. 50; and Santa Ana Polychrome, p. 51.
Zuni Wares: Heshotauthla Polychrome, pp. 118, 142; Kwakina Polychrome, p. 142; Pinnawa Glaza-on-white, p. 142; Pinnawa Red-on-white, p. 142; Kechipawan Polychrome, pp. 118,
142; Matsaki Polychrome, p. 123; Hawikuh Polychrome, p. 118;
Ashiwi Polychrome, p. 131; Kiapkwa Polychrome, p. 118; and
Zuni Polychrome, p. 40.
Acoma Ware: Kwakina Polychrome, p. 143; Kechipawan
Polychrome, p. 143; Hawikuh Glaze-on-red, p. 122; Ako Poly-
chrome, p. 143; Acomita Polychrome, p. 143; McCarthys Poly-
chrome, p. 142; Acoma Polychrome, p. 143; and Laguna Poly-
chrome, p. 122.
Illustrations of contemporary, village specific wares: Hopi:
D. Q. Nampeyo, p. 35; Fannie Nampeyo, p. 34; Helen Naja,
Black-on-cream, p. 37; Joy Navasi, polychrome, p. 38; and
Al Colton, Sculptured applique, p. 40.

Acoma Pueblo: Lucy Lewis, Black-on-white, p. 46; Marie
Chino, Black-on-white, p. 46; and Pablita Concho, polychrome,
p. 47.
Other pueblos: Medina, Zia acrylic, p. 51; Santa Clara
Black, pp. 59-60; Santa Clara Polychrome, pp. 62-63; Santa
Clara Red, pp. 61-62, 68-69. San Ildefonso Black-on-black,
p. 66; San Ildefonso Polychrome, p. 68; San Juan Incised, p.
72; San Juan Polychrome, p. 71; San Juan Red/Tan, p. 72;
and Picuris Micaceous, p. 72.

228. Dixon, Keith A. 1956 "The Archaeological Significance of Certain Unusual Pottery Shapes of the Prehistoric Southwest."
Ph.D. dissertation, University of California, Los Angeles, California.
Unusual forms included in this study are agave boxes and
pottery imitations, pp. 14-17; animal shaped vessels, 17 sites,
pp. 18-24; bail handle vessels, 10 sites, pp. 26-30; bird
shaped jars, fairly common, pp. 32-47; bird shaped pitchers,
pp. 53-57; culinary shoe-pots, 12 sites, pp. 58-70; double
bodied communicated vessels, pp. 70-73; double-flare vessels,
pp. 75-79; double neck vessels, pp. 80-83; human effigy vessels, pp. 83-91; legged vessels, 11 sites, pp. 93-96; lobed
jars, 14 sites, pp. 97-100; multi-gobular jars, 24 sites, pp.
102-109; multiple bowls, 7 sites, pp. 109-110; ring vessels,
12 sites, pp. 115-121; stirrup spouted vessels, 23 sites, pp.
123-129; submarine vessels, 10 sites, pp. 131-134; and vege-
table effigies, 11 sites, pp. 134-136.

229. Dixon, Keith A. 1956a "Hidden House, A Cliff Ruin in Syca-
more Canyon, Central Arizona." Museum of Northern Arizona,
Bulletin 29, pottery, pp. 63-65, Flagstaff, Arizona.
Illustrations of Walnut Black-on-white bowl, Fig. 31, and
Walnut Black-on-white bird effigy jar, Fig. 32. Sherds found
on surface were Walnut Black-on-white, Moenkopi Corrugated,
Verde Black-on-gray, and Tusayan Black-on-red (trace).

230. Dixon, Keith A. 1964 "The Acceptance and Persistence of
Ring Vessels and Stirrup-Spout Handles in the Southwest."
American Antiquity, Vol. 29, No. 4, pp. 455-460.
"In the Southwest they first appeared in the San Juan area
around AD 500. Later they were accepted by other Anasazi
and Anasazi-influenced attitudes and persisted to the historic
period. The apparent interest of the early Anasazi in odd
vessel shapes may account for their acceptance of these two
shape concepts by the Anasazi rather than by the Hohokam or
Mogollon. The ring vessels and stirrup tubes may have continued into the historic period because unlike most of the
other odd forms, these had come to be traditional in certain
persisting ceremonial contexts," p. 455. List and map of distribution and references to 12 ring vessels and 25 stirrup spout
handles.

231. Dixon, Keith A. 1976 "Shoe-Pots, Patojos and the Principle
      of Whimsy." American Antiquity, Vol. 41, No. 3, pp. 386-391.
          "The traditional broad category of shoe-shaped pots (or
      bird forms or patojos) is invalid for analytic purposes. It is a
      catchall category for vessels which may have different his-
      tories, uses, and meanings. One kind, the culinary shoe-pot,
      does form a distinctive class with a special use in cooking and
      was widely distributed in space and time.... The following
      recommendations are explained: (1) culinary shoe-pots should
      not be classified with bird or foot effigies, although they some-
      times become effigies as visual puns; (2) they should not be
      grouped with other asymmetrical pots on the single criterion
      of horizontal body elongation without considering the other ves-
      sels attributes; (3) further ethnographic and linguistic field
      investigation should be done while culinary shoe-pots are still
      used; (4) primary and secondary uses of culinary shoe-pots
      should not be confused," p. 386.

232. Dobson, Masil S. 1967 "A Survey of Indian Art with an Em-
      phasis on Southwest Pottery Design." Masters thesis, West
      Virginia University, Morgantown, West Virginia.
          A very general study of limited use. Includes illustrations
      of pottery from Aztec Ruin, Tsankawi, Otowi Pueblo, Sikyatki,
      the Mimbres area, Shuminkya Ruin, Ojo Caliente, Snaketown,
      Elden Pueblo, Little Colorado River, and a few color photo-
      graphs of pottery in the Smithsonian Institution.

233. Dobyns, Henry F. 1959 "A Mohave Potter's Experiment,
      Parker Black-on-red." Kiva, Vol. 24, p. 24.
          Schroeder, 1952, described pottery called Parker Black-on-
      red. This article indicates Dobyns found sherds which sub-
      stantiate the pottery named by Schroeder. Nineteen sherds
      of this type were found; no restorable vessels. Concludes
      that black paint as an experiment was neither widespread nor
      long lived. It is possible that it was the experiment of one
      individual or family.

234. Dobyns, Henry F. and Euler, R. C. 1958 "Tizon Brown Ware."
      Pottery Types of the Southwest Museum of Northern Arizona,
      Ceramic Series, 3D, Ware No. 15, Museum of Northern Arizona,
      Flagstaff, Arizona.
          Descriptions and illustrations of Cerbat Brown, D15-1;
      Cerbat Red-on-brown, D15-2; Cerbat Black-on-brown, D15-3;
      Sandy Brown, D15-4; Aquarius Brown, D15-5; Aquarius Black-
      on-brown, D15-6; and Tizon Wiped, D15-7.

235. Douglas, Frederic H. 1932 Indian Leaflet Series. Vol. 1,
      1930-32, Denver Art Museum, Leaflet No. 6, Pueblo Indian
      Pottery Making, Denver, Colorado.
          Brief description of production and use of Pueblo pottery.
      One photograpy of pottery from historic pueblos.

1931 <u>Leaflet No. 35</u>, Denver Art Museum, Santa Clara and
San Juan Pottery. Short presentation of production and shapes
of pottery from Santa Clara and San Juan Pueblos. One photo
of pottery.
1932 <u>Leaflet No. 47</u>, Denver Art Museum, Hopi Indian Pottery.
Description of manufacture of Hopi pottery. One photo of
pottery.

236. Douglas, Frederic H. 1941 "Santo Domingo Pottery of the
'Aguilar' Type." <u>Clearing House for Southwestern Museums
Newsletter</u>, No. 37, pp. 133-134.
    Describes a type of pottery made at Santo Domingo Pueblo
starting in the early 1900s. This pottery had a black base
with narrow white or red and white lines in geometric designs.
Two sisters, Felipita Garcia and Asuncion Cate, made this
type of pottery until about 1916 when they ceased their pottery
making. The writer states these vessels are often mistaken
for pottery made at Nambe Pueblo.

237. Douglas, Frederic H. and D'Harnoncourt, René. 1941 <u>Indian
Art of the United States</u>. Museum of Modern Art, New York,
New York.
    A few illustrations of historic and prehistoric pottery.
Types illustrated are Acoma Polychrome, p. 26; Mohave Ware,
p. 32; Mesa Verde Black-on-white, p. 99; Sacaton Red-on-
buff, p. 101; Santa Cruz Red-on-buff, p. 102; Socorro Black-
on-white, p. 107; Fourmile Polychrome, p. 108; Sikyatki Polychrome, p. 109; Jeddito Black-on-yellow, p. 110; Zuni Polychrome, p. 123; Santa Clara Black, p. 124; Santo Domingo
Polychrome, p. 125; and San Ildefonso Polished Black and
Papago Black-on-red, p. 204.

238. Douglas, Frederic H. and Raynolds, F. R. (compilers). 1941
"Pottery Design Terminology--Final Report on Questionnaires."
<u>Clearinghouse for Southwest Museums Newsletter</u>, No. 35, pp.
120-124.
    Drawings of design elements with terminology that received
the most votes from a survey of Southwestern archaeologists.
This is the final report on the results of two questionnaires
sent out in an attempt to establish some definite terminology
for the description of Southwestern pottery designs. The first
questionnaire included some 50 designs selected from the most
common pottery decorations. With each design were listed all
the names for that design which could be found in the existing
literature. Only illustrated publications could be used for the
bibliography in order that there be no guesswork as to the
author's meaning. In addition to the designs, a list of definitions were included covering the terms "design," "element,"
"unit," "pattern," and their meanings. Persons to whom the
work was submitted indicated their choices of the names listed
or suggested new ones. The second questionnaire was compiled

from the results of the first. All names which received only
one or two votes or none were discarded and only those names
which seemed generally popular were resubmitted. In addition
some of the best and most pertinent suggestions were included
and some recommendations were made. Also, where names received very strong majorities this was noted. This questionnaire was checked in the same way as the first.

239. Dove, Donald E. 1970 "A Site Survey Along the Lower Agua
     Fria, Arizona." Arizona Archaeologist, No. 5, December, pp.
     1-36.
        Very few decorated sherds were found in this survey; 97%
     of all sherds were Wingfield Plain and 2% were Verde Brown.
     Most of the few painted sherds were Hohokam red-on-buff
     types. A small amount of Gila Plain was also present. Northern
     trade wares found in small numbers were Black Mesa Black-
     on-white, Holbrook Black-on-white, Tusayan Black-on-red, and
     Middleton Black-on-red. The similarity of Wingfield Plain to
     Gila Plain and Verde Brown is discussed. Sherds of the fol-
     lowing types are shown: Holbrook Black-on-white, Black Mesa
     Black-on-white, Aquarius Black-on-orange, Santa Cruz Red-
     on-buff, Sacaton Red-on-buff, and Casa Grande Red-on-buff.

240. Doyel, David E. 1976 "Revised Phase System of the Globe-
     Miami and Tonto Basin Areas, Central Arizona." Kiva, Vol.
     41, Nos. 3-4, pp. 241-266.
        "A proposed realignment of State Route 88 near Miami, Ari-
     zona, necessitated the excavation of eight small prehistoric
     sites. Material culture representative of the Salado, Hohokam,
     and Apache occupations were recovered," p. 241.
        Miami Phase ceramics included the indigenous types, Gila
     Plain and Gila Red, and several intrusive types from the
     north. Tonto Corrugated and Inspiration Red are mentioned
     in the discussion. Sherds of Snowflake Black-on-white, an
     intrusive type, are shown in Fig. 6.

241. Doyel, David E. 1977 "Excavations in the Middle Santa Cruz
     River Valley, Southeastern Arizona." Arizona State Museum
     Contribution to Highway Salvage Archaeology in Arizona, No.
     44, University of Arizona, Tucson, Arizona.
        Descriptions and illustrations of Rio Rico Polychrome, pp.
     38, 40, 82, 86, and Trincheras Purple-on-red, pp. 41-42, 34,
     39, 86. Illustrations of Trincheras Plain, p. 25; Gila Plain,
     p. 25; Rillito Red-on-brown, pp. 34-35, 83; Nogales Polychrome,
     p. 34; Rincon Red-on-brown, pp. 34-82, 83; Red-on-buff
     types, p. 39; and Rincon Red-on-brown (white slipped variant),
     p. 83. Worked sherds are shown on p. 86.

242. Doyel, David E. 1978 "The Miami Wash Project: Hohokam
     and Salado in the Miami-Globe Area, Central Arizona." Con-
     tributions to Highway Salvage Archaeology in Arizona No. 52,
     Arizona State Museum, University of Arizona, Tucson, Arizona.

Description and illustrations of Tonto Plain and Tonto Cor-
rugated. Tonto Plain encompasses Tonto Red (in part), Tonto
Rough and Tonto Brown. Tonto Corrugated includes Tonto
Ribbed and Obliterated Corrugated. Also descriptions of Gila
Plain and Inspiration Red and illustrations of Gila Polychrome
and Tonto Polychrome.

243. Doyel, David E. 1980 "Stylistic and Technological Analysis
of the Dead Valley Ceramic Assemblages." In David E. Doyel
and Sharon S. Debowski (eds.), Prehistory in Dead Valley
East-Central Arizona: The TG&E Springerville Project. Archaeological Series #144, pp. 141-188, Arizona State Museum,
University of Arizona, Tucson, Arizona.

The white ware assemblage at the sites examined in Dead
Valley consisted of primarily Puerco Black-on-white with Reserve Black-on-white, Red Mesa Black-on-white and Tularosa
Black-on-white also present. Sherds of all of three styles
are illustrated. Corrugated and plain sherds were mainly
those with gray paste. The remaining were brown paste types.
The problem of classifying similar white ware types from the
upper Little Colorado region is discussed.

It is concluded that Dead Valley ceramics are more similar
to the Puerco-Zuni region than the Reserve or Snowflake-
Vernon regions. Presence of Mogollon Brown and smudged
wares indicates much trade in this region.

244. Doyel, David E. 1980 "Functional Analysis of Ceramic As-
semblages from Dead Valley." In David E. Doyel and Sharon
S. Debowski (editors), Prehistory in Dead Valley, East-Central
Arizona: The TG&E Springerville Project. Archaeological
Series 144, pp. 205-221. Arizona State Museum, University
of Arizona, Tucson, Arizona.

Functional analyses from Foote Canyon and Coyote Creek
Pueblos, two nearby sites, are reported for comparison. Vessel forms were compared across artifact scatters, agricultural
field houses, and pueblos. No meaningful differences were
found. This is interpreted to mean that the field house sites
may have functioned as extensions of the habitation sites during the growing season.

245. Doyel, David E. 1984 "Stylistic and Petrographic Variability
in Pueblo II Period Cibola Whiteware from the Upper Little
Colorado." In A. P. Sullivan and J. L. Hartman, Prehistoric
Ceramic Variation: Contemporary Studies of Cibola Whiteware.
Anthropological Research Papers #31, Arizona State University,
Tempe, Arizona.

Abstract: "A discussion of two Pueblo II period Cibola
Whiteware design styles, known as Puerco and Reserve, as
they occur in the Springerville region is presented. The key
attributes which identify these styles are described with reference to previous research. Stylistic variation is then discussed

with respect to preliminary results obtained from petrographic
(thin-section) analysis. The results of this research suggest
that ceramic design style varied independently of technology.
Ceramic analysis also contributes to the refinement of perspec-
tives on spatially dispersed subsistence-settlement systems during the Pueblo II period in the Upper Little Colorado," p. 4.

246. Drucker, Phillip. 1941 "Culture Element Distributions XVII--
Yuma--Piman." University of California Anthropological Record,
Vol. 6, No. 3, pp. 107-176.
　　　Description of Pima ware, pp. 107, 176.

247. Dulany, Alan R. and Piggot, John D. 1977 "Preliminary
Technological Analysis of El Paso Brown Ware and Design for
Further Research." In Michael R. Beckes, Prehistoric Cultural
Stability and Change in the Southern Tularosa Basin, Ph.D.
dissertation, University of Pittsburgh, Pittsburgh, Pennsylvania.
　　　Abstract: "Brownware is analyzed by petrographic, X-Ray
diffraction and refiring techniques from selected sites of the
83 El Paso Brown ceramic sites. The results reveal mineralogic
and temperature characteristics which differ spatially related
to geologic provenance of the clay material. Firing tempera-
tures appear to be generally less than 650 degrees centigrade.
Differences in particle sizes and in types of rock fragments
distinguish subgroups within the brownware. Most brownware
is local in origin with only a few exceptions. Two methods of
inference, ethnographic analogy and the concept of mental
template, are used to interpret and reconstruct the technology
of prehistoric potters. A design for further research is suggested," p. 278.

248. Dutton, Bertha P. 1938 "Leyit Kin, A Small House Ruin,
Chaco Canyon, New Mexico, Excavation Report." Monograph
of the School of American Research, No. 7, Santa Fe.
　　　General discussion of types found. Unnamed black-on-white
and brown corrugated wares of Mogollon complex are described.
Most common types found were Kana-a Gray, Escavada Black-
on-white, Gallup Black-on-white, Exuberant Corrugated, and
Red Mesa Black-on-white. Illustrations of worked sherds and
pottery artifacts of various types, Pl. 2.

249. Dutton, Bertha P. 1965 Pocket Handbook: Indians of the
Southwest. Southwestern Association of Indian Affairs, Santa
Fe, New Mexico.
　　　Photographs of historic Pueblo pottery, pp. 88-89. Vessels
from Santa Clara, Santo Domingo, Zuni, Zia, San Juan, Hopi,
San Ildefonso, and Acoma.

250. Dutton, Bertha P. 1966 "Pots Pose Problems." El Palacio,
Vol. 73, No. 1, pp. 5-15.

Illustrations of shapes of Southwestern pottery and descriptions of these shapes.

251. Ebinger, Michael H. 1980 "New Information on Pottery Smudging." Pottery Southwest, Vol. 7, No. 4, October, pp. 1-2. Brief study of the chemical composition of the smudge on prehistoric pottery.

252. Eddy, Frank W. 1961 "Excavations at Los Pinos Phase Sites in the Navajo Reservoir District." Museum of New Mexico Papers, No. 4, Museum of New Mexico, Santa Fe, New Mexico. Ceramics occurring in primary association with the Los Pinos Phase were unfired gray ware probably of local manufacture and fired brown ware which was probably intrusive.

253. Egloff, B. J. 1973 "A Method for Counting Ceramic Rim Sherds." American Antiquity, Vol. 38, No. 3, pp. 351-353. Abstract: "Archaeologists rely upon sherd count to quantify ceramic data. A simple method for counting rim sherds uses the percentage of a vessel's orifice represented by each sherd. This technique can be used to estimate the minimum number of vessels represented by the sherds in any specific category," p. 351.

254. Eidenbach, Peter L. (Editor). 1983 The Prehistory of Rhodes Canyon, New Mexico: Survey and Mitigation. Human Systems Research, Tularosa, New Mexico. Study of four prehistoric sites at the mouth of Rhodes Canyon in the White Sands Missile Range. Documents the prehistoric sequence in the Tularosa Basin. Chapter 10--Rhodes Canyon Ceramics by Regge Wiseman. A section of notes on types and categories of the pottery found and an analysis.

255. Eighth Southwest Ceramic Seminar. 1966 "Rio Grande Glazes." Manuscript at Museum of Northern Arizona, Flagstaff, Arizona. It was agreed to use the alphabetical system devised by Mera to name the Rio Grande Glazes. The groups of types were lettered A through F. The new types described were Sanchez Glaze-on-red; Sanchez Glaze-on-yellow; Sanchez Glaze Polychrome; Pottery Mound Glaze Polychrome, Voll, 1961; Largo Glaze-on-red, Lange, 1968; Medio Glaze Polychrome; Lemitar Glaze-on-yellow, Honea, 1966; Lemitar Glaze Polychrome, Honea, 1966; Polvadera Glaze-on-red; and Polvadera Glaze Polychrome.

256. Ellis, Bruce T. 1953 "Vessel-lip Decoration as a Possible Guide to Southwestern Group Movements and Contacts." Southwestern Journal of Anthropology, Vol. 9, No. 4, pp. 436-457, Albuquerque, New Mexico. Indicates the following four styles of lip decoration: (1) striping with black or red paint; (2) ticking or embellishing with checkered, double linear, or other open design in black

or occasionally white paint; (3) red-slipping, in a slip distinct
from that of decorative zone; (4) leaving the lip undecorated;
it may be covered with body slip or left "in paste." Lip decoration is used to indicate possible movements and contact of
prehistoric people of the Southwest.

257. Ellis, Florence (Hawley). 1966 "On Distinguishing Laguna
      from Acoma Polychrome." El Palacio, Vol. 73, No. 3, pp. 37-
      39.
      Indicates Laguna vessels usually have heavier designs and
      can often be distinguished by temper which is obtained from a
      stone site near Laguna. The use of crushed sherds in smaller
      Laguna vessels complicates identifying some Laguna pottery.

258. Ellis, Florence H. and Brody, J. J. 1964 "Ceramic Strati-
      graphy and Tribal History at Taos Pueblo." American Antiquity,
      Vol. 29, No. 3, pp. 316-327.
      Described types are Taos Micaceous, p. 318; Taos Poge
      Black-on-white, p. 317; and Taos Plain Utility, pp. 317-318.
      "In the succession of pottery types here, heavy designed
      Tewa Polychrome is found in varying amounts from bottom to
      top of the refuse mound. Black-on-white ware disappeared
      and Taos Micaceous ware, developed between AD 1550 and 1600
      (earlier than hitherto thought), became the dominant type.
      Polished Black ware, closely resembling that from the Santa Fe
      Tewa area, but probably made locally, appears in Taos about
      1400 and was at least as common as Taos Micaceous there dur-
      ing the 17th century. Taos Micaceous is the only type made
      today," p. 316.

259. Elwood, Priscilla B. 1978 "Ceramics of Yellow Jacket, Colo-
      rado." Masters thesis, University of Colorado, Boulder, Colo-
      rado.
      An analysis of the ceramic material from three sites near
      Yellow Jacket, Colorado: 5MT-1, Porter Pueblo, and 5MT-3,
      House 3. This includes 49,023 black-on-white sherds and 40
      whole vessels. The major types described from the samples
      were Chapin Gray; Mancos Corrugated; Mesa Verde Corrugated;
      Chapin Black-on-white; Twin Trees Black-on-white; Mancos
      Black-on-white, Types A, B, and C; McElmo Black-on-white,
      and Mesa Verde Black-on-white. Sherds are illustrated in
      Figs. 32-36, and all of the types listed above are illustrated.
      An unusual Mancos Black-on-white anthromorphic vessel from
      Porter Pueblo is described in detail and illustrated.

260. Enger, Walter D. 1950 "Archaeology of Black Rock 3 Cave."
      University of Utah Anthropological Papers, Nos. 1-8, Salt Lake
      City, Utah.
      The investigators found the following three wares in this
      cave site: Shoshoni ware (Stewart), 12.5%; Promontory Ware,
      14%; and Puebloid, 73%.

261.   Erickson, Jonathon E.; Read, Dwight; and Burke, Cheryl.
       1972 "Research Design: The Relationships Between the Pri-
       mary Functions and Physical Properties of Ceramic Vessels and
       Their Implications for Ceramic Distributions on an Archaeologi-
       cal Site." Anthropology UCLA, Vol. 3, pp. 84-95.
       "This paper proposes a method by which relationships be-
       tween primary function(s) of pottery and their physical proper-
       ties can be established. Such information can be combined
       with contextual data within an archaeological site which will
       allow the archaeologist to use the pottery to indicate certain
       kinds of past behavior within an archaeological site," p. 84.

262.   Erickson, John L. and DeAtley, Susan J. 1976 "Reconstruct-
       ing Ceramic Assemblages: An Experiment to Derive Morphology
       and Capacity of Parent Vessels from Sherds." American An-
       tiquity, Vol. 41, No. 1, pp. 484-489.
       Description of an experiment to use modern Tijuana vessels
       to determine the shape and capacity of ceramic vessels from
       their sherds. The results indicate it is possible to recon-
       struct the shape and volume of a vessel quite accurately from
       minimal remains using this technique.

263.   Euler, Robert C. 1959 "Pottery of Southern California Yu-
       mans Compared with Tizon Brown Ware of Arizona." In Ar-
       chaeological Resources of Borrego State Park, Archaeological
       Survey of University of California at Los Angeles, Annual
       Report for 1958-59, pp. 41-44.
       Because of the many similarities between Tizon Brown Ware
       and the pottery of the "Mountain Yumans" of Southern Cali-
       fornia and Northern Baja California, it is suggested that the
       Diegueno and Luiseno types can be included in Tizon Brown
       Ware but not be given the same type names. Illustrations of
       pottery from Borrego State Park, California.

264.   Euler, Robert C. 1971 "A Prehistoric Pottery Cache in Grand
       Canyon." Plateau, Vol. 43, No. 4, pp. 176-184.
       "The cache consisted primarily of four corrugated jars each
       covered with one or more sandstone covers. Inside one jar
       was a small twilled yucca basket; inside another were three
       small Black-on-white jars," p. 176. Types illustrated included
       Moenkopi and Tusayan Corrugated, p. 180; Black Mesa Black-
       on-white, Flagstaff Black-on-white?, and Walnut Black-on-white,
       p. 181.

265.   Euler, Robert C. 1982 "Ceramic Patterns of the Hakataya
       Tradition." Arizona Archaeologist, No. 15, pp. 53-70, Arizona
       Archaeological Society, Phoenix, Arizona.
       Conclusions include: "While many Southwestern peoples ob-
       viously made periodic stylistic changes in their ceramic produc-
       tion, the Patayan, except for some transculturation from the
       Kayenta Anasazi to the Cohonina, did not. The Cerbat, Prescott,

and Cohonina were internally conservative and pottery re-
mained essentially unchanged throughout the known history of
these groups," p. 63.

266.   Euler, Robert C. and Dobyns, H. F.   1961   "Excavations West
       of Prescott, Arizona."   Plateau, Vol. 3, pp. 69-84, Flagstaff,
       Arizona.
            Excavation of an oval rock outline and a masonry pueblo of
       the Chino Phase, 1025-1200 AD? on the Yolo Ranch between
       Bagdad and Camp Wood, Arizona.   Preface includes a discus-
       sion of Prescott Gray Ware in the region.   Sherds found were
       predominantly Prescott Gray Ware with a trace of Tizon Brown,
       Little Colorado White, and San Francisco Mountain Gray Wares.
       Illustrations of sherds: Verde Black-on-gray, Aquarius Black-
       on-gray, p. 77, and Aquarius Polychrome jar, p. 78.   Discus-
       sion of the relationship of this site to the King Ruin and a pit-
       house dug by Shutler in Williamson Valley.

267.   Euler, Robert C. and Dobyns, Henry F.   1985   "The Ethno-
       archaeology of Upland Arizona Yuman Ceramics."   In Charles
       H. Lange (ed.), Collected Papers in Honor of Albert H. Schroe-
       der, Papers of the Archaeological Society of New Mexico #10,
       Ancient City Press, Santa Fe, New Mexico.
            Description of four sites of historic Walapai camps with the
       types of pottery found at each.   Indicates that Walapai, Hava-
       supai, and Yavapai pottery has no significant differences.
            Describes and illustrates the following pieces of pottery:
       Tizon Wiped Jar, p. 80; Tizon Wiped Jar, Sharlot Hall Museum,
       p. 82; Cerbat Brown Jar, Peeples Valley, p. 85; Cerbat Brown
       Jar, Sharlot Hall Museum, p. 86; and Cerbat Brown Jar, p.
       88.
            "In summation, Walapai and Havasupai ceramics are both
       Tizon Brown Ware, distinguished only by a difference in sur-
       face treatment.   Yavapai pottery may have been Tizon Brown
       ware also, perhaps with minor differences, but this cannot as
       yet be stated with certainty," p. 88.

268.   Everitt, Cindy.   1973   "Black on White Mimbres Pottery: A
       Bibliography."   Artifact, The Mimbres Report, Vol. 11, No.
       4, pp. 69-89, El Paso Archaeological Society, El Paso, Texas.
            A good bibliography with a minimum of errors and omissions.
       This is useful for students of the Mimbres.   Brief annotations
       would have added a great deal to this bibliography.

269.   Farmer, Malcolm F.   1942   "Navajo Archaeology of Upper Blanco
       and Largo Canyons, Northwestern New Mexico."   American
       Antiquity, Vol. 8, No. 1, pp. 65-79.
            The two undecorated types recovered from these sites were
       Dinetah Scored and a plain brown ware which may be related
       to Gallina Utility ware.   The decorated type most prevalent was
       an outgrowth of Gobernador Polychrome.   It is red and black

on orange. The second decorated type found was a dull red
on tan, and the third a red and orange on buff. A possible
relationship with the makers of Promontory Ware in northern
Utah is mentioned. Conical bottom vessels suggest a relationship to plains people to the east.

270. Farwell, Robin E. 1981 "Pots, Lids, Plates, and Pukis."
Pottery Southwest, Vol. 8, No. 3, July, pp. 1-2.
Article on the possible functions of round, concave ceramic
"dishes" found at a Mogollon site near Angus, New Mexico.

271. Feder, Norman. 1965 American Indian Art. Harry N. Abrams,
New York, New York.
Pottery illustrations of Zuni Polychrome bowl, Pl. 3; Hopi
Pottery bowl, Polikmana or Butterfly Maiden, Pl. 66; Hopi
Pottery jar, modeled human face, Pl. 67; Hopi Pottery tiles,
Pl. 68; Owl figure, Zuni, Pl. 69; Pottery drum jar, Zuni?, Pl.
70; Acoma Polychrome jar, Pl. 71; Zia, seed bowl, Pl. 72;
Santo Domingo Black-on-cream jar, Pl. 73; Black, Santa Clara
double spout jar, Pl. 74; San Juan incised bowl, Pl. 75; Mo-
have clay doll, Pls. 108, 110; Cocopa pottery figure, Pl. 109;
Maricopa bowl and animal figure, Pl. 112; Pima shallow bowl,
Pl. 114; and Mohave doll in cradle, color Pl. 30.

272. Fenner, Gloria J. 1977 "Flare-Rimmed Bowls: A Sub-type of
Mimbres Black-on-white?" Kiva, Vol. 43, No. 2, pp. 129-140.
"The characteristics of field of decoration, framing lines,
and vessel shape of Mimbres Classic Black-on-white geometric
design bowls from two sites are presented and observations
are made on some of the more obvious correlations. Descriptions from one of the sites suggests that the vessels primary
function was of a utilitarian nature. Comparative data indicate
that the traits under discussion were wide spread in the American Southwest, in time and space, while taxonomic considerations should oblige the student to be circumspect in the way in
which they are used and interpreted," p. 129.

273. Ferg, Alan. 1978 "The Painted Cliffs Rest Area: Excava-
tions Along the Rio Puerco, Northeastern Arizona." Contri-
butions to Highway Salvage Archaeology in Arizona No. 50,
Arizona State Museum, University of Arizona, Tucson, Arizona.
A good discussion of the ceramics found at this Anasazi-
Mogollon site on the Rio Puerco of the west.

274. Ferg, Alan. 1980 "Forestdale Black-on-red: A Type Description and Discussion." Kiva, Vol. 46, Nos. 1-2, pp. 69-98.
A good description based on a number of recently excavated
vessels.
Abstract: "Forestdale Black-on-red was named as a ceramic
type in 1953 by Wendorf on the basis of two vessels. Based
on these vessels and an additional 11 bowls and three sherds

in the Arizona State Museum, a formal description of the type is presented along with a discussion of its chronological position and relationships to other types. Forestdale Black-on-red may be the earliest locally made decorated pottery in the Forestdale area and represents another example of the close interrelationships among painted, plainware, and redware pottery types within the Mogollon ceramic tradition," p. 69.

275. Ferg, Alan. 1981 "Response to Gomolak: Fugitive Red Washes on Early Black-on-white Types." Pottery Southwest, Vol. 8, No. 4, October, pp. 1-2.
    Annotated references to fugitive red treatments on early black-on-white types.

276. Ferg, Alan. 1986 "A Hopi Ceramic Finger Ring." Pottery Southwest, Vol. 13, No. 1, pp. 1-3.
    Description of an unusual historic finger ring made of fired clay from Hopi.

277. Ferg, Alan and Dixon, Keith A. 1983 "Double-Flare Bowls." Pottery Southwest, Vol. 10, No. 4, pp. 207.
    Presents information on the geographic and temporal distribution of double-flare bowls in the Southwest.

278. Ferg, Alan; Rozen, Kenneth C.; Deaver, William C.; Tagg, Martyn D.; Phillips, David A.; and Gregory, David A. 1984 "Hohokam Habitation Sites in the Northern Santa Rita Mountains." Arizona State Museum Archaeological Series, No. 147, Vol. 2, Arizona State Museum, Tucson, Arizona.
    Reports investigation on early Colonial to late Sedentary Hohokam sites in the Tucson Basin. Ceramics found were analyzed. Two new types described are Rincon Black-on-brown and Sahaurita Polychrome.

279. Fewkes, Jesse W. 1895 "Preliminary Account of an Expedition to the Cliff Villages of the Red Rock Country and the Tusayan Ruins of Sikyatki and Awatobi, Arizona in 1895." Annual Report to the Smithsonian Institution, 1895, Washington, D.C., pp. 557-588.
    Early report of Sikyatki and Awatobi with illustrations of Sikyatki Polychrome vessels.

280. Fewkes, Jesse W. 1898 "Archaeological Expedition to Arizona in 1895." 17th Annual Report, 1895-1896, Bureau of American Ethnology, Pt. 2, pp. 519-741, Washington, D.C. (Reprint Rio Grande Press, 1971).
    Good early report on Eastern Arizona ruins primarily Awatobi and Sikyatki. Photos of ruins and pottery from the area called Tusayan Province. Awatobi pottery; colored drawings, Pls. CXI, CXII, CXIII; Sikyatki pottery, colored drawings, Pls. CXI to CXLV. Pottery of Sikyatki, pp. 650-656; coiled

and indented pottery, Pl. CXIX; saucers and slipper bowls,
Pl. CXX; ornamented ladles from Sikyatki, Pl. CXXXI; vases,
bowl, and ladle with figures of feathers, Pl. CXLII; food bowls
with figures of sun, Pl. CLVII; and many drawings of designs
from Sikyatki and Awatobi. First description of what is now
named Jeddito Black-on-yellow, p. 652.

281. Fewkes, Jesse W. 1904 "Two Summers' Work in the Pueblo
Ruins." 22nd Annual Report, Pt. 1, Bureau of American Eth-
nology, Washington, D.C., pp. 3-195.
Illustration: Kwakina Polychrome, Fig. 42b from Fourmile
Ruin. Good illustrations of pottery from these areas: Little
Colorado Ruins, pp. 63-85; Old Shumopovi, pp. 113-118; Kin-
tiel, pp. 130-133; Fourmile Ruin, pp. 141-157; Pueblo Viejo,
pp. 181-191; and color drawing plates of pottery, Pls. XX-XLII.

282. Fewkes, Jesse W. 1909 Ancient Zuni Pottery. Putnam Anniversary Volume, pp. 43-82, G. E. Stechert and Co., New
York, New York.
Good color plates of painted pottery, Pls. 1-5. Illustrations
(color) of Heshotauthla Polychrome, Pls. IV, 8; V2, 4, 7, 8;
Heshotauthla Black-on-red, Pls. II, 10, III, 8; IV, 6; V, 6;
and Kwakina Polychrome, Pls. IV, 4, 5; V, 3. It is concluded
that the resemblance in the decoration and texture of prehistoric and modern Zuni pottery is not very close and the symbolism is radically different. Some possible explanations are
given for the lack of similarity.

283. Fewkes, Jesse W. 1911 "Antiquities of the Mesa Verde National Park." Bureau of American Ethnology, Bulletin 51, Washington, D.C.
Short section on pottery, pp. 67-72. Illustrations of sherds
and bowls, Pl. 23; Black-on-white bowls, Pl. 24; Black-on-
white jar and bowls, Pl. 25; Black-on-white mugs and ladle,
corrugated jar, Pl. 26; Black-on-white kiva jar, Pl. 27; and
yucca jar rests, Pl. 28.

284. Fewkes, Jesse W. 1912 "Casa Grande Arizona." Bureau of
American Ethnology 28th Annual Report, Washington, D.C.
Pottery, pp. 113-142. Very brief discussion. Illustrations
of plain vessels, Pl. 72; painted vessels, Pl. 73; polychrome
bowl, bird's head, p. 136; and bowl designs, pp. 140-141.

285. Fewkes, Jesse W. 1916 "Animal Figures on Prehistoric Pottery
from Mimbres Valley, New Mexico." American Anthropologist,
Vol. 18, No. 4, pp. 535-545, Lancaster, Pennsylvania.
Drawings of 11 Mimbres Black-on-white bowls and animal
figures.

286. Fewkes, Jesse W. 1919 "Designs on Prehistoric Hopi Pottery."
Bureau of American Ethnology, 33rd Annual Report, pp. 211-
283, Washington, D.C. (Dover reprint, 1973).

Good early report of designs on Hopi pottery primarily from
Sikyatki Ruin. Relates pottery designs to history of Hopi
Clans. Drawings of many designs including human, animals,
sky-band, insects, geometrical, rain clouds, sun and stars.
Large drawing of Sikyatki "butterfly bowl," Pl. 90.

287.   Fewkes, Jesse W.   1923   "Designs on Prehistoric Pottery from
the Mimbres Valley, New Mexico." Smithsonian Miscellaneous
Collections, Vol. 74, No. 6, Washington, D.C.
      Drawings of over 100 Mimbres bowls, pp. 27-47; descrip-
tions of human, animal, and geometric designs.

288.   Fewkes, Jesse W.   1924   "Additional Designs on Prehistoric
Mimbres Pottery." Smithsonian Miscellaneous Collections, Vol.
76, pp. 1-46, Washington, D.C.
      Drawings of 93 Mimbres Black-on-white bowls, pp. 29-45;
photo of Mimbres vessels, p. 46; some descriptions of designs
and conjecture about the age of Mimbres pottery.

289.   Fewkes, Jesse W.   1926   "An Archaeological Collection from
Young's Canyon Near Flagstaff, Arizona." Smithsonian Miscel-
laneous Collections, Vol. 77, No. 10, Washington, D.C.
      Illustrations of Redware, smudged interiors, and corrugated,
Pls. 1, 2, 3; Black-on-white ladle, Pl. 3; designs on Black-on-
white bowls, Pls. 4, 5; and unusual "cradle handle" ladles,
Pls. 6, 7.

290.   Fish, Paul R.   1976   "Replication Studies in Ceramic Classification." Pottery Southwest, Vol. 3, No. 4, pp. 4-6.
      Four archaeologists were asked to classify 90 Kayenta
Tusayan Gray and White Ware sherds and their classifications
were compared for agreement. Discrepancy in classification
ranged from 22% to 30% between any two of the participants.
This indicates that data in some studies may be inaccurate due
to the discrepancies among classifiers.

291.   Fitting, James E.   1971   "Burris Ranch Site, Dona Ana County,
New Mexico." Southwestern New Mexico Research Reports, No.
1, Case Western Reserve University, Cleveland, Ohio.
      Surface collections were done in four areas of this site. In
Area 1, sherds were found of the following types and frequencies: Brown utility (Mogollon)--1,281; Mimbres Classic
Black-on-white--19; El Paso Polychrome--5; and Chupadero
Black-on-white--3. Area 2: Brown utility comprised the bulk
of the collection; Mimbres Classic Black-on-white--1; Mimbres
Corrugated--3; Mogollon Red-on-brown--2; and one sherd each
of Mimbres Boldface Black-on-white and Chupadero Black-on-
white. Very few sherds were found in Areas 3 and 4 indicating probable preceramic occupations.

292.   Fitting, James E.   1971a   "Excavation at MC 110, Grant County,

New Mexico." Southwestern New Mexico Research Reports,
No. 2, Case Western Reserve University, Cleveland, Ohio.
Excavations and surface collections produced 2,646 sherds
and one complete brownware bowl.
Ceramics from this site were analyzed by Don Graybill during the spring and fall of 1970 and were classified according
to the types used for the 1967 Mimbres Survey. Painted types
present were Mimbres Classic Black-on-white, Mimbres Boldface Black-on-white, and a group of Mimbres sherds which did
not fit into either category. Also found were Mogollon Red-on-
brown and Three Circle Red-on-white. Chupadero Black-on-
white and El Paso Polychrome were found in lesser frequencies.
Unpainted ceramics were primarily Jornada Series Plain wares
including Jornada Brown, Jornada Red, and Jornada Red
Tooled, a red slipped Jornada type with both tool and string
impressions on the surface. It is similar to the type Playas
Red Incised but has the distinctive large particles of feldspar
in the tempering which Graybill believes mark the Jornada
Series.
Most of the plainwares have a much finer tempering and
were set apart from the Jornada Series. The surface treat-
ments among these plainwares included: scoured plain brown
ware, a clapboard corrugated surface, and a more elaborated
indented corrugated from. Twenty-seven worked sherds were
found at this site.

293.   Fitting, James E. 1971b "The Hermanas Ruin, Luna County,
New Mexico." Southwestern New Mexico Research Reports,
No. 3, Case Western Reserve University, Cleveland, Ohio.
Types found in descending order of frequency were:
Painted wares: Mimbres Classic Black-on-white, Mimbres Bold-
face Black-on-white, Chupadero Black-on-white, Three Circle
Red-on-white, and Mogollon Red-on-brown. Plain wares:
Clapboard Corrugated, Indented Corrugated, Red Slipped,
Plain Scored, and Plain. One small restorable brownware bowl
was found at this site.
Conclusions which can be drawn from the ceramics at the
Harmanas Site are very limited. The first conclusion would be
that the ceramics as a group represent a Mimbres occupation.
Probably an early stage within the Mimbres sequence and a
short intensive period of occupation. Forty-two worked sherds
were found.

294.   Fitting, James E. 1973 "An Early Mogollon Community: A
Preliminary Report on the Winn Canyon Site." Artifact, Vol.
11, Nos. 1, 2, 3, El Paso Archaeological Society, El Paso,
Texas.
The Alma Series, 94%, and the San Francisco Series, 6%,
were the only ceramic wares found at this early Mogollon site.
Finer classifications were not attempted. A total of 7,600 sherds
including 136 rim sherds were found. This report contains a
sketch map of sites in the Cliff-Gila Valley.

295. Fitzgerald, Gerald X. (Editor). 1973 "The Mimbres Report."
      Artifact, Vol. 11, No. 4, El Paso Archaeological Society, El
      Paso, Texas.
      This entire number is devoted to the Mimbres culture of
      southwest New Mexico. Articles include:
      (I.) Introduction: The Mimbres Branch of the Mogollon,
      Paul E. Palmer, Jr., pp. 1-4. (II.) A Mimbres Stone Effigy
      Vessel, Stephen Lekson and Timothy Klinger, pp. 5-7. (III.)
      A Major Mimbres Collection by Camera: Life Among the Mim-
      brenos as Depicted by the Designs on Their Pottery, O. T.
      Snodgrass (73 drawings of Mimbres pottery designs), pp. 8-
      65. (IV.) A Bead Cache from Saige-McFarland, A Mimbres Site
      in Southwestern New Mexico, Timothy Klinger and Stephen
      Lekson, pp. 66-68. (V.) Black-on-white Mimbres Pottery--A
      Bibliography, Cindi Everitt, pp. 69-98 (an excellent biblio-
      graphy).

296. Fontana, Bernard L.; Robinson, W. J.; Cormack, C. W.; and
      Leavitt, E. E. 1962 "Papago Indian Pottery." American
      Ethnological Society, Monograph 37, University of Washington
      Press, Seattle, Washington.
      A thorough study of modern Papago pottery. Section with
      illustrations on manufacture of pottery. Information gathered
      from current Papago potters. Comparison of Papago pottery
      with prehistoric Hohokam wares. Types of pottery described:
      Ceramic Complex, Period I (AD 1700-1860); Papago Red-on-
      brown, p. 104; Papago Red, p. 104; Papago Plain, p. 105.
      Ceramic Complex, Period 2 (AD 1860-1930): Papago Red-on-
      brown, p. 105; Papago Black-on-red, p. 106; Papago Red, p.
      109. Ceramic Complex, Period 3 (AD 1930-present): Papago
      Black-on-white, p. 109; and Papago Polychrome, p. 110. Brief
      description of contemporary pottery of the Pima, Maricopa,
      Mohave, Yuma, and Seri tribes. List of pottery types found
      in Papagueria and the Santa Cruz Valley.

297. Forde, C. Daryll. 1931 "Ethnography of the Yuma Indians."
      University of California Publications in Archaeology and Ethnol-
      ogy, Vol. 28, No. 4.
      Description of Yuma Ware, pp. 123-124.

298. Forsyth, Donald W. 1972 "A Preliminary Classification of
      Anasazi Ceramics from Montezuma Canyon, San Juan County,
      Southeastern Utah." Masters thesis, Department of Anthropology
      and Archaeology, Brigham Young University, Provo, Utah.
      "The results of a topological study of ceramic remains re-
      covered by the Department of Anthropology and Archaeology
      from Montezuma Canyon, San Juan County Southeastern Utah
      are herein reported. Background material concerning the ex-
      cavations undertaken by the Department in the Montezuma Can-
      yon is followed by description of the development of classifica-
      tion systems utilized in American archaeology to date. The

Type: Variety-Mode Conceptual Approach, which was used to order to Montezuma Canyon collections is described, and new ware categories for the northern San Juan drainage are defined. This is followed by the detailed description of the ceramic types and varieties identified in the collections. Finally, the cultural significance of the Montezuma Canyon ceramic content is discussed. It was found that the ceramic history of this region represents a consistent cultural development through time," Abstract.

The four new wares described are San Juan Red Ware, p. 43; Montezuma Gray Ware, p. 43; Monument White Ware, p. 43; and Dolores Basket-Impressed Ware, p. 44.

The new types described and illustrated are Tin Cup Polychrome, pp. 139-141; Devil Mesa Painted-Corrugated, pp. 143-145; Towaoc Painted-Smeared, p. 146; Cajon Painted-Gouged, p. 147; Coal Bed Gray, pp. 162-163; and Recapture Black-on-white, pp. 162-163.

The following new type names were assigned to ceramic materials from Montezuma Canyon. Synonyms in former systems are presented in parentheses after each new name.

San Juan Red Ware: Abajo Red-on-orange: Variety 1 (Abajo Red-on-orange), pp. 48-52; Hermano Polychrome: Variety 1 (Abajo Polychrome), p. 53; Bluff Black-on-red: Variety 1 (Bluff Black-on-red), pp. 54-57; and La Plata Black-on-red: Variety 1 (La Plata Black-on-red), pp. 58-61.

Montezuma Gray Ware: Chapin Gray: Variety 1 (Chapin Gray), pp. 62-67; Chapin Gray: Variety 2 (Twin Trees Plain), pp. 68-70; Bigwater Red: Variety 1 (Chapin Gray, fugitive red), p. 71; Moccasin Neckbanded: Variety 1 (Moccasin Gray, in part), pp. 72-75; Rincon Neckbanded: Variety 1 (Mancos Gray, in part), pp. 76-79; McCracken Tooled: Variety 1 (Mancos Gray, in part), p. 80; Ismay Black-on-gray: Variety 1 (Chapin Black-on-white), pp. 81-84; Ismay Black-on-gray: Variety 2 (Twin Trees Black-on-white), pp. 85-86; Mancos Corrugated: Variety 1 (Mancos Corrugated, in part), pp. 87-93; Mancos Corrugated: Variety 2 (Mancos Corrugated, in part), pp. 94-95; Mancos Corrugated: Variety 3 (Mancos Corrugated, in part), pp. 96-97; Cannonball Incised: Variety 1 (Mancos Corrugated, in part), pp. 98-99; Cannonball Incised: Variety 2 (Mancos Corrugated, in part), p. 100; Cannonball Incised: Variety 3 (Mancos Corrugated, in part), p. 101: Uncompahgre Smeared: Variety 1 (Mancos Corrugated, in part), pp. 102-103; Uncompahgre Smeared: Variety 2, p. 104; Uncompahgre Smeared: Variety 3, p. 105: Menefee Gouged: Variety 1 (Mancos Corrugated, in part), pp. 106-107; Menefee Gouged: Variety 2 (Mancos Corrugated, in part), pp. 108-109; Hatch Gouged-Incised (Mancos Corrugated, in part), p. 110; Dalton Corrugated: Variety 1 (Mesa Verde Corrugated, in part), pp. 111-117; Dalton Corrugated: Variety 1 (Mesa Verde Corrugated, in part), p. 118; Dalton Corrugated: Variety 3 (Mesa Verde Corrugated, in part), p. 119; Hovenweep Corrugated: Variety 2 (Hovenweep Corrugated, in part), pp.

120-125; Hovenweep Corrugated: Variety 3 (Hovenweep Corrugated, in part), p. 126; Hackberry Gouged: Variety 2 (Hovenweep Corrugated, in part), pp. 127-128; and Hackberry Gouged: Variety 3 (Hovenweep Corrugated, in part), p. 129.

Monument White Ware: Mustang Black-on-white: Variety 1 (Cortez Black-on-white), pp. 130-138; Mustang Black-on-white: Variety 2 (Mancos Black-on-white), pp. 130-138; Tin Cup Polychrome (new type), pp. 143-145; Towaoc Painted-smeared (new type), p. 146; Devil Mesa Painted-corrugated (new type), pp. 143-145; Mesa Verde Black-on-white: Variety 1 (McElmo Black-on-white), pp. 148-154; Mesa Verde Black-on-white, Variety 2 (Mesa Verde Black-on-white), pp. 155-161.

Dolores Basket-Impressed Ware: Coal Bed Gray (new type), pp. 162-163; and Recapture Black-on-white (new type), pp. 162-163.

An unnamed Exuberant Corrugated type is described on pp. 164-166.

299. Forsyth, Donald W. 1977 "Anasazi Ceramics of Montezuma Canyon, Southeastern Utah." Department of Anthropology and Archaeology, Brigham Young University Publications in Archaeology (new series), 2, Brigham Young University, Provo, Utah.

Descriptions of the pottery wares and types from Montezuma Canyon, Utah, listed above in Forsyth, 1972.

300. Fourth Southwestern Ceramic Seminar. 1962 Museum of Northern Arizona, Flagstaff, Arizona, 12 pp. Xerox.

Discussed Kayenta Area pottery. Types discussed are Kana-a Black-on-white, Black Mesa Black-on-white, Sosi Black-on-white, and Dogoszhi Black-on-white. "In the discussion these types were rapidly merged into a whole. This does not mean that the type descriptions were combined, but the occurence of these types appears to be a matter of style preference on the same time horizon," p. 4. Shato Black-on-white: consensus was to drop this type but to include it as an occasional addition to decoration in the type description. Dogoszhi Polychrome: It was decided to omit Dogoszhi as a type description except as a variety or descriptive category.

301. Fowler, Don D. 1963 "1961 Excavations, Harris Wash, Utah." University of Utah Anthropological Papers, No. 64, Glen Canyon Series No. 9, Salt Lake City, Utah.

The pottery types found were predominantly Turner Gray: Emery Variety, Tusayan Gray Ware of the following types: Tusayan Corrugated, Moenkopi corrugated, and Kiet Siel Gray. Small amounts of Tusayan White Ware, Tsegi Orange Ware, and San Juan Red Ware. Illustrations of North Creek Gray and a fugitive red olla, Fig. 32.

302. Fowler, Don D. and Aikens, C. M. 1963 "A Preliminary Report of 1961 Excavations, Kaiparowits Plateau, Utah." University

of Utah Anthropological Papers, No. 66, Glen Canyon Series,
No. 20, Salt Lake City, Utah.
    Pottery found was primarily Tusayan Gray Ware including
the following types: Tusayan Corrugated, Moenkopi Corrugated, Kiet Siel Gray, North Creek Corrugated, and North
Creek Gray; also Tusayan White Ware of the Kayenta Series
and of the Southern Utah Series, primarily southern Utah variety black-on-white. Some Tsegi Orange Ware was also found,
San Juan Orange Ware, Utah Desert Gray Ware primarily Turner
Gray: Emery Variety and Snake Valley Gray.

303. Fowler, Morris G. 1935 "Spectrographic Examination of Pot-
      sherds." In Louis R. Caywood and Edward H. Spicer, Tuzi-
      goot. National Park Service, Berkeley, California.
          Examined Jeddito Black-on-yellow and other types of sherds
      from several sites. It was found that Jeddito Black-on-yellow
      sherds were comparatively low in manganese content, quite
      low in calcium and copper and had "fair" amounts of sodium
      and chromium.

304. Fox, Nancy. 1975 "Potsuwi'i Incised Cylindrical Vessels."
      In Theodore R. Frisbie (Ed.), Collected Papers in Honor of
      Florence Hawley Ellis, Papers of the Archaeological Society of
      New Mexico, No. 2, pp. 88-97, Santa Fe, New Mexico.
          Descriptions and illustrations of two Potsuwi'i Incised ves-
      sels which shed new light on the range of vessel forms of this
      type.

305. Fox, Nancy. 1977 "Rose Gonzales." American Indian Art
      Magazine, Vol. 2, No. 4, Autumn, pp. 52-57.
          A brief history of the life and work of this expert, innova-
      tive pottery of Santa Clara Pueblo. Tells of her development
      of the carved black and carved red pottery styles. Photo-
      graphs of Mrs. Gonzales; carved red pieces, Figs. 2, 4; car-
      ved black pieces, Figs. 3, 5, 8; matte black-on-polished
      black, Fig. 6; and plain polished black, Fig. 7.

306. Frank, Larry. 1972 "The Art of Ancient Indian Pottery."
      Nimrod, Vol. 16, No. 2, University of Tulsa, Tulsa, Oklahoma,
      Spring/Summer, pp. 23-25.
          The owner of the pottery from the C. G. Wallace Collection
      presents a very brief history of Pueblo pottery. Artistic and
      cultural features are discussed. One paragraph on modern
      pottery and illustrations of an Acoma Polychrome pot, ca. 1910;
      a black bowl by Maria Martinez; and a carved black bowl by
      Margaret Tafoya, Santa Clara Pueblo.

307. Frank, Larry and Harlow, Francis H. 1974 Historic Pottery
      of the Pueblo Indians, 1600-1880. New York Graphic Society,
      Ltd., Boston, Massachusetts.
          A good book which describes almost 200 vessels from the

pueblos of the Southwest. Contains a brief introduction to
pueblo pottery. The body of the book is a listing of each
pueblo and illustrations of the various types of pottery ancestral to the more recent wares. Some of the distinctions
made among the types by Harlow are rather fine points of
decoration styles. These seem to be rather subjective characteristics and may not warrant as fine a type breakdown as is
made here. Nevertheless, this is a fine book.

The photos, some in color, are excellent and provide a much
needed complement to the type descriptions in Harlow's previous works. The glossary and annotated bibliography are
useful additions. The following types are illustrated and
briefly described: Picuris jars and pitchers (micaceous), p.
28; Tewa Polychrome jar, Pl. I, Figs. 6 and 7; Ogapoge Polychrome, Pl. II, Figs. 8, 9, 10, 13; Pojoaque Polychrome, Pl.
III. Figs. 11 and 12; San Ildefonso Polychrome, Pl. IV, Figs.
30-32; San Ildefonso Black-on-red, Pl. V, Figs. 35, 36; Tunyo
Polychrome, Pl. VI; Kiua Polychrome (Cochiti Variety), Pls.
VII and VIII, Figs. 61, 63, 65-72; Kiua Polychrome, Pl. IX;
Cochiti Polychrome, Pl. X, Figs. 80-88; Santo Domingo Poly-
chrome, Pl. XI, Figs. 89 and 90; Puname Polychrome, Pl. XII,
Figs. 91-95; Trios Polychrome, Pls. XIII-XIV, Figs. 98-104;
Zia Polychrome, Pl. XVI, Figs. 107-110; Santa Clara Black,
Fig. 2; San Juan (red and tan), Fig. 3; Sakona Polychrome,
Figs. 4 and 5; Powhoge Polychrome, Figs. 14-29; Kapo Black,
Fig. 21; Powhoge Black-on-red, Figs. 33-35; Powhoge Poly-
chrome (Tesuque Variety), Figs. 38-43; Tesuque Polychrome,
Figs. 44-47, 50-54; Tatungue Polychrome, Figs. 45, 55-56;
Tesuque Black-on-tan, Figs. 48-49; Nambe Polychrome, Figs.
58-60; Kiua Polychrome (Santo Domingo Variety), Figs. 64,
73, 75, 78; Kiua Black-on-red, Fig. 79; San Pablo Polychrome,
Figs. 96-97; Ranchitos Polychrome, Figs. 111-113, Pl. XVII;
Santa Ana Polychrome, Figs. 114-115, PL. XVIII; Jemez Black-
on-white, Fig. 117; Gobernador Polychrome, Fig. 118; Hawikuh
Polychrome, Fig. 119; Ako Polychrome, Figs. 120-121, Pls.
XIX and XX; Acomita Polychrome, Figs. 122-126, Pls. XXI to
XXIII; McCartys Polychrome, Figs. 127-130; Acoma Polychrome,
Pl. XXIV, Figs. 131-135; Laguna Polychrome, Pl. XXV, Figs.
136-140; Ashiwi Polychrome, Pl. XXVI and XXVII, Figs. 141-
145; Kiapkwa Polychrome, Pl. XXVIII; Zuni Polychrome, Pl.
XXIX and XXX, Figs. 152-156; Payupki Polychrome, Fig. 158,
Pl. XXXI, Figs. 146-151; Polacca Polychrome, Pl. XXXII, Figs.
159-164; San Bernardo Polychrome, Fig. 157, Walpi Polychrome,
Fig. 165; and Hano Polychrome, Fig. 166.

308. Franke, Paul R. 1932 "Incised Pottery Designs on Building
      Blocks of Mesa Verde Masonry." Mesa Verde Notes, No. 3,
      pp. 29-32.
            Shows a number of incised designs similar to pottery de-
      signs on building blocks from the ruins of Cliff Palace, Far
      View House, Sun Temple, and Spruce Tree House.

309. Franklin, Hayward H. 1978 "A Comparison of Ceramic Counts
      from Salmon and Aztec Ruins, New Mexico." Pottery South-
      west, Vol. 5, No. 3, July, pp. 1-4.
          "In sum, these data from Salmon and Aztec illustrate the
      close similarity of the two sites both qualitatively and quanti-
      tatively. This similarity extends to intrusive pottery as well
      as ceramics thought to be locally made," p. 3.

310. Franklin, Hayward H. 1979 "A Method of Determining Size
      and Density of Tempering Materials." Pottery Southwest,
      Vol. 6, No. 4, October, pp. 3-4.
          "Although the sample size in this example was clearly too
      small to include all the variability in the two pottery types,
      it illustrates that two classes of pottery, having the same
      tempers qualitatively, may differ quantitatively in terms of
      temper size and/or temper abundance," p. 4.

311. Franklin, Hayward H. 1980 "Excavations at Second Canyon
      Ruin, San Pedro Valley, Arizona." Contributions to Highway
      Salvage Archaeology in Arizona, No. 60, Arizona State Museum,
      University of Arizona, Tucson, Arizona.
          "In the descriptive section, types that are well described
      in the literature (not many) only have exceptional properties
      portrayed and discussed. Named but poorly described (or
      underdescribed) types, such as San Carlos Red for example,
      are fully described. One new type, Peppersauce Red, is also
      described, and balancing this addition, is the merging of two
      types, Cascabel and Galiuro Red-on-brown, into a single entry
      Cascabel/Galiuro Red-on-brown. Franklin's evidence for this
      is clearly presented and convincing. Then, based on studies
      of tempering material, trade wares are separated from locally
      produced wares, and in his comparative sections, Franklin
      makes good use of his ceramic (and other) clues to relation-
      ships. First it is done for the San Pedro Valley and sur-
      rounding areas. Then it is done for the whole of southeastern
      Arizona and bordering parts of New Mexico and Chihuahua,
      Mexico" (Sundt, Pottery Southwest, 1981).

312. Fraps, Clara Lee. 1935 "Tanque Verde Ruins." Kiva, Vol.
      1, No. 4, pp. 1-4.
          In 1925 an archaeology class from the University of Arizona
      reconnoitered the Southwestern slopes of the Tanque Verde
      Mountains near Tucson, Arizona. The Tanque Verde Ruins
      are situated on the top of a small prominence which extends
      southeast of the mountains. The clay used in the pottery
      varies considerably in its coarseness. Mica and quartzite are
      used for temper materials. Several wares are indicated by
      the sherds recovered. Red-on-buff pottery with a variety of in-
      teriors is predominant. Also Black-on-red and plain buff ex-
      teriors are present. Firing clouds are common. Description
      of Tanque Verde Red-on-brown, p. 4.

313. Frisbie, Theodore R. 1967 "The Excavation and Interpreta-
      tion of the Artificial Leg Basketmaker III--Pueblo I Sites near
      Corrales, New Mexico." Masters thesis, Department of Anthro-
      pology, University of New Mexico, Albuquerque.
           Ceramics found at these sites are described and illustrated.
      No whole vessels were found, but one restorable vessel of
      Tallahogan Red was excavated. Local types found were Lino
      Gray, Transitional Gray, Kana-a Neckbanded Gray, Lino Fu-
      gitive Red, Tallahogan Red, and Lino Smudged. Locally made
      painted wares: San Marcial Black-on-white and Red Mesa
      Black-on-white. Illustrations of Tallahogan Red and San Mar-
      cial Black-on-white and trade sherds.

314. Frisbie, Theodore R. 1973 "The Influence of J. Walter Few-
      kes on Nampeyo: Fact or Fancy?" In Albert E. Schroeder
      (Ed.), The Changing Ways of Southwestern Indians, Brand
      Book, Rio Grande Press, Glorieta, New Mexico.
           "On the basis of the available facts, however, it would seem
      that the major contribution of J. Walter Fewkes to the Hopi
      ceramic revival was simply that he, as the archaeologist in
      charge of the Sikyatki excavations, permitted Nampeyo and
      Lesou to examine recovered vessels and reproduce the de-
      signs. For this Fewkes does, indeed, deserve credit, for his
      actions not only facilitated the work which Nampeyo and Lesou
      had already begun, but also illustrate a fact worthy of recogni-
      tion and consideration by contemporary archaeologists and eth-
      nologists that the material objects recovered during an excava-
      tion can further enhance a native craft development already in
      process," pp. 139-240.

315. Frisbie, Theodore R. 1975a "On the Validity of Tamaya Red."
      Pottery Southwest, Vol. 2, No. 1, January, p. 4.
           Author suggests that Tamaya Red be deleted from the list
      of valid Southwestern pottery types because it does not differ
      significantly from Lino Gray.

316. Frisbie, Theodore R. 1975b "The Art of Ceramic Restoration"
      (concluded). Pottery Southwest, Vol. 2, No. 4, pp. 7-8.
           This is the conclusion of a three-part article. The first
      two sections are presented in numbers 2 and 3 of this volume
      of Pottery Southwest. These articles describe in detail a step-
      by-step method to restore pottery.

317. Frisbie, Theodore R. 1976 "Standards of Description and
      Analytical Procedure: Stirrup-Spouted Vessels." Pottery
      Southwest, Vol. 3, No. 2, April.
           Proposes descriptive elements that will more effectively
      describe and suggest the functions of these vessels.

318. Frisbie, Theodore R. 1976a "Open Forum: Ceramic Typology."
      Pottery Southwest, Vol. 3, pp. 1-12, Special Supplement, De-
      cember.

Good discussion of the problems in typology of Southwestern pottery. The author suggests:

"1. Identify major described types which provide the core in each area, region or district. This should be done by local specialists. (a) Use replication analyses to check type validity, (b) Use quantitative and qualitative tests to establish type validity, (c) Use ethno-archaeology for verification and understanding of ceramic dynamics and change, and (d) Delete any existing types which cannot be shown absolutely valid based on the above criteria.

2. Allow others to check the results obtained for each locale. The types should offer a chronological progression indicating change and variation within the locale. Provide a compendium of these major types which will offer a base from which a high degree of accuracy in typing is possible for anyone wishing to master the overall ceramic trends.

3. Identify the greatest ceramic problems within areas, districts, or locales and find the answers to them.

4. Be aware that any problem, no matter how large and complex is capable of solution if the human mind is in some way coaxed, coerced, or otherwise put into action. In this ceramic typological instance, a collective effort is definitely in order, and Pottery Southwest is a fine vehicle for that expression," p. 9.

319. Frisbie, Theodore R.   1984 "Teed Off." Pottery Southwest, Vol. 11, No. 4, pp. 4-5.
Notes the presence of rare T-shaped worked sherds which are present at several Tewa ancestral sites. Indicates these may have been used as counters in games requiring pieces of different shapes.

320. Frisbie, Theodore R.   1984a "San Marcial Black-on-white: The Paste Thickens." Pottery Southwest, Vol. 11, No. 4, pp. 1-3.
Points out the need for petrographic analysis to help resolve the problem of the relationship of San Marcial Black-on-white to White Mound Black-on-white.

321. Fritz, Gordon L.   1968 "Five Pottery Vessels from Near Casas Grandes." Artifact, Vol. 6, No. 2, El Paso Archaeological Society, El Paso, Texas.
Five pottery vessels from the Casas Grandes Ruin Area of Chihuahua, Mexico, are described. Associated artifacts and the exact origins of the vessels are not known. Possible uses of the vessels are postulated. Illustrations of Ramos Polychrome jar, Fig. 1, Ramos Black vessels, Figs. 2 and 3; Neck Corrugated vessels, Fig. 4; and an Incised jar, Fig. 5.

322. Fuller, Steven L.   1984 "Late Anasazi Pottery Kilns in the Yellowjacket District, Southwestern Colorado." CASA Papers, No. 4, Cortez, Colorado.

Describes, analyzes, interprets, and synthesizes perspec-
tives on the excavation of eight pottery kilns found near the
Yellowjacket Site.

323. Fulton, William S. 1928 "Pottery-Making in the Southwest."
University of California Publications in American Archaeology
and Ethnology, Vol. 23, No. 8, pp. 353-373, Berkeley, California.
There are two methods of making coiled pottery in the
Southwest. The principal criterion of method is the use or
nonuse of a wooden paddle and a stone or pottery anvil in
shaping the vessel. Illustrations of pottery anvils, Fig. 1.
There are some conclusions concerning Southwestern cultural
history suggested by these findings on the two pottery-making
techniques.

324. Fulton, William S. 1933-4 "Archaeological Notes on Texas
Canyon, Arizona." Contributions from the Museum of the
American Indian, Heye Foundation, Vol. 12, Nos. 1 and 2,
New York, New York.
A brief description of types found; includes Red-on-buff,
Mimbres Black-on-white, Gila Polychrome, and Chupadero Black-
on-white. Called a "Red-on-buff site." Illustration of brown
utility ware. A few drawings of designs and one color plate
in No. 2.

325. Fulton, William S. and Tuthill, Carr. 1940 An Archaeological
Site Near Gleeson, Arizona. Amerind Foundation, No. 2, Dra-
good, Arizona.
Types of pottery described are Dragoon Red, p. 45; and
Dragoon Red-on-brown, pp. 40-44.

326. Gaede, Marc. 1977 "The Makers." Plateau, Vol. 49, No. 3,
Winter, pp. 18-21.
Photographs of the following noted Hopi potters: Susie
Youvella, Garnet Pavatea, Rodina Huma, Mamie Nahoodyce,
Patty Maho, Grace Chapella, Wallace Youvella, Clarice Sahmie,
Sadie Adams, Beth Sakeva, Violet Huma, Anita Polacca, and
Rena Kavena.

327. Garrett, Betty. 1974 "Thin Sectioning of Pottery as an Aid
in Ceramic Identification." Pottery Southwest, Vol. 1, No. 3,
pp. 5-7.
Information derived from thin sectioning of ceramics can be
used to (1) accurately identify tempering materials, their size,
shape, and abundance; (2) separate local from trade wares;
(3) postulate the original source of temper; (4) aid in typological identification of body sherds; and (5) correlate tempering materials with functions.

328. Garrett, Betty. 1976 "A Petrographic Analysis of Thirty

Pottery Mound Polychrome, San Clemente Polychrome, and
Glaze C Sherds from Pottery Mound, New Mexico." Pottery
Southwest, Vol. 3, No. 1, pp. 4-8.
Petrographic examination resulted in petrographic descrip-
tion of the above mentioned types. It enabled the identifica-
tion of seven of the ten questionable sherds to be postulated.

329. Garrett, Elizabeth. 1983 "A Petrographic Analysis of Black
Mesa, Arizona Ceramics." Master's thesis, Western Michigan
University.
A petrographic analysis of seven ceramic types from sites
excavated on Black Mesa in the area leased by the Peabody
Coal Company. Tempering materials are described for each
type. The purpose was to determine if these types share a
common area of manufacture and to determine if these types
contain temper of local materials from the Wepo or Toreva
formations.
Each type studied appeared to have more than one place
of manufacture. Only Black Mesa Black-on-white has local
temper indicating manufacture in the vicinity. All other types
had non-local temper indicating they were made elsewhere and
inferring an organized prehistoric trade network.

330. Gauthier, Rory P. 1982 "Notes on Biscuit Wares and Some
General Trends in the Northern Rio Grande." Pottery Southwest, Vol. 9, Nos. 2 and 3, pp. 6-7 and 1-5.
"This discussion points out several weaknesses in the classification of biscuit wares. Clearly more research is needed in
this area, and defining the source areas should be a priority.
The evidence suggests wide-spread trading of large amounts
of decorated pottery and also indicates that certain source
areas are responsible for various ceramic types and possibly
even vessel forms," p. 4.

331. Geib, Phil R. and Callahan, M. M. 1983 Volcanic Ash Temper
and Ceramic Exchange in the Kayenta Anasazi Region. Manuscript, Archaeology Laboratory, Northern Arizona University,
Flagstaff.
"A microscopic examination of ceramic collections from nearly
300 sites, coupled with petrographic analysis of selected sherds,
conclusively establishes the presence of volcanic ash temper
in the white wares of the Kayenta Anasazi region. Using
distributional data, refiring experiments, and geologic sourc-
ing of both clays and the ash, the authors attempt a reconstruction of the prehistoric production zones of various wares
in the Kayenta tradition. The distribution of ash tempered
ceramics in time and space supports our contention that the
ash tempered white wares were being traded out of the Klethla
Valley region in exchange for the orange wares being produced
by the Anasazi group further north," p. 1.

332. Gerald, Rex E. 1957 "Appendix A, A Study of Brown Ware
      Pottery." In Edward B. Danson, An Archaeological Survey of
      West Central New Mexico and East Central Arizona, Papers of
      the Peabody Museum of Archaeology and Ethnology, Vol. 44,
      No. 1, pp. 123-124, Peabody Museum, Cambridge, Massachu-
      setts.
         "On the basis of the above experiments we may conclude
      that the rounded sand (form 1) may be distinguished from
      angular sand (form 3) and/or crushed rock by visual means
      when these extremes occur, but it is felt that all brown ware
      cannot be classified on this basis, and that crushed rock tem-
      per cannot be distinguished from sand temper," p. 124.

333. Gerald, Rex E. n.d. Description of Pottery Types of the El
      Paso Area. Manuscript on file, El Paso Archaeological Society,
      El Paso, Texas.
         Descriptions of El Paso Red-on-brown, El Paso Black-on-
      brown, Jornada Red-on-brown, Jornada Black-on-brown, and
      El Paso Polychrome.

334. Giammattei, Victor M. and Reichert, Nanci G. 1975 Art of a
      Vanishing Race: The Mimbres Classic Black-on-white. Dillon-
      Tyler Publishers, Woodland, California.
         A brief history of the Mimbres people and their pottery
      with two illustrative charts of the history. Forty plates of
      drawings of bowls of Mimbres Black-on-white. Most of these
      are from Fewkes, 1923, and Cosgrove, 1932.

335. Gifford, Edward W. 1928 "Pottery-Making in the Southwest."
      Publications in American Archaeology and Ethnology, Vol. 23,
      No. 8, University of California, Berkeley, California.
         Description of basic methods of pottery manufacture.

336. Gifford, Edward W. 1932 "The Southeastern Yavapai." Publi-
      cations in American Archaeology and Ethnology, Vol. 29, No.
      3, p. 220, University of California, Berkeley, California.
         Description of Yavapai (southeastern) ware, pp. 220.

337. Gifford, Edward W. 1936 "Northeastern and Western Yavapai."
      Publications in American Archaeology and Ethnology, Vol. 34,
      No. 4, pp. 280-281, University of California, Berkeley, Cali-
      fornia.
         Description of Yavapai (northeastern and western) ware,
      pp. 280-281.

338. Gifford, Edward W. 1940 "Culture Element Distributions:
      XII Apache-Pueblo." University of California Anthropological
      Records, Vol. 4, No. 1, pp. 50-141, Berkeley, California.
         Description of Apache ware, pp. 50-141.

339. Gifford, James C. 1957 "Archaeological Explorations in Caves

of Point of Pines Region." Masters thesis, University of Arizona, Tucson, Arizona.
Descriptions of McDonald Painted Corrugated, Pinto Black-on-red, Prieto Indented Corrugated, and Reserve Red: Point of Pines variety, pp. 372-375.

340. Gifford, James C. 1960 "The Type Variety Method of Ceramic Classification as an Indicator of Cultural Phenomenon." American Antiquity, Vol. 25, No. 3, January, pp. 341-347.
Abstract: "This discussion deals with the theoretical reasoning that underlies the type-variety method of ceramic analysis. Not only do pottery 'types' and 'varieties' embody sets of recognizable distinct attributes and impart particular cultural, areal, and temporal connotations, but they are also meaningful entities of cultural interpretation," p. 341.

341. Gifford, James C. 1980 "Archaeological Explorations in Caves of the Point of Pines Region, Arizona." Anthropological Papers of the University of Arizona, No. 36, Tucson, Arizona.
Red Bow Cliff Dwelling: Most common types found at this site were Point of Pines Plain Corrugated, Point of Pines Obliterated Corrugated, Point of Pines Indented Corrugated, Alma Plain, and Kinishba Red. Types described are Cedar Creek Polychrome, Point of Pines Corrugated, Point of Pines Indented Corrugated, and Point of Pines Obliterated Corrugated. Most of these types and others found are shown.
Tule Tubs Cave: Most common types found in this cave were Alma Plain, Point of Pines Indented Corrugated, Point of Pines Obliterated Corrugated, and Reserve Indented Corrugated. Illustrations of the types listed above and Gila Polychrome, McDonald Painted Corrugated, Encinas Red-on-brown, Sacaton Red-on-buff, Point of Pines Plain Corrugated, Reserve Plain corrugated, Reserve Incised Corrugated, Alma Knobby, and Point of Pines Punctate.
Pine Flat Cave: Alma Plain, Point of Pines Obliterated Corrugated, Plain Corrugated, and Indented Corrugated were the most common types found at this site. Descriptions of Reserve Red, Pine Flat Corrugated, and Apache Plain. All three of these types and others present are illustrated.

342. Gifford, James C. and Smith, Watson. 1978 "Gray Corrugated Pottery from Awatovi and Other Jeddito Sites in Northeastern Arizona." Papers of the Peabody Museum of Archaeology and Ethnology, Vol. 69, Harvard University, Cambridge, Massachusetts.
An excellent analysis of the often neglected corrugated types of pottery. The following new types of corrugated pottery and associated varieties are described and illustrated:
Tusayan Corrugated: Tusayan Variety, pp. 46-48, 61-65;
Tusayan Corrugated: Star Mountain Variety, pp. 65-69, 78-79; Tusayan Corrugated: Wipo Variety, pp. 79, 82-83; Tusayan

Corrugated: Kwatoko Variety, pp. 83-85; Bluebird Corrugated:
Bluebird Variety, pp. 85, 88-89, 94; Bluebird Corrugated:
Patni Variety, pp. 95-97, 100; Moenkopi Corrugated, pp. 110-
111, 114; Keams Corrugated, pp. 117-119, 126; Deadmans Corrugated, pp. 131, 133, 138; Bonsikya Corrugated, pp. 138-
139, 143; Pakiubi Corrugated, p. 143; and Honani Tooled, pp.
147, 151. Gifford names Nushaki Corrugated but it is not
described nor illustrated.

343. Gillin, John. 1955 "Archaeological Investigations in Nine Mile
      Canyon, Utah: A Replication." University of Utah Anthropo-
      logical Papers, No. 21, Salt Lake City, Utah.
          "Summarizing the pottery types of sites 17B, 17C, and 2,
      we were handicapped at the start first by the absence of
      whole pots; second by the relatively few sherds recovered in
      spite of thorough sifting methods during excavation. However,
      in variety of types the three sites stand in the above order.
      Since all sites show the fundamental diagnostic types, there
      seems to be no evidence to indicate priority. On the basis of
      the classical styles of the Southwest those pottery types fall
      into the period of late Pueblo I or early Pueblo II ("Develop-
      mental Pueblo") according to terminology suggested by Roberts
      (1935).... Crude but not elementary brushwork on an un-
      slipped grayish background characterized the painted sherds.
      Corrugated sherds occur with insignificant frequency and in
      the wrong shapes to indicate that they were parts of pots
      whose whole exterior surface was corrugated but rather they
      represent parts of corrugated, decorated necks," p. 14. Illus-
      trations of a few sherds.

344. Gladwin, Harold S. 1943 "A Review and Analysis of the Flag-
      staff Culture." Medallion Papers No. 31, Gila Pueblo, Globe,
      Arizona.
          Chapter 8: The pottery of the Coconino, Medicine Valley,
      Sunset, and Rio de Flag Phases. Types of pottery found dur-
      ing the above phases are listed. "The distribution of pottery
      seems to be perfectly clear and affords confirmation of the
      evidence of the architecture. It would, I think, be very dif-
      ficult to point to any detail of pottery or architecture which
      is not in harmony and on the strength of this evidence I shall
      with no hesitation say that the Flagstaff Culture shows a Pueblo
      I or Coconino Phase at the Baker Ranch and developed into a
      Pueblo II or Medicine Valley Phase in Medicine Valley," p. 54.

345. Gladwin, Harold S. 1957 A History of the Ancient Southwest.
      Bond Wheelwright Co., Portland, Maine.
          A general text on Southwest archaeology. Illustrations of
      pottery include a sherd board from Wingate area, p. 5; Basket-
      maker Black-on-white, p. 71; Hohokam designs, pp. 82-83, 88-
      89; Snaketown Red-on-buff, p. 90; White Mound Black-on-white,
      Plain and Red, pp. 108-110; Early Black-on-white, pp. 115-116;

Red-on-orange, Alkali Ridge, p. 117; Black-on-white Basketmaker, p. 122; Snaketown Red-on-buff, pp. 138-140; Verde
Black-on-gray, p. 150; fine hatched designs, p. 164; sherd
board, Wingate pithouse, p. 167; Red Mesa Ruin pottery, p.
173; Chaco-Kayenta Black-on-white, p. 175; bowl designs of
various types, pp. 186-189; Wingate Ruin pottery, p. 204;
Cibola Black-on-white, p. 205; Mimbres designs, pp. 225-230;
St. Johns Polychrome and Tularosa Black-on-white, p. 232;
Chaco Black-on-white, p. 238; Mesa Verde Black-on-white, p.
244; Salado and Cibola Black-on-white, p. 250; Pinto Polychrome, p. 252; Gila Polychrome, p. 262; Mesa Verde Black-
on-white, p. 276; Fourmile Polychrome, p. 289; Black-on-
yellow ware, p. 303; Casas Grandes pottery, pp. 333-335;
and Sikyatki Polychrome, p. 338.

346. Gladwin, Winifred and Gladwin, Harold S. 1928 "The Use of
      Potsherds in an Archaeological Survey." Medallion Papers No.
      2, Gila Pueblo, Globe, Arizona.
          Discussion of pottery classifications and survey methods.

347. Gladwin, Winifred and Gladwin, Harold S. 1930a "A Method
      for the Designation of Southwestern Pottery Types." Medallion
      Papers No. 7, Gila Pueblo, Globe, Arizona.
          Method devised at the Pecos Conference, 1929, and Gila
      Pueblo, 1930, to standardize the designation for new pottery
      types. Major points are:
          "1. The color combination or surface treatment of the pot-
      tery should determine the Genus, and the following Genera
      were selected: Black-on-white, Black-on-red, Brown-on-
      yellow, Red-on-buff, Polychrome, Corrugated, Incised, Slipped
      Plain ware, and Unslipped Plain ware.
          2. A geographical locality should determine the specific
      name. This locality need not necessarily be the spot where
      the first type was found or its area of greatest density but
      would simply serve as a label for reference. As for example:
      Mesa Verde Black-on-white.
          3. A specimen of the type should be deposited in a mu-
      seum with an appropriate label to indicate that it is the type-
      piece on which the description is based.
          4. Sherds of the type should be availabe for those persons
      who might request them.
          5. The type should be described in as much detail as pos-
      sible to show wherein it is distinct; its range, association and
      such other information as might assist in its identification.
          6. This description should be published," n.p.

348. Gladwin, Winifred and Gladwin, Harold S. 1930b "Some South-
      western Pottery Types: Series II." Medallion Papers No. 7,
      Gila Pueblo, Globe, Arizona.
          Salado Culture. Color plates and descriptions of Pinto Poly-
      chrome, pp. 4-5; Gila Polychrome, pp. 6-7; Tonto Polychrome,

pp. 8-9; Salado Red ware, pp. 10-11; Gila Red ware, pp. 12-
15; and Salado White-on-red (Tonto Red, in part), Pl. 12.

349.   Gladwin, Winifred and Gladwin, Harold S. 1930c "An Archa-
        eological Survey of Verde Valley." Medallion Papers No. 6,
        Gila Pueblo, Globe, Arizona.
        Description of Verde Black-on-gray, p. 140; illustration,
        Pl. 20 (color).

350.   Gladwin, Winifred and Gladwin, Harold S. 1931 "Some South-
        western Pottery Types, Series II." Medallion Papers No. 10,
        Gila Pueblo, Globe, Arizona.
        Descriptions and illustrations of Puerco Black-on-white, pp.
        24-26; Showlow Black-on-red, pp. 27-28; Wingate Black-on-
        red, pp. 29-30; Tularosa Black-on-white, pp. 32-35; St. Johns
        Polychrome, pp. 36-40; Pinedale Polychrome, pp. 41-42; Four-
        mile Polychrome, pp. 43-45; and Roosevelt Black-on-white, pp.
        47-49.

351.   Gladwin, Winifred and Gladwin, Harold S. 1933 "Some South-
        western Pottery Types, Series III." Medallion Papers, No.
        13, Gila Pueblo, Globe, Arizona.
        Description and illustrations of Red-on-buff types: Santa
        Cruz Red-on-buff, pp. 8-14; Sacaton Red-on-buff, pp. 16-20;
        Sacaton Buff, pp. 16-20; Casa Grande Red-on-buff, pp. 22-
        24; Sacaton Smudged, p. 28; Santan Red, pp. 28-29; and Gila
        Plain, pp. 25-27.

352.   Gladwin, Winifred and Gladwin, Harold S. 1938 "Excavations
        at Snaketown, Material Culture." Medallion Papers, No. 25,
        Gila Pueblo, Globe, Arizona (Reprint, 1965).
        A basic reference on study of Hohokam culture and pottery.
        Chapter on pottery by Haury, pp. 168-229. Types described
        and illustrations of Sacaton Red-on-buff, pp. 171-178; Sacaton
        Buff, pp. 178-179; Santa Cruz Red-on-buff, pp. 179-185;
        Santa Cruz Buff, p. 185; Gila Butte Red-on-buff, pp. 185-189;
        Snaketown Red-on-buff, pp. 189-192; Sweetwater Red-on-gray,
        pp. 192-198; Sweetwater Polychrome, p. 198; Estrella Red-on-
        gray, pp. 199-202; Sacaton Red, pp. 202-204; Vahki Red, pp.
        204-205; Gila Plain, pp. 205-211; and Vahki Plain, pp. 211-
        220. Pottery illustrated in Pls. CXXXIV-CCXIII. Chapters
        on petrography and clay figurines. Descriptions in this volume
        supercede descriptions in previous Gila Pueblo publications.

353.   Gladwin, Winifred and Gladwin, Harold S. 1945 "Chaco
        Branch: Excavations at White Mound and the Red Mesa Valley."
        Medallion Papers No. 33, Gila Pueblo, Globe, Arizona.
        A report of excavations at White Mound and Red Mesa Val-
        ley. Descriptions of Kiatuthlanna Black-on-white, p. 41;
        White Mound Black-on-white, pp. 22-23; and Red Mesa Black-
        on-white, p. 56. Illustrations of Red Mesa Black-on-white, p.
        56; and White Mound Black-on-white, p. 41.

354. Goddard, Pliny E. 1928 "Pottery of the Southwestern Indians."
      Guide Leaflet Series, American Museum of Natural History, New
      York (reprint Acoma Books, Ramona, California, 1971).
      A 30-page booklet. A description of pottery manufacture
      taken from Guthe, 1925. Discussion of prehistoric painted
      and corrugated ware with a few local design varieties. Short
      section on modern Pueblo wares. Illustrations of Corrugated
      vessel, Aztec, Fig. 10; Unfired, basketmolded fragment, Fig.
      11; Neckbanded vessels, Fig. 12; Corrugated, patterned bowl,
      Fig. 13; Mesa Verde Black-on-white bowls and mugs, Fig. 14;
      drawings of four Mesa Verde Black-on-white designs, Fig. 15;
      jars from Aztec, Chaco bowls, Fig. 16; Chaco bowls, pitchers
      and vases, Fig. 17; Mimbres bowls, Fig. 18; Polychrome jars
      and Tularosa pitchers, Fig. 19; and Zuni, San Ildefonso, La-
      guna, Zia, Santa Ana and Santo Domingo, Figs. 20-22.

355. Gomolak, Andrew R. and Ford, Dabney. 1976 Berrenda Creek
      LA 12992, 1976: Reclamation of a Vandalized Prehistoric Settle-
      ment Site. New Mexico State University, Las Cruces, New
      Mexico.
        A field report and analysis of the excavation of a pothunted
      Mimbres Site; 2,043 painted/slipped sherds and 9 whole or
      restorable vessels were recovered from the undisturbed por-
      tion of this site. Of the sherds, 97.75% were local Mimbres
      Black-on-white and the remaining 2.25% were intrusive types.
      No Mimbres Boldface Black-on-white sherds were found. Mim-
      bres Black-on-white vessels and sherds are illustrated. A
      total of 3,262 plain and corrugated sherds were recovered.
      Most of the plain sherds were a brownware variety of Alma
      Plain. The 763 corrugated sherds were not typed. Intrusive
      types were Jornada El Paso Brownware, Jornada/El Paso Bi-
      chrome, San Francisco Red, and Mogollon Red-on-brown.

356. Gooding, John D. 1980 "The Durango South Project: Archa-
      eological Salvage of Two Late Basketmaker III Sites in the Du-
      rango District." Anthropological Papers of the University of
      Arizona, No. 34, University of Arizona Press, Tucson, Arizona.
        Section on ceramics of Durango South by Priscilla Ellwood.
      Nearly 2,000 potsherds and 46 whole or restorable vessels
      were obtained from the excavations of these two sites. Types
      found and described are Lino Gray: Durango Variety, p. 79;
      Twin Trees Plain: Durango Variety, pp. 82, 84; Lino Black-
      on-gray: Durango Variety, pp. 84-85; and Twin Trees Black-
      on-white, pp. 85, 88. All of the above types and a Moccasin
      Gray jar are illustrated. A few sherds of Abajo Red-on-orange
      were also found. The occupation of this site was estimated at
      AD 775-800.

357. Gratz, Kathleen. 1970 "The M.N.A. Ceramic Repository: Its
      History and Status in 1970." Plateau, Vol. 44, No. 2, pp. 72-
      74.

"Potsherds or broken pieces of pottery have been thought important enough by archaeologists to be designated, accessioned, and deposited as type specimens according to Dr. H. S. Colton's rules of Type and Ware Classification. This service has been carried out by the Museum of Northern Arizona continuously for 38 years in the form of a ceramic repository," p. 74. In 1970, over 13,000 type specimen sherds were stored according to type and ware and accompanied by information, provenience, and special surface features. Sherds are also held as specimens to illustrate common and rare examples of surface treatment, manufacture, and finishing techniques. In this group are examples of basket imprinting, drilled holes, fugitive paint, tooled designs, textile impressions, coil, paddle and anvil methodology, scraping and polishing finishes and several trays of reworked sherds. This repository is very comprehensive and of great value to the student of Southwest ceramics.

358. Gratz, Kathleen. 1975 "A Presentation of a Possible Hypothesis Concerning the Wedding Jar Vessel Form and Function." Pottery Southwest, Vol. 2, No. 2, pp. 2-4.
      "Data records are being kept at the MNA on the ceramic Wedding Jar form. Several theories are here presented on the origin and initial functions of this vessel type. The practice of Christianity, prehistoric antecedents, and trade demand are investigated as possible sources," p. 2.

359. Gratz, Kathleen. 1975a "A Report on an Unusual Rain God Figurine Belonging to Mr. Jerry Jacka." Pottery Southwest, Vol. 2, No. 3, pp. 2-4.
      "After comparison of the figurine with Tesuque and other pueblo examples, it is concluded that the specimen is a Zuni tradition imitation of the Tesuque Rain God. The figurine probably dates in the early 1900s, perhaps between 1910 and 1920," p. 2. The figurine is shown in Fig. 1.

360. Gratz, Kathleen. 1976 "The Phallic Handle Attachment Point: A Problem in Prehistoric Ceremonialism." Pottery Southwest, Vol. 3, No. 4, p. 7.
      Brief description of six ladles which were made with a phallus shaped protrusion to which the hollow handle was attached.

361. Gratz, Kathleen. 1977 "Making Hopi Pottery: Techniques and Materials." Plateau, Vol. 49, No. 3, pp. 14-17.
      Good short article with sequential photos of Hopi pottery production.

362. Graves, Michael W. 1982 "Breaking Down Ceramic Variation: Testing Models of White Mountain Redware Design Style Development." Journal of Anthropological Archaeology, Vol. 1, No. 4, p. 305-354.

"Design styles in White Mountain Redware pottery from the American Southwest are analyzed, drawing on the ethnoarchaeological work conducted among the Kalinga of northern Luzon, the Philippines, to establish a strong relationship between distinct social groups and ceramic decoration. From this base regional production zones are identified for several White Mountain Redware design styles in eastern Arizona and Western New Mexico," p. 305.

363.   Graves, Michael W.   1984   "Temporal Variation Among White Mountain Redware Design Styles." Kiva, Vol. 50, No. 1, pp. 3-24.

Abstract: "Design styles on White Mountain Redware pottery from the American Southwest are time sensitive units whose application has been underexploited. Six named design styles are systematically defined in order to produce comparably distinct classes, and the occurrence of these styles is employed to chronologically order 31 prehistoric sites in east central Arizona and western New Mexico. This seriation also provides the basis for assessing the extent of contemporaneity between design styles, information that can be used to estimate the date of prehistoric occupation at settlements that contain White Mountain Redware. Temporal variation among design styles also has implications for Southwestern cultural historical interpretive frameworks, and these issues are briefly examined," p. 3.

364.   Graybill, Donald A.   1937   "Prehistoric Settlement Pattern Analysis in the Mimbres Region, New Mexico." Ph.D. dissertation, University of Arizona, Tucson, Arizona.

A 1971-72 survey of the Mimbres Valley north of the Mimbres Ranger Station and up the North, East, and West forks of the Mimbres River. Predominant types found were Plain Brown, Alma Scored, Alma Incised, Alma Punched, San Francisco Red, Alma Neckbanded, Mogollon Red-on-brown, Three Circle Red-on-white, Mimbres Boldface, and Mimbres Black-on-white. Graybill was unable to separate Three Circle Neck Corrugated sherds from Mimbres Corrugated so he formed five Clapboard corrugated types which include both types. The clapboard types based on surface treatment are Clapboard Corrugated, Clapboard Corrugated smoothed, Clapboard Corrugated indented, Clapboard smoothed and indented, and Clapboard Corrugated incised.

365.   Green, Robert C.   1956   "A Pithouse of the Gallina Phase." American Antiquity, Vol. 22, No. 2, pp. 188-193.

"The site contains sufficient trade ware of Chacoan types to suggest a more definite contact than was previously suspected between Chacoan and Gallina groups in this Southwestern Gallina area," p. 194.

366. Greenleaf, J. Cameron. 1975 "Excavations at Punta de Agua in the Santa Cruz River Basin, Southeastern Arizona." Anthropological Papers of the University of Arizona, No. 26, University of Arizona, Tucson, Arizona.
      Excavation of a site on the San Xavier Indian Reservation a few miles south of Tucson, Arizona. A good discussion of the pottery recovered on pp. 45-77. Descriptions of Rincon Red-on-brown, Rincon Red, and Rincon Polychrome. In addition to these three types, the local types illustrated are Canada del Oro Red-on-brown, Rillito Red-on-brown, Tanque Verde Red-on-brown, Tanque Verde Plain ware, Topawa Red-on-brown, and Rillito Plain ware. Sherds of intrusive types and ceramic artifacts including spindle whorls, figurines, effigies, and worked sherds are also described and illustrated.

367. Greer, John W. 1977 "Geometric Methods for Computing Vessel Diameters." Southwestern Lore, Vol. 43, No. 1, March, pp. 25-28.
      Abstract: "A method is presented to compute vessel diameter from sherd curvature," p. 25.

368. Greer, John W. 1977a "Some Simple Methods for Computing Vessel Diameters from Sherds." Pottery Southwest, Vol. 4, No. 1, January, pp. 6-9.
      "Geometric methods given involve intersecting chords to locate the center of the vessel and two formulas to compute vessel diameter using the width and depth of curvature of the sherds. Mechanical methods given involve use of cutout templates to match the curves of known diameters," p. 6.

369. Griffin, P. Bion. 1967 "A High Status Burial from Grasshopper Ruin, Arizona." Kiva, Vol. 33, No. 2, pp. 37-53.
      "Included in the two areas were 36 ceramic vessels, 128 projectile points, an incised bone wand, and many other items. The implication that burial 140 may represent a high status burial with a socially stratified society is discussed," p. 37. Types of pottery found were Pinedale Polychrome, Pinto-Gila Polychrome, Cibecue Polychrome, Grasshopper Polychrome, and Salado Red Ware. Unique pottery object was a Pinto Polychrome annular-base plate, Fig. 40.

370. Griset, Suzanne (editor). 1986 "Pottery of the Great Basin and Adjacent Areas." University of Utah Anthropological Papers, No. 111, University of Utah Press, Salt Lake City, Utah.
      Primarily deals with pottery outside the Southwest, the techniques and methods discussed may be applicable outside the Great Basin. Annotated bibliography contains references to articles on pottery of the Southwest. Descriptions of Desert gray, Great Salt Lake Gray, and Promontory Gray.

371. Gumerman, George J. 1969 "The Archaeology of the Hopi Buttes District, Arizona." Ph.D. dissertation, University of Arizona, Tucson, Arizona.
     Surveyed 211 sites and excavated in six of them. A total of 6,977 potsherds were recovered from 202 of the sites. Holbrook Black-on-white and Walnut Black-on-white were the most common types found. Types illustrated are Leupp Black-on-white, Showlow Black-on-red, Flagstaff Black-on-white, White Mound Black-on-white, Kana-a Black-on-white, Holbrook Black-on-white, Padre Black-on-white, Sunset Red, and Little Colorado Corrugated. Worked sherds of several types are shown.

372. Gumerman, George J. 1970 "Black Mesa: Survey and Excavation in Northeastern Arizona, 1968." Prescott College Studies in Anthropology, No. 2, Prescott, Arizona.
     Wares found were primarily Tusayan White, Tusayan Gray, and Tsegi Orange. Only possible intrusive was Abajo Black-on-orange. A total of 1,325 sherds were collected from all the Anasazi sites. Illustrations of sherds: Fig. 6, Kana-a Black-on-white, Black Mesa Black-on-white; Fig. 7, Abajo Red-on-orange, Tusayan Black-on-red, Medicine Black-on-red, and Tusayan Polychrome; Figs. 9-10, vessels of above types except Abajo Red-on-orange plus Tusayan Corrugated; Fig. 27, worked sherds.

373. Gumerman, George J.; Westfall, D.; and Weed, C. S. 1972 "Black Mesa: Archaeological Investigations on Black Mesa, the 1969-1970 Seasons." Prescott College Studies in Anthropology, No. 4, Prescott College Press, Prescott, Arizona.
     Description of Wepo Black-on-white.

374. Gumerman, George J. and Euler, Robert C. 1976 Papers on the Archaeology of Black Mesa, Arizona. Southern Illinois University Press, Carbondale, Illinois.
     Kayenta Anasazi Sites: In the survey of a coal slurry pipeline, 1,174 sherds were collected from the surface most of which were Tusayan White Ware and Tusayan Gray Ware. Illustrations include Lino Black-on-gray vessels and sherds, Tallahogan Red sherds, and worked sherds.

375. Gunnerson, James A. 1956 "Fremont Ceramics." University of Utah Anthropological Papers, No. 26, Salt Lake City, Utah, pp. 54-62.
     Illustrations of Turner Gray Variety II, Fig. 9; and Turner Gray Variety II, Fig. 10.

376. Gunnerson, James A. 1957 "An Archaeological Survey of the Fremont Area." University of Utah Anthropological Papers, No. 28, Salt Lake City, Utah.
     Ceramics, pp. 7-18. Illustrations of Turner Gray: Variety II, 3 vessels, Fig. 2; Turner Gray: Variety II sherds, painted

and surface treatment, Fig. 3; Turner Gray; Variety II, Figs.
4, 5; Turner Gray: Variety II portions of bowls, Fig. 6;
Turner Gray: Variety II vessels, Figs. 42-64; Turner Gray
sherds, Fig. 47; Turner Gray rim sherds with punching and
incising, Figs. 48-49; trade sherds from Old Woman Site, Fig.
51; and worked pot sherds, Fig. 52.

377. Gunnerson, James A. 1962 "Archaeological Survey in the Ham-
      mond Canyon Area, Southeastern Utah." In Miscellaneous Col-
      lected Papers, University of Utah Anthropological Papers, No.
      60, pp. 9-44, Salt Lake City, Utah.
      Survey uncovered only small numbers of sherds from these
      sites. These were primarily Chapin Gray, San Juan White
      Ware, San Juan Red Ware, and corrugated.

378. Gunnerson, James A. 1969 "Apache Archaeology in North-
      eastern New Mexico." American Antiquity, Vol. 34, No. 1,
      pp. 23-39.
      Abstract: "The predominant pottery, however, is a thin
      micaceous ware, herein described as Ocate Micaceous, accom-
      panied by trade sherds of Tewa Polychrome, plain black Pueblo
      ware, and Puebla (Mexico) blue and white majolica. Mid-19th
      century Apache sites in this area are "tipi-ring" sites yielding
      a thicker micaceous ware, herein described as Cimarron Mica-
      ceous, white man's trade goods, and a few stone artifacts.
      The relationship between Apache micaceous pottery, made from
      Ca. 1600 (or earlier) until the early 1900s and that made at
      Taos and Picuris is not clear," p. 23.

379. Guthe, Alfred K. 1949 "A Preliminary Report on Excavations
      in Southwestern Colorado." American Antiquity, Vol. 15, pp.
      144-154.
      A report on excavation of the Cahone Ruin during the sum-
      mer of 1947. Large amounts of pottery were found. Corru-
      gated ware was the most common and Mancos Black-on-white
      was the predominant painted type. Other types found were
      Lino Gray, Red Mesa Black-on-white, Tusayan Polychrome, and
      Citadel Polychrome.

380. Guthe, Carl E. 1925 Pueblo Pottery Making: A Study at the
      Village of San Ildefonso. Philips Andover Academy, Yale Uni-
      versity Press, New Haven, Connecticut.
      A good general discussion of how pottery is made in the
      Southwestern pueblos. Techniques can be considered similar
      to prehistoric methods. Illustrations include: raw materials,
      tools, molding, drying, scraping, slipping, polishing, paint-
      ing, firing, and design. Pottery types described are San Ilde-
      fonso Black-on-cream, San Ildefonso Polychrome, San Ildefonso
      Black-on-red, and San Ildefonso white-on-polished red. Illus-
      trations of pottery: Corrugated sherds, Pl. 2; Acoma, Zuni,
      Sia, Hopi, San Ildefonso, Tesuque, Santo Domingo and Cochiti,
      Pl. 3; San Ildefonso Black-on-buff and polished black, Pl. 4;

San Ildefonso Polychrome and Black-on-red, Pl. 5; Polychrome
by Maria Martinez, Pl. 6; San Ildefonso Black-on-red by Maria
Martinez, Pl. 7; and matte on polished black, Pl. 8.

381. Guthe, Carl E. 1927 "A Method of Ceramic Description."
Papers of the Michigan Academy of Science, Art and Letters,
Vol. 8, pp. 23-29, Ann Arbor, Michigan.
    Guthe suggests description based on four primary charac-
teristics of ceramic material: (I.) Paste: composition, texture,
hardness, color. (II.) Surface finish: surface manipulation,
smoothing, scraping, and polishing. (III.) Decoration: incised, engraved, punched, etc., application of paint. (IV.)
Form: shape (drawing best), dimension.

382. Hagstrum, Melissa. 1985 "Measuring Prehistoric Craft Specialization: A Test Case in the American Southwest." Journal of
Field Archaeology, Vol. 12, No. 1, pp. 65-75.
    "Standardization and efficiency in pottery decoration are
used to measure ceramic specalization in two ceramic wares
from the Upper Rio Grande Valley of the American Southwest.
Santa Fe/Wiyo Black-on-white from the coalition period (1200-
1325 AC) and Bandelier Black-on-gray (Biscuit B) from the
Classic Period, 1325-1600 AC. Vessels produced by specialists
should exhibit standarized and efficient methods of pottery
decoration. Standardization in vessel decoration is assessed
by gesture use and variability of design elements and efficiency
in vessel decoration is assessed by the number of gestures
and brush strokes. These measures demonstrate that the
decoration of Biscuit B is more standarized and efficiently exe-
cuted, and they suggest increased craft specialization in the
Classic period in the Upper Rio Grande Valley," Abstract, p.
65.

383. Hagstrum, Melissa B. and Hildebrand, John A. 1983 "Understanding the Curvature Measurement of Potsherds." Pottery
Southwest, Vol. 10, No. 3, pp. 3-7.
    "We have found that the radius of curvature measured on
sherds from cylindrical and hemispherical pots can vary significantly from the whole vessel radius. Although the average
measured sherd curvature is a good indicator of vessel size,
the standard deviation of the measured curvature increases
linearly with the vessel size. The observed errors are attributable to surface variations on the sherds, to slightly ellipti-
cal vessel cross-sections, and to the inability to visually dis-
criminate between neighboring radius of curvature values for
nearly flat sherds," p. 7.

384. Hales, Henry. 1892 "Prehistoric New Mexican Pottery." Annual Report to the Smithsonian Institution (1892), pp. 535-554.
    Early pottery found in excavations in Tula Rosa Canyon,
New Mexico. Found pottery described as: coil pots, plain
smooth red ware, black-on-white and black-on-red.

385. Halley, David. 1983 "Use Alteration of Pottery Vessel Sur-
      faces: An Important Source of Evidence for the Identification
      of Vessel Function." North American Archaeologist, Vol. 4,
      No. 1, pp. 3-26.
         Ceramic vessels from two Barnett phase sites in northwest
      Georgia were analyzed for surface alternation from use. Soot-
      ing, discoloration from oxidation, and pitting of the interior
      were found and the processes by which they were produced
      were identified. The relationships between the type of surface
      alteration and the form of the vessel are described and inter-
      preted. Because these surface alternations are a result of
      vessel use, they reliably identify the function of individual
      vessels and vessel forms.

386. Halseth, Odd S. 1926 "The Revival of Pueblo Pottery Making."
      El Palacio, Vol. 21, No. 6, pp. 135-154.
         A description of the revival of pottery manufacture in the
      pueblos of the Southwest United States. Illustrations of San
      Ildefonso Polychrome vessels, p. 142. "Good and bad" San
      Ildefonso pottery, plate following p. 143.

387. Halseth, Odd S. 1941 Portfolio of Hohokam Pottery Designs.
      Pueblo Grande Laboratory, Phoenix, Arizona.
         This portfolio contains 52 plates reproduced in color by silk
      screen process. The plates are accompanied by a brief printed
      introduction. The plates are unbound and are about 14" by
      10" in size. They have been chosen to illustrate the range in
      pottery design through the whole development of Hohokam
      pottery. The main work of preparing the plates was done by
      the Arizona W.P.A. under the direction of Odd Halseth.

388. Hall, Edward T., Jr. 1944 "Early Stockaded Settlements in
      the Gobernador, New Mexico. Columbia Studies in Archaeology
      and Ethnology, Vol. 2, Pt. 1.
         Illustrations of Bancos Black-on-white (Piedra-Gallina Tran-
      sition), Figs. 25 and 26. Descriptions of Rosa Black-on-white,
      Rosa Neck Coil, Rosa Plain, and Rosa Scored.

389. Hammack, Laurens C. 1969 "Highway Salvage Archaeology in
      the Forestdale Valley, Arizona." Kiva, Vol. 34, Nos. 2 and
      3, pp. 58-89.
         Excavation of Skiddy Canyon Ruin and Gobbler Tank Site
      in 1966. Many types of pottery were found. Illustrations of
      Red Mesa style black-on-white, p. 78; Snowflake Black-on-
      white, p. 80; Lino Gray, p. 83; and Alma Incised, p. 83.

390. Hammack, Laurens C. 1974 "Effigy Vessels in the Prehistoric
      Southwest." Arizona Highways, Vol. 50, No. 2, pp. 33-35.
         (See Arizona Highways, February 1974 for annotation)

391. Hammack, Laurens C. and Sullivan, Alan P. (Editors). 1981

"The 1968 Excavations at Mound 8, Las Colinas Ruins Group, Phoenix, Arizona." Cultural Resource Management Section, Archaeological Series No. 154, Arizona State Museum, University of Arizona, Tucson, Arizona.

Conclusion: "The Las Colinas assemblage has offered a rare, diachronic view of the Hohokam ceramic variability and manufacture from the end of the Sacaton phase to the end of the Civano phase. This comprehensive collection, well dated and with excellent records of provenience, has permitted a thorough examination of changes in ceramic style, technology, and manufacturing frequency through time," p. 168. Description of Santan Red-on-buff.

392-   Hammack, Nancy S.; Ferg, Alan; and Bradley, Bruce. 1983
93.   "Excavation at Three Developmental Period Sites Near Zia and Santa Ana Pueblos, New Mexico." CASA Papers, No. 2, Complete Archaeological Service Associates, Cortez, Colorado.

Chapter No. 2 by Ferg presents a section on the ceramics of the Sheep Chute Site. Extensive discussion of Lino Black-on-white, Kana-a Black-on-white and on related gray wares and on San Marcial Black-on-white and types related to it.

394.   Hammersen, Martha M. (Compiler). 1972 "The Prehistoric Mogollon Culture and its Regional Aspects in the El Paso Area." Artifact, Vol. 10, No. 1, El Paso Archaeological Society.

A good summary of the investigations of the Society concerning the Jornada Branch of the Mogollon Culture. Chronology of the pottery in the phases and regions of this area is given on p. 17. Trade wares in the area and maps indicating possible movements are included. Descriptions include: El Paso Polychrome, p. 42, ill., p. 22; El Paso Brown Ware, p. 41; Chupadero Black-on-white, p. 43, ill., p. 20; and Three Rivers Red-on-terra cotta, p. 44. Illustrations of Mimbres Polychrome and Plain ware jars, p. 16, and Gila Polychrome bowl, p. 36.

395.   Hammett, Julia. 1977 "Analysis of 1976 Ceramic Collections." In Joseph C. Winter, Hovenweep 1976, Archaeological Report No. 3, pp. 63-78, Anthropology Department, San Jose University, San Jose, California.

Description of ceramics recovered during the 1976 field season at Hovenweep National Monument. Ceramics were analyzed by type and feature association. A partial vessel of Hovenweep Gray was found indicating this may be a valid type. This type is described and illustrated. Other types recovered and illustrated are Mesa Verde Corrugated, Hovenweep Corrugated, Chapin Gray, Piedra Black-on-white, McElmo Black-on-white, Mesa Verde Black-on-white and unidentified black-on-white.

396. Hantman, Jeffrey L., and Lightfoot, Kent. 1978 "Analysis of
Ceramic Design: A New Method for Chronological Seriation."
In Fred Plog, An Analytical Approach to Cultural Resource
Management, Arizona State University Anthropological Research Papers, No. 13, Tempe, Arizona.
   Conclusion: "The above analysis demonstrates the utility
of design element studies in developing finer temporal control
of the prehistoric record of an area. Preliminary analyses
suggest that the sites in the Little Colorado Planning Unit reflect a fairly homogeneous adaptation to a high elevation region, occupied during one relatively short phase (Reserve/
Tularosa) of Southwestern prehistory. This study has demonstrated that there is significant variability within this traditionally defined phase. By utilizing the analytical technique
of seriating ceramic attributes, as opposed to the normative
types, a temporal sequence has been developed which allows
for the processual study of a short-term adaptation such as
that in the Little Colorado Planning Unit," p. 56.

397. Hantman, Jeffrey L.; Lightfoot, Kent; Steadman, Upham; Plog,
F.; Plog, S.; and Donaldson, B. 1984 "Cibola White
wares: A Regional Perspective." In A. P. Sullivan and J. L.
Hantman, Regional Analysis of Prehistoric Ceramic Variation:
Contemporary Studies of Cibola Whitewares, Anthropological
Research Papers, No. 31, Arizona State University, Tempe,
Arizona.
   Abstract: "Regional distributions of black-on-white decorated ceramics in east-central Arizona are examined. A variety
of analyses provides new data for revaluating the processes
that affect the spatial and temporal variability of stylistic and
technological attributes. We discuss, in turn, how such factors as variation in exchange patterns, vessel function, and
localization of ceramic production and distribution may affect
the composition of ceramic assemblages. The implications of
our analyses for Cibola Whiteware systematics are also explored,"
p. 17.

398. Hardin, Margaret Ann. 1983 Gifts of Mother Earth: Ceramics
of the Zuni Tradition. Heard Museum, Phoenix, Arizona.
   Catalog of a travelling collection of historic Zuni Pottery
sponsored by Zuni Pueblo and Heard Museum. Includes information on construction, decoration, use and symbolism of
Zuni ceramics over the past century. One hundred illustrations of Zuni pottery from prehistoric to contemporary. Many
illustrations of pottery collected in 1881 and 1884-85 by the
Museum of Natural History. Illustrations of recent ceramics
made by Jenny Laate, Anderson Peynetsa, Nellie Bica, Gunnison Natachu, Albert Eustace, Myra Eriacho, and Noreen Sim-
plicio. Illustration of Zuni Polychrome. Two teachers, in recent years, are Daisy Hooee (Hopi) and Jenny Laate originally
from Acoma.

Points out that although pottery making was traditionally a
woman's role, today many accomplished young potters are men.
Zuni pottery seems to be on the verge of a change. Pottery
is more varied.

399. Hargrave, L. Lyndon. 1931 "Recently Dated Pueblo Ruins in
      Arizona: Excavations at Kin Tiel and Kokopnyama." Smith-
      sonian Miscellaneous Collections, Vol. 82, No. 11, pp. 80-120,
      Washington, D.C.
          Description of Jeddito Black-on-orange, pp. 118-119. Illus-
      trations of Jeddito Black-on-orange bowls and late Black-on-
      white ollas from Kin Tiel Ruins.

400. Hargrave, L. Lyndon. 1932 "Guide to Forty Pottery Types
      from the Hopi Country and the San Francisco Mountains, Ari-
      zona." Museum of Northern Arizona Bulletin, No. 1, Flagstaff,
      Arizona.
          An early effort to bring together descriptions and illustra-
      tions of Southwestern pottery types. Methods of pottery mak-
      ing, pp. 5-7. Pottery types described: Lino Gray, p. 11,
      Kana-a gray, p. 11-12; Conconino Gray, p. 12; Lino Black-
      on-gray, p. 12; Deadmans Gray, pp. 12-13; Tusayan Cor-
      rugated, p. 13; Deadmans Corrugated, p. 14; Moenkopi Cor-
      rugated, p. 14; Deadmans Black-on-gray, p. 14; Deadmans
      Fugitive Red, pp. 14-15; Kana-a Black-on-white, p. 15; Dead-
      mans Black-on-white, pp. 15-16, Flagstaff Black-on-white, p.
      16; Jeddito Black-on-white, pp. 16-17; Rio de Flag Brown, p.
      17; Deadmans Black-on-red, p. 18; Sunset Red, pp. 18-19;
      Flagstaff Red, p. 19; Elden Corrugated, p. 19; Walnut Black-
      on-white, p. 20; Wupatki Black-on-white, p. 20; Tusayan
      Black-on-red, pp. 21-22; Tusayan Polychrome, p. 22; Kayenta
      Polychrome, p. 22; Tusayan Polychrome, p. 22; Kayenta Black-
      on-white, pp. 23-24; Homolovi Plain, pp. 24-25; Homolovi Cor-
      rugated, p. 25; Jeddito Plain, pp. 25-26; Jeddito Corrugated,
      pp. 26-27; Jeddito Tooled, p. 27; Kokop Black-on-orange, pp.
      28-29; Jeddito Black-on-yellow, pp. 29-30; Jeddito Black-on-
      yellow stippled, p. 30; Jeddito Black-on-yellow engraved, p.
      30; Bidahochi Polychrome, p. 30; Sikyatki Polychrome, p. 31.
      A map of the Hopi country and San Francisco Mountain Region
      on page 35.

401. Hargrave, L. Lyndon. 1932a "The Museum of Northern Ari-
      zona Archaeological Expedition, 1932." Museum of Northern
      Arizona Notes, Vol. 5, No. 5, Flagstaff, Arizona.
          Red-on-buff sherds were found associated with Pueblo II
      sherds in a small site at Turkey Tank. Excavation proved
      that Hohokam contact to Pueblo II was more than transitory.
      Excavation of the dwelling showed Hohokam influence and even
      plain red ware jars had a neck decoration of small white crosses.
      Some sherds also showed evidence of the "Gila shoulder."
      Some sherds with Red-on-buff surface characteristics but hav-
      ing volcanic cinder temper showed they were locally manufactured.

402.   Hargrave, L. Lyndon. 1935 "Concerning the Names of South-
        western Pottery Types." Southwestern Lore, Vol. 1, No. 3,
        pp. 17-23.
            A general discussion of pottery terms, reasons for pottery
        classification, and analysis. Rules for naming pottery types
        and rules of priority are listed.

403.   Hargrave, L. Lyndon. 1936 "Notes on a Red Ware from Bluff,
        Utah." Southwestern Lore, Vol. 2, No. 2, pp. 29-34.
            Sherds from site NA 2659 near Bluff, Utah. Red sherds
        from this site are similar to those found in Tsegi Canyon and
        Deadmans Black-on-red. Description of Bluff Black-on-red,
        pp. 31-32.

404.   Hargrave, L. Lyndon. 1961 Ceramics of the Prewitt District,
        New Mexico. Unpublished manuscript, Museum of Northern
        Arizona, Flagstaff, Arizona.
            Descriptions of Grants Black-on-white, pp. 37-38; Bluewater
        Black-on-white, pp. 41-42; Las Tusas Black-on-white, pp. 43-
        44; and San Mateo Plain, pp. 40-41.

405.   Hargrave, L. Lyndon. 1974 "Type Determinants in South-
        western Ceramics and Some of Their Applications." Plateau,
        Vol. 46, No. 3, pp. 76-95.
            A discussion of the reasons for formulating the present
        system of taxonomy as first presented in Colton and Hargrave,
        1937. This article presents facts and data to clarify the mean-
        ing and use of a pottery type. A pottery type is defined as
        follows: "A group of ceramic vessels displaying in common,
        a specific combination of objective characteristics which when
        taken collectively, refer to it and to nothing else," p. 78.
        Type determinants: "Any one or more objective characters oc-
        curring consistently on each of a group of pottery vessels
        which character, characters, or combination are distinctive of
        the group and may serve as a basis for identifying, describ-
        ing and naming the group." The following are listed as type
        determinants: (1) surface color, (2) exterior surface of ves-
        sel smudges, (3) smudging limited to interior surface, (4) un-
        altered surface, no material added, (5) undecorated surface
        covered with a slip, (6) local use of a slip (on a restricted
        area of the surface), (7) addition of paint, as a drawing, (8)
        two paint colors in design, one on interior, one on exterior,
        (9) more than one paint color in a drawing, (10) painted de-
        sign outlined with another paint color, (11) special use of a
        slipped area as a base for a painted design, (12) a variation
        of technique in applying paint in design, (13) a painted area
        altered by engraving in paint, (14) incising or "cutting" the
        surface, (15) gouged or punched depressions in the surface,
        (16) scored, scratched or wiped surface, (17) structural coils
        left relatively intact, (18) surface corrugated, and variations
        thereof, (19) surface altered by adding clay, (20) temper and/

or paste, (21) kind of paint mixture, (22) styles of design,
(23) layout, (24) polished over paint, (25) combinations of
two or more of these determinants. Polishing, "floating" and
vessel form are not considered to be type determinants.
This writer supports the addition of pottery types based
on the above determinants. This article contrasts with the
point of view presented in Martin and Plog, 1973, concerning
the adequacy of the Colton system of pottery taxonomy.

406.   Hargrave, L. Lyndon and Colton, Harold S. 1935 "What Do
        Potsherds Tell Us." Museum of Northern Arizona Notes, Vol.
        7, No. 12, Flagstaff, Arizona.
            Brief introduction and explanation of how potsherds are
        described and used. Gives rules of priority for naming and
        mentions handbook to be published.

407.   Hargrave, L. Lyndon and Smith, Watson. 1936 A Method for
        Determining the Texture of Pottery." American Antiquity, Vol.
        2, No. 1, pp. 32-36.
            Texture of the core of a pottery sherd is defined as: "The
        visual or tactile character of the core of a pottery vessel which
        results from the arrangement, size, shape, and relative quan-
        tity of the individual particles composing the core, regardless
        of color or chemical composition," p. 34. The following terms
        were suggested to describe sizes of the particles in the core:
        "Very coarse, coarse, medium, fine, very fine," p. 34.
        Sherds are kept on file at the Museum of Northern Arizona for
        a standard comparison of the above terms.

408.   Harlow, Francis H. 1965 "Recent Finds of Pajaritan Pottery."
        El Palacio, Vol. 72, No. 2, pp. 27-33.
            Description of eight vessels found in the summer of 1964
        by hikers in the White Rock Canyon near White Rock Housing
        Development, New Mexico. Illustrations of three Sankawi
        Black-on-cream jars, Espinosa Glaze Polychrome bowl, Sankawi
        Black-on-cream bowl, Figs. 2-5; Glaze ware bowl, and a Tewa
        Polychrome jar.

409.   Harlow, Francis H. 1965a "Tewa Indian Ceremonial Pottery."
        El Palacio, Vol. 72, No. 4, pp. 13-23.
            "The emphasis of this paper is on one section of the Tewa
        ceramic hitsory, that of the ceremonial or religious vessels,
        Only the objective properties of these ceremonial ceramics are
        discussed. No reference is made to the religious practice nor
        to the purposes for which these pieces were manufactured....
        The earliest ceremonial pottery ascribed to the Tewa is of the
        prebiscuit ware types: Santa Fe Black-on-white and Wiyo
        Black-on-white. Almost invariably the vessels are small squat
        jars with horizontal handles or with holes drilled for tying,"
        p. 13. Illustrations of the following Tewa ceremonial vessles:
        Tewa Polychrome jar and bowl, two Ogapoge Polychrome jars,

Pojoaque Polychrome jar, Fig. 1; Bandelier Black-on-gray bowl,
Tewa Black-on-tan jar, Ogapoge Polychrome jar, incised, Tewa
Black-on-tan jar, San Ildefonso, Terraced bowl Ca.
1890, San
Ildefonso Polychrome jar CA 1890, Fig. 3; and late Tesuque
Polychrome bowl, San Ildefonso Polychrome jar, Pojoaque Polychrome blow, Tesuque Black-on-tan jar, Ca. 1850, Tesuque
bowl 1850-1890, a pseudo ceremonial bowl of San Ildefonso Polychrome, Fig. 4.

410. Harlow, Francis H. 1970 Historic Pueblo Indian Pottery. Mu-
      seum of New Mexico, Santa Fe, New Mexico (revision of 1967).
      Covers pottery from the pueblos during the period AD 1600-
      1900. Brief description of designs and illustrations of the fol-
      lowing types: Northern Rio Grande Area: Tewa Pueblos, San-
      kawi Polychrome, p. 6; Tewa Polychrome, p. 6; Ogapoge Poly-
      chrome, p. 8; Powhoge Polychrome, p. 8; San Ildefonso Black-
      on-red, p. 10; San Ildefonso Polychrome, p. 10; Tesuque Poly-
      chrome 1830-1910, p. 10. Northern Rio Grande Area: Keres
      Pueblos, Kiua Polychrome 1780-1920, p. 12; Santo Domingo
      Polychrome 1900-present, p. 14; Cochiti Polychrome 1830-
      present, p. 14; Puname Area, Puname Polychrome 1700-1760,
      p. 16; San Pablo Polychrome 1750-1800, p. 18; Trio Polychrome
      1800-1850, p. 20; Zia Polychrome 1850-present, p. 20; Ran-
      chitos Polychrome 1780-1810, p. 22; Santa Ana Polychrome
      1810-1920, p. 22. Various Areas: Jemez Black-on-white to
      1700, p. 24; Tortugas Red-on-orange 1800?, p. 24; Kotyiti
      Glaze Polychrome 1650-1710, p. 24; Acoma-Laguna-Zuni; Haw-
      ikuh Polychrome 1600-1700, p. 26; Ako Polychrome 1700-1760,
      p. 26; Acomita Polychrome 1760-1830, p. 28; Laguna Polychrome
      1830-1920, p. 28; Acoma-Laguna Area, McCartys Polychrome
      1830-1890, p. 30; Acoma Polychrome 1890-present, p. 30; Zuni
      Area, Ashiwi Polychrome 1700-1770, p. 32; Kiapkwa Polychrome
      1770-1850, p. 34; Zuni Polychrome 1850-present, p. 36. Hopi
      Area: San Bernardo Polychrome 1600-1750, p. 38; Payupki
      Polychrome 1700-1780, p. 40; Polacca Polychrome 1760-1900, p.
      42; Walpi Polychrome 1750-present, p. 44; and Hano Polychrome
      1900-present, p. 44.

411. Harlow, Francis H. 1973 Matte-Paint Pottery of the Tewa,
      Keres and Zuni Pueblos. Museum of New Mexico, Santa Fe,
      New Mexico.
      A useful compilation of matte paint pottery from most of the
      New Mexico pueblos. Descriptions and illustrations of the fol-
      lowing types: Abiquiu Black-on-gray, p. 76; Bandelier Black-
      on-gray, p. 76; Cuyamungue Black-on-tan, p. 76; Sankawi
      Black-on-cream, p. 76; Sakona Black-on-tan, p. 77; Sakona
      Polychrome, p. 77; Pojoaque Polychrome, p. 77; Ogapoge Poly-
      chrome, p. 78; Powhoge Polychrome, p. 78; San Ildefonso
      Black-on-red, p. 78; San Ildefonso Polychrome, p. 79; Tunyo
      Polychrome, p. 79; Tatungue Polychrome, p. 79; Nambe Poly-
      chrome, p. 80; Potsuwi'i Incised, p. 80; Potsuwi'i Gray, p.
      80; Kapo Gray, p. 80; Kapo Black, p. 81; Santa Clara Black,

p. 81; Posuge Red, p. 81 (no illustration); Nambe Red, p. 82
(no illustration); San Juan Red-on-tan, p. 82; Kiua Polychrome,
p. 82; Cochiti Polychrome, p. 83; Santo Domingo Polychrome,
p. 83; Puname Polychrome, p. 83; San Pablo Polychrome, p.
84; Trios Polychrome, p. 84; Zia Polychrome, p. 84; Santa Ana
Polychrome, p. 85; Hawikuh Polychrome, p. 85 (no illustra-
tion); Ako Polychrome, p. 86 (cover); Acomita Polychrome, p.
86; McCartys Polychrome, p. 86; Acoma Polychrome, p. 87;
Laguna Polychrome, p. 87; Ashiwi Polychrome, p. 87; Kiapkwa
Polychrome, p. 88; and Zuni Polychrome, p. 88. Appendix
I (pp. 69-74): a good glossary of pottery terms. Appendix
III (pp. 89-192): design styles and evolution with drawings.
Contemporary incised and polychrome pottery illustration in
Plate 18.

412.   Harlow, Francis H.   1976 "Glazed Pottery of the Southwest."
       American Indian Art Magazine, Vol. 2, No. 1, November, pp.
       64-70
       A brief description of the use of glaze paint decoration in
       the Southwest from AD 1250 to 1700. Good photos of these
       types: Hawikuh Polychrome, White Mountain Black-on-red,
       Hawikuh Glaze-on-red, Carretas Polychrome, Ramos Polychrome,
       and a glaze paint stirrup jar.

413.   Harlow, Francis H.   1977 Modern Pueblo Pottery, 1880-1960.
       Northland Press, Flagstaff, Arizona.
       A good introduction to modern pottery of the pueblos and
       other pottery producing tribes of the Southwest. Short sec-
       tion on the prehistoric era includes color photographs of a
       few vessels. Modern pueblo pottery is presented by language
       groups and pueblos. Major types are shown through excellent
       color photos. Also included is a one page section on the re-
       vival of prehistoric Chihuahua wares made by Juan Quezada.
       A glossary of pottery terms is appended.

414.   Harlow, Francis H. and Bartlett, Katherine.   1978 An Intro-
       duction to Hopi Pottery. Museum of Northern Arizona, Flag-
       staff, Arizona.
       A short presentation of the history and contemporary status
       of Hopi pottery. Included are color illustrations of prehistoric,
       historic, and contemporary Hopi pottery vessels.

415.   Harlow, Francis H. and Young, John V.   1965 Contemporary
       Pueblo Indian Pottery. Museum of New Mexico Press, Santa
       Fe, New Mexico.
       Popular booklet with black and white and color photos of
       contemporary Southwestern pottery. Illustrations of pottery
       from the following pueblos and tribes: Acoma, Picuris, San
       Juan, Santa Clara, San Ildefonso, Taos, Tesuque, Jemez, Zuni,
       Cochiti, Zia, Hopi, Maricopa, and Santo Domingo.

416. Harner, Michael J. 1957 "Potsherds and the Tentative Dating
      of the San Gorgonio-Big Marie Trail." In F. J. Johnson and
      Patricia H. Johnson, "An Indian Trail Complex of the Central
      Colorado Desert," University of California Archaeological Sur-
      vey No. 37, Papers on California Archaeology, pp. 47-49,
      Berkeley, California.
      Description and illustrations of Parker Buff: Fort Mohave
      variety, pp. 18-19, Pls. 5, 6, and 8; and Parker Red-on-buff:
      Fort Mohave variety, pp. 16-18, Pls. 1-8.

417. Harrill, Bruce G. 1972 "Archaeological Salvage in a Prehis-
      toric Campsite, Petrified Forest National Park." Plateau, Vol.
      44, No. 4, pp. 163-175.
      The ceramics consisted of slightly over 1,000 sherds which
      suggest an intermittent occupation between AD 1150-1300.
      Sixty-three percent of the sherds were textured Mogollon Brown
      ware. The most numerous painted ware is Snowflake Black-on-
      white. No whole or restorable vessels were found.

418. Harrill, Bruce G. 1973 "The Do Bell Site: Archaeological
      Salvage Near the Petrified Forest." Kiva, Vol. 39, No. 1,
      pp. 35-67.
      Excavation at a small pithouse village south of Petrified
      Forest National Park. Twenty-six whole vessels and over
      10,000 sherds were collected and analyzed in this 1968 salvage
      project. Painted types found were Snowflake Black-on-white,
      Showlow, St. Johns, and Puerco Black-on-red types; and St.
      Johns, Springerville, and Wingate polychromes.

419. Harrington, Mark R. 1937 "Excavations of Pueblo Grande de
      Nevada." Texas Archaeological and Paleological Society Bulletin,
      Vol. 9, pp. 130-145.
      Excavations recovered appear to be Pueblo type dwellings
      and corrugated and painted pottery. Illustrations of a corru-
      gated jar, seven black-on-white bowls, a corrugated canteen,
      and a plain canteen.

420. Harris, Arthur H.; Schoenwetter, James; and Warren, A. H.
      1967 "An Archaeological Survey of the Chuska Valley and the
      Chaco Plateau, New Mexico." Museum of New Mexico Research
      Records, No. 4, Santa Fe; "Petrographic Analysis of Pottery
      and Lithics," A. H. Warren, pp. 104-134.
      "The rock used for temper in all local pottery types and in
      all localities, almost without exception, was a fine-grained vol-
      canic rock which is classified herein as trachyte," p. 107.
      Twenty-three new gray, white, and red ware types are named.
      (These are described in Wilson and Peckham, 1964). A de-
      tailed analysis is made of the different tempers, and it is con-
      cluded that: "Trachyte tempered pottery is unique to the
      Chuska Valley or Chuska Mountains vicinity."

421. Hartman, Russell P. and Musial, Jan. 1987 Navajo Pottery: Traditions and Innovations. Northland Press, Flagstaff, Arizona.
      A good book on the cultural significance, technology, history, decline, and revival of Navajo pottery making. Potters making traditional pitch covered pottery included are Lorena Bartlett, Bertha and Silas Claw, Alice Cling, Kate Davis, Penny Emerson, Louise Goodman, Betty Manygoats, Faye Tso, Cecelia Whiterock, Rose Williams, and Jimmy Wilson.
      The following potters who have developed new styles are discussed and pictured: Chris McHorse, Lucy McKelvey, Ida Sahmie, Blanche and David Sales, and John Whiterock. Historic pottery types illustrated and briefly described are Dinetah Gray, Gobernador Polychrome, Navajo Polychrome, and Navajo Gray. Pinyon Gray is also mentioned.

422. Haury, Emil W. 1930 "A Sequence of Decorated Redware from Silver Creek Drainage." Museum of Northern Arizona, Museum Notes, Vol. 2, No. 11, Flagstaff, Arizona.
      The trend of pottery development in the Silver Creek area was from a very generalized stage represented by Little Colorado Polychrome to an extreme specialized stage represented by Fourmile Polychrome.

423. Haury, Emil W. 1932 "Roosevelt: 9:6, A Hohokam Site of the Colonial Period." Medallion Papers, No. 9, Gila Pueblo, Globe, Arizona.
      Types described are Pinedale Polychrome, p. 41; and Fourmile Polychrome.

424. Haury, Emil W. 1932a "The Age of Lead Glaze Decorated Pottery in the Southwest." American Anthropologist, Vol. 34, No. 3, pp. 418-425.
      Discussion of glaze pigments in the Zuni Region and their use in the dating of sites.

425. Haury, Emil W. 1934 "The Canyon Creek Ruin and the Cliff Dwellings of Sierra Ancha." Medallion Papers, No. 14, Gila Pueblo, Globe, Arizona.
      An extensive report of work done in this area. Type described is Cibicue Polychrome, pp. 131-134. Illustrations in plate following p. 133. Fourmile Polychrome and other types are illustrated.

426. Haury, Emil W. 1936 "Some Southwestern Pottery Types: Series IV." Medallion Papers, No. 14, Gila Pueblo, Globe Arizona.
      Descriptions of Mogollon and early Mimbres types. Types described are Alma Scored, p. 38; Alma Punched, p. 39; Alma Incised, p. 40; Alma Neckbanded, p. 35; Three Circle Neck Corrugated, p. 36; San Francisco Red, p. 28; San Lorenzo

Red-on-brown, p. 6; Mogollon Red-on-brown, p. 10; Three
circle Red-on-white, p. 103; and Mangus Black-on-white (Mimbres Boldface), p. 22.

427. Haury, Emil W. 1937 "Material Culture in Excavations at
      Snaketown." Medallion Papers, No. 25, Gila Pueblo, Globe,
      Arizona.
      Comprehensive descriptions and illustrations of Hohokam
      Red-on-buff types. The types described are Estrella Red-on-
      gray, p. 199; Sweetwater Red-on-gray, p. 192; Sweetwater
      Polychrome, p. 198; Snaketown Red-on-buff, p. 189; Gila Butte
      Red-on-buff, p. 179; Sacaton Buff, p. 78; Sacation Red-on-
      buff, p. 171; Vahki Plain, pp. 211-212; Vahki Red, pp. 204-
      205; Gila Plain, pp. 205-211; Sacaton Red, pp. 202-204; and
      Santan Red, pp. 202-204.

428. Haury, Emil W. 1940 "Excavations in the Forestdale Valley,
      East-Central Arizona." University of Arizona Social Science
      Bulletin, No. 12, Tucson, Arizona.
      Types described are Forestdale Plain (Woodruff Brown),
      p. 24; Forestdale Red (Woodruff Red), p. 11; and Forestdale
      Smudged (Woodruff Smudged), p. 73.

429. Haury, Emil W. 1945 Painted Cave in Northern Arizona.
      Amerind Foundation, No. 3, Dragoon, Arizona.
      "The main impression gained from a review of Painted Cave
      pottery is its cosmopolitan nature. Perhaps only little more
      than half of the pottery was locally derived, while the source
      of the remainder must be sought elsewhere.... The meaning
      of this is simply that the Four Corners region was far from iso-
      lated and that the people were receiving culture elements,
      probably not restricted to pottery, rather than contributing
      them to adjacent centers," pp. 59-60. Illustrations of Mesa
      Verde Black-on-white, Pl. 27; Mesa Verde Black-on-white jar,
      Pl. 28; Little Colorado White Ware, Pl. 29; Tusayan Black-on-
      red and Kintiel Black-on-orange, Pl. 30.
      Sherd of an undescribed type, Chinle Rough, shown in Pl.
      31.

430. Haury, Emil W. 1945a "The Excavation of Los Muertos and
      Neighboring Ruins in the Salt River Valley, Southern Arizona."
      Papers of the Peabody Museum, Vol. 24, No. 1, Cambridge,
      Massachusetts.
      Good report of this culture and description and illustration
      of pottery types. Types described are Gila Polychrome, pp.
      80-100; Gila Black-on-red, p. 98; Tonto Polychrome, pp. 80-
      100; Casa Grande Red-on-buff, pp. 15-62; Gila Smudged, p.
      81; Gila Red, p. 91; Salt Smudged, p. 81; and Salt Red, p.
      81.

431. Haury, Emil W. 1947 "An Early Pithouse Village of the Mogollon

Culture, Forestdale Valley, Arizona." University of Arizona Bulletin, Vol. 18, No. 4; Social Science Bulletin, No. 16, Tucson, Arizona.
Description of Alma Plain: Bluff Variety, pp. 49-50.

432. Haury, Emil W. 1950 The Stratigraphy and Archaeology of Ventana Cave, Arizona. University of Arizona and University of New Mexico Presses.
Descriptions of Vamori Red-Brown, p. 12; Tanque Verde Red-Brown, pp. 348-349; Sells Plain, p. 344; and Sells Red, p. 346.

433. Haury, Emil W. and Gifford, C. 1959 "A 13th Century Strong Box." Kiva, Vol. 24, No. 4, pp. 1-11.
Description of Tanque Verde Red-on-brown jar, background is light brown with fireclouds. Rectilinear designs in a deep red paint on exterior. Paragraph indicates articles on Tanque Verde pottery from University Ruin, Martinez Hill Ruin, Hodges Ruin, and Tanque Verde Ruin.

434. Haury, Emil W. and Hargrave, Lyndon L. 1931 "Recently Dated Pueblo Ruins in Arizona." Smithsonian Miscellaneous Collections, Vol. 82, No. 11, Publication 3069, Washington, D.C.
Types described are Showlow Black-on-red, p. 27, and Pinedale Black-on-white, p. 62. Illustrations of Fourmile Polychrome and Pinedale Polychrome.

435. Harvey, Doris L. 1935 "The Pottery of the Little Colorado Culture Area." Masters thesis, University of Arizona, Tucson, Arizona.
Pottery of this area is compared to that from San Juan, Upper Gila, Kinishba, and other areas. Types illustrated are Turkey Hill Black-on-white ware, Puerco Black-on-white, Tularosa Black-on-white, Hopi stippled bowls, Zuni olla, Fourmile Polychrome, and Pinedale Polychrome.

436. Hawley, Florence M. 1929 "Prehistoric Pottery Pigments in the Southwest." American Anthropologist, Vol. 31, pp. 731-754, Menasha, Wisconsin.
Data on chemical composition of pottery pigments.

437. Hawley, Florence M. 1930 "Prehistoric Pottery and Culture Relations in Middle Gila." American Anthropologist, N.S., Vol. 32, No. 3, pp. 522-536.
Red-on-buff, black-on-white, and polychrome types of the Middle Gila, three plates. Illustrated are polished red-on-buff, smudged interior, Pl. 8; slipped and unslipped red-on-buff, Pl. 8; Little Colorado Black-on-red, Pl. 9; Tularosa Black-on-white, Pl. 9; and Gila Polychrome, Pl. 10.

438. Hawley, Florence M. 1930a "Chemical Examination of Prehistoric Wares." American Anthropologist, Vol. 32, No. 3, July-September, pp. 500-502.
Early study of tests of the chemical composition of the black smudge on some prehistoric pottery of the Southwest.

439. Hawley, Florence M. 1934 "The Significance of the Dated Prehistory of Chetro Ketl, Chaco Canyon, New Mexico." University of New Mexico Bulletin, Vol. 1, No. 1, Albuquerque.
Three types of Chaco Black-on-white ware and the typical Mesa Verde Black-on-white were found at Chetro Ketl. The three Chaco Black-on-whites are illustrated in Pl. 15. The Mesa Verde Black-on-white designs are shown in Pl. 16, and the one black-on-red type is illustrated in Fig. 14, Pl. 16. These unnamed types are well described. Statistical significance of the potsherd data, pp. 47-57.

440. Hawley, Florence M. 1936 "Field Manual of Prehistoric Southwestern Pottery Types." University of New Mexico Bulletin, Anthropology Series, Vol. 1, No. 4 (revised 1950).
First major effort to compile a comprehensive volume of pottery descriptions. Good early descriptions of many pottery types. Best on Eastern Arizona and New Mexico areas. No illustrations, good bibliography. Types are organized by chronological periods, culture areas, districts, and wares:
Southwestern Pottery Types
Basketmaker III
San Juan Area: Rosa Black-on-white, Rosa Smoothed, Lino Gray, Lino Black-on-gray; Little Colorado; La Plata Black-on-white, White Mound Black-on-white, Adamana Brown, Woodruff Brown, Woodruff Red, and Woodruff Smudged; Rio Grande: San Marcial Black-on-white.
Pueblo I
San Juan: Kana-a Gray, Deadmans Gray, Deadmans Fugitive Red, Rio de Flag Brown, Deadmans Black-on-red, Deadmans Black-on-white, Kana-a Black-on-white; Little Colorado: Dead River Black-on-white, Kiatuthlanna Black-on-white, Deadmans Black-on-red, Piedra Black-on-white.
Pueblo II
San Juan: Deadmans Black-on-white, Tusayan Black-on-red, Coconino Gray, Deadmans Gray, Deadmans Fugitive Red, Rio de Flag Brown, Sunset Red, Tusayan Corrugated, Deadmans Corrugated, Moenkopi Corrugated, and McElmo Black-on-white.
Little Colorado: Escavada Black-on-white, Gallup Black-on-white, Pueblo II Exuberant Corrugated, Holbrook Black-on-white, and Puerco Black-on-white. Rio Grande: Kwahe'e Black-on-white, Taos Black-on-white, Gallina Black-on-white, Gallina Plain and Indented, Socorro Black-on-white, Los Lunas Smudged, and Pitoche Rubbed-ribbed.
Pueblo III
San Juan: Mesa Verde Black-on-white, Tusayan Black-on-white,

Kayenta Black-on-white, Wupatki Black-on-white, Tusayan
Black-on-red, Tusayan Polychrome, Kayenta Polychrome, Flagstaff Black-on-white, Walnut Black-on-white, Sunset Red, Flagstaff Red, and Elden Corrugated. Little Colorado: Gallup
Black-on-white, Chaco Black-on-white, Chaco Corrugated, Mancos Black-on-white, Tularosa Black-on-white, Puerco Black-on-
red, Showlow Black-on-red, Showlow Corrugated, Showlow
Smudged, Showlow Corrugated Smudged, Wingate Black-on-
red, Wingate Corrugated, Wingate Polychrome, St. Johns Poly-
chrome, Houck Polychrome, Querino Polychrome, Jeddito Black-
on-white, Bidahochi Black-on-white, Jeddito Black-on-orange,
Kokop Black-on-orange, Jeddito Corrugated, Tularosa Black-
on-white, Upper Gila Corrugated, Roosevelt Black-on-white,
Salado Red, and Gila Red. Verde Valley: Verde Brown,
Prescott Gray, Tuzigoot Red, Verde Red-on-buff, Prescott
Black-on-gray, Tuzigoot Black-on-gray, Prescott Polychrome,
Tuzigoot White-on-red. Sonora: Trincheras Purple-on-red,
Trincheras Polychrome, and Santa Cruz Polychrome. Chi-
huahua: Carmen Red-on-gray, Medanos Red-on-brown, Ma-
dera Black-on-red, Playas Red, and Ramos Black. Mimbres:
Mimbres Bold Face Black-on-white, Mimbres Classic Black-on-
white, Mimbres Plain, Mimbres Incised, Mimbres Plain Brown,
and Mimbres Corrugated. Rio Grande: El Paso Polychrome,
Three Rivers Red-on-terra cotta, Lincoln Black-on-red, Chu-
padero Black-on-white, Casa Colorado Black-on-white, Corona
Rubbed-ribbed, Corona Rubbed-indented, Santa Fe Black-on-
white, Galisteo Black-on-white, Wiyo Black-on-white, and Jemez
Black-on-white.
Pueblo IV
Little Colorado: Pinedale Polychrome, Fourmile Polychrome,
Cibique Polychrome, Homolovi Polychrome, Homolovi Black-on-
red, Jeddito Black-on-yellow, Jeddito Black-on-yellow engraved,
Jeddito Black-on-yellow stippled, Bidahochi Polychrome, Sik-
yatki Polychrome, Kawaioku Polychrome, Jeddito Plain, Homo-
lovi Corrugated, Heshotauthia Polychrome, Pinto Polychrome,
Gila Polychrome, Tonto Polychrome. Rio Grande: Los Padillos
Glaze Polychrome, Agua Fria Glaze-on-red, Rayo Glaze-on-red,
Arenal Glaze Polychrome, San Clemente Glaze Polychrome,
Cieneguilla Glaze-on-yellow, Largo Glaze-on-yellow, Espinosa
Glaze Polychrome, Kuaua Glaze Polychrome, San Lazaro Glaze
Polychrome, Puaray Glaze Polychrome, Pecos Glaze Polychrome,
Trenaquel Glaze Polychrome, Tiquex Glaze Polychrome, Kotyiti
Glaze Polychrome, Cicuye Glaze Polychrome, Bandelier Black-
on-gray, Sankawi Black-on-cream, Tewa Polychrome, Potsuwi'i
Incised, Tesuque Smeared-indented, Cundiyo Micaceous Smeared-
indented, Cordova Micaceous ribbed, and Sapawe Micaceous
Washboard. Chihuahua: Babicora Polychrome, Huerigos Poly-
chrome, Carretas Polychrome, Villa Ahumada Polychrome, Dub-
lan Polychrome, Corralitos Polychrome Incised, Ramos Poly-
chrome, Carmen Red-on-gray, Medanos Red-on-brown, Madera
Black-on-red, Cloverdale Gouged Red. Northern Peripheral:

Great Salt Lake Gray, Sevier Gray, Sevier Corrugated, Sevier
Black-on-gray, Great Salt Lake Black-on-gray, Promontory
Black, Uintah Gray. Mogollon: San Lorenzo Red-on-brown,
Mogollon Red-on-brown, Three Circle Red-on-white, Mimbres
Bold Face Black-on-white, San Francisco Red, Alma Plain, Alma
Neckbanded, Three Circle Neck Corrugated, Alma Punched,
Alma Scored, and Alma Incised.
Hohokam Pottery Types
Santa Cruz Red-on-buff, Gila Plain Ware, Sacaton Red-on-
buff, Gila Plain Ware, Santan Red, Casa Grande Red-on-
buff, and San Carlos red-on-brown. Glossary of terms, p.
110.

441. Hayden, Julian D. 1957 "Excavations, 1940, at University
      Indian Ruin." Southwestern Monument Association Technical
      Series, Vol. 5.
          Appendix in 1954 by E. B. Danson describes: Tanque
      Verde red-on-brown, pp. 220-223; Pantano red-on-brown,
      pp. 224-226; Tucson Polychrome, pp. 226-231; and Tucson
      Plain.

442. Hayden, Julian D. 1959 "Notes on Pima Pottery Making."
      Kiva, Vol. 24, No. 3, pp. 10-16.
          Description with good photographs of a Pima Indian, Mrs.
      Annie O. Jackson, making pottery in 1937. Illustrations of
      Pima ware.

443. Hayes, Alden C. 1964 "The Archaeological Survey of Wethe-
      rill Mesa, Mesa Verde National Park." National Park Service
      Archaeology Series, No. 7A, Washington, D.C.
          Ceramics covered in section, pp. 42-75. Descriptions and
      clear photos of the following types: Chapin Gray, pp. 42-44;
      Moccasin Gray, pp. 44-45; Mancos Gray, pp. 45-48; Mancos
      Corrugated, pp. 48-49; Mesa Verde Corrugated, pp. 49-53;
      Hovenweep Corrugated, p. 53; La Plata Black-on-white, pp.
      53-55; Piedra Black-on-white, pp. 55-58; Cortez Black-on-
      white, pp. 58-59; Mancos Black-on-white, pp. 59-61; Wetherill
      Black-on-white, pp. 63-64; McElmo Black-on-white, pp. 65-69;
      and Mesa Verde Black-on-white, pp. 69-70. Some discussion
      and illustrations of San Juan Red ware, p. 74. Most common
      trade wares were Escavada Black-on-white and Red Mesa Black-
      on-white.

444. Hayes, Alden C. and Lancaster, James A. 1975 "Badger House
      Community." Publications in Archaeology, 7E Wetherill Mesa
      Studies, National Park Service, Washington, D.C.
          Pottery, pp. 98-104. Descriptions of sherds and vessels
      recovered at this mesa top site in Mesa Verde National Park.
      Local types described and illustrated include Chapin Gray,

Moccasin Gray, Mancos Gray, Mancos Corrugated, Mesa Verde
Corrugated, Chapin Black-on-white, Cortez Black-on-white,
Piedra Black-on-white, Mancos Black-on-white, McElmo Black-
on-white, Mesa Verde Black-on-white, Bluff Black-on-red, and
Deadmans Black-on-red. Also shown are clay pipes and worked
sherds.

445. Hayes, Alden C.; Young, Jon Nathan; and Warren, A. H.
      1981 "Excavation of Mound 7, Gran Quivira National Monument,
      New Mexico." Publications in Archaeology, Vol. 16, National
      Park Service, Washington, D.C.
         The pottery recovered in the excavation of Mound 7 is
      described and analyzed in Chapter 3, pp. 63-103. There were
      nearly 100,000 sherds and over 300 whole or restorable pots
      recovered. The types recovered, described and illustrated
      are local brown wares: Corona Corrugated and Corona Plain;
      local whiteware: Chupadero Black-on-white, Tabira' Plain,
      Tabira' Polychrome, and Tabira' Black-on-white; Rio Grande
      Glaze ware: 12 types and Salinas Red. Many types of other
      exotic pottery were found including brown and gray wares,
      white wares, yellow and cream wares, red wares, and types
      introduced by Europeans. A total of 936 worked sherds were
      found. This is the largest number reported from any site in
      the Southwest. They are completely described on pp. 158-
      161. The overall description and discussion of the pottery at
      Mound 7 is one of the best and most complete of any Salinas
      site. Appendix 1, pp. 179-182, presents a description of the
      tempering materials in the local pottery written by A. Helene
      Warren.

446. Hedges, Ken and Dittert, Alfred. 1984 "Heritage in Clay."
      San Diego Museum Papers, No. 17, San Diego, California.
         Description of the southwestern pottery collection in the San
      Diego Museum of Man obtained in 1912 by Wesley Bradfield and
      Thomas Dozier.

447. Hedrick, John A. 1971 "Investigations of Tigua Potters and
      Pottery at Ysleta de Sur, Texas." Artifact, Vol. 9, No. 2,
      El Paso Archaeological Society, El Paso, Texas.
         Description of pottery making at this Tigua community near
      El Paso. The work of three potters--Isidor Piarote, Juana
      Munoz, and Nestora Piarote Granillo--is briefly discussed in-
      cluding their techniques of manufacture and sources of materials.
      Pottery illustrations: Tortilla flatteners, Juana Munoz, Fig.
      10; large bowl decorations in red, Juana Munoz, Fig. 11;
      small fire-blackened brown ware bowl, Andres Granillo, fig.
      12; bowl with reddish brown paste, possibly made on a potter's
      wheel, Fig. 13; brown ware bowl, Juana Munoz, Fig. 14; stones
      for smoothing used by Tigua potters, Fig. 16. At the time

this article was written, Mr. and Mrs. Pablo Silvas were experimenting with pottery making in hopes they could develop
a good product.

448. Hedrick, John A. 1982 "An Experiment in the Replication of
El Paso Brown Pottery." Collected Papers in Honor of John
W. Runyan, Papers of the Archaeological Society of New Mexico,
7, Albuquerque Archaeological Society, Albuquerque, New
Mexico.
     An experimental study of the characteristics of fired bricks
and small vessels made of clays from two sources in the El
Paso area. The bricks and vessels were painted with hematite
or limonite paint made from local samples of red ochre and
yellow ochre. They were fired in an oxidizing, partially con-
trolled mesquite fire below 600 degrees C. The characteristics
of the fired vessels and bricks are compared to samples of El
Paso Brown sherds.

449. Hester, James J. and Shiner, Joel L. 1963 "Studies at Navajo
Period Sites in the Navajo Reservoir District." Museum of New
Mexico Papers in Anthropology, No. 9, Santa Fe, New Mexico.
     Description of Frances Polychrome, a variant of Goberna-
dor Polychrome.

450. Hewett, Edgar L. 1938 Pajarito Plateau and Its Ancient People. University of New Mexico Press, Albuquerque, New Mexico.
     General book with a short section on pottery. Color illus-
trations of Glaze Ware vessels, Pls. B and C. The pottery is
better described in Kidder, 1915.

451. Hibben, Frank C. 1949 "The Pottery of the Gallina Complex."
American Antiquity, Vol. 14, No. 3, pp. 194-202.
     Good article on the pottery of this complex in North Central
New Mexico. Descriptions and illustrations of the following
pottery types of the Gallina complex: Gallina Black-on-gray,
pp. 194-195; Gallina Plain undecorated, pp. 195-197; Gallina
Plain utility, pp. 197-198; Gallina Coarse utility, p. 198; Gallina Plain unfired, pp. 198-199; and Gallina Punched ware, p.
199. The undecorated wares of the Gallina Complex suggest
other than Pueblo connections. Among such possibilities are
connections with the Navajo and Woodland contact or origin.

452. Hill, David V. 1985 "Pottery Making at the Ewing Site (5
MT 927)." Southwestern Lore, Vol. 51, No. 1, pp. 19-31.
     A comparison of historic pottery making tools and techni-
ques with the prehistoric pottery materials and tools found at
the Ewing Site. Except for perishable tools, all the tools and
materials were found at this site. Tools included molding
trays formed from vessel bases, smoothing and scraping tools
made from recycled potsherds, polishing stones, manos, and
metates.

Conclusions were that each habitation area at the Ewing
Site had one or more potters in residence, during both building phases, and the majority of vessels in everyday use were
probably produced locally.

453. Hill, Gertrude. 1942 "Notes on Papago Pottery Manufacture
at Santa Rosa, Arizona." American Anthropologist, Vol. 44,
No. 3, pp. 531-533, Menasha, Wisconsin.
Good description of Papago pottery manufacture and uses
of pottery forms.

454. Hill, James N. 1966 "A Prehistoric Community in Eastern Arizona." Southwestern Journal of Archaeology, Vol. 22, No. 1,
pp. 9-30.
Broken K Pueblo located 11 miles east of Snowflake, Arizona, was excavated by personnel from the Chicago Natural
History Museum. It is a rectangular 95 room, single-storied,
surface masonry pueblo, dating from about AD 1150-1280. It
is the largest and latest site in the Hay Hollow Valley.
"The factor analysis of pottery types was particularly interesting in that it indicated each type of room was dominated by
a different constellation or cluster of pottery types. Of the
13 types analyzed, five of them were dominant in habitation
rooms; two of them were dominant in storage rooms; and two
largely peculiar to ceremonial rooms. The four remaining types
were common to both habitation and ceremonial rooms," p. 14.
Thirteen pottery types are listed and the room types in which
they were dominant are indicated.

455. Hill, Mac. 1971 "Preliminary Report of an El Paso Brown Ware
Site, El Paso County, Texas." Transactions of the Sixth Regional Archaeological Symposium from Southeastern New Mexico
and Western Texas, El Paso Archaeological Society, El Paso,
Texas.
Several small El Paso Brown ware vessels were found at the
Little Pot Site on a shifting sand dune area. Illustrations of
small El Paso brown vessels, Figs. 3, 6, 7, and 8; and Mimbres Bold Face (Mangus) sherds, Fig. 5.

456. Hill, W. W. 1937 "Navajo Pottery Manufacture." University
of New Mexico Bulletin Anthropological Series, Vol. 2, No. 3,
pp. 1-23, Albuquerque, New Mexico.
Description of the manufacture of Navajo ware.

457. Hitchcock, Ann. 1977 "A Consumer's Guide to Hopi Pottery."
Plateau, Vol. 49, No. 3, Winter, pp. 22-31.
Good article with advice on sources of information, judging
quality, care, product documentation, and related subjects
pertaining to Hopi pottery. Photos of a jar by Elizabeth White,
bowl with a firecloud, damaged vessels, bowl by Priscilla
Namingha, Polychrome bowl by Carol Namoki, and a polychrome
pot by Fanny Polacca.

458. Hobler, Philip M. 1974 "The Late Survival of Pithouse Ar-
      chitecture in the Kayenta Anasazi Area." Southwestern Lore,
      Vol. 40, No. 2, pp. 1-44.
         Description of the excavation of Neshaki Village (NA7719)
      on Paiute Mesa in southeastern Utah. "The uniqueness of
      Neshaki Village lies in the manner in which over the years a
      village plan had evolved which incorporated into a unified
      whole both above-ground masonry rooms and subterranean pit-
      houses," pp. 4-5. Pottery: the pottery analysis was based
      on 74 whole or restorable vessels and 29,537 sherds.
         Tusayan Gray Ware is the most common ware found and
      makes up 47% of the total sherd collection. Other major wares
      were Tsegi Orange Ware (31%) and Tusayan White Ware (19%).
      There were small amounts of intrusive types from the Mesa
      Verde region. Types illustrated: Sherds in Fig. 18: Black
      Mesa Black-on-white, Sosi Black-on-white, Dogoszhi Black-on-
      white, Flagstaff Black-on-white, Tusayan Black-on-white, and
      Kayenta Black-on-white. Whole vessels of Tusayan White Ware
      Fig. 19: Black Mesa Black-on-white, Sosi Black-on-white,
      Dogoszhi Black-on-white, Flagstaff Black-on-white, Tusayan
      Black-on-white, and Flagstaff Black-on-white. Sherds of
      Tsegi Orange Ware, Fig. 20: Kiet Siel Black-on-red, Medicine
      Black-on-red, Tusayan Black-on-red, Cameron Polychrome,
      Citadel Polychrome, Tusayan Polychrome, Kiet Siel Polychrome,
      Tsegi Black-on-orange, Tsegi Red-on-orange, and Tsegi Orange.
      Whole vessels of Tsegi Orange ware Fig. 21: Tsegi Orange;
      Tsegi Black-on-orange, Medicine Black-on-red, and Tusayan
      Black-on-red. Whole vessels of Tusayan Gray ware, Fig. 22:
      Tusayan Corrugated and Moenkopi Corrugated. Worked sherds,
      Fig. 23. Miniature pottery vessels, Fig. 24. Conclusion:
      "Analysis of the ceramics and artifacts within the total collec-
      tion show few deviations from the norm for Kayenta Anasazi
      peoples," p. 40.

459. Hodge, Frederick W. 1923 "Circular Kivas Near Hawikuh,
      New Mexico." Contributions from the Museum of the American
      Indian, Vol. 7, No. 1, pp. 1-37, New York, New York.
         Illustrations of Heshotauthla Black-on-red, Pl. XXIV, a-c,
      and Hawikuh Polychrome, Pl. XXXIX, a.

460. Hodge, Frederick W. 1924 "Pottery of Hawikuh." Indian
      Notes, Museum of the American Indian, Heye Foundation, Vol.
      1, No. 1, pp. 8-15, New York, New York.
         General descriptions of types of pottery found at Hawikuh.

461. Hodge, Frederick W. 1950 "Those Small Pottery Discs."
      Master Key, Vol. 24, No. 5, pp. 171-172, Southwestern Mu-
      seum, Los Angeles, California.
         According to a Zuni elder, Manchalito, the small pottery
      discs of which thousands were found at Hawikuh, were used
      by early hunters. They were placed in the tracks of deer to
      prevent them from backtracking while being pursued.

462. Holmes, Walter H. 1886 "Pottery of the Ancient Pueblos."
      Fourth Report of the Bureau of Ethnology, 1882-1883, pp.
      257-360, Washington, D.C.
          Very early study of pottery from the Southwest. Good
      black and white illustrations of surface treatments and pottery
      from the following areas: Saint George Utah Area, Fig. 16;
      Zuni, Fig. 2; Tusayan Province, 42 vessels; Cibola Province,
      4,vessels; San Juan Valley, 12 vessels; Kanab, Utah, 2 ves-
      sels; and Montezuma Canyon, 2 vessels.

463. Honea, Kenneth. 1966 "A Proposed Revision of Rio Grande
      Glaze Paint Pottery." Eighth Southwestern Ceramic Seminar,
      Museum of New Mexico.
          No formal report was prepared. Honea proposed the follow-
      ing new types: Glaze A--Pottery Mound Glaze Polychrome
      (AD 1400+); Sanchez Glaze-on-red (AD 1400+); and Sanchez
      Glaze Polychrome (AD 1400+). Glaze B--Medio Glaze Polychrome
      (AD 1425+). Glaze C--(no new types). Glaze D--(no new
      types). Glaze E--Escondida Glaze Polychrome (AD 1515+);
      Encierro Glaze Polychrome (AD 1625+). Glaze F--Polvadera
      Glaze Polychrome (AD 1625+) and Yunque Black-on-red (AD
      1650-1750).

464. Honea, Kenneth. 1968 "Material Culture of the Herrera and
      North Bank sites." Research Records, Vol. 6, pp. 111-169,
      Museum of New Mexico, Santa Fe, New Mexico.
          Description of the pottery types found at Red Hill Site
      (LA 6461), North Bank site (LA 6462), and Alfred Herrera
      Site (LA 6455).

465. Honea, Kenneth. 1973 "The Technology of Eastern Puebloan
      Pottery on the Llano Estacado." Plains Anthropologist, Vol.
      18, No. 59, pp. 73-88.
          "Presented in summary form are morphological descriptions
      of the principal kinds of eastern Anasazi decorated pottery
      found on the Llano Estacado and adjacent regions. Empha-
      sized is glaze-paint pottery which seems to occur more fre-
      quently than earlier black-on-white types. Anasazi pottery has
      generally been accurately dated by the dendrochronological
      method in its area of manufacture. Because of this, it is an
      invaluable tool in the cross dating of some Plains sites to the
      east and northeast. Descriptions have been recently revised
      for many of the types and a number of new types defined by
      the author. Still lacking are firm redefinitions of Eastern
      Anasazi culinary types, which also often occur on the Plains,
      sometimes not accompanied by decorated types," p. 73.

466. Hough, Walter. 1903 "Archaeology of Northeastern Arizona."
      Museum-Gates Expedition of 1901, Annual Report of the U.S.
      National Museum for 1901, pp. 270-358, Washington, D.C.
          Description of Salado traits and sites in the northern area.

Good color plates of Arizona pottery. Black and white and
color illustrations of pottery from the following regions: Mc
Donalds Canyon, Pls. 24-29; Scorse Ranch, Le Roux Wash,
Pls. 31-36; Canyon Butte Wash, Petrified Forest, Pls. 45-51;
Stone Axe Ruin, Petrified Forest, Pls. 57-64; Biddahoochee,
Cottonwood Wash, Pls. 68-80; and Jettyto Valley Ruins, Pls.
92-101. Illustrations of Kwakina Polychrome, Pl. 75; Pinnawa
Glaze-on-white, Pl. 76; upper and lower, Pl. 77; Pinnawa Red-
on-white, Pl. 77, Fig. 1.

467.   Hough, Walter. 1928 "The Lead Glaze Decorated Pottery of
the Pueblo Region." American Anthropologist, Vol. 30, No.
2, pp. 243-249.
Short discussion of the history of glaze ware.

468.   Hough, Walter. 1930 "Explorations of Ruins in the White
Mountain Apache Indian Reservation, Arizona." Proceedings
of the U.S. National Museum, Vol. 78, Article 13, pp. 1-21,
Washington, D.C.
Pottery found at Grasshopper Ruin was gray ware, Black-
on-white, Gila ware, Chevelon ware, red ware, and coil ware.

469.   Hough, Walter. 1932 "Decorative Designs on Elden Pueblo
Pottery, Flagstaff, Arizona." Proceedings of the U.S. National
Museum, Vol. 81, Article 7, pp. 1-11, Washington, D.C.
Illustrations of Roosevelt Black-on-white, Pls. 3 and 4.
Descriptions of the band and quadrant types of designs on
the pottery excavated by Fewkes at Elden Pueblo in 1926.
Illustrations of Tusayan White Ware, Tusayan Red Ware, cor-
rugated vessels and two animal figurines.

470.   Howard, Richard M. 1968 The Mesa Verde Museum. Mesa
Verde Association, KC Publications, Flagstaff, Arizona.
Illustrations of San Juan Black-on-white ware. Mesa Verde
Black-on-white double mug--cover photo; Wetherill Mesa Black-
on-white pottery--inside cover; Basketmaker pottery, p. 10;
Developmental Pueblo pottery, p. 16; Classic Pueblo pottery,
p. 10; (Mesa Verde Black-on-white); Corrugated jar, p. 24;
Black-on-white jar, p. 25; pictures of Pueblo pottery making
by Maria Martinez, p. 36; and Black-on-white bowl with painted
horned toad, back cover.

471.   Howard, Richard M. 1975 "The Mesa Verde Mug." American
Indian Art Magazine, Vol. 1, No. 1, November, pp. 20-25.
Popular article describing the pottery mugs typical of the
Mesa Verde area. Covers designs, possible use, and unusual
mugs with window handles, rattle bottoms, and painted bases.
Includes black and white photos of 16 mugs and color photos
of 5 others.

472.   Howard, Richard M. 1976 "A Magnificent Acoma Pot."

American Indian Art Magazine, Vol. 1, No. 2, February, pp. 16-19.
Description of a large well-executed Acoma Polychrome olla collected at Acoma circa 1898-1902 by photographer Henry G. Peabody. Includes several good color photographs of this vessel.

473. Hubbell, Lyndi and Traylor, Diane (editors). 1982 Bandelier; Excavations in the Flood Pool of Cochiti Lake, New Mexico. National Park Service, Southwest Cultural Resources Center, Santa Fe, New Mexico.
Excavation at 23 sites in 1974-75 yielded 34,651 sherds. These sherds were used to aid in establishing the chronology of the project sites. Illustrations of representative sherds and tables of sherd frequencies are presented.

474. Huckell, Bruce B. 1978 "The Oxbow Hill-Payson Project: Archaeological Excavations South of Payson, Arizona." Anthropological Papers of the University of Arizona, No. 36, University of Arizona, Tucson, Arizona.
Description of archaeological Apache pottery recovered during these excavations.

475. Hudson, Dee Travis. 1980 "White Goat House: A Prehistoric Anasazi Community in Northeastern Arizona." Arizona Archaeologist, No. 12, May, Phoenix, Arizona.
Many types of pottery were found during the excavations. The dominant ware was Little Colorado Gray, next was Cibola White Ware, and Tusayan Gray was the least common. Three complete and five partial vessels were found. Illustrations of a Kiet Siel bowl and jar, a Wide Ruin White dipper, and worked sherds.

476. Human Systems Research, Inc. 1973 Technical Manual: 1973 Survey of the Tularosa Basin. Three Rivers, New Mexico.
This is a useful compilation for workers in this area of New Mexico. Fifty pottery types present in the Tularosa Basin of south central New Mexico are described. These descriptions are primarily paraphrasings of previous descriptions.
Types described are Jornada Plain, Jornada Bichrome, Jornada Polychrome, El Paso Brown, El Paso Bichrome, El Paso Polychrome, San Andres Red-on-terra cotta, Three Rivers Red-on-terra cotta, Lincoln Black-on-red (Glaze-on-red variety), Chupadero Black-on-white, Tabira' Black-on-white, Tabira' White Plain, Tabira' Polychrome, Corona Rubbed-Ribbed, Corona Rubbed-Indented, Ochoa Brown Indented, Ochoa Brown Smudged Indented, Three Circle Red-on-white, Mimbres Boldface Black-on-white, Mimbres Classic Black-on-white, Alma Plain, Alma Neckbanded, Alma Neck Indented, Alma Punched, Alma Scored, Alma Incised, San Lorenzo Red-on-brown, Mogollon Red-on-brown, San Francisco Red, San

Marcial Black-on-white, Socorro Black-on-white, Pitoche Rubbed-
Ribbed, Los Lunas Smudged, Wingate Black-on-red, St. Johns
Polychrome, Heshotauthla Polychrome, Agua Fria Glaze-on-red,
Gila Polychrome, Playas Red, Playas Red Incised, Ramos
Black, Medanos Red-on-brown, Madera Black-on-red, Babicora
Polychrome, Villa Ahumada Polychrome, Carretas Polychrome,
Dublan Polychrome, Corralitos Polychrome, and Ramos Poly-
chrome. Illustrations of Chupadero Black-on-white.

477. Hunt, Alice. 1953 "Archaeological Survey of the La Sal Moun-
      tain Area." University of Utah Anthropological Papers, No.
      14, Salt Lake City, Utah.
         Illustrations of Pinyon Utility, called "Navajo" and "gray-
      ware," p. 172, fig. 74c.

478. Hurst, C. T. 1936 "Some Interesting Mimbres Bowls." El
      Palacio, Vol. 40, Nos. 7, 8, and 9, pp. 37-41, Santa Fe, New
      Mexico.
         The author believes that this type of pottery was the work
      of "a genius and her pupils." The Roger Springer Collection
      at Western State has about 50 pieces of Mimbres pottery; all
      but four are bowls. One of the bowls has a Kokopelli painted
      figure on it. The bowls are briefly described and five with
      naturalistic designs are illustrated. One of these is the logo
      for the Colorado Archaeological Society. This bowl is now at
      the University of Colorado Museum, Boulder, Colorado.

479. Hurst, C. T. 1948 "The Cottonwood Expedition 1947, A Cave
      and Pueblo Site." Southwestern Lore, Vol. 14, No. 1, pp. 4-
      19.
         Site on Hill Ranch, 16 miles east of Nucla, Colorado, on
      the north side of Cottonwood Creek. Found sherds of Mancos
      Black-on-white and Wingate Black-on-red.

480. Hurst, C. T. and Lotrich, V. F. 1932 "An Unusual Mug from
      Yellow Jacket Canyon." El Palacio, Vol. 33, pp. 195-198,
      Santa Fe, New Mexico.
         Yellow Jacket Spring Ruin: "The most remarkable find was
      a perfectly preserved and beautifully decorated square mug.
      Each face of the mug is divided into two triangles by a di-
      agonal line. Each triangle is enclosed in a second triangle
      with its sides parallel to those of the first triangle. Into each
      of the inside triangles projects a 'bat wing' from its sides.
      On the bottom of the mug are two diagonal black lines that
      cross in the middle and thus divide the space into four tri-
      angles. The decoration on the handle consists of two triangles
      in solid black," p. 196.
         This mug measures 6.5 cm in height by 5.5 by 5.8 cm in
      cross section. The strap handle is wide and extends the full
      height of the mug. The inside of the mug is blackened as if
      something was burned in it. One other square mug has been
      reported according to the writer.

481. Hurst, C. T. and Lotrich, V. F. 1934 "Another Unusual
    Bowl from Yellow Jacket Canyon." El Palacio, Vol. 34 (15-16),
    pp. 111-115, Santa Fe, New Mexico.
        Description of an unusual Mesa Verde bowl of the Pueblo
    I or II period. It is oval in shape and has a black background
    with a design in white paint on the interior.

482. Hurst, C. T. and Lotrich, V. F. 1935 "The Gunnison Col-
    lection II." Southwestern Lore, Vol. 1, No. 2, pp. 6-11.
        Descriptions of Pueblo II vessels from Yellow Jacket Canyon.
    Vessels are illustrated in drawings, Pls. I-III.

483. Hurst, Winston; Bond, Mark; and Schwindt, Sloan E. 1985
    "Piedra Black-on-white, White Mesa Variety: Formal Descrip-
    tion of a Western Mesa Verde Anasazi Pueblo I White Ware
    Type." Pottery Southwest, Vol. 12, No. 3, pp. 1-7.
        Description of a new variety of Piedra Black-on-white from
    the western Anasazi region. Photographs of sherds.

484. Huscher, Harold and Bette. 1943 "The Hogan Builders of
    Colorado." Southwestern Lore, Vol. 9, No. 2.
        Descriptions of sherds found on the Uncompahgre Plateau
    at ruined hogan sites.

485. Huse, Hannah. 1976 "The Identification of the Individual in
    Archaeology: A Case Study from the Prehistoric Hopi Site
    of Kawaika-A." Doctoral dissertation, Department of Anthro-
    pology, University of Colorado, Boulder, Colorado.
        This is a case study of pottery excavated by Earl Morris
    at the Hopi site of Kawaika-a in 1928. The pottery studied
    consisted of 115 decorated yellow ware bowls from 44 burials,
    primarily in the talus slopes below Kawaika-a.
        Characteristics of the bowls were studied to attempt a clas-
    sification by individual potters. The author's classification
    was compared to a previous, independent classification done
    by Roy Carlson. A good agreement between the two classifi-
    cations was obtained. A cluster analysis supported the author's
    classification as did distributional and burial associational data.
    The major conclusion was that "it is possible to isolate an in-
    dividual's products from archaeological materials," p. iv.
        Pottery types studied and illustrated are Awatovi Black-on-
    yellow, Jeddito Black-on-yellow, Kawaika-a Spattered, Plain
    Jeddito Yellow, and Sikyatki Polychrome.

486. Husted, William M. 1964 "Pueblo Pottery from Northern Colo-
    rado." Southwestern Lore, Vol. 30, No. 2, pp. 21-25.
        "Sherds of coiled pottery nearly identical to Indented Blind-
    Corrugated ware have been found on several sites in northern
    Colorado. The Plains Apache probably received the pottery
    in trade at Pecos or the Upper Rio Grande Pueblos and trans-
    ported it to their camps further north and east," p. 21. Photos
    of some of the sherds found in Rocky Mountain National Park.

487. Hyde, Hazel. 1973 Maria Pottery Making. Sunstone Press,
      Santa Fe, New Mexico, 27 pp.
          Picture story of Maria and Julian Martinez. Written origi-
      nally in the 1930s. Text is sparse but good photos of pottery
      making at San Ildefonso.

488. Ipshording, Wayne C. 1974 "Combined Thermal and X-ray
      Diffraction Technique for Identification of Ceramic Ware Tem-
      per and Paste Minerals." American Antiquity, Vol. 39, No.
      3, pp. 477-483.
          "The identification of the original paste and temper minerals
      present in ceramic ware fragments can often be useful in de-
      termining if they are indigenous to the area or whether they
      represent tradeware.... A new technique is described that
      permits the investigator to often identify both temper and the
      fine grain paste material as well," p. 477. This technique is
      described.
          "Examples are shown for the clay materials, kaolinite, mont-
      morillonite, and polygorskite. Diffractions are also presented
      for the comparison of ceramic fragments from Mexico and Ala-
      bama that contain the above minerals as original constituents,"
      p. 477.

489. Jacka, Jerry and Gill, Spencer. 1976 Pottery Treasures.
      Graphic Arts Center Publishing Co., Portland, Oregon.
          This book is almost entirely composed of photographs of
      Southwestern pottery with data concerning types, dates, and
      makers of the vessels. The color photographs are excellent.
          Prehistoric types illustrated are Tularosa Black-on-white,
      p. II; Mimbres Black-on-white, p. 5; Gila and Tonto Poly-
      chromes, p. 6; Sacaton and Santa Cruz Red-on-buff, p. 7;
      Sikyatki Polychromes, p. 8; Mesa Verde Black-on-white, p. 9;
      Polacca Polychrome, pp. 14-15; Tularosa Black-on-white, p.
      58; Mimbres Black-on-white, p. 65; Salado Red, human effigy
      figurine, p. 81; Kinishba Polychrome, p. 82; Hopi yellow ware,
      p. 83; Tonto Polychrome, p. 84; and Kayenta Black-on-white,
      p. 85.
          Historic types illustrated are San Ildefonso Black, p. 10;
      San Ildefonso Polychrome, p. 13; Hopi Polychrome (Nampeyo),
      p. 16; Acoma Polychrome, p. 17; Tesuque "Rain god" figurines,
      p. 18; Acoma Polychrome, p. 19; Hopi Polychrome (Nampeyo),
      p. 21; Zuni Polychrome, p. 22; Tesuque Polychrome, p. 23;
      Santo Domingo Polychrome, p. 24; Zuni Polychrome, pp. 25-
      26; Zia Polychrome, p. 2; Santa Ana Polychrome, p. 28; Santa
      Clara Black, p. 29; Zuni Polychrome, p. 30; Hopi Polychrome
      and Cochiti Polychrome, p. 31; Zia Polychrome and San Ilde-
      fonso Polychrome, p. 32; Zia Polychrome, p. 33; San Juan
      Red-on-tan, p. 34; and Zia Polychrome, p. 76.
          Contemporary pottery types shown are San Ildefonso Poly-
      chrome, pp. 35-36; San Ildefonso Black-on-red and San Ilde-
      fonso Black (Maria), p. 37; Gun metal black (Maria), p. 38;

Maria and Popovi Da, p. 39; Hopi black-on-white (Feather
Woman), p. 42; Hopi (Wallace Youvella), p. 43; Hopi Poly-
chrome (Fawn), p. 44; Hopi (Elizabeth White), p. 45; Hopi
Polychrome, p. 46; Santo Domingo Polychrome, p. 47; Hopi
(Thomas Polacca Nampeyo), p. 48; Hopi (Frog Woman), p. 49;
Hopi (Fannie Nampeyo), p. 50; Hopi (Garnet Pavatea), p. 51;
miniatures, p. 52; Santa Clara (Camilla Tafoya), p. 53; Santa
Clara Polychrome (Margaret and Luther), p. 54; Santa Clara
Red and Black (Margaret Tafoya), p. 55; Acoma figurines, p.
56; Acoma Black-on-white (Lucy Lewis), p. 57; Acoma (Juana
Leno), p. 58; Cochiti figure (Helen Cordera), p. 59; Cochiti
Polychrome (Laurencita Herrera), p. 60; Santa Clara Black,
p. 61; Acoma (Rose Chino and Marie Z. Chino), p. 62; Santa
Clara (Grace Medicine Flower), p. 63; Santa Clara (Margaret
and Luther), p. 64; Joseph Lonewolf, p. 65; Tony Da, pp.
66-67; Blue Corn, p. 68; Grace Medicine Flower, p. 69; San-
tana and Adam, p. 70; Rose Gonzales, p. 711; Mohave (Elmer
Gates), p. 72; San Juan (Tomasita and Dominguita), p. 73;
Maricopa (Ida Redbird and Barb Johnson), p. 74; Navajo (Fae
Tso), p. 75; Tesuque and Taos (Virginia Romero), p. 77;
and Minnie Vigil, Santa Clara, p. 80.

490. Jackson, Earl and Van Valkenburg, Sallie. 1954 "Montezuma
      Castle Archaeology, Part I: Excavations." Southwestern
      Monuments Association Technical Series, Vol. 3, No. 1, Gila
      Pueblo, Globe, Arizona.
          A general report of the results of the excavations directed
      by Earl Jackson in 1933-34. Pottery recovered in decreasing
      order of abundance: Verde Brown, Tuzigoot Red, Walnut
      Black-on-white, Jeddito Black-on-yellow, Bidahochi Polychrome,
      Tusayan Black-on-red, Citadel Polychrome, Winslow Polychrome,
      Tusayan Corrugated, Flagstaff Black-on-white, Dogoszhi Black-
      on-white, Kayenta Black-on-white, Tonto Polychrome, Homolovi
      Polychrome, Deadmans Black-on-red, Fourmile Polychrome, and
      Verde Red-on-buff. An unnamed white-on-red type is de-
      scribed.

491. Jacobs, Mike. 1979 "The St. Mary's Hospital Site." Kiva,
      Vol. 45, Nos. 1-2, pp. 119-130.
          "Findings of the AAHS, 1974-1975 investigations at the St.
      Mary's Hospital Site (ARIZ.:16:26) are discussed. The basic
      conclusions of the research are that the site's boundaries can
      be roughly defined and that the major period of occupation
      was during Rillito-Rincon times," p. 119.
          Local types of pottery found were Rincon Red-on-brown,
      Rillito Red-on-brown, Snaketown Red-on-buff, Canada del Oro
      Red-on-brown, and Rincon Polychrome. Intrusive types were
      Santa Cruz Red-on-buff, Sacaton Red-on-buff, and Gila Poly-
      chrome? All local types except Rincon Polychrome are illus-
      trated by photos of sherds.

492. Jacobs, Mike. 1986 "A Lost Pot from the Keam Collection of
      Historic Hopi Pottery." Pottery Southwest, Vol. 13, No. 4,
      pp. 3-5.
         A Polacca Polychrome bowl from the collection at the Arizona
      State Museum was traced through an old catalog number to the
      Keam Collection. This bowl was collected between 1875 and
      1884. It is noted that old catalog numbers should be retained
      because they may provide valuable information.

493. James, George. 1909 Indian Basketry. Henry Malkan (Dover
      reprint, 1972), Chapter II, "Basketry, The Mother of Pottery,"
      pp. 17-20.
         Descriptions of how pottery may have developed from
      basketry. Illustrations show how baskets were used as molds
      for early pottery and how coiled pottery may have developed
      as a copy of coiled basketry.

494. James, Marjorie. 1937 "A Note on Navajo Pottery Making."
      El Palacio, Vol. 43, pp. 13-15.
         Description of Navajo ware, pp. 85-86.

495. Jeancon, Jean A. 1923 "Excavations in the Chama Valley,
      New Mexico." Bureau of American Ethnology, Bulletin No. 81,
      Washington, D.C.
         Pottery, pp. 34-65. Drawings of biscuit ware bowls, pp.
      48-55; drawings of incised designs, pp. 56-59; Red ware bowl
      designs, pp. 60-62; miniature vessels, Pl. 37; Bird pots, Pl.
      38; Biscuit ware bowls, Pls. 41, 42, 45, 46; Incised ware,
      Pls. 43, 44, 48; Glazed red ware bowls, Pls. 46, 47; worked
      sherds, Pls. 49, 50; and Biscuit ware sherds and handles,
      Pls. 52, 53.

496. Jeancon, Jean A. 1924 "Pottery of the Pagosa-Piedra Region."
      In Further Archaeological Research on the Northeastern San
      Juan Basin of Colorado, During the Summer of 1922, Colorado
      Magazine, Vol. 1, Nos. 6 and 7; pp. 260-276, 301-307.
         Description and illustrations of pottery found in the Pagosa-
      Piedra area of southern Colorado.

497. Jeancon, Jean A. 1929 "Archaeological Investigations in the
      Taos Valley, New Mexico During 1920." Smithsonian Miscel-
      laneous Collections, Vol. 81, No. 12, Washington, D.C.
         Describes Bagley Ranch Ruin, Pot Creek Ruin, and the
      Llano Site in the Taos Valley. Illustrations of culinary jars
      with incised necks, two black-on-white seed bowls, black-on-
      white sherds, and pottery handles from these sites.

498. Jellinek, Arthur J. 1952 "Pottery of the Rio Bonita Area of
      Lincoln County, New Mexico." Texas Archaeological and
      Palentological Society Bulletin, Vol. 23, pp. 247-267.
         Illustrations: Three Rivers Red-on-terra cotta, Lincoln

Black-on-red, and Agua Fria Glaze-on-red, Pl. 20; Jornada Brown, Chupadero Black-on-white, El Paso Polychrome, Mimbres Black-on-white, Pl. 21.

499. Jellinek, Arthur J. 1961 "Mimbres Warfare?" Kiva, Vol. 27, No. 2, pp. 28-30, Tucson, Arizona.
Abstract: "A Mimbres bowl, recovered from excavations at the Mattocks Ruin, is decorated with realistic designs which indicate that violent death and perhaps warfare was a part of Mimbres culture," p. 28. A portion of a Mimbres Black-on-white bowl is illustrated with what appears to be a woman being killed in a battle.

500. Jellinek, Arthur J. 1967 "A Prehistoric Sequence in the Middle Pecos Valley, New Mexico." Anthropological Papers, Museum of Anthropology, No. 31, University of Michigan, Ann Arbor, Michigan.
Middle Pecos Ceramics, pp. 47-87. Descriptions of Jornada Brown, pp. 47-49; Middle Pecos Micaceous Brown, pp. 49-50; Roswell Brown, pp. 50-51; McKenzie Brown, pp. 51-52; South Pecos Brown, pp. 53-54; Chupadero Black-on-white, pp. 54-55; Crosby Black-on-gray, pp. 55-56; ills., Pl. IV; Middle Pecos Black-on-white, pp. 56-58; ills. Pl. V; and intrusive sherds, Pl. VI. Good study of a neglected area in east central New Mexico during 1956-1960.

501. Jenks, Albert E. 1932 "Architectural Plans of Geometric Art on Mimbres Bowls." El Palacio, Vol. 33, Nos. 3-6, pp. 21-64.
Discusses Mimbres bowls in regard to the number of design units present. These bowls range in complexity from one to six units. Asymmetric designs are also briefly described. Mimbres unit plans are compared to earlier Basketmaker and Hohokam pottery designs. Thirty-two Mimbres bowls are illustrated.

502. Jennings, Jesse. 1978 "Prehistory of Utah and the Eastern Great Basin." Anthropological Papers of the University of Utah, No. 98, University of Utah, Salt Lake City, Utah.
Overview of the prehistory of this area with several maps. The pottery types illustrated are Moenkopi Corrugated: Coombs Variety, Fig. 119; Citadel Polychrome: Coombs Variety and Cameron Polychrome: Coombs Variety, Fig. 120; Black Mesa Black-on-white, Flagstaff Black-on-white, and Sosi Black-on-white, Fig. 121; Ivie Creek Black-on-white, Fig. 125; Tusayan Gray: Emery Variety, Fig. 126; Corrugated ware, Fig. 138; Six worked sherds, Mancos Black-on-white ladle, Chapin Gray, La Plata Black-on-red effigy vessel and olla, Mesa Verde Black-on-white, and Morfield Black-on-white, Fig. 139; and Gray ware from Caldwell Village, Fig. 170.

503. Jernigan, E. Wesley. 1986 "A Non-hierachical Approach to

Ceramic Decoration Analysis." American Antiquity, Vol. 51,
No. 1, pp. 3-20.
    "The element-motif-layout framework of design analysis
which has dominated the study of Southwestern ceramic decoration since the late 1930s is shown to be ambiguous as a means
of understanding and comparing such decoration. A new analytical approach is presented involving the isolation of design
units based on a comparative study of how design configura-
tions are used in a style corpus of whole vessels. Application of the method and its usefulness in comparative stylistic
studies, as well as potential usefulness in ceramic dating, are
discussed," Abstract, p. 3.

504.   Jett, Stephen and Moyle, Peter B.   1986 "The Exotic Origins
       of Fishes Depicted on Prehistoric Mimbres Pottery from New
       Mexico." American Antiquity, Vol. 51, No. 4, pp. 628-720.
           Fishes on classic Mimbres Black-on-white pottery are identi-
       fied in 20 fish taxa, 18 of which are marine. Thses species
       indicate a provenience in the Gulf of California near Guaymas,
       Mexico. Apparently, Mimbres traders travelled 1,500 miles
       from the Mimbres Valley to the Gulf and back, probably to ob-
       tain shells and other materials for use in trade. During these
       trips they observed the marine fishes depicted on the Mimbres
       pottery.

505.   Johnson, Alfred E.   1964 "Archaeological Excavations in Ho-
       hokam Sites of South Arizona." American Antiquity, Vol. 30,
       No. 2, Part 1, pp. 146-161, Salt Lake City, Utah.
           Mentions types of pottery found and has a few photos of:
       Sacaton Red-on-buff, p. 148; Gila Butte Red-on-buff, p. 148;
       Tanque Verde Red-on-brown, p. 152; Casa Grande Red-on-
       buff, p. 152; and Gila Smudged Plain and Red, p. 152.

506.   Johnson, Alfred E. and Thompson, R. H.   1968 "The Ringo
       Site, Southeastern Arizona." American Antiquity, Vol. 28,
       No. 4, pp. 465-481, Salt Lake City, Utah.
           "Locally made pottery was primarily plain red and brown
       with both smudging and texturing. Most of the painted pottery
       was traded into the site from the surrounding Chihuahua, White
       Mountain, Tonto Basin, and Tucson areas," p. 465.

507.   Johnson, Alfred E. and Wasley, William.   1966 "Archaeologi-
       cal Excavations Near Bylas, Arizona." Kiva, Vol. 31, No. 4,
       pp. 205-253.
           Pottery, pp. 223-228. A summary of descriptions of all
       ceramic and nonceramic artifacts found at Arizona B16:10. Il-
       lustrations of mortuary vessels, Fig. 13, p. 224; Corrugated
       ware; San Carlos Red-on-buff, Fig. 14, p. 225; Roosevelt
       Black-on-white, McDonald Painted Corrugated, Reserve Black-
       on-white, Tularosa Black-on-white, Reserve Indented Corrugated,

Casa Grande Red-on-buff and Plain ware vessel. "Casa Grande
Red-on-buff: Safford variety was the most common painted
pottery found at Arizona B16:10, accounting for 9.4% of the
sample of locally made pottery. In addition to the large sample of sherds, there were 22 complete or restorable vessels.
Casa Grande Red-on-buff: Safford variety has not been previously described but is apparently a development of the earliest Sacaton Red-on-buff: Safford variety which has been reported from the Point of Pines area. A detailed description of
the variety will have to await petrographic analysis that should
allow the establishment of objective criteria for distinguishing
this variety from its counterpart in the Gila Basin," pp. 224,
226. A list of intrusive pottery types on p. 227 with references to recent dates and descriptions.

508. Johnson, Chester R. 1963 "Tohalina Bikitsiel: A Pueblo
Ruin at Toadlena, New Mexico," El Palacio, Vol. 70, No. 4,
pp. 21-32.
    Salvage archaeology on a pueblo site near Toadlena Board-
ing School, New Mexico. Many pottery types were recovered
including Toadlena Black-on-white and a local corrugated ware
which are illustrated on p. 28. Author proposes the names
Toadlena Black-on-white and Chuska Black-on-white.

509. Judd, Niel M. 1926 "Archaeological Observations North of
the Rio Colorado." Bureau of American Ethnology, Bulletin
82, Washington, D.C.
    Pottery, p. 143. Short section on small collection of sherds
and a few vessels. Illustrations of corrugated and plain
sherds, Pl. 37; Black-on-white sherds and bowls, Pls. 38-39;
Plain and corrugated vessels, Pls. 40-43; Clay pipes, Pl. 47;
and drawing of designs on food bowls, Pl. 61. An early survey of sites in Utah.

510. Judd, Niel M. 1954 "The Material Culture of Pueblo Bonito."
Smithsonian Miscellaneous Collections, Vol. 124, Washington,
D.C.
    Section on pottery, pp. 174-239. A great deal of pottery
was excavated, and it is well described in this section. Pre-
pueblo and transitional Black-on-white sherds, Pl. 48; Chaco
San Juan sherds, Pl. 49; Corrugated pots, Pl. 51; Painted
pot and corrugated, Pl. 52; Black-on-white bowls, Pl. 53;
38 Black-on-white bowls, Pl. 54; 30 Black-on-white bowls, Pl.
55; 22 Black-on-white bowls, Pl. 56; 15 Black-on-white pitchers,
Pl. 57; bird, animal, and human figures on bowls, Fig. 50;
intrusive bowls, some Mesa Verde, p. 58; 9 Black-on-white
ladles, p. 61; handles and covers, p. 62; pitchers and "duck
jars," Pl. 63; ollas and water jars, Pl. 64; Black-on-white
canteen, Pl. 65; fragments of animal effigy vessels, Figs. 54-
62; cylindrical Black-on-white vessels, pls. 67-68; and miniature Black-on-white, Pl. 69.

511. Judd, Niel M.   1959   "Pueblo del Arroyo, Chaco Canyon, New
      Mexico." Smithsonian Institute Miscellaneous Collections, Vol.
      138, No. 1, Washington, D.C.
          Pottery, pp. 145-171. Description of Red Mesa Black-on-
      white, pp. 145-146. Points out similarities between the Chaco
      San Juan Black-on-white pottery and the McElmo Black-on-
      white from Mesa Verde. Descriptions and illustrations of the
      following ceramics: Transitional and solid type Black-on-white
      sherds, Pl. 20; Chaco San Juan ware sherds, Pl. 21; Black-
      on-white bowls and other vessels, Pls. 22-24; bowl with pol-
      ished black interior and design, Pls. 25; Eccentric Black-on-
      white ladle, Pl. 26; ladles and fragments, Pl. 27; Black-on-
      white canteens and pitchers, Pl. 28; Black-on-white seed bowls
      and water jars, Pls. 29-30; Black-on-white ollas and storage
      jars, Pls. 31-32; corrugated vessels, Pls. 32-34; Prieta
      Smeared Indented, Pls. 34a, 34b; Pottery representations of
      bifurcated baskets, Pl. 35; pottery figurine fragments, Pl.
      36; Black-on-white bowls and corrugated pots, Pl. 47; red
      ware vases (color), Pl. 55; and Polychrome bowl from Houck
      district east-central Arizona (color), Pl. 54.

512. Kayser, David W.   1971   "Take a Pebble, Add Hard Work:
      That's Maricopa Pottery." El Palacio, Vol. 77, No. 1, pp.
      25-32, Museum of New Mexico, Santa Fe, New Mexico.
          Description and illustrations of modern Maricopa pottery.
      Description of the current method of manufacture of this pot-
      tery. Maricopa pottery is an amalgamation of old forms brought
      with them from the Colorado River area, designs taken from
      old sherds and techniques recently borrowed from neighboring
      Pima and Papago potters.

513. Kelly, Isabel T.   1978   "The Hodges Ruin, a Hohokam Com-
      munity in the Tucson Basin." Anthropological Papers of the
      University of Arizona, No. 30, University of Arizona, Tucson,
      Arizona.
          Report of excavations conducted by the author in 1936-
      1938.
          Chapter 4--Ceramics. Descriptions and illustrations of
      Sweetwater Red-on-gray, pp. 18-20; Snaketown Red-on-buff,
      pp. 20-21; Canada del Oro Red-on-brown, pp. 22-27; Rillito
      Red-on-brown, pp. 32-37; Picacho Red-on-brown, p. 39-48;
      Tanque Verde Red-on-brown, pp. 48-59; Rincon Red, p. 67;
      San Carlos Redware, pp. 67-69; and Gila Redware, p. 69.
      There is a photo of a vessel named "Cortaro Red-on-brown,"
      an undescribed transitional type. Chapter 5--Ceramic Arti-
      facts. Description of clay figurines, worked sherds, and
      worked objects, pp. 78-85.

514. Kelly, Roger E.   1968   "Fourteen Prehistoric Sites in Nanko-
      weap Canyon, Grand Canyon National Park." Arizona Archeo-
      logist, No. 3 December, Phoenix, Arizona.

Of 530 sherds recovered from seven sites in Nankoweap Canyon, 46.5% were Tusayan and Moenkopi Corrugated types and 14.6% were Dogoszhi or Sosi Black-on-white types. No Nankoweap Polychrome was found. Other less common types were Tusayan White Ware, Tusayan Black-on-red, Tusayan Gray Ware, Citadel Polychrome, and Tsegi Orange Ware. Small amounts of Virgin Branch of the Anasazi pottery types were present at these sites.

515. Kelly, Roger E. 1969 "An Archaeological Survey in the Payson Basin." Plateau, Vol. 42, No. 2, pp. 46-65.
Survey in the area to be used for an enlarged seismological station. Most of the collected sherds (87.5%) are representatives of "tonto Red," a type included within Salado Red Ware.

516. Kelley, Jane Holden. 1979 "The Sierra Blanca Restudy Project." In Jornada Mogollon Archaeology: Proceedings of the First Jornada Conference, Beckett, Patrick H. and Wiseman, Regge N., pp. 107-132, New Mexico State University, Las Cruces, New Mexico.
Ceramic studies: pp. 121-130. A study of the interrelationships among sites in the Sierra Blanca. The testing of a hypothesis of specialized manufacturing centers of Chupadero Black-on-white.

517. Kent, Susan. 1981 "A Recent Navajo Pottery Manufacturing Site, Navajo Indian Irrigation Project, New Mexico." Kiva, Vol. 46, No. 3, pp. 189-196.
"A site originally reported as an Anasazi sherd scatter is interpreted, upon excavation and analysis, as an historic Navajo pottery manufacturing site," p. 189.

518. Kent, Susan. 1986 "New Dates for Old Pots: A Comment on Cortez Black-on-white." Kiva, Vol. 51, No. 4, pp. 255-262.
Abstract: "The traditional end date for the Pueblo II ceramic type, Cortez Black-on-white, may be as much as 50 years too early. Several independent dates from a recently excavated Mesa Verde Anasazi site in Colorado--5 MT 1786-- suggest a modified end date of AD 1050 for this ceramic. This revision is significant to type-dependent survey and excavation temporal interpretations, particularly in cultural resource management and for sites with only limited testing," p. 255.

519. Kidder, Alfred V. 1915 "Pottery of the Pajarito Plateau and of Some Adjacent Regions in New Mexico." Memoirs, American Anthropological Association, Vol. II, Part 6, Lancaster, Pennsylvania.
Brief description and drawings of biscuit ware and red ware (glazed decoration) from ruins in the Pajarito region.

520. Kidder, Alfred V. 1916 "The Pottery of the Casas Grandes
District, Chihuahua." Holmes Anniversary Volume, pp. 253-
268, Washington, D.C.
Illustrations and descriptions of vessels in the Phillips collection in the Peabody Museum. There are 190 pieces of pottery excavated primarily at Janos, Ramos, and Corralitos all
of which are localities in the Casas Grandes Area. The pieces
fall into the following general classifications: (1) Rough,
dark ware, (2) Polished black ware, (3) Red ware, and (4)
Painted red ware. Photographs of Casas Grandes vessels of
the above types, Pls. I, II, and III. Drawings of designs,
Pls. IV-VII.

521. Kidder, Alfred V. 1920 "Ruins of the Historic Period in the
Upper San Juan Valley, New Mexico." American Anthropologist,
Vol. 22, No. 4, pp. 322-329.
This study deals with the Gobernador pottery period in
the early 18th century. Pottery recovered was of three wares:
(1) Black ware, large ollas with outer surfaces textured by
scraping, no corrugations; (2) Thick two and three color
painted ware, bowls with high recurved rims, decorated surfaces have thick yellowish and grayish slips, and undecorated
surfaces well polished, illustrated, Fig. 20; (3) Thin three
color painted ware, ollas and bowls, hard surface, walls dark
gray in cross section, surface smoothed but not polished, surface color yellow to orange, rim edges painted, red wash on
lower walls and bases, and design in red and/or black.

522. Kidder, Alfred V. 1924 "An Introduction to the Study of
Southwestern Archaeology." Papers of the Phillips Academy
Southwestern Expedition, No. 1, Yale University Press, New
Haven, Connecticut (revised 1962).
First regional synthesis of Southwestern archaeology. De-
scriptions and illustrations in first edition: Tularosa Patterned
Corrugated, p. 98; Tularosa Fillet Rim (V), p. 98; Gila Poly-
chrome, Kayenta Polychrome, p. 71; Kayenta Black-on-white,
p. 71; Named Mesa Verde Black-on-white, p. 63-66. Illustra-
tions: (page numbers from 1962 revision): Modern pueblo
vessels, p. 156; Chaco Canyon Black-on-white ware, p. 183;
Mesa Verde Black-on-white ware, pp. 200-201; Proto Mesa
Verde pottery, p. 208; Kayenta Black-on-white pottery, p.
221. Pre-Pueblo pottery, p. 233; Pecos pottery chronological
series, p. 258; Little Colorado pottery, p. 269; Upper Gila
Black-on-white Corrugated, pp. 286-287; Mimbres Black-on-
white, p. 292; Lower Gila pottery, p. 307; and Chihuahua
Basin pottery, p. 320.

523. Kidder, Alfred V. 1932 The Artifacts of Pecos. Robert S.
Peabody Foundation for Archaeology, Yale University Press,
New Haven, Connecticut.
A good section on recovered objects of clay including 842
worked sherds.

524. Kidder, Alfred V., and Amsden, C. A. 1931 Pottery of
     Pecos: Volume I. Yale University Press, New Haven, Con-
     necticut.
        Descriptions of Galisteo Black-on-white, pp. 25-28 (syno-
     nym Crackle Black-on-white); Abiquiu Black-on-white, pp.
     74-100 (Biscuit A); and Bandelier Black-on-gray, pp. 101-
     150 (Biscuit B). Illustrations of all three types.

525. Kidder, Alfred V., and Cosgrove, C. B. 1949 "The Pendle-
     ton Ruin, Hidalgo County, New Mexico." Contributions to
     American Anthropology and History, No. 50, pp. 107-152,
     Carnegie Institute of Washington Publication 585, Washington,
     D.C.
        Report of excavations done in 1933. Pottery types found
     were Plain ware, described, p. 131, illustration, Fig. 13;
     Cloverdale Corrugated, described, p. 132, illustrated, Figs.
     12, 13, 15; and Incised ware, described, p. 132; illustrated,
     Figs. 5, 7, 18. Other types found in smaller amounts and il-
     lustrated: Chihuahua Polychrome, Figs. 5, 10, 14; Gila, Tonto,
     and Tucson Polychromes, Fig. 11; and Cord marked vessels,
     Fig. 16. Map of Hidalgo County and Mimbres sites, p. 123.

526. Kidder, Alfred V. and Guernsey, Samuel J. 1919 "Archaeo-
     logical Explorations in Northeastern Arizona." Bureau of
     American Ethnology, Bulletin No. 65, Washington, D.C.
        Pottery section, pp. 129-144. Illustrations of Black-on-
     white ollas and other vessels, Pls. 53-54; Black-and white pot-
     sherds, Pl. 55; Black-on-white designs, pp. 132-135; Red
     ware jugs, p. 136; Red ware decorations, p. 137; Polychrome
     designs, p. 140, Pl. 56; Corrugated ware, Pls. 57-58; Plain
     bowl, Sunflower Cave, Pl. 59; and Black-on-white sherds, Pl.
     63. First description of pottery later named Kana-a Black-on-
     white. Found pottery typical of the cliff dwellings and pueb-
     los of the region but none in the Basketmaker debris typical
     of that period. The reason for this surprising absence was
     not determined. Tusayan Black-on-white, pp. 130-134 and
     Kayenta Black-on-white, pp. 130-134.

527. Kidder, Alfred V. and Shepard, A. O. 1936 The Pottery of
     Pecos: Volume II. Yale University Press, New Haven, Con-
     necticut.
        Shepard's chapters good in detailed description of labora-
     tory methods of pottery study. Descriptions and illustrations
     of Arenal Glaze Polychrome (Glaze 1, Red), pp. 1-36; Agua
     Fria Glaze-on-red (Glaze 1-A), pp. 1-36; San Clemente Glaze
     Polychrome (Glaze 1-A), pp. 1-36; Cieneguilla Glaze-on-yellow
     (1), pp. 39-71; Cieneguilla Glaze Polychrome (Glaze 1, yellow),
     p. 69; Largo Glaze Polychrome (Glaze II), pp. 79-107; Espinosa
     Glaze Polychrome (Glaze III), pp. 108-160; San Lazaro Glaze
     Polychrome (Glaze IV), pp. 161-213; Pecos Glaze Polychrome
     (Glaze V), pp. 214-250; Kotyiti Glaze Polychrome (Glaze VI),

pp. 254-258; Gobernador Polychrome, p. 373 (named only); San Bernardo Polychrome (Awatovi Polychrome), p. 368 (named only); Walpi Polychrome, p. 368 (named only) (Mishongnovi Polychrome); Galisteo Black-on-white (synonym Crackle ware), and Santa Fe Black-on-white.

528. Kidder, M. A. and Kidder, A. V. 1917 "Notes on the Pottery of Pecos." American Anthropologist, Vol. 19, No. 3, pp. 325-360, Lancaster, Pennsylvania.
      Early discussion of characteristics of Pecos pottery. Description of wares and profiles of vessel rims. Following wares described: (1) Dull Paint Ware: Black-on-white, Biscuit, Modern; (2) Glaze Paint Ware (6 types); (3) Undecorated Smooth Ware: Polished Black, Plain Red; and (4) Black Ware (6 types).

529. King, Dale S. 1949 "Nalakihu: Excavations at a Pueblo III Site on Wupatki National Monument, Arizona." Museum of Northern Arizona, Bulletin 23, Flagstaff, Arizona.
      Pottery, pp. 109-132. Illustrations of Walnut Black-on-white mug, Flagstaff Black-on-white pitcher, Tusayan Black-on-red ladle, p. 126; Verde Black-on-gray jar, Dogoszhi Black-on-white jar, Padre Black-on-white bowl, p. 127; and Sunset Red vessels, p. 129. Most common wares found were Alameda Brown, Prescott Gray, Tusayan Gray, and Tusayan White. Jars constituted 90% of all sherds. Almost all pottery from Nalakihu and the pits falls in Colton's Ceramic Group 7, 1130-1210 AD. Map of sites in the area.

530. Kintigh, Keith W. 1985 "Settlement, Subsistence, and Society in Late Zuni Prehistory." Anthropological Papers of the University of Arizona, No. 44, Tucson, Arizona.
      Ceramic Chronology, pp. 12-20.
      Based primarily on surface collections, the author formulates 12 ceramic complexes including two transitional complexes and two historic complexes for sites in the Zuni area. The late prehistoric pottery types recovered in the Zuni area are listed with their dates in Table 3.1. The method of dating sites through the ceramics recovered is explained. (Only one site, the Scribe S Site, has adequate tree-ring dating.)

531. Kintigh, Keith W. 1985 "Social Structure, the Structure of Style and Stylistic Patterns in Cibola Pottery." In Ben Nelson (Ed.), Decoding Prehistoric Ceramics, pp. 35-174, Southern Illinois University Press, Carbondale, Illinois.
      A study to attempt to relate stylistic patterns to social structure at several prehistoric sites in the El Morro Valley, east of the Zuni Reservation. There is an indication that careful study of stylistic patterns in ceramics may lead to a better understanding of the social structure within and between sites.

532. Kirk, Ruth. 1943 "Introduction to Zuni Fetishism." El Pala-
      cio, Vol. 50, Nos. 6-10, Santa Fe, New Mexico.
          Descriptions and illustrations of Zuni fetish bowls studded
      with turquoise, and description of a Zuni bowl used as a re-
      pository for scalps.

533. Kluckhohn, Clyde and Reiter, Paul. 1939 "Preliminary Re-
      port on the 1937 Excavations, BC 50-51 Chaco Canyon, New
      Mexico." University of New Mexico Bulletin, Anthropology
      Series, Vol. 3, No. 2, Albuquerque, New Mexico.
          Hawley, Florence, "Additions to Descriptions of Chaco Pot-
      tery Types." Descriptions of Galisteo Black-on-white, pp. 69-
      70; Exuberant Corrugated, Sandstone Black-on-orange (La
      Plata Black-on-red), and Red Mesa Black-on-white.

534. Knight, Terry L. and Gomolak, A. R. 1981 The Ceramics
      of LA1178, Gallinas Springs, New Mexico. Cibola National
      Forest, Albuquerque, New Mexico.
          Description of Magdalena Black-on-white, a local type very
      similar to Mesa Verde Black-on-white. Other local types de-
      scribed: Magdalena Black-on-red, Magdalena Polychrome, Mag-
      dalena Plain Utility, Magdalena Indented Corrugated, Magdalena
      Finger Smeared, and Magdalena Punched Corrugated.

535. Kroeber, Alfred L. 1925 "The Mohave." In Indians of Cali-
      fornia, Bureau of American Ethnology Bulletin, 78, Washing-
      ton, D.C.
          Descriptions of Mohave Ware, pp. 737-738.

536. Kroeber, Alfred L. and Harner, M. J. 1955 "Mohave Pottery."
      Anthropological Records, University of California Press, Vol.
      16, No. 1, Berkeley, California.
          Good description and illustrations of Mohave pottery. De-
      scribes manufacture and decoration on vessels. Types de-
      scribed are Parker Red-on-buff (Fort Mohave variant), and
      Parker Buff (Fort Mohave variant).

537. Krowne, Clifford M. and Sidrys, Raymond, V. 1976 "Centro-
      graphic Means for the Distribution of the Chevelon Drainage
      Ceramics." Monograph II, Archaeological Survey, University
      of California, Los Angeles, California.
          "A computer-aided method has been used to calculate the
      centrographic means and standard deviations for the areal
      distribution of 18 Chevelon ceramic classes. In general these
      mean points are widely distributed and exhibit a lack of areal
      localization. This suggests either a high degree of local
      ceramic exchange or the widespread imitation of ceramic standard
      pottery classes. However, we did note a definite southerly
      movement into higher elevations (wetter regions) for the cera-
      mic classes throughout their chronological history. The maxi-
      mum southern movement, reached in 1250-1325 AD, may have

been effected by the Great Drought of the 13th Century,"
p. 80.

538.   Lambert, Marjorie F.   1966 Pueblo Indian Pottery: Materials,
       Tools and Techniques.   Museum of New Mexico Press, Santa
       Fe, New Mexico.
       A booklet describing and illustrating techniques of pottery
       manufacture.

539.   Lambert, Marjorie F.   1966a "A Unique Kokopelli Jar."   El
       Palacio, Vol. 73, No. 2, pp. 21-25, Santa Fe, New Mexico.
       Description of a rare Gallup Black-on-white effigy jar re-
       covered from a burned room in a stone masonry site south-
       east of Chaco Canyon.   The jar is in the form of a bird pot
       with a handle from the rim to the tail forming Kokopelli's flute
       and two molded arms extending from the body of the jar to
       the flute.   The arms are banded and the body has hatched
       Chaco designs plus two anthromorphic figures, one male and
       one female.
       "Perhaps the most unique feature of this vessel is that it
       combines a traditional prehistoric bird from with the typical
       Kokopelli attributes, both painted and sculptured," p. 23.

540.   Lambert, Marjorie F.   1981 "Spanish Influences on the Pottery
       of San Jose de los Jemez and Giusewa, Jemez State Monument
       (LA679), Jemez Springs, New Mexico."   In Albert H. Schroeder,
       Collected Papers in Honor of Erik Kellerman Reed, Papers of
       the Archaeological Society of New Mexico, No. 6, pp. 215-
       236, Albuquerque, New Mexico.
       Surprisingly few European artifacts were found at this site.
       There appears to have been little Spanish influence on pottery
       produced at this site.

541.   Lancaster, James A.; Pinkley, J. M.; Van Cleave, P. F.; and
       Watson, Don.   1954 "Archaeological Excavations in Mesa Verde
       National Park, Colorado, 1950."   Archaeological Research
       Series, No. 2, National Park Service, Washington, D.C.
       Illustrations of Lino Gray jar, p. 18; La Plata Black-on-
       white sherds, p. 20; La Plata Black-on-white, Black-on-red
       sherds, p. 71; Mancos Black-on-white sherds, pp. 72-79;
       Pueblo II Corrugated sherds, p. 81; Pueblo II Corrugated Jars,
       p. 82; Mesa Verde Black-on-white bowl, p. 104; Mesa Verde
       Black-on-white, p. 107; and Corrugated sherds, p. 108.

542.   Lang, Richard W.   1982 "Transformation in White Ware Pot-
       tery of the Northern Rio Grande."   Arizona Archaeologist,
       No. 15, pp. 153-200, Arizona Archaeological Society, Phoenix,
       Arizona.
       Discussion of 10 ceramic districts in the northern Rio
       Grande and development and change in Black-on-white pottery
       in this region from AD 700 to 1700.   Designs and vessel forms
       of the types mentioned are illustrated.

"This paper has three basic purposes beyond that of con-
tributing elements of information useful to Schroeder's summa-
tion and conclusions. These are the review of both particular
events and basic trends in the transformation of the long lived
whiteware tradition in the Rio Grande, the delineation of po-
tentially effective cultural and historical correlations of change
within the tradition, and the examination of the data for con-
textual patterning of continuity and change. I have attempted
to maintain a compromise throughout between synthesis and
particularism but have found it necessary to regularly provide
some highly detailed information. This is, I believe, war-
ranted by my concern that the reader have a precise understanding of the attributes which are being singled out for
comparison in the development of genealogical arguments, and
by the sketchy nature of published description of certain pottery types which--as they stand--are sometimes misleading,"
p. 154.

543. Lange, Charles. 1968 "The Cochiti Dam Archaeological Salvage Project, Part I, Report on the 1963 Season." Museum of
New Mexico Research Records, No. 6, Santa Fe, New Mexico.
      Descriptions of the following pottery types: Borrego Black-
on-white, p. 323; Cholla Black-on-white, p. 324; Santa Fe
Black-on-white: Pajarito Variety, p. 325; and Wiyo Black-on-
white: Seguro Variety, p. 326.

544. Larson, Daniel O. and Olson, Katharyne. 1984 A Refined
Ceramic Chronology for the Southern Great Basin. Paper
presented at the 19th Great Basin Anthropology Conference,
Boise, Idaho.
      Statistically examines ceramic characteristics and compares
traditional Virgin ceramic chronologies with carbon dated sites.

545. Leavitt, Ernest E. 1961 "Technical Differences in the Painted
Decoration of Anasazi and Hohokam Pottery." Masters thesis,
University of Arizona, Tucson, Arizona.
      "The thesis proposes a system for establishing comparable
classes of data formulated on a study of the total decoration,
using whole or restorable vessels. Pottery types prior to AD
1300 found in the Mesa Verde Branch of Anasazi culture and
the River Branch of the Hohokam culture are analyzed and
compared to illustrate the operation of the method. Decorations are analyzed and recorded following the approach of the
painter in decoration construction through an understanding
of the internal mechanics of geometric design. It is concluded
that no direct relationship is exhibited in the pottery decoration of the two areas. Qualities which are inherent to design
and those which are culturally determined or selected are discussed. The basic tenet of the paper is that similarities
between the ceramic groups, not through individual traits but
through like complexes of traits, will suggest relationships

which should be followed up by further archaeological investigations," pp. ii-iii.
Designs on Mesa Verde and Hohokam ceramics are illustrated.

546. LeBlanc, Steven A. 1975 "Mimbres Archaeological Center:
Preliminary Report of the Second Season of Excavation 1975."
Journal of New World Archaeology, Vol. 1, No. 6, June, University of California, Los Angeles, California.
    The relationship of the growth of Chaco and the Casas
Grandes as population centers and the possible effects the
trade route through the Mimbres country may have had on
the Mimbres population, ceramics, and other characteristics
are discussed.
    The 1975 excavations were conducted at the Beauregard
Site (Z:1:27), the Mattocks Site (LA 676), the Janss Site (LA
12077), and the Stailey Site (Z:1:78), a non-Mimbres site.
    The Beauregard Site is a pithouse village with "pottery
more similar to Mimbres Classic than any other pithouse village
known to date." Types found in the seven pithouses excavated were Three Circle Red-on-white, San Francisco Red,
Bold Face Black-on-white, Mogollon Red-on-brown, and corrugated. These types were found in significantly different
frequencies indicating possibly several different dates of occupation of the pithouses.
    Excavations at the Mattocks Ruin recovered a Chupadero
Black-on-white canteen, Playas Red Incised sherds, and seven
Classic Mimbres Black-on-white bowls, one of which is shown
in the frontispiece and the others in Figure 1.
    At the Stailey Site, a Cliff Phase site not closely related
to the Mimbres culture, the most frequent pottery was plainware, much of which had a burnished interior. Locally made
Gila Polychrome was the dominant painted type. Intrusives
with low frequencies were Chupadero Black-on-white, Ramos
Polychrome, and El Paso Polychrome.
    Pottery Analysis: As a result of these excavations, two
important aspects of Mimbres pottery have come to light: (1)
Described a variant of the Mimbres Boldface to Mimbres Classic
Black-on-white sequence that represents a transition, both
stylistically and chronologically between these two types. This
is not a new type but a transitional variant. Boldface, transitional and Classic sherds are shown for comparison in Pl.
3; (2) Flare-rim bowls and hemispherical bowls have different
design fields and seem to have been used differently.

547. LeBlanc, Steven A. 1975a "Micro-Seriation: A Method for
Fine Chronological Differentiation." American Antiquity, Vol.
40, No. 1, pp. 22-38.
    "The value and need for micro-seriation of archaeological
data are discussed, and a nontopological approach is described.
Excavated and surface material from the Cibola Region of New
Mexico are seriated by two different techniques: factors

scores and multidimensional scaling. The results are compared
with stratigraphic and dendrochronological data. It is argued
that the methods produce useful results and that time differences of about a decade can be determined," p. 22.

548. LeBlanc, Steven A. 1976 "Temporal and Ceramic Relationships Between Some Late Pueblo III Sites in the Zuni Area."
Plateau, Vol. 48, Nos. 3-4, Spring, pp. 75-82.
      An attempt to use contract and problem oriented archae-
ology at sites in two areas, Nutria Road and El Morro Valley,
to determine if the contemporaneity of these sites could be
established. Suggests using more objective characteristics
such as average width of painted lines in comparisons rather
than the more subjective type classifications.

549. LeBlanc, Steven A. 1978 "Mimbres Pottery." Archaeology,
May-June, pp. 6-13.
      Popular article with overview of Mimbres prehistory and the
development of their distinctive pottery. Photos of 13 Mimbres
Black-on-white bowls and a map of the Mimbres area.

550. LeBlanc, Steven A. 1982 "Temporal Change in Mogollon Ceramics." Arizona Archaeologist, No. 15, pp. 107-128, Arizona
Archaeological Society, Phoenix, Arizona.
      A good overview of the temporal changes in the ceramics of
the Mogollon.
      "It has hopefully been shown that Mogollon ceramics were
not homogeneous within the area, but that several long term
trends (or traditions) did exist. Ceramic similarity existed
with the Hohokam and to a lesser extent with the Anasazi.
After AD 1100 there was a very considerable change in ceramics over the entire area. The northern Mogollon became
ceramically related to the Little Colorado-east central New Mexico region; the Jornada area produced several independent
traditions unrelated to each other and unrelated to the rest
of the Mogollon; and the southern division ceased to exist as
Mogollon in the usual meaning of the term. Thus, it is hard
to speak of general Mogollon patterns over the entire range of
either space or time. What is clear is that there is much to
be explained about the Mogollon, and ceramics are an extremely
important tool in finding the answers," p. 124.

551. LeBlanc, Steven A. 1982a "The Advent of Pottery in the
Southwest." Arizona Archaeologist, No. 15, pp. 27-54, Arizona Archaeoloigcal Society, Phoenix, Arizona.
      An excellent summary of the earliest ceramics in the South-
west.
      "The present evaluation of the evidence for the inception
of ceramics in the Southwest is that it was a rapid, practically
synchronous phenomenon over most of the area. It occurred
sometime between AD 200-300 in most areas and may well have

begun by 400 in the north (see Schroeder, this volume). More significantly, ceramics were part of a rapidly spreading trait complex which apparently allowed for a rapid shift in adaptive strategy. This trait complex included new dwelling construction techniques, and probably associated tools (axes); new food preparation procedures and equipment (trough metates and ceramics); and perhaps new storage techniques (at least it allowed for significant intramural storage); it may have been associated with new cultigens," p. 46.

552. LeBlanc, Steven A. and Khalil, C. L. 1976 "Flare-Rimmed Bowls: A Sub-Type of Mimbres Classic Black-on-white. Kiva, Vol. 41, Nos. 3-4, pp. 289-298.

   "Mimbres classic Black-on-white bowls are shown to be divisible into two classes on the basis of shape and design layouts. It is demonstrated that flare-rim bowls have different patterns of design layout than do hemispherical bowls. The similarity of these design canons to those found on Gila Polychrome is discussed. Implications from this study concerning the analysis of Southwestern pottery are also considered," p. 289.

   Illustrations of rim profiles of flare-rimmed bowls, and six Mimbres Black-on-white bowls, both hemispherical and flare-rimmed, Figs. 1-2.

553. LeFree, Betty. 1975 Santa Clara Pottery Today. University of New Mexico Press, published for the School of American Research, No. 29, Albuquerque, New Mexico.

   A good study begun in 1968 of contemporary Santa Clara pottery. Types described and illustrated are Santa Clara Black, pp. 71-78, 84-87; Santa Clara Red, pp. 79-80; Micaceous Ware, pp. 80-82, 87-88; and Buff Polychrome, p. 89. Illustrations of Santa Clara Black, Cover, Pls. 1, 3-6, 8-10, 14-16, 19-20, 22-23; Santa Clara Red, Pls. 11-12, 21; and Santa Clara Buff Polychrome, Pls. 17-18. Very good description of the manufacture of Santa Clara pottery, pp. 6-69. Illustrations of pottery making, Figs. 1-52. Design analysis, Appendix B, pp. 91-99. Potters active at Santa Clara in 1968, Appendix C, pp. 101-103. Glossary, pp. 105-107.

554. Leh, Leonard L. 1942 "A Preliminary Report of the Monument Ruins in San Juan County, Utah." University of Colorado Series in Social Science, Vol. 1, No. 3, pp. 261-295, Boulder, Colorado.

   Pottery found included: corrugated culinary jars, corrugated bowls, basket molded bowls, plain ware, black-on-white ware, and red-on-orange ware. Illustrations: unusual basket molded bowl with painted figures of a man and a quadruped, Fig. 16. Black-on-white (probably Mesa Verde Black-on-white and McElmo Black-on-white).

555. Lehmer, Donald J.   1948   "The Jornada Branch of the Mogol-
      lon." University of Arizona Social Science Bulletin, No. 17,
      Vol. 19, No. 2, pp. 9-99, Tucson, Arizona.
         A good general discussion of the phases of the Jornada
      Branch. Lists indicate pottery types found at the sites studied
      and in the various phases. Map shows distribution of El
      Paso Polychrome in the excavated sites. Also mentions El
      Paso Black-on-brown and El Paso Red-on-brown.

556. Lekson, Stephen H.   1978   "Settlement Patterns in the Red-
      rock Valley, Southwestern, New Mexico." Masters thesis,
      Eastern New Mexico University, Portales, New Mexico.
         Abstract: An archaeological survey of 22 square miles
      along the Gila River in the Redrock Valley of Southwestern
      New Mexico was undertaken to accomplish two objectives: first,
      to extend the Upper Gila survey conducted by James Fitting
      and the author; and secondly, to locate a series of small habi-
      tation sites of all time periods within a very restricted geo-
      graphic area, comparable to the Villareal sites excavated by
      the author in the Cliff Valley. Descriptions of the ceramics
      recovered during this survey are presented in Appendix F.

557. Lekson, Stephen H.   1986   "Mesa Verde-Like Ceramics Near
      T or C, New Mexico." Pottery Southwest, Vol. 13, No. 4,
      pp. 1-3.
         Description of pottery similar to Magdalena Black-on-white,
      a southern variety of Mesa Verde Black-on-white. Rather
      than add another type, Lekson prefers to call this type, found
      in Sierra County, New Mexico, "affinis Magdalena Black-on-
      white."

558. Leslie, Robert H.   1979   "The Eastern Jornada Mogollon in Ex-
      treme Southeastern New Mexico." In Jornada Mogollon Archae-
      ology: Proceedings of the First Jornada Conference, Patrick
      H. Beckett and Regge Wiseman, pp. 179-199, New Mexico State
      University, Las Cruces, New Mexico.
         A list of types and variants with their suggested dates in
      this area, Fig. 4. Local brownwares are grouped into North-
      ern Area Brown, Central Area Brown, and Southern Area
      Brown with three maps showing their geographical distribution.
      Another local type, Ochoa Indented Brown, is discussed and
      its distribution is shown on a map. Rim sherds found are
      classified according to profile by types, Figs. 6-8.

559. Lightfoot, Kent.   1978   "The Impact of Casual Collecting on
      Archaeological Interpretation Through Regional Surface Sur-
      veys." In Fred Plog, An Analytical Approach to Cultural Re-
      sources Management, Arizona State University Anthropological
      Research Papers, No. 13, pp. 92-113, Tempe, Arizona.
         Conclusion: "Evaluation of pothunting's impact on the dis-
      persal of surface material is a complex procedure. The multiple

processes which affect the pattern of material on a site surface preclude a simple causal relationship between pothunting
and the dispersal of surface material.
   "In order to facilitate the testing of casual collecting, variables can be developed which predict the impact of pothunting
on sites. Two major predictive variables tested in this paper
are accessibility and visibility of sites," p. 112.

560. Lightfoot, Kent G. and Jewett, Roberta. 1984 "Late Prehis-
      toric Ceramic Distributions in East-Central Arizona: An Ex-
      amination of Cibola White Mountain and Salado Wares." In A.
      P. Sullivan and Hantman, J. L., Regional Analysis of Prehis-
      toric Ceramic Variation: Contemporary Studies of Cibola White-
      wares, Anthropological Research Papers No. 31, Arizona State
      University, Tempe, Arizona.
         Abstract: "Cibola Whitewares and White Mountain Redwares
      are characterized by a widespread spatial distribution over
      much of the prehistoric Southwest during the period AD 1100
      to AD 1400. Archaeologists have proposed a number of hy-
      potheses to account for these broad areal patterns. These
      interpretations range from local household production and dis-
      tribution to large-scale exchange networks involving ceramic
      specialists and restricted access to political elites. Some al-
      ternative explanations are examined in this paper using cera-
      mic data from the Little Colorado and Tonto Basin regions of
      East-central Arizona. Specifically, we analyzed local clay
      sources, White Mountain Redwares, Cibola Whitewares, and
      Salado wares using X-ray diffraction. Mineralogical and dis-
      tributional information suggests that several mechanisms pro-
      duced the broad geographic range of these wares," p. 36.

561. Lindsay, Alexander J. and Jennings, Calvin. 1968 "Salado
      Red Ware Conference, Ninth Southwestern Ceramic Seminar."
      Museum of Northern Arizona, Ceramic Series, No. 4, Flagstaff,
      Arizona.
         Some valuable information on Salado Red Ware. No illustra-
      tions or complete descriptions.

562. Linne', Sigvald. 1946 "Prehistoric and Modern Hopi Pottery."
      Ethnos, Vol. 11, Nos. 1 and 2, pp. 89-98.
         Summary of a description of the history of pottery making
      among the Hopi based on published literature and study of the
      pottery collection of Carl Oscar Borg. Borg donated his col-
      lection to a museum in Stockholm, Sweden, in 1945.

563. Linton, Ralph. 1944 "North American Cooking Pots." Ameri-
      can Antiquity, Vol. 9, No. 4, pp. 369-380, Menasha, Wisconsin.
         A general discussion of the types of ceramic cooking pots
      used throughout North America including the history of the
      development of utility vessels in the Southwest.

564. Lister, Florence C. 1960 "Pottery of the Coombs Site." Uni-
      versity of Utah Anthropology Papers, No. 41, Part II, pp.
      182-238, Salt Lake City, Utah.
            As reported earlier (Lister, 1959), the pottery of the
      Coombs Site is overwhelmingly of Kayenta tradition, the bulk
      of the types being of Tusayan Gray and White Ware, with
      Tsegi Orange Ware of Pueblo II to mid-Pueblo III times also
      being represented.
            Illustrations of Coombs Gray vessels, Fig. 48; worked
      sherds, Fig. 50; Tusayan Corrugated: Coombs Variety, Fig.
      51; Moenkopi Corrugated: Coombs Variety, Fig. 52; Garfield
      Black-on-white, Figs. 53-54; Cameron Polychrome: Coombs
      Variety and Citadel Polychrome: Coombs Variety, Fig. 55.
      Descriptions of Coombs Gray (new type), p. 225; Tusayan
      Corrugated: Coombs Variety, p. 227; Moenkopi Corrugated:
      Coombs Variety, p. 227; Garfield Black-on-white, p. 228; Mid-
      dleton Polychrome, p. 230; Ivie Creek Black-on-white, p. 231;
      Turner Gray: Emery Variety, p. 232; and Turner Gray:
      San Francisco Variety, p. 233.

565. Lister, Florence C. 1964 "Kaiparowits Plateau and Glen Can-
      yon Prehistory: An Interpretation Based on Ceramics." Uni-
      versity of Utah Anthropology Papers, No. 71, Salt Lake City,
      Utah.
            This report presents geographical distributions of the follow-
      ing ceramic cultures: Fremont pottery, Sevier-Fremont pot-
      tery, Kayenta pottery, Southern Utah Kayenta pottery, Hopi
      pottery, and Southern Paiute pottery. Part II, p. 76, good
      discussion of a cultural interpretation based upon ceramic evi-
      dence of this area.

566. Lister, Robert H. 1958 "Archaeological Excavations in the
      Northern Sierra Madre Occidental, Chihuahua and Sonora."
      University of Colorado Studies, Series in Anthropology, No.
      7, Boulder, Colorado.
            Short section on pottery, pp. 69-77. Pottery from 11 caves
      in the Northern Sierra Madre Occidental. Most of the material
      in the ceramic area was found in the form of sherds. One
      complete Red-on-brown bowl, a partially restorable Villa Ahum-
      ada Polychrome olla, and an almost complete Alma Neckbanded
      jar were found. The sherds found were primarily Alma Plain
      and its varieties.

567. Lister, Robert H. 1964 "Contributions to Mesa Verde Archae-
      ology: I Site 499, Mesa Verde National Park, Colorado." Uni-
      versity of Colorado Studies, Series in Anthropology, No. 9,
      Boulder, Colorado.
            Chapter V on pottery by Florence Lister, pp. 47-63. Found
      Mesa Verde Gray, San Juan White, and San Juan Red wares.
      Illustrations of a few vessels of the above wares, pp. 52-55.
      Good descriptions of complete or partial vessels found, p. 59-
      62.

568. Lister, Robert H. 1964a "Contributions to Mesa Verde Ar-
      chaeology: II Site 875, Mesa Verde National Park, Colorado."
      University of Colorado Studies, Series in Anthropology, No.
      11, Boulder, Colorado.
          Chapter on pottery, pp. 62-87. Types found were primarily
      Mancos Corrugated, Mancos Black-on-white, and McElmo Black-
      on-white. In addition to the above types, the following types
      are illustrated: Chapin Gray, Moccasin Gray, Cortez Black-
      on-white, and Piedra Black-on-white. All complete or partial
      vessels are fully described.

569. Lister, Robert H. 1966 "Contributions to Mesa Verde Archae-
      ology: III Site 866, and the Cultural Sequence at Four Vil-
      lages in the Far View Group, Mesa Verde National Park, Colo-
      rado." University of Colorado Studies, Series in Anthropology,
      No. 12, Boulder, Colorado.
          Chapter on pottery by Florence Lister, pp. 33-59. Pottery
      found at site 866 was nearly pure Pueblo II types. An es-
      timated 97% of the 25,000 sherds are Mancos Corrugated or
      Mancos Black-on-white. Illustrations of San Juan White Ware
      and Mesa Verde Gray. Descriptions of the few vessels found,
      pp. 38, 39-49.

570. Lister, Robert H. 1968 "Contributions to Mesa Verde Archae-
      ology: V Emergency Archaeology in Mesa Verde National Park,
      Colorado, 1948-1966." University of Colorado Studies, Series
      in Anthropology, No. 15, Boulder, Colorado.
          Site 1088, Morfield Canyon. Pottery, pp. 20-23, 80% was
      Mancos Black-on-white or Mancos Corrugated. Illustrations of
      Chapin Gray, Mancos Corrugated, Mancos Black-on-white, pp.
      21-22, and Mesa Verde White Ware. Site 1104, Pottery, pp.
      82-84; Mesa Verde Gray Ware, p. 83. Site 1107, Mancos Black-
      on-white seed jar and pitcher, p. 93. Site 1926, Wetherill
      Mesa, Mesa Verde Black-on-white, and McElmo Black-on-white
      sherds, p. 99.

571. Lister, Robert H.; Ambler, J. R.; and Lister, Florence C.
      1960 "The Coombs Site, Part II." University of Utah Anthro-
      pological Papers, No. 41, Glen Canyon Series, No. 8, Part 3,
      Salt Lake City, Utah.
          Pottery, Florence Lister, pp. 182-202. The pottery at the
      Coombs Site has many similarities to Tusayan Gray Ware and
      Tusayan White Ware of the Kayenta area. The non-Tusayan
      characteristics include the use of igneous rock temper rather
      than temper of quartz sand. The Coombs potters crushed the
      temper particles. This may have been necessitated by the
      lack of sufficiently decomposed rock in the area. This practice
      may have been copied from the pottery of the Fremont area.
      It may be that three influences were involved in the production
      of the pottery at the Coombs Site: diffusion of P II Kayenta
      pottery practices, retention of the use of crushed rock temper

from Basketmaker II times, and an influence from the P II San Juan area in the use of crushed rock temper. The presence of fugitive red on Coombs pottery may have come from the Virgin Branch Kayenta or from the Fremont area.

"To summarize, it can be said that the ancient folk who dwelt in the verdant Boulder valley possessed a variety of gray cooking and storage pots, some plain and some elaborated with corrugations, and created both black-on-white and red vessels for special purposes. Although none of this was excellent pottery when contrasted with later ceramics of surrounding regions, it was favorably comparable to that created during the same period in the San Juan. It must be presumed to have been adequate for the community's needs. Nonetheless, a taste for their neighbor's pottery seems to have been cultivated from the beginning. Trade sherds and complete vessels have come from all portions of the settlement," p. 201.

572. Lister, Robert H. and Lister, Florence C. 1961 "The Coombs Site, Part III, Summary and Conclusions." University of Utah Anthropological papers, No. 41, Glen Canyon Series, No. 8, Salt Lake City, Utah.
    Pottery, pp. 32-90. Found mainly Tusayan Gray Ware and other types in small amounts. Drawing of designs and vessel forms. Good maps of distributions of temper, paint and slips during Basketmaker III to Pueblo III periods. Pottery covered in Part II (see Lister et al., 1960).

573. Lister, Robert H. and Lister, Florence C. 1969 "The Earl H. Morris Memorial Pottery Collection, An Example of Ten Centuries of Prehistoric Art in the Four Corners Country of the Southwestern U.S." University of Colorado Studies, Series in Anthropology, No. 16, Boulder, Colorado.
    Very good photos and descriptions of vessels, mostly from the San Juan Region. Illustrations and descriptions of pottery vessels from the following areas and periods: San Juan, Basketmaker II, Fig. 3; San Juan Basketmaker III, Figs. 4-9; San Juan Pueblo I, Figs. 10-18; San Juan Pueblo II, Figs. 19-24; San Juan Pueblo III, Figs. 25-40; Little Colorado, Pueblo III-IV, Figs. 42-44; and Casas Grandes, Mimbres, Middle Gila Pueblo III-IV, Fig. 45. Map of the San Juan region and a color photo of a Puerco Black-on-red pitcher.

574. Lister, Robert H.; Hallisy, S. J.; Kane, M. H.; and McLellan, G. E. 1970 "Site 5LP11, A Pueblo I Site Near Ignacio, Colorado." Southwestern Lore, Vol. 35, No. 4, pp. 57-67, Boulder, Colorado.
    Sherds mainly Rosa Gray, Rosa Neckbanded, Piedra Gray, Arboles Gray, and Lino Gray. Illustrations of Rosa Gray and Arboles Gray restored vessels, p. 65.

575. Litzinger, William J. 1979 "Ceramic Evidence for the Prehistoric

Use of Datura in Mexico and Southwestern United States."
Kiva, Vol. 44, Nos. 2-3, pp. 145-156.
   A study of "spiked" ceramic vessels which resemble the
fruit of Datura shows they were widespread in the Southwest.
Further study of these vessels is suggested for understanding
of cultural and historical relationships in this area. Several
"spiked" vessels are illustrated.

576. Longacre, William A. 1964 The Ceramic Analysis and Sociologi-
      cal Implications of the Ceramic Analysis. In "Chapters in the
      Prehistory of Eastern Arizona, II," Paul Martin et al., Chicago
      Natural History Museum, Fieldiana: Anthropology, Vol. 55,
      pp. 110-125, 155-170, Chicago, Illinois.
         Description and illustrations of Snowflake Black-on-white,
      pp. 110-123, Figs. 49-58, 61-64.

577. Love, Suzann. 1973 "Hopi Tiles." Masters thesis, Univer-
      sity of Denver, Denver, Colorado.
         A descriptive study of Hopi ceramic tiles made from 1890
      to 1973. A total of 176 from the Denver Art Museum, Museum
      of Northern Arizona, Milwaukee Public Museum, and private
      collections were studied. The tiles are described by shape,
      design, color, and style. Designs include geometric forms,
      kacinas, humans, birds, and other animals. A few pieces
      have trader inspired hallmarks such as ears of corn and
      flowers. Tiles can be traced back to prehistoric origins and
      the earliest found are those from Awatovi Ca. 1700. This
      study deals with one more aspect of the minor arts and be-
      liefs of the Hopis.

578. Lucius, William A. 1982 "Some Propositions Concerning North-
      ern Anasazi Ceramics." Arizona Archaeologist, No. 15, pp.
      149-151, Arizona Archaeological Society, Phoenix, Arizona.
         "During the course of analysis of the ceramics obtained
      from the first two field sessions of the Dolores Archaeological
      Program, some ideas regarding the prehistoric pottery of the
      Four Corners Anasazi, in general, and the Mesa Verde Region
      specifically, have been formulated. Primarily, the definition
      of the ceramic divisions of the northern Anasazi and the re-
      sultant sources of ceramic influence into the Mesa Verde Region
      up to AD 950 can be addressed," p. 149.

579. Lucius, William A. and Breternitz, David A. 1981 "The Cur-
      rent Status of Redwares in the Mesa Verde Region." In Al-
      bert Schroeder (Ed.), Collected Papers in Honor of Erik Keller-
      man Reed, Papers of the Archaeological Society of New Mexico,
      No. 6, pp. 99-111.
         Discusses the question of whether redwares in the Mesa
      Verde Region were traded in or locally produced. Although
      no pat answer is warranted, it appears that the redwares are
      indigenous to the Mesa Verde region and that they moved east

from the Blanding/Montezuma Creek area. The original impetus probably came from the Kayenta region (Tallahogan Red)
rather than from the Mogollon.

580. Lucius, William A. and Wilson, Dean. 1981 "Formal Descrip-
tions of Mesa Verde Region Ceramic Types: Three New, One
Old." Pottery Southwest, Vol. 8, No. 3, July, pp. 4-7.
Descriptions and illustrations of two new pottery types
found during the Dolores Archaeological Project in southwestern
Colorado. These types are named Dolores Corrugated and
Dolores Red.

581. Lucius, William A. and Wilson, Dean. 1981a "Formal Descrip-
tions of Mesa Verde Region Ceramic Types: Three New, One
Old." Pottery Southwest, Vol. 8, No. 4, October, pp. 2-5.
Description and illustrations of a new pottery type, Dolores
Brown. Illustration of a previously described type, Tallahogan
Red. Both of these types were recovered in the Dolores Ar-
chaeological Project in southwestern Colorado.

582. Luebben, Ralph A. 1953 "Leaf Water Site." In Fred Wen-
dorf, Salvage Archaeology in the Chama Valley, New Mexico,
Monograph of the School of American Research, No. 17, Santa
Fe, New Mexico.
Description of excavations of Leaf Water Site in 1951. Con-
sidering the size of this site, little pottery was recovered.
Indigenous pottery found was Santa Fe Black-on-white, Wiyo
Black-on-white, Corrugated Indented, Biscuit A and Biscuit
B, and Micaceous Corrugated ware, pp. 29-30.

583. Luebben, Ralph; Rohn, Arthur; and Owens, R. Dale. 1960
"An Unusual Pueblo II Ruin, Mesa Verde, Colorado." Ameri-
can Antiquity, Vol. 16, No. 1, pp. 11-20.
Only a total of 70 sherds were found in the excavation of
Site 52. The unpainted types in order of decreasing frequency
were Unclassified Corrugated, Chapin Gray, Mancos Corrugated,
Mancos Gray, and Moccasin Gray. The painted types in the
same order were Mancos Black-on-white, Unclassified Black-on-
white, Chapin Black-on-white, McElmo Black-on-white, and La
Plata Black-on-red.
This site may have had a platform mound of ceremonial,
rather than domestic, significance.

584. Luhrs, Dorothy L. 1937 "The Identification and Distribution
of the Ceramic Types in the Rio Puerco Area, Central New
Mexico." Masters thesis, University of New Mexico, Albuquer-
que, New Mexico.
A ceramic survey of the lower Rio Puerco of the East. The
following transitional pottery types are described and illustrated:
Affinis Red Mesa Black-on-white, p. 41; Red Mesa Kiatuthlanna
Black-on-white, pp. 41-42; "Kawanesa" Basket Impressed Black-

on-white, pp. 42-43; Kwahe'e Survival Black-on-white, pp. 43-44; Socorro-Chaco Black-on-white, p. 45; Socorro Survival Black-on-white, p. 47; Mesa Verde Black-on-white, pp. 47-49; Mesa Verde Chaco Black-on-white, pp. 49-51; Mesa Verde Santa Fe Black-on-white, p. 51; Zuni Red-on-buff Burnished Interior, p. 52; "Humming Bird" Red-on-buff, pp. 52-53; Cieneguilla-Zuni Glaze I, p. 53; Glaze III Polychrome, p. 54; and "Tierra Verde" Redware, pp. 54-55.

585. Lyon, Dennis. 1976 "The Polychrome Plates of Maria and Popovi." American Indian Art Magazine, Vol. 1, No. 2, February, pp. 76-79.
    Short article with information on Maria Martinez of San Ildefonso indicating how she and her son, Popovi, revived the polychrome style of pottery at their pueblo. Color photos of six polychrome plates made by Maria and Popovi.

586. MacCallum, Spencer H. 1977 "A Ceramic Arts Revival in Northern Mexico." American Indian Art Magazine, Vol. 3, No. 1, November, pp. 35-39.
    A good article with 10 color illustrations of the pottery of Juan Quezada and other potters of Chihuahua, Mexico, who are producing contemporary copies of prehistoric pottery from the Chihuahua site of Casas Grandes.

587. Madsen, David B. and Lindsay, LaMar W. 1977 "Backhoe Village." Antiquities Section Selected Papers, Vol. 6, No. 12, Antiquities Section, Division of State History, State of Utah, Salt Lake City, Utah.
    Description and illustrations of Sevier Black-on-gray and Ivie Creek Black-on-white found at this site in Richfield, Utah, on the west side of the central Sevier River Valley.

588. Madsen, Rex E. 1977 "Prehistoric Fremont Ceramics." Museum of Northern Arizona Ceramic Series, No. 6, Flagstaff, Arizona.
    The best single source of descriptions and illustrations of Fremont pottery types. Pottery types fully described and illustrated are Snake Valley Gray, pp. 1-2; Snake Valley Black-on-gray, pp. 5-6; Snake Valley Corrugated, pp. 9-10; Paragonah Coiled, pp. 13-14; Sevier Gray, pp. 15-16; Great Salt Lake Gray, pp. 19-20; Promontory Gray, pp. 23-24; Uinta Gray, pp. 27-28; Emery Gray, pp. 31-32; and Ivie Creek Black-on-white, pp. 35-36. A map of the Fremont regional variants is included.

589. Maerz, A. and Paul, M. Rea. 1930 A Dictionary of Color. McGraw-Hill Co., New York, New York.
    Commonly used in early years to describe colors of prehistoric pottery.

590. Malouf, Carling; Dibble, Charles E.; and Smith, Elmer R.
      1950 "The Archaeology of the Deep Creek Region, Utah."
      University of Utah Anthropology Papers, Nos. 1-8, pp. 43-
      68, Salt Lake City, Utah.
         Descriptions of Knolls Gray, p. 48, and Deep Creek Buff,
      p. 50.

591. March, B. 1934 "Standards of Pottery Description." Oc-
      casional Contributions from the Museum of Anthropology, No.
      3, University of Michigan, Ann Arbor, Michigan.
         A good early explanation of terms and characteristics of
      pottery description. Topics included are: body description,
      hardness, color, surface texture, crackle, a ceramic panto-
      graph, and record keeping methods. Illustrations of texture
      of glazed and unglazed surfaces and crackle. Also illustra-
      tions of a ceramic pantograph and ceramic record cards.

592. Mariott, Alice. 1948 Maria: The Potter of San Ildefonso.
      University of Oklahoma Press, Norman, Oklahoma.
         Biography of the most famous Indian potter. Description
      of the development of matte black on polished black type of
      pottery. Illustrations of pottery: Black-on-black jar, "Maria
      and Julian," p. 9; Black and red-on-cream meal bowl, p. 23;
      Old San Ildefonso Micaceous jug, p. 42; Old San Ildefonso
      Micaceous bowl, p. 55; Black-on-cream olla, p. 62; Black-on-
      cream jar, "Maria," p. 75; Black-on-cream olla, p. 86; Black
      and red-on-cream, "Julian and Maria," p. 105; Black-on-cream
      water jar, Tesuque, p. 114; Black and red-on-cream jar,
      "Maria and Julian," p. 162; Black and red-on-cream seed bowl,
      "Maria," p. 178; Black and red-on-cream jar, "Maria," p. 185;
      Black and red-on-cream olla, "Maria," p. 199; Black and red-
      on-cream food bowl, "Maria," p. 206; Black-on-red slip, yeast
      bowl, "Maria," p. 215; Black-on-black jar, "Maria and Julian,"
      p. 218; Black-on-black jar, "Maria and Julian," p. 244; Black-
      on-black olls, "Maria and Julian," p. 270; Black-on-black bowl,
      "Maria," p. 276; and descriptions of vessels, pp. 283-287.

593. Marshall, Michael. 1980 "Descriptive Notes." In Reconnais-
      sance Study of the Archaeological and Related Resources of
      the Lower Puerco and Salado Drainages, Central New Mexico,
      Mark Wimberly and Peter Eidenbach, Human Systems Research,
      Tularosa, New Mexico.
         Brief descriptions of pottery types found during these
      studies. San Marcial Black-on-white is more fully described
      and illustrated.

594. Martin, Paul S. 1936 "Lowry Ruin in Southwestern Colorado."
      Field Museum of Natural History, Anthropology Series, Vol.
      23, No. 1, Chicago, Illinois.
         Pottery, pp. 79-114, 23 plates. Description of Mancos
      Black-on-white, pp. 80-94. Illustrations of Mancos Black-on-

white, many vessels; plain and indented corrugated jars; Mesa
Verde Black-on-white sherds; McElmo Black-on-white mugs,
bowls; Red Mesa Black-on-white bowls; Chaco Black-on-white
bowls; Kana-a Black-on-white bowl, ladle; and Tusayan Black-
on-red bowl.

595. Martin, Paul S. 1939 "Modified Basketmaker Sites, Ackmen-
Lowry Area, Southwestern Colorado." Field Museum of Natural
History, Anthropology Series, Vol. 23, No. 3, Chicago, Il-
linois.
Types described are Abajo Red-on-orange, p. 431; Abajo
Polychrome, p. 431; and La Plata Black-on-orange, p. 432.

596. Martin, Paul S., et al. 1952 "Mogollon Cultural Continuity
and Change: The Stratigraphic Analysis of Tularosa and Cordova Caves." Chicago Museum of Natural History, Fieldiana:
Anthropology, Vol. 40, Chicago, Illinois.
Pottery, pp. 51-101. Types illustrated are: Tularosa
Cave: San Francisco Red jar, Fig. 14; Mogollon Red-on-
brown sherds, Fig. 15; Reserve Black-on-white sherds, Fig.
16; textured ware sherds, Fig. 18; indented corrugated bowl,
Fig. 19; Tularosa Black-on-white sherds, Fig. 20; minority
type sherds, Figs. 21-22; and unfired type sherds, Fig. 23.
Cordova Cave: Three Circle Neck Corrugated jar, Fig. 27;
Puerco Black-on-white bowl, Fig. 28; Mimbres Black-on-white
bowl, Fig. 29; and Mimbres Boldface Black-on-white bowl,
Fig. 30.

597. Martin, Paul S. and Plog, Fred. 1973 The Archaeology of
Arizona: A Study of the Southwest Region. Doubleday, Natural History Press, Garden City, New York.
Chapter XIV, Portable Containers, pp. 239-260. A valuable
discussion of the problems inherent in the most commonly used
current classification method of Southwestern ceramics (Colton).
Problems with Colton's typology:
(1) The number of types is proliferating rapidly and it is
very difficult for the archaeologist to keep track of them; (2)
Morphological attributes of a vessel are confused with its space-
time coordinates; (3) The archaeologist's inability to say just
how different two types are from each other.
"A typology that will facilitate precise communication would:
(1) be based on formal attributes of the artifacts, not their
spatial or temporal locus; (2) be based on attributes that
closely reflect distinctions that might have been made by prehistoric peoples, (3) define a limited number of types; (4)
permit statistical confirmation of the existence of types; and
(5) allow precise statements of the degree of difference between types," p. 252.
Spatial distributions of major wares of the Southwest are
presented in maps, Fig. 34. A short section on explaining
patterns of ceramic variability gives a different point of view

from most current studies. Fig. 33: A tree diagram of major pottery wares based on the presence or absence of particular attributes. Some illustrations of pottery from previous publications are presented in this volume.

598. Martin, Paul S. and Rinaldo, John B. 1943 "The S. U. Site: Excavations at a Mogollon Village, Western New Mexico, Second Session, 1941." Field Museum of Natural History, Anthropology Series, Vol. 32, No. 2, Chicago, Illinois.
Types described are Alma Rough, p. 238, and San Francisco Red: Saliz Variety, p. 240.

599. Martin, Paul S. and Rinaldo, John B. 1947 "The S. U. Site, Excavations at a Mogollon Village Western New Mexico, 1939." Field Museum of Natural History, Anthropology Series, Vol. 32, No. 3, Chicago, Illinois.
Chapter IV, "Pottery," by Leonard G. Johnson, pp. 362-375. Sherds recovered this season totaled 15,263. Types recovered included mostly Alma Plain, Alma Rough, San Francisco Red, and Three Circle Neck Corrugated. Most common were the plain wares and least were painted wares. Sherds illustrated Fig. 130. Red Mesa Black-on-white and Mimbres bowls, p. 129. Plain ware restored jars, Figs. 131, 132 (Alma Plain, San Francisco Red, and Three Circle Neck Corrugated).

600. Martin, Paul S. and Rinaldo, John B. 1960 "Excavations in the Upper Little Colorado Drainage, Eastern Arizona." Chicago Museum of Natural History, Fieldiana: Anthropology, Vol. 51, No. 1, Chicago, Illinois.
Descriptions of these types: Alma Plain polished, Heshotauthla Polychrome, p. 200; Pinnawa Red-on-white, Fig. 111; Kwakina Polychrome, Fig. 108; and Kechipawan Polychrome, Fig. 112.

601. Martin, Paul S. and Rinaldo, John B. 1960a "Table Rock Pueblo Arizona." Chicago Museum of Natural History, Fieldiana: Anthropology, Vol. 51, No. 2, Chicago, Illinois.
Illustrations of Pinnawa Glaze-on-white bowl, Fig. 89; Puerco Black-on-white jar, Fig. 90; Alma Plain jars, St. Johns variation, Fig. 91; White Mound Black-on-white bowl, Fig. 92; Tonto Polychrome ladle, Fig. 93; White-on-red ladle, Fig. 94; San Francisco Red bowl, Fig. 95; Gila Polychrome bowl, Fig. 96; Plain brown plate, Fig. 97; White-on-red, Fig. 98; Kwakina Polychrome bowl, Fig. 99; Gila Polychrome effigy bowl, Fig. 100; sherds of Belford perforated rims, Fig. 101; sherds of Tularosa Black-on-white, Fig. 102; sherds of Gila Polychrome, Fig. 103; sherds of Tonto Polychrome bowls, Figs. 104-105; sherds of Gila-Tonto Polychrome bowls, Fig. 106; sherds of Tonto Polychrome, Fig. 107; sherds of Kwakina Polychrome bowls, Fig. 108; sherds of Pinnawa Glaze-on-white, Fig. 110; sherds of Pinnawa Red-on-white, Fig. 111; and sherds of Kechipawan Polychrome, Fig. 112.

602. Martin, Paul S. and Rinaldo, John B. 1967 Pottery in "Chap-
      ters in the Prehistory of Arizona, Ill." Paul S. Martin et al.,
      Field Museum of Natural History, Fieldiana: Anthropology,
      Vol. 57, pp. 126-138, Chicago, Illinois.
         Discussion and illustrations of Snowflake Black-on-white,
      Figs. 89, 96-104; Springerville Polychrome, Figs. 91-93; Pinto
      Polychrome, Fig. 94; and Querino Polychrome, Fig. 95. Ex-
      cavations at Broken K Pueblo, Carter Ranch, Eastern Arizona,
      recovered a total of 26,082 sherds and 28 whole or restorable
      vessels.

603. Martin, Paul S.; Rinaldo, John B.; and Antevs, E. 1949 "Co-
      chise and Mogollon Sites, Pine Lawn Valley, Western New Mexi-
      co." Chicago Natural History Museum, Fieldiana: Anthropology,
      Vol. 38, No. 3, Chicago, Illinois.
         Types described and illustrated: Reserve Plain Corrugated,
      p. 526; Reserve Incised Corrugated, pp. 500-501, 529; Re-
      serve Punched Corrugated, pp. 526-529; Reserve Indented
      Corrugated, p. 526; Tularosa Patterned Corrugated, p. 529;
      Reserve Fillet Rim, p. 501; and Reserve Black-on-white, pp.
      502-503.

604. Martin, Paul S.; Rinaldo, John B.; and Barter, Eloise R.
      1957 "Late Mogollon Communities: Four Sites of the Tularosa
      Phase, Western New Mexico." Chicago Natural History Museum,
      Fieldiana: Anthropology, Vol. 49, No. 1, Chicago, Illinois.
         Two chapters on pottery by Eloise R. Barter. Pottery of
      the Jewett Gap Site, pp. 106-125. Illustrations of Tularosa
      Black-on-white, Fig. 56. A large collection of pottery was
      made. Pottery is characteristic of Tularosa Phase sites.
      Forty-three Tularosa Black-on-white vessels were identified.
      Pottery of the Reserve area, pp. 89-102. Pottery from Hig-
      gins Flat Pueblo, Apache Creek Site and Valley View Site.
      Illustrations of Reserve Indented Corrugated (unusual form,
      looks like jar set on bowl), Fig. 53; Tularosa Black-on-white
      jar, Fig. 54; and list of pottery types and reference to de-
      scriptions, pp. 100-102.

605. Martin, Paul S.; Rinaldo, John B.; and Bluhm, E. A. 1954
      "Caves of the Reserve Area." Chicago Natural History Museum,
      Fieldiana: Anthropology, Vol. 42, Chicago, Illinois.
         Pottery, pp. 53-86. Four caves excavated in season of
      1952. No new pottery types discovered. Illustrations of Re-
      serve Black-on-white and Tularosa Black-on-white sherds,
      Fig. 26; various minority sherds, Fig. 27; textured sherds,
      Fig. 28; smudged decorated sherds, Fig. 29; Puerco Black-on-
      white sherds, Fig. 30; Alma Plain bowl, Fig. 31; Incised Cor-
      rugated jar, Fig. 32; Indented Corrugated smudged interior
      bowl, Fig. 34; Reserve smudged bowl, Fig. 36; Three Circle
      Neck Corrugated jar, Fig. 37; Tularosa Indented Corrugated
      jar, Fig. 38; and Tularosa White-on-red, Fig. 40.

606. Martin, Paul S.; Rinaldo, John B.; Bluhm, E. A.; and Cutler,
      H. C. 1956 "Higgins Flat Pueblo, Western New Mexico."
      Chicago Natural History Museum, Fieldiana: Anthropology,
      Vol. 45, Chicago, Illinois.
          Pottery, pp. 137-173. Illustrations: Reserve Black-on-
      white jar, Fig. 72; St. Johns Polychrome bowls, Figs. 73-74;
      and Tularosa Black-on-white vessels, Figs. 75-77. Some 40,000
      sherds and 88 whole or restorable vessels were excavated from
      rooms, the midden, and exploratory trenches. "About 90% of
      the pottery from Higgins Flat Pueblo was assigned to Mogollon
      Brown ware. The remainder ('trade' sherds; about 10%) were
      assigned to White Mountain Red ware ... and to the following
      Black-on-white series: Kiatuthlanna, Mimbres Boldface, Mim-
      bres Classic, Puerco and Red Mesa," pp. 148-149. "On the
      basis of these ceramic data we conclude that Higgins Flat
      Pueblo would fall within the Tularosa Phase and was probably
      occupied about AD 1200-1250," p. 149.

607. Martin, Paul S.; Rinaldo, John B.; and Longacre, W. A. 1961
      "Mineral Creek Site and Hooper Ranch Site, Eastern Arizona."
      Chicago Natural History Museum, Fieldiana: Anthropology,
      Vol. 52, Chicago, Illinois.
          Descriptions of Heshotauthla Polychrome, p. 140; Kwakina
      Polychrome, Fig. 95; and illustrations of Tularosa Black-on-
      white, Figs. 78, 84-85, 90.

608. Martin, Paul S.; Rinaldo, John B.; and Longacre, W. A. 1967
      "Chapters on the Prehistory of Eastern Arizona I." Chicago
      Natural History Museum, Fieldiana: Anthropology, Vol. 53,
      Chicago, Illinois.
          Pottery illustrations of Snowflake Black-on-white vessels,
      Fig. 43, p. 78; and Corrugated bowl (McDonald), Fig. 45, p.
      79.

609. Martin, Paul S. and Willis, E. S. 1940 Anasazi Painted Pottery
      in the Field Museum of Natural History. Field Museum of
      Natural History, Anthropology Memoir, Vol. 5, Chicago, Il-
      linois.
          Good photos of Southwestern pottery. Vessels described
      and sites given but some not specifically typed. Brief de-
      scription of one type: Chevelon Corrugated Polychrome, p.
      238. Illustrations of 900 vessels in the following 43 types:
      I. Kayenta Branch
          Kana-a Black-on-white, pp. 14-19; Black Mesa Black-on-
      white, pp. 20-29; Tusayan Black-on-white, pp. 30-37; Tusayan
      Black-on-red, pp. 38-39; Tusayan, Kayenta, Kiet Siel Poly-
      chromes, pp. 40-41; Sagi (Tsegi) Black-on-white, pp. 36-37,
      42-49; Bidahochi Black-on-white, pp. 50-57; Jeddito Black-on-
      orange, pp. 58-69; Jeddito Black-on-yellow, pp. 70-97; Bida-
      hochi Polychrome, pp. 98-105; Sikyatki Polychrome, pp. 106-
      119; Post Conquest Sikyatki Polychrome, pp. 120-121; and Post
      Conquest Hopi Pottery, pp. 122-123.

II.   Mesa Verde Branch
    Abajo Red-on-orange, pp. 126-127; La Plata Black-on-orange,
pp. 126-127; Mancos Black-on-white, pp. 128-131; McElmo
Black-on-white, pp. 132-135; and Mesa Verde Black-on-white,
pp. 136-139.
III. Chaco Branch
    Kiatuthlanna Black-on-white, pp. 142-145; Red Mesa Black-
on-white, pp. 146-149; Chaco Black-on-white, pp. 150-153;
Puerco Black-on-white, pp. 154-161; and Puerco Black-on-
red, pp. 162-163.
IV.   Cibola Branch
    Reserve Black-on-white, pp. 166-177; Tularosa Black-on-
white, pp. 178-193; Wingate Black-on-red, pp. 194-209; St.
Johns Polychrome (variations), pp. 210-219; Querino and Houck
Polychromes, pp. 220-233; Pinedale Polychrome, pp. 222-223;
Fourmile Polychrome, pp. 266-233; Showlow Polychrome, pp.
234-235; Pseudo Black-on-white, pp. 236-237; Painted and Corrugated types, pp. 238-239; and Homolovi Polychrome, pp.
240-251. Zuni Glazes: Heshotauthla Polychrome, pp. 252-253;
Arauca Polychrome, pp. 254-255; Hawikuh Glaze-on-white, pp.
254-255; Adamana Polychrome, pp. 256-257; and Wallace Polychrome, pp. 256-257.
V.   Salado Branch
    Snowflake Black-on-white, pp. 260-263; Roosevelt Black-on-
white, pp. 244-267; and Pinto, Gila, and Tonto Polychrome,
pp. 268-269.
    Also included in this volume are: a map of southwest sites
mentioned in this report, p. 10; a bibliography of all references used in sorting vessels, p. 271; a table of all major sites
represented with references to vessels illustrated, p. 276; a
numerical index of the illustrated specimens with collector's
names, p. 280; and an alpha index including the names of
most sub-types and synonyms for illustrated types as well as
type names used in this volume.

610.   Marwitt, John P. 1968 "Pharo Village." Anthropological
    Papers, University of Utah, No. 91, April, Salt Lake City,
    Utah.
        Pottery, p. 33-40. A total of 12,273 sherds and 24 partially
    restorable vessels were found. Types found and proportion
    of occurrence: Sevier Gray, 86.8%; Snake Valley Gray, 5.61%;
    Snake Valley Black-on-gray, 4.75%; and Ivie Creek Black-on-
    white, 2.72%. Descriptions of the following types from other
    sources: Sevier Gray, Rudy, 1953; Snake Valley Gray, Rudy,
    1953; Snake Valley Black-on-gray, Rudy, 1953; and Ivie Creek
    Black-on-white, Lister et al., 1960. Illustrations: Sevier
    Gray vessels, Figs. 39-43; Snake Valley Black-on-gray, Figs.
    44-46; pottery and unfired clay objects, Fig. 50; pottery discs
    and smoothers, Fig. 51; and Ivie Creek Black-on-white, Figs.
    47-49.

611. Marwitt, John P. 1970 "Median Village and Fremont Culture
      Regional Variation." University of Utah, Anthropological
      Papers, No. 95, Salt Lake City, Utah.
          Section on ceramics by David B. Madsen, pp. 54-77. "The
      ceramic material recovered from Median Village is unusually
      uniform in both ceramic type and vessel form. Over 90% of
      the total sherds recovered are either Snake Valley Gray or
      Snake Valley Black-on-gray types first described by Rudy,
      1953. The rest of the collection consisted mainly of Tsegi
      Black-on-orange, North Creek gray and Black-on-gray, Para-
      gonah Coiled and Sevier Gray," p. 54. Descriptions of Great
      Salt Lake Gray, p. 72; Sevier Gray, p. 72; Snake Valley Gray,
      p. 73, Fig. 38-39; Uinta Gray, p. 73; Emery Gray, p. 74;
      Snake Valley Black-on-gray, Fig. 40; and Paragonah Coiled,
      Fig. 41. A map showing the distribution of the following types
      of Fremont Gray Ware: Emery Gray, Great Salt Lake Gray,
      Sevier Gray, Snake Valley Gray, and Uinta Gray, pp. 70-71.

612. Masse, W. Bruce. 1982 "Hohokam Ceramic Art." Arizona
      Archaeologist, No. 15, pp. 71-107, Arizona Archaeological So-
      ciety, Phoenix, Arizona.
          "This paper attempts to bring together a new body of
      largely unsynthesized data resulting from recent contract re-
      search projects throughout southern and central Arizona. The
      focus of this paper is to elucidate the continuities in Hohokam
      ceramic art through time and among the different regional popu-
      lations; continuities that along with a few other traits reflect
      the binding fabric of the Hohokam culture. At the same time,
      attention will be given to the unique ceramic qualities that
      provide each regional population with its own distinctive charac-
      ter. As the title of this paper suggests, changes in Hohokam
      ceramic art through space and time reflect the ebb and flow of
      the society as a whole," p. 71.

613. Matson, Frederick R. (Editor). 1965 "Ceramics and Man."
      Viking Fund Publications in Anthropology, No. 41, pp. 61-82,
      Aldine Publishing Co., Chicago, Illinois.
          Section on "Rio Grande Glaze-Paint Pottery: A Test of
      Petrographic Analysis," by Anna O. Shepard, pp. 63-87.
      Descriptions of a petrographic study that illustrates the use-
      fulness of this technique for the archaeologist.

614. Mauer, Michael M. 1970 "Cibicue Polychrome: A Fourteenth
      Century Ceramic Type from East-Central Arizona." Masters
      thesis, University of Arizona, Tucson, Arizona.
          Good description and illustration of Cibicue Polychrome, pp.
      7-14. The following varieties of this type are described and
      illustrated: Fishscale variety, Smooth or plain variety, Plain
      Corrugated variety, and Obliterated corrugated. Small Cibicue
      Polychrome jars are shown in Fig. 12. This type is dated at
      AD 1300-1350.

615. Maxwell Museum of Anthropology. 1974 <u>Seven Families in</u>
      <u>Pueblo Pottery</u>. University of New Mexico, Albuquerque, New
      Mexico.
          A catalog of Pueblo pottery made by members of seven
      prominent pottery making families from various pueblos in the
      Southwest. Photographs of a number of contemporary vessels
      and a few of the noted potters. Family trees of the families
      and glossary of terms, pp. 108-111. Families included are:
      (1) Chino, Acoma; (2) Lewis, Acoma; (3) Nampeyo, Hopi; (4)
      Gutierrez, Santa Clara; (5) Tafoya, Santa Clara; (6) Gonzales,
      San Ildefonso; and (7) Martinez, San Ildefonso. Types illus-
      trated are Santa Clara Black, pp. 45, 49, 52, 64; Zia Poly-
      chrome, p. 82; San Ildefonso Polychrome, pp. 85, 88, 90, 95;
      Chaco Black-on-white, p. 108; Hano Polychrome, p. 108; Mim-
      bres Black-on-white, p. 108; Polacca Polychrome, p. 108;
      Sikyatki Polychrome, p. 109; and Tularosa Black-on-white, p.
      109.

616. McCluney, Eugene. B. 1962 "A New Name and Revised De-
      scription for a Mogollon Pottery Type from Southern New Mex-
      ico." <u>Southwestern Lore</u>, Vol. 27, No. 4, pp. 49-55, Boulder,
      Colorado.
          Description and illustrations of San Andres Red-on-terra
      cotta (wide lined), pp. 49-55.

617. McGregor, John C. 1938 "How Some Important Northern Ari-
      zona Pottery Types Were Dated." <u>Museum of Northern Arizona</u>
      <u>Bulletin</u>, No. 13, Flagstaff, Arizona.
          Data on a few pottery types from Northern Arizona.

618. McGregor, John C. 1951 <u>The Cohonina Culture of Northwestern</u>
      <u>Arizona</u>. University of Illinois Press, Urbana, Illinois.
          Best available report of ceramics from excavated sites in
      this area. Ceramics, pp. 30-54. From 14 sites, including four
      caves, 7,212 sherds were obtained. San Francisco Mountain
      Gray Ware was the most common native ware found in several
      types. Also recovered were Black Mesa Black-on-white, Tusa-
      yan Black-on-red, San Juan Orange, Tusayan Corrugated, and
      Tusayan White. Illustrations of Deadmans Black-on-gray ves-
      sels and Deadmans Gray, Fugitive Red; and Tusayan Corru-
      gated, Figs. 5-6.

619. McGregor, John C. 1965 <u>Southwestern Archaeology</u> (2nd ed.).
      University of Illinois Press, Urbana, Illinois.
          Good general text on archaeology of the Southwest. Chap-
      ter VI on pottery, pp. 91-110. Chapter includes descriptions
      of methods of pottery manufacture, technical application, forms,
      glossary of ceramic terms, and a list of 78 dated pottery types.
          Drawing of shapes and designs of the following types:
      Roosevelt Black-on-white, p. 94; Alma Rough, Alma Plain, San
      Francisco Red, p. 144; Estrella Red-on-gray, Vahki Red and
      Plain, Gila Polychrome, p. 151; Dos Cabezas Red-on-brown,

p. 163; Snaketown Red-on-buff, Sweetwater Red-on-gray, p.
167; Alma Neckbanded, p. 194; Basketmaker forms and designs, p. 211; Mogollon Red-on-brown and Three Circle Red-
on-white, p. 227; Tusayan Corrugated, p. 281; Black Mesa
Black-on-white, p. 282; Chaco Black-on-white, p. 284; Sunset
Red and Winona Brown, p. 297; Verde Black-on-gray, p. 307;
Moenkopi Corrugated and Tusayan White ware, p. 325; Kayenta Black-on-white, p. 327; Tularosa Black-on-white, p. 330;
St. Johns Polychrome and Mesa Verde Black-on-white, p. 332;
Gila Polychrome, p. 369; Gallina Black-on-gray, p. 383; Jeddito Black-on-yellow, p. 404; Fourmile Polychrome, p. 408;
and Kinishba Red and McDonald Corrugated, p. 425. Descriptions of Kinishba Red, p. 424, and Los Pinos Brown, p. 174.
"Very rare, has sand temper and is almost certainly derived
from the Mogollon area either directly or indirectly," p. 174.
   Pottery is the most useful single trait in the Southwest
because: "(1) pottery once made and fired is practically in-
destructible; (2) in any site (of pottery bearing periods)
which was inhabited for more than a few years it is relatively
abundant; (3) it was made throughout the entire Southwest
during most periods of cultural development and is therefore
widespread; (4) it reflects minute changes (which may consti-
tute definite types or subtypes) both temporally and spatially,
and (5) it is relatively easy to collect, handle, store, and
study," p. 91.

620. McGuire, Randall H. and Schiffer, Michael B.   1982 Hohokam
      and Patayan: Prehistory of Southwestern Arizona. Academic
      Press, New York. Ceramics, pp. 180-184. A broad overview
      of periods, phases, and regions of Hohokam ceramics. Indi-
      cates Vamori and Topaw Red-on-brown cannot be distinguished
      from Rillito, Rincon and Cortaro Red-on-brown. Therefore,
      these are synonyms.
        Lowland Patayan Ceramic Tradition, Michael R. Waters, pp.
      275-297. Good discussion of history of the typology and de-
      velopment of Colorado Buffware. Indicates much work needs
      to be done on precise dating of Patayan pottery types to ad-
      dress important questions about development of the Patayan
      culture such as origins, interactions with other Southwestern
      peoples, and adaptive changes.
        Lowland Patayan Ceramic Typology, Michael R. Waters, pp.
      558-570. Descriptions of the following 17 pottery types based
      primarily on the criteria of lip forms, vessel shapes, and diag-
      nostic traits introduced, continued or discontinued during each
      period. Types described: Black Mesa Buff, p. 558; Black
      Mesa Red-on-buff, p. 559; Colorado Beige, p. 560; Colorado
      Red-on-beige, p. 561; Colorado Red, p. 562; Tumco Buff, p.
      562; Tumco Red-on-buff, p. 563; Salton Buff, p. 564; Salton
      Red-on-buff, p. 565; Topoc Buff, p. 566; Topoc Red-on-buff,
      p. 566; Parker Buff, p. 567; Parker Red-on-buff, p. 567;
      Palomas Buff, p. 568; Palomas Red-on-buff, p. 569; Colorado
      Buff, p. 569; and Colorado Red-on-buff, p. 570.

621. McKenna, Peter J. and Toll, H. Wolcott. 1981 Ye Ceramics
      from Shabik'eschee (29SJ1659). Manuscript on file at the
      Chaco Center, Albuquerque, New Mexico.
      Discusses the Basketmaker pottery excavated from this
      Chaco Canyon site in 1974 by Alden Hayes.

622. McKenna, Peter J. and Toll, H. Wolcott. 1984 "The Archi-
      tecture and Material Culture of 29SJ1360." Reports of the
      Chaco Center, No. 7, National Park Service, Denver, Colorado.
      Quantified description, analysis, and discussion of the pri-
      mary pottery types found at this Chaco Canyon site. Primary
      types recovered here were Basketmaker Black-on-white, Early
      Red Mesa Black-on-white, Red Mesa Black-on-white, wide and
      narrow neckbanded, neck corrugated, and Pueblo II corrugated.

623. NcKenna, Peter J. and Windes, Thomas C. 1977 "Historic
      Navajo and Puebloan Ceramics." In Charles A. Reher (Ed.),
      Settlement and Subsistence Along the Lower Chaco River, pp.
      557-565, CGP Survey, University of New Mexico, Albuquerque,
      New Mexico.
      "Ceramics of historic Indian manufacture, both Navajo and
      Puebloan in origin, were recovered in small quantities from the
      lease.... The scarcity of historic pottery (60 sherds total
      sample) precluded an accurate assessment of Navajo ceramic
      practices within the lease area. The scant evidence does, how-
      ever, allow some tentative suggestions about local ceramic tech-
      nology. Eleven sherds collected were classified as Puebloan,
      but were included here because they were felt to represent
      items traded to the Navajo," p. 557. Types illustrated are
      Dinetah Utility, Navajo Painted, Pinyon Utility, Puname Poly-
      chrome, Cochiti/Domingo Polychrome, and Jeddito Black-on-
      yellow.

624. McLean, David R. and Larson, Stephen M. 1979 "Inferences
      from the Distribution of Plainware Sherd Attributes on Tuma-
      moc Hill." Kiva, Vol. 45, Nos. 1-2, pp. 83-94.
      Abstract: "The spatial distribution of plainware sherd at-
      tributes is studied as a possible means of identifying use areas
      as well as intersite relationships. The results show a relative
      lack of pottery for cooking at the top of the hill as compared
      with the sites at the base. Differences from area to area on
      the hill indicate segregation of activities and possible changes
      in patterns with time. The method used in this study, with
      refinements, offers a quantitiative statistical approach that may
      prove useful at other types of sites," p. 83.

625. McNutt, Charles H. 1969 "Early Puebloan Occupations at
      Tesuque By-Pass and the Upper Rio Grande Valley." Uni-
      versity of Michigan Museum of Anthropology, Anthropological
      Papers, No. 40, Ann Arbor, Michigan.
      "Excavations of Tesuque By-Pass site north of Santa Fe,

New Mexico, disclosed three distinct Puebloan components (Red Mesa, Kwahe'e, and Santa Fe) and two pithouse occupations which could be neither assigned to, nor distinguished from, the Red Mesa component," p. 111. Illustrations: Plate I: sherds of painted pottery from Area A, Kwahe'e Black-on-white, Red Mesa Black-on-white, Gallup Black-on-white, Chaco Black-on-white, Santa Fe Black-on-white, and Wingate Black-on-red. Plate II: painted potsherds from Area B, Santa Fe Black-on-white, Kwahe'e Black-on-white, and Red Mesa Black-on-white. Plate VIII: Corrugated Neckbanded vessels from Areas A and B.

626. McPherson, Gale. 1975 "White Mountain Redware from NA 11,527 and NA 11,530." Pottery Southwest, Vol. 2, No. 3, pp. 4-5.
    Abstract: "Two pueblo sites near lower Nutria Village, New Mexico, were excavated by Museum of Northern Arizona personnel. Analysis of the 13,000 sherds recovered substantiates many of the suggested dating indicators believed by Roy L. Carlson (1970) to occur in White Mountain Red Ware. One further potential temporal indicator, the occurrence of glaze and subglaze paint, was discovered during the course of the analysis," p. 4.

627. Meighan, Clement W., et al. 1956 "Archaeological Excavations in Iron Country, Utah." University of Utah Anthropological Papers, No. 25, Salt Lake City, Utah.
    Description of Paragonah Coiled.

628. Mera, Harry P. 1931 "Chupadero Black-on-white." Laboratory of Anthropology Technical Series, Bulletin No. 1, Santa Fe, New Mexico.
    Description and illustration of Chupadero Black-on-white, pp. 1-4.

629. Mera, Harry P. 1932 "Wares Ancestral to Tewa Polychrome." Laboratory of Anthropology Technical Series, Bulletin No. 4, Santa Fe, New Mexico.
    Descriptions of Los Padillas (Glaze) Polychrome, p. 31; Arenal Glaze Polychrome (synonym Glaze I, Red), pp. 3-4; Agua Fria Glaze-on-red (synonym Glaze I-A), pp. 3-4; Rayo Glaze-on-red, p. 10; San Clemente Glaze Polychrome (synonym Glaze I-A), p. 4; and Cieneguilla Glaze-on-yellow (synonym Glaze I), pp. 3-4.

630. Mera, Harry P. 1934a "A Survey of the Biscuit Ware Area in Northern New Mexico." Laboratory of Anthropology Technical Series, Bulletin No. 6, Santa Fe, New Mexico.
    Description of the following types: Abiquiu Black-on-gray (Biscuit A) and Bandelier Black-on-gray (Biscuit B). "The characteristics of certain pottery types of the Rio Grande

drainage of Northern New Mexico, known generally to archaeologists of the Southwest field as Biscuits A and B, have been
thoroughly described but little has been done toward defining
the limits of the area in which these wares were produced or
the number and situation of villages concerned in their manufacture. The object of this paper is to define the Biscuit
Area; to discuss the locations of pueblos producing these
wares; and to present such information as has been obtained
through a study of sherd collections obtained in a surface survey of the region," p. 1. Three maps are included showing
Biscuit Ware sites of the 15th, 16th and 17th centuries. Also
an analytical chart of Biscuit Ware sites is presented. Types
discussed in addition to Biscuit Ware A and B are Wiyo Black-
on-white, Sankawi Black-on-cream, Potsuwi'i Incised, and Tewa
Polychrome.

631. Mera, Harry P. 1934b "Observations on Archaeology of the
      Petrified Forest National Monument." Laboratory of Anthropo-
      logy Technical Series, Bulletin No. 7, Santa Fe, New Mexico.
          Description of Dead River Black-on-white, p. 8; Adamana
      Brown, p. 4; Adamana Fugitive Red, p. 4; Woodruff Brown,
      p. 6 (synonym Forestdale Plain); Woodruff Red, p. 6 (synonym
      Forestdale Red); Woodruff Incised, p. 6; Woodruff Smudged
      (synonym Forestdale Smudged) and Homolovi Polychrome, pp.
      17-19.

632. Mera, Harry P. 1935 "Ceramic Clues to the Prehistory of
      North Central New Mexico." Laboratory of Anthropology Tech-
      nical Series, Bulletin No. 8, Santa Fe, New Mexico.
          Types described are Pajarito Gray Ware, Vallecitos Black-on-
      white, p. 23; Jemez Black-on-white, p. 22; Santa Fe Black-on-
      white, p. 11; Wiyo Black-on-white, p. 16; and Cibola White
      Ware. Illustrations of Basketmaker III to Chaco I decorated
      and utility wares, Pl. 1; Chaco II decorated and utility wares,
      Pl. 2; Kwahe'e Black-on-white, Pl. 3; Taos Black-on-white,
      Pl. 4; Mesa Verde white ware, Galisteo Black-on-white, pp.
      20-21; Gallina Black-on-white vessels, Pl. 5; Gallina utility
      ware, Pl. 6; Gallina Conical bottomed vessel, Pl. 7; Wiyo Black-
      on-white, Pl. 9; Cordova Micaceous Ribbed, Pl. 10; Galisteo
      Black-on-white, Pl. 11; Jemez Black-on-white, Pl. 13; San
      Marcial Black-on-white, Pl. 14; Socorro Black-on-white, Pl.
      15; Los Lunas Smudged, Pl. 16; Los Padillas Polychrome, Pl.
      17; and Colorado Black-on-white, Corona (rubbed) Ribbed.
      Also Tesuque Smeared-indented, Pl. 8; Cundiyo Micaceous-
      indented, Pl. 10; Sapawe' Micaceous-washboard, Pl. 10; Val-
      lecitos Black-on-white, Pl. 12; and Pitoche Rubbed-ribbed, Pl.
      16. Maps showing distributions of types listed above.

633. Mera, Harry P. 1939 "Style Trends in Pueblo Pottery in the
      Rio Grande and Little Colorado Cultural Areas from the 16th
      Century." Laboratory of Anthropology Memoirs, Vol. 3, Santa
      Fe, New Mexico.

Good descriptions and illustrations of the following types of pottery: Upper Rio Grande Ceramic Province: Sankawi Black-on-cream, pp. 9-11, Pls. 11-13; Biscuit ware (Bandelier Black-on-gray), Pls. 1-3; Tewa Polychrome, pp. 11-12, Pls. 14-15; Posuge Red, pp. 12-13 (no illustration); Ogapoge Polychrome, pp. 13-14, Pls. 16-20, 27; Pojoaque Polychrome, p. 14, Pls. 21-23; and Kapo Black, pp. 14-16, Pls. 14-15. Middle Rio Grande Ceramic Province: Kotyiti Glaze Polychrome, pp. 17-18, Pls. 30-37, and Puname Polychrome, p. 18, Pls. 38-46. Little Colorado Ceramic Province: Hawikuh Polychrome, pp. 19-20, Pls. 47-49, 52-53; Hawikuh Glaze-on-red, Pls. 50-51; Ashiwi Polychrome, pp. 20-21, Pls. 54-66; and Hopi feather and bird motifs, Pl. 67. Other types illustrated are Rio Grande Glaze Polychrome, Pls. 4-6; Jemez Black-on-white, Pls. 7-8; and Little Colorado Glaze Polychrome, Pls. 9-10. A map of the five regional divisions of Pueblo Ceramic Styles in the 16th century is presented on p. 1.

634. Mera, Harry P. 1943 "An Outline of Ceramic Developments in Southern and Southeastern New Mexico." Laboratory of Anthropology Technical Series, Bulletin No. 11, Santa Fe, New Mexico.

Types described are Jornada Brown, p. 12; Jornada Red-on-brown, p. 12; Jornada Polychrome, p. 12; and Broadline Red-on-terra cotta.

635. Mera, Harry P. and Stallings, W. S., Jr. 1931 "Lincoln Black-on-red." Laboratory of Anthropology Technical Series, Bulletin No. 2, Santa Fe, New Mexico.

Two types described are Three Rivers Red-on-terra cotta, p. 1, and Lincoln Black-on-red, p. 5. Illustration of sherds and a bowl.

636. Miller, Donald S. 1974 "A Synthesis of Excavations at Site 42SA863, Three Kiva Pueblo, Montezuma Canyon, San Juan County, Utah." Masters thesis, Department of Anthropology and Archaeology, Brigham Young University, Provo, Utah.

"In 1969, the BYU Field School of Archaeology began intensive excavations at Site 42SA863, Three Kiva Pueblo in Montezuma Canyon, San Juan County, Utah. Four seasons of fieldwork, including analysis of architecture, ceramics, lithic, and skeletal materials are herein reported. Three occupational components represented by successive building constructions are apparent in 863. A total of 14 rooms and three kivas were delineated. All but two rooms were excavated. A trash mound containing voluminous cultural material and burials was located southwest of the main house structure. West of the house mound is another shallow mound representing a ramada use area which was utilized by all three component occupations. This site was occupied, abandoned, reoccupied, perhaps seasonally, from late Pueblo I to late Pueblo III times," Abstract.

The ceramics are reported in accordance with Forsyth's
(1972) classification. Two new types described are Bradford
Corrugated, pp. 76-77, Fig. 14a-b, and Monticello Gray, pp.
75-76.

637. Mills, Jack P. and Mills, Vera M. 1971 "The Slaughter Ranch
Site: A Prehistoric Village Near the Mexican Border in Southeastern Arizona." Artifact, Vol. 9, No. 3, El Paso Archaeological Society, El Paso, Tecas.
The report of the excavation of the Slaughter Ranch Site,
a four house Salado village with more than 22 rooms, located
in Cochise County, Arizona, near the Mexican border. The
site exhibited strong evidence of Mexican influence from the
south (the painted pottery was approximately 50% Saladoan and
50% Mexican) and tended to confirm the theory that the Salado
people mingled peacefully and in harmony with their neighbors.
An unusual feature of the site was the presence of enclosures
for Pisttacene birds.
Illustrations of Gila Polychrome bird effigy jar, Fig. 8;
Ramos Polychrome jar, Fig. 9; Ramos Polychrome and Madera
Black-on-red jar, Fig. 10. Total sherds excavated were 4,471:
65% Plain ware, 28% Cloverdale Corrugated, 2% Gila Polychrome,
3% Mexican, and 26% miscellaneous.

638. Mills, Jack P. and Mills, Vera M. 1972 "The Dinwiddie Site:
A Prehistoric Salado Ruin on Duck Creek, Western New Mexico."
Artifact, Vol. 10, No. 2, El Paso Archaeological Society, El
Paso, Texas.
Ceramic, pp. 46-48. "El Paso Polychrome was a popular
type at this village," p. 46. A White-on-red type similar to
Salado Red Ware in form was found at this site. It has been
locally called "Cliff White-on-red." The 20,549 sherds found
are grouped in the following percentages: 69% Plain ware,
14% Polished red ware, 6.5% Gila Polychrome, .9% White-on-red,
2% Gila Black-on-red, 2.6% Corrugated, .5% Tonto Polychrome,
and .1% Mexican, mostly Ramos. Illustrations of Tonto Polychrome, Fig. 3; Gila Black-on-red bowl, Tucson Polychrome,
Fig. 13; and Gila Polychrome, White-on-red, El Paso Polychrome, Fig. 15.

639. Mobley, Charles M. 1978 Archaeological Research and Manage-
ment at Los Esteros Reservoir, New Mexico. Archaeological
Research Program, Department of Anthropology, Southern
Methodist University, Dallas, Texas.
Appendix III: Descriptions of the following aboriginal
ceramic types: Blind Indented Corrugated, Chupadero Black-
on-white, Corona Corrugated, Faint Striated Utility (Pecos),
Jornada Brown, Kapo Black, Pecos Glaze Polychrome, and
Smeared Indented Corrugated.

640. Mooney, James. 1893 "Recent Archaeological Find in Arizona."
American Anthropologist, Vol. 6, No. 3, pp. 28-84.

Description and photograph of ancient mortuary vessels
from neighborhood of Kawaika Spring, Hopi Reservation.

641. Monthan, Guy and Monthan, Doris.   1977 "Dextra Quotskuyva
Nampeyo." American Indian Art Magazine, Vol. 2, No. 4,
Autumn, pp. 63-68.
Discussion and illustrations of the ceramic production of
this member of the noted Hopi Nampeyo family. Color photo-
graphs of 10 vessels by Dextra.

642. Monthan, Guy and Monthan, Doris.   1977a "Helen Cordera."
American Indian Art Magazine, Vol. 2, No. 4, Autumn, pp. 72-
76.
The story of how this Cochiti potter developed the storyteller figurine. Illustrations of storytellers and other figurines
by this innovative artist.

643. Morris, Don P.   1986 Archaeological Investigations at Antelope
House. National Park Service, Washington, D.C.
Decorated ceramics and unfired clay objects, pp. 398-431.
Descriptions and distribution of pottery types found in the
excavation of Antelope House, Canyon de Chelly. Thirty-six
decorated types were found at Antelope House. The types illustrated are Mesa Verde Black-on-white, Medicine Black-on-
red, Black Mesa Black-on-white, Sosi Black-on-white, Kana-a
Black-on-white, Wingate Polychrome, Dogoszhi Black-on-white,
McElmo Black-on-white, Puerco Black-on-red, Tusayan Black-
on-white, and a number of unfired clay objects and miniature
clay vessels. A ladle identified as Reserve Black-on-white
appears to be Flagstaff Black-on-white, Fig. 214.
Questions concerning the changes in social groups or im-
migration of new people could not be answered due to the lack
of Pre-Pueblo III ceramics and undisturbed refuse evidence.
Recycled sherds and repaired vessels are described on pp.
409-416.
Ceramics vary significantly from Tse-ta'a, the only other
excavated site reported from Canyon de Chelly. These differences are due to a different pottery classification system.
More "lumping" was done by the investigators at Tse-ta'a
producing fewer type categories.

644. Morris, Earl H.   1917 "The Place of Coiled Ware in Southwestern Pottery." American Anthropologist, Vol. 19, No. 1,
pp. 24-29, Lancaster, Pennsylvania.
Conclusion: "Coiled pottery is not always older than smoothed
forms," p. 28.

645. Morris, Earl H.   1919 "The Aztec Ruin." Anthropological
Papers, Vol. 26, Part 1, Museum of Natural History, New York,
New York.
Extensive report on the excavation of this ruin, 1916-1918

seasons. Pottery is discussed on pp. 65-92. There are good
photos of black-on-white, polychrome, and corrugated vessels.
The vessels appear to be predominantly Mesa Verde White and
Gray Ware and some San Juan and Tsegi Orange Ware pieces.

646. Morris, Earl H. 1927 "The Beginnings of Pottery Making in
the San Juan Area: Unfired Prototypes and the Wares of the
Earliest Ceramic Periods." Anthropology Papers, Vol. 28,
Part II, American Museum of Natural History, New York, New
York.
    Discussion of the pottery sequence from unfired types to
true pottery. Post-Basketmaker wares, p. 161 (Lino gray).
Illustrations of Kana-a gray, Figs. 26a and b. Described and
named: La Plata Black-on-white, p. 23.

647. Morris, Earl H. 1936 "Archaeological Background of Dates in
Early Arizona Chronology." Tree Ring Bulletin, Vol. 2, No.
4, Flagstaff, Arizona.
    Types of pottery briefly described are Obelisk Gray, pp.
35-36, and Twin Trees Gray, pp. 35-36.

648. Morris, Earl H. 1939 Archaeological Studies in the La Plata
District in Southwestern Colorado and Northwestern New Mexico.
Carnegie Institution of Washington, Publication No. 519, Wash-
ington, D.C.
    Very good plates and descriptions of Basketmaker II to
Puebo III pottery. Description of La Plata Black-on-red, p.
222, and La Plata Black-on-white, pp. 153-156, illustrated.
Section on Technology of La Plata pottery by Anna Shepard,
pp. 249-287.

649. Morris, Elizabeth Ann. 1957 "Stratigraphic Evidence for a
Cultural Continuum at the Point of Pines Ruin." Masters thesis,
University of Arizona, Tucson, Arizona.
    Descriptions of Point of Pines Polychrome, p. 20; Maverick
Mountain Black-on-red, Maverick Mountain Polychrome, and
Prieto Polychrome.

650. Morris, Elizabeth Ann. 1959a "Basketmaker Caves in the Prayer
Rock District, Northeastern Arizona." Doctoral dissertation,
University of Arizona, Tucson, Arizona.
    Description of Lino Smudged.

651. Morris, Elizabeth Ann. 1959b "A Pueblo I Site Near Bennett's
Peak, Northwestern New Mexico." El Palacio, Vol. 66, No. 5,
pp. 169-175.
    The majority of pottery found was plain gray globular seed
jars, probably a variant of Lino Gray, and plain gray neckbanded jars, probably a variant of Kana-a Gray. One Black-
on-white pear shaped Pueblo I jar and a Black-on-red seed
jar were found, probably Abajo Red-on-orange or an early
Black-on-red.

652. Morris, Elizabeth Ann. 1980 "Basketmaker Caves in the Prayer Rock District, Northeastern Arizona." <u>Anthropological Papers of the University of Arizona</u>, No. 35, Tucson, Arizona.
     A shortened and updated revision of Morris' 1959 doctoral dissertation. Earl Morris escavated these sites in 1931. He recovered 211 whole or restorable vessels and thousands of sherds, predominantly Basketmaker III.
     Types of pottery found were Lino Gray, Chapin Gray, Plain gray ware, Obelisk Gray, Lino Fugitive Red, Lino Smudged, La Plata Black-on-white, Lino Black-on-gray, Polished Red Ware, Fiber tempered ware, and Untempered mud vessels. A few vessels of later Pueblo types were also recovered.
     The author concludes that Basketmaker ceramic technology could have been derived from the Mogollon area to the south. Crude fiber tempered vessels were probably not independently invented prototypes of true fired types. They are interpreted as short lived products of the diffusion of an idea rather than a method or response to a specific need.

653. Morss, Noel. 1931a "Notes on the Archaeology of the Kaibito and Rainbow Plateaus in Arizona." <u>Papers of the Peabody Museum of American Archaeology and Ethnology</u>, Vol. 12, Harvard University, Cambridge, Massachusetts.
     Descriptions of Black Mesa Black-on-white, p. 4. Illustrations of Black Mesa Pueblo II Black-on-white (synonym Sosi Black-on-white), Pl. 2, and (synonym Dogoszhi Black-on-white), Pl. 2.

654. Morss, Noel. 1931b "The Ancient Culture of the Fremont River in Utah." <u>Papers of the Peabody Museum of American Archaeology and Ethnology</u>, Vol. 12, No. 3, Harvard University, Cambridge, Massachusetts.
     Descriptions of Fremont Plain, p. 42, and Fremont Corrugated, p. 45.

655. Morss, Noel. 1954 "Clay Figurines of the American Southwest." <u>Papers of the Peabody Museum of American Archaeology and Ethnology</u>, Vol. 49, No. 1, Harvard University, Cambridge, Massachusetts.
     The first aim of this paper is to present 11 clay figurines which were discovered in March 1950 by Mr. Clarence Pillings of Price, Utah. The Pillings figurines are illustrated in photographs as are other figurines with which they are compared.

656. Moulard, Barbara L. 1984 <u>Within the Underworld Sky: Mimbres Ceramic Art in Context</u>. Twelve Trees Press, Pasadena, California.
     Discussion of Mimbres pottery as it relates to pottery of the Hohokam, Anasazi, and Casas Grandes. There is a section on icongraphic interpretation of Mimbres painted pottery including form, function, line, color, geometric compositions,

representational compositions: animals and humans, and major
themes. A map of prehistoric sites in the Southwest and a
time chart comparing pottery of the major cultures to Mimbres-
Mogollon. One hundred black and white plates contain excellent full page photos of the following types: Classic Mimbres
Black-on-white, Pls. 1-55; Hohokam Red-on-buff, Pls. 56-65;
Tularosa Black-on-white, Pls. 66-67, 76, 78; Snowflake Black-
on-white, Pls. 68, 77; Roosevelt Black-on-white, Pls. 69, 73;
Reserve Black-on-white, Pls. 72, 74, 75; Socorro Black-on-
white, Pls. 79-80; Villa Ahumada Polychrome, Pls. 81-82, 85,
88; Huerigos Black-on-white, Pls. 83, 91-92; Ramos Polychrome,
Pls. 84, 86, 89, 90; Salado White-on-red, Pl. 93; Salado Red,
Pl. 94; Pinto Polychrome, Pls. 95-96; Gila Polychrome, Pls.
97-99; and Tonto Polychrome, Pl. 100.
Detailed descriptions of all pieces and interpretation of
some on pp. 105-151.

657.   Muench, David and Pike, Donald G. 1974 Anasazi: Ancient
       People of the Rock. American West Publishing, Palo Alto,
       California.
       Good color photos of the ruins of the major prehistoric cul-
       ture regions of the Southwest and contemporary pueblos. A
       few photos of pottery including Mesa Verde Black-on-white,
       Kayenta Black-on-white, Gila Polychrome, Tonto Polychrome,
       Hohokam Buff ware, Corrugated ware, McElmo Black-on-white,
       Chaco Black-on-white, Mimbres Black-on-white, and modern
       Zuni Polychrome owl figurines. Two old photos of Nampeyo
       making pottery.

658.   Mulberger, Michael. 1980 Ageless Images of Southwestern Pre-
       historic Pottery. Land O'Sun Printers, Scottsdale, Arizona.
       Good photos of the following types from the Mulberger Col-
       lection: Reserve Black-on-white effigy, Mimbres Black-on-
       white, Sikyatki Polychrome, Bidahochi Polychrome, Tularosa
       Black-on-white snake effigy, Fourmile Polychrome, Hohokam
       Red-on-buff, Jeddito Black-on-yellow, Sinagua Plainware hu-
       man effigy, and Salado Corrugated human effigy.

659.   Museum of the American Indian. 1972 Naked Clay: 3000 Years
       of Unadorned Pottery of the American Indian. Museum of the
       American Indian, Heye Foundation, New York, New York.
       Illustrated catalog of an exhibition of Indian pottery. Em-
       phasizes the unpainted types from north, south, and central
       portions of the hemisphere. Short section on the technology
       of American Indian pottery by Lewis Krevolin, pp. 11-20.
       Photographs of pottery making and tools, pp. 21-25. South-
       western vessels illustrated in photographs are: Red ware
       pitcher from Yavapai County, Arizona, p. 36; Gila Red vessel,
       Maricopa County, Arizona, p. 36; Corrugated bowl, Apache
       County, Arizona, p. 37; Tularosa Corrugated bowl, Socorro
       County, New Mexico, p. 37; Maricopa red bowl, p. 38 (by

Mary Juan, 1950); Isleta, plain orange vessel, p. 39 (made by
Francis Jamarillo, 1962); Santa Clara Black jar (1925), p. 39;
Santa Clara black carved bowl, p. 40 (made by Grace Medicine
Flower, 1963); Santa Clara wedding jar, p. 40 (made about
1900); and three Casa Grandes vessels, pp. 41-42.

660. Neely, James A. and Olson, Alan P. 1977 "Archaeological
Reconnaissance of Monument Valley in Northeastern Arizona."
Museum of Northern Arizona Research Paper 3, Museum of
Northern Arizona, Flagstaff, Arizona.
Appendix III contains a table showing the types of pottery
found at each ceramic site. A map of the sites in the area is
part of this report.

661. Neitzel, Jill E. 1984 "The Organization of the Hohokam Regional System." American Archaeology, Vol. 4, No. 3, pp.
207-216.
Analysis of the designs of Hohokam Red-on-buff sherds
from different river valleys show that they can be with vary-
ing success distinguished on the basis of designs. Interaction
among peoples of adjacent valleys provided internal structure
for the Hohokam regional system. The development of this
system was influenced by the environmental and locational advantages of the Salt/Gila River Valley which permitted intensive
agriculture and control of long distance trade.

662. Nelson, Ben A. (Editor). 1985 Decoding Prehistoric Ceramics.
Southern Illinois University Press, Carbondale, Illinois.
Five chapters deal directly with ceramics of the Southwestern
United States. These articles are listed under the names of
their authors. They are Brunson, Judy L.; Kintigh, Keith
W.; Nelson, Ben A.; Plog, Stephen; and Washburn, Dorothy
and Matson, R. G. Other chapters using data from other
areas may be of interest to Southwesternists.

663. Nelson, Ben A. 1985 "Reconstructing Ceramic Vessels and
Their Systemic Contexts." In Ben Nelson (Ed.), Decoding
Prehistoric Ceramics, pp. 310-329, Southern Illinois University
Press, Carbondale, Illinois.
A technique is described for estimating vessel capacities
from images of whole or partial vessel profiles. A sample of
partial vessels from a prehistoric Mimbres site and observations of vessels in use in a Guatemalan village are studied to
indicate the feasibility of using this method of determining
vessel capacity with prehistoric remains and ethnological specimens.

664. Nelson, Charles M. 1966 "Prehistoric Pottery Trails of Colorado." Southwestern Lore, Vol. 31, No. 4, pp. 84-85.
Very brief statement on a project proposed to study Colorado's prehistoric ceramic cultures. Sherds submitted primarily

from Weld, Adams, and Morgan counties were 90% Woodland,
7% Dismal River, 3% upper Republican and Pueblo. Small map
of Colorado with types of ceramic sites marked.

665. Nelson, Nels C. 1914 "Pueblo Ruins, the Galisteo Basin, New
Mexico." Anthropology Papers, American Museum of Natural
History, Vol. 15, Part 1, pp. 1-124.
A description of the first use of stratigraphy in the study
of Southwestern pottery. Excavations were done in 1912 in
the Galisteo Basin. The following ruins are described with
drawings of plans: Pueblo San Cristobal, Pueblo Colorado,
Pueblo She', Pueblo Blanco, Pueblo San Lazaro, Pueblo Largo,
and Pueblo Galisteo. A map of the Galisteo Basin shows the
locations of the pueblos listed above. No descriptions or illustrations of pottery types.

666. Nequatewa, E. 1939 "Miniature Pottery." Plateau, Vol. 12,
No. 1, Museum of Northern Arizona, Flagstaff, Arizona.
A brief explanation of the use of miniature pots to prevent
further calamities in a potter's work.

667. Nesbitt, Paul H. 1931 The Ancient Mimbrenos. Bulletin No.
4, Logan Museum, Beloit College, Beloit, Wisconsin.
Good illustrations and photos of Mimbres pottery found at
the Mattock's Ruin. Illustrations of the following types with
descriptions: Mimbres Black-on-white, pp. 52-54, 58, 61, 63-
64; Mimbres Polychrome, p. 57; Mimbres Red-on-white, p. 66;
Mimbres Corrugated, pp. 69-70; and Three Rivers Red-on-
terra cotta ware, p. 97.

668. Nesbitt, Paul H. 1939 Starkweather Ruin, A Mogollon Pueblo
Site in the Upper Gila Area of New Mexico. Bulletin No. 6,
Logan Museum Publications in Anthropology, Beloit, Wisconsin.
Descriptions of the following types: Alma Plain, p. 137;
Reserve Corrugated, p. 140; Alma Scored, p. 138; Reserve
Smudged, p. 139; Alma Punched, p. 138; Starkweather Smudged
Decorated (synonym Reserve Polychrome), p. 139; Alma In-
cised, p. 138; Reserve Black-on-white, p. 138; Tularosa White-
on-red (synonym Reserve Polychrome), p. 139; Mogollon Red-
on-brown, p. 137; and Three Circle Red-on-white, p. 137.

669. New Mexico Quarterly. 1957 "Designs from Ancient Mimbres
Pottery." New Mexico Quarterly, Vol. 37, Nos. 1-2, pp. 36-
44.
Drawings of 16 Mimbres Black-on-white bowls by Mrs. C. B.
Cosgrove.

670. New Mexico University. 1967-8 Pueblo Pottery: AD 400-1967.
New Mexico University, Museum of Anthropology, Albuquerque,
New Mexico.
Brochure of an exhibit at the Museum of Anthropology, New

Mexico University. Photos of pottery making at Acoma. Il-
lustrations of Lino Gray, Basketmaker III, p. 16; Exuberant
Corrugated, Pueblo III, p. 17; Lino Black-on-gray, Basket-
maker III, p. 18; La Plata Black-on-white, Pueblo III, p. 29;
Mesa Verde and McElmo Black-on-white bowls, p. 21; Mancos
Black-on-white, Pueblo III, p. 22; San Ildefonso Black-on-red,
Ca. 1900, p. 23; Gallup Black-on-white and Escavada Black-
on-white, Pueblo II, p. 24; Tularosa Black-on-white, Pueblo
III, p. 25; Mimbres Black-on-white, Pueblo III, p. 26; Sosi
and Dogoszhi Black-on-white bowls, Pueblo II-III, p. 27; Tusa-
yan Black-on-red, Pueblo III and Abajo Red-on-orange, Pueblo
I, p. 28; St. Johns Polychrome, Pueblo III, p. 29; Puerco
Black-on-red, Pueblo II, p. 30; Hano Polychrome, Ca. 1955,
p. 32; and Acoma Black-on-white, 1967, p. 34.

671. Nordenskiold, Gustav. 1893 The Cliff Dwellers of the Mesa
Verde Southwestern, Colorado. Their Pottery and Implements.
Translated by D. L. Morgan, P. A. Norstedt, and Soner,
Stockholm, Sweden (Reprint, Rio Grande Press, 1979).
    The first scientific study of the Mesa Verde. Good plates
of pottery and Mesa Verde Ruins. First description of Mesa
Verde Black-on-white, p. 82 (not named).

672. O'Bryan, Deric. 1950 "Excavations in Mesa Verde National
Park." Medallion Papers, No. 39, Gila Pueblo, Globe, Arizona.
    Descriptions and illustrations of the following types: Cha-
pin Gray (synonym Twin Trees Plain), p. 91, Pl. 39; Twin
Trees Black-on-white, p. 91, Pl. 39; and McElmo Black-on-
white, pp. 93-98, Pls. 46-47. Illustrations of Lino Black-on-
gray, Pls. 39, 42; Lino Gray, Pls. 39-41; Kana-a Gray, Pl.
41; La Plata Black-on-white, Pl. 42; Piedra Black-on-white,
Pl. 42; White Mound Black-on-white, Pl. 42; La Plata Black-
on-red, Pl. 42; Abajo Red-on-orange, Pl. 42; Abajo Polychrome, Pl. 42; Mancos Black-on-white, Pls. 43-44; Chaco
Black-on-white wares, Pl. 44; Corrugated wares of Mancos
Mesa and McElmo phase, Pl. 45; and Mesa Verde Black-on-
white, Pls. 48-49. Intrusive pottery illustrated in Pl. 50;
Wingate Black-on-red, Houck Polychrome, St. Johns Polychrome,
Tusayan Polychrome, and Mogollon Red-on-brown.
    Good introductory section on previous excavations at Mesa
Verde National Park. Detailed descriptions of excavations at
sites 145, 102, and 34. Associated pottery from above three
sites, pp. 89-100. Pottery from Site 145 was predominantly
Lino Gray and Twin Trees Plain. Village pottery found at
Sites 102 and 1 was 59% Lino Gray and 35% Kana-a Gray.
Pueblo pottery from Site 102 was found in the following amounts:
Lino Gray, 50%; Kana-a Gray, 23.5%; Mancos Black-on-white,
11%; and Corrugated, 9.5%. Site 34 Pueblo pottery included:
Corrugated, 56%; Mesa Verde Black-on-white, 23%; Mancos
Black-on-white, 10%; and McElmo Black-on-white, 7.5%.

168   Southwestern Pottery

673. Oleman, Minnie. 1968 "Lucy Lewis, Acoma's Versatile Potter."
     El Palacio, Vol. 75, No. 2, pp. 10-12.
     Illustrations of four Lucy Lewis vessels. Brief discussion
     of her life and work.

674. Olson, Allan P. 1959 "Evaluation of the Phase Concept as
     Applied to 11th and 12th Century Occupations at Point of Pines,
     East Central Arizona." Ph.D. dissertation, University of Ari-
     zona, Tucson, Arizona.
     Descriptions of McDonald Patterned Corrugated, McDonald
     Painted Corrugated, and Prieto Indented Corrugated.
     "The phase concept, one of the most useful taxonomic de-
     vices for the classification of archaeologic cultures was traced
     in the Southwest from its inception in the early 1930s to the
     present. The use of ceramic taxonomy as the major determinant
     in phase assignment is evident in these various applications....
     It is obvious that ceramic indicators are most effective in
     terms of the spatial and temporal definition of phases but that
     pottery has been over-emphasized in its application as a de-
     vice used in cultural synthesis," abstract.

675. Olson, Allan P. 1971 "Archaeology of the Arizona Public
     Service Company 345 KV Line." Museum of Northern Arizona
     Bulletin, No. 46, Flagstaff, Arizona.
     Descriptions of sherds found at various sites of the sur-
     vey. Cross Canyon Group, NA 8013: Types found were
     Abajo Black-on-red, Black Mesa Black-on-white, Gallup Black-
     on-white, Kana-a Black-on-white, Kiatuthlanna Black-on-white,
     La Plata Black-on-white, McElmo Black-on-white, Pinedale
     Black-on-red, Puerco Black-on-red, Puerco Black-on-white,
     Red Mesa Black-on-white, Sosi Black-on-white, St. Johns Poly-
     chrome, Tusayan Polychrome, White Mound Black-on-white,
     Wingate Black-on-red, corrugated, Plain brown ware, Kana-a
     Gray, Kana-a Neckbanded, Lino Fugitive Red, Lino Gray, Re-
     serve Smudged, and Cibola White Ware. Ceramics of Kinlichee
     Ruin are described.
     Payson Site NA 8082: Pottery complex from this site is
     very simple. Twenty decorated sherds included Tonto Poly-
     chrome, Pinedale Polychrome, and one sherd of Cibola White
     Ware. Tonto Brown and Tonto Smudged comprised most of
     the sherds found. Illustrations: Modified sherds, Fig. 43,
     p. 38; Gallup Black-on-white sherds, p. 40; White Mound
     Black-on-white and Kiatuthlanna Black-on-white, p. 41; Puerco
     Black-on-white sherds, p. 41; and Red Mesa Black-on-white
     sherds, p. 42.

676. Opler, Marvin K. 1939 "Southern Ute Pottery." Master Key,
     Vol. 13, No. 5, pp. 161-163.
     Brief and incomplete description of Southern Ute pottery.

677. Oppelt, Norman T. 1976 "The Use of Sculptamold as a Patching

Material in the Restoration of Pottery." Pottery Southwest,
Albuquerque Archaeological Society, Vol. 3, No. 2, April,
p. 8.
An explanation of the use and advantages of Sculptamold
in place of plaster of Paris in restoring pottery.

678. Oppelt, Norman T. 1984 "Worked Potsherds of the Southwest: Their Forms and Distribution." Pottery Southwest,
Vol. 11, No. 1, pp. 1-6.
The most common forms of worked sherds are described
and illustrated. These forms include unperforated discs, perforated discs, spindle whorls, pendants, pottery tools, gam-
ing pieces, scoops, pukis, and potrests. The methods of
manufacture are briefly discussed. It is suggested that in the
Anasazi culture worked potsherds increased from Basketmaker
times to Pueblo IV. In geographical distribution, worked
sherds are more common in the Anasazi culture than in the
Mogollon culture and are least common among the Hohokam.
Possible causes of these temporal and geographic differences
are mentioned. The results of this exploratory study should
be validated, and the writer recommends that worked sherds
be more carefully documented in future excavations so their
potential for determining social structure can be fulfilled.

679. Orchard, William C. 1925 "Fine Line Decoration of Ancient
Southwestern Pottery." Indian Notes, Museum of American
Indian, pp. 24-31, Heye Foundation, New York, New York.
Describes the methods used to paint fine-line pottery, pri-
marily Mimbres. Illustrations of two Mimbres bowls.

680. Pattison, Natalie B. 1968 "Nogales Cliff House: A Largo-
Gallina Site." Masters thesis, University of New Mexico, Al-
buquerque, New Mexico.
Description and illustrations of Gallina Black-on-gray, Gal-
lina Coarse Utility, and Gallina Plain Utility. Descriptions of
Gallina Plain Undecorated and Gallina Utility Punched.

681. Peck, Fred. 1956 "An Archaeological Reconnaissance of the
East Verde River in Central Arizona." Masters thesis, Uni-
versity of Arizona, Tucson, Arizona.
Descriptions of Hardscrabble Brown and Pine Brown.

682. Peckham, Steward and Reed, Erik K. 1963 "Three Sites
Near Ranchos de Taos, New Mexico." Highway Salvage Ar-
chaeology, New Mexico, Vol. 4, pp. 1-29.
Illustrations of Taos Black-on-white. Description of Kwahe'e
Black-on-white.

683. Pendergast, David M. 1960 "The Frei Site, Santa Clara, Utah."
Utah Anthropological Papers, No. 60, pp. 127-163, University
of Utah, Salt Lake City, Utah.

"With the exception of two sherds of Washington Black-on-gray identified as Pueblo I type by Colton and 167 sherds of Boulder Gray which Colton believes to be Basketmaker III or Pueblo I type, all of the pottery recovered at the Frei Site appears to fall in the Pueblo II to Pueblo III range," p. 142. Major types of pottery found were North Creek Gray, 44.6%; Boulder Gray, 9.08%; North Creek Corrugated, 24.36%; Washington Corrugated, 4.1%; North Creek Black-on-gray, 6.1%; and Virgin Black-on-white, 4.73%. Painted pottery illustrated in Fig. 5: three Middleton Black-on-red bowls, one Middleton Black-on-red squash pot, and a double Black-on-white vessel with Pueblo II design. Vessels illustrated in Fig. 6: two Virgin Black-on-white bowls, one Black-on-gray Pueblo I-III bowl, one fragment of Snake Valley Black-on-gray bowl, and one Toquerville Black-on-white bowl. Vessels illustrated in Fig. 7: one North Creek Gray canteen, two North Creek Gray ollas, one North Creek Gray handled bowl or cup, and one Snake Valley Gray handled bowl or cup.

684. Pendleton, Michael and Washburn, Dorothy. 1977 "Comparative Analysis of the Surface Treatment of Pueblo II-III Corrugated Wares from Hovenweep National Monument, 1975 Survey." In Joseph C. Winter, Hovenweep 1976, Archaeological Report No. 3, pp. 79-92, Anthropology Department, San Jose State University, San Jose, California.

A total of 3,635 corrugated sherds were recovered and analyzed: 1,981 were typed as Hovenweep Corrugated and the remainder as Mancos/Mesa Verde Corrugated. The characteristics of coil width, sherd thickness, wave form, primary angle, vessel construction and surface treatment were examined. It was found that the surface treatment decorative characteristics are not useful in discriminating between Hovenweep and Mancos/Mesa Verde Corrugated. Total vessel form may still need to be examined to determine if rim shape, temper, and patterning of surface treatment may distinguish between these two types.

685. Pepper, G. H. 1920 "Pueblo Bonito." Anthropology Papers of American Museum of Natural History, Vol. 26, New York, New York.

Plates showing typical Chaco shapes and designs. Types illustrated include Chaco Black-on-white, Escavada Black-on-white, Gallup Black-on-white, and Mesa Verde Black-on-white.

686. Pepper, George H. 1924 "A Strange Type of Pottery from Utah." Indian Notes, Vol. 1, No. 4, pp. 167-184, Museum of the American Indian, New York, New York.

Description and illustrations of Basketmaker pottery from Grand Gulch, southeastern Utah.

687. Peterson, Susan. 1978 Maria Martinez: Five Generations of

Potters. Smithsonian Institution Press for the Renwick Gallery
of the National Collection of Fine Arts, Washington, D.C.
Catalog of an exhibit of pottery by Maria Martinez and
other members of her family from San Ildefonso Pueblo. One
hundred pieces are described and 33 are illustrated. Also
there are photos of Maria, Julian, Santana, Adam, and others.

688. Phelps, Alan L. 1968 "A Recovery of Purslane Seeds in an
Archaeological Context." Artifact, Vol. 6, No. 4, El Paso
Archaeological Society, El Paso, Texas.
A Chupadero Black-on-white pitcher containing Purslane
seeds found at a site near Coe Lake, Dona Ana County, New
Mexico, is described and illustrated. Other types found at
this site were El Paso Polychrome, Three Rivers Red-on-terra
cotta, El Paso and/or Jornada Brown, Alma Plain, Mimbres
Black-on-white, Playas Red Incised, Villa Ahumada Polychrome,
and Ramos Polychrome.

689. Phelps, Alan L. 1974 "An Analysis of the Ceramics of the
Guadalupe Mountains National Park." Bulletin of the Texas
Archaeological Society, Vol. 45, pp. 121-150.
"The pottery sherds collected by the Texas Archaeological
Society Field School from the Guadalupe Mountains National
Park are identified and classified. The sherds are tabulated
by site and sites are assigned a date span through the use of
ceramic cross-dating. Ceramic attributes are examined for the
purpose of identifying the occupants and isolating possible
settlement patterns; the latter being attempted by using various
site groupings. An hypothesis is proposed that places a
Jornada-Mogollon occupation in the Guadalupe Mountains National Park between AD 850 and AD 1350," p. 121.

690. Philbrook Art Center. 1963 Indian Pottery of the Southwest
Post Spanish Period. Clark Field Collection, revised edition,
Tulsa, Oklahoma.
Photos and very brief descriptions of historic vessels.
Provenience and some dates given but not typed.

691. Pilles, Peter J. and Danson, Edward B. 1974 "The Prehistoric Pottery of Arizona." Arizona Highways, Vol. 50, No.
4, Tucson, Arizona.
(See Arizona Highways, February 1974, for annotation.)

692. Pippin, Lonnie C. 1973 "The Archaeology and Paleoecology of
Guadalupe Ruin, Sandoval County, New Mexico." Ph.D. dissertation, Department of Anthropology, Washington State University, Pullman, Washington.
Excavation of a Chaco outlier occupied AD 900-1200 and reoccupied by San Juan Anasazi in the late 13th and early 14th
centuries. In addition to the established types listed below,
a locally made type similar to McElmo Black-on-white is named

Guadalupe Black-on-white. Local corrugated and indented
types are called Guadalupe Corrugated and Guadalupe Smeared
Indented, respectively. These three local types are described
in Appendix I, p. 405.
In addition to those local types mentioned above, the types
recovered at this site were Puerco Black-on-red, Wingate Black-
on-red, Wingate Polychrome, St. Johns Black-on-red, St.
Johns Polychrome, *Santa Fe Black-on-white, *Red Mesa Black-
on-white, *Puerco Black-on-white, *Gallup Black-on-white,
*Chaco Black-on-white, *Kwahe'e Black-on-white, Socorro
Black-on-white, Tularosa Black-on-white, Incised plainware,
Tohatchi Banded, Exuberant Corrugated, Prieto Smeared, and
Tesuque Smeared Indented. *These types are described in
Appendix I, p. 405.

693. Plog, Fred. 1976 "Ceramic Analysis." Monograph II, Archaeo-
      logical Survey, pp. 58-78, University of California, Los An-
      geles, California.
      "Surface finish, temper, and paint form the basis of the
      ceramic typology. These attributes occur together in relatively
      homogeneous, non-overlapping categories. The black-on-white
      types cluster into six groups that appear to have temporal
      significance," p. 59.

694. Plog, Fred. 1978 "An Analytical Approach to Cultural Re-
      source Management." Arizona State University Anthropologi-
      cal Research Papers, No. 13, Tucson, Arizona.
      (See Hantman and Lightfoot, 1978.)

695. Plog, Stephen. 1976 "The Inference of Prehistory Social Or-
      ganization from Ceramic Design Variability." Michigan Discus-
      sions in Anthropology, Vol. 1, Winter, pp. 1-47.
      "The goal of this paper is to evaluate the proposal that as-
      pects of prehistoric social organization can be inferred through
      stylistic analysis," abstract.

696. Plog, Stephen. 1977 "A Multivariate Approach to the Explana-
      tion of Ceramic Design Variation." Ph.D. dissertation, Univer-
      sity of Michigan, Ann Arbor, Michigan.
      "Using archaeological information from the Chevelon Canyon
      area in east-central Arizona, the importance of four variables--
      ceramic exchange, subsistence-settlement systems, vessel form,
      and temporal variation--in explaining design variation in the
      Chevelon area are evaluated. Designs are described using a
      hierarchical, attribute based system that emphasizes the dif-
      ferent decisions made by prehistoric artisans in the process
      of painting a vessel. Analysis of the mineral and chemical
      composition of black-on-white pottery along with stylistic
      analysis of the designs demonstrates that a large percentage
      of the black-on-white pottery was imported into the Chevelon
      area, probably from the region around Winslow. This ceramic

exchange accounts for the most statistically significant difference in the relative frequencies of design attribute states. Design change through time is studied using tree-ring dated sites. Analysis indicates that the temporal variation accounts for the second highest number of statistically significant differences. Design differences between different vessel forms accounts for the lowest number of statistically significant differences," abstract.

"Theories of stylistic variation are evaluated using the results of the design analysis and design information from other areas of the American Southwest. It is argued that the social interaction-learning cannot explain the temporal and spatial variations in ceramic designs in the Southwest. An information exchange theory can explain this variation as could increasing specialization in ceramic production the development of exchange networks. It is argued that additional information on ceramic manufacture and use is needed to test these explanations," abstract.

697. Plog, Stephen. 1980 Stylistic Variation in Prehistoric Ceramics: Design Analysis in the American Southwest. Cambridge University Press, Cambridge, Massachusetts.
    A study designed to examine possible explanations for stylistic variations in prehistoric ceramics. Topics included are design classification, ceramic exchange, subsistence-settlement systems, vessel form, and temporal variation.

698. Plog, Stephen. 1985 "Estimating Vessel Orifice Diameters: Measurement Methods and Measurement Error." In Ben Nelson (Ed.), Decoding Prehistoric Ceramics, pp. 243-253, Southern Illinois University Press, Carbondale, Illinois.
    Two methods of estimating vessel orifice diameters are compared with a sample of 63 potsherds. One is a curve fitting method where technicians match sherd curvatures to a series of concentric circles. The second uses a Starrett dial indicator to measure sherd curvature. Both methods were shown to inject significant amounts of measurement error. This study indicates that the measurement error is likely to increase as the number of technicians increases. It is suggested that minimizing measurement error should be an objective of researchers in archaeological studies.

699. Pomeroy, John A. 1962 "A Study of Black-on-white Pottery in the Tonto Basin, Arizona." Masters thesis, University of Arizona, Tucson, Arizona.
    Description and illustrations of: Chaco Black-on-white, Tularosa Black-on-white, Reserve Black-on-white, Puerco Black-on-white, Showlow Black-on-white, and Tusayan Black-on-white. Abstract: "A collection of 165 Black-on-white vessels from the Tonto Basin has been studied. These vessels were found in association with the remains of the Cherry

Creek and Roosevelt phases of the Salado Culture and the
southern extension of the Western Pueblo culture. The collection was divided into two groups, foreign or trade ware
and a ware assumed to be locally made Roosevelt Black-on-
white. The latter was then analyzed in terms of style of design and found to consist of two major styles termed Pinedale
and Roosevelt. The style analysis was done by first dividing
the material into form classes such as bowls, jars, and pitchers
and then analyzing each class in terms of design modes. Layout, pattern, and component modes were determined. The
styles were then defined in terms of these modes. The major
difference between the Pinedale and Roosevelt styles is that
Pinedale has opposed solid and hatch decoration whereas Roosevelt has mainly solid elements."

700. Randall, Mark E. 1978 "Ceramic Marbles." Pottery Southwest,
     Vol. 5, No. 2, April, pp. 4-7.
         Short article on ceramic marbles. Describes glazed and un-
     glazed marbles, how they were made, and where they were
     found.

701. Reed, Erik K. 1938a Preliminary Study of Pottery of Room
     7, Wupatki Pueblo. U.S. National Park Service, Region III,
     Special Report, Manuscript, Santa Fe, New Mexico.
         Types described: Wupatki Polychrome, p. 20; Tsegi Red-
     washed, p. 22; and Sunset Corrugated, p. 26.

702. Reed, Erik K. 1938b "Archaeology of the Mimbres Valley,
     New Mexico." Central Texas Archaeologist, No. 4, pp. 9-20.
         General article on Mimbres archaeology. "The popularity
     of this Mimbres pottery is due to the distinctiveness and high
     quality already referred to of the decoration. The brush work
     of Mimbres Black-on-white is accurate and precise to an ex-
     treme not equalled by any other Southwest pottery except per-
     haps that of Chihuahua, and the designs include a far greater
     emphasis on life forms than is found in any other prehistoric
     Southwestern ware. The typical Mimbres Black-on-white bowl
     is, as is unually the case with bowls in the Southwest, deco-
     rated only on the interior usually with a band or zone of geo-
     metric ornament around the top of the interior just below the
     rim, and typically with an animal figure in the middle of the
     open space. Birds, fishes, insects, and mammals including
     men, are portrayed. Often there is a composition, either
     schematic or active, of two or more figures. Not all Mimbres
     bowls have zoomorphic designs; sometimes the field below the
     zone of the geometric ornament is left entirely open, and many
     bowls have an overall geometric pattern covering the entire
     interior. Exterior decoration of the bowl does occur but is
     very restricted. The elements composing the geometric decora-
     tions are typical Southwestern motif-stepped or terraced ele-
     ments, solid triangles, thin horizontal parallel lines, lozenge

shaped figures, checkering, key figures, etc. Jars of Mimbres
Black-on-white also occur, usually with only the geometric
decoration. In addition to this fine decorated ware which may
have been used as 'table service' food bowls as well as for
mortuary purposes, the Mimbres people made a great deal of
unpainted pottery for cooking and storage purposes. Most of
this is corrugated ware; the structural coils not scraped and
smoothed down to a flat surface but emphasized. There is also
a good deal of plain pottery, ornamented neither by painting
or corrugating, red to brown in color, often with bowl interiors
smudged and polished to a glossy black," pp. 11-12. A
sketch map of southwestern New Mexico shows locations of
some of the Mimbres sites.

703. Reed, Erik K. 1944 "Pottery Types of Manuelito District."
American Antiquity, Vol. 10, No. 2, pp. 161-172.
    Study of surface sherd collections from Manuelito Wash south
of Highway 66 between Gallup, New Mexico, and Lupton, Arizona. Photos of sherds.

704. Reed, Erik K. 1944a "Archaeological Work in Mancos Canyon,
Colorado." American Antiquity, Vol. 10, No. 1, pp. 48-58.
    Brief report of salvage archaeology in lower Mancos Canyon
in 1942. More complete report in Reed, 1958.

705. Reed, Erik K. 1944b "The Place of Citadel Polychrome in
San Juan Orange Ware." Southwestern Lore, Vol. 9, No. 4,
pp. 5-7.
    Description of Citadel Polychrome, San Juan Orange Ware,
pp. 5-7.

706. Reed, Erik K. 1944c "Late Red Ware Intrusives in the Mesa
Verde Focus." Southwestern Lore, Vol. 9, No. 4, pp. 7-9.
    Discussion of red trade wares in various sites in the South-
west.

707. Reed, Erik K. 1947 "Review of Archaeological Survey Potsherd Collections, Petrified Forest National Monument, Arizona." Special Report of the Regional Archaeologist, U.S.
National Park Service, Region III, Santa Fe, New Mexico.
    A list of the types found in museum sherd collections. The
ceramic horizons of different sites in this area range from Adamana Brown to Homolovi Polychrome.

708. Reed, Erik K. 1954 "Test Excavations at San Marcos Pueblo."
El Palacio, Vol. 61, No. 10 October, pp. 323-343.
    Predominant painted pottery recovered from Building #38
was Glaze A Red, Glaze A Yellow, and Galisteo Black-on-white.
Also Abiquiu Black-on-gray and a small amount of Wiyo Black-
on-white. Pottery found at Building #37 was Glaze A Yellow,
Cieneguilla; Glaze b, Largo; Rough black utility; Glaze Polychrome; Glaze A Red; Galisteo Black-on-white; and Biscuit A.

709.   Reed, Erik K.   1955   "Painted Pottery in Zuni History."   South-
       west Journal of Anthropology, Vol. 11, No. 2, pp. 178-193.
          Very brief descriptions of Heshotauthla Glaze Polychrome,
       p. 184; Pinnawa Glaze-on-white, p. 186; Kwakina Glaze Poly-
       chrome, p. 186; Pinnawa Glaze Polychrome, p. 187; Matsaki
       Brown-on-buff, p. 186; Matsaki Polychrome, p. 186; and Con-
       cepcion Polychrome, p. 188.   Names here differ from similar
       types in Watson et al., 1966.

710.   Reed, Erik K.   1958   "Excavations in Mancos Canyon, Colo-
       rado."   University of Utah Anthropology Papers, No. 35, Salt
       Lake City, Utah.
          Pottery, pp. 69-136.   Good discussion of Mesa Verde White
       Ware.   Illustrations of La Plata Black-on-white, p. 76; Piedra
       Black-on-white, p. 76; Mancos Black-on-white, p. 82; McElmo
       Black-on-white, p. 105; Rosa Gray and Rosa Black-on-gray,
       p. 113; and Corrugated jars, p. 120.   Description of Piedra
       Black-on-white, pp. 78-81.   Identifying statements and refer-
       ences on Abajo Red-on-orange (Brew), pp. 127-128; La Plata
       Black-on-orange (Martin), p. 128; and La Plata Black-on-red,
       p. 129.

711.   Reher, Charles A. (Editor).   1977   Settlement and Subsistence
       Along the Lower Chaco River.   The CPG Survey, University
       of New Mexico Press, Albuquerque.
          (See Windes, 1977.)

712.   Reid, J. Jeffrey.   1984   "What is Black-on-white and Vague
       All Over?"   In Regional Analysis of Prehistoric Ceramic Varia-
       tion: Contemporary Studies of the Cibola Whitewares, Anthro-
       pological Research Papers No. 31, Arizona State University,
       Tempe, Arizona.
          Abstract: "Inadequacies in conventional approaches to
       Southwestern ceramic classification are presented as five prob-
       lem areas which warrant further attention.   Thoughts on ce-
       ramic variability, expressed within a linguistic model of ce-
       ramic information, point the direction to more informative analy-
       sis and nomenclature.   Examples and alternative approaches
       are presented.   Emphasis throughout the discussion is on re-
       thinking taxonomic procedures for achieving the full analytic
       potential of ceramic materials," p. 135.

713.   Reiley, Anita M.   1974   "Petrographic Studies of Mimbres
       Sherds."   Pottery Southwest, Vol. 1, No. 3, pp. 9-11.
          Mimbres sherds from LA 6083 were tempered with rhyolite
       tuff or glassy rhyolite tuff.   Rhyolite flakes and artifacts were
       found at the site but it is not known whether it is local or in-
       trusive.

714.   Reiter, Paul.   1938   "The Jemez Pueblo of Unshagi, New Mexico
       with Notes on the Earlier Excavations at Amoxiumqua and

Giusewa." Monographs of the School of American Research,
Nos. 5-6, Albuquerque, New Mexico.
    Illustrations of Jemez culinary vessels, Pls. 14, 15A;
Jemez culinary bowls, Pls. 15B, 16-19 (jars), 20; and Glaze
decorated bowls, Pl. 21.

715.   Reyman, Jonathan E. 1981 "An Unusual Basket-Handle Bowl
        from Central New Mexico." Pottery Southwest, Vol. 8, No. 1,
        January, pp. 1-6.
            It is concluded that bowls of this type incorporate the
        ideas and symbols of the Mexican Quetzalcoatl cult. There-
        fore, this is another example of contact between Mexico and
        the Southwest pueblos, probably during the Pueblo IV period.

716.   Rice, Glen; Wilcox, David; Rafferty, Kevin; and Schoenwetter,
        James. 1979 "An Archaeological Test of Sites in the Gila
        Butte-Santan Region, South Central Arizona." Anthropological
        Research Papers, No. 18, Arizona State Museum, Tucson, Ari-
        zona.
            A study of style and function in the Hohokam ceramics
        found in tests of sites in south-central Arizona by Glen Rice
        and Kevin Refferty.

717.   Rice, Prudence M. 1976 "Rethinking the Ware Concept."
        American Antiquity, Vol. 41, No. 4, pp. 538-543.
            Abstract: "The type-variety system of ceramic taxonomy
        is widely accepted, but some difficulties exist in the identifi-
        cation and interpretation of wares in the study of Mayan pot-
        tery. Although ware concept was formulated to incorporate
        technological data, such as paste composition, into the classifi-
        catory scheme, in practice ware definitions are frequently
        limited to variables of surface treatment. A redefinition of the
        ware concept and the creation of a new unit of paste composi-
        tion analysis which crosscuts types is suggested. This will
        realign theory closer to what is current practice and will en-
        hance the potential and actual contributions of the type-
        varieties system to the anthropological study of pottery,"
        p. 538.

718.   Richert, Roland. 1962 "Excavation of a Portion of the East
        Ruin, Aztec National Monument, New Mexico." Southwest
        Monument Association, Technical Series, Vol. 4, Globe Arizona.
            Most pottery found was Mesa Verde or McElmo Black-on-
        white. Illustrations of sherds of Mesa Verde Black-on-white,
        pp. 27-28.

719.   Riley, Carroll. 1952 "San Juan Anasazi and the Galisteo
        Basin." El Palacio, Vol. 59, No. 3, pp. 77-82, Santa Fe, New
        Mexico.
            The author suggests a relationship between Mesa Verde and
        the Galisteo Basin based on apparent spread of Mesa Verde

pottery to Galisteo. Also similarities between kiva characteristics from these two areas are discussed.

720. Rinaldo, John B. 1959 "Foote Canyon Pueblo, Eastern Arizona." Chicago Natural History Museum, Fieldiana: Anthropology, Vol. 49, No. 2, pp. 149-187, Chicago, Illinois.
Description of St. Johns Polychrome. Illustrations of Reserve Indented Corrugated, p. 188; Tularosa Black-on-white, p. 189; Tularosa Fillet Rim, p. 190; Tularosa White-on-red, pp. 192-193; Pinedale Polychrome, pp. 193, 202-203; Querino Polychrome and St. Johns Polychrome, p. 195; Querino Polychrome, p. 205; Kwakina Polychrome, p. 206; and Pinnawa Polychrome, p. 207. Tabulation of tree ring dates for St. Johns Polychrome, Pinedale Polychrome, Pinnawa Polychrome, Heshotauthla Polychrome, Kwakina Polychrome, and Fourmile Polychrome.

721. Rinaldo, John B. 1964 "Notes on the Origin of Historic Zuni Culture." Kiva, Vol. 29, No. 4, pp. 86-98, Tucson, Arizona.
"Surveys and excavations in the Zuni area have indicated that the culture of the early periods of this district was broadly Puerco-Chaco in character and was strongly influenced in late periods by the Mogollon pueblos of the northern branches. Evidence for this relationship is noted in the continuum between these areas. Not only in styles of ceramic design and complexes of pottery types but also architectural traits such as types of masonry construction, settlement patterns, and types of stone artifacts of the San Juan region. The relationship is outlined as having developed in three stages beginning with trade in pottery and axes of Puerco-Chacoan character to the Mogollon village and culminating in a period when the Zuni were making Black-on-white and Black-on-red polychrome pottery in the Tularosa style and building a characteristic type of rectangular kiva," p. 86. A good discussion of the relationship of early Zuni and surrounding types of pottery with the later types. A bibliography on this subject.

722. Rinaldo, John B. and Bluhm, Elaine A. 1956 "Late Mogollon Pottery Types of the Reserve Area." Chicago Natural History Museum, Fieldiana: Anthropology, Vol. 36, No. 7, pp. 149-187, Chicago, Illinois.
Descriptions and illustrations of Reserve Plain Corrugated, p. 155; Reserve Indented Corrugated, p. 159; Reserve Punched Corrugated, p. 162; Reserve Incised Corrugated, p. 164; Tularosa Patterned Corrugated, p. 196; Starkweather Smudged Decorated, p. 171; Tularosa White-on-red, p. 173; and Tularosa Black-on-white, p. 177.

723. Ripley, Don. 1967 The ABC's of Pueblo Designs. Beaber Printing Co., Cortez, Colorado.
Drawings of typical designs on Mesa Verde pottery.

724. Rixey, Ray and Voll, C. B. 1962 "Archaeological Materials from Walnut Canyon Cliff Dwellings." Plateau, Vol. 34, No. 3, pp. 85-96.
     Types found in this site were primarily Flagstaff Black-on-white, 17%; Wupatki Black-on-white, 10%; Tusayan Black-on-red, 3%; and Showlow Black-on-red, 2%. The vast bulk of the sherd material consisted of culinary wares which were nearly all Winona Brown or Sunset Red. Nine complete or restorable vessels were found. These vessels were of Sunset Red, Elden Corrugated, and Walnut Black-on-white.

725. Roberts, Frank H. H. 1925 "Report on Archaeological Reconnaissance in Southwestern Colorado in the Summer of 1920." Colorado Magazine, Vol. 2, No. 1, April.
     Description of a survey in the areas of Arboles, Piedra River, Allison, and Tiffany, Pine River Valley, Animas Valley, Johnson Canyon Region, Mancos Canyon, Mesa Verde, and Montezuma Valley. Some descriptions and photos of pottery vessels found and a sketch map of sites.

726. Roberts, Frank H. H. 1929 "Shabik'eschee Village: A Late Basketmaker Site in Chaco Canyon, New Mexico." Bureau of American Ethnology, Bulletin 92, Washington, D.C.
     Illustrations and description of Basketmaker III pottery, pp. 107-124. Vessels are gray, white, or orange-red in color. Temper protrudes causing slightly pebbled surface. Decorated vessels have a thin wash, marked use of dots, tipped, stepped lines and solid triangular figures in the designs together with an "O" in the bottom of the bowl. Illustrations of types later named are Lino Gray, Pls. IIa and b, 17a; Lino Fugitive Red, p. 176; and Lino Black-on-gray, p. 175. Description of La Plata Black-on-white, pp. 119-124.

727. Roberts, Frank H. H. 1930 "Early Pueblo Ruins in the Piedra District Southwest Colorado." Bureau of American Ethnology, Bulletin 96, Smithsonian Institute, Washington, D.C.
     Pottery on pages 74-140. Illustrations of neckbanded vessels, Pls. 13-14; plain vessels, Pls. 15-16; seed jars, Pl. 20; pitchers, Pls. 22-23; Black-on-white Basketmaker bowls, Pls. 25-31; cylindrical and eccentric forms, Pl. 33; miniature vessels, Pls. 34-35; designs on black-on-white bowls, pp. 113-136; and clay pipes, stoppers and pot lids, Pls. 37-38.

728. Roberts, Frank H. H. 1931 "The Ruins at Kiatuthlanna." Bureau of American Ethnology, Bulletin 100, Washington, D.C.
     Pottery, pp. 114-149. Illustrations and description of Kiatuthlanna Black-on-white, p. 114, Pls. 13, 15, 17-22. Illustrations of Basketmaker pottery from pithouses and some from Pueblo Neckbanded culinary, p. 121.

729. Roberts, Frank H. H. 1941 "Archaeological Remains in the

Whitewater District Eastern Arizona." Bureau of American
Ethnology, Bulletin 126, Part II, Artifacts and Burials, Washington, D.C.
    Pottery discussed, pp. 3-109.   "The collection from the
Whitewater sites contains a few examples of the Modified Basketmaker wares, a large number of Developmental Pueblo pieces,
and some from the Great Pueblo horizon," p. 9.   Percentages
for different wares show gray or utility group, 64.1%; black-
on-white, 32.7%; black interior with dull and burnished forms
combined, 2.5%; black-on-red, 2%; and fugitive red treatment,
5%.   Illustrations of vessels: Basketmaker and Developmental
Pueblo plain wares, Pl. 2; neckbanded pitchers, Pls. 3-5;
corrugated vessels, Pls. 6-8; plain miniature vessels, Pl. 9;
black-on-white pitchers and canteen, Pls. 10-13, 15-16; bird
shaped and ring-bottomed pitchers, Pl. 14; black-on-white
canteens, Pl. 17; ladles and scoops, Pls. 18-19; Modified
Basketmaker and Great Pueblo black-on-white bowls, Pl. 29;
worked potsherds, Pls. 30-31; and clay pipes, Pl. 32.
    "The significant feature about the pottery evidence is that
it demonstrates an early Southwest extension of influence from
the Chaco Canyon area with a subsequent spread toward the
Northwest from Little Colorado centers and toward the Southwest from the Kayenta or Tusayan region.   The movement was
contrary to that postulated by many southwestern workers
and tends to show that the traits appearing in the Chaco that
have been attributed to influence penetrating from the Little
Colorado Region actually belong in the Chaco and diffused from
there toward the Little Colorado," p. 138.

730. Roberts, Marcia. 1977 "Mimbres Pottery." All Points Bulletin,
      Vol. 14, No. 6, June, Denver Chapter, Colorado Archaeologi-
      cal Society.
          Brief introduction to Mimbres pottery with drawings of three
      Classic Mimbres Black-on-white and one Mimbres Boldface bowl.

731. Robinson, William J. 1958 "A New Type of Pottery Killing at
      Point of Pines." Kiva, Vol. 23, No. 3, pp. 12-14.
          Bowls and jars used to hold cremations were commonly
      notched in four places at the rims.   The notches were aligned
      with the cardinal points of the compass.   This is known only
      in the Showlow area.

732. Rodeck, Hugo G. 1976 "Mimbres Painted Pottery." American
      Indian Art Magazine, Vol. 1, No. 4, August, pp. 44-53.
          A popular article with several generalizations.   Black and
      white photos of 12 Mimbres bowls and color plates of seven
      bowls including three polychrome vessels.

733. Rogers, Malcolm J. 1936 "Yuman Pottery Making." San Diego
      Museum Papers, No. 2, San Diego, California (reprint by Bal-
      lena Press, 1973).

Description of pottery making among the Yuman tribes of
Southern California and Western Arizona. Comparisons of pottery made by the following tribes: Seri, Kiliwa, Southern Digueno, Northern Digueno, Luiseno and Cupeno, Kamia, Yuma,
Maricopa, Cocopa, Mohave, Havasupai, Walapai, Yavapai, also
some Shoshonean tribes of this region. Illustrations of Kamia
seed jar, Pl. I; Southern Digueno pottery making, Pls. II,
III, IV; pottery making tools, Pl. V; Southern Digueno pottery vessels, Pl. VI; tobacco pipes, Pl. VII; Kamia pottery,
Pl. VIII; tribal distributions Ca. 1800 map I; and Yuman Shoshonean pottery shapes, Pl. IX.

734. Rogers, Malcolm J. 1945 Final Yuman Pottery Types Nomen-
clature with Synonyms. Manuscript on file, San Diego Museum
of Man, San Diego, California.
First descriptions of 15 Patayan pottery types including:
Black Mesa Buff, Black Mesa Red-on-buff, Colorado Beige,
Colorado Red-on-beige, Colorado Red, Tumco Buff, Tumco
Red-on-buff, Salton Buff, Salton Red-on-buff, Topoc Buff,
Topoc Red-on-buff, Parker Buff, Parker Red-on-buff, and
Palomas Buff. Rogers did not publish these type descriptions.
They were eventually published by Michael Waters in 1982.

735. Rogers, Rose Mary. 1972 "Ceramics, Pecos River Drainage,
Pecos and Crockett Counties, Texas." Transactions of the 7th
Regional Archaeological Symposium on Southwestern New Mexico
and Western Texas, pp. 47-70.
Report of sherds found in two western Texas counties.
"Sherds described in this report reflect evidence of inter-
cultural contacts between groups in northeast trans-Pecos and
peoples to the east, southeast, plains and south into Chihuahua, Mexico," p. 55. Types found included Jornada Brownware, local brownware, Caddoan types, and one sherd of Chupadero Black-on-white.

736. Rogers, R. N. 1980 "The Chemistry of Pottery Smudging."
Pottery Southwest, Vol. 7, No. 2, April, pp. 2-4.
Abstract: "The processes involved in the smudging of pottery are somewhat more complex than originally assumed. An
understanding of the chemistry involved may make it possible
to draw some inferences concerning the function of smudging,"
p. 2.

737. Rohn, Arthur H. 1970 "Mug House, Mesa Verde National
Park (Wetherill Mesa Excavations)." National Park Service
Archaeological Research Series, 7-D, Washington, D.C.
Chapter on pottery, pp. 131-200. The total number of re-
storable vessels from 1960-1961 excavations was 439. Major
types were Mesa Verde Corrugated jars and McElmo-Mesa Verde
Black-on-white. Illustrations of Mesa Verde Corrugated, pp.
131-132, 134-143; McElmo-Mesa Verde Black-on-white, pp. 148,

150-184; Mancos Black-on-white, p. 187; Chapin Gray, p. 188;
and vessel repairs, pp. 188-189. Good discussion of San Juan
White Ware types.

738. Rohn, Arthur H. 1977 <u>Cultural Change and Continuity on
      Chapin Mesa</u>. Regents Press, Lawrence, Kansas.
          "A comprehensive archaeological survey of Chapin Mesa,
      Mesa Verde National Park, Colorado. During the past two
      decades field work in the 10 square miles comprising Chapin
      Mesa has revealed approximately 950 separate sites, or loca-
      tions of unquestioned human activity including habitations,
      field houses, shrines, petrographs, terraces, reservoirs, and
      ditches covering the time span from 600 to 1300 AD. Rohn
      presents a synthesis of previous archaeological research--most
      of it never published--and presents the substantial findings of
      his own excavations in the area from 1958 to the present,"
      dust jacket.
          Chapter IV, "Ceramics," pp. 192-215. Types and wares
      described and illustrated are Mesa Verde White Ware, pp. 136-
      137; Chapin Black-on-white, pp. 139-142; Piedra Black-on-
      white, pp. 145-147; Cortez Black-on-white, pp. 149-151; Man-
      cos Black-on-white, pp. 153-157; Mesa Verde Black-on-white,
      pp. 159-161; Mesa Verde Black-on-white: Mesa Verde Variety,
      pp. 163-165; Mesa Verde Black-on-white: McElmo Variety, pp.
      167-168; Mesa Verde Gray Ware, pp. 169-170; Chapin Gray,
      pp. 171-172; Chapin Gray: Chapin Variety, pp. 175-176;
      Chapin Gray: Moccasin Variety, pp. 179-180; Chapin Gray:
      Mummy Lake Variety, pp. 183-185; Mancos Gray, pp. 187-188;
      Mesa Verde Corrugated Ware, pp. 189-190; Mesa Verde Cor-
      rugated: Mesa Verde Variety, pp. 193-194; and Mesa Verde
      Corrugated: Mancos Variety, pp. 197-199.
          Discussion of all pottery recovered, pp. 201-215.

739. Rohn, Arthur H. and Swannack, J. D. 1965 "Mummy Lake
      Gray: A New Pottery Type." In Memoirs of the Society for
      American Archaeology, No. 19, <u>American Antiquity</u>, Vol. 31,
      Part 2, pp. 14-18.
          Description of Mummy Lake Gray, pp. 14-18. "A formal
      description is presented for a new type of plain gray pottery
      made during the late Pueblo II and early Pueblo III at Mesa
      Verde and its surrounding territory. Significant characteris-
      tics include jar and pitcher shapes, small size, and the pres-
      ence of a single unobliterated fillet around the rim. This type
      is seen as a continuation of the plain gray pottery tradition in
      the Northern San Juan region," p. 14. Illustrations of ves-
      sels of Mummy Lake Gray, Figs. 1-2.

740. Rosenthal, E. Jane; Brown, Douglas R.; Severson, Marc; and
      Clonts, John B. 1978 <u>The Quijotoa Valley Project</u>. Cultural
      Resources Management Division, Western Archaeological Center,
      National Park Service, Tucson, Arizona.

"Ceramics" by Marc Severson, pp. 84-134. "The pottery recovered along PIR 1 and PIR 34 during the Quijotoa Valley Project represents an indigenous tradition of vessel manufacture from local ingenous clays. Over 30,000 potsherds from 42 sites were analyzed in the laboratory; less than 2% of these were decorated or slipped wares. Several partially restorable vessels were also found. The evidence supports Ezell's hypothesis that most Papaguerian ceramic sites have pottery belonging to the 'Sonoran Brownware Tradition.' Our sample did not contain a high percentage of intrusive types.... In this manuscript the pottery types, their attributes, uses and cultural affiliation are discussed," p. 84.

741. Ruby, Jay W. 1966 "Southwest Pottery in Los Angeles County, California: A Correction." American Antiquity, Vol. 31, p. 440.
   Reports a minor error in an article by Ruby and Blackburn, 1964. On page 209, column 1, line 9. Reads ... "Cibola Black-on-white of the White Mountain Series from Eastern Arizona." It should read: ... "black-on-white too small to type; probably falls within the range of Cibola White Ware as presently described (White Mountain Series?)," p. 440.

742. Ruby, Jay W. and Blackburn, Thomas. 1964 "Occurrence of Southwestern Pottery in Los Angeles County, California." American Antiquity, Vol. 30, pp. 209-210.
   Brief report that small numbers of sherds of Cibola White Ware, Sacaton Red-on-buff, and Jeddito Ware were recovered from several sites in Los Angeles County, California. Probable trade routes from the Southwest to southern California are discussed. (See Ruby, 1966.)

743. Rudy, Jack R. 1953 "Archaeological Survey of Western Utah." University of Utah Anthropology Papers, No. 12, Salt Lake City, Utah.
   Descriptions of the following wares and types: Utah Desert Gray Ware, p. 79; Great Salt Lake Gray, p. 85; Snake Valley Black-on-gray (synonym Sevier Black-on-gray), p. 91; Snake Valley Corrugated (Sevier Corrugated), p. 88; Knolls Gray, p. 92; Deep Creek Buff, p. 98; Promontory Ware, p. 93; and Shoshoni Ware, p. 94.

744. Rugge, Dale and Doyel, David E. 1980 "Petrographic Analysis of Ceramics from Dead Valley." In David E. Doyel and Sharon S. Debowski (Eds.), Prehistory in Dead Valley, East-Central Arizona: The T G & E Springerville Project, Archaeological Series #144, pp. 189-203, Arizona State Museum, University of Arizona, Tucson, Arizona.
   The pilot study on ceramic technology of the material recovered in this study consisted of petrographic analysis of all major ceramic classes at A2Q:12:16. A total sample of 55 thin

sections of sherds representing all major ceramic classes and
styles were examined. The tempering materials are reported
for painted and plainware types. This analysis did not provide
definite information on locally and nonlocally produced types
at this site.

745. Runyan, John W. n.d. Pottery Analysis for the Texas Archaeological Society. Manuscript on file at Texas A & M Anthropological Laboratory, College Station, Texas.
Description of El Paso Brown and other types.

746. Runyan, John W. and Hedrick, John A. 1973 "Pottery Types
of the SWFAS Area." Transactions of the Eighth Regional
Archaeological Symposium for Southeastern New Mexico and
Western Texas, pp. 19-45, Lea County Archaeological Society,
Hobbs, New Mexico.
"The purpose of this paper, with pottery identification
sheets, is to aid and better aquaint [sic] members (and others)
with most of the pottery types found in their areas, and to
correct parts of early Jornada pottery descriptions, basically
temper, and includes some other pertinant [sic] data found in
the course of our sherd studies. Areas of distrubution [sic]
of Jornada potterys [sic] based on temper content is not included; this will be the subject of another report in the future by Hedrick and myself," p. 19.
Types described are El Paso Brown, Jornada Brown, El
Paso Red-on-brown, El Paso Polychrome, Three Rivers Red-
on-terra cotta, Lincoln Black-on-red, Ochoa Indented Brown
Ware, Mimbres Boldface Black-on-white, Mimbres Classic Black-
on-white, Chupadero Black-on-white, Gila Polychrome, St.
Johns Polychrome, Ramos Polychrome, Playas Red Incised, and
Rio Grande Glaze A Red. (This report has many obvious
typographical errors and should be used with caution.)

747. Ruppe, Reynold J. and Dittert, A. E., Jr. 1953 "Acoma Archaeology: A Preliminary Report of the First Season in the
Cebolleta Mesa Region, New Mexico." El Palacio, Vol. 60, No.
7, pp. 259-273, Santa Fe, New Mexico.
"Acoma ceramics have not yet been studied in detail. Until
the present investigation little was known of early Acoma pottery so the analysis of the material has been of a pioneering
nature. From superficial study it is clear that the earliest
Acoma polychromes are a direct outgrowth of the late Pueblo
III periods. Ceramics in the Pueblo III period in the Cebolleta
Mesa region show resemblances to the Zuni ceramics. Some
are decorated with glazed paint, the origin of which is not yet
known. Glaze paint may have started in the Cebolleta region
as Socorro Black-on-white of the early Pueblo III period often
possessed this glazed paint decoration," p. 264. Site 24D:
"The ceramics are uniform throughout the site except for the
lowest level of trench B which contained a late Pueblo III

assemblage. There were none of the early Pueblo IV types
such as the Zuni glazes in this level. However late determinants like the carbon paint ware known as Galisteo Black-on-
white with Mesa Verde influence are present and the practice
of smearing the corrugations of Northern gray corrugated vessels had started. The ceramic situation in the lowest levels
of the Acoma trenches is very similar to that of Site 24 D
aside from the fact that both sites have identical types. The
materials from both places suggest a certain amount of freedom with ceramic techniques. It is possible that the area of
glaze paint received impetus from the Zuni area along with the
idea of freedom of decorative styles," p. 269.

748. Russel, Frank. 1908 "The Pima Indians." Annual Report of
the Bureau of American Ethnology, No. 26, Washington, D.C.
      Description and illustrations of Pima pottery, pp. 124-131.

749. Sapir, Edward and Sandoval, A. G. 1930 "A Note on Navajo
Pottery." American Anthropologist, Vol. 32, pp. 575-576.
      Description of Navajo ware, pp. 575-576.

750. Sauer, Carl and Brand, D. 1930 "Pueblo Sites in Southeastern
Arizona." University of California Publications in Geography,
Vol. 3, No. 7, Berkeley, California.
      Descriptions of Santa Cruz Polychrome, p. 445, and Arma-
dilla Ware.

751. Sauer, Carl and Brand, D. 1931 "Prehistoric Settlements in
Sonora with Special References to Cerros de Trincheras."
University of California Publications in Geography, Vol. 5,
No. 3, Berkeley, California.
      Descriptions and illustrations of Trincheras Polychrome, p.
18; Trincheras Purple-on-red, p. 18; and Cloverdale (gouged
red).

752. Sauer, Carl and Brand, D. 1953 "Excavations at Cave Creek
and in the San Simon Valley, I Material Culture." Medallion
Papers, No. 34, Gila Pueblo, Globe, Arizona.
      Descriptions and illustrations of the following types: San
Francisco Red, p. 39; Dos Cabezas Red-on-brown, p. 42, Pl.
20; Pinaleno Red-on-brown, p. 42, Pls. 21, 26-27; Galiuro
Red-on-brown, p. 42, Pls. 22, 27-28; Cerros Red-on-white,
p. 43; and Encinas Red-on-brown, p. 43.

753. Sayles, Edward B. 1936 "Some Southwestern Pottery Types,
Series V." Medallion Papers, No. 21, Gila Pueblo, Globe, Arizona.
      The following types of Chihuhua Red Ware are described and
illustrated: Dublan Polychrome, pp. 7-12; Medanos Red-on-
brown, pp. 1-6; Villa Ahumada Polychrome, pp. 13-18; Babicora Polychrome, pp. 19-22; Madera Black-on-red, pp. 23-26;

Carretas Polychrome, pp. 27-30; Playas Red, pp. 31-34; Playas Red Incised, pp. 35-38; Corralitos Polychrome Incised, pp. 39-42; Ramos Black, pp. 43-44; Ramos Polychrome, pp. 45-49; and Conchos Red-on-brown, p. 55. Illustration of Mimbres Corrugated, Pl. 8.

754.   Sayles, Gladys and Sayles, Ted. 1948 "The Pottery of Ida Redbird." Arizona Highways, Vol. 24, No. 1, pp. 28-31, Phoenix, Arizona.
       Photographs of Ida Redbird making Maricopa pottery with illustrations of vessels.

755.   Scantling, Frederick H. 1940 "Excavations at the Jackrabbit Ruin, Papago Indian Reservation, Arizona." Masters thesis, University of Arizona, Tucson, Arizona.
       Descriptions of the following types: Tanque Verde Red-on-brown, pp. 27-30; Sells Plain, pp. 33-35; and Sells Red, pp. 30-33.

756.   Schaefer, P. D. 1969 "Prehistoric Trade in the Southwest and Distribution of Pueblo IV Hopi Jeddito Black-on-yellow." Kroeber Anthropological Papers, No. 41, pp. 54-77.
       A study of the distribution of Jeddito Black-on-yellow throughout the Southwest. "Thus, intrusive pottery by no means is a necessary indication of trade. It is quite conceivable that one sherd could be evidence of any number of forms of contact between two peoples or it may represent no connection whatsoever, or an indirect one at best.
       "Actually, however, the answer to Jeddito's distribution is probably a composite of the above. No doubt the Hopi were traders who also sought ties with other tribes and accorded prestige to those who maintained and broadened such ties. No doubt also that there were at least scattered instances of Hopi migration through Pueblo IV times. No one explanation will, or should be, allowed to suffice, at least not until a far more extensive analysis of interculture contacts in the prehistoric Southwest has been accomplished," p. 65.

757.   Scheans, Daniel J. 1957 "An Addition to the Anasazi Ceremonial Bifurcate Basket Complex," Kiva, Vol. 22, No. 4, June, pp. 10-12.
       Description of a Wingate Black-on-red pitcher with an unusual handle which resembles a bifurcate basket. It is part of the S. F. Trew Collection of Southwestern pottery, Museum of Natural History, University of Oregon. This pitcher is compared to pitchers illustrated in Martin and Willis, 1940. The pitcher is shown in Fig. 5.

758.   Scheick, Cherie (compiler). 1983 "The Gamerco Project: Flexibility as an Adaptive Response." Report No. 071 of the Archaeology Division of the School of American Research, Santa Fe, New Mexico.

Study by Richard Lang of the ceramics from the Pueblo III sites in the Gamerco area of the Rio Puerco of the West. Includes methods of analysis and ceramic types, site discussions and conclusions. Illustrates use of Lang's typology.

759. Schmidt, E. F. 1928 "Time-relation of Prehistoric Pottery Types in Southern Arizona." Anthropology Papers of the American Museum of Natural History, Vol. 30, Part 5, pp. 247-302, New York, New York.
Description of Gila Red, p. 298. Illustrations of Hohokam Red-on-buff Ware, Figs. 20-22; Gila and Tonto Polychrome, Fig. 25; Little Colorado Black-on-white, Fig. 26; San Carlos Red-on-buff, Fig. 31; and "Onion ware" urn, Fig. 36.

760. Schroeder, Albert H. 1940 "A Stratigraphic Survey of Pre-Spanish Mounds of the Salt River Valley." Masters thesis, University of Arizona, Tucson, Arizona.
Descriptions of Salt Red, pp. 183-186, and Gila Smudged, pp. 184-185.

761. Schroeder, Albert H. 1952a "The Bearing of Ceramics on Developments in the Hohokam Classic Period." Southwest Journal of Anthropology, Vol. 8, No. 3, pp. 320-335, Albuquerque, New Mexico.
"Several new traits appear in the Gila basin at the beginning of the Classic Period, around 1150 AD, all of which appear to be similar to the pattern of the Sinaqua of 1125 AD in the Verde Valley. The ceramic evidence of that time of the introduction of these traits points to a very close relationship with Sinaqua pottery and cannot be related to the Salado ceramic pattern.... The ceramic evidence, in fact, tends to suggest that Sinaqua elements were more important than Salado influence even in the Tonto basin," p. 334.

762. Schroeder, Albert H. 1952b A Brief Survey of the Lower Colorado River from Davis Dam to the International Border. Bureau of Reclamation, Region III, Boulder City, Navada.
Descriptions of the following types: Gila Bend Plain, pp. 24-25; Topoc Buff, pp. 29-30; Topoc Fugitive Red, p. 30; Topoc Stucco, p. 30; Palomas Buff, p. 31; Tumco Buff, pp. 26-27; Needles Buff, p. 32; Needles Buff-on-red, Fig. 5; Parker Buff, pp. 19-20; illustrations Fig. 1, Parker Black-on-red, p. 21; illustration Fig. 5, Parker Stucco, pp. 20-21; Colorado Beige, p. 22; Colorado Red-on-beige, p. 22; Colorado Red, pp. 23-24; illustration Fig. 5, Gila Bend Stucco, p. 25; Gila Bend Beige, p. 25; Tumco Red-on-buff, pp. 27-28; illustrations Figs. 1, 4; Black Mesa Red, p. 29; and Needles Red-on-buff, Fig. 3.

763. Schroeder, Albert H. 1955 "The Archaeology of Zion Park." University of Utah Anthropological Papers, No. 22, Salt Lake City, Utah.

Map of sites in Zion Park on p. 2. Ceramic materials, pp.
103-130. Illustrations and brief descriptions of the following
types: North Creek Corrugated, illus., p. 102; North Creek
Tooled, illus., p. 102; North Creek Gray, illus., p. 102;
North Creek Tooled, illus., p. 102; and St. George Black-on-
gray. Brief descriptions of Middleton Polychrome, Washington
Black-on-gray, and Snake Valley Gray. Types found in addition to the above were Hurricane Black-on-gray, Middleton
Black-on-gray, Toroweap Black-on-gray, Trumbull Black-on-
gray, Virgin Black-on-gray, Toquerville Black-on-gray, Washington Corrugated, Moapa Gray, Moapa Corrugated, and Moapa
Tooled.

764.   Schroeder, Albert H. 1958 "Lower Colorado Buff Ware." In
        Pottery Types of the Southwest, Museum of Northern Arizona,
        Ceramic Series 3D, Ware 16 (Colton, ed.), Flagstaff, Arizona.
        Good descriptions and illustrations of the following types
        of Lower Colorado Buff Ware: Parker Buff, D16-1; Parker Red-
        on-buff, D16-2; Parker Red-on-buff: Fort Mohave Variant,
        D16-2a; Parker Black-on-red, D16-3; Parker Stucco, D16-4;
        Colorado Beige, D16-5; Colorado Red-on-beige, D16-6; Colo-
        rado Red, D16-7; Gila Bend Plain, D16-8; Gila Bend Stucco,
        D16-9; Gila Bend Beige, D16-10; Gila Bend Red, D16-11; Tumco
        Buff, D16-12; Tumco Red-on-buff, D16-13; Tumco Stucco,
        D16-14; Black Mesa Beige, D16-15; Black Mesa Red, D16-16;
        Black Mesa Polychrome, D16-17; Topoc Buff, D16-18; Topoc
        Red-on-buff, D16-19; Topoc Fugitive Red, D16-20; Topoc
        Stucco, D16-21; Palomas Buff, D16-22; Palomas Stucco, D16-
        23; Needles Buff, D16-24; Needles Stucco, D16-25; Needles
        Red-on-buff, D16-26; Needles Beige, D16-27; Needles Red-
        on-beige, D16-28; Needles Red, D16-29; and Needles Black-on-
        red, D16-30; and Pyramid Gray, D16-31.

765.   Schroeder, Albert H. 1960 "The Hohokam, Sinagua, and the
        Hakataya." Society for American Archaeology Archives in
        Archaeology, No. 5, Society for American Archaeology, Madison,
        Wisconsin. (Reprint 1975, Imperial Valley College Museum So-
        ciety, El Centro, California.)
        Descriptions of Hohokam Plain Ware, Beaver Creek Series:
        Verde Brown and Verde Red; Alameda Brown Ware, Verde
        Series: Tuzigoot Plain and Tuzigoot Red; Rio de Flag Series:
        Beaver Creek Red (variety of Sunset Red); and Apache Plain
        Ware, Verde Series: Rimrock Plain.

766.   Schroeder, Albert H. 1961 "An Archaeological Survey of the
        Painted Rocks Reservoir, Western Arizona." Kiva, Vol. 27,
        No. 1, pp. 1-28, Tucson, Arizona.
        Descriptions of the following types: Palomas Red, Palomas
        Beige, and Palomas Red-on-buff.

767.   Schroeder, Albert H. 1966 "Pattern Diffusion from Mexico

into the Southwest after AD 600." American Antiquity, Vol.
31, No. 5, pp. 683-704.

"The introduction of the colonial period culture of the Hohokam of southern Arizona derived from northern Mexico, and
its diffusion in one form or another is traced north and east
through Arizona. On the basis of change in settlement patterns, architectural structures, and other material traits, a
tentative reconstruction of sociological, ceremonial and other
intangible aspects of the early cultural developments in southern
Arizona is attempted," p. 683.

768. Schroeder, Albert H. 1968 "Collected Papers in Honor of
Lyndon Lane Hargrave." Papers of the Archaeological Society
of New Mexico, No. 1, Museum of New Mexico, Santa Fe, New
Mexico.
Chapter by Herbert Dick on six historic pottery types from
Spanish-type sites, pp. 77-94. Describes and illustrates the
following types: Casitas Red-on-brown, pp. 80-81, Fig. 23a-
c; Powhoge Polychrome, pp. 81-82, Fig. 26, 28; Kapo Black,
pp. 82-83, Fig. 27e-g; El Rito Micaceous Slipped, pp. 83-84;
Fig. 27a-b; Carnue Plain, pp. 84-85, Fig. 28a-j, 29a-b; and
Petaca Micaceous, pp. 85-86, Fig. 29c-d.

769. Schroeder, Albert H. 1967-8 "An Archaeological Survey Ad-
jacent to Hovenweep National Monument." Southwestern Lore,
Vol. 33, Nos. 3-4, Boulder, Colorado.
A survey of this little studied area with a small map of
sites. Drawings of sherds of Mancos Black-on-white, McElmo
Black-on-white, and possible new types.

770. Schroeder, Albert H. 1982 "Historical Overview of Southwestern Ceramics." Arizona Archaeologist, No. 15, pp. 1-26,
Arizona Archaeological Society, Phoenix, Arizona.
An excellent, concise overview of the characteristics, horizons, and new traits of Southwestern ceramics from the 700s
to the historic period.
"It is obvious that various factors and/or events affected
Southwestern potters (as well as cultures), some more strongly
than others. The type diffusion in turn may well have depended
on the nature of contact and existing trade channels. The
introduction of various ceramic innovations on occasion was
accompanied by other material culture traits, raising the possibility that some of the ceramic changes might have been part
of a complex of related traits, but this is a subject beyond the
scope of this paper," p. 19.

771. Schroeder, Albert H. (Editor). 1982 "Southwestern Ceramics:
A Comparative Overview." A School of American Research Advanced Seminar, Arizona Archaeologist, No. 15, Arizona Archaeological Society, Phoenix, Arizona.
This volume contains 11 papers written for a School of

American Research Advanced Seminar held February 26 through
March 2, 1979. The objective of this seminar was to obtain
and sort as much ceramic data as possible in order to search
for Pan-Southwestern ceramic origins, directions of influence,
and changes. This was admirably accomplished making this
the best comparative overview of Southwestern ceramics available at this time.

Topics covered in the papers and their authors are his-
torical overview (Schroeder), advent of pottery in the South-
west (LeBlanc), ceramic patterns of the Hakataya (Euler),
Hohokam ceramic art (Masse), temporal change in Mogollon
ceramics (Le Blanc), Four Corners Anasazi ceramic tradition
(Breternitz), propositions concerning northern Anasazi ceramics
(Lucius), transformation in white pottery of the northern Rio
Grande glaze, matte paint, and plainware tradition (Snow),
Apache and Navajo ceramics (Brugge), and summary thoughts
(Schroeder). Each of these papers are cited and annotated
under the author's name in this bibliography.

772.   Schroeder, Gail. 1954 "San Juan Pottery: Methods and In-
       centives." El Palacio, Vol. 71, No. 1, pp. 45-51.
       A good discussion of the art of contemporary pottery mak-
       ing, its commercial incentives, and conditions at San Juan
       Pueblo.

773.   Schwartz, Douglas W.; Marshall, Michael P.; and Kepp, Janet.
       1979 "Archaeology of the Grand Canyon: The Bright Angel
       Site." School of American Research, Grand Canyon Archaeology
       Series, Vol. 1, Santa Fe, New Mexico.
       Description by M. Marshall of two new wares and three new
       types. Walhalla Gray Ware, pp. 97-98; Walhalla Corrugated,
       pp. 98-100; Walhalla Plain, pp. 100-101; Walhalla White Ware,
       pp. 101-104; and Walhalla Black-on-white, pp. 101-104. All
       of these are illustrated.

774.   Scott, Stuart D. 1960 "Pottery Figurines from Central Ari-
       zona." Kiva, Vol. 26, No. 2, December, pp. 11-26.
       An analysis of 400 ceramic figurines from the Prescott,
       Arizona, area. They were found in the Bradshaw Mountains
       by J. W. Simmons. These figurines are from Pueblo II or
       Pueblo III. The figures are primarily humans and animals,
       some of which are illustrated in Fig. 2-3.

775.   Seaberg, Stevens F. F. 1964 "Some Formal Relationships
       Among the Designs on Snowflake Black-on-white Pottery from
       the Carter Ranch Site." In "Chapters on Prehistory of Eastern
       Arizona, Chapter II," Paul S. Martin et al., Chicago Natural
       History Museum, Fieldiana: Anthropology, Vol. 55, pp. 235-
       241, Chicago, Illinois.
       Illustrations of Snowflake Black-on-white, Figs. 76-78 (lay-
       outs and motifs); drawings.

776. Second Southwestern Ceramic Conference. 1959 "Concordance
of Opinion Reached at the Second Southwestern Ceramic Conference, 1959." Museum of Northern Arizona, Flagstaff, Arizona, 16pp, Xerox.
"The main topics discussed were the White Mountain Red
Ware and Shiwanna Red Ware," p. 1. Agreements: "The
Maverick Mountain 'Series' should not be listed under White
Mountain Red ware; delete the term 'Maverick Mountain Series'
and types 3 through 6 ... and put Point of Pines Polychrome
into the White Mountain Series," p. 3.
Showlow Red. "It was decided to eliminate Showlow Red as
a named type as it is considered synonymous with Kinishba
Red. Haury stated that when black and white are added the
result is Fourmile Polychrome (as also Pinedale Polychrome).
Haury also mentioned that the type occurred with white decoration only and could be called Kinishba White-on-red although
the type has not been described," p. 4. Changes in description of Kinishba Red are stated. "The type with the longest
history (San Francisco Red) ... is modified through time but
remains essentially similar; later additions to the basic design
include smudging, painting, and slipping as well as changes
in vessel form," p. 5.
Puerco Black-on-red: descriptions appended by Vivian.
Wingate Black-on-red: changes in the description of this type.
Wingate Polychrome: Minor additions to the description. St.
Johns Polychrome: Minor additions to the description. Pinedale Black-on-red: changes in the type description. Showlow
Glaze-on-white: Brief description of this type.

777. Seventh Southwestern Ceramic Seminar. 1965 "Acoma-Zuni
Pottery Types." Museum of Northern Arizona, Flagstaff, Ari-
zona, 14pp., Xerox.
The following types were discussed. Zuni pottery types:
Heshotauthla Polychrome, Heshotauthla Black-on-red, favored
this name over Pinnawa Black-on-red which should be dropped.
Kwakina Polychrome, Pinnawa Glaze-on-white, Pinnawa Red-
on-white, Kechipawan Polychrome, "originally named Arauca
Polychrome (Colton & Hargrave, 1937), it was renamed Pinnawa
Polychrome (Reed, 1955) and has now been changed to Kechip-
awan by the Woodburys (1965) and accepted by Martin and
Rinaldo (1960)," p. 4. Matasaki Polychrome and Hawikuh Poly-
chrome were discussed. Acoma pottery types: Dittert and
Ruppe' presented temporary type designations for pottery
found at Acoma.

778. Shaafsma, Curt. 1968 "Funeral Bowls from a Spanish-contact
Compasanto." El Palacio, Vol. 75, No. 2, pp. 40-43.
Illustrations of Rio Grande Glaze C and D bowls, p. 43.

779. Shaeffer, James D. 1956 Kinishba: A Classic Site of the
Western Pueblos. Bureau of Indian Affairs, Chilocco Indian
School, Chilocco, Oklahoma.

Photographs of Kinishba Ruin and artifacts found at this
site. Photos of White Mountain Red Ware, Gila Polychrome,
and corrugated ware.

780. Sharrock, Floyd and Keane, E. G. 1962 "Carnegie Museum
      Collection from Southeastern Utah." University of Utah An-
      thropology Papers, No. 57, Glen Canyon Series, No. 16, Salt
      Lake City, Utah.
          Carnegie Museum expedition of 1945-47 to the part of South-
      eastern Utah lying between the San Juan and Colorado Rivers.
      Pottery, pp. 10-16. The pottery is overwhelmingly of the Mesa
      Verde Tradition. There are 1,387 Mesa Verde sherds (93.2%),
      99 Kayenta sherds (6.7%), and 2 Chaco sherds (.1%). Wares
      found include Tusayan Gray Ware, Tusayan White Ware, Tsegi
      Orange Ware, Mesa Verde White Ware, San Juan Red Ware,
      San Juan White Ware, and Cibola White Ware. Illustrations of
      Mesa Verde Black-on-white jar, Fig. 5; Mancos Corrugated
      Jar, McElmo Black-on-white jar, and Sosi Black-on-white jar
      fragment.

781. Sharrock, Floyd W.; Day, K. C.; and Dibble, D. S. 1961
      "1961 Excavations, Glen Canyon Area." University of Utah
      Anthropological Papers, No. 63, Glen Canyon Series, No. 18,
      University of Utah Press, Salt Lake City, Utah.
          Section on pottery, pp. 162-168. Pottery found at Ivy
      Shelter. Types found and illustrated in one figure, p. 168;
      Tusayan Black-on-red, McElmo Black-on-white, Mesa Verde
      Black-on-white, Tsegi Black-on-orange, and Moenkopi Corru-
      gated. "The Moqui Canyon ceramic inventory varied from past
      collections in that Mesa Verde affiliates predominate at most
      sites. Until now, Mesa Verde ceramic predominance from even
      a single site was quite rare (i.e., Lipe, 1960, p. 133). Mo-
      qui Canyon then can evidently be considered the boundary
      between Kayenta and Mesa Verde ceramic predominance," p.
      162.

782. Shepard, Anna O. 1964 "Temper Identification: Technologi-
      cal Sherd-splitting or an Unanswered Challenge." American
      Antiquity, Vol. 2, No. 4, pp. 518-520.
          "Two recent publications offer stimulating generalizations
      about pottery analysis (Weaver, 1963; Fontana et al., 1962).
      A broader view of contemporary potters' techniques shows that
      paste composition may or may not have cultural significance.
      Simple rules of analysis are misleading because of the com-
      plexity of pottery and the varied role it has played in cul-
      ture." p. 518.

783. Shepard, Anna O. 1965 "Ceramics for the Archaeologist.
      Carnegie Institute of Washington, Publication 609, Washington,
      D.C.
          A good study of the technical aspects of ceramics as they

pertain to the archaeologist's study of pottery. Explains the need for collaboration and understanding between the archaeologist and the ceramic technologist. Photographs of Mesa Verde Black-on-white, p. 296. Some of this volume may be too technical for the non-scientist, but there are many valuable broad concepts which are very useful to all persons with a deep interest in prehistoric pottery.

784. Shepard, Anna O. 1965 (See Matson, Frederick R., Ceramics and Man.)

785. Shiner, Joel L. 1961 "A Room in Gila Pueblo." Kiva, Vol. 27, No. 2, pp. 3-11.
Description of Tonto Ribbed.

786. Shutler, Dick, Jr. 1951 "Two Pueblo Ruins in the Verde Valley, Arizona." Plateau, Vol. 24, No. 1, pp. 1-9, Flagstaff, Arizona.
The first ruin excavated was Panarama Ruin, NA5111. Pottery found was predominantly Alameda Brown Ware (88%), Tusayan Gray Ware (6%), and Hohokam plain (5%). Tentatively AD 1125-1160. The second ruin excavated was the Kittridge Ruin, NA4490. Less Tusayan Gray Ware and more Hohokam plain ware than NA5111. Majority was Alameda Brown Ware (81%) and Hohokam Plain Ware (8%). This places the date of this ruin at AD 1210-1240.

787. Shutler, Dick, Jr. 1961 "The Pueblo Indian Occupation of the Southern Great Basin." Doctoral dissertation, University of Arizona, Tucson, Arizona.
Lost City pottery, pp. 186-238. No new types were recovered and the lack of data on the collections makes the contributions of ceramics very limited. Types found and illustrated are Washington Black-on-gray, St. George Black-on-gray, Moapa Black-on-gray, North Creek Black-on-gray, Boulder Black-on-gray, Lino Black-on-gray, Virgin Black-on-gray, Medicine Black-on-red, Citadel Polychrome, Washington Corrugated, Moapa Corrugated, North Creek Corrugated, Hurricane Black-on-gray, Tusayan Black-on-red, Pyramid Gray, Washington Gray, Boulder Gray, and North Creek Gray. Rim forms of 13 types are shown in Figs. 80-81; and 13 pottery handles are shown in Fig. 82.

788. Sikorski, Kathryn A. 1968 "Modern Hopi Pottery." Monograph Series, Vol. 15, No. 2, Utah State University Press, Logan.
Illustrations of contemporary Hopi pottery exhibited at the 1959 Craftsman show. Each vessel is critiqued and the potter identified. Sections on pottery making, design layout, elements, and shapes.

789. Simpson, De Ette R. 1953 "The Hopi Indians." Southwest
      Museum Leaflet No. 25, Southwest Museum, Los Angeles, Cali-
      fornia.
        Hopi pottery making briefly discussed, pp. 75-80.

790. Skinner, S. Alan. 1968 "Further Excavations at the Sedillo
      Site, Albuquerque, New Mexico." Southwestern Lore, Vol.
      34, No. 3, pp. 69-78, Boulder, Colorado.
        Previously unreported brown ware types at this site are
      Alma Plain: Northern Variety, p. 74; Pilares Fine Banded,
      p. 74; and Corona Rubbed Indented, p. 74. Majority of pot-
      tery found was gray body sherds, indented gray corrugated,
      and Kana-a Gray.

791. Smiley, Nancy K. 1977 "An Analysis of Ceramic Materials
      from McGregor Range." In Prehistoric Culture Stability and
      Change in the Southern Tularosa Basin, Michael Beckes, Ph.D.
      dissertation, University of Pittsburgh, Pittsburgh, Pennsyl-
      vania.
        Abstract: "Description and analysis was performed on the
      nearly 22,000 ceramic sherds collected on the McGregor Range.
      Twenty-seven previously described ceramic types are recognized
      in the material and are categorized according to vessel shape,
      rim styles, miscellaneous forms, and unusual characteristics
      of firing and finishing. El Paso Polychrome is singled out
      and dealt with extensively; information on wall thickness,
      paste and surface colors, surface finishing, design styles,
      paints and geological constituents are included. Post firing
      modifications, i.e., worked sherds and repair holes are an-
      alyzed for all types. A tabulation of ceramic types by site is
      made.... Functional explanations for various ceramic types
      and vessel shapes are put forward as well as ideas on the
      place of various types and shapes in the overall trade net-
      work of the area. Finally, comparisons are made with ceramic
      data gathered by others in the general vicinity of McGregor
      Range," p. 221.
        A table of tentative dates for ceramic types found on Mc-
      Gregor Range, p. 225. Illustrations of El Paso Polychrome,
      El Paso Brown, Three Circle Red-on-white, San Francisco Red,
      Alma Plain: Corrugated Variety, Chupadero Black-on-white,
      Tucson Polychrome, Seco Corrugated, and Ochoa Brown
      Smudged Indented.

792. Smiley, Nancy K. 1978 "Prehistoric Ceramics of the Lower
      Tularosa Basin, Southeastern New Mexico." Masters thesis,
      University of Texas, Austin, Texas.
        Descriptions and illustrations of El Paso Brown, El Paso
      Polychrome, El Paso Brown: Tooled Variety, El Paso Brown:
      Corrugated Variety, and Chupadero Black-on-white. Types
      illustrated but not described are Three Circle Red-on-white,
      San Francisco Red, Alma Plain: Corrugated Variety, Mimbres

Black-on-white, Mimbres Boldface, San Andres Red-on-terra
cotta, Three Rivers Red-on-terra cotta, Tucson Polychrome,
Seco Corrugated, Ochoa Brown Smudged Indented, Playas
Red, and Convento Patterned Incised Corrugated.

793. Smiley, Nancy K. 1979 "Evidence for Ceramic Trade Specialization in the Southern Jornada Branch." In Jornada Mogollon
Archaeology: Proceedings of the First Jornada Conference,
pp. 53-60, Patrick H. Beckett and Regge Wiseman, New Mexico
State University, Las Cruces, New Mexico.
"Examination of ceramic sherds collected on a recent archaeological survey in the lower Tularosa Basin, Southern Jornada
Branch, has shown evidence that a limited number of vessel
forms were imported from other areas involved in a prehistoric
trade network. This specialization was seen in the shapes and
sizes of vessels of several ceramic types," p. 53.

794. Smiley, Terah. 1949 "Pithouse No. 2, Mesa Verde National
Park." American Antiquity, Vol. 14, No. 3, pp. 167-171,
Menasha, Wisconsin.
Found Lino ware sherds, two bowls and one clay pipe.

795. Smiley, Terah L.; Stubbs, Stanley A.; and Bannister, Bryant.
1953 "A Foundation for the Dating of Some Late Archaeological Sites in the Rio Grande Area, New Mexico." Laboratory of
Tree-Ring Research Bulletin, No. 6, University of Arizona,
Tucson, Arizona.
This valuable work includes 56 prehistoric sites and 26
modern pueblos and missions in Northern New Mexico.

796. Smith Exploring Company, H. H. 1893 The Cliff Dwellers.
Pamphlet for the World's Columbian Exposition, 1893, pp. 1-19,
Chicago, Illinois.
Illustrates some of the pottery collected at Mesa Verde for
this exposition.

797. Smith, Landon D. 1977 "Archaeological and Paleoenviron-
mental Investigations in the Cave Buttes Area North of Phoenix, Arizona." Arizona Archaeologist, No. 22, December,
Phoenix, Arizona.
Wingfield Plain constituted 73% to 85% of the pottery recovered. Other wares present were Hohokam buff, red wares,
and a few Gila Plain sherds. Wingfield Plain is shown in Plate
X.

798. Smith, Watson. 1952 Excavations in Big Hawk Valley: Wu-
patki National Monument. Museum of Northern Arizona, Flag-
staff, Arizona.
Painted types were mainly Tusayan White Ware and Tusayan
Black-on-red. Unpainted types found were predominantly
Deadmans Gray and Fugitive Red. Illustrations of Black Mesa

and Flagstaff Black-on-white, pp. 84, 88; Walnut Black-on-white, p. 95; Alameda Brown Ware, p. 99; Winona Brown, p. 101; Deadmans Fugitive Red, p. 103; and Tusayan Gray Ware, p. 105.

799. Smith, Watson. 1962 "Schools, Pots and Potters." American Anthropologist, Vol. 64, pp. 1165-1178, Menasha, Wisconsin.
An excellent article discussing the problems of ceramic taxonomy. Shows the pitfalls in the extremes of discarding classification or over classifying Southwestern pottery. Supports the view that ceramic "schools" be used as a compromise to over and under emphasizing taxonomy in the study of pottery.

800. Smith, Watson. 1971 "Painted Ceramics of the Western Mound at Awatovi." Papers of the Peabody Museum of Archaeology and Ethnology, No. 38, Harvard University, Cambridge, Massachusetts.
Detailed report of a portion of the ceramic material excavated from the Western Mound in 1936-1939. Many black and white photos and drawings. One color plate of characteristic sherds showing color variations. Also a very useful Munsell Chart for identification of ceramic color designations.
Types described and illustrated are new types: Antelope Black-on-straw, pp. 540-549, and Antelope Polychrome, pp. 549-554. The following types are described and well illustrated: Tusayan Black-on-white, pp. 185-244; Little Colorado White Ware: Walnut Black-on-white, pp. 248-249; Bidahochi Black-on-white, pp. 254-259; Cibola White Ware: Tularosa Black-on-white, pp. 263-266; Mesa Verde White Ware, pp. 283-292 (very little found); Orange Polychromes (northern), Tsegi, Tusayan Dogoszhi, Kayenta, and Kiet Siel Polychromes, pp. 206-320; Jeddito Polychrome, pp. 320-347; Jeddito Black-on-orange, pp. 352-441; Jeddito Black-on-orange (slipped variety), pp. 442-452; Kwaituki Black-on-orange, pp. 453-461; Kokop Black-on-orange, pp. 462-465; Jeddito Polychrome (slipped), Kwaituki and Kokop Polychrome, pp. 465-469; Kwaituki Black-on-orange and Kwaituki Polychrome (maroon slipped), pp. 469-471; Awatovi Black-on-yellow, pp. 474-527; Huckovi Black-on-orange, pp. 533-540; Bidahochi Polychrome, pp. 561-570; and Kiet Siel Black-on-red, pp. 570-572. Also good sections on: (1) field procedures and stratigraphy, (2) analysis and distribution features of painted decoration, (3) evolution of ceramic technology at Awatovi, and (4) dating the Western Mound.

801. Smith, Watson. 1973 "The Williams Site: A Frontier Mogollon Village in West-Central New Mexico." Peabody Museum Papers, Vol. 39, No. 2, Harvard University, Cambridge, Massachusetts.
Excavation of a small site near Quemado, New Mexico, in the summer of 1951 by the Upper Gila Expedition of the Peabody Museum.

"While the ceramic remains at UG636 were meager, totaling only about 1,700 sherds from the site as a whole, they were sufficient to provide a reasonably certain placement of the occupation both culturally and chronologically. The majority of the sherds were clearly affiliated with the generality of the Mogollon culture of the late 10th and 11th centuries albeit with some minor characteristics that might distinguish them as local variants of the norms. Along with these were much smaller quantities of quite different sherds characteristic of the Anasazi culture of the Upper Little Colorado area during about the same time period. Mogollon sherds numbered 1,408 (83% of the total), while Anasazi sherds numbered 286 (17% of the total)," p. 27.

Types recovered and illustrated were Alma Plain, Reserve Smudged, San Francisco Red, Reserve Plain Corrugated, Reserve Punched Corrugated, Reserve Incised Corrugated, Reserve Indented Corrugated, and Tularosa Patterned Corrugated.

Mimbres Boldface Black-on-white was the one local painted type found. The four exotic painted types were Kiatuthlanna Black-on-white, Kiatuthlanna Red Mesa Black-on-white, Red Mesa Black-on-white, and Reserve Black-on-white.

802. Smith, Watson; Woodbury, R. B.; and Woodbury, N. F. S. 1966 "The Excavation of Hawikuh by Frederick W. Hodge, 1917-1923." Contributions from the Museum of the American Indian, Heye Foundation, Vol. 20, New York, New York.

Good material on the Zuni Series of White Mountain Red Ware. The following types are described and illustrated: Heshotauthla Polychrome, p. 304, illus., Figs. 39-40; Pinnawa Glaze-on-white, p. 315, illus., Figs. 43-49; Pinnawa Red-on-white, p. 319, illus., Fig. 41; Kwakina Polychrome, p. 311, illus., Figs. 47-50; Kechipawan Polychrome, p. 321, illus., Figs. 41-42; Matsaki Brown-on-buff, p. 330, illus., Figs. 51-71; and Hawikuh Polychrome, p. 331, illus., Figs. 74-79. Illustrations also of Gila Polychrome, Figs. 45-46; Jeddito Black-on-yellow, Fig. 80; and Sikyatki Polychrome, Fig. 80.

803. Snodgrass, O. T. 1973 "A Major Mimbres Collection--By Camera." Artifact, Vol. 11, No. 4, El Paso Archaeological Society, El Paso, Texas.

Life among the Mimbrenos as depicted by realistic designs on their pottery. Drawings of 78 Mimbres vessels from several collections are used to illustrate a somewhat fictionalized account of the lives of the ancient Mimbrenos.

804. Snodgrass, O. T. 1977 Realistic Art and Times of the Mimbres Indians. Privately printed, 6200 Caprock Court, El Paso, Texas.

This is an expanded edition of the author's 1975 work of the same title. Includes over 350 illustrations of Mimbres Black-on-white bowls.

805. Snow, David H. 1973 "Some Economic Considerations of His-
      toric Rio Grande Pueblo Pottery." In The Changing Ways of
      Southwestern Indians, El Corral de Santa Fe, Westerners
      Brand Book, Rio Grande Press, Glorieta, New Mexico.
      "The discussion presented here is a preliminary attempt to
      show that the exchange of pottery was a fully developed pat-
      tern whose existence for more than 300 years of Pueblo his-
      tory implies an economic complexity somewhat above the level
      of gift exchange and subsistence farming. Furthermore, the
      production of Pueblo pottery, for inter-village and inter-ethnic
      use was an economic specialization of considerable importance,
      considering the fact that the Spaniards were dependent upon
      the Pueblos for the bulk of their household ceramic utensils,"
      p. 56.

806. Snow, David H. 1974 "The Excavations of Saltbush Pueblo,
      Bandelier National Monument, New Mexico." Laboratory of
      Anthropology Notes, No. 97, Santa Fe, New Mexico.
      The excavation of a small pueblo with 11 rooms and one
      kiva. Some of the kiva characteristics may indicate influence
      from the Mesa Verde area. Indigenous painted pottery types
      recovered were Kwahe'e Black-on-white, Santa Fe Black-on-
      white, Galisteo Black-on-white, and Wiyo Black-on-white.
      Culinary wares were indented corrugated, slapboard corrugated,
      and plain surfaced types. Exotic types were of White Moun-
      tain Red Ware.

807. Snow, David H. 1982 The Rio Grande Glaze, Matte Paint,
      and Plainware Tradition." Arizona Archaeologist, No. 15, pp.
      235-278, Arizona Archaeological Society, Phoenix, Arizona.
      "The purpose of this essay is to provide a summary, with
      relevant details, of the origins, directions, and extent of
      transmittal of attributes characteristic of the Rio Grande glaze
      and matte-paint ceramic traditions. Specifically, I attempt to:
      (a) present a case for the Mexican origins of diagnostic tech-
      nology attributes and their ultimate combinations which resulted
      in the White Mountain Redware sequence; (b) to provide the
      reader with a synthesis of the sub-regional variations in the
      development of the Rio Grande traditions from about AD 1250
      to Ca. 1875-1900; (c) to discuss the principal attributes which
      I believe relate the Rio Grande glaze tradition to the historic
      matte-paint wares; and (d) to provide a brief review of the
      highlights of the development of the latter," p. 235.

808. Snow, David H. and Fullbright, H. J. 1976 "Strontium/
      Ribidium Occurrence Pattern in Apachean Sherds." SAMAC
      Analytical Notes I, Pottery Southwest, Vol. 3, No. 2, April,
      pp. 3-4.
      The analysis by X-ray fluorescence spectometry indicated
      significant differences in Sr/Rb/Zr in sherds from different
      time periods. These may be used to identify the source of the
      clay used in making the pottery.

809.   Solheim, Wilhelm G., III.   1960   "The Use of Sherd Weights
       and Counts in the Handling of Archaeological Data."   Current
       Anthropology, Vol. 1, No. 4, pp. 325-329, Chicago, Illinois.
       Author indicates how sherd weight and sherd counts can
       be used to make inferences.   Sherd count divided by sherd
       weight gives the number of ounces per sherd for the type.
       This can be used to determine the ceramic homogeneity of a
       site.

810.   Soule, Edwin C.   1976   "Lost City II."   Masterkey, Vol. 50,
       No. 1, January-March, pp. 10-19.
       Brief description of the excavations at the Weinmann Site
       in the Moapa Valley of extreme southeastern Nevada.   The site
       is primarily from Basketmaker III period.   Pottery recovered
       and illustrated is Logandale Plainware, Black-on-gray: Lino
       type, and Plain ware, Lino Gray type.

811.   Soule, Edwin C.   1978   "Pottery Types of the Moapa Valley."
       Masterkey, Vol. 52, No. 3, pp. 101-104.
       Description of Logandale Gray Ware and Logandale Black-
       on-gray, Virgin Branch Anasazi pottery from southern Utah.

812.   Soule, Edwin C.   1979   "Pottery Types of the Moapa Valley:
       Moapa Gray Ware."   Masterkey, Vol. 53, No. 1, pp. 27-33.
       Brief discussion of Moapa Gray Ware.

813.   Southward, Judith A.   1979   "A Summary of Ceramic Technology,
       Plant Remains and Shell Identification Analyses from LA4921,
       Three Rivers, New Mexico."   In Jornada Mogollon Archaeology:
       Proceedings of the First Jornada Conference, pp. 91-102, New
       Mexico State University, Las Cruces, New Mexico.
       A petrographic analysis of the pottery recovered at the
       Three Rivers Site.   The temper of six traditionally recognized
       types is described.   The source of these tempering materials
       is tentatively suggested to be the San Andres Mountains.

814.   Spencer, J. E.   1934   "Pueblo Sites of Southwestern Utah."
       American Anthropologist, Vol. 36, No. 1, pp. 70-80.
       Descriptions of the following types and photos of sherds:
       North Creek Gray, p. 74; North Creek Fugitive Red, p. 74;
       North Creek Corrugated, p. 74; North Creek Black-on-gray,
       p. 74; North Creek Black-on-gray Corrugated, p. 74; Shina-
       rump Brown, p. 75; Shinarump Brown Coiled, Middleton Black-
       on-red, p. 75; Middleton Red, p. 75; Virgin Black-on-white,
       p. 75; Virgin Corrugated, Virgin Tooled, and Washington
       Black-on-cream.

815.   Spicer, Edward H. and Caywood, L. P.   1936   "Two Pueblo
       Ruins in West Central Arizona."   University of Arizona Social
       Science Bulletin, No. 10, Vol. 7, No. 1, Tucson, Arizona.

Pottery, pp. 29-49. Discussion and photographs of Verde
Black-on-gray. Drawing of designs and photos of vessels.
Illustrations of an unusual brown ware pitcher in the form of
a child, p. 45. One plate of intrusive Black-on-white, p. 47.

816. Spicer, Leslie. 1917 "An Outline for a Chronology of Zuni
Ruins." American Museum of Natural History, Anthropology
Papers, Vol. 18, Part 3, New York, New York.
Pottery types in section, pp. 306-325. Sherd collections
from the Zuni area around Ramah, New Mexico. Most sherds
were glazed ware and black-on-white with a small amount of
corrugated and red ware. Photo of three black-on-white vessels and one corrugated vessel, p. 321. Series of wares are
presented but study was conducted before specific type names
were devised so comparisons are difficult.

817. Spicer, Leslie. 1919 "Notes on Some Little Colorado Ruins."
American Museum of Natural History, Anthropology Papers,
Vol. 18, Part 4, pp. 333-362, New York, New York.
States that random surface collections of sherds at a site
are often representative of types of pottery in lower layers
and of time span of the site. Brief description and one photograph of pottery found at ruins in the Little Colorado area.

818. Spicer, Leslie. 1928 "Havasupai Ethnography." American
Museum of Natural History, Anthropology Papers, Vol. 29,
Part 3, New York.
Description of Havasupai Ware, pp. 138-140.

819. Spicer, Leslie. 1933 Yuman Tribes of the Gila River. University of Chicago Press, Chicago, Illinois.
Description of Yuma Ware, pp. 104-110. Illustrations, Pls.
6-7 and Fig. 7.

820. Spinden, Herbert J. 1911 "The Making of Pottery at San
Ildefonso." American Museum Journal, Vol. 9, No. 6, pp. 192-
196.
A brief illustrated description of pottery manufacture at
this Tewa pueblo.

821. Stallings, W. S. 1931 "El Paso Polychrome." Technical Series
Bulletin, No. 3, Archaeological Survey, Laboratory of Anthro-
pology, Santa Fe, New Mexico.
Description of El Paso Polychrome, pp. 1-13.

822. Stallings, W. S. 1932 "Notes on the Pueblo Culture of South
Central New Mexico and in the Vicinity of El Paso, Texas."
American Anthropologist, Vol. 34, No. 1, pp. 67-78, Menasha,
Wisconsin.
Data on pottery types from Southern New Mexico. Conclu-
sion of the survey: "The extreme south-central part of New

Mexico and immediate vicinity of El Paso, Texas, constitutes
a pueblo ceramic district which may be called the El Paso District. This is characterized by two definite native wares,
Black-on-white and a decorated brown ware. There were apparently Mimbres settlements in the district and possibly others
of the Casas Grandes culture," p. 78. Illustrations of native
(Chupadero Black-on-white) sherds and vessels, Pls. 1-2, and
brown ware, Fig. 1.

823. Stanislawski, Michael B. 1969 "The Ethno-Archaeology of
Hopi Pottery Making." Plateau, Vol. 42, No. 1, pp. 27-33.
Description of a study in progress on Hopi pottery.

824. Stanislawski, Michael B. 1969a "What Good Is a Broken Pot?
An Experiment in Hopi-Tewa Ethnoarchaeology." Southwestern
Lore, Vol. 35, No. 1, pp. 11-18, Boulder, Colorado.
Hopi and Hopi Tewa potsherds are used in the following
manner:
1. Manufacturing other pottery: (a) cover pottery during
firing, (b) ground sherds used for temper, and (c) designs
used for painting. 2. Household uses: chinking of masonry
in adobe buildings and bread ovens. 3. Ceremonial uses:
sherds from pipes and ceremonial meal bowls are sometimes
blessed and buried in separate locations.

825. Stanislawski, Michael B. 1978 "If Pots Were Mortal." In
Explorations in Ethnoarchaeology, pp. 201-227, Richard A.
Gould (Ed.), School of American Research, Santa Fe, New
Mexico.
A good article on models for ethnoarchaeologists using South-
western ceramics as examples.

826. Stanislawski, Michael B.; Hitchcock, Ann; and Stanislawski,
Barbara. 1976 "Identification Marks on Hopi and Hopi-Tewa
Pottery." Plateau, Vol. 48, Nos. 3-4, Spring, pp. 47-60.
Abstract: "We know of only four Hopi and Hopi-Tewa potters who were using identification marks before 1930. They
were encouraged to use such marks by the personnel of MNA
and by artists and traders. Perhaps they used marks rather
than personal names because of the typical Pueblo reticence to
identify individuals, or because of their unfamiliarity with Eng-
lish script. Hopi-Tewa individuals in particular seem to have
encouraged clanmates and in-laws to take up the practice during the 1930s and 1940s. A minimum of 33 potters have used
such marks since 1930, 8 Hopi and 15 Hopi-Tewa potters, only
13% of the potters. Most of these potters live close together
in three major villages and are related by clan membership or
marriage to two Hopi-Tewa clans. At least five different associations and meanings for the marks are now known to us,
i.e., the potter's personal name, husband's name, clan, and
clan linked, or mother's name; but the first use of such marks
seems to have symbolized the native personal name," p. 47.

827.   Steadman, Upham. 1982 Politics and Power: An Economic
       and Political History of the Western Pueblo. Academic Press,
       New York, New York.
           Ceramic exchange, pp. 125-142. An examination of ex-
       change between nine 14th century settlements for four ceramic
       groups: Jeddito Yellow Ware, White Mountain Redware, Win-
       slow Orange Ware, and Zuni Glaze Ware. The sites from which
       ceramic data were obtained were: Nuvaqueotaka; Homolovi I,
       II, and IV; Chevelon Ruin; Awatovi; Puerco Ruin; Fourmile
       Ruin; Hooper Ranch; Table Rock; Hawikku; and Acoma.

828.   Steen, Charlie R. 1966 "Excavations at Tse-ta'a, Canyon de
       Chelly National Monument, Arizona." Archaeological Research
       Series, No. 9, National Park Service, Washington, D.C.
           Pottery found was from Basketmaker III to Pueblo III
       periods. Basketmaker sherds were predominantly Lino Gray,
       one-fourth have Fugitive Red. Pueblo II pottery is mainly
       Mancos Black-on-white. The three types of Pueblo III pottery
       are McElmo Black-on-white, Tusayan Polychrome, and St. Johns
       Polychrome. Pottery illustrated by photos: Flagstaff Black-
       on-white bowl, p. 42; Kana-a Black-on-white, bowl, p. 35;
       Mancos Black-on-white vessel, pp. 41-89; Payupki (Hopi) Poly-
       chrome bowl, p. 57; Navajo clay figurines and cooking pot,
       pp. 63, 69; plain gray handled jar, Pueblo II-III, p. 80; Kana-
       a Black-on-white vessels, p. 87; Mesa Verde Black-on-white
       bowl, p. 90 and cover; Betatakin Black-on-white pitcher, p.
       93; Mesa Verde Black-on-white pitcher, p. 94; sherd, discs,
       p. 97; and two pottery pipes, p. 99.

829.   Steen, Charlie; Pierson, L. M.; Bohrer, V. L.; and Kent,
       Kate P. 1962 Archaeological Studies in Tonto National Monu-
       ment. Technical Series, Vol. 2, Southwestern Monuments
       Association, Globe, Arizona.
           A general summary of the Salado question. Upper Ruin
       Pottery, pp. 16-19. Description of San Carlos Red by Irene
       Vickery from specimens at Besh-Ba-Gowa, p. 19. Painted pot-
       tery found was predominantly Gila Polychrome (71%) and Salado
       Red (25%). Tonto Red is in the majority (86%) among the un-
       painted pottery. Illustrations of Gila Polychrome and Tonto
       Red vessels, p. 17. Sherds of Tonto Red and Salado Red, p.
       19. Lower Ruin and Annex pottery, pp. 61-64. Types found
       were primarily Tonto Red and Gila Polychrome. Description of
       Tonto Red, p. 62, illus., p. 63.

830.   Stein, Pat H. 1978 "New Data on the Lower Colorado Buff
       Wares from Palo Verde Hills." Pottery Southwest, Vol. 5, Nos.
       1-2, January, April.
           New information on Lower Colorado Buff Wares including
       data on the dates of these types. Palo Verde Nuclear Station
       is located six miles northwest of Arlington, in western Maricopa
       County, Arizona.

831. Stevenson, James. 1880 "Illustrated Catalogue of the Collec-
      tions Obtained from the Indians of New Mexico in 1880." 2nd
      Annual Report, Bureau of American Ethnology, Smithsonian
      Institute, pp. 429-465, U.S. Government Printing Office, Wash-
      ington, D.C.
          Illustrations of the following clay articles: pitcher, red
      micaceous ware (Pojoaque), p. 440; polished black olla (Santa
      Clara), pp. 443-444; polished black bowl and figure (Santa
      Clara), p. 445; polished meal bowl and pipe (Santa Clara), p.
      446; canteen with bird heads (Santa Clara), p. 447; polychrome,
      stirrup canteen (Santa Clara), p. 449; large jar, appears
      black-on-cream (Santo Domingo), p. 451; polychrome jar, wavy
      rim (Jemez), p. 453; polychrome canteen, animal (Silla), p.
      455; black-on-white jar (San Juan), p. 457; black-on-cream
      (San Ildefonso), p. 461; and polychrome meal bowl (Taos), p.
      465.

832. Stevenson, James. 1883 "Illustrated Catalogue of the Collec-
      tion Obtained from the Indians of New Mexico and Arizona in
      1879." Second Report of the Bureau of American Ethnology,
      pp. 307-465, U.S. Government Printing Office, Washington,
      D.C.
          Illustrations: Zuni water vases, Figs. 359-378; Black-on-
      red Zuni vessels, Figs. 379-384; Zuni canteens, Figs. 385-402;
      Zuni pitchers, cups and bowls, Figs. 403-412; Zuni bowls,
      Figs. 413-430; Zuni (plain) cooking vessels, Figs. 431-436;
      Zuni ladles, Figs. 437-441; Zuni clay baskets (meal bowls),
      Figs. 442-453; Zuni paint and condiment cups, Figs. 454-459;
      Zuni effigies, Figs. 460-483; Wolpi vessels, Figs. 514-534; La-
      guna water vases, Figs. 585-596; Laguna effigies, Figs. 597-
      609; Laguna pottery, Figs. 610-615; Acoma water vases, Figs.
      618-633; Cochiti pottery, Figs. 623-647; Santo Dominto, Figs.
      648-649; Tesuke pottery, Figs. 651-659; Santa Clara pottery,
      Figs. 660-672; San Juan pottery, Figs. 673-675; and ancient
      pottery from Canyon de Chelly, Figs. 677-696.

833. Stevenson, James. 1884 "Illustrated Catalogue of the Collec-
      tions Obtained from the Pueblos of Zuni, New Mexico and Wolpi,
      Arizona in 1881." Third Annual Report of the Bureau of Ameri-
      can Ethnology, pp. 511-594, U.S. Government Printing Office,
      Washington, D.C.
          Many brief descriptions of clay articles but only one pottery
      illustration: Zuni meal bowl (rectangular) duck pot and un-
      usual canteen described as "representing in form the reproduc-
      tiveness of water (the phallic frog) and in decoration, water,
      its inhabitants, and a star of reflection," p. 538.

834. Stewart, Joe D. 1979 The Formal Definition of Decorative
      Traditions in the Jornada Area: A Case Study of Lincoln
      Black-on-red Designs." In Jornada Mogollon Archaeology:
      Proceedings of the First Jornada Conference, Patrick H.

Beckett and Regge N. Wiseman, pp. 295-344, New Mexico State
University, Las Cruces, New Mexico.
A study of the rotational designs and other types of designs on Lincoln Black-on-red from sites in the Jornada Branch
of the Mogollon culture. Includes many drawings of designs.

835. Stewart, Joe D. 1983 "Structural Analysis of Three Rivers
Redware Designs." Kiva, Vol. 49, Nos. 1-2, pp. 39-65.
Abstract: Structural analysis of complete and fragmentary
designs on prehistoric Three Rivers Red-on-terra cotta and
Lincoln Black-on-red bowls from south central New Mexico de-
fines more specifically the long recognized continuity in decorative tradition between them. The resulting classification of
design lays the groundwork for future research on archaeological problems to which they are pertinent, including the nature of exchange interaction within the region and relationships to other regions," p. 39.
Illustrations of Lincoln Black-on-red and Three Rivers Red-
on-terra cotta.

836. Stewart, Joe D. 1984 "Jornada Ceramics at Casas Grandes:
Chronology and Interaction." Pottery Southwest, Vol. 11, No.
2, pp. 1-3.
Abstract: "Ceramic cross-ties demonstrate interaction of
the Jornada area with Casas Grandes and Mimbres area during
the Viejo Period of Casas Grandes. Jornada-Casas Grandes
interaction continued through the Medio Period. Jornada ceramics at Casas Grandes tend to support Le Blanc's (1980) revised dating of the Viejo-Medio transition and also (but very
tenuously) suggest an earlier inception of the Three Rivers
Red-on-terra cotta in the Jornada area than has usually been
thought," p. 1.

837. Stewart, Julian H. 1936 "Pueblo Material Culture of Western
Utah." University of New Mexico Anthropology Series, Vol.
1, No. 3, Albuquerque, New Mexico.
Descriptions of the following types of Utah Desert Gray
Ware: Great Salt Lake Gray, p. 6; Great Salt Lake Black-on-
gray, p. 16; Sevier Gray, p. 10; Sevier Black-on-gray, p.
13; and Sevier Corrugated, p. 11.

838. Stewart, Julian H. 1941 "Archaeological Reconnaissance of
Southern Utah." Bureau of American Ethnology, Bulletin 128,
pp. 275-356, Washington, D.C.
Descriptions of Johnson Corrugated, Johnson Gray and Johnson Gray-tan. Illustrations of Black-on-white sherds. Map
and list of sites in Johnson Canyon and Paria River Region.
Also some sites in Glen Canyon.

839. Stewart, Omer C. 1942 "Culture Element Distributions, XVIII
Ute-Southern Paiute." University of California Anthropology
Records, Vol. 6, No. 4, Berkeley, California.

Description of Southern Paiute ware, pp. 272, 341; Ute Ware, pp. 272, 341; and Navajo Ware, pp. 272, 341.

840. Stubbs, Stanley A. 1950 Birds Eye View of the Pueblos.
University of Oklahoma Press, Norman, Oklahoma.
Primarily brief descriptions of the architecture with descriptions of the following types:
Santa Ana Polychrome: "Distinctive pottery was produced for many years in this village and recently an attempt was made to revive the craft after a period of years when none was made. The brick-red pottery was finished with a thick white slip and decorated with red and black designs; unlike conventional practice in most pueblo pottery design, the red areas were often not outlined in black," p. 78.
Isleta Polychrome: "A plain red cooking ware has been made for domestic use, but the pottery called Isleta sold in curio stores and at the railroad station in Albuquerque is almost exclusively the product of the Laguna colony. This pottery is brick-red in color with a white slip and black and red designs, usually the vessels are in the form of small bowls," p. 38.

841. Stubbs, Stanley A. and Stallings, W. A. 1953 "The Excavations of Pindi Pueblo." New Mexico School of American Research and Laboratory of Anthropology, Monograph 18, Santa Fe, New Mexico.
Descriptions and illustrations of sherds of the following types: Santa Fe Black-on-white, p. 48; Galisteo Black-on-white, Pindi Black-on-white, p. 50; and Poge Black-on-white, p. 50. Illustrations of Heshotauthla Polychrome, Figs. 57a-c, e, Pl. 12.

842. Sudar-Murphy, Toni; Laumbach, Karl W.; and Ford, Dabney. 1977 "Analyses of Ceramic, Lithic, Bone and Flotation Materials." Chapter 2 in Archaeological Investigations in Cochiti Reservoir, New Mexico, Volume 2: Excavation and Analysis 1975 Season, pp. 19-25, edited by Richard Chapman and Jan Biella, Office of Contract Archaeology, University of New Mexico, Albuquerque, New Mexico.
Analysis of the ceramics associated with five prehistoric sites located in White Rock Canyon. Descriptions of the utility ware recovered and three painted types: Kwahe'e Black-on-white, Santa Fe Black-on-white, and Wiyo Black-on-white.

843. Sullivan, Alan P. 1984 "Design Styles and Cibola Whiteware: Examples from the Grasshopper Area, East-Central Arizona." In A. P. Sullivan and J. L. Hantman (Eds.), Regional Analysis of Prehistoric Ceramic Variation: Contemporary Studies in Cibola Whitewares, Anthropological Research Papers, No. 31, Arizona State University, Tempe, Arizona.
Abstract: "An attribute-based taxonomy of eleven styles of

whiteware decoration is presented. The taxonomy clarifies the
relations of the Cibola Whiteware types to each other and shows
how they, in turn, are related stylistically to Little Colorado
Whiteware and Tusayan Whiteware types. Several revisions of
the White Mountain Series are suggested," p. 74.

844. Sullivan, Alan P. and Hantman, Jeffrey L. (Editors). 1984
      "Regional Analysis of Prehistoric Ceramic Variation: Contem-
      porary Studies of the Cibola Whitewares." Anthropological Re-
      search Papers, No. 31, Arizona State University, Tempe, Ari-
      zona.
          Abstract: "The papers in this volume demonstrate how dif-
      ferent approaches may be profitably employed to understand
      regional patterns of ceramic stylistic and technological varia-
      tion. These papers are unified, however, in their focus on
      the Cibola Whitewares, a common group of black-on-white ce-
      ramic types found throughout east-central Airzona, west-
      central and northwestern New Mexico.
          "A variety of methods, including design attribute analysis,
      symmetry analysis, petrography, and X-ray diffraction, may
      be found in these studies. New data are presented regarding
      the distribution and interpretation of Cibola Whitewares. Equally
      important, the contributions in this volume illustrate the value
      of both typological and nontypological data in ascertaining how
      regional factors affect prehistoric ceramic variation. Although
      methods and data bases differ, common conclusions reached in
      these diverse studies indicate that (1) a great deal of techno-
      logical variation occurs within a single ceramic ware, (2) ce-
      ramic style and technology vary independently, and (3) the
      study of regional distributions of stylistic and technological
      attributes is a valuable means of investigating patterns of pre-
      historic ceramic production, interaction, and exchange," p. 1.

845. Sundt, William M. 1977 "How Big? How Much?" Pottery
      Southwest, Vol. 4, No. 3, October, pp. 8-9.
          Method for estimating the size of temper particles by use of
      probes made of varying sizes of piano wire is described. A
      scale for estimating the density of temper is also proposed.

846. Sundt, William M. 1984 "Design Analysis of a Pure Variety
      of Santa Fe Black-on-white." In Collected Papers in Honor of
      Harry L. Hadlock, Nancy L. Fox (Ed.), Papers of the Archae-
      ological Society of New Mexico, No. 9, Albuquerque, New
      Mexico.
          Presents a brief history of the descriptions and study of
      Santa Fe Black-on-white. Analysis of Santa Fe Black-on-white
      sherds from the Artifical Leg Site (LA 35493), excavated by
      Regge Wiseman in 1968-69 and 1971. Describes paste composi-
      tion, vessel identification, test for unmixed strata, and de-
      sign analysis. Illustrations of three partial Santa Fe Black-on-
      white bowls and band designs from medium and smaller vessels.

The author concludes that the sample of Santa Fe Black-on-
white exhibits two sets of band patterns, one for small and
medium vessels and another for larger vessels. Artistry is
rather mediocre and lack of control of firing cause tan-gray
surfaces rather than the usual light gray. Slipped surfaces
are uncommon; 90% are jars and 7-10% are bowls. This article
provides valuable additional information on Santa Fe Black-on-
white.

847. Sunset Magazine. 1972 "Southwestern Indian Art in 1972."
      Sunset Magazine, April, pp. 86-94.
          Color illustrations of Santa Clara Black, Navajo utility cook-
      ing pot, Maricopa Black-on-red, Cochiti Polychrome figurine,
      Margaret and Luther jar (Santa Clara), and turtle figurine by
      Tony Da.

848. Swannack, Jervis D. 1969 "Big Juniper House, Mesa Verde
      National Park (Wetherill Mesa Excavations)." National Park
      Service Archaeological Research Series, Wetherill Mesa Studies,
      7-C, U.S. Government Printing Office, Washington, D.C.
          A late Pueblo II and early Pueblo III site. Pottery types
      illustrated in good photos include sherds and vessels of the
      following types: Mancos Gray, p. 65; Moccasin Gray, p. 65;
      Mummy Lake Gray, pp. 66-67; Mancos Corrugated, pp. 66-69,
      72; Mesa Verde Corrugated, p. 72; Piedra Black-on-white, p.
      73; Cortez Black-on-white, pp. 74-77; Mancos Black-on-white,
      pp. 79-94; McElmo Black-on-white, pp. 94-96; and Redware:
      Bluff, Abajo, Puerco, p. 97. Types of worked sherds, pp.
      98-103; miniatures and other eccentrics, pp. 104-107. "Several
      features of the ceramics of Big Juniper House are indicative
      of the transition from Pueblo II to Pueblo III. The early style
      of McElmo Black-on-white was introduced at this time. On
      present evidence this pottery seems to be limited to this stage
      and to be superceded after 1150 by other styles of McElmo, or
      pre-Mesa Verde Black-on-white, and by 'classic' Mesa Verde
      Black-on-white.... The evidence indicates that Mancos Black-
      on-white, still the dominant decorated pottery type of the
      transitional stage, declined after 1150. In the realm of utility
      pottery, Mummy Lake Gray reached the zenith of its popularity
      during this time. Mesa Verde Corrugated began to be made
      but Mancos Corrugated was the principal corrugated type until
      about 1150. The greater percentage of flaring rims on Mancos
      Corrugated pottery may be an indicator of change to Pueblo III
      style of sharply everted rims on Mesa Verde Corrugated," p.
      180.

849. Swarthout, Jeanne and Dulaney, Alan. 1982 "The Coronado
      Project Archaeological Investigations: A Description of Ceramic
      Collections from the Railroad and Transmission Line Corridors."
      MNA Research Paper 26, Museum of Northern Arizona, Flag-
      staff, Arizona.

208 Southwestern Pottery

Abstract: "Ceramics from more than 148 sites produced a wide range of decorated and undecorated whitewares, red wares, and brown wares from the construction of the railroad and transmission lines at the Coronado Generating Plant near St. Johns, Arizona.

"A discussion of cultural affiliation, exchange, and chronology of the study area through ceramic evidence from several sites is presented; and the larger problem of southwestern ceramic typology is addressed, both in narration of traditional problems, and in a typological consensus test employing Cibola whitewares. A thorough petrographic study of ceramic thin sections was made to test specific theses."

850. Switzer, Ronald R. 1969 "An Unusual Late Red Mesa Effigy Pitcher." Plateau, Vol. 42, No. 7, pp. 39-45, Museum of Northern Arizona, Flagstaff, Arizona.
Descriptions and illustrations of an effigy pitcher of a man, Red Mesa Black-on-white type. Comparisons with similar vessel forms in other types of pottery.

851. Tanner, Clara Lee. 1968 Southwest Indian Craft Arts. University of Arizona Press, Tucson, Arizona.
Pottery, Chapter IV, pp. 85-114. Illustrations and brief descriptions of prehistoric vessels Chaco, Tularosa, and Hohokam, Fig. 41; modern Hopi bowls and jars, Figs. 4.4-4.5; Zuni vessels, Figs. 4.7-4.8 (owl); San Ildefonso Polychrome, Fig. 4.9; Matte Black-on-polished black (Maria), Fig. 4.10; polished carved red jar, Fig. 4.11; Santa Clara Black, Figs. 4.12-4.13; contemporary Santa Clara Polychrome (Lela and Van), Fig. 4.14; San Juan incised, Fig. 4.15; Santo Domingo Polychrome, Fig. 4.16; Zia Polychrome, Fig. 4.17; Acoma Polychrome, Fig. 4.18; Acoma Black-on-white, Fig. 4.19; Santa Ana Polychrome, Fig. 4.20; Cochiti Polychrome, Figs. 4.12, 4.22; Taos bean pot and bowl, Fig. 4.23; Tesuque Polychrome (poster paint), Fig. 4.24; Mohave Red-on-buff ware, Figs. 4.24, 4.26; Maricopa Black-on-red, Fig. 4.22; old Navajo Polychrome, Fig. 4.29; Navajo plain ware cooking pot, Fig. 4.30; and Papago Black-on-red bowls, Fig. 4.31. A good general introduction.

852. Tanner, Clara Lee. 1976 Prehistoric Southwestern Craft Arts. University of Arizona Press, Tucson, Arizona.
Pottery chapter, pp. 93-146. Good introduction to Southwestern prehistoric pottery. Topics included are: technical background--materials, methods, and form; decoration--design layout, types of decoration, and design analysis; and regional styles of decoration--Anasazi, Hohokam, and Mogollon. The following forms and shapes are illustrated: modeled decorations, basket impressed Basketmaker III bowl, smudged interior indented exterior bowl, neckbanded jar, gourd shaped pots, and varieties of corrugated wares. A number of Anasazi,

Hohokam and Mogollon types of pottery are well described and illustrated in excellent color and black and white photographs.

853. Taylor, Walter W. 1958 "Two Archaeological Studies in Northern Arizona, Part II, A Brief Survey Through the Grand Canyon." Museum of Northern Arizona Bulletin, No. 30, Flagstaff, Arizona.
      Description of Nankoweap Polychrome (similar to Citadel Polychrome).

854. Third Southwestern Ceramic Seminar. 1961 Museum of Northern Arizona, Flagstaff, 5 pp., Xerox.
      "The main topic of discussion was brown ware throughout the Southwest and particularly the brown ware that is the ceramic expression of the Mogollon. The initial portion of the seminar was spent in a rather general investigation of this technology in the Southwest as well as its antecedents. While generally accepting the priority of a Southern source, several historical possibilities were considered. It may be safely stated that the problem of brown ware/gray ware successions yet remains to be solved.... Few majority concurrences and no fiats regarding these problems are offered herein," p. 1.

855. Thompson, Ray A. 1971 Grand Canyon National Monument Archaeological Survey Preliminary Report. Museum of Southern Utah, Cedar City, Utah.
      Descriptions of Kanab Brown, pp. 57-58; Tuweep Brown, pp. 53-58; Tuweep Corrugated, pp. 59-60; and Tuweep Gray, pp. 53-58.

856. Toll, H. Wolcott. 1984 "Trends in Ceramic Import and Distribution in Chaco Canyon." In James W. Judge and John D. Schelberg, Recent Research in Chaco Prehistory, Reports of the Chaco Center, No. 8, pp. 115-135, Chaco Center, National Park Service, Albuquerque, New Mexico.
      Ceramic samples from Pueblo Alto and four smaller sites from the 10th to 13th century are examined in regard to the redistribution model developed for the Chaco Anasazi. Through time and increasing proportion of these ceramics can be identified as having been made in the Chuska area. The proportion reaches a maximum of 60%. There is some evidence that specialization in ceramic production may have occurred in the Chuska area. While this supports some aspects of the redistribution model it cannot be said that this study supports the redistribution of ceramics in the Chaco area.

857. Toll, H. Wolcott and McKenna, Peter J. 1981 The Testimony of the Spadefoot Ceramics, Description and Analysis of the 29SJ629 Sherds. Manuscript on file, Chaco Center, National Park Service, Albuquerque, New Mexico.
      Analysis and discussion of ceramics from a Pueblo III "Mc-Elmo" kiva in Chaco Canyon.

858. Toll, H. Wolcott and McKenna, Peter J. 1981 Ceramics of
      628. Manuscript on file, Chaco Center, National Park Service,
      Albuquerque, New Mexico.
          Description of the pottery found at this late Basketmaker
      III to early Pueblo I site composed of seven pithouses.

859. Toll, H. Wolcott and McKenna, Peter J. 1982 The Rhetoric
      and the Ceramics, Discussion of Types, Functions, Distribu-
      tion, and Sources of the Ceramics at 29SJ27. Manuscript on
      file, Chaco Center, National Park Service, Albuquerque, New
      Mexico.
          Diversity in paste and surface treatment increases with
      time. The diversity of sources through time is discussed.
      Chuskan vessels are the most frequent imports.

860. Toll, H. Wolcott and McKenna, Peter J. 1983 The Ceramo-
      graphy of Pueblo Alto. Manuscript on file, Chaco Center,
      National Park Service, Albuquerque, New Mexico.
          Description and analysis of ceramics from nine major spatially
      and temporally discrete occupational and trash proveniences.

861. Toulouse, Betty. 1977 Pueblo Pottery of the New Mexico In-
      dians. Museum of New Mexico Press, Santa Fe, New Mexico.
          An excellent introduction to the history of historic and con-
      temporary pueblo pottery. History is presented from the open-
      ing of the Santa Fe Trail to 1940 and to 1976 when Pueblo
      pottery became an art form. Very good photos of represen-
      tative ceramics from the historic pottery producing pueblos
      and works of many of the noted contemporary potters.

862. Toulouse, Joseph H. 1949 "The Mission of San Gregario de
      Abo: A Report on the Excavation and Repair of a 17th Cen-
      tury New Mexico Mission." School of American Research,
      Monograph No. 13, Santa Fe, New Mexico.
          Descriptions of Salinas Red (synonym Salinas Red Ware),
      p. 14; Tabira' Black-on-white, p. 19; and Tabira' Polychrome,
      p. 19.

863. Toulouse, Joseph H. and Stephenson, R. L. 1960 "Excava-
      tions at Pueblo Pardo." Papers in Anthropology, No. 2, Mu-
      seum of New Mexico, Santa Fe.
          Description and illustrations of Tabira' Black-on-white. A
      few illustrations of Chupadero Black-on-white and Rio Grande
      Glaze Ware.

864. Travis, Scott E. 1984 "Modeling Levels of Socio Economic
      Interaction Within the Dolores River Valley: A Tentative As-
      sessment." In David A. Breternitz, Dolores Archaeological
      Project: Synthetic Report 1978-1981, pp. 105-128, Bureau of
      Reclamation, Denver, Colorado.
          "The following discussion examines the potential of DAP

ceramic assemblages in relation to more recent techniques of exchange system analysis and outlines some aspects of a tentative distributional patterning. The ultimate utility of the investigation may then be viewed in terms of an increasing sensitivity towards data variability, and clarification of the unique role of the Dolores River occupation played in prehistoric Anasazi exchange systems," pp. 105-106.

865. Traylor, Diane E. and Scaife, Robert P. 1980 "Ceramics." In Lyndi Hubbell and Diane Traylor (Eds.), Bandelier: Excavations in the Flood Pool of Cochiti Lake, New Mexico, pp. 239-294, National Park Service, Southwest Cultural Resources Center, Santa Fe, New Mexico.

A descriptive study of ceramics found at 23 sites in the project area. A total of 34,561 sherds were excavated. The common types found and illustrated are: Kwahe'e Black-on-white, Santa Fe Black-on-white, Wiyo Black-on-white, Galisteo Black-on-white, Agua Fria Glaze-on-red, and San Clemente Glaze Polychrome. Common unpainted wares were: utility pottery, plain surface, ribbed surface, washboard surface, indented corrugated surface and smeared indented surface; 87% of the sherds recovered came from one site, LA12119. Only one whole vessel, a Tesuque Corrugated jar, was found. Other restorable vessels recovered were of the following types: Tesuque Corrugated, Wiyo Black-on-white, Santa Fe Black-on-white, Lino Gray, San Clemente Glaze Polychrome, Cieneguilla Glaze-on-yellow, and Agua Fria Glaze-on-red.

866. Trimble, Stephen. 1987 Talking with the Clay: The Art of Pueblo Pottery. School of American Research Press, Santa Fe, New Mexico.

An excellent summary of contemporary Pueblo pottery and its makers. Based primarily on personal interviews with 60 potters representing all of the pottery making pueblos. Very good photographs of the potters and their pottery from each pueblo. Emphasizes the close relationship between the lives and beliefs of the potters and the pottery they produce. The traditions of pottery making and the economics of present day production are discussed.

867. Trost, Willy. 1970 "An El Paso Polychrome Bowl Used as a Mortuary Vessel." Artifact, Vol. 8, No. 3, El Paso Archaeological Society, El Paso, Texas.

"The description of a killed El Paso Polychrome bowl that was used to cover the remains of an infant burial focuses upon the design element and suggests temporal and spatial contacts using associated ceramics as data. It is believed that this is the first report of a complete El Paso Polychrome vessel which was used as a mortuary offering," p. 1. Description of El Paso Polychrome, p. 17. Color illustrations of El Paso Polychrome, cover, Figs. 5-10 (found near Rincon, New Mexico).

868. Tryk, Shelia. 1979 "Solving the Pecos Pottery Mystery."
      New Mexico Magazine, Vol. 57, No. 7, July, pp. 20-23.
      Popular article on the reproduction of Pecos glaze ware
      pottery by Evelyn Vigil of Jemez Pueblo. Presents photos of
      vessels made by Vigil and Juanita T. Toleda and indicates the
      materials and methods they used.

869. Tschopik, Harry K., Jr. 1938 "Taboo as a Possible Factor
      Involved in the Obsolescence of Navajo Pottery and Basketry."
      American Anthropologist, Vol. 40, No. 2, pp. 257-262, Menasha,
      Wisconsin.
      As pottery and baskets lost their utilitarian function among
      the Ramah Navajo, they became nearly entirely ceremonial in
      use. The taboos surrounding their manufacture caused so
      many restrictions that, as of 1938, they were obsolete and
      nearly extinct.

870. Tschopik, Harry K., Jr. 1941 "Navajo Pottery Making: An
      Inquiry into the Affinities of Navajo Painted Pottery." Papers
      of the Peabody Museum of American Archaeology and Ethnology,
      Vol. 27, No. 1, Cambridge, Massachusetts.
      Comprehensive description and illustrations of Navajo Ware
      including painted types and utility ware. Navajo Painted ves-
      sels, Pls. 8-15; Navajo cooking vessels, Pl. 9; Navajo pipes,
      Pl. 16; and pottery manufacture, Pls. 1-7.

871. Turner, Christy G. and Lofgren, Laurel. 1966 "Household
      Size of the Prehistoric Western Pueblo Indians." Southwestern
      Journal of Anthropology, Vol. 22, pp. 117-132.
      "This paper presents a trial method of estimating Anasazi
      household size, independent of ethnographic or census observa-
      tions, by the use of the ratio of the capacities of individual
      serving bowls and cooking jars belonging to the Kayenta
      branch (Western Pueblo of Erik Reed, 1955) between AD 500
      and 1900," p. 117.

872. Tuthill, Carr. 1947 "The Tres Alamos Site on the San Pedro
      River, Southeastern Arizona." Amerind Foundation, Publica-
      tion No. 4, Dragoon, Arizona.
      Descriptions of the following types of Pimeria Brown Ware:
      Cascabel Red-on-brown, pp. 50-51; Tres Alamos Red-on-brown,
      pp. 51-53; Deepwell Red-on-brown, p. 53; Benson Red-on-
      brown, p. 47; and Tres Alamos Red, p. 55.

873. Underhill, Ruth. 1944 Pueblo Crafts. U.S. Department of
      Interior, Bureau of Indian Affairs, Haskell Institute, Lawrence,
      Kansas.
      Photographs and descriptions of historic pueblo pottery, p.
      79-105. Descriptions and illustrations of Maria Martinez mak-
      ing pottery, pp. 79-89. Photos of pottery from these pueblos:
      Santo Domingo Black-on-cream, p. 92; Cochiti Black-on-cream,

p. 94; Santa Ana Polychrome, p. 95; Zia Polychrome, p. 96; Acoma Polychrome, p. 97; Zuni Polychrome, p. 98; Hopi Black-on-orange, p. 99; Polished Black or Red, Santa Clara, p. 100; polished Black-on-red, San Juan, p. 101; San Ildefonso Black-on-cream, p. 102; unpainted micaceous, Taos, Picuris, p. 103; and modern variegated, several pueblos, pp. 104-105.

874. Upham, Steadman; Lightfoot, Kent G.; and Feinman, Gary M. 1981 "Explaining Socially Determined Ceramic Distributions in the Prehistoric Plateau Southwest." American Antiquity, Vol. 46, No. 4, pp. 822-833.

"We examine the process of political development in relation to selected social and economic variables in the plateau region of the American Southwest. We argue that political development was closely associated with strategies of agricultural intensification, surplus production, changes in the organization and management of labor, and expanding regional exchanges. We draw supporting data from several settlement systems and attempt to demonstrate that both exotic and labor-intensive commodities were restricted to political and economic centers. We then examine the distribution of one category of these materials, ceramics, through application of the 'production step' measure. Our analysis suggests that access to highly decorated ceramic items was restricted to individuals residing at the largest centers. Traditional interpretations of the political organization of plateau region prehistoric groups stress their egalitarian qualities. We suggest that such interpretations be re-examined in the light of data and arguments presented here," p. 822.

875. Valehrach, Emil M. and Valehrach, Bruce S. 1971 "Excavations at Brazeletes Pueblo." Arizona Archaeologist, No. 6, December, Phoenix, Arizona.

The local types found were Verde Red, Verde Smudged, Verde Brown, and Tuzigoot White-on-red. A number of local vessels were restored and some are illustrated. One Flagstaff Black-on-white and a few Snowflake Black-on-white, Tularosa Black-on-white and Hohokam Red-on-buff sherds were recovered.

876. Vickery, Irene. 1939 "Besh-ba-gowah." Kiva, Vol. 4, No. 5, pp. 19-22, Tucson, Arizona.

Description of a ruin in city of Globe, Arizona. Pottery was abundant. Early phase types: Roosevelt Black-on-white, Pinto Polychrome, Pinto Black-on-red, Salado Red Ware, Gila Red Ware, San Carlos Red-on-brown, Coiled ware and plain ware. Later phase types: Gila Polychrome and Gila Black-on-red. Trade wares: Tularosa Black-on-white, Pinedale Polychrome, Fourmile Polychrome, Tucson Polychrome, and Chihuahua Polychrome.

877. Vivian, Gordon R. 1959 "Hubbard Site and Other Tri-Wall

Structures in New Mexico and Colorado." U.S. National Park
Service Archaeological Research Series, No. 5, Washington,
D.C.
　　Pottery, pp. 19-23. Descriptions and illustrations of the
following types: Escavada Black-on-white, Pueblo del Arroyo
(cross section of sherd), pp. 20-22; Gallup Black-on-white,
Pueblo del Arroyo, pp. 23-24 (sherd cross section, p. 25);
Chaco Black-on-white, Pueblo del Aroyo, pp. 26-27 (sherd
cross section, p. 25); Mancos Black-on-white, Pueblo del Ar-
royo, pp. 29-30 (sherd cross section, p. 31); McElmo Black-
on-white, Pueblo del Arroyo, pp. 32-33; McElmo Black-on-white,
Hubbard Site, p. 34 (sherd cross section, p. 35); Mesa Verde
Black-on-white, Hubbard Site, pp. 36-37 (sherd cross section, p. 38); Puerco Black-on-red, Pueblo del Arroyo, pp.
39-40 (sherd cross section, p. 41); and Wingate Black-on-red,
Pueblo del Arroyo, p. 42.

878.　Vivian, Gordon R.　1964　"Excavations in a 17th Century Ju-
　　mano Pueblo, Gran Quivira." U.S. National Park Service
　　Archaeological Research Series, No. 8, Washington, D.C.
　　　Ceramics discussed on pages 95-114. Types found include
　　culinary ware, Tabira' Black-on-white, Glaze (late), and
　　Tabira' Plain. Description of Tabira' Black-on-white (a late
　　variety of Chupadero Black-on-white, Toulose). Illustrations
　　of Tabira' Black-on-white, pp. 104-107, 94, 121; Tabira' Poly-
　　chrome, p. 108; Tabira' plain, pp. 108-109; and glaze paint
　　sherds, p. 112.

879.　Vivian, Gordon R.　1965　"The Three-C Site an Early Pueblo
　　II Ruin in Chaco Canyon, New Mexico." University of New
　　Mexico Publications in Anthropology, No. 13, University of
　　New Mexico Press, Albuquerque.
　　　Pottery discussed on pp. 24-35. Indigenous types found
　　were Lino Gray, Neckbanded, Indented Corrugated, La Plata
　　Black-on-white, Lino Black-on-gray, Kiatuthlanna/Red Mesa
　　Black-on-white (described), and Escavada Black-on-white.
　　Illustrations of sherds: La Plata Black-on-white, variations,
　　Fig. 6, and Kiatuthlanna/Red Mesa Black-on-white, Figs. 7-
　　10. Discusses problem of distinguishing Red Mesa Black-on-
　　white/Kiatuthlanna Black-on-white from La Plata Black-on-white
　　on the basis of either design or temper.

880.　Vivian, Gordon and Mathews, Tom.　1964　"Kin Kletso, A
　　Pueblo III Community in Chaco Canyon, New Mexico." South-
　　western Monuments Association Technical Series, vol. 6, Part
　　I, Globe, Arizona.
　　　Pottery, chapter IV, pp. 65-83. "There were 6,061 non-
　　culinary sherds and 16 whole or restorable vessels recovered,"
　　p. 65. Most pottery found was local Black-on-white types in-
　　cluding McElmo Black-on-white, Escavada Black-on-white, Chaco
　　Black-on-white, and Gallup Black-on-white. Red ware imports

were also found in small amounts. Illustrations of McElmo
Black-on-white designs on pp. 66, 68, 70, 72, 74, 76, 78, 80,
and 82.

881. Vivian, Gwinn. 1965 "An Archaeological Survey of the Lower
      Gila River, Arizona." Kiva, Vol. 30, No. 4, pp. 95-146.
      "During January and February of 1964, an archaeological
      survey of the lower Gila River was undertaken by the Arizona
      State Museum to locate sites endangered by future Gila River
      channel alterations. The 85 sites located in the survey re-
      flected occupation of the Gila River Valley by several cul-
      turally distinct groups. Anglo American, Modern Papago,
      historic Western Yavapai, historic and prehistoric Yuman and
      prehistoric Hohokam sites were represented," p. 95. Pottery
      discussed on pp. 116-125. Data indicating types of sherds
      found and a ceramic analysis given in Table II, pp. 118-119.

882. Vivian, Gwinn and Clendenen, Nancy W. 1965 "The Denison
      Site: Four Pithouses Near Isleta, New Mexico." El Palacio,
      Vol. 72, No. 2, pp. 9-15.
      Ceramics found in the following amounts: White ware, 43.4%;
      Gray ware, 32.9%; and Brown ware, 22.8%. White ware was
      primarily Red Mesa Black-on-white and Gallup Black-on-white.
      Description of the sample of Red Mesa Black-on-white, p. 11.
      Description of the sample of Gallup Black-on-white, p. 12. Il-
      lustrations of the above two types, Fig. 4. The most unusual
      feature of these sites and the Sedillo pithouses is the occur-
      rence of primarily Pueblo II and III ceramics. In most sites
      of these periods the dwellers had abandoned pithouses for the
      large communal pueblo type of habitation.

883. Voll, Charles B. 1961 "The Glaze Paint Ceramics of Pottery
      Mound, New Mexico." Masters thesis, University of New
      Mexico, Albuquerque, New Mexico.
      Good short study of the pottery found during the excava-
      tions at Pottery Mound Pueblo in the lower Puerco River Valley.
      Description and illustrations of San Clemente Glaze-Polychrome
      and Pottery Mount Glaze Polychrome, pp. 57-60. Other types
      illustrated are Agua Fria Glaze-on-red, Cieneguilla Glaze-on-
      yellow, Largo Glaze Polychrome, Espinosa Glaze Polychrome,
      Heshotauthla Glaze Polychrome, Kwakina Glaze Polychrome, Pin-
      nawa Glaze-on-white, and an unnamed Zuni Glaze paint type.

884. Wade, Edwin L. 1980 "The Thomas Keam Collection of Hopi
      Pottery, A New Typology." American Indian Art Magazine,
      Vol. 5, No. 3, Summer, pp. 55-61.
      Descriptions of several types of Hopi pottery in the Keams
      Collection at the Peabody Museum. The author presents a new
      system of classification of these pieces. This system empha-
      sizes ceramic styles as a subvariety of a general design tradi-
      tion or school.

885. Wade, Edwin L. 1980a America's Great Lost Expedition: The
      Thomas Keam Collection of Hopi Pottery from the Second Hemen-
      way Expedition, 1890-94. Heard Museum, Phoenix, Arizona.
      Hopi pottery in this 1980-82 exhibition is described and illus-
      trated. Types illustrated and described are San Bernardo
      Polychrome, Sikyatki Polychrome, Polacca Polychrome, Payupki
      Polychrome, Jeddito Polychrome, and Mishongnovi Polychrome.
      Prehistoric Hopi and other Tusayan types are also shown.

886. Wade, Edwin L. and McChesney, Lea S. 1981 Historic Hopi
      Ceramics: The Thomas V. Keam Collection of the Peabody Mu-
      seum of Archaeology and Ethnology, Harvard University, Pea-
      body Museum Press, Cambridge, Massachusetts.
      This study of an extensive collection of Hopi pottery ob-
      tained from the pioneer trader, Thomas Keam in 1892, includes
      a short history of the collection, an ethnographic profile of
      the Hopi, statements on traditional Hopi pottery manufacture
      and use, and a review of 500 years of Hopi history as evi-
      dence by the pottery in the Keam collection. The total num-
      ber of vessels included is 1,412 in the following type per-
      centages: Sikyatki Polychrome, 28%; San Bernardo Polychrome,
      5.1%; Payupki Polychrome, 2%; Polacca Polychrome, 61.8% and
      Eccentric painted ware, 4.5%.
      New types are described using variants of the established
      names: Sikyatki Polychrome and variants (AD1375-1625), p.
      20, illus., pp. 21-41. San Bernardo Polychrome and variants
      (AD 1625-1740), p. 44, illus., pp. 48-81. Payupki Polychrome
      and variants (AD 1680-1780), p. 84, illus., pp. 85-100. Po-
      lacca Polychrome and variants (AD 1780-1900), pp. 102-103;
      illus., Style A (AD 1780-1820), pp. 105-118; Style B (AD
      1820-1860), pp. 121-143; Style C (AD 1860-1890), pp. 145-454;
      Style D (AD 1890-1900), pp. 457-509. Eccentric Painted Ware
      (AD 1800-1900). Includes: Mishongave Polychrome-on-white,
      Polychrome-on-gray, Black-on-gray, Polychrome-on-buff, Brown-
      on-buff, and Red-on-pink, illus., pp. 513-545. Sikyatki, San
      Bernardo and Payupki Polychromes from Awatovi, illus., pp.
      547-557.

887. Walker, Willard and Wyckoff, Lydia L. 1983 Hopis, Tewas
      and The American Road. Wesleyan University, Middleton,
      Connecticut.
      Descriptions of pottery collected by Prof. and Mrs. Carey
      F. Melville in 1927. These were collected in the Hopi region
      during a nationwide auto tour. The 86 pieces are included in
      the following types: Polacca Polychrome (Style D), Sikyatki
      Revival Polychrome (Style A), Sikyatki Revival Polychrome
      (Style B), Polished Red Ware, Red and Buff Ware, Red and
      White Ware, and White Ware. Other types illustrated: Zuni
      Polychrome, Kiapkwa Polychrome, Laguna Polychrome, and
      Isleta Polychrome.
      Santa Clara Black, San Juan Polychrome, Tunyo Polychrome,
      San Ildefonso Matte Black-on-black by Maria Martinez and by

Isabel. One Pima Black-on-red bowl.

888. Walling, Barbara; Thompson, Richard A.; Dalley, Gardiner
F.; and Weder, Dennis G. 1986 "Excavations at Quail Creek."
Cultural Resource Series, No. 20, Bureau of Land Management,
Salt Lake City, Utah.
Western Anasazi ceramics by Thompson, pp. 351-380.
Points out the inadequacy of Colton's early classification of
ceramics from the western Anasazi area. New type names are
proposed for western analogs of the Tusayan Series. For the
Virgin Series these names are given to indicate the western
source of manufacture: Mesquite Gray, Mesquite Black-on-
gray, Hildale Black-on-gray, Glendale Black-on-gray, Orderville Black-on-gray, Pipe Springs Black-on-gray, and Parashant Black-on-gray. For the Moapa Series the following new
names are presented: Boysag Black-on-gray, Slide Mountain
Black-on-gray, Poverty Mountain Black-on-gray, Whitemore
Black-on-gray, Fern Glen Black-on-gray, and Tuckup Black-
on-gray. Kanab Black-on-red is suggested for a local slipped
black-on-red type with a sand temper. A polychrome type is
named Kanab Polychrome. Types illustrated are Washington
Black-on-gray, Mesquite Gray, North Creek Gray, Parashant
Black-on-gray, St. George Black-on-gray, Mesquite Black-on-
gray, Orderville Black-on-gray, Trumbull Black-on-gray, Hildale Black-on-gray, Kanab Black-on-red, Hurricane Black-on-
gray, Pipe Spring Black-on-gray, Glendale Black-on-gray,
Middleton Black-on-red, Nankoweap Polychrome, Tusayan Black-
on-red, North Creek Corrugated, North Creek Black-on-gray,
and Moapa Black-on-gray.

Ward, Albert A. See entry No. 900.

889. Warren, A. Helene. 1968 "Petrographic Notes on Glaze-Paint
Pottery." In Charles H. Lange, The Cochiti Dam Archaeological Salvage Project, Part I, Report on the 1963 Season, Museum of New Mexico Research Records, No. 6, pp. 184-197,
Santa Fe, New Mexico.
"The petrographic studies of temper materials at LA6455,
the Alfred Herrera Site, in the Cochiti area indicates that at
least three major successive ceramic traditions developed during the period of occupation. These traditions were related
to specific pottery types and may reflect either local or outside influences. The importance of defining chronologically
the centers of production and source material usage becomes
apparent when attempting to establish the nature and direction
of these influences," p. 196.
"The variation of temper material in the Glaze A pottery
types, particularly Agua Fria Glaze-on-red, is consistent with
the concept of a new and developing tradition. Local potters
were experimenting with new materials or adapting the old.
The scattering occurrence of non-local temper varieties indicates that there was diverse, if not abundant, trade with

neighboring areas. From the data now available, there is no
way of determining if the intrusive wares preceded or were
contemporary with the production of local pottery," p. 197.
"The Cieneguilla and Largo Glaze-on-yellow types reflect a
temper use differing from the earlier Glaze A types.... Although the specific source of the temper has not been located,
the 'augite latite' appears to be from the Espinaso volcanic
series. Outcrops are within five or ten miles of the Cochiti
area, a reasonable distance for importing raw materials," p.
197.
"During the Glaze C period, 'hornblende tuff' becomes the
predominant temper variety, while other varieties fall into dis-
use.... Since the number of Glaze C, D and E sherds at
LA6455 is small, they probably represent trade wares at this
particular site. This disappearance of other temper varieties
at this time points to a temporary abandonment of the site.
Subsequent occupation of the third architectural component was
probably intermittent, with little or no pottery being made at
this site," p. 197.

890. Warren, A. Helene. 1970 "Notes on Manufacture and Trade
      of Rio Grande Glazes." Artifact, Vol. 8, No. 4, pp. 1-7, El
      Paso Archaeological Society, El Paso, Texas.
      "Glaze paint began to replace carbon and mineral paints in
      the Rio Grande Valley shortly after AD 1300 when skilled pot-
      ters arrived from the west. Extensive trade was carried out
      from the beginning of manufacture through the 400 years of
      production of glaze wares. Determination of the centers of
      manufacture and trade of the glazes was made by establishing
      distribution patterns of wares containing a particular temper-
      ing material. The Tonque Pueblo was the major trading center
      in the 15th and 16th centuries, with small centers at San
      Lazaro and Abo. Pueblo trade continued with the Plains In-
      dians well into the 19th century and was evidently an integral
      and indispensable part of the prehistoric and historic economy
      of the Southwest," p. 1.

891. Warren, A. Helene. 1974 "Tonque, One Pueblo's Glaze Pot-
      tery Industry." El Palacio, Vol. 76, No. 2, pp. 36-42.
      "For nearly 200 years, a large prehistoric pueblo on the
      Arroyo Tonque, east of Bernalilo, New Mexico, was the site
      of a flourishing ceramic industry that dominated the economy
      of the Middle Rio Grande Pueblos, particularly in the Santo
      Domingo Valley. During the 15th and 16 centuries, the skilled
      potters of Tonque Pueblo (LA2401) supplied well over half and
      sometimes nearly all of the glaze decorated pottery used in con-
      temporary villages," p. 36.
      A map of the distribution of Glaze C Tonque Wares in the
      middle Rio Grande is presented on page 40. Classification of
      Rio Grande Glaze wares modified from Mera (1933) is included.

892. Warren, A. Helene. 1977a "Eighteenth Century Historic Pottery of the Cochiti District." Pottery Southwest, Vol. 4, No.
1, January, pp. 2-3.
    Discusses influences from the Spanish on Pueblo pottery of
the late 18th century and the possibility of Mesa-American potters among the settlers from the south. Author indicates Glaze
F pottery recovered in this district was probably produced at
Galisteo Pueblo.

893. Warren, A. Helene. 1977b "Appendix I: New Dimensions in
the Study of Prehistoric Pottery." In Richard Chapman and
Jan Biella (Eds.), Archaeological Investigations in Cochiti
Reservoir, New Mexico, Volume 2: Excavation and Analysis
1975 Season, pp. 363-374, Office of Contract Archaeology,
University of New Mexico, Albuquerque, New Mexico.
    "Observations concerning manufacturing practices and eco-
nomic considerations of prehistoric ceramics in the Middle Rio
Grande have been made, and guidelines and hypotheses for
further studies have been made. New methods or techniques
for applying petrographic analyses to the study of archaeological materials were used and are described in this report....
More than anything else the results of the more recent studies
of the Rio Grande glazes in the Cochiti district emphasize the
need for use of multiple or varied classification systems within any research project," p. 364.

894. Warren, A. Helene. 1977c "Chapter 5, Prehistoric and Historic Ceramic Analysis." In Richard Chapman and Jan Biella
(Eds.), Archaeological Investigations in Cochiti Reservoir,
New Mexico, Volume 2: Excavation and Analysis 1975 Season,
pp. 97-100, Office of Contract Archaeology, University of New
Mexico, Albuquerque, New Mexico.
    "The pottery from 24 excavated sites in Cochiti Reservoir
indicate almost continuous occupation of the area from about
AD 1175 to the present day," p. 100. A useful list of dates
and distinguishing features for the following types is included:
Santa Fe Black-on-white, Galisteo Black-on-white, Wiyo Black-
on-white, Abiquiu Black-on-gray, Bandelier Black-on-gray,
Agua Fria Glaze-on-red, San Clemente Glaze Polychrome, Ciene-
guilla Glaze-on-yellow, Cieneguilla Glaze Polychrome, Largo
Glaze-on-yellow, Largo Glaze Polychrome, Espinozo Glaze Polychrome, San Lazaro Glaze Polychrome, Puaray Glaze Polychrome,
Kotyiti Glaze-on-yellow, Kotyiti Glaze-on-red, Kotyiti Glaze
Polychrome, Kwahe'e Black-on-white, Tewa Polychrome, Posuge
Red, "Tewa" Black-on-red, Kapo Black, Potsui'i Incised, Ogapoge Polychrome, Powhoge Polychrome, Puname Polychrome,
and Casitas Red-on-black.

895. Warren, A. Helene. 1979a "Chapter 12, Historic Pottery of
the Cochiti Reservoir Area." In Richard Chapman and Jan
Biella (Eds.), Archaeological Investigations in Cochiti Reservoir,

New Mexico, Volume 4; Adaptive Change in the Northern Rio
Grande Valley, pp. 235-245, Office of Contract Archaeology,
University of New Mexico, Albuquerque, New Mexico.
   This study of pottery in the Cochiti area includes a sum-
mary of previous studies, pottery of the exploration and colo-
nization phases, Pueblo revolt and reconquest phase, colonial
Mexican and territorial phases, and a summary of pottery
classifications of the Cochiti study area.

896. Warren, A. Helene. 1979b "Glaze Paint Wares of the Upper
      Middle Rio Grande." In Richard Chapman and Jan Biella (Eds.),
      Archaeological Investigations in Cochiti Reservoir, New Mexico,
      Volume 4: Adaptive Change in the Northern Rio Grande Val-
      ley, pp. 187-216, Office of Contract Archaeology, University
      of New Mexico, Albuquerque, New Mexico.
         "For nearly 400 years, the Pueblo Indians living on the
      mesas and in the canyons of the southern Pajarito Plateau,
      Mesa Negra, and the upper Santo Domingo Basin used Rio
      Grande glaze paint pottery for every day culinary wares.
      Intermittent mineralogical studies during the past 10 years of
      glaze paint pottery from 47 archaeological sites in the upper
      middle Rio Grande region are summarized and reviewed in
      this report. By observing the variables between two inter-
      related pottery and temper classification systems, it has been
      possible to make observations about numerous aspects of the
      behavior of the populations who produced the pottery," p. 187.
         Major topics included in this valuable study are origins of
      the Rio Grande Glazes, estimated dates of manufacture of all
      major glaze types, and a list of Rio Grande glaze paint sites
      in the Upper Middle Rio Grande Valley. Also presented are
      a map showing the locations of 47 sites used in this study and
      maps showing the sites with Glaze A through Glaze F types of
      pottery.

897. Warren, A. Helene. 1981 "The Micaceous Pottery of the Rio
      Grande." In Albert H. Schroeder (Ed.), Collected Papers in
      Honor of Erik Kellerman Reed, Papers of the Archaeological
      Society of New Mexico, No. 6, pp. 149-167, Albuquerque, New
      Mexico.
         Reviews previous research on micaceous pottery in the Rio
      Grande region and discusses problems related to technology,
      cultural affiliations and origins. Lists time span, manufactur-
      ing technology, source of mica, and distribution of 20 South-
      western pottery types.

898. Warren, A. Helene. 1981a "A Petrographic Study of the Ce-
      ramics of Four Historic Sites of the Galisteo Basin, New Mexi-
      co." Pottery Southwest, Vol. 8, No. 2, April, pp. 2-4.
         "In summary, the pottery of the four pueblos indicates that
      potters were in residence at each of the pueblos, but that only
      San Marcos became a major ceramic producer. Economics and

social interaction among the four pueblos and to a limited extent with Pecos Pueblo is suggested by the distribution of the temper types at the sites. Temper studies at these sites and numerous other Rio Grande pueblos have enabled certain chronological refinements within the Rio Grande Glaze wares, which in turn can be used to estimate periods of occupation and abandonment of a site on the basis of presence or absence of a certain trade pottery," p. 4.

899. Warren, A. Helene. 1985 "San Marcial Problem." Pottery Southwest, Vol. 12, No. 4, pp. 1-2.
     Points out the importance of petrographic analysis to determine the constituents of pottery paste and temper.

900. Ward, Albert A. 1971 "A Multicomponent Site with a Desert Culture Affinity, Near Window Rock, Arizona." Plateau, Vol. 43, No. 3, pp. 120-131.
     "A wide range of ceramics suggests the site consists of two components: (1) a non-ceramic occupation represented by the Pinto Basin complex finds and (2) a long Anasazi occupation represented by the ceramics," p. 120. Types found were mainly Tusayan Gray Ware and Tusayan Corrugated.

901. Washburn, Dorothy K. 1976 "Symmetry Analysis of Ceramic Design." Pottery Southwest, Vol. 3, No. 3, July, pp. 3-5.
     The use of the analysis of the symmetry of pottery design to determine the closeness of potters in time and space.

902. Washburn, Dorothy K. 1977 "A Symmetry Analysis of Gila Area Ceramic Design." Papers of the Peabody Museum of Archaeology and Ethnology, No. 68, Cambridge, Massachusetts.
     Description and classification of pottery from four sites of the Upper Gila based on design analysis. Types analyzed and illustrated are Wingate Black-on-red, St. Johns Black-on-red, Tularosa Black-on-white, St. Johns Polychrome, Pinedale Polychrome, Springerville Polychrome, Showlow Polychrome, St. Johns Black-on-orange, and Reserve Black-on-white.
     "In conclusion, the method of symmetry analysis of ceramic design is suggested to be a highly systematic analytical tool," p. 188.

903. Washburn, Dorothy K. 1984 "The Usefulness of Typological Analysis for Understanding Aspects of Southwestern Pottery: Some Conflicting Returns from Design Analysis." In A. P. Sullivan and J. L. Hantman, Regional Analysis of Prehistoric Ceramic Variation: Contemporaries of the Cibola Whitewares, Anthropological Research Papers, No. 31, Arizona State University, Tempe, Arizona.
     Abstract: "This paper investigates typologically-defined ceramic sequences by analyzing how designs vary temporally and spatially. The assumption which implicitly underlies a

typological sequence taken from a stratigraphic sequence--that
types evolve into one another--will be shown from design
analysis to be qualified by the fact that (1) identical designs
crosscut ware sequences and (2) design layout discontinuities
exist within a ware sequence," p. 120.

904. Washburn, Dorothy K. and Matson, R. G. 1985 "Use of
      Multidimensional Scaling to Display Sensitivity of Symmetry
      Analysis of Patterned Design to Spatial and Chronological
      Change."   In Ben Nelson (Ed.), Decoding Prehistoric Ceramics,
      pp. 75-101, Southern Illinois University Press, Carbondale,
      Illinois.
          The authors' analysis "exhibits the ability of symmetry analy-
      sis to define stylistic relationships among sites. They employ
      unstandardized metric multidimensional scaling techniques to
      compare frequencies of use of symmetry classes that structure
      Puebloan ceramic design. They suggest that their units of
      measurement-geometric motions that generate repeated pat-
      terns--may be better suited to the ranking assumptions of
      scaling programs than are types, design elements, or other
      forms of data. Their data are selected from previously in-
      vestigated sites so that the scaling results can be compared
      with and checked against those of other methods. Three tests
      show that the combined analyses can accurately map site loca-
      tions over broad regions as well as within more localized areas
      and can order sites through time," p. 8.

905. Wasley, William W. 1959 "Cultural Implications of Style Trends
      in Southwestern Prehistoric Pottery: Basketmaker III to
      Pueblo II in West Central New Mexico." Ph.D. dissertation,
      University of Arizona, Tucson, Arizona.
          Descriptions of Cerro Colorado Red and Cerro Colorado
      Plain. "Ceramic material recovered during the excavation of
      the Cerro Colorado site near Quemado in west central New
      Mexico ... has been analyzed in terms of the normal techni-
      ques for differentiating pottery types and ceramic varieties.
      This analysis was used as the basis for dating the occupation
      of this site from about AD 600-1100 and for building an in-
      ternal chronology based on five ceramic periods," abstract.
      The nine styles represented in the pottery of the Cerro Colo-
      rado are Lino, Kana-a, Black Mesa, Sosi, Dogoszhi, Puerco,
      Tularosa, Dos Cabezas, and Three Circle. The three stylistic
      traditions defined are Kana-a and Tularosa belonging to the
      Anasazi culture and the Three Circle which belongs to the
      Mogollon culture.

906. Wasley, William W. 1960 "Temporal Placement of Alma Neck-
      banded." American Antiquity, Vol. 25, No. 4, pp. 599-603,
      Salt Lake City, Utah.
          "Alma Neckbanded is a horizon marker for Mogollon 3....
      Apparently first appeared in Southwestern U.S. in AD 600-700
      and continued to be made to about 950," p. 599.

907. Wasley, William W. and Johnson, Alfred E. 1965 "Salvage Archaeology in Painted Rocks Reservoir, Western Arizona." Anthropology Papers of the University of Arizona, No. 9, Tucson, Arizona.
    Discussion and illustrations of the following types of pottery: Gila Butte Red-on-buff, sherds, p. 12; Gila Plain: Gila Bend Variety, pp. 12-13, 54; Santa Cruz Red-on-buff, p. 26; Sacaton Red-on-buff, p. 26; and Tanque Verde Red-on-brown, p. 55. Native pottery very similar to Snaketown plain ware, lacks mica found in Snaketown. Appendix A-- Norton Allen Collection, Gila Butte Red-on-buff, p. 93; Santa Cruz Red-on-buff, pp. 94-95; and Sacaton Red-on-buff, pp. 95-98; Black Mesa Black-on-white, p. 101; Sacaton Buff, p. 101; Tanque Verde Red-on-brown, p. 106; and Roosevelt Black-on-white, p. 106.

908. Waterman, Robert M. R. and Blinman, Eric. 1986 "Modified Sherds, Unidirectional Abrasion, and Pottery Scrapers." Pottery Southwest, Vol. 13, No. 2, pp. 4-7.
    Report of an analysis of over 900 reworked sherds from the Dolores Archaeological Project. Drumlins on the edges of pottery scrapers are shown to indicate unidirectional use of these artifacts. Thus, the presence of pressing drumlins can be used to identify fragments or whole modified sherds as pottery scrapers.

909. Waters, Michael R. 1982 "The Lowland Patayan Ceramic Typology." In Randall H. McGuire and Michael B. Schiffer, Hohokam and Patayan: Prehistory of Southwestern Arizona, pp. 537-570, Academic Press, New York, New York.
    Revisions of 17 Patayan pottery types named or described by Malcolm Rogers in 1945. Types described are Black Mesa Buff, Black Mesa Red-on-buff, Colorado Beige, Colorado Red-on-beige, Colorado Red, Tumco Buff, Tumco Red-on-buff, Salton Buff, Salton Red-on-buff, Topoc Buff, Topoc Red-on-buff, Parker Buff, Parker Red-on-buff, Palomas Buff, Palomas Red-on-buff, Colorado Buff, and Colorado Red-on-buff. A discussion of the disagreement between Malcolm Rogers and Albert Schroeder on Patayan ceramic typology. Waters points out Schroeder's typology is based primarily on differences in temper. He believes temper materials are not different enough to distinguish types. He follows Rogers typology which is based on form differences such as rim shape.

910. Watson, Don. 1961 Indians of the Mesa Verde. Mesa Verde Museum Association, Mesa Verde National Park, Colorado.
    Illustrations of Mesa Verde pottery. Mesa Verde Black-on-white, pp. 51-55, corrugated jar.

911. Watson, Patty Jo. 1977 "Design Analysis of Painted Pottery." American Antiquity, Vol. 42, No. 3, pp. 381-393.

"She reviews painted pottery analyses in the Near East
and Southwestern United States and makes a strong plea for
an approach which combines recovery and analysis of archaeological data with ethnographic and sociological observations of
living societies. It is clear that this approach offers considerable promise in achieving and understanding of ceramic
design and transmission of design elements in prehistoric pottery," p. 381.

912. Watson, Patty Jo; LeBlanc, Steven; and Redman, Charles L.
      1980 "Aspects of Zuni Prehistory: Preliminary Report on Ex-
      cavations and Survey in the El Morro Valley of New Mexico."
      Journal of Field Archaeology, Vol. 7, No. 2, pp. 201-218.
      Stylistic analysis of the painted pottery from the El Morro
      sites by Keith Kintigh.

913. Way, Karen L. 1979 "Early Pueblo Occupation in Southern
      Tularosa Basin, New Mexico." In Jornada Mogollon Archaeology:
      Proceedings of the First Jornada Conference, pp. 41-45, New
      Mexico State University, Las Cruces, New Mexico.
      A description of the pottery found in this area. Based on
      the pottery present, the occupation span for the recorded
      sites in the area is concluded to be from AD1100-1150 to AD
      1230-1260. An illustration of El Paso Polychrome jar rim pro-
      files.

914. Way, Kathy Ann. 1975 "An Introduction to Pueblo Pottery."
      In Portrait of the Earth, Art of the Pueblo Potter, catalog of
      an exhibit at Chaffey College, Alta Loma, California, June 1-
      July 3, 1975.
      This exhibit catalog gives a brief introduction and descrip-
      tion of the methods of manufacture of Pueblo pottery. Nine
      pueblos are included, the outstanding potters and a photo of
      one vessel from each pueblo. The pueblos represented are
      Acoma, Cochiti, San Ildefonso, San Juan, Santa Clara, Santo
      Domingo, Zia, Zuni, and Hopi.

915. Weaver, Donald E. 1977 "Investigations Concerning the Ho-
      hokam Classic Period in the Lower Salt River Valley, Arizona."
      Arizona Archaeologist, No. 9, March, Phoenix, Arizona.
      Gila Plain was the dominant type at Pueblo del Monte. Salt
      Red was frequent with decorated types of Casa Grande Red-on-
      buff, Gila Polychrome, and Tonto Polychrome infrequent. Casa
      Grande Red-on-buff and Gila Polychrome are illustrated.

916. Weed, Carol S. 1970 "Two Twelfth Century Burials from the
      Hopi Reservation." Plateau, Vol. 43, No. 1, pp. 27-38.
      "The site produced two burials dating from Ca. AD 1125,
      associated funeral offerings and a mealing and massed sherd
      area. The funeral offerings consist of some 16 whole and re-
      storable vessels, many of which prove to be variants on

Tusayan White Ware and Little Colorado White Ware themes,"
p. 27. Vessels of the following types are illustrated: Aberrant Black Mesa Black-on-white and Sosi Black-on-white design
jar, p. 35; Flagstaff Black-on-white, pp. 35-36; Sosi Black-on-
white, p. 35; Verde Black-on-gray, p. 36; and Tusayan Applique, p. 36.

917. Weide, David L. 1978 "Temper Analysis of Southern Nevada
      Prehistoric Ceramics: A test Case of X-ray Diffraction." In
      Richard A. Thompson (Ed.), Western Anasazi Reports, Vol.
      1, No. 3, pp. 177-183, Museum of Southern Utah, Cedar City,
      Utah.
          "X-ray analysis of a very small sample (three types) of
      potsherds from southwestern Utah and southern Nevada and
      one sample of fluvial sand from Muddy River indicates that the
      green and red temper component of the ceramics is olivine with
      minor amounts of iron-stained quartz," p. 181.

918. Weigand, Phil C. 1976 "Suggestions on the Cleaning of
      Striated, Brushed, and Corrugated Ceramics." Pottery South-
      west, Vol. 3, No. 3, pp. 2-3.
          Layers of mud on some vessels are post firing coverings
      purposely used to make cooking heat more even and prolong
      life of the vessel. Mud layers such as this should not be
      cleaned from vessels until they have been mapped and measured.

919. Weigand, Phil C. 1977 "Rio Grande Glaze Sherds in Western
      Mexico." Pottery Southwest, Vol. 4, No. 1, January, pp. 3-5.
          A few Largo Glaze-on-yellow sherds were found at Atitlan-
      Las Cuevas Citadel located in the highland lake valleys due
      west of Guadalajara, Jalisco, Mexico. This is the furthest
      south record of this type.

920. Wendorf, Fred. 1950 "A Report on the Excavation of a Small
      Ruin Near Point of Pines, East Central Arizona." University
      of Arizona Social Science Bulletin, No. 19, Tucson, Arizona.
          Descriptions of the following pottery types: Kinishba Red,
      Kinishba Polychrome, and Point of Pines Polychrome (called
      Fourmile Polychrome: Point of Pines variety).

921. Wendorf, Fred. 1953 "Archaeological Studies in Petrified
      Forest National Monument." Museum of Northern Arizona Bul-
      letin, No. 27, Flagstaff, Arizona.
          Notes on color and paste composition by Anna Shepard, pp.
      177-193. Description of Adamana Brown.

922. Wendorf, Fred. 1953a "Excavations at Te'ewi." In F. Wen-
      dorf, Salvage Archaeology in the Chama Valley, New Mexico,
      School of American Research Monograph, No. 17, Santa Fe,
      New Mexico.
          Description of salvage excavations in 1950-51. Types found

were Santa Fe Black-on-white, Wiyo Black-on-white, Biscuit A,
Biscuit B, Sankawi Black-on-cream, Potsuwi'i Incised, and mica
culinary. Illustrations of Biscuit ware doughnut vessel, Potsuwi'i Incised, worked sherds, and clay pipes. Based on excavations some relationships among early Tewa types are
brought out. Discussion of possible relationships of some
types to plains pottery.

923. Wendorf, Fred; Fox, Nancy; and Lewis, O. L. (Editors). 1956
Pipeline Archaeology. Laboratory of Anthropology and Museum
of Northern Arizona, Santa Fe and Flagstaff.
Description of Tohatchi Banded. A ceramic analysis is pre-
sented of the pottery recovered in the various projects. New
Mexico Section, Fig. 8. Illustration of sherds from LA2498:
Kana-a Gray, Kiatuthlanna Black-on-white, Red Mesa Black-on-
white, Kana-a Black-on-white; Fig. 15, sherds from LA2520,
Mesa Verde Black-on-white; Fig. 18, sherds from LA2480,
Pueblo: Gallup Black-on-white, and Indented Gray Corrugated;
Fig. 28, sherds from LA2491: Lino gray, Kana-a gray, Kana-
a Black-on-white, Black Mound Black-on-white, Piedra Black-
on-white and Rosa Black-on-white; Fig. 36, McElmo Black-on-
white ladle from LA2497, Pueblo house unit; Fig. 38, Fig. 38,
sherds from LA2497; Red Mesa Black-on-white, Gallup Black-
on-white, Escavada Black-on-white and McElmo Black-on-white.
Sherds of the above types in Figs. 47 and 48. Fig. 56,
sherds from LA2507: La Plata Piedra Black-on-white, Twin
Trees Black-on-white and Forestdale Smudged; Fig. 69, pottery vessels from LA2508: Red Mesa Black-on-white and Kana-
a Neckbanded; Fig. 73, two modern Navajo jars; Fig. 118,
sherds of Red Mesa Black-on-white; Fig. 119, sherds of Escavada Black-on-white and Gallup Black-on-white; Fig. 120,
McElmo Black-on-white; Fig. 200, sherds from LA2640: Socorro
Black-on-white, North Plains Black-on-red and Wingate Black-
on-red; Fig. 201, vessels, Pilares Fine Banded and Northern
Gray Corrugated; Fig. 227, sherds, Puerco Black-on-white
and early Klageto Black-on-white; Fig. 228, pitchers from
LA2675, Gallup Black-on-white and McElmo Black-on-white;
Fig. 140, Puerco Black-on-white sherds; Fig. 241, Gallup
Black-on-white sherds; Fig. 258, vessels of Red Mesa Black-
on-white from burial LA2701; and Fig. 260, banded sherds of
Kana-a Gray and Tohatchi Banded.

924. Wendorf, Fred and Peckham, Stewart. 1957 "A Mimbres Pueblo Near Glenwood, New Mexico." Highway Salvage Archaeology, No. 13, pp. 71-84, New Mexico State Highway Department, Museum of New Mexico, Santa Fe, New Mexico.
Pithouse pottery types found were Alma Plain, Alma Rough,
San Francisco Red, Reserve Smudged, and possible Mimbres
Plain Corrugated. Painted types recovered were Mogollon Red-
on-brown, Three Circle Red-on-white, Mimbres Boldface Black-
on-white, and Classic Mimbres Black-on-white. Sherds from

the pueblo and kiva were Mimbres Boldface Black-on-white,
Mimbres Plain Corrugated, Alma Plain, and Reserve Smudged.
Photos of sherds of all the above types.

925. Wetherington, Ronald K. 1968 Excavations at Pot Creek
      Pueblo. Fort Burgwin Research Center, No. 6, Taos, New
      Mexico.
          Report of excavations done at Pot Creek Pueblo during
      1957-1967 seasons. Section C: Ceramics, pp. 45-60. Types
      described and illustrated: Talpa Black-on-white, p. 51, Figs.
      26, 33-36; Taos Black-on-white, p. 51, Figs. 26-30; Santa Fe
      Black-on-white, p. 54, Figs. 31-32; Taos Gray, p. 59, Figs.
      40-42; Taos Corrugated, p. 60, Figs. 26, 38; Taos Incised,
      p. 60, Fig. 39; and Taos Punctate, p. 60, Fig. 39. Illustra-
      tion of worked sherds, Fig. 43; rim profiles, Fig. 37; and
      tubular clay pipes, Fig. 44.

926. Weymouth, John W. 1973 "X-Ray Diffraction Analysis of Pre-
      historic Pottery." American Antiquity, Vol. 30, No. 3, pp.
      339-344.
          "This is a preliminary report on a quantitative method for
      grouping prehistoric pottery using X-ray diffraction techni-
      ques. Of the various analytical methods that have been applied
      to the analysis of pottery, X-ray diffraction techniques have
      been among the least used, and then usually to obtain qualita-
      tive information. Most analytic methods measure the relative
      abundance of chemical elements, but diffraction patterns give
      information on the crystalline substance in the pottery. In
      this study, attention is directed to the crystalline components
      of the temper rather than the clays or their derivatives. The
      method groups pottery according to the relative concentrations
      of such minerals as quartz and calcite. Thus, success depends
      on a reasonable consistency in the use of tempering material
      by pottery makers at one time and place. I have examined a
      number of sherds from different sites in Iowa and Missouri
      supplied by Dale R. Henning, University of Nebraska. The
      results so far indicate that it is possible to group prehistoric
      pottery by a quantitative analysis of the X-ray diffraction pat-
      terns of the temper in the pottery," p. 339.

927. Whallon, Robert. 1972 "A New Approach to Pottery Typology."
      American Antiquity, Vol. 37, No. 1, pp. 13-33.
          A good technical article that suggests a different typology
      for eastern U.S. ceramics.

928. Wheat, Joe Ben. 1948 "A Double Walled Jar from Chihuahua."
      Kiva, Vol. 14, Nos. 1-4, pp. 8-10.
          An unusual double walled Ramos Polychrome jar is described
      and illustrated.

929. Wheat, Joe Ben. 1954 "Crooked River Village." University
      of Arizona Social Science Bulletin, No. 24, Tucson, Arizona.

A pithouse of Black River Branch of Mogollon Culture.
Pottery discussed on pp. 81-104. Descriptions of Alma Plain:
Point of Pines variety, pp. 82-85, and Alma Plain: Black River
variety, pp. 85-86.

930. Wheat, Joe Ben. 1955 "Mogollon Culture Prior to AD 1000."
      American Anthropologist, Vol. 57, No. 2, Part 3, Memoir 82,
      Menasha, Wisconsin.
         Chapter on Mogollon pottery with drawings of vessel shapes
      and frequency of shapes by types. Good summary of Mogollon
      culture.

931. Wheat, Joe Ben. 1955a "Prehistoric People of the Northern
      Southwest." Grand Canyon Natural History Association Bulletin,
      No. 12, Grand Canyon, Arizona.
         Pottery photographs: Basketmaker III bowl and jar, p. 18;
      early developmental Pueblo pitchers, Black-on-white and neck-
      banded, p. 23; and late developmental Black-on-white olla, p.
      29.

932. Wheat, Joe Ben; Gifford, J. C.; and Wasley, W. W. 1958
      "Ceramic Variety, Type Cluster, Ceramic System in Southwest
      Pottery Analysis." American Antiquity, Vol. 24, No. 1, pp.
      34-46.
         Supports point of view that types and varieties should be
      combined into clusters and systems.

933. White, Leslie A. 1932 "The Acoma Indians, People of the Sky
      City." 47th Annual Report of the Bureau of American Eth-
      nology, Washington, D.C. (reprint by Rio Grande Press, 1979).
         Color illustrations of Acoma Polychrome vessels Ca. 1970
      in Pls. 25-30, in reprint.

934. Whittlesey, Stephanie M. 1974 "Identification of Imported Ce-
      ramics Through Functional Analysis of Attributes." Kiva, Vol.
      40, Nos. 1-2, pp. 101-112.
         "The use of technical ceramic analysis is not always feasible
      for the archaeologist seeking information concerning the locale
      of ceramic production. An alternative method for differentiat-
      ing imported from locally produced ceramics utilizing stylistic
      and functional attributes is suggested. This method is opera-
      tionalized in a functional analysis of three ceramic types from
      the Grasshopper Pueblo. The results of this analysis provide
      some cautionary implications for archaeologists interpreting be-
      havioral interactions by means of ceramic data," p. 101.

935. Wilkinson, Nancy M. 1977 "Arts and Crafts of the Gallina
      Culture." El Palacio, Vol. 65, No. 5, pp. 189-196.
         Described and illustrated are Gallina Utility and Gallina
      Black-on-white, subtypes of Gallina Plain Polished and Gallina
      Smudged.

936. Willey, Gordon R. 1966 An Introduction to American Archae-
      ology, Vol. I, North and Middle America. Prentice Hall, New
      York, New York.
           A general archaeology text with some discussion and illustra-
      tion of ceramics. Map of archaeological regions, p. 180. Illus-
      trations of San Francisco Red, p. 185; Alma Neckbanded, p.
      185; Tularosa Black-on-white, p. 194; Reserve Black-on-white,
      p. 195; Mimbres Black-on-white, p. 196; Kana-a Neckbanded,
      p. 213; Kana-a Black-on-white, p. 213; Kiatuthlanna Black-
      on-white, p. 214; Mancos Black-on-white, p. 214; Tusayan
      Polychrome, p. 215; Chaco Black-on-white, p. 216; Acoma Poly-
      chrome, p. 219; Santa Ana Polychrome, p. 218; Vahki Plain,
      p. 222; Sacaton Red-on-buff, p. 223; Santa Cruz Red-on-buff,
      p. 223; Casa Grande Red-on-buff, p. 223; Tonto Polychrome,
      p. 228; Ramos Polychrome, p. 240; and Playas Red, p. 241.

937. Wilson, C. Dean and Errickson, Mary P. 1985 "Formal De-
      scription and illustration of a new variety of Bluff Black-on-
      red from the Dolores Archaeological Program."

938. Wilson, John P. 1969 "Introduction to Ceramics of the Survey
      Area, Excerpted from the Sinagua and Their Neighbors." Ph.D.
      dissertation, Harvard University, Cambridge, Massachusetts.
           A good discussion of pottery collections from the Sinagua
      Culture. Descriptions of Diablo Black-on-white (mentioned)
      and Snowflake Black-on-white, pp. 308-315, Fig. 56. Illustra-
      tion of pottery discs, Fig. 55. Descriptions, Appendix III.
      "Early" Black Mesa Black-on-white, pp. 576-579, Fig. 68;
      Diablo Brown: Yaeger Variety, pp. 580-584; Diablo Brown,
      pp. 585-589; Diablo Red, pp. 590-592; Sunset Brown: Variety
      "B," pp. 593-597; Type II Corrugated, pp. 598-602, Fig. 75;
      Type IV Corrugated, pp. 603-607, Fig. 75; Type VII Corru-
      gated, pp. 608-611, Fig. 75; and Type VIII Corrugated, pp.
      612-615, Fig. 75.

939. Wilson, John P. and Peckham, Stewart. 1964 Type Descrip-
      tions of Chuska Valley Wares. Unpublished manuscript, Mu-
      seum of New Mexico, Santa Fe, New Mexico.
           Descriptions of new types of pottery found in the Chuska
      Valley including Bennett Gray, Hunter Corrugated, Sheep
      Springs Gray, Crozier Black-on-white, Tocito Gray, Drolet
      Black-on-white, Gray Hills Banded, Naschitti Black-on-white,
      Capt. Tom Corrugated, Taylor Black-on-white, Newcomb Cor-
      rugated, Brimhall Black-on-white, Blue Shale Corrugated,
      Theodore Black-on-white, Pena Black-on-white, Tunicha Black-
      on-white, Newcomb Black-on-white, Burnham Black-on-white,
      Chuska Black-on-white, Toadlena Black-on-white, Nava Black-
      on-white, Crumbled House Black-on-white, and Sanostee Red-
      on-orange. The primary distinguishing characteristic of Shu-
      ska Ware is the presence of a dark igneous rock (trachyte)
      in the temper.

940. Wilson, John P. and Warren, A. Helene. 1973 "New Pottery
      Type Described: Seco Corrugated." Awanyu, Vol. 1, No. 1,
      Archaeological Society of New Mexico, Albuquerque, New Mexico.
      Description of Seco Corrugated, pp. 12-13.

941. Wilson, L. W. W. 1918 "Hand Sign or Avanyu, A Note on a
      Pajaritan Biscuit-Ware Motif." American Anthropologist, n.s.,
      Vol. 20, No. 3, pp. 310-317, Lancaster, Pennsylvania.
          Concludes that this figure on pottery is not an Avanyu but
      is much more probably a hand sign. Hand signs are common
      on the rocks of Otowi, and this hand sign is universal across
      the ages and throughout the world.

942. Wilson, Olive. 1920 "The Survival of an Ancient Art." Art
      and Archaeology, Vol. 9, No. 1, pp. 25-29.
          Photographs of Tewa pottery making and polychrome, black-
      on-white, and polished black vessels, pp. 24-29.

943. Wimberly, Mark and Rogers, Alan. 1977 "Cultural Succes-
      sion, A Case Study: Archaeological Survey, Three Rivers
      Drainage, New Mexico." Artifact, Vol. 15, El Paso Archae-
      ological Society, El Paso, Texas.
          Summary: "We have suggested that from the earliest occupa-
      tions of the Three Rivers drainage to the present, there is
      evidence that human culture has repeatedly undergone succes-
      sional change. The response of human culture has invariably
      been to attempt to predict through succeedingly more complex
      systematic structures and relationships, the stresses which
      threaten it. However, it is also clear that invariably as cul-
      ture solutions to stress become more exact, and therefore com-
      plex, and adaptations represented by the culture become more
      specialized and therefore more susceptible to selection," p.
      462.
          Ceramics from 35 of the 55 sites surveyed were analyzed
      in the field. The authors state: "A somewhat modified ver-
      sion of the traditional typology was used in sorting the local
      ceramics." The types included in Native Brownware were
      Plain Brownware, Red Slipped Brownware, Native Black/Brown,
      and Native Red/Brown. Three Rivers Redware included Plain
      Three Rivers Redware, Red Slipped Redware, San Andres Red/
      Terra cotta, Three Rivers Red/Terra cotta, and Lincoln Black/
      Red. Three other probable local types were Corona or Ochoa
      Corrugated and Chupadero Black-on-white. Plain Brownware
      made up 75% and Plain Three River Redware 14% of the total
      of 5,612 sherds collected from all sites. The local ceramics
      are divided into seven time periods with tentative dates for
      each period. Analysis of the ceramics in this area supports
      the authors' conclusions: "Although one variable, composition
      of the clay, remains uncontrolled, it seems likely that the fre-
      quency of well-oxidized local pottery in the Three Rivers area
      was effected by change through time in the technology of ce-
      ramic manufacture, as well as availability of fuel," p. 416.

944. Windes, Thomas C. 1977 "Typology and Technology of Ana-
     sazi Ceramics." In Charles A. Reher (Ed.), Settlement and
     Subsistence Along the Lower Chaco River, pp. 279-369, CGP
     Survey, University of New Mexico, Albuquerque, New Mexico.
     A good chapter on the ceramics of this area, particularly
     the Chuska Valley types. The following types from the Chuska
     ceramic traditions are well described and illustrated:
        Chuska Gray Wares: Bennett Gray, pp. 299-300; Tocito
     Gray, pp. 300-302; Gray Hills Banded, p. 302; Newcomb Cor-
     rugated, pp. 302-305; Captain Tom Corrugated, p. 305; Blue
     Shale Corrugated, pp. 305-307; and Hunter Corrugated, p.
     307.
        Chuska White Ware--Mineral Paint Series: Drolet Black-on-
     white, p. 310; Naschitti Black-on-white, pp. 319; Taylor Black-
     on-white, pp. 310-312; and Brimhall Black-on-white, pp. 312-
     313.
        Chuska White Ware--Carbon Paint Series: Tunicha Black-
     on-white, pp. 313-315; Newcomb Black-on-white, pp. 315-317;
     Burnham Black-on-white, pp. 317-318; Chuska Black-on-white,
     p. 319; Toadlena Black-on-white, pp. 319-322; and Nava Black-
     on-white, pp. 322-324.
        Mesa Verde types: Mancos Gray, pp. 329-332; Mesa Verde
     Corrugated, pp. 332-333; Cortez Black-on-white, p. 333; Man-
     cos Black-on-white, pp. 333-335; McElmo Black-on-white, pp.
     335-337; and Mesa Verde Black-on-white, pp. 337-340.
        Cibola Ceramics: Red Mesa Black-on-white, p. 342; Esca-
     vada Black-on-white, pp. 342-345; Gallup Black-on-white, p.
     345; and Chaco Black-on-white, pp. 345-346.
        Illustration of a Tohatchi Banded jar. San Juan Red Ware,
     White Mountain Red Ware, and Tsegi Orange Ware were also
     found in small amounts.

945. Windes, Thomas C. 1984 "A View of the Cibola Whiteware
     from Chaco Canyon." In A. P. Sullivan and J. L. Hantman,
     Regional Analysis of Prehistoric Ceramic Variation: Contem-
     porary Studies of the Cibola Whitewares, Anthropological Re-
     search Papers, No. 31, p. 94, Arizona State University, Tempe,
     Arizona.
        "Previous Chaco Series typologies are reviewed, and the
     periods of popularity are questioned for those types found dur-
     ing the Pueblo II and III periods in Chaco Canyon. Based on
     recent work in Chaco Canyon, a revised Chaco Series is
     presented that reflects greater temporal sensitivity than past
     typologies," p. 94.
        Map of suggested area of greatest popularity for Bonita
     Phase Ceramic types. Illustrations of Gallup Black-on-white,
     Red Mesa Black-on-white and Chaco-McElmo Black-on-white.

946. Winter, Joseph C. 1975 "Hovenweep 1974." Archaeological
     Report No. 1, San Jose State University, San Jose, California.
        Chapter VI by Dorothy Washburn. Report of sherds

collected from the surface of 140 sites at Hovenweep. Types
found in descending frequency are Gray ware: Hovenweep
Gray, Mancos Gray, Moccasin Gray, and Chapin Gray; Corrugated ware: Hovenweep Corrugated and Mancos-Mesa Verde
Corrugated; Black-on-white wares: McElmo-Mesa Verde Black-
on-white, Mancos Black-on-white (mineral and carbon paint),
Cortez Black-on-white, Piedra Black-on-white, and Chapin
Black-on-white; Redware: Deadmans Black-on-red, Abajo Red-
on-orange, and Bluff Black-on-red. Illustrations of Mancos
Black-on-white designs and McElmo/Mesa Verde Black-on-white
designs, sherds, and a partial mug.

947.   Wiseman, Regge N. 1971 "A Mountain Lion Effigy Pipe from
       Southern New Mexico." Artifact, Vol. 9, No. 3, El Paso Ar-
       chaeological Society, El Paso, Texas.
          A mountain lion effigy pipe was excavated from the Smokey
       Bear Site (LA2112) in Lincoln County, New Mexico. The ce-
       ramic pipe is described and illustrated, Figs. 1 and 2.

948.   Wiseman, Regge N. 1981 "Playas Incised, Sierra Blanca Va-
       riety: A New Pottery Type in Jornada Mogollon." Trans-
       actions of the 16th Regional Symposium for Southeastern New
       Mexico and Western Texas, El Paso, Texas.
          Description of Playas Incised: Sierra Blanca Variety, not
       illustrated.

949.   Wiseman, Regge N. 1984 "Chupadero and Tabira' Black-on-
       white: Continuum or Dichotomy?" Kiva, Vol. 50, No. 1, pp.
       41-54.
          Abstract: "Alden C. Hayes and A. H. Warren, in recent
       publications on excavations at Gran Quivira in the Medano re-
       gion of New Mexico, suggest that Tabira Black-on-white pot-
       tery represents a break from the earlier Chupadero Black-on-
       white tradition. They further suggest, on the basis of ce-
       ramic, architectural, and burial data, that a migration of new
       peoples, possibly from the Zuni-White Mountains-Hopi region,
       was responsible for the inception of Tabira. New data and a
       reassessment of old data are used to question the validity of
       the Hayes-Warren interpretation," p. 41.

950.   Wiseman, Regge N. 1986 "An Initial Study of the Origins of
       Chupadero Black-on-white." Albuquerque Archaeological So-
       ciety Technical Note No. 2, January, Albuquerque, New Mexico.
          Analysis of black-on-white sherds from the Kite Site, cen-
       tral New Mexico. Chupadero Black-on-white sherds were
       separated on the basis of scoring of the nondecorated surfaces.
       Some non-scored sherds were classified as smooth Chupadero.
       This type is described in detail. Sherds are illustrated and
       forms are described. The relationship of Chupadero Black-on-
       white to contemporary and antecedent types is discussed.
          It was found that the regular and smooth Chupadero Black-

on-white have some systematic differences: undecorated surface treatment, design affinities, frequency of slipping and
bowl-jar ratios. The question of the usefulness of the variety
name "Casa Colorado Black-on-white" is discussed.

951. Withers, Arnold M. 1973 "Excavations at Valshni Village,
Arizona." Arizona Archaeologist, No. 7, W. T. Duering (Ed.),
Arizona Archaeological Society, Phoenix, Arizona.
        A report of the 1939-40 excavation of Valshni Village (ARIZ.
DD:1:11), a surface ruin 14 miles southwest of Sells, Arizona,
on the Papago Indian Reservation. "Owing to the total lack of
knowledge of the earlier phases in Papagueria, most of the
pottery types have never been recognized, and none have
ever been described. On the following pages are the technological analyses of these types as they occur in the Vamori
and Topawa Phases at Valshni Village. These include the two
local red-on-brown types and one redware type," p. 22.
        Local types described and illustrated are Vamori Red-on-
brown, pp. 22-23; Topawa Red-on-brown, pp. 27-32; and
Valshni Red, pp. 33-36. Sells Plain was also present but is
not described. Intrusive types recovered are described and
illustrated: Trincheras Purple-on-red: Specular iron paint
variety, pp. 37-41; Trincheras Purple-on-red: nonspecular
paint variety, pp. 42-43; Trincheras Polychrome, pp. 43-46;
and Altar Polychrome, pp. 46-48. Miscellaneous clay objects
described on pp. 53-55.

952. Withers, Arnold M. 1985 "Three Circle Red-on-white: An
Alternate to Oblivion." In Charles H. Lang (Ed.), Southwest
Culture History, Collected Papers in Honor of Albert H. Schroeder, Papers of the Archaeological Society of New Mexico, No.
10, Ancient City Press, Santa Fe, New Mexico.
        A good discussion of the dates of Three Circle Red-on-
white. Indicates dates for Three Circle Red-on-white may be
wrong and that it was contemporaneous with Mogollon Red-on-
brown in the Mogollon villages during the 8th and 9th centuries.
This type is probably the earliest in the Southwest to have a
white slip. Author suggests Three Circle Red-on-white is a
legitimate type but is a variant of Mogollon Red-on-brown.

953. Wolff, Eldon G. 1960 "Pottery Restoration." Curator, Vol.
3, No. 1, pp. 75-87.
        A good article with detailed descriptions and illustrations
for restoring either small or large portions of broken pottery
vessels.

954. Worman, F. C. V. 1969 Archaeological Investigations at the
U.S. Atomic Energy Commission's Nevada Test Site and Nuclear
Rocket Development Station. Los Alamos Scientific Laboratory
of the University of California, Los Alamos, New Mexico.
        Primary pottery found was Southern Paiute Brownware
which is briefly described and illustrated.

955. Wormington, H. Marie. 1955 "A Reappraisal of the Fremont
      Culture with a Summary of the Archaeology of the Northern
      Periphery." Denver Museum of Natural History Proceedings,
      No. 1, Denver, Colorado.
          Descriptions of Uinta Plain (synonym Turner Gray: Variety
      I) and Turner Gray (synonym Turner Gray: Variety II, gray
      rock temper).

956. Wormington, H. Marie. 1964 "Prehistoric Indians of the
      Southwest." Denver Museum of Natural History Series, No.
      7, Denver, Colorado.
          Illustrations of Developmental pottery, p. 67; Neckbanded,
      p. 68; Chaco Black-on-white, p. 88; Kayenta Black-on-white,
      p. 100; Mesa Verde Black-on-white, p. 95; Rio Grande Glaze,
      p. 112; Biscuit Ware, p. 113; Red-on-buff, p. 133; Salado
      Polychrome, p. 138; and Mimbres Black-on-white, p. 160.

957. Wormington, H. Marie and Neal, Arminta. 1951 The Story of
      Pueblo Pottery. Denver Museum of Natural History, Museum
      Pictorial No. 2, Denver, Colorado.
          Good brief introduction to prehistoric and historic pottery.
      Illustrations of unfired Basketmaker bowls, pp. 9-10; Basket-
      maker III Black-on-gray, p. 13; clay pipe, p. 14; Basket-
      maker figurines, p. 16; Neckbanded vessels, p. 17; Corrugated
      bowl, p. 18; Developmental Pueblo Black-on-white bowl, p. 19;
      Developmental Pueblo Black-on-white ladle, p. 20; Chaco
      Black-on-white pitcher, p. 21; Chaco Corrugated jar, p. 22;
      Mesa Verde Black-on-white bowl, p. 23; Mesa Verde Black-on-
      white mugs, p. 24; Kayenta Black-on-white bowl, p. 25; Tula-
      rosa Black-on-white jars, p. 26; Soccoro Black-on-white, p.
      27; Mimbres Black-on-white bowls, pp. 28-29; Puerco Black-on-
      red bowl, p. 30; Wingate Black-on-red bowl, p. 31; St. Johns
      Polychrome bowl, p. 32; Tonto Polychrome jar, p. 33; Jeddito
      Black-on-yellow, p. 34; Sikyatki Polychrome, p. 34; Abiquiu
      Black-on-gray, p. 35; and Rio Grande Glaze bowl, p. 35.
          Historic period: Photos of pottery making at San Ildefonso,
      pp. 38-42; San Lorenzo (Picuris) jar, p. 43; San Juan red
      and tan incised jar, p. 44; Santa Clara polished black, pp.
      45-46; San Ildefonso Polychrome jar, p. 47; San Ildefonso
      carved bowl, p. 48; Tesuque poster paint bowl, p. 49; Tesu-
      que figurine, p. 50; Cochiti Black-on-cream jar, p. 51; Santo
      Domingo Black-on-cream, p. 52; Santo Domingo bird effigy, p.
      53; Zia Polychrome jar, p. 54; Santa Ana Polychrome jar, p.
      54; Acoma Polychrome, p. 55; Isleta Polychrome jar, p. 55;
      Zuni Polychrome jar, p. 56; Zuni owl effigy, p. 57; Hopi Poly-
      chrome jar, p. 58; and Hopi tile, p. 59.

958. Wright, Barton. 1977 "Hopi Tiles." American Indian Art
      Magazine, Vol. 2, No. 4, Autumn, pp. 64-70.
          Descriptions of a little known and scarce ceramic form and
      illustration of a number of tiles.

959. Young, John N. 1972 "The Garden Canyon Site." Artifact, Vol. 10, No. 3, pp. 3-19, El Paso Archaeological Society, El Paso, Texas.
   Sixty whole or restorable vessels and a human clay figurine were found at this site. Types found were Babicomari Polychrome, Gila Polychrome, Tanque Verde, Rincon, and Rillito types. A human figurine and a Babicomari funerary bowl are illustrated.

960. Young, John N. 1982 "Salado Polychrome Pottery." In Collected Papers in Honor of John W. Runyan, Papers of the Archaeological Society of New Mexico, No. 7, Albuquerque Archaeological Society, New Mexico.
   A summary of some of the observations in the author's 1967 dissertation, The Salado Culture in Southwestern Prehistory. Observations on designs are made concerning dual-balanced designs, undecorated centers, life lines, life forms, and hachure. Observations are compared to the descriptions of Salado redware by Colton and Hargrave (1937) and Haury (1945). The major observations are that the red-based vessels are a variant of Tonto Polychrome rather than Gila Polychrome; some Gila Polychrome vessels cannot be distinguished from Pinto Polychrome, and the presence of intentional imperfections in the designs of Salado vessels are discussed. Drawings of designs on Gila, Pinto, and Tonto Polychromes are included.

961. Zahniser, Jack L. 1966 "Late Prehistoric Villages Southeast of Tucson, Arizona." Kiva, Vol. 31, No. 3.
   Rincon Valley southeast of Tcuson, Arizona. Sherd collections indicate the presence of Tucson Hohokam in the Rincon Valley from late colonial to middle classic times. Arizona BB14:44 site: Pottery, pp. 136-148. Primary types: 72% Gila, 8.8% Tanque Verde Red-on-brown. Four restorable vessels. Illustrations of Tanque Verde Red-on-brown jar, p. 137; Tanque Verde Red-on-brown jar and bowl, p. 138; Tanque Verde bowls and tray, p. 139; sherds, Tanque Verde Red-on-brown, p. 141; Rincon Rillito Red-on-brown, Roosevelt Black-on-white, and Playas Incised. Spindle whorls and sherd disc, p. 147.

962. Zaslow, Bert. 1977 "A Guide to Analyzing Prehistoric Ceramic Decorations by Symmetry and Pattern Mathematics and Archaeology." Pattern Mathematics and Archaeology, Anthropological Research Papers, No. 2, Arizona State University, Tempe, Arizona.
   Abstract: "An approach is presented for examining painted designs that are systematically repeated on ceramic vessels. The approach uses symmetry elements, which are defined mathematically, and presents the methods for covering band and surface areas with units of design to yield patterns. Symmetry and patterns are distinctive components of the decorative

art of prehistoric peoples and undergo evolutionary development. Knowledge about patterns is shown to lead to an understanding of the mechanics of constructing decorations. The
development and spread of different types of patterns among
prehistoric peoples represents important archaeological information. Specific suggestions are given for research in this field
of study."

963. Zaslow, Bert. 1986 "Symmetry and Contemporary Hopi Art."
      Kiva, Vol. 51, No. 4, pp. 233-253.
      Abstract: "One hundred fifty-eight contemporary Hopi
      ceramic decorations, dated ca. 1900-1983, have been analyzed,
      and their symmetry characteristics are described and tabulated.
      Against this background, relationships between symmetry fea-
      tures of contemporary Hopi designs and the Hopi world view,
      which were advanced by Greenberg (1975), are reexamined.
      No basis is found for relating the designs to the structure of
      the Hopi cosmos.
      Symmetry groups having three space dimensions, although
      not previously employed in archaeology or anthropology, are
      introduced in this paper. These groups are useful in describ-
      ing certain ceramic decorations, in studying three-dimensional
      concepts, such as cosmology, and in characterizing weaves,"
      p. 233.

964. Zaslow, Bert and Dittert, Alfred E. 1977 "Pattern Theory
      Used as an Archaeological Tool: A Preliminary Statement."
      Southwestern Lore, Vol. 43, No. 1, March, pp. 18-24.
      Abstract: "It is reported that the painted ceramic decora-
      tions of the prehistoric Indians of the American Southwest can
      be classified by mathematics. The Hohokam developed one-
      dimensional patterns or bands during the Pioneer Period, and
      characteristic two dimensional patterns appear on ceramics from
      the Colonial Period. A brief introduction to the mathematics
      of design repetition is given; and subsequently, a pattern
      analysis is presented. The ceramic painting selected for analy-
      sis reveals the mechanics by which plaited Hohokam patterns
      evolved in the early Sedentary Period," p. 18.

965. Zier, Christian J. 1976 "Excavations Near Zuni, New Mexico:
      1973." Museum of Northern Arizona Research Paper, No. 2,
      Anthropology Research Report 2, Flagstaff, Arizona.
      A report of the excavation and/or testing of seven archae-
      ological sites on the Zuni Indian Reservation. The sites are
      located within the right-of-way boundaries of a realigned sec-
      tion of Zuni Route 5 (Nutria Road) between New Mexico High-
      way 53 and Lower Nutria Village.
      Appendix B, "Ceramics," by Gale McPhearson: "A total of
      14,813 sherds and 20 restored vessels was recovered from the
      six Anasazi sites in the Nutria Z-5 excavations.... Analysis
      of the ceramics is based on established typologies. A descriptive

approach is used in cases where pottery varies from established definitions," p. 57.

All sherds were placed in five major groupings: White Mountain Redware, Cibola White Ware (Puerco-Chaco); Cibola White Ware (White Mountain Series); Corrugated Gray ware; Unclassified gray ware; and Mogollon Brown Ware. Any sherd not falling in one of these groups was placed in a "miscellaneous" category. A St. Johns Polychrome jar with an effigy handle, sherds, and Tularosa dippers and a bowl are shown in photographs.

LIST OF SOUTHWESTERN POTTERY
TYPES AND WARES

Following is a list of all published, and most unpublished, names of South-western pottery types, varieties, and wares in alphabetical order. This list is current as of 1986. The types listed cover a time span of 2,000 years from the beginnings of pottery making in the Southwest before the start of the Christian era to the contemporary Pueblo ceramics.

Dates are given for all dated types, wares, and varieties. The reader is referred to the descriptions cited for discussion of how these dates were determined. The best single source for tree-ring dates of prehistoric South-western pottery is An Appraisal of Tree-Ring dated Pottery in the Southwest (1966) by David Breternitz.

Synonyms (Syn.) are listed for all types and varieties with more than one name. The reader may refer to citations for the synonyms for complete information on the most widely accepted name.

Descriptions (Des.), both published and unpublished, are listed in chronological order. The few types and wares for which no descriptions could be found have citations to the references in which they were named.

Complete citations for each description may be found in the foregoing annotated bibliography. Descriptions that include illustrations of the pottery described are indicated by an asterisk.

Most of the published illustrations (Illus.) are listed in chronological order. These include photographs or drawn illustrations of whole vessels or sherds of the pottery type, variety, or ware.

LIST OF POTTERY TYPES AND WARES

Note: *=includes illustration

ABAJO BLACK-ON-GRAY
AD 700-850
Des. Brew, 1946; *Abel, 1955, 5A-1

ABAJO BLACK-ON-RED
Des. Olson, 1971

ABAJO POLYCHROME
AD 700-850
Des. *Martin, 1939; *Brew, 1946;
Abel, 1955, 5A-3; *Breternitz et
al., 1974; Dittert and Plog,
1980.
Illus. O'Bryan, 1950.

ABAJO RED-ON-ORANGE
AD 700-850
Syn. Abajo Black-on-gray, Abel,
1955; Abajo Polychrome, Abel,
1955.
Des. *Martin, 1939; *Brew, 1946;
*Abel, 1955, 5A-I; *Breternitz
et al., 1974; *Dittert and Plog,
1980.
Illus. Martin and Willis, 1940; Gladwin, 1957; Dittert and Eddy,
1963; Hayes, 1964; New Mexico
Univ., 1967; Lister and Lister,
1969; Gumerman, 1970.

ABAJO RED-ON-ORANGE: VARIETY
I
AD 700-850
Syn. Abajo Red-on-orange, Brew,
1946.
Des. *Forsyth, 1972.

ABIQUIU BLACK-ON-GRAY
AD 1375-1450
Syn. Biscuit A, Mera, 1934a.
Des. Kidder and Amsden, 1931;
Mera, 1934a; Hawley, 1936;
*Harlow, 1973; Warren, 1977c;
Dittert and Plog, 1980.
Illus. Kidder, 1915; Hewett, 1938;
Wormington, 1951; Barnett,
1973b.

ACOMA POLYCHROME
AD 1890-present
Des. *Bunzel, 1929; Kidder and
Shepard, 1936; Chapman, 1936b;
*Chapman, 1938; Ellis, 1966;
*Harlow, 1970; *Frank and Har-
low, 1974; *Dittert and Plog,
1980.
Illus. Stevenson, 1883; Underhill,
1944; Wormington, 1951; Feder,
1965; Willey, 1966; Tanner,
1968; White, 1932 (rep. 1973);
Arizona Highways, May 1974;
Dillingham, 1977; Barry, 1981;
Trimble, 1987.

ACOMITA POLYCHROME
AD 1750-1850
Des. *Harlow, 1970; Frank and
Harlow, 1974; Dittert and Plog,
1980.
Illus. Dillingham, 1977; Harlow,
1977.

ADAMANA BROWN
Early AD 300's
Des. Mera, 1934b; Hawley, 1936;
Colton and Hargrave, 1937; Wen-
dorf, 1953.

ADAMANA FUGITIVE RED
Pre AD 700-Ca. 800
Des. Mera, 1934b; Colton and Har-
grave, 1937.

ADAMANA POLYCHROME
Ca. AD 1300-1400
Des. Colton and Hargrave, 1937.
Illus. Martin and Willis, 1940.

AGUA FRIA GLAZE-ON-RED
AD 1315-1425
Syn. Glaze I-A, Kidder and Shep-
are, 1936.
Des. Mera, 1933; Hawley, 1936;
Eighth SW Ceramic Conf., 1966;
Human Systems Research, 1973;
Warren, 1977c; Dittert and Plog,
1980.
Illus. Jellinek, 1952; Voll, 1961;
Ambler, 1977; Traylor and
Scaife, 1980.

AGUA FRIA GRAY-ON-RED
Des. Stubbs and Stallings, 1952;
Honea, 1968.

AKO POLYCHROME
AD 1700-1750
Des. *Harlow, 1970; Harlow, 1973;
Frank and Harlow, 1974; *Dil-
lingham, 1977.

ALAMEDA BROWN WARE
Pre AD 700-ca. 1400
Des. Colton and Hargrave, 1937;
Colton, 1958, 14; Schroeder,
1960.
Illus. Smith, 1940.

ALAKALI BLACK-ON-RED
Hargrave notes at MNA, Named
by J. O. Brew, no published
description.

ALLENTOWN BLACK-ON-WHITE
Colton, 1952. Named in supple-
mentary pottery keys at MNA.

ALLENTOWN CORRUGATED
Colton, 1952. Named in supple-
mentary pottery keys at MNA.

ALMA GROOVED
AD 300-950
Des. Breternitz, 1959.

ALMA INCISED
AD 300-925
Des. Haury, 1936; Hawley, 1936;
Nesbitt, 1938; Human Systems
Research, 1973.
Illus. Bluhm, 1957; Hammack,
1963; Hammack, 1969.

ALMA KNOBBY
Illus. Gifford, 1980.

ALMA NECKBANDED
AD 665-910
Des. Haury, 1936; Hawley, 1936;
Wasley, 1960a; Human Systems
Research, 1973.
Illus. Lister, 1958; Dittert, 1959;
McGregor, 1965; Willey, 1966.

ALMA NECK INDENTED
Des. Human Systems Research,
1973.

ALMA PLAIN
AD 300-950
Des. Haury, 1936; Hawley, 1936;
Nesbitt, 1938; Gladwin, 1939;
Human Systems Research, 1973.
Illus. Martin, 1947; Martin, et al.,
1954; Bluhm, 1957; McGregor,
1965; DiPeso, 1967; Smith, 1973;
Smiley, 1978.

ALMA PLAIN: FORESTDALE VARIETY
AD 300-950
Des. Haury, 1940.

ALMA PLAIN: BLUFF VARIETY
AD 300-950
Des. Haury, 1947; Wheat, 1954.

ALMA PLAIN: BLACK RIVER VARIETY
Des. *Wheat, 1954.

ALMA PLAIN: POINT OF PINES VA-
RIETY
Des. Wheat, 1954.

ALMA PLAIN: POLISHED
Des. Martin and Rinaldo, 1960.

ALMA PUNCHED
AD 300-925
Des. Haury, 1936; Hawley, 1936;
Nesbitt, 1938; Human Systems
Research, 1973.

ALMA ROUGH
Ca. AD 750-800
Des. Martin and Rinaldo, 1940;
Martin 1943.
Illus. McGregor, 1965; Martin,
1957.

ALMA SCORED
AD 300-925
Des. Haury, 1936; Hawley, 1936;
Nesbitt, 1938; Human systems
Research, 1973.

ALMA SMUDGED
Des. *Wheat, 1954.

ALTAR POLYCHROME
Des. Withers, 1941; Withers, 1973.

AMUSOVI POLYCHROME
AD 1250-1300
(Similar to Kayenta Polychrome)
Des. *Colton, 1956, 5A-10; Dit-
tert and Plog, 1980.

ANCHONDO RED-ON-BROWN
Des. DiPeso, 1969; *DiPeso, 1974.

ANGEL GRAY-ON-WHITE
Des. Colton, 1940, personal files
at MNA.

ANGELL BROWN
AD 1075-1150
Des. *Colton, 1941a; Colton,
1958, 14-5.

ANIMAS POLYCHROME
AD 1275-1400
Syn. Escondida Polychrome.
Des. DiPeso, 1969; *DiPeso, 1974.

ANTELOPE BLACK-ON-STRAW
Des. *Smith, 1971.

ANTELOPE POLYCHROME
Des. *Smith, 1971.

APACHE PLAIN
Des. *Gifford, 1980.

APACHE WARE
Des. Gifford, 1940.
Illus. Brugge, 1963.

APODACA GRAY
Des. Dick, 1965.

AQUARIUS APPLIQUE
AD 1000-1100
Des. Colton, 1958, 17-4; Euler,
1957.

AQUARIUS BLACK-ON-BROWN
AD 900-1890
Des. Colton, 1939; *Dobyns
and Euler, 1958, 15-6.

AQUARIUS BLACK-ON-GRAY
AD 1050-1200
Syn. Verde Black-on-gray.

Des. Colton, 1939; Colton, 1958.
Illus. Euler and Dobyns, 1962.

AQUARIUS BLACK-ON-ORANGE
AD 1000-1100
Des. Colton, 1939; Colton, 1958,
17-3.
Illus. Dove, 1970.

AQUARIUS BROWN
AD 900?-1890
Syn. Yuma Plain, Gladwin, 1930.
Des. Colton, 1939; Dobyns and
Euler, 1958, 15-5.

AQUARIUS ORANGE
AD 1000-1100
Des. Colton, 1939; Colton, 1958,
17-2.

ARAUCA PLAIN
AD 1250-1400
Syn. Black Axe Plain.
Des. Colton and Hargrave, 1937;
Colton, 1956, 6B-6.

ARAUCA POLYCHROME
AD 1350-1425
Syn. Pinnawa Polychrome, Reed,
1955; Kechipawan Polychrome,
Martin and Rinaldo, 1960.
Des. Hodge, 1923; Colton and Har-
grave, 1937.
Illus. Martin and Willis, 1940.

ARBOLES BLACK-ON-WHITE
Ca. AD 900-1050
Des. *Dittert et al., 1961; *Dittert
and Plog, 1980.
Illus. Dittert and Eddy, 1963.

ARBOLES GRAY
AD 900-1050
Des. Dittert et al., 1961.
Illus. Dittert and Eddy, 1963; Lis-
ter et al., 1970.

ARBOLES NECKBANDED
Des. Dittert et al., 1963b.
Illus. Dittert and Eddy, 1963.

ARENAL GLAZE POLYCHROME
AD 1315-1350?
Syn. Glaze I, Red.
Des. Mera, 1933; Hawley, 1936;
*Kidder and Shepard, 1936;
Eighth SW Ceramic Conf., 1966;
Dittert and Plog, 1980.

ARMADILLO WARE
Des. Sauer and Brand, 1930.

ASH CREEK BROWN
Des. Breternitz, 1960.

ASHIWI POLYCHROME
AD 1700-1770
Des. *Mera, 1939; *Carlson, 1965;
Harlow, 1970; *Harlow, 1973;
*Frank and Harlow, 1974; *Carl-
son, 1977; Dittert and Plog, 1980.

ASHIWI WHITE-ON-RED
Des. *Carlson, 1965.

AWATOVI BLACK-ON-YELLOW
AD 1300-2400
Des. Smith, 1971.
Illus. Huse, 1976.

AWATOVI POLYCHROME
AD 1400-1625
Des. Colton and Hargrave, 1937;
*Colton, 1965, 7B-10:*Frank and
Harlow, 1974; Dittert and Plog, 1980.
Illus. Ambler, 1977.

AWATOVI YELLOW WARE
AD 1300-1700
Des. Colton and Hargrave, 1937;
Colton, 1956, 7A.

BABICOMARI PLAIN
Des. *DiPeso, 1951.

BABICOMARI POLYCHROME
AD 1450-1450
Des. *DiPeso, 1951.
Illus. Young, 1972.

BABICORA POLYCHROME
AD 1275-1400
Des. *Amsden, 1928; *Carey, 1931;
Brand, 1935; Hawley, 1936; *Sayles,
1936; *DiPeso, 1974; Human Sys-
tems Research, 1973; *DiPeso, 1974.
Illus. Lister and Lister, 1969; Bice, 1975.

BANCOS BLACK-ON-WHITE
AD 850-1000
Syn. Piedra-Gallina Transitional,
*Hall, 1944.
Des. Dittert et al., 1961; *Dittert
and Plog, 1980.
Illus. Dittert and Eddy, 1963.

BANDELIER BLACK-ON-GRAY

AD 1400-1550
Syn. Biscuit B.
Des. Kidder and Amsden,
1931; Mera, 1934a; Hawley,
1936; Lange, 1968; Harlow,
1973; Warren, 1977c; *Dittert
and Plog, 1980.
Illus. Hewett, 1938; Mera, 1939;
Harlow, 1965a; Carlson, 1965;
Barnett, 1973b.

BATKI PLAIN WARE
Des. *Fontana et al., 1962.

BEAR RIVER BROWN
Madsen, n.d., a variety of Promontory Gray with shell temper.

BEAVER CREEK RED
(Variety of Sunset Red)
Des. Schroeder, 1960.

BELFORD BURNISHED
Des. *DiPeso, 1958.

BELFORD CORRUGATED
Des. *DiPeso, 1958.

BELFORD PERFORATED RIM
Des. *DiPeso, 1958.

BELFORD PLAIN
Des. *DiPeso, 1958.

BELFORD RED
Syn. Gila Polychrome without paint.
Des. *DiPeso, 1958.

BELFORD SMUDGED
(Similar to Gila Polychrome)
Des. *DiPeso, 1958.

BELFORD-SOPBAIPURI PLAIN
Des. *DiPeso, 1958.

BELFORD-WHETSTONE PLAIN
Des. *DiPeso, 1958.

BENNETT GRAY
Ca. AD 700-850
Des. Wilson and Peckham, 1964;
*Windes, 1977.

BENSON RED-ON-BROWN
Des. Tuthill, 1947.

BETATAKIN BLACK-ON-WHITE
AD 1260-1300

Des. *Colton and Hargrave, 1937;
*Colton, 1955; 8B-8; *Dittert
and Plog, 1980.
Illus. Steen, 1966.

BIDAHOCHI BLACK-ON-WHITE
AD 1300-1400
Des. *Caywood and Spicer, 1935; Haw-
ley, 1936; Colton and Hargrave,
1937; Colton, 1955, 8B-14; Smith,
1971; *Dittert and Plog, 1980.
Illus. Martin and Willis, 1940;
Bice, 1975; Barry, 1981.

BIDAHOCHI POLYCHROME
AD 1320-1400
Des. *Hargrave, 1932; Hawley,
1936; *Colton and Hargrave,
1937; *Colton, 1956, 7B-5;
Smith, 1971.
Illus. Martin and Willis, 1940; Ari-
zona Highways, Feb. 1974;
Barry, 1981.

BIGWATER RED: VARIETY I
AD 575-900
Syn. Chapin Gray (Fugitive red
paint), Abel, 1955; Chapin Gray,
fugitive decoration, Rohn, 1966.
Des. *Forsyth, 1972.

BISCUIT A
AD 1375-1450
Syn. Abiquiu Black-on-gray.
Des. Kidder, 1931; Mera, 1934a;
Hawley, 1936; Kidder and Shep-
ard, 1936; *Harlow, 1973; Dit-
tert and Plog, 1980.
Illus. Kidder, 1915; Jeancon, 1923;
Chapman, 1936; Ambler, 1977.

BISCUIT B
AD 1400-1550
Syn. Bandelier Black-on-gray,
Mera, 1934a.
Des. Kidder, 1931; Mera, 1934a;
Hawley, 1936; Kidder and
Shepard, 1936; *Harlow, 1973;
*Dittert and Plog, 1980.
Illus. Kidder, 1915; Jeancon, 1923;
Hewett, 1938; Mera, 1939; Carlcon
1964; Harlow, 1965a; Ambler, 1977

BLACK AXE PLAIN
AD 1250-1400
Syn. Arauca Plain.
Des. Colton and Hargrave, 1937;
Colton, 1956, 6B-6; Dittert

and Plog, 1980.

BLACK AXE POLYCHROME
AD 1300-1400
Des. Colton and Hargrave, 1937;
*Colton, 1956, 6B-8; Dittert and
Plog, 1980.

BLACK FALLS CORRUGATED
(A variety of Tusayan Corrugated)
Post AD 1065
Des. Colton, 1943, notes at MNA.

BLACK MESA BEIGE
Post AD 1150?
Des. Schroeder, 1952; *Schroeder,
1958, D16-15.

BLACK MESA BLACK-ON-WHITE
AD 875-1130
Syn. Deadmans Black-on-white,
Hargrave, 1932.
Des. *Morss, 1931a; Colton, 1932;
Hawley, 1936; Colton and Har-
grave, 1937; *Colton, 1955, 8B-
21; Wilson, 1969; *Dittert and
Plog, 1980.
Illus. Martin and Willis, 1940; Beals,
Brainerd and Smith, 1945; Col-
ton, 1946; Smith, 1952; Colton,
1953; Ambler et al., 1964; Mc-
Gregor, 1965; Anderson, 1969;
Lister and Lister, 1969; Weed,
1970; Gumerman, 1970; Dove,
1970; Euler, 1971; Hobler, 1974;
Bice, 1975; Ambler, 1977.

BLACK MESA BUFF
Ca. AD 700-1000
Des. Rogers, 1945; Waters, 1982.

BLACK MESA POLYCHROME
Post AD 1150-?
Des. Schroeder, 1952b; *Schroeder,
1958, D16-17.

BLACK MESA RED
Post AD 1150-?
Des. Schroeder, 1952b; *Schroeder,
1958, D16-16.

BLACK MESA RED-ON-BUFF
Ca. AD 800-1000
Des. Rogers, 1945; Waters, 1982.

BLIND INDENTED CORRUGATED
AD 1300-1700
Des. Kidder, 1936; Honea, 1968;

Warren, 1976; Mobley, 1978.

BLUEBIRD CORRUGATED: BLUE-
BIRD VARIETY
Des. *Gifford and Smith, 1978.

BLUEBIRD CORRUGATED: PATNI
VARIETY
Des. *Gifford and Smith, 1978.

BLUE SHALE CORRUGATED
Ca. AD 950-1150
Des. Wilson and Peckham; 1964;
*Windes, 1977.

BLUEWATER BLACK-ON-GRAY
AD 850-1125
Syn. Red Mesa Black-on-white.
Des. Colton, 1953, ms. at MNA;
Hargrave, 1961.

BLUFF BLACK-ON-RED
AD 750-900
Syn. Sandstone Black-on-orange,
in part; LaPlata Black-on-red,
in part; LaPlata Black-on-orange
in part.
Des. Roberts, 1930; Guernsey,
1931; Hargrave, 1936; *Abel,
1955; 5A-4; *Breternitz, 1974;
Dittert and Plog, 1980.
Illus. Colton et al., 1940; Lan-
caster et al., 1954; Dittert and
Eddy, 1963; Swannack, 1969;
Hayes and Lancaster, 1975.

BLUFF BLACK-ON-RED: MCPHEE
VARIETY
Ca. AD 875-920
Des. *Wilson and Errickson, 1985;
Blinman and Wilson, 1986.

BLUFF BLACK-ON-RED: VARIETY I
AD 750-900
Syn. LaPlata Black-on-red, in
part, Martin and Rinaleo, 1939;
Bluff Black-on-red, Colton and
Hargrave, 1937.
Des. *Forsyth, 1972.

BONITO BLACK-ON-WHITE
O'Bryan, 1950, mentioned as a
Chaco ware.

BONSIKYA CORRUGATED
Des. *Gifford and Smith, 1978.

BORREGO BLACK-ON-WHITE

Des. Lange, 1968.

BOULDER BLACK-ON-GRAY
Des. *Colton, 1952.
Illus. Shutler, 1961.

BOULDER GRAY
Des. Colton, 1939; Colton, 1952.
Illus. Shutler, 1961; Worman, 1969.

BOYSAG BLACK-ON-GRAY
AD 725-900
Des. Thompson, 1986.

BRADFORD EXUBERANT CORRUGATED
Syn. Unamed Exuberant Cor-
rugated, Forsyth, 1972.
Des. *Miller, 1974.
Illus. Brew, 1946.

BRIMHALL BLACK-ON-WHITE
Ca. AD 900-1075
Des. Wilson and Peckham, 1964;
*Windes, 1977.

BROADLINE RED-ON-TERRA COTTA
AD 1150-1300
Syn. San Andres Red-on-terra cotta;
Three Rivers Red-on-terra cotta.
Des. *Mera and Stallings, 1931; *Nes-
bitt, 1931; Mera, 1943; Jellinek,
1952; Holden, 1952; *McCluney,
1962.

BURNHAM BLACK-ON-WHITE
AD 850-1000
Des. Wilson and Peckham, 1964;
*Windes, 1977.

CAJON PAINTED-GOUGED
(Similar to Devil Mesa Painted Corrugated except for surface manipulation)
Des. *Forsyth, 1972.

CAMERON POLYCHROME
AD 1057-1175
Des. *Colton, 1956, 5B-3; Dittert
and Plog, 1980.
Illus. Ambler et al., 1964; Anderson,
1969; Hobler, 1974.

CAMERON POLYCHROME: COOMBS
VARIETY
Illus. Lister, 1960; Jennings, 1978.

CAMERON RED-ON-GRAY
Des. Brand, 1935; Hawley, 1936.

CANADA DEL ORO RED-ON-BROWN
Des. *Kelly, 1978.
Illus. DiPeso, 1956; Greenleaf,
1975.

CANELO BROWN-ON-YELLOW
Des. Danson, 1946, manuscript
at Univ. of Arizona.

CANNONBALL INCISED: VARIETY 1
Des. *Forsyth, 1972.

CANNONBALL INCISED: VARIETY 2
Des. *Forsyth, 1972.

CANNONBALL INCISED: VARIETY 3
Les. *Forsyth, 1972.

CAPT. TOM CORRUGATED
Ca. AD 875 or 900-1000
Des. Wilson and Peckham, 1964;
*Windes, 1977.

CARMEN RED-ON-GRAY
Des. Brand, 1935; Hawley, 1936.

CARNUE PLAIN
Des. Dick in Schroeder, 1968.

CARRETAS POLYCHROME
AD 1350-1450
Syn. Huerigos Polychrome, in
part, Brand, 1935; Peripheral
Casas Grandes, in part, Ams-
den, 1928; Nacozari Polychrome,
Gladwin, 1934.
Des. Amsden, 1928; Brand, 1935;
*Sayles, 1936; Hawley, 1936;
DiPeso, 1969; Human Systems
Research, 1973; *DiPeso, 1974.
Illus. Harlow, 1976; DiPeso, 1977.

CASA COLORADO BLACK-ON-WHITE
AD 1150-1400
Des. Hawley, 1936; Atwood, 1974;
*Dittert and Plog, 1980.

CASA GRANDE RED-ON-BUFF
Des. *Gladwin, 1933; Hawley, 1936;
*Haury, 1945a; Antieau, 1981.
Illus. Johnson and Wasley, 1966;
Willey, 1966; Arizona Highways,
Feb. 1974; Dove, 1970; Weaver
1977.

CASAS GRANDES ARMADILLO
Des. *DiPeso, 1974.

CASAS GRANDES BROAD COIL
Des. *DiPeso, 1974.

CASAS GRANDES CORRUGATED
Des. *DiPeso, 1974.

CASAS GRANDES INCISED
Des. Brand, 1935; *DiPeso, 1974.

CASAS GRANDES PATTERNED INCISED
CORRUGATED
Des. *DiPeso, 1974.

CASAS GRANDES PATTERNED SCORED
Syn. Alma Plain Patterned
Des. *DiPeso, 1974.

CASAS GRANDES PLAINWARE
AD 1050-1525
Des. Carey, 1931; Sales, 1936;
*DiPeso, 1974.

CASAS GRANDES RUBBED CORRU-
GATED
Des. *DiPeso, 1974.

CASAS GRANDES RUBBED INCISED
Des. *DiPeso, 1974.

CASAS GRANDES RUBBED SCORED
Des. *DiPeso, 1974.

CASAS GRANDES SCORED
Des. *DiPeso, 1974.

CASAS GRANDES TOOL PUNCHED
Des. *DiPeso, 1974.

CASCABEL RED-ON-BROWN
Des. Tuthill, 1947.

CASCABEL/GALIURO RED-ON-BROWN
Des. *Franklin, 1980.

CASITAS RED-ON-BROWN
AD 1740-1900?
Des. *Dick in Schroeder, 1968;
Warren, 1977c.

CEBOLLETA BLACK-ON-WHITE
AD 950-1100
Des. *Dittert and Ruppe, 1951;
Dittert and Plog, 1980.
Illus. Dittert, 1959; Bice, 1975.

CEDAR CREEK POLYCHROME
AD 1300-1375.
Des. Haury, 1952; Gifford, 1957;

Carlson, 1970; *Gifford, 1980;
Dittert and Plog, 1980.

CERBAT BLACK-ON-BROWN
Des. *Dobyns and Euler, 1958, 15-3.

CERBAT BROWN
Ca. AD 700-1890
Des. Colton, 1939; *Dobyns and
Euler, 1958, 15-1.

CERBAT RED-ON-BROWN
Des. Colton, 1939; *Dobyns and
Euler, 1958, 15-2.

CERRO COLORADO PLAIN
Des. Wasley, 1959.

CERRO COLORADO RED
Des. Wasley, 1959.

CERRO RED-ON-WHITE
Des. *Sayles, 1945.

CHACO BLACK-ON-WHITE
AD 1050-1200
Des. Hawyley, 1936; *Vivian, 1959;
*Windes, 1977; *Dittert and
Plog, 1980.
Illus. Pepper, 1920; Kidder, 1924;
Goddard, 1928; Hawley, 1934;
Martin, 1936; Martin and Willis,
1940; O'Bryan, 1950; Worming-
ton, 1951; Cummings, 1953;
Gladwin, 1957; Vivian, 1959;
Corbett, 1962; Pomeroy, 1962;
Wormington, 1964; McGregor,
1965; Willey, 1966; Lister and
Lister, 1969; Arizona Highways,
Feb. 1974; Maxwell Museum,
1974; Bradley, 1974; Bice,
1975; Ambler, 1977.

CHACO CORRUGATED
AD 1050-1110
Des. Hawley, 1936; *Bice and
Sundt, 1972.
Illus. Wormington and Neal, 1951.

CHAMBERS BLACK-ON-WHITE
Des. *Colton, 1941a.

CHAPIN BLACK-ON-WHITE
AD 575 or 600 to 875-900
Syn. LaPlata Black-on-white, in
part; Lino Black-on-gray, in
part; Twin Trees Black-on-
white, Abel, 1955.

Des. *O'Brien, 1950; Reed, 1958;
*Abel, 1955, 12A-1; Fifth SW
Ceramic Conf., 1963; *Breter-
nitz et al., 1974; *Rohn, 1977;
*Dittert and Plog, 1980.
Illus. Morris, 1939; Lancaster, 1954;
Hayes, 1964; Ambler, 1977.

CHAPIN GRAY
AD 575-900
Syn. Twin Trees Plain
Des. *Morris, 1939; *Brew, 1946;
*O'Bryan, 1950; Abel, 1955, 10A-
1; *Rohn, 1959; *Hayes, 1964;
*Breternitz et al., 1974; Rohn,
1977.
Illus. Lister, 1965; Lister, 1968;
Lister and Lister, 1969; Hayes
and Lancaster, 1975.

CHAPIN GRAY: CHAPIN VARIETY
AD 575-900
Des. *Rohn, 1977.

CHAPIN GRAY: MOCCASIN VARIETY
AD 800-900
Des. *Rohn, 1977.

CHAPIN GRAY: MUMMY LAKE VARIETY
Ca. AD 950-1200
Des. *Rohn, 1977.

CHAPIN GRAY: VARIETY 1
AD 575-900
Syn. Chapin Gray: Chapin
Variety, Rohn, 1977.
Des. *Forsyth, 1972.

CHAPIN GRAY: VARIETY 2
AD 575-900
Syn. Twin Trees Plain, O'Bryan,
1950; Chapin Gray: Chapin
Variety, Rohn, 1977.
Des. *Forsyth, 1972.

CHAVEZ BROWN
AD 1200-1400
Des. *Colton, 1941; Colton, 1958,
14-16.

CHAVEZ PASS BLACK-ON-RED
AD 1300-1400
Des. Colton and Hargrave, 1937;
*Colton, 1956, 6B-4; Dittert and
Plog, 1980.

CHAVEZ PASS POLYCHROME
AD 1300-1400

Des. *Colton and Hargrave, 1937;
Colton, 1956, 6B-5; Dittert and
Plog, 1980.

CHETA BLACK-ON-WHITE
AD 1100-1250
Syn. Tularosa Black-on-white,
Martin and Bluhm, 1965.
Des. *Colton, 1941a.

CHEVELON BLACK-ON-WHITE
AD 1070-1125
Des. Colton, 1941; *Colton, 1955,
9B-4.

CHEVELON CORRUGATED POLYCHROME
Des. *Martin and Willis, 1940.

CHIHUAHUA RED WARE
Des. *DiPeso, 1974.
Illus. Kidder, 1916; Kidder, 1924;
Kidder and Cosgrove, 1949; Cum-
mings, 1953; Gladwin, 1957; Mu-
seum of American Indian, 1972.

CHINLE RED
Des. *Haury, 1945 (no complete
description).

CHOLLA BLACK-ON-WHITE
(Similar to Kwahe'e Black-on-
white)
Des. Lange, 1968.

CHUPADERO BLACK-ON-WHITE
AD 1150-1550
Des. *Mera, 1931; Hawley, 1936;
Kidder and Shepard, 1936; Lehmer, 1948; Smiley, Stubbs and
Bannister, 1953; *Jellinek, 1967;
*Hammerson, 1972; *Human Sys-
tems Research, 1973; Runyan
and Hedrick, 1973; Warren,
1976; Mobley, 1978; *Smiley,
1978; *Dittert and Plog, 1980;
Hayes et al., 1981; Wiseman,
1986.
Illus. Stallings, 1932, Jennings,
1940; Jellinek, 1952; Toulouse
and Stephenson, 1960; DiPeso,
1967; Phelps, 1968; Brody, 1977.

CHUSKA BLACK-ON-WHITE
AD 1000-1125
Des. Wilson and Peckham, 1964;
*Windes, 1977.
Illus. Johnson, 1963; Brody, 1977.

CHUSKA GRAY WARE
Des. Wilson and Peckham, 1964;
Windes, 1977.

CHUSKA WHITE WARE
Des. Wilson and Peckham, 1964;
Windes, 1977

CIBUCUE POLYCHROME
Ca. AD 1300-1350
Des. *Haury, 1934; Hawley, 1936;
Mauer, 1970.

CIBOLA WHITE WARE
Des. Mera, 1935; Colton, 1941a.
Illus. Gladwin, 1957.

CICUYE GLAZE-ON-RED
Des. Mera, 1933; Hawley, 1936.

CICUYE GLAZE POLYCHROME
AD 1650-1750
Des. Mera, 1933; Hawley, 1936;
Dittert and Plog, 1980.

CIENEGUILLA GLAZE POLYCHROME
AD 1325-1425
Syn. Glaze I, Yellow, Kidder and
Shepard, 1936.
Des. Mera, 1933; Hawley, 1936;
Lange, 1968; Warren, 1977c;
Dittert and Plog, 1980.

CIENEGUILLA GLAZE-ON-YELLOW
AD 1325-1425
Syn. Glaze I, Yellow, *Kidder and
Shepard, 1936.
Des. Mera, 1933; Hawley, 1936;
Lange, 1968; Atwood, 1974; War-
ren, 1977c; Dittert and Plog, 1980.
Illus. Voll, 1961; Barnett, 1973;
Bice, 1975.

CIMARRON MICACEOUS
AD 1750?-1900?
Des. Ellis and Brody, 1964; Dick,
1958; Skinner, 1968; Gunnerson,
1969; Wilson and Warren, 1974;
Warren, 1976.

CITADEL POLYCHROME
AD 1115-1200
(Similar to Nankoweap Polychrome)
Des. *Colton and Hargrave, 1937;
Reed, 1944b; Colton, 1956, 5B-4;
*Dittert and Plog, 1980.
Illus. Colton et al., 1940; Shutler,
1961; Ambler et al., 1964; An-

derson, 1969; Hobler, 1974;
Bartlett, 1977.

CITADEL POLYCHROME: COOMBS
VARIETY
Illus. Lister, 1960; Lister et al.,
1960; Jennings 1978.

CIVANO PLAIN
Des. Schroeder in communication
to Southwest Archaeological
Center, Globe, AZ, Ref. Chen-
hall, 1967.

CIVANO SMUDGED
Des. Schroeder in Communication
to Southwest Archaeological
Center, Globe, AZ, Ref. Chen-
hall, 1967.

CLEAR CREEK BROWN
AD 1000-1200?
Des. Colton, 1941; Colton, 1958;
14-22.

CLAPBOARD CORRUGATED
Des. Wendorf, 1950.

CLAPBOARD CORRUGATED
(Upper Mimbres)
Des. Graybill, 1973.

CLAPBOARD CORRUGATED INCISED
(Upper Mimbres)
Des. Graybill, 1973.

CLAPBOARD CORRUGATED INDENTED
(Upper Mimbres)
Des. Graybill, 1973.

CLAPBOARD CORRUGATED SMOOTHED
(Upper Mimbres)
Des. Graybill, 1973.

CLAPBOARD CORRUGATED SMOOTHED
AND INDENTED
(Upper Mimbres)
Des. Graybill, 1973.

CLIFF BLACK-ON-WHITE
Des. Bussey, 1975.

CLIFF FILLET RIM
No Published description.
Named by Richard Ellison for ma-
terial found at Kwilleleykia Ruins.

CLIFF RED

No published description.
Named by Richard Ellison for material
found at Kwilleleykia Ruins.

CLIFF WHITE -ON-RED
No published description.
Named by Richard Ellison for material
found at Kwilleleykia Ruins.

CLOVERDALE CORRUGATED
Syn. Cloverdale Gouged Red Ware,
Hawley, 1936.
Des. Kidder and Cosgrove, 1949.

CLOVERDALE GOUGED RED
Syn. Cloverdale Corrugated, Kidder and Cosgrove, 1949.
Des. *Sauer and Brand, 1931; Hawley, 1936.

COAL BED GRAY
(basket impresed)
Des. *Forsyth, 1972.

COCHITI BLACK-ON-CREAM
Des. Chapman, 1933; *Chapman,
1938.
Illus. Underhill, 1944; Wormington,
1965.

COCHITI BLACK-ON-RED
Des. *Chapman, 1935; *Chapman,
1938.
Illus. Harlow, 1977.

COCHITI POLYCHROME
AD 1830-present
Des. *Chapman, 1933; Chapman,
1938; *Harlow, 1970; *Harlow,
1973; *Frank and Harlow, 1974.
Illus. Arizona State Museum, 1959;
Tanner, 1968; Arizona Highways,
May 1974; Barry, 1981.

COCONINO BUFF WARE
AD 1050-1150
Des. Colton and Hargrave, 1937.

COCONINO GRAY
AD 890-1060
Des. *Hargrave, 1932; Hawley,
1936; *Colton and Hargrave,
1937; *Colton, 1955.

COCONINO RED-ON-BUFF
AD 1050-1150
Des. *Colton and Hargrave, 1937;
Colton, 1941.

COLORADO BEIGE
Ca. AD 700-1050
Des. Rogers, 1945; Waters, 1982.

COLORADO BEIGE
AD Post 1150-historic?
Des. Rogers, 1945; Schroeder,
1952b; Schroeder, 1958, D16-
5; Waters, 1982.

COLORADO BUFF
Ca. AD 1500-post 1900
Des. Waters, 1982.

COLORADO RED
Ca. AD 700-1000
Des. Rogers, 1945; Waters, 1982.

COLORADO RED-ON-BEIGE
AD Post 1150-?
Des. Rogers, 1945; Schroeder,
1952b; *Schroeder, 1958, D16-
6; Waters, 1982.

COLORADO RED-ON-BEIGE
Ca. AD 800-1050
Des. Rogers, 1945; Waters, 1982.

COLORADO RED-ON-BUFF
Ca. AD 1500-post 1900
Des. Waters, 1982. (Colton's
Topoc Red-on-buff and Needles
Red-on-buff are varieties of
this type.)

CONCEPCION POLYCHROME
Ca. AD 1475-late 1600s
Syn. Matsaki Polychrome
Des. Reed, 1955.

CONCHOS RED-ON-BROWN
Des. *Sayle, 1936.

CONVENTO BROAD COIL
Des. DiPeso, 1969; *DiPeso, 1974.

CONVENTO CORD MARKED
Named, *DiPeso, 1974.

CONVENTO CORRUGATED
Des. DiPeso, 1969; *DiPeso, 1974.

CONVENTO INCISED
Des. DiPeso, 1969; *DiPeso, 1974.

CONVENTO PATTERNED INCISED
CORRUGATED
AD 900-1060

Des. DiPeso, 1969; *DiPeso, 1974;
  *DiPeso et al., 1976.
Illus. Smiley, 1978.

CONVENTO PATTERNED SCORED
Des. *DiPeso, 1974.

CONVENTO PLAINWARE
Des. DiPeso, 1969; *DiPeso, 1974.

CONVENTO RED
Des. DiPeso, 1969; *DiPeso, 1974.

CONVENTO RUBBED CORRUGATED
Des. *DiPeso, 1974.

CONVENTO RUBBED INCISED
Des. *DiPeso, 1974.

CONVENTO SCORED
Des. DiPeso, 1969; *DiPeso, 1974.

CONVENTO RUBBED SCORED
Des. *DiPeso, 1974.

CONVENTO TOOLED PUNCHED
Des. DiPeso, 1969; *DiPeso, 1974.

CONVENTO VERTICAL CORRUGATED
Des. *DiPeso, 1974.

COOLIDGE CORRUGATED
A Pueblo II corrugated-indented type
of Cibola Gray Ware. Mentioned
in Wendorf, 1953 and Marshall
et al., 1979.

COOMBS GRAY
Des. *Lister, 1960.

CORDOVA (MICACEOUS RIBBED) COIL
Des. *Mera, 1935; Hawley, 1936.

CORDUROY BLACK-ON-WHITE
AD 800-900
Des. Breternitz, 1959.

CORONA CORRUGATED
AD 1450-1672
Des. Warren, 1976; Mobley, 1978;
  Hayes, 1981.

CORONA PLAIN
AD 1450-1672
Des. *Hayes, 1981, from Gran
  Quivira.

CORONA (RUBBED) INDENTED

Des. Mera, 1935; Hawley, 1936;
  Human Systems Research, 1973.

CORONA RUBBED-RIBBED
Des. Mera, 1935; Human Systems
  Research, 1973.

CORRALES RED
Des. Frisbie, 1967.

CORRALITOS POLYCHROME
AD 1060-1340
Syn. Chihuahua Red Ware, Hodge,
  1916; Corralitos Polychrome In-
  cised, in part, Sayles, 1936.
Des. *Carey, 1931; *Sayles, 1936;
  Hawley, 1936; DiPeso, 1969,
  Human Systems Research, 1973.
  *DiPeso, 1974; DiPeso et al.,
  1976.
Illus. Chapman, 1923.

CORTARO RED-ON-BROWN
Syn. Rincon Red-on-brown
Illus. Kelly, 1978.

CORTEZ BLACK-ON-WHITE
AD 900-1000
Syn. Mancos Black-on-white, in
  part.
Des. *Abel, 1955, 12A-3; Fifth SW
  Ceramic Conf., 1963; *Hayes,
  1964; *Breternitz et al., 1974;
  *Rohn, 1977; *Windes, 1977;
  Dittert and Plog, 1980.
Illus. Morris, 1939; Dittert and
  Eddy, 1963; Lister, 1965; Lis-
  ter and Lister, 1969; Swan-
  nack, 1969; Bice, 1975; Hayes
  and Lancaster, 1975.

CRACKLE WARE (A TYPE)
AD 1300-ca. 1375
Syn. Galisteo Black-on-white,
  Abel, 1955, 10B-4.
Des. *Mera, 1935.
(The name Crackle Ware is also used
  for Polacca Polychrome, but this
  Hopi type is very distinct from
  the type found at Galisteo.)

CROSBY BLACK-ON-GRAY
Des. *Jellinek, 1967.

CROZIER BLACK-ON-WHITE
Des. Wilson and Peckham, 1964.

CRUMBLING HOUSE BLACK-ON-WHITE

AD 1150-1300
Des. Wilson and Peckham, 1964;
*Windes, 1977.

CUBERO POLYCHROME
(Mentioned as a copy of Gila Polychrome made at Acoma in the
1300s) LeBlanc and Nelson, 1976.

CUMMINGS POLYCHROME
Des. Colton Manuscript at MNA,
similar to Tusayan Polychrome.

CUNDIYO (MICACEOUS) SMEARED
INDENTED
Des. *Mera, 1935; Hawley, 1936.

CUYAMUNGUE BLACK-ON-TAN
AD 1450-1550
Des. *Harlow, 1973; Dittert and
Plog, 1980.

DALTON CORRUGATED: VARIETY I
Syn. Mesa Verde Corrugated, in
part, Brew, 1946; Mesa Verde
Corrugated, Abel 1955; Hayes,
1964; Swannack, 1969; Mesa
Verde Corrugated: Mesa Verde
Variety, Rohn, 1966.
Des. *Forsyth, 1972.

DALTON CORRUGATED: VARIETY 2
Des. Forsyth, 1972.
(Differs from Dalton Corrugated:
Variety 1 only in respect to sur-
face manipulation.)

DALTON CORRUGATED: VARIETY 3
Des. *Forsyth, 1972.
(Differs from Dalton Corrugated:
Variety 1 only in respect to sur-
face manipulation.)

DAVIS RED-ON-WHITE
DiPeso, 1958, mentioned as a local
type at Bidegain Ruin.

DEADMANS BLACK-ON-GRAY
AD 900-1115
Des. Colton, 1931; *Hargrave, 1932;
Hawley, 1936; *Colton and Har-
grave, 1937; *Colton, 1958, 18-5.
Illus. Kidder and Guernsey, 1919;
Colton, 1933; McGregor, 1951.

DEADMANS BLACK-ON-RED
AD 800-1066

Syn. LaPlata Black-on-red, Abel,
1955; Sandstone Black-on-
orange, in part, Martin, 1939.
Des. *Colton, 1932; *Hargrave,
1932; Hawley, 1936; *Colton
and Hargrave, 1937; Roberts,
1939; *Colton, 1956; 5A-6;
*Breternitz, 1974; *Dittert
and Plog, 1980.
Illus. Colton et al., 1940; Hayes
and Lancaster, 1975.

DEADMANS BLACK-ON-WHITE
Ca. AD 875-Ca. 1100
Syn. Black Mesa Black-on-white.
Des. Colton, 1932; Hargrave,
1932; Hawley, 1936; Colton
and Hargrave, 1937.
Illus. Colton, 1933.

DEADMANS CORRUGATED
AD 950-1300
Syn. Tusayan Corrugated, Col-
ton, 1955, 8A-11.
Des. *Hargrave, 1932; Hawley,
1936; *Gifford and Smith, 1978.

DEADMANS FUGITIVE RED
AD 775-1200
Des. Colton, 1931; *Hargrave,
1932; Hawley, 1936; *Colton
and Hargrave, 1937; *Colton,
1958, 18-4.
Illus. Colton, 1946; McGregor,
1951; Smith, 1952.

DEADMANS GRAY
AD 775-1200
Des. Colton, 1931; Hargrave,
1932; Hawley, 1936; Colton
and Hargrave, 1937; Reed,
1938; *Colton, 1958, 18-3.
Illus. Colton, 1946; McGregor, 1951.

DEAD RIVER BLACK-ON-WHITE
AD 750-800
Des. Mera, 1934b; Hawley, 1936;
Colton and Hargrave, 1937.
(A Variety of Kiathuthlanna black-
on-white, Cibola White Ware
Conf., 1958.)

DEEP CREEK BUFF
Des. Malouf, 1946; Malouf, 1950,
Reed, 1953.

DEEP CREEK GRAY
AD 900-1200

Syn. Snake Valley Gray, Rudy,
1953; *Marwitt, 1970.
Des. Malouf, Dibble and Smith, 1940.

DEEPWELL RED-ON-BROWN
Des. Tuthill, 1947.

DEVIL MESA PAINTED-CORRUGATED
Des. *Forsyth, 1972.

DIABLO BLACK-ON-WHITE
Des. Fenenga in Wendorf, 1956.

DIABLO BROWN
Des. Wilson, 1969.

DIABLO BROWN: YEAGER VARIETY
Des. Wilson, 1969.

DIABLO RED
Des. Wilson, 1969.

DINETAH GRAY
Ca. AD 1700-1800
Syn. Dinetah Utility.
Des. *Brugge, 1981; *Hartman and
Musial, 1987.

DINETAH SCORED
Des. *Carlson, 1965.

DINETAH UTILITY
Ca. AD 1700-1800
Syn. Dinetah Gray, Brugge, 1981.
Des. *Dittert et al., 1961; Brugge,
1963.

DOGOSZHI BLACK-ON-WHITE
AD 1085-1200
Des. *Colton and Hargrave, 1937;
*Colton, 1955, 8B-4; *Dittert
and Plog, 1980.
Illus. Beals, Brainerd and Smith,
1945; King, 1949; Colton, 1953;
Colton, 1956; Ambler et al., 1964.
New Mexico Univ., 1967; Lister
and Lister, 1969; Gumerman,
1970; Arizona Highways, Feb.
1974; Hobler, 1974; Wade, 1980.

DOGOSZHI POLYCHROME
AD 1050-1300
(Considered by some to be in-
completely slipped Tusayan
Black-on-red, Breternitz, 1966.)
Des. Colton and Hargrave, 1937;
*Colton, 1956, 5B-10; *Smith,
1971; Dittert and Plog, 1980.

Illus, Colton et al., 1940.
(Fourth SW Ceramic Seminar,
1959, dropped this type.)

DOLORES BASKET-IMPRESSED WARE
Des. *Forsyth, 1972.

DOLORES BROWN
Des. *Lucius and Wilson, 1981a;
Blinman and Wilson, 1986.

DOLORES CORRUGATED
AD 1050-1250
Des. *Lucius and Wilson, 1981;
Blinman and Wilson, 1986.
Illus. Breternitz et al., 1984.

DOLORES RED
Des. *Lucius and Wilson, 1981;
Blinman and Wilson, 1986.

DOS CABEZAS RED-ON-BROWN
Des. *Sayles, 1945.
Illus. McGregor, 1965; Brody, 1977.

DRAGOON PLAIN
Des. *Fulton and Tuthill, 1940.

DRAGOON RED
Des. *Fulton and Tuthill, 1940.
Illus. DiPeso, 1956

DRAGOON RED-ON-BROWN
Des. *Fulton and Tuthill, 1940.
Illus. DiPeso, 1967; Haury, 1976.

DROLET BLACK-ON-WHITE
Ca. AD 825-900
Des. Wilson and Peckham, 1964;
Windes, 1977.

DUBLAN POLYCHROME
?AD 1275-1400
Syn. Casas Grandes Polychrome.
Des. Hawley, 1936; *Sayles, 1936;
DiPeso, 1969; Human Systems
Research, 1973; *DiPeso, 1974.

ELDEN CORRUGATED
AD 1085-1200
Des. Colton, 1932; Hawley, 1936;
*Colton and Hargrave, 1937.

ELDEN RED-ON-BUFF
Des. Colton, 1945, manuscript at
MNA.

ELMENDORF BLACK-ON-WHITE

Des. Peckham files at Laboratory
of Anthropology. (Similar to
Casa Colorado Black-on-white
except for carbon paint.)

ELPASO BICHROME
AD 900-1000
Syn. El Paso Red-on-brown; El
Paso Black-on-brown.
Des. Lehmer, 1948; Human Systems
Research, 1973.

EL PASO BLACK-ON-BROWN
Syn. El Paso Bichrome
Des. Lehmer, 1948; Human Systems
Research, 1973.

EL PASO BROWN
AD 500-1350
Des. Cosgrove, 1947; Lehmer, 1948;
*Hammerson, 1972; Runyan and
Hedrick, 1973; Human Systems
Research, 1973; Dulany and
Pigott, 1977; *Smiley, 1978.
Illus. Hill, 1971.

EL PASO BROWN: TOOLED AND COR-
RUGATED VARIETIES
AD 500-1350
Des. Lehmer, 1948; *Smiley, 1978.

EL PASO POLYCHROME
AD 1100-1350
Des. Alves, 1931; Stallings, 1931;
Brand, 1935; Hawley, 1936; Leh-
mer, 1948; *Trost, 1970; *Ham-
merson, 1972; Human Systems Re-
search, 1973; Runyan and Hed-
rick, 1973; DiPeso et al., 1974;
Dulaney and Pigott, 1977;
*Smiley, 1978.
Illus. Cosgrove, 1932; Jellinek, 1952;
Bilbo, 1969; Mills and Mills, 1972;
Brook, 1977; Way, 1979.

EL PASO RED-ON-BROWN
AD 900-1100
Syn. El Paso Bichrome.
Des. Stallings, 1931; Lehmer, 1948;
Jellinek, 1967; Runyan and Hed-
rick, 1973; Human Systems Re-
search, 1973.

EL RITO MICACEOUS
Des. *Dick in Schroeder, 1968.

EL RITO RED-ON-BROWN

Dick, 1965, mentioned but not
described.

EMERY GRAY
Ca. AD 700-1200?
Syn. Turner Gray: Variety II,
Wormington, 1955; Turner
Gray: Emery Variety, Lister,
1960; Escalante Gray, Gunner-
son, 1969.
Des. *Lister, 1960; Madsen, 1970;
Marwitt, 1970; Madsen, 1972;
*Madsen, 1977.

ENCIERRO GLAZE POLYCHROME
AD 1650-1750
Des. Kidder, 1936; Honea, 1966;
Eighth SW Ceramic Conf.,
1966; Dittert and Plog, 1980.

ENCINAS RED-ON-BROWN
Des. *Sayles, 1945.
Illus. Breternitz, 1959; Gifford,
1980.

ESCALANTE GRAY
Ca. AD 700-1200?
Syn. Emery Gray, Madsen, 1977.
Des. Gunnerson, 1969.

ESCAVADA BLACK-ON-WHITE
AD 925-1125
Des. Hawley, 1934; Hawley, 1936;
*Vivian, 1959; *Windes, 1977;
*Dittert and Plog, 1980.
Illus. Pepper, 1920; Wendorf et
al., 1956; Lister and Lister,
1969; Bice, 1975.

ESCONDIDA POLYCHROME
AD 1275-1400
Syn. Animas Polychrome; Imitation
Gila Polychrome, Kidder in
Hodge, 1916; Ramos Polychrome
with Salado influence, Sayles,
1936; Local Gila Polychrome,
Gladwin, 1957.
Des. DiPeso, 1969; *DiPeso, 1974.
Illus. Hodge, 1916; Chapman, 1923;
Chapman, 1931; Gladwin, 1957.

ESCONDIDO GLAZE POLYCHROME
AD 1515-1650
Des. Honea, 1966; Dittert and
Plog, 1980.

ESPINOZO GLAZE POLYCHROME
AD 1425-1500

Syn. Glaze III, *Kidder, 1936.
Des. Mera, 1933; Hawley, 1936, War-
ren, 1977c; *Dittert and Plog,
1980.
Illus. Harlow, 1956; Caywood, 1966;
Ambler, 1977.

ESTRELLA RED-ON-GRAY
100 BC-AD 100
Des. *Gladwin et al., 1937: *Haury,
1937; *Haury, 1976.
Illus. McGregor, 1965; Arizona
Highways, Feb. 1974.

EXUBERANT CORRUGATED
AD 890-1075
Des. Kluckhohn and Rieter, 1939;
Dittert, 1959.

FAIRBANK PLAIN
Des. DiPeso, 1953.

FERNANDO RED-ON-BROWN
Des. DiPeso, 1969; *DiPeso, 1974.

FERN GLEN BLACK-ON-GRAY
AD 1080-1130
Des. Thompson, 1986.

FLAGSTAFF BLACK-ON-WHITE
AD 1085-1275
Des. *Hargrave, 1932; Hawley, 1936;
*Colton and Hargrave, 1937;
*Colton, 1955, 8B-6; *Dittert
and Plog, 1980.
Illus. Colton, 1946; King, 1949;
Smith, 1952; Colton, 1953; Lister
et al., 1960; Steen, 1966; Ander-
son, 1969; Barnett, 1970; Gumer-
man, 1970; Weed, 1970; Hobler,
1974; Ambler, 1977.

FLAGSTAFF RED
AD 1065-1200
Syn. Sunset Red, Colton, 1932.
Des. Colton, 1932; *Hargrave, 1932;
Hawley, 1936.

FLOYD BLACK-ON-GRAY
AD 775-940
Des. McGregor, Manuscript; *Col-
ton, 1958, 18-2.
Illus. Haury, 1976.

FLOYD GRAY
AD 700-900
Des. *Colton, 1958, 18-1.

FLYING-V BROWN
Des. Dittert, n.d., manuscript
at ASU.
(Plain brownware from the Vosberg Valley.)

FORESTDALE BLACK-ON-RED
Ca. AD 800-1000
Des. Wendorf, 1953; *Ferg, 1981.

FORESTDALE PLAIN
AD 600-800+
Syn. Woodruff Brown, Mera, 1934b.
Des. Haury, 1940.

FORESTDALE RED
Ca. late 600s-early 700s.
Syn. Woodruff Red, Mera, 1934b.
Des. Haury, 1940.

FORESTDALE SMUDGED
Ca. AD 300-1150
Syn. Woodruff Smudged.
Des. Haury, 1940; Gladwin, et
al., 1937.
Illus. Dittert and Ruppe, 1951;
Wendorf et al., 1956.

FOURMILE POLYCHROME
AD 1325-1400
Des. Haury, 1930; *Gladwin, 1931;
Haury, 1932; Hawley, 1936;
Baldwin, 1937; *Colton and
Hargrave, 1937; Smiley, Stubbs
and Bannister, 1953; Carlson,
1962; *Carlson, 1970; *Dittert
and Plog, 1980.
Illus. Haury, 1934; Baldwin, 1939;
Martin and Willis, 1940; Cum-
mings, 1953; Gladwin, 1957;
McGregor, 1965; Lister and Lis-
ter, 1969; Arizona Highways,
Feb. 1974; Barry, 1981.

FOURMILE POLYCHROME: KINISHBA
VARIETY
Des. *Cummings, 1940.

FRANCES POLYCHROME
AD 1700-1750
Syn. Gobernador Polychrome
Variant, *Carlson, 1965.
Des. Hester and Shiner, 1963.

FREDONIA BLACK-ON-GRAY
Des. Colton, 1952.

FREMONT BLACK-ON-WHITE

Ca. AD 700-1200?
Syn. Sevier Black-on-gray, Stewart,
1936; Great Salt Lake Gray,
Stewart, 1936; Ivy Creek Black-
on-gray, Madsen, 1977.
Des. Morss, 1931; Gunnerson, 1956.

FREMONT CORRUGATED
Ca. AD 1100-1200
Syn. Sevier Corrugated, Stewart,
1936; Snake Valley Corrugated,
Madsen, 1977.
Des. Morss, 1931b; Malouf, Dibble
and Smith, 1950.

FREMONT GRAY WARE
No published description.

FREMONT PLAIN
Des. Morss, 1931b.

GALISTEO BLACK-ON-WHITE
AD 1300-1400
Syn. Crackle Ware (see note).
Des. Kidder and Amsden, 1931;
*Mera, 1935; Kidder and Shepard,
1936; Hawley, 1936; Kluckhohn
and Reiter, 1939; Stubbs and
Stallings, 1953; *Abel, 1955,
10B-4; Dittert and Plog, 1980.
Illus. Bice and Sundt, 1972; Bice,
1975; Traylor and Scaife, 1980.

GALIURO RED-ON-BROWN
Des. *Sayles, 1945.
Illus. Gladwin, 1948.

GALLINA BLACK-ON-GRAY
Ca. AD 1250
Syn. Gallina Black-on-white.
Des. *Hibben, 1949; *Pattison, 1968.
Illus. McGregor, 1965.

GALLINA BLACK-ON-WHITE
AD 1050-1300
Syn. Gallina Black-on-gray, Patti-
son, 1968.
Des. *Mera, 1935; Hawley, 1936;
Smiley, Stubbs and Bannister,
1953; *Wilkinson, 1958; *Dittert
and Plog, 1980.
Illus. Bice, 1975.

GALLINA COARSE
Des. *Pattison, 1968.

GALLINA GRAY (WASHBOARD)
Ca. AD 1250

Syn. Gallina Washboard?
Des. *Mera, 1935.

GALLINA PLAIN
Ca. AD 1250
Syn. Gallina Plain Utility.
Des. *Hibben, 1949.

GALLINA PLAIN INDENTED
Des. Mera, 1935; Hawley, 1936.

GALLINA PLAIN POLISHED
Des. Wilkinson, 1958.

GALLINA PLAIN UNDECORATED
Des. Pattison, 1968.

GALLINA PLAIN UNFIRED
Des. *Hibben, 1949.

GALLINA PLAIN UTILITY
Ca. AD 1250
Syn. Gallina Plain.
Des. *Hibben, 1949; *Pattison,
1968; Wilkinson, 1958.
Illus. Mera, 1935.

GALLINA PUNCHED WARE
Ca. AD 1250
Des. *Hibben, 1949.

GALLINA SMUDGED
Des. Wilkinson, 1958.

GALLINA UTILITY PUNCHED
Des. Pattison, 1968.

GALLINA WASHBOARD
Ca. AD 1250
Syn. Gallina Gray (Washboard)?
Des. *Mera, 1935.

GALLUP BLACK-ON-WHITE
AD 1000-1150
Des. Hawley, 1936; *Vivian, 1959;
*Windes, 1977; *Dittert and
Plog, 1980.
Illus. Pepper, 1920; Brand et al.,
1937; Wendorf et al., 1956;
Vivian and Clendenen, 1965;
Lambert, 1966; New Mexico
Univ., 1967; Lister and Lister,
1969; McNutt, 1969; Olson,
1971; Bice, 1975.

GARFIELD BLACK-ON-WHITE
Des. *Lister, 1960.

GILA BEND BEIGE
Des. Schroeder, 1952b; *Schroeder,
1958, D16-10.

GILA BEND PLAIN
Post AD 1150-?
Des. Schroeder, 1952b: *Schroeder,
1958, D16-8.

GILA BEND RED
Post AD 1150-?
Des. Schroeder, 1952b; Schroeder,
1958, D16-11.

GILA BEND STUCCO
Post AD 1150-?
Des. Schroeder, 1952b; *Schroeder,
1958, D16-9.

GILA BLACK-ON-RED
Ca. AD 1300-1350
Des. *Haury, 1945a; Wendorf, 1950;
*DiPeso, 1958.
Illus. Clarke, 1935; Mills and Mills,
1972.

GILA BUTTE RED-ON-BUFF
AD 550-700
Des. *Haury, 1937; *Haury, 1976;
*Antieau, 1981.
Illus, Gladwin, 1948; Wasley and
Johnson, 1965; Tanner, 1976;
Brody, 1977.

GILA PLAIN
AD 300-1300
Des. *Gladwin, 1933; *Haury, 1937;
*Haury, 1976; Doyel, 1978; An-
tieau, 1981.
Illus. Norton, 1953; DiPeso, 1956.

GILA PLAIN: GILA BEND VARIETY
Illus. Wasley and Johnson, 1965.

GILA PLAIN: PERRY MESA VARIETY
Des. Barnett, 1974a.

GILA PLAIN: TUCSON VARIETY
Des. Danson in Hayden, 1957.

GILA PLAIN WARE
Des. *Gladwin, 1933; Hawley, 1936.

GILA POLYCHROME
AD 1300-1600
Des. *Kidder, 1924; *Gladwin,
1930b; Hawley, 1936; Colton and

Hargrave, 1937; *Haury, 1945a;
*DiPeso, 1958; Human Systems
Research, 1973; Kelly, 1978;
Doyel, 1978.
Illus. Fewkes, 1912; Hawley, 1930;
Baldwin, 1937; Cummings, 1940;
Kidder and Cosgrove, 1949;
Cummings, 1953; Shaeffer,
1956; Gladwin, 1957; Martin
and Rinaldo, 1960a; Steen et
al., 1962; McGregor, 1965;
Smith et al., 1966; Lister and
Lister, 1969; Mills and Mills,
1971; Hammerson, 1972; Ari-
zona Highways, Feb. 1974;
Brody, 1977; Weaver, 1977.

GILA RED
Pre AD 1200-post 1400
Des. *Schmidt, 1928; *Gladwin,
1930b; Hawley, 1936; Schroe-
der, 1940; *Haury, 1945a;
Schroeder, 1952; Steen et al.,
1962.
Illus. DiPeso, 1956; Museum
American Indian, 1972; Bice,
1975.

GILA RED-ON-BROWN
Des. *DiPeso, 1958.

GILA SMUDGED
Ca. AD 1300s
Des. Schroeder, 1940; *Haury,
1945a.

GILA WHITE-ON-RED
AD 1300-1350
Des. Gladwin, 1930; Colton and
Hargrave, 1937.

GLAZE I
AD 1325-1425
Syn. Cieneguilla Glaze-on-yellow.
Des. *Kidder and Shepard, 1936.

GLAZE I-A
AD 1315-1425
Syn. Agua Fria Glaze-on-red;
San Clemente Glaze Polychrome.
Des. *Kidder and Shepard, 1936;
Hawley, 1936; Warren, 1977c.

GLAZE I, RED
AD 1315-1350?
Syn. Arenal Glaze Polychrome.
Des. *Kidder and Shepard, 1936;
Hawley, 1936

GLAZE I, YELLOW
AD 1325-1425
Syn. Cieneguilla Glaze Polychrome.
Des. *Kidder and Shepard, 1936.

GLAZE II
AD 1400-1450
Syn. Largo Glaze Polychrome.
Des. *Kidder and Shepard, 1936.

GLAZE III
AD 1425-1500
Syn. Espinosa Glaze Polychrome.
Des. *Kidder and Shepard, 1936.

GLAZE IV
AD 1470-1515
Syn. San Lazaro Glaze Polychrome.
Des. *Kidder and Shepard, 1936.
Illus. Bice, 1975.

GLAZE V
AD 1600-1700
Syn. Pecos Glaze Polychrome.
Des. *Kidder and Shepard, 1936.
Illus. Barry, 1981.

GLAZE VI
AD 1650-1700
Syn. Kotyiti Glaze Polychrome.
Des. *Kidder and Shepard, 1936.

GLENDALE BLACK-ON-GRAY
AD 1125-1250
Syn. Flagstaff Black-on-white
Des. *Thompson, 1986.

GOBERNADOR BLACK-ON-YELLOW
Des. *Carlson, 1965.

GOBERNADOR FILLETED
Des. *Carlson, 1965.

GOBERNADOR INDENTED
Des. Dittert et al., 1961.
Illus. Carlson, 1965.
(Similar to Dinetah Utility Indented
variety, Brugge, 1963.)

GOBERNADOR POLYCHROME
AD 1700-1750
Syn. Frances Polychrome, Hester
and Shiner, 1973.
Des. Kidder and Shepard, 1936;
Keur, 1941; Brugge, 1963; Carl-
son, 1965; *Frank and Harlow,
1974; *Carlson, 1977; *Dittert

and Plog, 1980; *Brugge, 1981;
*Hartman and Musial, 1987.
Illus. Dittert et al., 1961.

GOBERNADOR RED-ON-YELLOW
Des. *Carlson, 1961.

GORDON BLACK-ON-WHITE
Des. *Colton, 1941a.
(A Red Mesa derivative, not ade-
quately described, Cibola White
Ware Conf., 1958.)

GRANTS BLACK-ON-WHITE
Des. Hargrave, 1961.

GRAPEVINE BROWN
AD 1150-1350
Des. *Colton, 1958, 14-17.

GRAPEVINE RED
AD 1150-1300
(Variety of Grapevine Brown)
Des. *Colton, 1958, 14-18.

GRAPEVINE SMUDGED
AD 1150-1300
(Variety of Grapevine Brown)
Des. *Colton, 1958, 14-18.

GRASSHOPPER POLYCHROME
Des. Colton, 1943, manuscript at
MNA.

GRAY HILLS BANDED
Ca. AD 850-950
Des. Wilson and Peckham, 1964;
*Windes, 1977.

GREAT SALT LAKE BLACK-ON-GRAY
AD 700-1200
Syn. Fremont Black-on-white,
Morss, 1931; Sevier Black-on-
gray, Stewart, 1936; Ivie
Creek Black-on-white, Madsen,
1977.
Des. Stewart, 1936; Hawley,
1936.

GREAT SALT LAKE GRAY
Ca. AD 400-1350
Syn. Deep Creek Gray, Malouf
et al., 1950; Knolls Ware,
Malouf et al., 1950; Great Salt
Lake Plain Gray, Enger, 1950;
Knolls Gray, Rudy, 1953.
Des. Stewart, 1936; Hawley, 1936;

List of Types and Wares

Malouf et al. , 1950; Rudy, 1953;
Aikens, 1967; Marwitt, 1970;
Madsen 1970; Madsen, 1972;
*Madsen, 1977; Griset, 1986.

GREAT SALT LAKE PUNCHED
Des. Stewart, 1936; Hawley, 1936.
Illus. Aikens, 1967.

GUADALUPE SMEARED INDENTED
Des. Pippin, 1978.

HACKBERRY GOUGED: VARIETY 2
Des. *Forsyth, 1972.

HACKBERRY GOUGED: VARIETY 3
Des. *Forsyth, 1972.

HANO BLACK-ON-YELLOW
AD 1896-present
Des. *Colton, 1956, 7B-21.
Illus. Dittert and Plog, 1980.

HANO POLYCHROME
AD 1896-present
(Mentioned in Kidder and Shepard,
1936)
Des. *Colton, 1956, 7B-20; *Harlow, 1970; Frank and Harlow,
1974; *Dittert and Plog, 1980.
Illus. New Mexico Univ. , 1967;
Maxwell Museum, 1974; Harlow,
1977; Barry, 1981; Trimble,
1987.

HANO POLYCHROME
AD 1885-present
Des. Adams, 1979.

HANO POLYCHROME: VARIETY A
(Unslipped Style)
AD 1895-present
Des. Adams, 1979.

HANO POLYCHROME: VARIETY B
(Red slipped variety)
AD 1920-present
Des. Adams, 1979.

HANO POLYCHROME: VARIETY C
(White slipped variety)
AD 1950-present
Des. Adams, 1979.

HARDSCRABBLE BROWN
AD 1050-1100?
Des. Peck, 1956; Colton, 1958,
14-28.

HARTLEY BLACK-ON-BROWN
Des. Colton, 1958, 14-24.

HARTLEY PLAIN
Des. Colton, 1958, 14-23.

HATCH GOUGED-INCISED: VARIETY
I
Des. *Forsyth, 1972.

HAVASUPAI WARE
Des. Spicer, 1928.

HAWIKUH BROWN-ON-BUFF
Ca. AD 1475-late 1600s
Syn. Matsaki Brown-on-buff.
Des. *Hodge, 1923; Reed, 1955;
*Smith, Woodubry and Wood-
bury, 1966.
Illus. Carlson, 1965.

HAWIKUH GLAZE POLYCHROME
AD 1630-1680
Syn. Hawikuh Polychrome
Des. Reed, 1955; Harlow, 1973.

HAWIKUH GLAZE-ON-RED
Des. *Mera, 1939; *Dittert and
Plog, 1980.

HAWIKUH GLAZE-ON-WHITE
AD 1350-1425
Syn. Pinnawa Glaze-on-white.
Des. Colton and Hargrave, 1937;
Reed, 1955; Smith, Woodbury
and Woodbury, 1966.
Illus. Martin and Willis, 1940;
Martin et al., 1961; Harlow,
1976.

HAWIKUH POLYCHROME
AD 1630-1680
Syn. Hawikuh Glaze Polychrome.
Des. *Mera, 1939; Reed, 1955;
Smith, Woodbury and Wood-
bury, 1966; Harlow, 1970;
Harlow, 1973; *Frank and Har-
low, 1974; *Dittert and Plog,
1980.
Illus. Hodge, 1923; Kidder, 1936;
Bushnell and Digby, 1955;
Harlow, 1976; Harlow, 1977.

HERMANO POLYCHROME: VARIETY 1
AD 700-850
Syn. Abajo Polychrome, Brew;
1946; Abajo Red-on-orange:

Polychrome deviation.
Des. *Forsyth, 1972.

HESHOTA BLACK-ON-RED
AD 1275 or 1300-1400
Syn. Heshotauthla Black-on-red.
Des. *Smith, Woodbury and Wood-
bury, 1966; Carlson, 1970.

HESHOTA POLYCHROME
AD 1275-1400
Syn. Heshotauthla Polychrome.
Des. Carlson, 1970.

HESHOTAUTHLA BLACK-ON-RED
AD 1275 or 1300-1400
Syn. Heshota Black-on-red.
Des. *Smith, Woodbury and Wood-
bury, 1966; Carlson, 1970.
Illus. Fewkes, 1909; Hodge, 1923.

HESHOTAUTHLA GLAZE POLYCHROME
AD 1275-1400
Syn. Heshotauthla Polychrome.
Des. Reed, 1955.
Illus. Smith, Woodbury and Wood-
bury, 1966.

HESHOTAUTHLA POLYCHROME
AD 1275-1400
Syn. Heshotauthla Glaze Polychrome;
Heshota Polychrome, Carlson,
1970.
Des. Hodge, 1923; Hawley, 1936;
Kidder, 1936; Colton and Har-
grave, 1937; Smiley, Stubbs and
Bannister, 1953; *Martin and
Rinaldo, 1960; *Martin et al.,
1961; Carlson, 1962; *Smith,
Woodbury and Woodbury, 1966;
Human Systems Research, 1973;
*Dittert and Plog, 1980.
Illus. Hough, 1903; Fewkes, 1909;
Martin and Willis, 1940; Stubbs
and Stallings, 1953.

HIBBARD CORRUGATED
Des. Colton, manuscript at MNA.

HIGLEY RED
Des. Schroeder, n.d., manuscript
at Pueblo Grande.

HILDALE BLACK-ON-GRAY
AD 1100-1225
Syn. North Creek Black-on-gray,
Type B.
Des. *Thompson, 1986.

HOHOKAM BUFF WARE
Des. Colton, 1941.
Illus. Cummings, 1953.

HOHOKAM PLAIN WARE: BEAVER
CREEK SERIES
Des. Schroeder, 1960.

HOLBROOK BLACK-ON-WHITE
AD 1075-1130
(Black Mesa and Sosi style)
Des. Mera, 1934; Hawley, 1936;
Colton and Hargrave, 1937;
*Colton, 1955, 9B-2; Dittert
and Plog, 1980.
Illus. Dove, 1970.

HOMOLOVI BLACK-ON-RED
AD 1300-1400
Des. Mera, 1934; Hawley, 1936;
*Colton and Hargrave, 1937;
*Colton, 1956, 6B-7; Dittert
and Plog, 1980.

HOMOLOVI CORRUGATED
AD 1300-1400
Des. *Hargrave, 1932; Hawley,
1936; Colton and Hargrave,
1937; Colton, 1956, 6A-1.

HOMOLOVI ORANGE WARE
AD 1300-1400
Des. Colton and Hargrave, 1937;
Colton, 1956, 6A.

HOMOLOVI PLAIN
AD 1300-1400
Des. *Hargrave, 1932; Colton and
Hargrave, 1937; Colton, 1956,
6A-2.

HOMOLOVI POLYCHROME
AD 1300-1400
Syn. Winslow Polychrome; Tuwiuca
Polychrome.
Des. Mera, 1934; Hawley, 1946;
Colton and Hargrave, 1937;
*Colton, 1965, 6B-2; Dittert
and Plog, 1980.
Illus. Martin and Willis, 1940;
Arizona Highways, Feb. 1974;
Barry, 1981.

HONANI TOOLED
Ca. AD 900
Des. *Colton and Hargrave, 1937;
*Colton, 1955, 8A-8; *Gifford
and Smith, 1978.

HOSTA BUTTE BLACK-ON-WHITE
Des. Colton, manuscript on Cibola
White Ware at MNA. Mentioned
as a Chaco white ware in O'Bryan,
1950.

HOUCK POLYCHROME
AD 1125-1200
Syn. Wingate Polychrome.
Des. *Roberts, 1932; Mera, 1934;
Hawley, 1936; Colton and Har-
grave, 1937; Carlson, 1962;
Carlson, 1970.
Illus. Martin and Willis, 1940; O'
Bryan, 1950.

HOVENWEEP CORRUGATED
AD 1250-1300
Des. Colton, 1932; *Abel, 1955,
10A-8; *Hayes, 1964.
Illus. Hammett, 1977.

HOVENWEEP CORRUGATED: VARI-
ETY 2
Des. *Forsyth, 1972.

HOVENWEEP CORRUGATED: VARI-
ETY 3
Des. *Forsyth, 1972. (Differs from
Variety 2 only in respect to sur-
face manipulation.)

HOVENWEEP GRAY
AD 1250-1300
Des. *Abel, 1955, 10A-7.
Illus. Hammett, 1977.

HOYAPI BLACK-ON-WHITE
AD 1250-1300
Des. *Colton and Hargrave, 1937;
*Colton, 1955, 8B-13.

HUAMANUI RED
Des. Hayden, 1957. (Local variety
of Santan Redware found at Pueblo Grande.)

HUCKOVI BLACK-ON-ORANGE
AD 1250-1300
Des. Colton, 1956, 7B-2; *Smith,
1971; Dittert and Plog, 1980.

HUCKOVI POLYCHROME
AD 1275-1325
Des. *Colton, 1956, 7B-1; Dittert
and Plog, 1980.

HUERIGOS POLYCHROME
AD 1350-1450
Syn. Carretas Polychrome.
Des. *Amsden, 1928; *Carey,
1931; Brand, 1935; Hawley,
1936; Sayles, 1936; DiPeso,
1969; *DiPeso, 1974.

HUNTER CORRUGATED
AD 1100-1300
Des. Wilson and Peckham, 1964;
*Windes, 1977.

HURRICANE BLACK-ON-GRAY
Des. Colton, 1952; Anderson,
1960.
Illus. Shutler, 1961.

INDENTED BLIND-CORRUGATED
Des. Kidder and Shepard, 1936.

INSPIRATION RED
Pre AD 1200-post 1400
Syn. Gila Red.
Des. *Doyel, 1978.

ISLETA POLYCHROME
Des. Stubbs, 1950.
Illus. Wormington, 1951; Barry,
1981; Trimble, 1987.

ISMAY BLACK-ON-GRAY: VARIETY
1
AD 575-900
Syn. Chapin Black-on-white,
abel, 1955; Swannack, 1969,
in part; Rohn, 1966.
Des. Forsyth, 1972.

ISMAY BLACK-ON-GRAY: VARIETY
2
AD 575-900
Syn. Chapin Black-on-white,
in part, Rohn 1966; Twin
Trees Black-on-white, O'Bryan,
1950.
Des. Forsyth, 1972.

IVIE CREEK BLACK-ON-WHITE
Ca. AD 700-1200
Syn. Fremont Black-on-white,
Morss, 1931; Sevier Black-on-
gray, Stewart, 1936; Great
Salt Lake Black-on-gray,
Stewart, 1936.
Des. Gunnerson, 1956; *Lister,

1960; Madsen, 1972; *Madsen,
1977.
Illus. Aikens, 1967; Marwitt, 1968.

JEDDITO BLACK-ON-ORANGE
AD 1275-1400
Des. Hargrave, 1931; Hawley, 1936;
Colton and Hargrave, 1937;
*Colton, 1956, 5B-14; Dittert
and Plog, 1980.
Illus. Martin and Willis, 1940; Bice,
1975.

JEDDITO BLACK-ON-WHITE
Ca. AD 1275-1350
Des. Hargrave, 1932; Hawley, 1936;
Colton and Hargrave, 1937.
Illus. Bice, 1975; Barry, 1981.

JEDDITO BLACK-ON-YELLOW
AD 1300-1600
Des. Fewkes, 1898; *Hargrave,
1932; Hawley, 1936; *Colton
and Hargrave, 1937; *Colton,
1956, 7B-6; Smith, 1971; *Dittert and Plog, 1980.
Illus. Hough, 1903; Martin, 1940;
Wormington, 1951; McGregor,
1965; Smith et al., 1966; Lister
and Lister, 1969; Arizona Highways, Feb. 1974; Huse, 1976;
Windes, 1977; Wade, 1980; Barry,
1981.

JEDDITO CORRUGATED
AD 1300-1400
Des. *Hargrave, 1932; Hawley,
1936; Colton and Hargrave,
1937; *Colton, 1956, 7A-1.
Illus. Lister and Lister, 1969.

JEDDITO ENGRAVED
AD 1350-1600
Des. *Hargrave, 1932; Hawley,
1936; Colton and Hargrave,
1937; *Colton, 1956, 7B-8; Dittert and Plog, 1980.

JEDDITO PLAIN
AD 1300-present
Des. *Hargrave, 1932; Hawley,
1936; Colton and Hargrave,
1937; *Colton, 1956, 7A-2.
Illus. Huse, 1976.

JEDDITO POLYCHROME
AD 1250-1300

Des. Colton and Hargrave, 1937;
*Colton, 1956, 5B-15; *Smith,
1971; Dittert and Plog, 1980.
Illus. Wade, 1980; Barry, 1981.

JEDDITO STIPPLED
AD 1350-1600
Syn. Jeddito Black-on-yellow
stippled, Hawley, 1936.
Des. *Hargrave, 1932; *Colton
and Hargrave, 1937; *Colton,
1956, 7B-7; Dittert and Plog,
1980.

JEDDITO TOOLED
AD 1300-recent
Des. *Hargrave, 1932; Hawley,
1936; *Colton and Hargrave,
1937; Colton, 1956, 7A-3.

JEDDITO YELLOW WARE
Ca. AD 1250-1700
Des. Colton and Hargrave, 1937;
Colton, 1956, 7B.

JEMEZ BLACK-ON-WHITE
AD 1300-1750
Des. *Mera, 1935; Hawley, 1936;
*Reiter, 1938; Harlow, 1970;
Frank and Harlow, 1974; *Dit-
tert and Plog, 1980.
Illus. Mera, 1939; Carlson, 1965;
Barnett, 1973; Barry, 1981.

JOHNSON CORRUGATED
Des. Stewart, 1941.

JOHNSON GRAY
Syn. Johnson Gray-Tan, Stewart,
1941.
Des. Stewart, 1941; Colton, 1952;
Anderson, 1960.
Illus. Lister et al., 1960.

JOHNSON GRAY-TAN
Syn. Johnson Gray, Colton, 1952.
Des. Stewart, 1941; Colton, 1952;
Anderson, 1960.
Illus. Lister et al., 1960.

JORNADA BICHROME
(Red-on-brown and Black-on-
brown)
Des. Human Systems Research,
1973.

JORNADA BLACK-ON-BROWN

Des. Mera, 1943; Human Systems
Research, 1973.

JORNADA BROWN (PLAIN)
Ad 900-1350
Des. Mera, 1943; Lehmer, 1948;
Jellinek, 1967; Human Systems
Research, 1973; Runyan and
Hedrick, 1973; Warren, 1976;
Mobley, 1978.
Illus. Jellinek, 1952.

JORNADA CORRUGATED
Mentioned in Jellinek, 1967.

JORNADA POLYCHROME
Des. Mera, 1943; Human Systems
Research, 1973.

JORNADA RED
Des. Bussey et al., 1976.

JORNADA RED-ON-BROWN
Des. Mera, 1943; Human Systems
Research, 1973.

JORNADA RED TOOLED
Mentioned in Fitting, 1971.

KANA-A BLACK-ON-WHITE
AD 725-950
Des. *Kidder and Guernsey, 1919;
*Hargrave, 1932; Hawley, 1936;
*Colton and Hargrave, 1937;
*Colton, 1955, 8B-2; *Dittert
and Plog, 1980.
Illus. Martin, 1936; Martin and
Willis, 1940; Beals, Brainerd
and Smith, 1945; Colton, 1946;
Colton, 1953; Wendorf et al.,
1956; Steen, 1966; Willey, 1966;
Lister and Lister, 1969; Gumer-
man, 1970; Brody, 1977.

KANA-A GRAY
AD 760-900
Syn. Kana-a Neckbanded, Colton,
1955.
Des. Kidder and Guernsey, 1919;
*Hargrave, 1932; Hawley, 1936;
*Colton and Hargrave, 1937;
*Colton, 1955, 8A-5.
Illus. Kidder, 1924; Morris, 1927;
Brew, 1946; Colton, 1946;
O'Bryan, 1950; Dittert and
Ruppe, 1951; Wendorf et al.,
1956; Dittert and Eddy, 1963;

Lister and Lister, 1969; Bice,
1975; DiPeso, 1967; Ambler, 1977.

KANA-A BLACK-ON-WHITE: FUGI-
TIVE RED VARIETY
Des. *Gomolak, 1980.

KANA-A NECKBANDED
AD 760-900
Syn. Kana-a Gray.
Des. *Colton, 1955; Olson, 1971.

KANAB BLACK-ON-RED
Des. *Thompson, 1986.
(Name suggested for a slipped
black-on-red type with quartz
and sand temper from the
western Anasazi area.)

KANAB BROWN
Des. Thompson, 1971.

KANAB POLYCHROME
Syn. Middleton Polychrome
Des. Thompson, 1986.

KAPO BLACK
AD 1650-1800
Syn. Tewa Polished Black, Carlson, 1965.
Des. *Mera, 1939; *Dick in
Schroeder, 1968; Harlow,
1973; *Frank and Harlow,
1974; Mobley, 1978; Dittert
and Plog, 1980.

KAPO GRAY
AD 1650-1720
Des. *Harlow, 1973; Dittert and
Plog, 1980.

KAWAIOKU (KAWAIKA-A) POLY-
CHROME
AD 1400-1625
Des. *Hargrave, 1932; Hawley,
1936; Colton and Hargrave,
1937; *Colton, 1956, 7B-11;
Dittert and Plog, 1980.
Illus. Fewkes, 1898; Martin and
Willis, 1940.

KAWAIKA-A SPATTERED
Des. *Huse, 1976.

KAYENTA BLACK-ON-WHITE
AD 1260-1300
Des. *Kidder and Guernsey,

1919; *Kidder, 1924; *Hargrave,
1932; Hawley, 1936; Colton and
Hargrave, 1937; *Colton, 1956,
8B-10; *Dittert and Plog, 1980.
Illus. Cummings, 1935; Brainerd
and Smith, 1945; Colton, 1946;
Wormington, 1951; Colton, 1953;
Cummings, 1952; Lister et al.,
1960; Wormington, 1964; McGregor, 1965; Arizona Highways,
Feb. 1974; Bice, 1975; Hobler,
1974; Wade, 1980.

KAYENTA POLYCHROME
AD 1250-1300
Des. Kidder and Guernsey, 1919;
*Kidder, 1924; *Hargrave, 1932;
Hawley, 1936; *Colton and Har-
grave, 1937; *Colton, 1956,
5B-12; *Smith, 1971; Dittert
and Plog, 1980.
Illus. Martin and Willis, 1940; Cum-
mings, 1953; Colton et al., 1940;
Wade, 1980.

KEAMS CORRUGATED
Des. *Gifford and Smith, 1978.

KECHIPAWAN POLYCHROME
AD 1375-1475
Syn. Arauca Polychrome, Colton
and Hargrave, 1937; Pinnawa
Polychrome, Reed, 1955.
Des. *Martin and Rinaldo, 1960;
*Smith, Woodbury and Wood-
bury, 1966; *Dittert and Plog,
1980.
Illus. Martin and Willis, 1940; Rin-
aldo, 1959; Martin and Rinaldo,
1960a.

KIA-KO BLACK-ON-WHITE
Ca. AD 1100-1150
Syn. Sosi Black-on-white.
Des. Colton and Hargrave, 1937;
*Colton, 1956, 8B-11.

KIAPKWA POLYCHROME
AD 1700-1850
Des. *Harlow, 1970; Harlow, 1973;
*Frank and Harlow, 1974; *Dit-
tert and Plog, 1980.
Illus. Wade, 1980.

KIATUTHLANNA BLACK-ON-WHITE
AD 825-910

Syn. Kiatuthlanna/Red Mesa Black-
on-white, Vivian, 1965.
Des. *Roberts, 1931; Hawley,
1936; Gladwin, 1945; Cibola
White Ware Conf., 1958; Dit-
tert and Plog, 1980.
Illus. Martin and Willis, 1940;
Adams 1949; Wendorf et al.,
1956; Willey, 1966; Lister and
Lister, 1969; Olson, 1971;
Barnett, 1974a; Bice, 1975;
Brody, 1977; Andrews, 1980.

KIET SIEL BLACK-ON-RED
AD 1250-1300
Syn. Tusayan Black-on-red.
Des. *Colton, 1956, 5B-13; *Smith,
1971; Dittert and Plog, 1980.
Illus. Ambler et al., 1964; Hob-
ler, 1974; Hudson, 1980.

KIET SIEL GRAY
Ca. AD 1200-1300
Des. Hargrave, 1932; Colton and
Hargrave, 1937; *Colton,
1955, 8A-13.
Illus. Ambler et al., 1964; Hud-
son, 1980.

KIET SIEL POLYCHROME
AD 1225-1300
Des. *Colton and Hargrave, 1937;
*Colton, 1956, 5B-12; *Smith,
1971; Dittert and Plog, 1980.
Illus. Colton et al., 1940; Martin
and Willis, 1940; Beals, Brain-
erd and Smith, 1945; Ambler
et al., 1964; Hobler, 1974;
Ambler, 1977.

KINISHBA POLYCHROME
Ca. AD 1300-1350
Des. Baldwin, 1938; Wendorf,
1950; *Dittert and Plog, 1980.
Illus. Cummings, 1940; Arizona
Highways, Feb. 1974; Jacka
and Hill, 1976.

KINISHBA RED
Ca. AD 1300-1350
Syn. Showlow Red.
Des. Wendorf, 1950; Second SW
Ceramic Conf., 1959; *McGre-
gor, 1965.
Illus. Gifford, 1980.

KINISHBA WHITE-ON-RED
AD 1300-1350
Haury at Second SW Ceramic Conf.,
1959.
(Not described except as Kinishba
Red with white decoration.)
Illus. Asch, 1960.

KINNIKINNICK BROWN
Ca. AD 1300
Des. *Colton, 1941; Colton, 1958,
14-14.

KINNIKINNICK RED
AD 1130-1350?
Des. *Colton, 1941; Colton, 1958,
14-15.

KINTIEL BLACK-ON-ORANGE
AD 1275-1300
Syn. Black-on-yellow.
Des. Colton and Hargrave, 1937;
*Colton, 1956, 5B-18; Dittert
and Plog, 1980.
Illus. Haury, 1945.

KINTIEL POLYCHROME
Ca. AD 1250-1300
Des. Colton and Hargrave, 1937;
*Colton, 1956, 5B-19; Dittert
and Plog, 1980.

KIRKLAND GRAY
Syn. Yavapai Plain, Gladwin, 1934.
Des. Colton, 1939; Colton, 1958,
18-6.

KIUA BLACK-ON-RED
Ca. AD 1780-1880?
Des. *Frank and Harlow, 1974.

KIAU POLYCHROME
AD 1780-present
Des. *Harlow, 1970; Harlow, 1973;
*Frank and Harlow, 1974; *Dit-
tert and Plog, 1980.

KLAGETO BLACK-ON-WHITE
Ca. AD 1250-1300
Des. *Colton and Hargrave, 1937;
*Smith, 1971.
Illus. Wendorf et al., 1956; Dan-
son, 1957; Andrews, 1980.

KLAGETO BLACK-ON-YELLOW
Ca. AD 1250
Des. Colton, 1932; Colton and

Hargrave, 1937; *Colton, 1956,
5B-16; Dittert and Plog, 1980.

KLAGETO POLYCHROME
Ca. AD 1250
Des. Colton and Hargrave, 1937;
*Colton, 1956, 5B-17; Dittert
and Plog, 1980.

KNOLLS GRAY
AD 400-1350
Des. Malouf, 1946; Malouf, 1950;
Rudy, 1953. (A variant of
Great Salt Lake Gray)

KOKOP BLACK-ON-ORANGE
AD 1250-1300
Des. *Hargrave, 1932; Hawley,
1936; Colton and Hargrave,
1937; *Colton, 1956, 7B-4;
*Smith, 1971.

KOKOP BLACK-ON-WHITE
Ca. AD 1300
Des. Colton and Hargrave, 1937;
Cibola White Ware Conference,
1958.

KOKOP POLYCHROME
AD 1250-1325
Des. Hargrave, 1932; Colton and
Hargrave, 1937; *Colton, 1956,
7B-3; *Smith, 1971; Dittert
and Plog, 1980.

KOTYITI GLAZE-ON-RED
AD 1650-1700
Des. Mera, 1933; Hawley, 1936;
Eighth SW Ceramic Sem. 1966;
Warren, 1979; Dittert and
Plog, 1980.

KOTYITI GLAZE-ON-YELLOW
AD 1650-1700
Des. Warren, 1979; Dittert and
Plog, 1980.

KOTYITI GLAZE POLYCHROME
AD 1650-1700
Syn. Glaze VI, *Kidder and
Shepard, 1936.
Des. Mera, 1933; Hawley, 1936;
*Mera, 1939; Harlow, 1970;
Warren, 1979.
Illus. Carlson, 1965.

KOWINA BANDED
Des. Dittert, 1959.

KOWINA BLACK-ON-RED
Des. Dittert, 1959.

KOWINA BLACK-ON-WHITE
AD 1200-1400
Des. Dittert, 1959.

KOWINA INDENTED
Des. Dittert, 1959.

KOWINA POLYCHROME
Des. Dittert, 1959.

KUAUA GLAZE POLYCHROME
Des. Mera, 1933; Hawley, 1936;
Eighth SW Ceramic Seminar,
1966.
Illus. Barry, 1981.

KWAHE'E BLACK-ON-WHITE
AD 1125-1200
Des. *Mera, 1935; Hawley, 1936;
Peckham, 1963; *McNutt, 1969;
Sudar-Murphy and Laumbach,
1977; Dittert and Plog, 1980.
Illus. Bice and Sundt, 1972; Tray-
lor and Scaife, 1980.

KWAITUKI BLACK-ON-ORANGE
Des. *Smith, 1971.

KWAITUKI POLYCHROME
AD 1250-1300
Des. Colton and Hargrave, 1937;
Second SW Ceramic Seminar,
1959.

KWAITUKI POLYCHROME
(Maroon Slipped variant)
Des. *Smith, 1971.

KWAKINA GLAZE POLYCHROME
AD 1285-1300
Syn. Kwakina Polychrome.
Des. Reed, 1955.
Illus. Voll, 1961; Carlson, 1970.

KWAKINA POLYCHROME
AD 1285-1300
Syn. Kwakina Glaze Polychrome,
Reed, 1955; Wallace Polychrome,
Colton and Hargrave, 1937.
Des. *Martin and Rinaldo, 1960;
*Martin et al., 1963; *Smith,
Woodbury and Woodbury, 1966;
*Carlson, 1970; *Dittert and Plog,
1980.

Illus. Hough, 1903; Fewkes,
1904; Fewkes, 1909; Rinaldo,
1959; Martin and Rinaldo,
1960a; Carlson, 1962.

LAGUNA POLYCHROME
AD 1830-1940
Des. Ellis, 1966; *Harlow, 1973;
*Frank and Harlow, 1974; *Dit-
tert and Plog, 1980.
Illus. Stevenson, 1883; Bahti,
1964; Barry, 1981; Trimble,
1987.

LA PLATA BLACK-ON-ORANGE
Des. *Martin, 1939.
Illus. Martin and Willis, 1940.

LA PLATA BLACK-ON-RED
AD 800-1000
(May be a regional variety of
Deadmans Black-on-red)
Syn. Sandstone Black-on-orange,
Kluckhohn and Reiter, 1939.
Des. Morris, 1939; Shepard, 1939;
Reed, 1943; *Abel, 1955, 5A-
5.
Illus. Guernsey, 1931; O'Bryan,
1950; Lister and Lister, 1969;
Morris, 1980.

LA PLATA BLACK-ON-RED: VA-
RIETY 1
AD 800-1000
Syn. Sandstone Black-on-orange,
in part, Kluckhohn and Rei-
ter, 1939; La Plata Black-on-
orange, in part, Martin and
Rinaldo, 1939; La Plata Black-
on-red, in part, Reed, 1943;
Bluff Black-on-red; La Plata
Variety (slipped), Rohn, 1966.
Des. *Forsyth, 1972.

LA PLATA BLACK-ON-WHITE
AD 575-875
Des. Morris, 1927; Roberts, 1929;
Hawley, 1936; *Morris, 1939;
Cibola White Ware Conf., 1958;
*Hayes, 1964; *Dittert and
Plog, 1980.
Illus. Brew, 1946; Adams, 1949;
O'Bryan, 1950; Lancaster et
al., 1954; Peckham, 1957;
Reed, 1958; Vivian, 1965; New
Mexico Univ., 1967; Lister and
Lister, 1969; Bice, 1970.

LAPSTREAK CORRUGATED
AD 1100-1200
Syn. Fremont Corrugated, Morris,
1931b.
Des. Morris, 1931b.

LARGO GLAZE-ON-RED
Des. Honea, 1966; Dittert and
Plog, 1980.

LARGO GLAZE-ON-YELLOW
AD 1400-1450
Des. Mera, 1933; Hawley, 1936;
Warren, 1977c.

LARGO GLAZE POLYCHROME
AD 1400-1450
Syn. Glaze II, *Kidder and Shep-
ard, 1936.
Des. Mera, 1933; Hawley, 1936;
Warren, 1977c; Dittert and Plog,
1980.
Illus. Voll, 1961.

LAS MADRES BLACK-ON-WHITE
Mentioned in Honea, 1968.

LAS TUSAS BLACK-ON-GRAY
AD 915-1125
Syn. Escavada Black-on-white,
Vivian, 1959.
Des. Hargrave, 1961.

LEMITAR GLAZE POLYCHROME
Des. Mera, 1933; *Vivian, 1964;
Honea, 1966.

LEAL RED-ON-BROWN
Des. DiPeso, 1969; *DiPeso, 1974.

LEUPP BLACK-ON-WHITE
AD 1200-1300
Syn. Walnut Black-on-white, in
part.
Des. *Colton, 1955, 9B-6.

LINCOLN BLACK-ON-RED
AD 1300-1400
Des. *Mera and Stallings, 1931;
Hawley, 1936; Human Systems
Research, 1973; Runyan and
Hedrick, 1973.

LINCOLN BLACK-ON-RED GLAZE
Des. Hawley, 1936; Smiley, Stubbs
and Bannister, 1953; Human Systems Research, 1973.

Illus. Jellinek, 1952; Smiley, 1978;
Stewart, 1979.

LINDEN CORRUGATED
AD 1050-1250
Des. Haury, 1931; *Colton and
Hargrave, 1937.

LINO BLACK-ON-GRAY
AD 575-875
Des. Morris, 1927; *Hargrave,
1932; Hawley, 1936; *Colton
and Hargrave, 1937; Colton,
1956, 8A-4; *Carlson, 1963.
Illus. Roberts, 1919; Colton,
1946; Brew, 1946; *O'Bryan,
1950; Colton, 1953; Daifuku,
1961; Shutler, 1961; New Mexico Univ., 1967; Bice, 1970;
Dittert and Plog, 1980.

LINO FUGITIVE RED
AD 572-775
Des. Morris, 1927; Colton and
Hargrave, 1937; Colton, 1956,
8A-3.
Illus. Roberts, 1919; Morris,
1980.

LINO GRAY
AD 575-875
Des. Kidder and Guernsey, 1919;
*Hargrave, 1932; Hawley,
1936; Colton and Hargrave,
1937; *Colton, 1956, 8A-2;
Dittert and Plog, 1980.
Illus. Roberts, 1928; Roberts,
1929; Brew, 1946; Colton,
1946; O'Bryan, 1950; Wendorf
et al., 1956; Lancaster et al.,
1964; New Mexico Univ., 1967;
Hammack, 1969; Bice, 1970;
Soule, 1976; Ambler, 1977.

LINO GRAY: DURANGO VARIETY
Des. Carlson, 1963.

LINO POLISHED
AD 500-750
Syn. Obelisk Gray, Abel, 1955,
8A-1.
Des. Morris, 1936.

LINO RED
AD 620-775
Syn. Tallahogan Red, Daifuku,
1961.

Des. Wendorf, 1953; Daifuku,
1961.

LINO SMUDGED
AD 620-775
Des. Haury, 1940a; E. Morris,
1959a.
Illus. Morris, 1980.

LITTLE COLORADO CORRUGATED
AD 1080-1275
Des. Colton and Hargrave, 1937;
*Colton, 1955, 9A-5.

LITTLE COLORADO GRAY WARE
AD 700-1200
Des. Colton, 1956, 9A.

LITTLE COLORADO WHITE WARE
AD 1000-1375
Des. Colton and Hargrave, 1937;
Colton, 1955, 9B.
Illus. Haury, 1945; Arizona High-
ways, Feb. 1974.

LOGANDALE GRAY
Des. Colton, 1952.
Illus. Worman, 1949; Soule, 1976;
Soule, 1978.

LOGANDALE GRAY WARE
Des. Colton, 1952.

LOPEZ MICACEOUS
Des. Honea, 1966.
(Similar to Cundiyo Micaceous and
Cordova Micaceous)

LOS LUNAS COIL
Mentioned in Breternitz, 1966.

LOS LUNAS INCISED
Des. Mera, 1935.

LOS LUNAS PUNCTATE
Des. Mera, 1935.

LOS LUNAS SMUDGED
AD 1270-1370
Des. *Mera, 1935; Hawley, 1936;
Human Systems Research, 1973;
Atwood, 1974.

LOS PADILLAS GLAZE POLYCHROME
AD 1300-1315?
Des. Mera, 1933; Hawley, 1936; Atwood, 1974; Dittert and Plog,
1980.

Illus. Mera, 1935.

LOS PINOS BROWN
AD 1-400
Des. Dittert et al., 1963; McGregor, 1965; Dittert and Plog,
1980.

LOWER COLORADO BUFF WARE
Ca. AD 800-post 1900
Syn. Topoc Buff, Colton, 1939.
Des. Schroeder, 1952; Schroeder,
1958, 16.

LUPTON BROWN
Des. Wasley, 1960.

MACHONPI POLYCHROME
AD 1250
Des. *Colton, 1956, 5A-11; Dittert and Plog, 1980. (Similar
to Kayenta Polychrome)

MADERA BLACK-ON-RED
Syn. Black-on-red, Carey, 1931;
Chihuahua Black-on-red,
Brand, 1935.
Des. Brand, 1935; *Sayles, 1936;
Hawley, 1936; DiPeso, 1969;
Human Systems Research,
1973; *DiPeso, 1974.
Illus. Martin et al., 1947; Mills
and Mills, 1971; Bice, 1975.

MAGDALENA BLACK-ON-RED
Des. Knight and Gomolak, 1981.

MAGDALENA BLACK-ON-WHITE
Syn. Similar to Mesa Verde Black-
on-white.
Des. Warren, 1974; Knight and
Gomolak, 1981.

MAGDALENA FINGER SMEARED
Des. Knight and Gomolak, 1981.

MAGDALENA INDENTED CORRUGATED
Des. Knight and Gomolak, 1981.

MAGDALENA PLAIN CORRUGATED
Des. Knight and Gomolak, 1981.

MAGDALENA PLAIN UTILITY
Des. Knight and Gomolak, 1981.

MAGDALENA POLYCHROME
Des. Knight and Gomolak, 1981.

MAGDALENA PUNCHED CORRUGATED
Des. Knight and Gomolak, 1981.

MANCOS BLACK-ON-WHITE
AD 900-1150
Syn. Piedra Black-on-white, Haw-
ley, 1936; Chaco Pueblo III
Black-on-white, Morris, 1939.
Des. *Martin, 1936; Hawley, 1936;
Colton and Hargrave, 1937;
Smiley, Stubbs and Bannister,
1953; *Abel, 1955, 12A-5; Fifth
SW Ceramic Conf., 1963; *Hayes,
1964; *Breternitz et al., 1974;
*Rohn, 1977; *Windes, 1977;
*Dittert and Plog, 1980.
Illus. Fewkes, 1911; Martin and
Willis, 1940; Brew, 1946; O'Bryan,
1950; Reed, 1958; Vivian, 1959;
Lancaster et al., 1964; Lister,
1965; Steen, 1966; Willey, 1966;
New Mexico Univ., 1967; Lister,
1968; Lister and Lister, 1969;
Rohn, 1970; Bice, 1975; Barry,
1981.

MANCOS CORRUGATED
AD 900-1200
Syn. Pueblo II Exuberant Corru-
gated, in part, Roberts, 1935;
Variable Corrugated, in part,
Reed, 1958; Mesa Verde Corru-
gated: Mancos Variety, Rohn;
Payan Corrugated, in part, Dit-
tert and Eddy, 1963.
Des. *Morris, 1939; *Brew, 1946;
*Abel, 1955, 10A-5; *Reed, 1958;
*Hayes, 1964; *Breternitz et al.,
1974.
Illus. Martin, 1938; O'Bryan, 1950;
Lancaster, 1954; Sharrock and
Keane, 1962; Dittert and Eddy,
1963; Lister, 1965; Lister, 1968;
Lister and Lister, 1969; Swan-
nack, 1969.

MANCOS CORRUGATED: VARIETY 1
AD 900-1200
Syn. Mancos Corrugated, in part,
Abel, 1955; Hayes, 1964; Swan-
nack, 1969; Mesa Verde Corru-
gated: Mancos variety, Rohn,
1966.
Des. *Forsyth, 1972.

MANCOS CORRUGATED: VARIETY 2
AD 900-1200

Des. *Forsyth, 1972.
(Differs from Mancos Corrugated:
Variety I only with respect to
decoration and surface treatment.)

MANCOS CORRUGATED: VARIETY 3
AD 900-1200
Des. *Forsyth, 1972.
(Differs from Mancos Corrugated:
Variety 1 only with respect to
decoration and surface treat-
ment.)

MANCOS GRAY
Ca. AD 875-950
Syn. Clapboard Corrugated, Kid-
der and Shepard, 1936; Plain
Corrugated, Martin, 1938.
Des. *Martin, 1938; *Abel, 1955,
10A-4; *Hayes, 1964; Breter-
nitz et al., 1974; *Rohn, 1977;
*Windes, 1977.
Illus. Morris, 1939; Brew, 1946;
Lister, 1965; Lister and Lister,
1969; Swannack, 1969.

MANGUS BLACK-ON-WHITE
AD 775-927
Syn. Mimbres Boldface, *Cos-
grove, 1932.
Des. *Cosgrove, 1932; Haury,
1936; Hawley, 1936; Human
Systems Research, 1973;
*Brody, 1977.
Illus. Martin et al., 1952; Breter-
nitz, 1959; Lister and Lister,
1969; Hill, 1971.

MANZANO THIN RED-ON-BROWN
Mentioned in Dick, 1965.

MARICOPA WARE
Des. Spier, 1933; *Kayser, 1971.
Illus. Sayles and Sayles, 1948;
Bahti, 1964; Feder, 1965; Tan-
ner, 1968; Museum of American
Indian, 1972; Sunset Magazine,
1972; Arizona Highways, May
1974; Barry, 1981.

MATA POLYCHROME
AD 1050-1275
Des. DiPeso, 1969; *DiPeso, 1974.

MATA RED-ON-BROWN TEXTURED
Des. DiPeso, 1969; *DiPeso, 1974;
DiPeso et al., 1976.

MATSAKI BROWN-ON-BUFF
  Ca. AD 1475-late 1600s
  Syn. Hawikuh Brown-on-buff,
    Smith, Woodbury and Wood-
    bury, 1966.
  Des. Reed, 1955; *Smith, Wood-
    bury and Woodbury, 1966.
  Illus. Carlson, 1965.

MATSAKI POLYCHROME
  Ca. AD 1475-late 1600s
  Des. Reed, 1955; *Smith, Wood-
    bury and Woodbury, 1966;
    *Dittert and Plog, 1980.
  Illus. Bushnell and Digby, 1955.

MAVERICK MOUNTAIN BLACK-ON-RED
  AD 1265-1290
  Des. Morris, 1957.
  (Now considered to be part of
    Maverick Mountain Polychrome)
  Illus. Brown, 1974.

MAVERICK MOUNTAIN POLYCHROME
  AD 1265-1290
  Des. E. Morris, 1957; DiPeso,
    1958; Wasley, 1962
  Illus. Brown, 1974.

MCCARTYS POLYCHROME
  AD 1850-1875
  Des. *Harlow, 1970; *Harlow,
    1973; *Frank and Harlow, 1974;
    *Dillingham, 1977; *Dittert and
    Plog, 1980.
  Illus. Harlow, 1977.

MCCRACKEN TOOLED: VARIETY 1
  Syn. Mancos Gray, in part, Abel,
    1955; Hayes, 1964; Rohn, 1966;
    Swannack, 1969.
  Des. *Forsyth, 1972.

MCDONALD CORRUGATED
  AD 1100-1300
  Syn. St. Johns Corrugated, *Col-
    ton and Hargrave, 1937.
  Des. *Haury, 1931.
  Illus. Hough, 1903; Schmidt, 1928;
    McGregor, 1965; Martin, 1967.

MCDONALD GROOVED CORRUGATED
  AD 1100-1300
  Syn. McDonald Grooved, Colton,
    1955.
  (Variant of McDonald Corrugated

with grooving.)
    Danson, 1952 manuscript, named
    but not described.
  Illus. Breternitz et al., 1957;
    Gifford, 1980.

MCDONALD INDENTED
  AD 1100-1300
  Danson, 1952 manuscript, named
    but not described.
  (Mariant of McDonald Corrugated
    with punched indentations.)

MCDONALD PAINTED CORRUGATED
  AD 1200-1300
  Syn. McDonald Corrugated, Col-
    ton and Hargrave, 1937.
  Des. Gifford, 1957; Olson, 1959.
  Illus. Breternitz et al., 1957;
    Johnson and Wasley, 1966;
    Gifford, 1980.

MCDONALD PATTERNED CORRUGATED
  AD 1100-1300
  Syn. McDonald Indented, Colton,
    1955.
  Des. Olson, 1959.
  Illus. Breternitz et al., 1957.

MCELMO BLACK-ON-WHITE
  AD 1075-1275
  Syn. Proto-Mesa Verde Black-on-
    white, in part, Kidder, 1927.
  Des. Kidder, 1924; Hawley, 1936;
    Brew, 1946; *O'Bryan, 1950;
    *Abel, 1955, 10B-1; Fifth SW
    Ceramic Conf., 1963; *Hayes,
    1964; *Breternitz et al., 1974;
    *Windes, 1977; Dittert and
    Plog, 1980.
  Illus. Fewkes, 1911; Martin,
    1936; Brand et al., 1937;
    Martin and Willis, 1940; Wen-
    dorf et al., 1956; Reed, 1958;
    Sharrock and Keane, 1962;
    Sharrock et al., 1963; Ambler
    et al., 1964; Vivian, 1964;
    Lister, 1965; New Mexico Univ.,
    1967; Lister and Lister, 1969;
    Swannack, 1969; Rohn, 1970;
    Bice, 1975; Rohn, 1977; Am-
    bler, 1977.

MCELMO BLACK-ON-WHITE: CHACO
  VARIETY
  Des. Vivian, 1959.

MCELMO BLACK-ON-WHITE: CHACO
VARIETY-PRIETA VISTA
Des. *Bice and Sundt, 1972.

MCELMO BLACK-ON-WHITE: GUA-
DALUPE VARIETY
Des. *Pippen, 1978.

MCKENZIE BROWN
Des. Jellinek, 1967.

MCKINLEY BLACK-ON-WHITE
Des. Colton manuscript MNA.

MEDANOS RED-ON-BROWN
Des. Haury, 1936; *Sayles, 1936;
Hawley, 1936; Human Systems
Research, 1973.

MEDICINE BLACK-ON-RED
AD 1075-1125
Des. *Colton and Hargrave, 1937;
*Colton, 1956, 5B-1; Dittert
and Plog, 1980.
Illus. Colton et al., 1940; Shutler,
1961; Ambler et al., 1964; An-
derson, 1969; Gumerman, 1970;
Hobler, 1974; Ambler, 1977.

MEDICINE GRAY
AD 890-1060
Des. *Colton and Hargrave, 1937;
*Colton, 1955, 8A-9.

MEDIO GLAZE POLYCHROME (HONEA)
AD 1425-1475
Des. Eighth SW Ceramic Conf.,
1966; Dittert and Plog, 1980.

MENEFEE GOUGED: VARIETY 1
Des. *Forsyth, 1972.
(Differs from Mancos Corrugated
only in respect to surface manipulation.)

MENEFEE GOUGED: VARIETY 2
Des. *Forsyth, 1972.
(Differs from Menefee Gouged:
Variety 1 only in respect to
decorative effect and surface
manipulation.)

MESA VERDE BLACK-ON-WHITE
AD 1200-1300
Syn. Mesa Verde Polychrome, Abel,
1955.
Des. *Nordenskiold, 1893; *Kidder,

1924; Kidder and Shepard,
1936; Hawley, 1936; Colton
and Hargrave, 1937; *Abel,
1955, 10B-2; Rohn, 1971;
Hayes, 1964; *Breternitz et
al., 1974; *Rohn, 1977;
*Windes, 1977; *Dittert and
Plog, 1980.
Illus. Barber, 1876; Fewkes, 1911;
Pepper, 1920; Goddard, 1928;
Martin, 1936; Morris, 1939;
Martin and Willis, 1940, Haury,
1945; Brew, 1946; O'Bryan,
1950; Wormington, 1951; Lan-
caster et al., 1954; Wendorf
et al., 1956; Gladwin, 1957;
Reed, 1958; Vivian, 1959;
Watson, 1961; Corbett, 1962;
Richert, 1962; Sharrock and
Keane, 1962; Sharoock et al.,
1963; Wormington, 1964; Mc-
Gregor, 1965; Steen, 1966;
New Mexico Univ., 1967; Di-
Peso, 1967; Howard, 1968;
Lister and Lister, 1969; Bice,
1975; Brody, 1977; Barry,
1981.

MESA VERDE BLACK-ON-WHITE:
VARIETY 1
Syn. McElmo Black-on-white, Haw-
ley, 1936; Reed, 1943; Brew,
1946; Hayes, 1964; Swannack,
1969; Abel, 1955; Mesa Verde
Black-on-white: McElmo
Variety, Rohn, 1966.
Des. *Forsyth, 1972.

MESA VERDE BLACK-ON-WHITE:
VARIETY 2
Syn. Mesa Verde Black-on-white,
Kidder, 1924; Abel, 1955;
Matheny, 1962; Hayes, 1964;
Colton and Hargrave, 1937;
Mesa Verde Black-on-white:
Mesa Verde Variety, Rohn,
1966.
Des. *Forsyth, 1972.

MESA VERDE BLACK-ON-WHITE:
MESA VERDE VARIETY
Ca. AD 1150-1300
Des. *Rohn, 1977.

MESA VERDE BLACK-ON-WHITE:
MCELMO VARIETY
Ca. AD 1050 or 1100-1300
Des. *Rohn, 1977.

MESA VERDE CORRUGATED
AD 1200-1300
Syn. Hovenweep Corrugated, Abel,
1955; Gray Corrugated, in part,
Colton, 1932; Standardized Corrugated, Reed, 1958.
Des. Morris, 1939; Abel, 1955,
10A-6; *Reed, 1958; *Rohn,
1959; *Hayes, 1964; *Rohn,
1971; *Breternitz et al., 1974;
*Rohn, 1977; *Windes, 1977.
Illus. Brew, 1946; Lister and Lister, 1969; Barry, 1981.

MESA VERDE CORRUGATED: MESA
VERDE VARIETY
Ca. AD 1100-1200
Des. *Rohn, 1977.

MESA VERDE CORRUGATED: MAN-
COS VARIETY
Ca. AD 900-1100
Syn. Mancos Corrugated, Breternitz
et al., 1974.
Des. Colton, 1932; *Abel, 1955,
10A-6; *Rohn, 1977.
Illus. Swannack, 1969.

MESA VERDE GRAY WARE
Ca. AD 450-1300
Des. Abel, 1955, 10A; Rohn, 1977.
Illus. Morris, 1919; Lister, 1966.

MESA VERDE POLYCHROME
Ca. AD 1200-1300
Syn. Mesa Verde Black-on-white,
Abel, 1955.
Des. Brew, 1946; *Abel, 1955,
10B-3; Dittert and Plog, 1980.
(Name dropped at the Fifth SW
Ceramic Seminar, 1963.)

MESA VERDE WHITE WARE
Ca. AD 600-1300
Des. Colton and Hargrave, 1937;
Abel, 1955, 10B; Rohn, 1977.
Illus. Morris, 1919.

MESQUITE BLACK-ON-GRAY
AD 525-750
Syns. Lino Black-on-gray and
Kana-a Black-on-gray.
Des. *Thompson, 1986.

MESQUITE GRAY
AD 525-775
Syn. Lino Gray
Des. *Thompson, 1986.

MIDDLE PECOS BLACK-ON-WHITE
Des. *Jellinek, 1967.

MIDDLE PECOS MICACEOUS BROWN
Des. Jellinek, 1967.

MIDDLETON BLACK-ON-RED
AD 1050-1130
(Similar to Tusayan Black-on-
red)
Des. *Spencer, 1934; Colton, 1952;
*Colton, 1956, 5A-7; Dittert
and Plog, 1980.
Illus. Lister et al., 1960; Pen-
dergast, 1960.

MIDDLETON POLYCHROME
Des. Schroeder, 1955; *Lister,
1960.

MIDDLETON RED
AD 900-1130
Des. *Spencer, 1934; Colton,
1952; Colton, 1956, 5A-8.

MIMBRES BLACK-ON-WHITE
AD 1000-1250
Des. *Cosgrove, 1932; Hawley,
1936; Reed, 1938b; Smiley,
Stubbs and Bannister, 1953;
Human Systems Research,
1973; Runyan and Hedrick,
1973; *Brody, 1977; Le Blanc,
1983.
Illus. Anonymous, 1914; Fewkes,
1916; Fewkes, 1923; Fewkes,
1924; Kidder, 1924; Ochard,
1925; Goddard, 1928; Bradfield, 1929; Nesbitt, 1931;
Martin, 1947; Wormington,
1951; Jellinek, 1952; Martin
et al., 1952; Martin et al.,
1954; Bluhm, 1957; Gladwin,
1957; New Mexico Quarterly,
1957; Denver Art Museum,
1969; Jellinek, 1961; Wormington, 1964; McGregor, 1965;
Alexander, 1966; Willey, 1966;
New Mexico Univ., 1967; Lister and Lister, 1969; Snodgrass, 1973; Arizona Highways, Feb. 1974; Maxwell
Museum, 1974; Bice, 1975;
DiPeso, 1967; LeBlanc and
Khalil, 1976; Brody, 1977a;
Snodgrass, 1977; LeBlanc,
1978; Barry, 1981.

MIMBRES BOLDFACE
AD 775-927
Syn. Mangus Black-on-white, Cosgrove, 1932.
Des. *Cosgrove, 1932; Human Systems Research, 1973; *Brody,
1977; Runyan and Hedrick,
1973; LeBlanc, 1983.
Illus. Bradfield, 1929; Martin et
al., 1952; Lister and Lister,
1969; Dennis, 1977; Smiley,
1978.

MIMBRES CORRUGATED
Des. *Cosgrove, 1932; Hawley,
1936; *LeBlanc, 1983.
Illus. Nesbitt, 1931; Sayles, 1936;
Brody, 1977.

MIMBRES INCISED
Des. *Cosgrove, 1932; Hawley,
1936; *LeBlanc, 1983.

MIMBRES PLAIN
Des. *Cosgrove, 1932; Hawley,
1936; *LeBlanc, 1983.

MIMBRES POLYCHROME
AD 1000?-1150
Des. *Cosgrove, 1932; *Brody,
1977; *LeBlanc, 1983.
Illus. Nesbitt, 1931; Hammerson,
1972; Bice, 1975; Gomolak,
1976.

MIMBRES RED-ON-WHITE
Des. *Nesbitt, 1931.

MIMBRES SPIRAL RUB
Des. *Cosgrove, 1932.

MISHONGNOVI POLYCHROME
Syn. Walpi Polychrome
Des. *Wade, 1980.

MOAPA BLACK-ON-GRAY
Des. Colton, 1952.
Illus. Shutler, 1961; Worman,
1969.

MOAPA BROWN
Des. Colton, 1952.

MOAPA CORRUGATED
Des. Colton, 1952.
Illus. Shutler, 1961.

MOAPA FUGITIVE RED
Des. Colton, 1951.

MOAPA GRAY
Des. Colton, 1951.

MOAPA GRAY WARE
Des. Colton, 1951; Soule, 1979.

MOAPA TOOLED
Mentioned in Schroeder, 1955.

MOCCASIN GRAY (NECK BANDED)
AD 775-900
Des. *Morris, 1939; *Brew, 1946;
*O'Bryan, 1950; *Abel, 1955,
10A-3; Rohn 1959; *Hayes,
1964; *Breternitz et al.,
1974.
Illus. Dittert and Eddy, 1963;
Lister, 1965; Swannack, 1969;
Lister, 1969; Hayes and Lan-
caster, 1975; Gooding, 1980.

MOCCASIN NECK-BANDED: VARIETY
1
Syn. Moccasin Gray, Abel, 1955;
Chapin Gray: Moccasin Va-
riety, Rohn, 1966.
Des. *Forsyth, 1972.

MOENKOPI CORRUGATED
AD 1075-1285
Des. *Hargrave, 1932; Hawley,
1936; *Colton and Hargrave,
1937; *Colton, 1955, 8A-12;
*Gifford and Smith, 1978.
Illus. Lister et al., 1960; Shar-
rock et al., 1963; Ambler et
al., 1964; McGregor, 1965;
Euler, 1971; Hobler, 1974.

MOENKOPI CORRUGATED: COOMBS
VARIETY
Des. *Lister, 1960.
Illus. Jennings, 1978.

MOGOLLON BROWN WARE
Pre AD 700-ca. 1150
Des. Colton and Hargrave, 1937.
Illus. Alexander, 1966; Arizona
Highways, Feb. 1974.

MOGOLLON RED-ON-BROWN
AD 775-950
Des. Haury, 1936; Hawley, 1936;

Colton and Hargrave, 1937; Nesbitt, 1938; Human Systems Research, 1973; *LeBlanc, 1983.
Illus. O'Bryan, 1950; Martin, et al., 1952; McGregor, 1965; Brody, 1977.

MOHAVE WARE
Des. Kroeber, 1925.
Illus. Bahti, 1964; Feder, 1965; Tanner, 1968; Arizona Highways, May 1974; Barry, 1981.

MONTEZUMA GRAY WARE
Syn. Mesa Verde Gray Ware, Abel, 1955 plus Chapin Black-on-white and Twin Trees Black-on-white.
Des. *Forsyth, 1972.

MONTEZUMA RED-ON-ORANGE
Syn. Abajo Red-on-orange. Mentioned in Martin, 1936.

MONTICELLO GRAY
Des. Miller, 1974.

MONUMENT WHITE WARE
Des. *Forsyth, 1972.

MORFIELD BLACK-ON-WHITE
Syn. Mancos Black-on-white, in part; Morfield Black-on-gray.
Des. *Abel, 1955, 12A-4.
(This name was discarded from the Mesa Verde pottery typology by the Fifth SW Ceramic Conf., 1963.)

MUMMY LAKE GRAY
AD 950-1200
Des. Rohn, 1959; *Rohn and Swannack, 1965; *Breternitz et al., 1974.
Illus. Morris, 1939; Swannack, 1969; Lister, 1965.

MUSTANG BLACK-ON-WHITE: VARIETY 1
Syn. Mancos Black-on-white, Abel, 1955; Cortez Black-on-white, Abel, 1955; Hayes, 1964; Rohn, 1966; Swannack, 1969.
Des. *Forsyth, 1972.

MUSTANG BLACK-ON-WHITE: VARIETY 2
Syn. Mancos Black-on-white, in

part, Martin, 1936; Mancos Black-on-white, Abel, 1955; Hayes, 1964; Rohn, 1966; Swannack, 1969;
Des. *Forsyth, 1972.

NACOZARI POLYCHROME
Syn. Carretas Polychrome, Di-Peso, 1974.
Des. *Gladwin, 1934.

NAMBE POLYCHROME
AD 1760-1825
Des. *Harlow, 1973; *Frank and Harlow, 1974.

NAMBE RED
AD 1760-1950
Des. *Harlow, 1973.

NANKOWEAP POLYCHROME
AD 1125-1175
Des. *Colton, 1956, 5A-9; Taylor, 1958; Dittert and Plog, 1980.
(Similar to Citadel Polychrome)

NANTACK POLYCHROME
AD 1265-1290
Des. E. Morris, 1957.

NANTACK RED-ON-BROWN
Des. *Breternitz, 1959.

NASCHITTI BLACK-ON-WHITE
Ca. AD 900-1000
Des. Wilson and Peckham, 1964; *Windes, 1977.

NAVA BLACK-ON-WHITE
AD 1100-1250 or 1300
Des. Wilson and Peckham, 1964; *Windes, 1977.

NAVAJO GRAY
Ad 1800-present
Syn. Navajo Utility.
Des. *Brugge, 1981; *Hartman and Musial, 1987.

NAVAJO GRAY: DEL MUERTO VARIETY
Des. James, 1976.

NAVAJO PAINTED
AD 1750-mid 1950s
Syn. Painted Wares, Hill, 1937;

Navajo Polychrome, Keur, 1941;
Dittert et al., 1961.
Des. Tschopik, 1941; Brugge,
1963; *Brugge, 1981; *Hantman
and Musial, 1987.
Illus. Tanner, 1968; Windes, 1977;
Harlow, 1977.

NAVAJO POLYCHROME
AD 1750-mid 1950s
Syn. Navajo Painted, Burgge, 1963.
Des. Keur, 1941; Dittert et al.,
1961.

NAVAJO UTILITY
AD 1800-present
Syn. Navajo Gray, Brugge, 1981.
Des. Tschopik, 1941; Brugge, 1963.
Illus. Bahti, 1964; Tanner, 1968;
Windes, 1977; Barry, 1981.

NAVAJO WARE
Des. Sapir and Sandoval, 1930;
Hill, 1937; James, 1937; *Tsch-
opik, 1941; Stewart, 1942; Bea-
ver, 1952.
Illus. Bahti, 1964; Steen, 1966.

NEEDLES BEIGE
AD 1150-?
Des. Schroeder, 1952; *Schroeder,
1958; D16-27.

NEEDLES BLACK-ON-RED
Des. *Schroeder, 1952b; *Schroeder, 1958, D16-30.

NEEDLES BUFF
AD 1150-?
Des. Schroeder, 1952b; *Schroe-
der, 1958, D16-24.

NEEDLES RED
Des. *Schroeder, 1958, D16-29.

NEEDLES RED-ON-BEIGE
Des. Schroeder, 1958, D16-28.
(Same as Needles Red-on-buff, but
polished.)

NEEDLES RED-ON-BUFF
Des. Colton, 1939; Schroeder,
1952; *Schroeder, 1952b; *Schroeder, 1958, D16-26.

NEEDLES STUCCO
Ca. AD 1150-?

Des. Schroeder, 1952; *Schroeder,
1958, D16-25.

NEWCOMB BLACK-ON-WHITE
Ca. AD 875-1000
Des. Wilson and Peckham, 1964;
*Windes, 1977.

NEWCOMB CORRUGATED
Ca. AD 875-900 or 950
Des. Wilson and Peckham, 1964;
*Windes, 1977.

NOGALES POLYCHROME
Syn. Trincheras Polychrome,
Sauer and Brand, 1931.
Des. *Clark, 1935.
Illus. Cummings, 1953; DiPeso,
1956.

NOGALES PURPLE-ON-RED
Des. *DiPeso, 1956.

NORTH CREEK BLACK-ON-GRAY
Des. *Spencer, 1934; Colton,
1952; *Schroeder, 1955; Worman, 1969.

NORTH CREEK CORRUGATED
Des. *Spencer, 1934; Colton,
1952; Schroeder, 1955.
Illus. Lister et al., 1960; Shutler, 1961; Worman, 1969.

NORTH CREEK FUGITIVE RED
Des. *Spencer, 1934; Colton,
1952; *Schroeder, 1955.
Illus. Fowler, 1963; Barry, 1981.

NORTH CREEK GRAY
Des. *Spencer, 1934; Colton,
1952; *Schroeder, 1955; Anderson, 1960.
Illus. Pendergast, 1960; Shutler,
1961; Dalley and McFadden,
1981.

NORTH CREEK TOOLED
Des. *Schroeder, 1955.

NORTH PLAINS BLACK-ON-RED
Des. *Olson and Wasley in Wendorf et al., 1956; Dittert,
1959.

NORTH PLAINS POLYCHROME
Des. Dittert, 1959.

NORTHERN GRAY CORRUGATED
Des. *Dittert, 1959; Wendorf et
al., 1956.

NUSHAKI CORRUGATED
Gifford and Smith, 1978 (not fully
described).

NUTRIOSO BLACK-ON-RED (MINERAL
PAINT)
Des. Colton, manuscript at MNA.

NUTRIOSO CORRUGATED
Des. Colton, manuscript at MNA.

OBELISK GRAY
AD 620-750
Syn. Lino Polished, Morris, 1936.
Des. Abel, 1955, 8A-1; Dittert and
Plog, 1980.
Illus. Morris, 1980.

OCATE MICACEOUS
AD 1550?-1750
(Jicarilla Apache type)
Des. Gunnerson, 1969.

OCHOA BROWN INDENTED
Des. Human Systems Research,
1973.

OCHOA BROWN SMUDGED INDENTED
AD 1250-1450
Des. Human Systems Research,
1973; Runyan and Hedrick,
1973.
Illus. Smiley, 1978.

OCHOA INDENTED CORRUGATED
AD 1375-1425
Des. Lea County Archaeological
Society, unpublished manuscript,
Leslie, 1965.

OGAPOGE BLACK-ON-CREAM
Des. *Mera, 1939.

OGAPOGE POLYCHROME
AD 1725-1800
Des. *Mera, 1939; Harlow, 1973;
*Frank and Harlow, 1974; War-
ren, 1979.
Illus. Carlson, 1965; Harlow, 1965a;
Harlow, 1970; Carlson, 1977.

O'LEARY TOOLED
AD 850-900

Des. *Colton and Hargrave, 1937;
*Colton, 1955, 8A-7.

ORDERVILLE BLACK-ON-GRAY
Ca. AD 1080-1130
Syn. Shato Black-on-white,
Black Mesa style.
Des. *Thompson, 1986.

ORME RANCH PLAIN
Des. Breternitz, 1960.

PAA-YU POLYCHROME
Des. Adams (in press); from
Homolovi Ruins.

PADRE BLACK-ON-WHITE
AD 1085-1200
(Dogoszhi Style)
Des. Colton and Hargrave, 1937;
Colton, 1941; *Colton, 1955,
9B-3; Dittert and Plog, 1980.
Illus. King, 1949.

PAINTED WARES (NAVAJO)
AD 1750-present
Syn. Navajo Painted, Brugge,
1963; Navajo Polychrome, Dit-
tert et al., 1961.
Des. Hill, 1937; Tschopik, 1950.
Illus. Tanner, 1968.

PAJARITO BLACK-ON-WHITE
(See Santa Fe Black-on-white:
Pajarito Variety.)

PAJARITO GRAY WARE
(No published description.)

PAJARITO SMEARED INDENTED
Des. *Bice and Sundt, 1972.

PAKIUBI CORRUGATED
Des. *Gifford and Smith, 1978.

PALOMAS BEIGE
Des. Schroeder, 1961.

PALOMAS BUFF
Ca. AD 1000-post 1800/1900
Des. Rogers, 1945; Waters, 1982.

PALOMAS BUFF
Post AD 1150-?
Des. Rogers, 1945; Schroeder,
1952b; *Schroeder, 1958; D16-
22; Waters, 1982.

PALOMAS RED
Des. Schroeder, 1961.

PALOMAS RED-ON-BUFF
Ca. AD 1000-post 1900
Des. Waters, 1982.

PALOMAS RED-ON-BUFF
Des. Schroeder, 1961; Waters,
1982.

PALOMAS STUCCO
Post AD 1150-?
Des. Schroeder, 1952; *Schroeder,
1958, D16-23.

PALOPARDO PLAIN
Des. *DiPeso, 1956.

PANTANO RED-ON-BROWN
Syn. Tanque Verde Red-on-brown,
Kelly, 1978.
Des. *Danson in Hayden, 1957.
Illus. DiPeso, 1956.

PAPAGO BLACK-ON-RED
Late AD 1800s-present
Des. Haury et al., 1950; *Fontana
et al., 1962.
Illus. Bahti, 1964; Tanner, 1968;
Barry, 1981.

PAPAGO BLACK-ON-WHITE
Des. *Fontana et al., 1962.
Illus. Bahti, 1964.

PAPAGO GLAZE
Des. Caywood, 1950; Haury et al.,
1950; *Fontana et al., 1962.

PAPAGO PLAIN
Des. *Fontana et al., 1962.

PAPAGO POLYCHROME
Des. *Fontana et al., 1962.
Illus. Barry, 1981.

PAPAGO RED
Des. Schroeder, 1940; Gerald,
1951; *Fontana et al., 1962.
Illus. Bahti, 1964.

PAPAGO RED-ON-BROWN
Des. Haury et al., 1950; *Fontana
et al., 1962.

PAPAGO WARE
Des. *Boggs, 1936; Gifford, 1940;
Hill, 1942; *Fontana et al.,
1962.

PAPAGO WHITE-ON-RED OR BROWN
Des. Haury et al., 1950; *Fontana et al., 1962.

PARAGONAH COILED
Ca. AD 900-1200
Des. Meighan et al., 1956; Mad-
sen, 1970; Madsen, 1972;
*Madsen, 1977.
Illus. Marwitt, 1970.

PARASHANT BLACK-ON-GRAY
Ca. AD 1080-1130
Syn. Shato Black-on-white, Flag-
staff style.
Des. *Thompson, 1986.

PARIA GRAY
Des. Stewart, 1941; Colton, 1952;
Anderson, 1960.

PARKER BLACK-ON-RED
Post AD 1150-?
Des. *Schroeder, 1952b; Schroeder, 1958; D 16-3; Dobyns,
1959.

PARKER BUFF
Ca. AD 1000-post 1900
Des. Rogers, 1945; Waters, 1982.

PARKER BUFF
Pre AD 900-post 1900
Des. Rogers, 1945; *Schroeder,
1952b; *Kroeber and Harner,
1959; *Harner, 1957; *Schroeder, 1958, D16-1; Waters,
1982.

PARKER RED-ON-BUFF
Ca. AD 1000-post 1900
Des. Rogers, 1945; Waters, 1982.

PARKER RED-ON-BUFF
Pre. AD 900-post 1900
Des. Rogers, 1945; *Schroeder,
1952b; *Kroeber and Harner,
1955; Harner, 1957; *Schroeder, 1958, D16-2; Waters,
1982.

PARKER STUCCO
  Pre AD 1000?-1840
  Des. Schroeder, 1952b; *Schroeder,
    1958, D16-4.

PAYAN CORRUGATED
  Ca. AD 950-1100
  Syn. Mancos Corrugated, in part
    Abel, 1955.
  Des. *Dittert and Eddy, 1963.

PAYUPKI BLACK-ON-YELLOW
  AD 1700-1800
  Des. Colton, 1956, 7B-16.
  (A variant of Payupki Polychrome.)

PAYUPKI POLYCHROME
  AD 1700-1800
  Des. *Colton, 1956, 7B-15; *Carl-
    son, 1965; *Harlow, 1970;
    *Frank and Harlow, 1974; Dit-
    tert and Plog, 1980; *Wade,
    1980, *Wade and McChesney,
    1981.
  Illus. Steen, 1966.

PAYUPKI POLYCHROME
  AD 1680-1820
  Des. Adams, 1979.

PAYUPKI POLYCHROME: VARIETY
  A
  AD 1680-1800
  Des. Adams, 1979.

PAYUPKI POLYCHROME: VARIETY
  B
  AD 1750-1820
  Des. Adams, 1979.

PAYUPKI POLYCHROME: VARIETY
  C
  AD 1780-1820
  Des. Adams, 1979.

PECK RED
  Des. *DiPeso, 1956.
  Illus. Brown and Grebinger, 1969.

PECOS FAINT STRIATED UTILITY
  AD 1600-1700
  Des. Kidder, 1936; Warren, 1967;
    Warren, 1976; Mobley, 1978;
    Hayes, 1981.

PECOS GLAZE POLYCHROME
  AD 1600-1700

Syn. Glaze V, *Kidder and Shep-
    art, 1936; Mobley, 1978.
  Des. Mera, 1933; Honea, 1973;
    Warren, 1976; Mobley, 1978;
    Dittert and Plog, 1980.

PENA BLACK-ON-WHITE
  Des. Wilson and Peckham, 1964.

PENASCO MICACEOUS
  Des. Dick, 1965.

PEPPERSAUCE RED
  Des. *Franklin, 1980.

PERALTA BLACK-ON-WHITE
  (See Santa Fe Black-on-white:
    Peralta Variety.)

PETACA MICACEOUS
  Des. *Dick in Schroeder, 1968.

PHOENIX RED
  Des. Schroeder, n.d. manuscript
    at Pueblo Grande.
  (Unsmudged Gila Red from Pueblo
    Grande.)

PICACHO RED-ON-BROWN
  Des. *Kelly, 1978.

PIEDRA BLACK-ON-WHITE
  AD 750-900
  Syn. Pueblo I Black-on-white,
    Morris, 1930; Mancos Black-
    on-white, in part, Martin,
    1939.
  Des. Hawley, 1936; Morris, 1939;
    Abel, 1955; 12A-5; *Reed,
    1958; *Hayes, 1964; *Breter-
    nitz et al., 1974; *Rohn, 1977;
    *Dittert and Plog, 1980.
  Illus. Roberts, 1930; Martin,
    1938; O'Bryan, 1950; Wendorf
    et al., 1956; Dittert et al.,
    1961; Dittert and Eddy, 1963;
    Fifth SW Ceramic Conf., 1963;
    Lister, 1965; Lister and Lis-
    ter, 1969; Swannack, 1969;
    Bice, 1974; Hayes and Lan-
    caster, 1975.
  (Removed from Cibola White Ware
    and placed in San Juan White
    Ware by Cibola White Ware
    Conference, 1958.)

PIEDRA BLACK-ON-WHITE: WHITE
MESA VARIETY
Ca. AD 825-925
Des. *Hurst, Bond and Schwind,
1965.

PIEDRA BROWN
Des. *Dittert et al., 1936b.
Illus Dittert and Eddy, 1963.

PIEDRA-GALLINA TRANSITIONAL
BLACK-ON-WHITE
Ca. AD 900
Syn. Bancos Black-on-white, Dit-
tert et al., 1961.
Des. Hall, 1944.

PIEDRA GRAY
AD 850-975
Des. Dittert et al., 1963b.
Illus. Dittert and Eddy, 1963.

PILARES BANDED
Des. Wendorf et al., 1956.

PILARES FINE BANDED
Des. Dittert, 1959; Skinner, 1968.
Illus. Wendorf et al., 1956.

PILON RED-ON-BROWN
Des. DiPeso, 1969; *DiPeso, 1974.

PILON RED RIM
Des. DiPeso, 1969; *DiPeso, 1974.

PIMA WARE
Des. *Russell, 1908; Drucker,
1941; *Hayden, 1959; *Haury,
1976.
Illus. Bahti, 1964; Feder, 1965;
Barry, 1981.

PIMERIA BROWN WARE
Des. Haury and Wasley, 1961.
(Unpublished description.)

PINALENO RED-ON-BROWN
Des. *Sayles, 1945.

PINDI BLACK-ON-WHITE
AD 1300-1350
Des. Smiley, Stubbs and Bannister, 1953; *Stubbs and Stallings,
1953; Atwood, 1974.

PINE BROWN
AD 1050-1100

Des. Peck, 1956; Colton, 1958,
14-30.

PINEDALE BLACK-ON-RED
AD 1275-1350
Des. Colton and Hargrave, 1937;
Second SW Ceramic Conf.,
1959; Carlson, 1962; *Carlson,
1970; Dittert and Plog, 1980.
Illus. Cummings, 1940; Barnett,
1974a; Gifford, 1980.

PINEDALE BLACK-ON-WHITE
AD 1290-1375
Des. *Gladwin, 1931; *Haury,
1931; Colton and Hargrave,
1937; Second SW Ceramic
Conf., 1959.

PINEDALE POLYCHROME
AD 1275-1350
Des. *Haury, 1930; Haury, 1932;
Hawley, 1936; *Colton and
Hargrave, 1937; Carlson, 1962;
*Carlson, 1970; Dittert and
Plog, 1980.
Illus. Martin and Willis, 1940;
Cummings, 1953; Rinaldo,
1959; Arizona Highways, Feb.
1974; Barnett, 1974a; Gifford,
1980; Barry, 1981.

PINE FLAT NECK CORRUGATED
Des. *Breternitz, 1959; *Gifford
1980.
Illus. Breternitz, 1957; Gifford,
1957; Haury, 1957.

PINNAWA BLACK-ON-RED
AD 1200-1250
Des. Hodge, 1923; Colton and
Hargrave, 1937.
(Seventh SW Ceramic Conference
in 1965 suggested this name
be dropped in favor of He-
shotauthla Black-on-red.)

PINNAWA GLAZE-ON-WHITE
AD 1350-1450
Syn. Hawikuh Glaze-on-white,
Colton and Hargrave, 1937.
Des. Reed, 1955; *Martin and
Rinaldo, 1960; *Smith, Wood-
bury and Woodbury, 1966;
*Dittert and Plog, 1980.
Illus. Hough, 1903; Hodge, 1923;
Martin and Willis, 1940; Martin

and Rinaldo, 1960a; Martin et
al., 1961; Voll, 1961.

PINNAWA GLAZE POLYCHROME
AD 1300-1400
Syn. Pinnawa Polychrome, Dittert,
1959.
Des. Reed, 1955; *Rinaldo, 1959.

PINNAWA POLYCHROME
AD 1300-1400
Syn. Pinnawa Glaze Polychrome,
Reed, 1955; *Rinaldo, 1959.
Des. Colton and Hargrave, 1937;
Dittert, 1959.

PINNAWA RED-ON-WHITE
AD 1350-1450
Des. Colton and Hargrave, 1937;
*Martin and Rinaldo, 1960;
*Smith, Woodbury and Wood-
bury, 1966; Dittert and Plog,
1980.
Illus. Hough, 1903; Martin and
Rinaldo, 1960a.

PINTO BLACK-ON-RED
AD 1265-1350
Des. Gifford, 1957; *DiPeso, 1958.
Illus. Gifford, 1980.

PINTO POLYCHROME
AD 1275-1400
Des. *Gladwin, 1930b; Hawley,
1936; Colton and Hargrave,
1937; *DiPeso, 1958.
Illus. Martin and Willis, 1940; Gladwin, 1957; McGregor, 1965; Gifford, 1957; Martin, 1967; Arizona Highways, Feb. 1974; Bice,
1975.

PINYON GRAY
AD 1800-present
Syn. Pinyon Utility.
Des. *Brugge, 1981; Hartman and
Musial, 1987.

PINYON UTILITY
AD 1800-present
Sym. Pinyon Gray, Brugge, 1981.
Des. Brugge, 1963.
Illus. Hunt, 1953.

PIPE SPRING BLACK-ON-GRAY
Ca. AD 1080-1130
Syn. Shato Black-on-white, Dogo-
szhi style.

Des. *Thompson, 1986.

PIRO RED-ON-BROWN
Stubbs, named, but no known
description.

PITOCHE RIBBED COIL
Syn. Pitoche (Rubbed) Ribbed,
Mera, 1935.
Des. *Mera, 1935.

PITOCHE (RUBBED) RIBBED
Syn. Pitoche Ribbed Coil, Mera,
1935.
Des. *Mera, 1935; Hawley, 1936;
Human Systems Research,
1973.

PLAIN AND INDENTED CORRUGATED
AD 1050-1250
Syn. Tularosa Patterned Corrugated: Reserve Variety, Rinaldo and Bluhm, 1956.
Des. Martin and Rinaldo et al.,
1952.

PLAYAS RED
Syn. Casas Grandes Redware,
Brand, 1935; Chihuahua Red-
ware, Kidder, 1916; Playas
Red Incised, Sayles, 1936.
Des. Kidder, 1916; *Sayles, 1936;
Hawley, 1936; DiPeso, 1969;
Runyan and Hedrick, 1973;
Human Systems Research, 1973;
*DiPeso, 1974; DiPeso et al.,
1976.
Illus. Chapman, 1923; Mera,
1945; Willey, 1966; Bice, 1975;
DiPeso, 1977; Smiley, 1978.

PLAYAS RED INCISED
AD 1060-1340
Des. *Sayles, 1936; Hawley,
1936; DiPeso, 1969; Human
Systems Research, 1973.
Illus. Zahniser, 1966.

PLAYAS INCISED: SIERRA BLANCA
VARIETY
Des. Wiseman, 1981.

POGE BLACK-ON-WHITE
AD 1300-1350
Des. Smiley, Stubbs and Ban-
nister, 1953; *Stubbs and
Stallings, 1953; Atwood, 1974;
Dittert and Plog, 1980.

POINT OF PINES INDENTED CORRU-
GATED
Syn. Indented Corrugated.
Des. Wendorf, 1950; *Gifford, 1980.

POINT OF PINES OBLITERATED COR-
RUGATED
Des. Wendorf, 1950; *Gifford, 1980.
Illus. Breternitz, et al., 1957.

POINT OF PINES PATTERNED COR-
RUGATED
Des. Wendorf, 1950.
Illus. Breternitz et al., 1957.

POINTS OF PINES PLAIN CORRUGATED
Syn. Clapboard Corrugated, Wen-
dorf, 1950.
Des. Wendorf, 1950; *Gifford, 1980.
Illus. Breternitz et al., 1957.

POINT OF PINES POLYCHROME
AD 1400-1450
Syn. Fourmile Polychrome: Point
of Pines Variety.
Des. Wendorf, 1950; Haury, 1952;
Gifford, 1957; E. Morris, 1957;
Olson, 1959; Carlson, 1962; *Carl-
son, 1970; Dittert and Plog, 1980.
Illus. Asch, 1960.

POINT OF PINES PUNCTATE
Des. Olson, 1959.
Illus. Gifford, 1980.

POJOAQUE POLYCHROME
AD 1720-1760
Des. *Mera, 1939; Harlow, 1973;
*Frank and Harlow, 1974; Dit-
tert and Plog, 1980.
Illus. Harlow, 1965a; Carlson, 1965;
Carlson, 1977; Harlow, 1977.

POLACCA BLACK-ON-WHITE
Ca. AD 1250-1300
Des. *Colton, 1956, 8B-12; Dittert
and Plog, 1980.

POLACCA PLAIN WARE
Des. *Wade, 1980.

POLACCA POLYCHROME
AD 1800-1900
Syn. Crackle Ware, not Galisteo
Black-on-white.
Des. *Colton, 1956, 7B-17; *Frank
and Harlow, 1974; *Dittert and

Plog, 1980; *Wade and McChesney, 1981.
Illus. Harlow, 1970; Breed, 1972;
Collins, 1974; Maxwell Museum,
1974; Harlow and Bartlett, 1978.

POLACCA POLYCHROME
AD 1780-1910
Des. Adams, 1979.

POLACCA POLYCHROME, STYLE A
AD Early 1780-1820
Des. *Wade and McChesney, 1981.

POLACCA POLYCHROME, STYLE B
WESTERN PUEBLO MODIFIED
AD 1820-1860
Des. *Wade and McChesney, 1981.

POLACCA POLYCHROME, STYLE C
ZUNI MODIFIED
AD 1860-1890
Des. *Wade and McChesney, 1981.

POLACCA POLYCHROME, STYLE D
SIKYATKI REVIVAL
AD 1890-1900
Des. *Wade and McChesney, 1981.

POLACCA POLYCHROME: VARIETY
A (Payupki Variety)
AD 1780-1850
Des. Adams, 1979.

POLACCA POLYCHROME: VARIETY
B (Arabesque Variety)
AD 1820-1880
Des. Adams, 1979.

POLACCA POLYCHROME: VARIETY
C (Zuni Variety)
AD 1850-1920
Des. Adams, 1979.

POLACCA POLYCHROME: VARIETY
D (Sikyatki Revival)
AD 1885-1910
Des. Adams, 1979.

POLACCA YELLOW WARE
AD 1680-present
Des. Adams, 1979.

POLVADERA GLAZE-ON-RED
Des. Eighth SW Ceramic Confer-
ence, 1966.
Illus. Vivian, 1964.

POLVADERA GLAZE POLYCHROME
Des. Eighth SW Ceramic Confer-
ence, 1966.
Illus. Vivian, 1964.

POLLES BROWN
AD 1050-1100?
Des. Peck, 1956; Colton, 1958, 14-29.

POSUGE RED
AD 1650-1750
Des. Mera, 1939; *Harlow, 1973;
Warren, 1979.

POTSUWI'I GRAY
AD 1500-1650
Des. *Harlow, 1973; Dittert and
Plog, 1980.

POTSUWI'I INCISED
Ca. AD 1425-1525
Des. *Mera, 1932; Hawley, 1936;
*Harlow, 1973; Dittert and Plog,
1980; Warren, 1979.
Illus. Fox, 1975; Ambler, 1977.

POTTERY MOUND GLAZE POLYCHROME
AD 1400-1490
Des. Voll, 1961; Eighth SW Ceramic
Conf., 1966; Honea, 1973; Dit-
tert and Plog, 1980.
Illus. Barnett, 1973b.

POVERTY MOUNTAIN BLACK-ON-
GRAY
AD 1125-1250
Syn. Flagstaff Black-on-white.
Des. Thompson, 1986.

POWHOGE BLACK-ON-RED
AD 1830-1850
Des. *Frank and Harlow, 1974;
Dittert and Plog, 1980.

POWHOGE POLYCHROME
AD 1760-1850
Des. *Dick in Schroeder, 1968;
*Harlow, 1970; *Harlow, 1973;
Frank and Harlow, 1974.

PRESCOTT BLACK-ON-BROWN
AD 1250-1400
Syn. Verde Black-on-gray, Colton,
1958; 17-1; Verde Black-on-
white, Gladwin, 1930; Verde
Polychrome, Colton, 1958.
Des. *Caywood, 1936; Colton and
Hargrave, 1937; Colton, 1958.

PRESCOTT GRAY WARE
AD 1025-1200
Des. Caywood and Spicer, 1935;
Hawley, 1936; Colton and Har-
grave, 1937; Colton, 1958, 17.

PREWITT BLACK-ON-WHITE
Des. Colton, 1953, manuscript at
MNA.

PRIETA SMEARED INDENTED
Des. *Bice and Sundt, 1972.
Illus. Judd, 1959.

PRIETO INDENTED CORRUGATED
Post AD 1300
Des. Wendorf, 1950; Gifford,
1957; Olson, 1959.
Illus. Breternitz et al., 1957;
Gifford, 1980.

PRIETO POLYCHROME
Ca. AD 1265-1290
Des. E. Morris, 1957.

PROMONTORY BLACK
AD 1000-1300
Syn. Promontory Ware, Enger,
1950.
Des. Stewart, 1936; Hawley, 1936.

PROMONTORY GRAY
Ca. AD 1000-1300
Syn. Promontory Black, Stewart,
1936.
Des. Madsen, 1972; *Madsen,
1977; Griset, 1986.

PROMONTORY WARE
Ca. AD 1000-1300
Syn. Promontory Black; Promon-
tory Gray.
Des. Stewart, 1937; Enger, 1950;
Rudy, 1953.
Illus. Aikens, 1967.

PUARAY GLAZE-POLYCHROME
AD 1515-1650
Des. Mera, 1933; Hawley, 1936;
Warren, 1977c.

PUEBLO GRANDE RED
Des. Schroeder, n.d. manuscript
at Pueblo Grande.
(Similar to Gila Red without the
smudged interior.)

PUERCO BLACK-ON-RED
  AD 1030-1175
  Des. *Gladwin, 1934; Hawley,
    1936; *Colton and Hargrave,
    1937; Second SW Ceramic Conf.,
    1959; Carlson, 1962; Carlson,
    1970; *Dittert and Plog, 1980.
  Illus. Martin and Willis, 1940;
    Wormington, 1951; Wendorf et
    al., 1956; Vivian, 1959; New
    Mexico Univ., 1967; Lister and
    Lister, 1969; Barnett, 1974a;
    Bice, 1975.

PUERCO BLACK-ON-WHITE
  AD 1010-1125
  Syn. Escavada Black-on-white,
    Hawley, 1936; Chaco Black-on-
    white, Hawley, 1936; Chambers
    Black-on-white, Colton, 1941a.
  Des. *Gladwin, 1931; Hawley, 1936;
    Colton and Hargrave, 1937;
    *Colton, 1941a; Cibola White
    Ware Conference, 1958; *Dit-
    tert and Plog, 1980; Pippin,
    1978.
  Illus. Martin and Willis, 1940;
    Martin et al., 1952; Martin et
    al., 1954; Martin and Rinaldo,
    1960a; Pomeroy, 1962; Olson,
    1971; Bice and Sundt, 1972;
    Bice, 1975; Andrews, 1980.

PUNAME POLYCHROME
  AD 1680-1740
  Des. *Mera, 1939; *Carlson, 1965;
    *Harlow, 1973; *Frank and Harlow,
    1974; Warren, 1976; Carlson,
    1977; Warren, 1979; *Dittert
    and Plog, 1980.
  Illus. Windes, 1977.

PYRAMID GRAY
  Des. Colton, 1939; *Schroeder,
    1958.
  Illus. Shutler, 1961.

QUERINO POLYCHROME
  AD 1250-1300
  Syn. Wingate Polychrome, Carl-
    son, 1970.
  Des. *Roberts, 1932; Hawley,
    1936; Colton and Hargrave,
    1937.
  Illus. Martin and Willis, 1940;
    Rinaldo, 1959; Martin, 1967.

RAINBOW GRAY
  Ca. AD 1200-1280
  Des. *Callahan and Fairley, 1983.

RAMANOTE PLAIN
  Des. *DiPeso, 1956.

RAMANOTE PURPLE-ON-RED
  Des. DiPeso, 1956.
  (A local variant of Trincheras
    Purple-on-red in which the
    potters rubbed over the de-
    sign; in general, a thicker
    type.)

RAMANOTE RED-ON-BROWN
  Des. *DiPeso, 1956.
  Illus. Brown and Grebinger,
    1969.

RAMANOTE SCORED
  Des. DiPeso, 1956.

RAMOS BLACK (PLAIN)
  Des. *Sayles, 1936; Hawley,
    1936; DiPeso, 1969; Human
    Systems Research, 1973;
    *DiPeso, 1974.
  Illus. Chapman, 1923; Fritz,
    1968.

RAMOS BLACK-ON-RED
  Des. *DiPeso, 1974.

RAMOS BLACK TEXTURED
  Des. DiPeso, 1969.

RAMOS BLACK-ON-WHITE
  Des. *DiPeso, 1977.

RAMOS PLAINWARE
  Des. *DiPeso, 1974.

RAMOS POLYCHROME
  AD 1350-1450
  Syn. Chihuahua Painted Ware,
    in part, Kidder, 1916; Fine
    Polychrome, Carey, 1931;
    Casas Grandes Polychrome, in
    part, Brand, 1935.
  Des. *Carey, 1931; Brand, 1935;
    *Sayles, 1936; Hawley, 1936;
    DiPeso, 1969; Human Systems
    Research, 1973; *DiPeso,
    1974; DiPeso et al., 1976.
  Illus. Hewett, 1908; Hodge, 1916;

Chapman, 1931; Willey, 1966;
Fritz, 1968; Lister and Lister,
1969; Mills and Mills, 1971; Di-
Peso, 1967; Bice, 1975; DiPeso,
1977; Brody, 1977.

RANCHITOS POLYCHROME
AD 1760-1825
Des. *Harlow, 1970; *Harlow, 1973;
*Frank and Harlow, 1974.

RAYO GLAZE-ON-RED
Des. Mera, 1933; Hawley, 1936.

RECAPTURE BLACK-ON-WHITE
Des. *Forsyth, 1972.
(Black-on-white type with basket
impressions.)

RED MESA BLACK-ON-WHITE
AD 850-1125
Syn. Kiatuthlanna/Red Mesa Black-
on-white, Vivian, 1956.
Des. Kluckhohn and Reiter, 1939;
*Gladwin, 1945; Cibola White
Ware Conf., 1958; Judd, 1959;
Bradley, 1971; *Windes, 1977;
*Dittert and Plog, 1980.
Illus. Martin, 1936; Brand et al.,
1937; Martin and Willis, 1940;
Martin, 1947; Dittert and Ruppe,
1951; Wendorf et al., 1956;
Hammack, 1963; Vivian and
Clendenen, 1965; New Mexico
Univ., 1967; Lister and Lister,
1969; McNutt, 1969; Switzer,
1969; Olson, 1971; Arizona High-
ways, Feb. 1974; Barnett, 1974a;
Bice, 1975; Brody, 1977.

REDINGTON PLAIN (VARIANT)
DiPeso, 1958, mentioned as a local
variant at Bidegain Ruin.

RESERVE BLACK-ON-WHITE
AD 940-1125
Syn. Whipple Black-on-white, Col-
ton, 1941a.
Des. Nesbitt, 1938; *Martin, and
Rinaldo, 1950; Cibola White
Ware Conf., 1958; *Smith, 1971;
*Dittert and Plog, 1980.
Illus. Martin and Willis, 1940; Mar-
tin et al., 1952; Martin et al.,
1954; Martin et al., 1956; Bluhm,
1957; Danson, 1957; Pomeroy,
1962; Johnson and Wasley, 1966;

Willey, 1966; Arizona Highways, Feb. 1974; Barnett,
1974a; Bice, 1975; Brody,
1977; Barry, 1981.

RESERVE FILLET RIM
Des. *Martin and Rinaldo, 1950.

RESERVE INCISED CORRUGATED
Des. *Martin and Rinaldo, 1950;
*Rinaldo and Bluhm, 1956.
Illus. Breternitz et al., 1957;
Smith, 1973.

RESERVE INCISED CORRUGATED:
PUNCHED VARIANT
Des. *Martin and Rinaldo, 1950;
Rinaldo and Bluhm, 1956.

RESERVE INDENTED CORRUGATED
Syn. Upper Gila Corrugated,
Hawley, 1936.
Des. Nesbitt, 1938; *Martin and
Rinaldo, 1950; Rinaldo and
Bluhm, 1956.
Illus. Martin et al., 1957; Breter-
nitz et al., 1957; Rinaldo,
1959; Johnson and Wasley,
1966; Smith, 1973.

RESERVE PLAIN
Des. Nesbitt, 1938.

RESERVE PLAIN CORRUGATED
AD 1000-1200
Des. *Martin and Rinaldo, 1950;
*Rinaldo and Bluhm, 1956.
Illus. Breternitz et al., 1957;
Bluhm, 1957; Gifford, 1980.

RESERVE POLYCHROME
Ca. AD 1100-1200
Syn. Starkweater Smudged Deco-
rated, Martin et al., 1949;
Tularosa White-on-red, Martin
and Rinaldo, 1952.
Des. Nesbitt, 1938; Rinaldo and
Bluhm, 1956.

RESERVE PUNCHED CORRUGATED
Des. *Martin and Rinaldo, 1950;
*Rinaldo and Bluhm, 1956.
Illus. Breternitz et al., 1957;
Smith, 1973.

RESERVE RED
Des. Nesbitt, 1938.

RESERVE RED: POINT OF PINES
   VARIETY
   Des. Gifford, 1957; *Gifford,
   1980.
   Illus. Breternitz, 1959.

RESERVE SMUDGED
   Ca. AD 750-800
   Des. Nesbitt, 1938; Martin et al.,
   1949; Martin and Rinaldo, 1950.
   Illus. Martin et al., 1954; Barnett,
   1974a; Bice, 1975.

RILLITO RED-ON-BROWN
   Des. *Kelly, 1978.
   Illus. DiPeso, 1956; Zahniser,
   1966; Greenleaf, 1975.

RIMROCK PLAIN
   (Western Apache type)
   Des. Schroeder, 1960.

RINCON BLACK-ON-BROWN
   Des. Deaver, 1984.

RINCON NECK-BANDED: VARIETY 1
   Syn. Mancos Gray, in part, Abel,
   1955; Hayes, 1964; Rohn, 1966;
   Swannack, 1969.
   Des. *Forsyth, 1972.

RINCON POLYCHROME
   Des. *Greenleaf, 1975.
   Illus. Doyel, 1977; Jacobs, 1979.

RINCON RED
   Des. *Greenleaf, 1975; Kelly, 1978.

RINCON RED-ON-BROWN
   Des. *Greenleaf, 1975; Doyel,
   1977; *Kelly, 1978.
   Illus. DiPeso, 1956; Zahniser, 1966;
   Jacobs, 1979.

RIO DE FLAG BROWN
   AD 775-1065
   Des. Colton, 1932; *Hargrave,
   1932; Mera, 1934; Hawley, 1936;
   *Colton and Hargrave, 1937;
   *Colton, 1958, 14-1.
   Illus. Colton, 1946; Breternitz,
   1957.

RIO DE FLAG SMUDGED
   AD 850-1050
   Des. Colton and Hargrave, 1937;
   Colton, 1958; 14-2.

RIO DE FLAG TOOLED
   AD 850-1050?
   Des. Colton, 1941; *Colton, 1958,
   14-3.

RIO GRANDE GLAZE WARE
   (Not described in print.)
   Illus. Hewett, 1938; Reiter, 1938;
   Mera, 1939; Wormington, 1951;
   Toulouse and Stevenson, 1960;
   Wormington, 1964; Alexander,
   1966; Schaafsma, 1968; Ben-
   nett, 1969; Dittert and Plog,
   1980.

RIO GRANDE GLAZE A
   AD 1315-1425
   Syn. Arenal Glaze Polychrome;
   Agua Fria Glaze-on-red; San
   Clemente Glaze Polychrome;
   Cieneguilla Glaze-on-yellow;
   Cieneguilla Glaze Polychrome.
   Des. Mera, 1933; *Eighth SW
   Ceramic Seminar, 1966.

RIO GRANDE GLAZE B
   AD 1400-1450
   Syn. Largo Glaze-on-yellow,
   Largo Glaze Polychrome.
   Des. Mera, 1933; *Eighth SW
   Ceramic Seminar, 1966.

RIO GRANDE GLAZE C
   AD 1425-1490
   Syn. Espinoso Glace Polychrome;
   Pottery Mound Glaze Poly-
   chrome.
   Des. Mera, 1933; *Eighth SW
   Ceramic Seminar, 1966.
   Illus. Warren, 1974.

RIO GRANDE GLAZE D
   AD 1490-1515
   Syn. San Lazaro Glaze Polychrome.
   Des. Mera, 1933; *Eighth SW
   Ceramic Seminar, 1966.
   Illus. Warren, 1974.

RIO GRANDE GLAZE E
   AD 1515-1600
   Syn. Puaray Glaze Polychrome
   (early); Pecos Glaze Polychrome.
   Des. Mera, 1933; *Eighth SW
   Ceramic Seminar, 1966.

RIO GRANDE GLAZE F
   AD 1600-1700 or 1750

Syn. Puaray Glaze Polychrome
(late); Pecos Glaze Polychrome,
Kotyiti Glaze-on-yellow; Kotyiti
Glaze Polychrome.
Des. Mera, 1933; *Eighth SW Ce-
ramic Seminar, 1966.

RIO GRANDE GRAY WARE
(Not described in print.)

RIO GRANDE MATTE PAINT WARE
AD 1375-present
Des. *Harlow, 1973.

RIO RICO POLYCHROME
Des. *Doyel, 1977.

ROOSEVELT BLACK-ON-WHITE
AD 1300-1350
Des. *Gladwin, 1931; Hawley, 1936;
*Pomeroy, 1962.
Illus. Hough, 1932; Martin and
Willis, 1940; McGregor, 1965;
Johnson and Wasley, 1966; Zah-
niser, 1966; DiPeso, 1967.

ROOSEVELT RED WARE
Ca. AD 1150-1400
Des. Colton and Hargrave, 1937.

ROSA BLACK-ON-WHITE
AD 700-900
Des. Mera, 1935; Hawley, 1936;
Hall, 1944; *Dittert and Plog,
1980.
Illus. Wendorf et al., 1956; Reed,
1958; Dittert et al., 1961; Dittert and Eddy, 1963; Brody,
1977.

ROSA BROWN
AD 700-950
Des. Dittert et al., 1961; Dittert
and Plog, 1980.
Illus. Dittert and Eddy, 1963.

ROSA GRAY
AD 700-900
Des. Hall, 1944; Dittert et al.,
1961.
Illus. Reed, 1958; Dittert and
Eddy, 1963; Lister et al., 1970.

ROSA NECK BANDED
AD 700-900
Des. Dittert et al., 1961.
Illus. Dittert and Eddy, 1963;
Carlson, 1964.

ROSA NECK COIL
AD 700-900
Des. Hall, 1944.

ROSA PLAIN
AD 700-900
Syn. Rosa Smoothed.
Des. Hawley, 1936; *Hall, 1944.

ROSA SCORED
AD 700-900
Des. Hall, 1944.

ROSA SMOOTHED
AD 700-900
Syn. Rosa Plain.
Des. Mera, 1935; Hawley, 1936;
*Hall, 1944.

ROSWELL BROWN
Des. Jellinek, 1967.

ROWE BLACK-ON-WHITE
Late AD 1300s
Des. *Mera, 1935; Hawley, 1936.
(Subtype of Galisteo Black-on-
white.)

SACATON BUFF
Ca. AD 950-1150
Des. Gladwin, 1933; *Haury,
1937; *Gladwin et al., 1973;
*Haury, 1976; Antieau, 1981.

SACATON RED
Des. Gladwin et al., 1937; *Haury,
1976; *Antieau, 1981.

SACATON RED-ON-BUFF
Ca. AD 950-1150
Des. Gladwin, 1931; *Gladwin
and Gladwin, 1933; Hawley,
1936; *Gladwin et al., 1937;
*Haury, 1937; *Haury, 1976.
Illus. DiPeso, 1956; Wasley and
Johnson, 1965; Willey, 1966;
Chenall, 1967; DiPeso, 1967;
Arizona Highways, Feb. 1974;
Bice, 1975; Brody, 1977.

SACRAMENTO BROWN
Des. Colton, 1939.

SAGUARO POLYCHROME
Des. Deaver in Los Morteros Re-
port (in press), Arizona State
Museum.

SAHAURITA POLYCHROME
Des. Deaver, 1984.

ST. GEORGE BLACK-ON-GRAY
Des. *Colton, 1952; *Schroeder,
1955.
Illus. Shutler, 1961; Dalley and
McFadden, 1981.

ST. GEORGE FUGITIVE RED
Des. Colton, 1952.

ST. JOHNS BLACK-ON-RED
Ca. AD 1175-1300
Des. Carlson, 1962; *Carlson,
1970.
Illus. Arizona Highways, Feb. 1974;
Barnett, 1974a; Dittert and
Plog, 1980.

ST. JOHNS POLYCHROME
AD 1175-1300
Des. *Gladwin, 1931; Haury, 1932;
Mera, 1935; Hawley, 1936; Kid-
der and Shepard, 1936; *Col-
ton and Hargrave, 1937; Smiley,
Stubbs and Bannister, 1953;
*Rinaldo, 1959; Carlson, 1962;
*Carlson, 1970; Human Systems
Research, 1973; Dittert and Plog,
1980.
Illus. Martin and Willis, 1940;
O'Bryan, 1950; Wormington,
1951; Cummings, 1953; Martin
et al., 1956; Gladwin, 1957;
McGregor, 1965; Martin, 1967;
New Mexico Univ., 1967; Lister
and Lister, 1969; Bice and
Sundt, 1972; Barnett, 1974a;
Bice, 1975; Washburn, 1977.

ST. JOSEPH BLACK-ON-WHITE
AD 700-900
(Kana-a style)
Des. *Colton, 1955, 9B-1; Dittert
and Plog, 1980.

SAKONA BLACK-ON-TAN
AD 1580-1650
Des. *Harlow, 1973; Dittert and
Plog, 1980.

SAKONA POLYCHROME
AD 1580-1650
Des. Harlow, 1973; *Frank and
Harlow, 1974; Dittert and Plog,
1980.

SALADO RED
AD 1350-1400
Des. Schmidt, 1928; *Gladwin,
1930b; Hawley, 1936; Colton
and Hargrave, 1937; Lindsay
and Jennings, 1968.
Illus. Steen et al., 1962; Arizona
Highways, Feb. 1974; Jacka
and Gill, 1976; Barry, 1981.

SALADO RED: VOSBERG VARIETY
Des. Rodgers and Weaver, n.d.,
Manuscript at ASU, Anthropo-
logy Dept.

SALADO WHITE-ON-RED
Ca. AD 1300
Des. *Schmidt, 1928; *Gladwin,
1930; Colton and Hargrave,
1937.

SALINAS RED
Syn. Salinas Red Ware.
Des. *Toulouse, 1949; *Hayes et
al., 1974.

SALIZ RED
AD 500-
Syn. San Francisco Red: Saliz
Variety, Martin, 1943.
Des. LeBlanc, 1982.

SALT RED
Des. Schroeder, 1940; *Haury,
1945a; Schroeder, 1952; Antieau, 1981.
Illus. DiPeso, 1956.

SALT SMUDGED
Des. *Haury, 1945a.

SALTON BUFF
Ca. AD 900-1500
Des. Rogers, 1945; Waters, 1982.

SALTON RED-ON-BUFF
Ca. AD 1000-1500
Des. Rogers, 1945; Waters, 1982.

SAMBRITO BROWN
AD 400-700
Des. Dittert et al., 1963; Dittert
and Plog, 1980.

SAN ANDRES RED-ON-TERRA COTTA
AD 1150-1300
(Wide lined)

Syn. Three Rivers Red-on-terra
cotta, Mera and Stallings, 1931;
Broad Line Red-on-terra cotta,
Jellinek, 1952.
Des. *McCluney, 1962; Human Sys-
tems Research, 1973; Bussey
et al., 1976.
Illus. Smiley, 1978.

SAN ANTONIO PLAINWARE
Des. *DiPeso, 1974.

SAN ANTONIO RED
Des. *DiPeso, 1974.

SAN ANTONIO RED-ON-BROWN
Named *DiPeso, 1974.

SAN BERNARDO BLACK-ON-WHITE
Des. Harlow, 1970.

SAN BERNARDO BLACK-ON-YELLOW
AD 1628-1680
Des. Dittert and Plog, 1980.

SAN BERNARDO PLAIN WARE
Des. *Wade, 1980.

SAN BERNARDO POLYCHROME
AD 1628-1680
Syn. Awatovi Polychrome, Kidder
and Shepard, 1936; Frank and
Harlow, 1974.
Des. Bunzel, 1929; *Colton, 1956,
7B-12; Harlow, 1970; *Frank
and Harlow, 1974; Dittert and
Plog, 1980; *Wade, 1980; *Wade
and McChesney, 1981.

SAN BERNARDO POLYCHROME:
YELLOW VARIETY
Des. *Brew, 1946; Colton, 1956.

SAN CARLOS BROWN SMUDGED
Des. DiPeso, 1956.

SAN CARLOS RED
Des. Vickery in Steen et al.,
1962; Kelly, 1978; Franklin,
1980.

SAN CARLOS RED-ON-BROWN (BUFF)
AD 1275-1400
Des. Hawley, 1930; Gladwin, 1934;
Hawley, 1936; Olson, 1959.
Illus. Jonson and Wasley, 1966;
Bice, 1975.

SAN CARLOS SMUDGED
Des. DiPeso, 1958.

SAN CLEMENTE GLAZE POLYCHROME
AD 1325-1425
Syn. Glaze I-A, Kidder and
Shepard, 1936.
Des. Mera, 1933; Hawley, 1936;
Voll, 1961; Atwood, 1974;
Warren, 1979; Dittert and
Plog, 1980.
Illus. Barnett, 1973; Bice, 1975;
Traylor and Scaife, 1980.

SAN CLEMENTE GLAZE-ON-YELLOW
No published description.
Illus. Voll, 1961; Brody, 1977.

SAN FRANCISCO MOUNTAIN GRAY
WARE
Pre AD 700-Ca. 1050
Des. Colton and Hargrave, 1937;
Colton, 1958, 18.
Illus. Schwartz et al., 1979.

SAN FRANCISCO RED
Ca. AD 750-950
Des. Haury, 1936; Hawley, 1936;
Colton and Hargrave, 1937;
Nesbitt, 1938; Sayles, 1945;
Human Systems Research,
1973.
Illus. Martin, 1947; Martin et al.,
1952; Martin and Rinaldo,
1960a; McGregor, 1965; Willey,
1966; Bice, 1970; Smiley, 1978.

SAN FRANCISCO RED: POINT OF
PINES VARIETY
Des. Wheat, 1954.

SAN FRANCISCO RED: SALIZ
VARIETY
Des. Martin, 1943; Martin and
Rinaldo, 1950.

SAN IGNACIO BLACK-ON-WHITE
Mentioned in Bice and Sundt,
1972.
Sherds from LA 880 series sites
in the Laboratory of Anthropology were given this name.
The authors believed this is
a late Chaco variety of Mc-
Elmo Black-on-white.

SAN ILDEFONSO BLACK-ON-CREAM
AD 1760-1850

Des. *Guthe, 1925; *Chapman,
1933; Chapman, 1938; *Chapman, 1970.
Illus. Underhill, 1944; Marriott,
1948.

SAN ILDEFONSO BLACK-ON-RED
AD 1880-1930
Des. *Guthe, 1925; *Chapman,
1933; *Chapman, 1938; *Chap-
man, 1970; *Harlow, 1973;
*Frank and Harlow, 1974.
Illus. New Mexico Univ., 1967; Har-
low, 1970; Sunset, 1972; Arizona
Highways, May 1974; Barry, 1981.

SAN ILDEFONSO POLYCHROME
AD 1880-1910
Des. *Guthe, 1925; *Chapman,
1933; Chapman, 1938; &Chapman,
1970; *Harlow, 1973; *Frank
and Harlow, 1974.
Illus. Halseth, 1926; Marriott, 1948;
Wormington, 1951; Harlow, 1965a;
Tanner, 1968; Arizona Highways,
May 1974; Dittert and Plog,
1980; Barry, 1981.

SAN ILDEFONSO WHITE-ON-POLISHED
RED
Des. *Guthe, 1925; *Chapman, 1933;
Chapman, 1938.

SAN ILDEFONSO WHITE AND PINK-
ON-POLISHED RED
Des. *Chapman, 1933; Chapman,
1938.
Illus. Maxwell Museum, 1974.

SAN JUAN ORANGE WARE
Des. Reed, 1944.

SAN JUAN RED WARE
Syn. San Juan Red Ware, San Juan
Series, Abel, 1955.
Des. *Forsyth, 1972.

SAN JUAN RED-ON-TAN
AD 1700?-present
Des. Dick, 1965; *Harlow, 1973;
*Frank and Harlow, 1974; *Dit-
tert and Plog, 1980.
Illus. Barry, 1981.

SAN JUAN WHITE WARE
Ca. AD 450-1150
Des. Abel, 1955, 12A.
Illus. Lister, 1966; Howard, 1968.

SAN LAZARO GLAZE POLYCHROME
AD 1470-1515
Syn. Glaze IV, Kidder and Shep-
ard, 1936.
Des. Mera, 1933; Hawley, 1936;
*Dittert and Plog, 1980; War-
ren, 1977c.

SAN LORENZO RED-ON-BROWN
Pre AD 900
Syn. Winona Red-on-tan, Colton
and Hargrave, 1937.
Des. Haury, 1936; Hawley, 1936;
Colton and Hargrave, 1937;
*Gladwin, 1948; Humsn Sys-
tems Research, 1973.

SAN MARCIAL BLACK-ON-WHITE
AD 750-950
Des. *Mera, 1935; Hawley, 1936;
Human Systems Research,
1973; Dittert and Plog, 1980;
*Marshall, 1980; Frisbie, 1984.
Illus. Frisbie, 1967.

SAN MARCOS GLAZE-ON-RED
Syn. San Marcos Polychrome.
Des. Mera, 1933; Hawley, 1936.

SAN MARCOS POLYCHROME
Syn. San Marcos Glaze-on-red.
Des. Mera, 1933; Hawley, 1936.

SAN MATEO PLAIN
Syn. Lino Gray; Kana-a Gray.
Des. Hargrave, 1961 manuscript
at MNA.

SAN PABLO POLYCHROME
AD 1740-1800
Des. *Harlow, 1970; *Harlow,
1973; *Frank and Harlow, 1974;
*Dittert and Plog, 1980.

SAN YSIDRO BLACK-ON-RED
Des. Warren, n.d., manuscript on
file Museum of New Mexico,
Santa Fe.
(Carbon painted, red slipped,
crushed rock tempered sherds
from the Zia area.)

SAN YSIDRO POLYCHROME
Des. Warren, n.d., manuscript
on file Museum of New Mexico,
Santa Fe.
(Carbon painted, red slipped,
crushed rock tempered sherds

from the Zia area.)

SANCHEZ GLAZE-ON-RED
AD 1350-1425
(Rio Grande Glaze A type)
Des. Eighth SW Ceramic Conf.,
1966; *Honea, 1966; Dittert and
Plog, 1980.

SANCHEZ GLAZE-ON-YELLOW
AD 1350-1425
(Rio Grande Glaze A type)
Des. Eighth SW Ceramic Conf.,
1966; *Honea, 1966; Dittert and
Plog, 1980.

SANCHEZ GLAZE POLYCHROME
AD 1350-1425
Des. Eighth SW Ceramic Conf.,
1966; *Honea, 1966; Dittert and
Plog, 1980.

SANDY BROWN
Ca. AD 700-1890
Des. Colton, 1939; Doyns and Eu-
ler, 1958, 15-4.

SANDSTONE BLACK-ON-ORANGE
AD 800-1000
Syn. LaPlata Black-on-red, *Mor-
ris, 1939.
Des. Kluckhohn and Reiter, 1939;
Colton, 1956.

SANKAWI BLACK-ON-CREAM
AD 1500-1600
Des. Mera, 1932; Hawley, 1936;
Kidder and Shepard, 1936; Mera,
1939; *Harlow, 1973; Dittert and
Plog, 1980.
Illus. Harlow, 1965; Caywood, 1966;
Barnett, 1969; Bice, 1975; Am-
bler, 1977.

SANKAWI POLYCHROME
Des. *Harlow, 1970.

SANOSTEE RED-ON-ORANGE
Ca. AD 825-875
Des. Wilson and Peckham, 1964.

SANTA ANA POLYCHROME
AD 1850-present
Des. Chapman, 1933; *Stubbs, 1950;
Harlow, 1970; *Harlow, 1973;
*Frank and Harlow, 1974; Dittert
and Plog, 1980.
Illus. Chapman, 1938; Underhill,

1944; Wormington and Neal,
1951; Willey, 1966; Tanner,
1968; Harlow, 1977; Barry,
1981; Trimble, 1987.

SANTA CLARA BLACK
AD 1760-1930
Des. *Underhill, 1944; *Harlow,
1973; *Frank and Harlow,
1974; *LeFree, 1975.
Illus. Stevenson, 1880; Chapman,
1938; Wormington and Neal,
1951; Bahti, 1964; Feder,
1965; Tanner, 1968; Sunset,
1972; Arizona Highways, May
1974; Maxwell Museum, 1974;
Dittert and Plog, 1980; Barry,
1981.

SANTA CLARA BUFF POLYCHROME
AD 1930-present
Des. *LeFree, 1975.
Illus. Arizona Highways, May
1974; Harlow, 1977; Barry,
1981.

SANTA CLARA POLYCHROME
Des. *Chapman, 1933; Chapman,
1938.
Illus. Stevenson, 1880; Dittert
and Plog, 1980.

SANTA CLARA RED
Des. *LeFree, 1975; *Dittert and
Plog, 1980.

SANTA CRUZ BUFF
Ca. AD 750-950
Des. *Gladwin et al., 1937;
*Haury, 1937; *Haury, 1976.

SANTA CRUZ POLYCHROME
AD 1350-1450
Des. Sauer and Brand, 1930;
Brand, 1935; Hawley, 1936;
DiPeso, 1956.

SANTA CRUZ RED-ON-BUFF
Ca. AD 750-950
Des. Haury, 1932; *Gladwin,
1933; Hawley, 1936; *Gladwin
et al., 1937; *Haury, 1937;
*Haury, 1976; Antieau, 1981.
Illus. DiPeso, 1956; Wasley and
Johnson, 1965; Willey, 1966;
Arizona Highways, Feb. 1974;
Chenall, 1967; Brody, 1977.

SANTA FE BLACK-ON-WHITE
AD 1200-1350
Des. Kidder and Amsden, 1931;
*Mera, 1935; Hawley, 1936; Kid-
der and Shepard, 1936; Smiley,
and Bannister, 1953; Stubbs
and Stallings, 1953; *Wetherington, 1968; *Bice and Sundt,
1972; Sudar-Murphy and Laumbach, 1977; Warren, 1977c;
Sundt, 1984.
Illus. McNutt, 1969; Barry, 1981;
Traylor and Scaife, 1980.

SANTA FE BLACK-ON-WHITE: PA-
JARITO VARIETY
Des. Lange, 1968.

SANTA FE BLACK-ON-WHITE:
PERALTA VARIETY
Des. Lange, 1968.

SANTAN RED
Ca. AD 900-1100
Des. *Gladwin, 1933; Hawley, 1936;
*Haury, 1937; Colton and Har-
grave, 1937.

SANTAN RED-ON-BUFF
Des. *Hammack and Sullivan, 1981.

SANTAN SMUDGED
Ca. AD 900-1100
Des. Gladwin, 1933.

SANTO DOMINGO BLACK-ON-CREAM
Des. Chapman, 1933; Chapman,
1936a; Chapman, 1938.
Illus. Stevenson, 1880; Underhill,
1944; Wormington, 1951; Feder,
1965; Arizona Highways, May
1974; Harlow, 1977.

SANTO DOMINGO MATTE BLACK-ON-
POLISHED BLACK
Des. Chapman, 1936a.

SANTO DOMINGO MATTE WHITE-ON-
RED
AD 1930-?
Des. Harlow, 1977.

SANTO DOMINGO POLYCHROME
AD 1900-present
Des. Chapman, 1933; Chapman,
1936a; *Chapman, 1938; *Harlow,
1973; *Frank and Harlow, 1974.

Illus. Bahti, 1964; Tanner, 1968;
Harlow, 1970; Arizona High-
ways, May 1974; Bice, 1975;
Toulouse, 1977; Barry, 1981;
Harlow, 1977; Trimble, 1987.

SAPAWE' MICACEOUS WASHBOARD
Des. *Mera, 1935; Hawley, 1936.

SECO CORRUGATED
AD 1100-1300
Des. Wilson and Warren, 1973.
Illus. Smiley, 1978.

SEGURO BLACK-ON-WHITE
See Wiyo Black-on-white: Seguro
Variety.

SELLS PLAIN
Des. Scantling, 1940; Haury,
1950.

SELLS RED
Des. Scantling, 1940; Haury,
1950; *DiPeso, 1956.

SEVIER BLACK-ON-GRAY
AD 900-1200
Syn. Snake Valley Black-on-
gray, *Madsen, 1977; Fre-
mont Black-on-gray, Malouf,
Dibble and Smith, 1950; Great
Salt Lake Black-on-Gray, Rudy,
1953.
Des. Stewart, 1936; Hawley, 1936.
Illus. Pendergast, 1960.

SEVIER CORRUGATED
Ca. AD 1100-1200
Syn. Snake Valley Corrugated,
*Madsen, 1977; Fremont Cor-
rugated, Malouf, Dibble and
Smith, 1950.
Des. Stewart, 1936; Hawley,
1936.

SEVIER GRAY
Ca. AD 800-1250
Des. Stewart, 1936; Hawley,
1936; Rudy, 1953; Marwitt,
1970; Madsen, 1970; Madsen,
1972; *Madsen, 1977.

SHATO BLACK-ON-WHITE
AD 1080-1130
Des. Colton, 1941; *Colton, 1955,
8B-5.

Illus. Dittert and Eddy, 1963.
(Fourth SW Ceramic Conf., 1962,
recommended this type be
dropped.)

SHEEPSPRINGS BROWN
Des. Wilson and Peckham, 1964.

SHINARUMP BROWN
Des. *Spencer, 1934; Colton, 1952;
Anderson, 1960; *Schwartz et
al., 1979.

SHINARUMP BROWN COILED
Des. Spencer, 1934.

SHINARUMP CORRUGATED
Des. Colton, 1952; *Schwartz et
al., 1979.

SHINARUMP GRAY WARE
Des. Colton, 1952; *Schwartz et
al., 1979.

SHINARUMP WHITE WARE
Des. Colton, 1953; *Schwartz et
al., 1979.

SHOSHONI WARE
Des. Rudy, 1953.

SHOWLOW BLACK-ON-RED
AD 1050-1200
Des. *Gladwin, 1931; Hawley, 1936;
*Colton and Hargrave, 1937.
Illus. Gumerman, 1969.

SHOWLOW BLACK-ON-WHITE
(No known description)
Illus. Pomeroy, 1962.

SHOWLOW CORRUGATED
Des. Mera, 1934; Hawley, 1936.

SHOWLOW CORRUGATED SMUDGED
Des. Mera, 1934; Hawley, 1936.

SHOWLOW GLAZE-ON-WHITE
Des. Second SW Ceramic Conference, 1959.

SHOWLOW POLYCHROME
AD 1325-1400
Des. *Haury, 1931; *Colton and
Hargrave, 1937; *Carlson, 1970;
*Dittert and Plog, 1980.
Illus. Clarke, 1935; Martin and

Willis, 1940; Arizona Highways,
Feb. 1974; Washburn, 1977;
Harlow, 1977.

SHOWLOW RED
Ca. AD 1300-1350
Syn. Kinishba Red.
Des. Haury, n.d.
(Name Showlow Red was dropped
in favor of Kinishba Red by
the Second SW Ceramic Con-
ference, 1959.)

SICHOMOVI BLACK-ON-RED
AD 20th century
Syn. Hopi Black-on-red.
Des. *Colton, 1956, 7C-2.

SICHOMOVI POLYCHROME
AD 20th century
Des. *Colton, 1956, 7C-1.
Illus. Harlow, 1977; Barry, 1981.

SICHOMOVI RED
AD 20th century
Des. *Colton, 1956, 7C-3.
Illus. Harlow and Bartlett, 1978.

SICHOMOVI RED WARE
AD 20th century
Des. Colton, 1956, 7C.

SIKYATKI POLYCHROME
AD 1400-1625
Des. *Fewkes, 1898; *Hargrave,
1932; Hawley, 1936; Kidder
and Shepard, 1936; Colton
and Hargrave, 1937; *Colton,
1956, 7B-9; Wade, 1980; Dittert and Plog, 1980; *Wade
and McChesney, 1981.
Illus. Hough, 1903; Fewkes, 1904;
Fewkes, 1919; Martin, 1940;
Martin and Willis, 1940; Wormington, 1951; Gladwin, 1957;
Smith et al., 1966; Lister and
Lister, 1969; Arizona Highways, Feb. 1974; Collins,
1974; Maxwell Museum, 1974;
Bice, 1975; Huse, 1976; Brody,
1977; Barry, 1981.

SILVER CREEK CORRUGATED
Ca. AD 1290-1400
Des. Haury, 1931; *Colton and
Hargrave, 1937; Connoly,
1940.

SILVER CREEK PLAIN
Des. Connolly, 1940.

SLIDE MOUNTAIN BLACK-ON-GRAY
AD 1100-1225
Syn. North Creek Black-on-gray,
Type B.
Des. Thompson, 1986.

SMEARED INDENTED CORRUGATED
AD 1175-1350?
Des. Mera, 1935; Warren, 1976;
Mobley, 1978.

SNAKE VALLEY BLACK-ON-GRAY
AD 900-1200
Syn. Sevier Black-on-gray, Ste-
wart, 1936; Paragonah Black-
on-gray, Corrugated exterior,
in part; Fremont Black-on-gray,
Malouf et al., 1950; Great Salt
Lake Black-on-gray, Rudy,
1953.
Des. Rudy, 1953; *Marwitt, 1970;
Madsen, 1972; *Madsen, 1977.
Illus. Pendergast, 1960; Aikens,
1967; Marwitt, 1968.

SNAKE VALLEY CORRUGATED
AD 1100-1200
Syn. Sevier Corrugated, Stewart,
1936; Fremont Corrugated Ware,
Malouf et al., 1950.
Des. Rudy, 1953; Madsen, 1970;
Madsen, 1972; *Madsen, 1977.

SNAKE VALLEY GRAY
AD 900-1200
Syn. Sevier Gray, Stewart, 1936.
Des. Rudy, 1953; *Marwitt, 1970;
Schroeder, 1955; Madsen, 1972;
*Madsen, 1977.

SNAKETOWN RED-ON-BUFF
Ca. AD 300-500
Des. *Haury, 1937; Gladwin et al.,
1937; Chenall, 1967; *Haury,
1976; *Kelly, 1978.
Illus. Gladwin, 1957; McGregor,
1965; Arizona Highways, Feb.
1974; Jacobs, 1979.

SNOWFLAKE BLACK-ON-WHITE
AD 1100-1200
Des. *Colton, 1941a; *Longacre,
1964; *Wilson, 1969; *Smith,
1971; *Dittert and Plog, 1980.

Illus. Martin and Willis, 1940;
Hammack, 1963; Martin, 1967;
Hammack, 1969; Seaberg, 1969;
Arizona Highways, Feb. 1974;
Bice, 1975; Doyel, 1967.

SOBAIPURI PLAIN
Des. *DiPeso, 1953.

SOBAIPURI RED
Des. DiPeso, 1953.

SOCORRO BLACK-ON-WHITE
AD 1050-1300
Des. *Mera, 1933; Hawley, 1936;
Smiley, Stubbs and Bannis-
ter, 1953; Dittert, 1959; Hu-
man Systems Research, 1973;
*Sundt, 1979; *Dittert and
Plog, 1980.
Illus. Wormington, 1951; Wen-
dorf et al., 1956; Bice and
Sundt, 1972; Bice, 1975;
Brody, 1977.

SONORA (RAKED) BROWN
Des. Brand, 1935.

SONORA RED-ON-BROWN
Syn. Trincheras Purple-on-red,
Sauer and Brand, 1931.
Des. Gladwin, 1931.
Illus. DiPeso, 1956.

SOSI BLACK-ON-WHITE
AD 1070-1200
Syn. Kia-ko Black-on-white,
*Colton, 1956, 8B-11.
Des. *Colton and Hargrave, 1937;
*Colton, 1955, 8B-3; *Dittert
and Plog, 1980.
Illus. Beals, Brainerd and Smith,
1945; Colton, 1946; Colton,
1953; Lister et al., 1960;
Sharrock and Keane, 1962;
Ambler et al., 1964; New
Mexico Univ., 1967; Lister
and Lister, 1969; Gumerman,
1970; Weed, 1970; Hobler,
1974; Ambler, 1977.

SOUTH PECOS BROWN
Des. Jellinek, 1967.

SOUTHERN PAIUTE WARE
Des. Stewart, 1941; *Baldwin,
1950; Worman, 1969.

SPRINGERVILLE POLYCHROME
AD 1250-1300
Des. Haury, 1952; Carlson, 1962;
*Carlson, 1970; Dittert and
Plog, 1980.
Illus. Martin, 1967; Bice, 1975;
Washburn, 1977.

STARKWEATHER SMUDGED DECO-
RATED
Ca. AD 1100-1200
Syn. Reserve Polychrome, Nesbitt,
1938; Tularosa White-on-red,
Martin and Rinaldo, 1952.
Des. Martin, Rinaldo and Antevs,
1949; Chapman, 1961.
Illus. Martin et al., 1949.

SUNSET APPLIQUE
AD 1125-1150
Des. *Colton, 1958, 14-13.

SUNSET BROWN
AD 1065-1200
Des. Colton, 1958, 14-11.

SUNSET BROWN: VARIETY B
Des. Wilson, 1969.

SUNSET CORRUGATED
Des. Reed, 1938a.

SUNSET PINCHED
Ad 1065-1200
Colton, 1958. (A variety of Sunset Red with pinched up nodes
on the surface.)

SUNSET PLAIN
AD 1065-1200
Des. Colton, 1958.

SUNSET RED
AD 1065-1200
Syn. Flagstaff Red, Colton, 1932.
Des. Colton, 1932; Hawley, 1936;
Colton and Hargrave, 1937;
*Colton, 1958, 14-10.
Illus. Hargrave, 1932; King, 1949;
McGregor, 1965; Gumerman,
1969.

SUNSET SMUDGED
AD 1065-1200
Des. Colton, 1958, 14-11.

SUNSET TOOLED
AD 1065-1200
Des. Colton, 1941a.

SUNSET WHITE-ON-RED
AD 1065-1200
Des. *Colton, 1941a; *Colton,
1958, 14-12.

SWEETWATER POLYCHROME
Ca. AD 100-300
Des. *Haury, 1937; Gladwin et
al., 1937; *Haury, 1976.

SWEETWATER RED-ON-GRAY
Ca. AD 100-300
Des. *Haury, 1937; *Gladwin et
al., 1937; Gladwin, 1948;
*Haury, 1976; *Kelly, 1978.
Illus. McGregor, 1965; Arizona
Highways, Feb. 1974; Brody,
1977; Antieau, 1981.

TABIRA' BLACK-ON-WHITE
AD 1550-1672
Des. Toulouse, 1949; *Vivian,
1964; *Toulouse and Stephen-
son, 1960; Human Systems
Research, 1973; *Hayes et al.,
1981.
Illus. Brody, 1977.

TABIRA' PLAIN
AD 1545-1672
Des. Toulouse and Stephenson,
1960; Human systems Re-
search, 1973; *Hayes et al.,
1981.
Illus. Vivian, 1964.

TABIRA' POLYCHROME
AD 1650-1672
Des. *Toulouse, 1949; Human
Systems Research, 1973.
Illus. Vivian, 1964; Briggs, 1973;
*Hayes et al., 1981.

TALLAHOGAN RED
AD 620-775
Syn. Lino Red, Wendorf, 1953.
Des. Wendorf, 1953a; Daifuku,
1961; *Lucius and Wilson,
1981a.
Illus. Frisbie, 1967.

TALPA BLACK-ON-WHITE
   Des. Dick, 1965; *Wetherington,
   1968.

TAMAYA RED
   Des. Allen and McNutt, 1955;
   Frisbie, 1975.

TANNER BLACK-ON-WHITE
   Des. Wendorf, 1956.

TANQUE VERDE RED-ON-BROWN
   Syn. Pantano Red-on-brown, Dan-
   son in Hayden, 1957.
   Des. Fraps, 1935; *Scantling, 1940;
   Withers, 1941; *DiPeso, 1956;
   *Danson in Hayden, 1957; Haury
   and Gifford, 1959; *Kelly, 1978.
   Illus. Wasley and Johnson, 1956;
   Zahniser, 1966; DiPeso, 1967;
   Greenleaf, 1975.

TANQUE VERDE BLACK-ON-BROWN
   Des. Deaver in Los Morteros Re-
   port (in press), Arizona State
   Museum.

TANQUE VERDE POLYCHROME
   Des. Deaver in Los Morteros Report (in press). ASM.

TAOS BLACK-ON-WHITE
   AD 1150-1250
   Des. *Mera, 1935; Hawley, 1936;
   Smiley, Stubbs and Bannister,
   1953; Dick, 1965; *Wethering-
   ton, 1968; Dittert and Plog,
   1980.
   Illus. Peckham, 1963.

TAOS CORRUGATED
   Des. *Wetherington, 1968.

TAOS GRAY
   Des. Dick, 1965; *Wetherington,
   1968.

TAOS INCISED
   AD 1000-1300
   Des. Gunnerson, 1959; Peckham,
   1963; Dick, 1965; *Wetherington, 1968.

TAOS MICACEOUS
   Des. Ellis and Brody, 1964.
   Illus. Underhill, 1944; Tanner, 1968;

Arizona Highways, May 1974;
   Trimble, 1987.

TAOS PLAIN UTILITY
   Des. Ellis and Brody, 1964.

TAOS-POGE BLACK-ON-WHITE
   Des. Ellis and Brody, 1964.

TATUNGUE POLYCHROME
   AD 1890-1910
   Des. *Harlow, 1973; *Frank and
   Harlow, 1974; Dittert and
   Plog, 1980.

TAYLOR BLACK-ON-WHITE
   Ca. AD 1000-1100
   Des. Wilson and Peckham, 1964;
   Windes, 1977.

TESUQUE BLACK-ON-CREAM
   Syn. Black-on-tan, *Frank and
   Harlow, 1974.
   Des. *Chapman, 1933; Chapman,
   1938.
   Illus. Underhill, 1944; Harlow,
   1965a; Frank and Harlow,
   1974.

TESUQUE POLYCHROME
   1930-present?
   Des. *Chapman, 1933; *Chapman,
   1938; *Harlow, 1973; *Frank
   and Harlow, 1974.
   Illus. Harlow, 1965a; Harlow,
   1970; Jacka and Gill, 1976;
   Barry, 1981.

TESUQUE SMEARED INDENTED
   Des. *Mera, 1935; Hawley, 1936.

TEWA BLACK-ON-WHITE
   (No known description)
   Illus. Carlson, 1977.

TEWA POLISHED BLACK
   AD 1650-1800
   Syn. Kapo Black, Dick in Schroe-
   der, 1968.
   Des. Carlson, 1965.

TEWA POLYCHROME
   AD 1650-1725
   Syn. Tewa Style, Smiley, Stubbs
   and Bannister, 1953.
   Des. Mera, 1932; Hawley, 1936;

*Mera, 1939; *Harlow, 1973;
Warren, 1976; *Frank and Harlow, 1974; Carlson, 1977; Warren, 1979; Dittert and Plog,
1980.

THEODORE BLACK-ON-WHITE
Des. Wilson and Peckham, 1964.

THREE CIRCLE NECK CORRUGATED
AD 775-950
Des. Haury, 1936; Hawley, 1936.
Illus. Martin, 1947; Martin et al.,
1952; Martin et al., 1954; Smiley,
1978; Gifford, 1980.

THREE CIRCLE RED-ON-WHITE
AD 750-950
Des. Haury, 1936; Hawley, 1936;
Nesbitt, 1938; Human Systems
Research, 1973; LeBlanc, 1983.
Illus. McGregor, 1965; Brody, 1977;
Smiley, 1978.

THREE RIVERS RED-ON-TERRA COTTA
AD 1125-1300
Syn. San Andres Red-on-terra
cotta, McCluney, 1962; Broad
Line Red-on-terra cotta, Jel-
linek, 1952.
Des. *Mera and Stallings, 1931;
Cosgrove, 1932; Hawley, 1936;
Kidder and Shepard, 1936; Hol-
den, 1952; Hammerson, 1972;
Human Systems Research, 1973;
Runyan and Hedrick, 1973; Bus-
sey et al., 1976.
Illus. Nesbitt, 1931; Jellinek, 1952;
Smiley, 1978.

TIN CUP POLYCHROME
Syn. Pueblo II (Mancos) Polychrome,
Brew, 1946.
Des. *Forsyth, 1972; Forsyth,
1977; Bond, 1983.

TIQUEX GLAZE POLYCHROME
Des. Mera, 1933; Hawley, 1936.

TIZON BROWN WARE
Ca. AD 700-1890
Des. Colton, 1939; Dobyns and
Euler, 1958, 15.

TIZON WIPED
Prehistoric ?-pre 1900
Des. Dobyns, 1956; *Dobyns and
Euler, 1958; 15-7.

TOADLENA BLACK-ON-WHITE
AD 975-1125
Des. Wilson and Peckham, 1974;
*Windes, 1977.
Illus. Johnson, 1963.

TOCITO GRAY
Ca. AD 825-875
Des. Wilson and Peckham, 1974;
*Windes, 1977.

TOHATCHI BANDED
Ca. AD 900-1050
Des. *Wendorf et al., 1956.
Illus. Windes, 1977.

TONTO BROWN
AD 1150-1400
Syn. Tonto Red, Colton, 1958,
14-31.
(No known description for this
type name.)

TONTO CORRUGATED
Des. Windmiller, 1972; *Doyel,
1978.

TONTO PLAIN
AD 1150-1400
Syn. Tonto Red, in part, Colton,
1958; Tonto Brown; Tonto
Rough, Colton, n.d., manu-
script at MNA.
Des. *Doyel, 1978.

TONTO POLYCHROME
AD 1350-1600
(May be considered a subtype of
Gila Polychrome.)
Des. *Gladwin, 1930; Hawley,
1936; Colton and Hargrave,
1937; *Haury, 1945a; *DiPeso,
1958.
Illus. Baldwin, 1939; Martin and
Willis, 1940; Kidder and Cos-
grove, 1949; Wormington, 1951;
Martin and Rinaldo, 1960a;
Willey, 1966; Mills and Mills,
1972; Arizona Highways, Feb.
1974; Bice, 1975; Doyel, 1978;
Barry, 1981.

TONTO RED
AD 1150-1400
Syn. Tonto Plain.
Des. *Gladwin, 1930b; Colton and
Hargrave, 1937; Colton, 1958;

14-31; *Steen et al., 1962; Pierson, 1962; Windmiller, 1972.

TONTO RIBBED
Des. Shiner, 1961.

TONTO ROUGH
AD 1150-1400
Syn. Tonto Plain.
Des. Colton, n.d., manuscript at
MNA.

TONTO SMUDGED
Des. Colton, 1941.

TOPAWA RED-ON-BROWN
Des. Withers, 1941; *Withers, 1973.
Illus. Greenleaf, 1975.

TOPOC BUFF
Ca. AD 1000-1400
Syn. Pyramid Red.
Des. Rogers, 1945; Waters, 1982.
(Not the same as Schroeder's Topoc
Buff.)

TOPOC BUFF
Post AD 1150-?
Syn. Lower Colorado Buff Ware,
Schroeder, 1958.
Des. Rogers, 1945; Schroeder,
1952b; *Schroeder, 1958; D16-
18; Waters, 1982.

TOPOC FUGITIVE RED
Post AD 1150-?
Des. Schroeder, 1952b; *Schroeder,
1958, D16-20.

TOPOC RED-ON-BUFF
Ca. AD 1000-1400
Des. Rogers, 1945; Waters, 1982.
(Not the same as Schroeder's Topoc
Red-on-buff.)

TOPOC RED-ON-BUFF
Des. Colton, 1939; Rogers, 1945;
*Schroeder, 1958; D16-19; Waters,
1982.

TOPOC STUCCO
Post AD 1150-?
Des. Schroeder, 1952b; *Schroeder,
1958, D16-21.

TOQUERVILLE BLACK-ON-WHITE
Des. Colton, 1952.
Illus. Pendergast, 1960.

TOROWEAP BLACK-ON-GRAY
Des. Colton, 1952.

TORTUGAS RED
Mentioned by Stubbs; no known
description.

TOTUGAS RED-ON-BROWN
Mentioned by Stubbs; no known
description.
Illus. Harlow, 1970.

TORTUGAS RED-ON-ORANGE
Des. *Harlow, 1970.

TOWAOC PAINTED-SMEARED
Des. *Forsyth, 1972.
(Differs from Devil Mesa Painted
Corrugated only with respect
to surface manipulation.)

TRAMPAS BLACK-ON-WHITE
Des. Dick, 1965.

TRENAQUEL GLAZE POLYCHROME
Des. Mera, 1933; Hawley, 1936.

TRES ALAMOS RED
Des. Tuthill, 1947.

TRES ALAMOS RED-ON-BROWN
Des. Tuthill, 1947.

TRINCHERAS POLYCHROME
Syn. Nogales Polychrome, *Clarke,
1935.
Des. *Sauer and Brand, 1931;
Hawley, 1936; Withers, 1941;
Withers, 1973.
Illus. Cummings, 1953.

TRINCHERAS PURPLE-ON-RED
Syn. Sonora Red-on-brown, Gladwin, 1931.
Des. *Sauer and Brand, 1931;
Brand, 1935; Hawley, 1936;
Withers, 1941.
Illus. DiPeso, 1956; DiPeso, 1967;
Chenall, 1967.

TRINCHERAS PURPLE-ON-RED
(Specular paint variety)
Des. *Withers, 1973.

TRINCHERAS PURPLE-ON-RED
(nonspecular paint variety)
Des. *Withers, 1973.

TRINCHERAS RED
  Syn. Trincheras Plain.
  Des. *DiPeso, 1956.

TRIOS POLYCHROME
  AD 1175-1875
  Des. *Harlow, 1970; *Harlow, 1973;
  *Frank and Harlow, 1974; *Dil-
  lingham, 1977; Dittert and Plog,
  1980.

TRUMBULL BLACK-ON-GRAY
  Des. Colton, 1952.

TSEGI BLACK-ON-ORANGE
  AD 1125-1300
  Des. Kidder and Guernsey, 1919;
  *Colton and Hargrave, 1937;
  *Colton, 1956, 5B-7; Dittert and
  Plog, 1980.
  Illus. Colton et al., 1940; Beals,
  Brainerd and Smith, 1945; Shar-
  rock et al., 1963; Hobler, 1974.

TSEGI CORRUGATED
  Mentioned by Lindsay in Gumerman, 1970.

TSEGI ORANGE
  AD 1150-1300
  Des, Kidder and Guernsey, 1919;
  *Colton and Hargrave, 1937;
  *Colton, 1956, 5B-5; Dittert
  and Plog, 1980.
  Illus. Colton et al., 1940; Hobler,
  1974.

TSEGI ORANGE WARE
  Ca. AD 1150-1300
  Des. Colton and Hargrave, 1937;
  Colton, 1956, 5B.
  Illus. Ambler et al., 1964; Lister
  and Lister, 1969; Worman, 1969;
  Hobler, 1974.

TSEGI POLYCHROME
  AD 1225-1300
  Des. Colton and Hargrave, 1937;
  *Colton, 1956, 5B-8; *Smith,
  1971; Dittert and Plog, 1980.
  Illus. Colton et al., 1940.

TSEGI RED-ON-ORANGE
  AD 1150-1300
  Des. *Colton and Hargrave, 1937;
  *Colton, 1956, 5B-6; Dittert and
  Plog, 1980.

Illus. Clarke, 1935; Colton et al.,
  1940; Beals, Brainerd and
  Smith, 1945.

TSEGI RED WASHED
  Des. Reed, 1938a.

TSEH-SO CORRUGATED
  Syn. Exuberant Corrugated.
  Des. Hargrave, 1962, manuscript
  at MNA.

TUCKUP BLACK-ON-GRAY
  Ca. AD 1080-1125
  Syn. Shato Black-on-white, Flag-
  staff Style.
  Des. Thompson, 1986.

TUCSON BLACK-ON-RED
  Des. *DiPeso, 1958.

TUCSON PLAIN
  Des. Hayden, 1957.

TUCSON POLYCHROME
  Post AD 1300-1400
  Des. *Clarke, 1935; *Hayden,
  1957; *DiPeso, 1958.
  Illus. Cummings, 1953; Mills and
  Mills, 1972; Smiley, 1978.

TULAROSA BLACK-ON-WHITE
  AD 1100-1200
  Syn. Upper Gila Black-on-white,
  Haury, 1931; Cheta Black-on-
  white, Colton, 1940.
  Des. *Kidder, 1924; *Gladwin,
  1931; Hawley, 1936; Colton
  and Hargrave, 1937; Smiley,
  Stubbs and Bannister, 1953;
  *Rinaldo and Bluhm, 1956;
  *Smith, 1971; Bice, 1975; *Dit-
  tert and Plog, 1980.
  Illus. Goddard, 1928; Martin and
  Willis, 1940; Wormington, 1951;
  Martin et al., 1952; Cummings,
  1953; Martin et al., 1956; Glad-
  win, 1957; Martin et al., 1957;
  Rinaldo, 1959; Martin and Rinaldo, 1960a; Martin et al.,
  1961; McGregor, 1965; Willey,
  1966; New Mexico Univ., 1967;
  Lister and Lister, 1969; Bice
  and Sundt, 1972; Arizona Highways, Feb. 1974; Maxwell Museum, 1974; Barnett, 1974a;
  Brody, 1977; Barry, 1981.

TULAROSA CORRUGATED PATTERNED
AD 1050-1250
Syn. Tularosa Corrugated Patterned,
    *Rinaldo and Bluhm, 1956.
Des. *Martin and Rinaldo, 1950;
    Martin et al., 1952; *Martin and
    Bluhm, 1956.
Illus. Museum of American Indian,
    1972.

TULAROSA FILLET RIM
Ca. AD 1100-1300
Des. Kidder, 1924; Gladwin, 1934;
    Wendorf, 1950; Martin et al.,
    1952.
Illus. Rinaldo, 1959.

TULAROSA PATTERNED CORRUGATED
AD 1050-1250
Syn. Tularosa Corrugated Patterned,
    Martin and Rinaldo, 1950.
Des. *Rinaldo and Bluhm, 1956.
Illus. Smith, 1973; Smiley, 1978.

TULAROSA PATTERNED CORRUGAT-
    ED: RESERVE VARIETY
Syn. Plain and Indented Corrugat-
    ed, Martin et al., 1952.
Des. *Martin and Rinaldo, 1950;
    *Rinaldo and Bluhm, 1956.
Illus. Kidder, 1924; Martin et al.,
    1954.

TULAROSA PATTERNED CORRUGATED:
    SMUDGED INTERIOR VARIETY
Ad 1050-1250
Des. *Rinaldo and Bluhm, 1956.

TULAROSA PLAIN
Des. Kidder, 1924.

TULAROSA WHITE-ON-RED
Ca. AD 1100-1200
Syn. Reserve Polychrome, Nesbitt,
    1938; Starkweather Smudged
    Decorated, Martin et al., 1959.
Des. Martin et al., 1952; *Rinaldo
    and Bluhm, 1956.
Illus. Martin et al., 1954; Rinaldo,
    1959.

TUMCO BUFF
Ca. AD 1000-1500
Des. Rogers, 1945; Waters, 1982.

TUMCO BUFF
Pre AD 900-post 1400

Des. Rogers, 1945; *Schroeder,
    1952b; *Schroeder, 1958, D16-
    12; Waters, 1982.

TUMCO RED-ON-BUFF
Ca. AD 1000-1500
Des. Rogers, 1945; Waters, 1982.

TUMCO RED-ON-BUFF
Pre AD 900-1150 plus
Des. Rogers, 1945; *Schroeder,
    1952b; *Schroeder, 1958; D16-
    13; Waters, 1982.

TUMCO STUCCO
Pre AD 900-1150 plus
Des. *Schroeder, 1952b; *Schroe-
    der, 1958; D16-14.

TUNICHA BLACK-ON-WHITE
AD 850-900
Des. Wilson and Peckham, 1964;
    *Windes, 1977.
Illus. Brody, 1977.

TUNYO POLYCHROME
AD 1907-present
Des. *Harlow, 1973; *Frank and
    Harlow, 1974.
Illus. Harlow, 1977.

TURKEY HILL RED
AD 1090-1200
Des. Colton and Hargrave, 1937;
    *Colton, 1958, 14-7.

TURKEY HILL SMUDGED
AD 1120-1200
Des. *Colton, 1958; 15-8.

TURKEY HILL WHITE-ON-RED
Ca. AD 1100-1200
Des. *Colton, 1941a; *Colton,
    1958; 14-9.

TURNER GRAY
Ca. AD 700-1200?
Syn. Turner Gray: Variety II,
    Wormington, 1955.
Des. Wormington, 1955; Anderson,
    1960; *Gunnerson, 1965.
Illus. Gunnerson, 1957.

TURNER GRAY: CISCO VARIETY
Ca. AD 650-950
Syn. Turner Gray: Variety I,
    Wormington, 1955; Uinta Gray,
    *Madsen, 1977.

Des. *Lister, 1960.
Illus. Aikens, 1967.

TURNER GRAY: EMERY VARIETY
Ca. AD 700-1200?
Syn. Emery Gray, *Madsen, 1977;
Turner Gray: Variety II, Worm-
ington, 1955; Escalante Gray,
Gunnerson, 1969.
Des. *Lister, 1960.
Illus. Aikens, 1967.

TURNER GRAY: VARIETY I
Ca. 650-950
Syn. Uinta Gray, *Madsen, 1977;
Turner Gray: Cisco Variety,
Lister et al., 1960; Uinta Plain,
Wormington, 1955.
Des. Wormington, 1955.

TURNER GRAY: VARIETY II
Ca. AD 700-1200?
Syn. Turner Gray: Emery Variety,
Lister et al., 1960; Escalante
Gray, Gunnerson, 1969; Emery
Gray, *Madsen, 1977.
Des. Wormington, 1955.

TUSAYAN APPLIQUE
AD 1050-1100
Syn. Tusayan Pinched, Colton,
1955.
Des. *Colton, 1955, 8A-10.
Illus. Weed, 1970.

TUSAYAN BLACK-ON-RED
AD 1050-1200
Des. Kidder and Guernsey, 1919;
Kidder, 1924; Gladwin, 1931;
*Hargrave, 1932; Hawley, 1936;
&Colton, 1956, 5B-2; *Dittert
and Plog, 1980.
Illus. Martin, 1936; Colton et al.,
1940; Martin and Willis, 1940;
Beals, Brainerd and Smith, 1945;
Haury, 1945; King, 1949; Lister
et al., 1960; Shutler, 1961;
Sharrock et al., 1963; New Mexi-
co Univ., 1967; Lister and Lis-
ter, 1969; Gumerman, 1970; Hob-
ler, 1974; Ambler, 1977.

TUSAYAN BLACK-ON-WHITE
AD 1125-1300
Des. Kidder and Guernsey, 1919;
Gladwin, 1930; *Hargrave, 1932;
Hawley, 1936; Colton and Har-

grave, 1937; *Colton, 1955;
8B-9; *Smith, 1971.
Illus. Martin and Willis, 1940;
Beals, Brainerd and Smith,
1945; Ambler et al., 1964;
Anderson, 1969; Arizona Highways, Feb. 1974; Hobler,
1974; Barry, 1981.

TUSAYAN CORRUGATED
AD 950-1300
Syn. Deadmans Corrugated, Gifford and Smith, 1978.
Des. *Hargrave, 1932; Hawley,
1936; *Colton and Hargrave,
1937; *Colton, 1955, 8A-11.
Illus. Colton, 1946; McGregor,
1951; Lister et al., 1960; Ambler et al., 1964; McGregor,
1965; Gumerman, 1970; Euler,
1971; Arizona Highways, Feb.
1974; Hobler, 1974; Harlow
and Bartlett, 1978.

TUSAYAN CORRUGATED: COOMBS
VARIETY
Des. Lister, 1960.
Illus. Lister et al., 1960.

TUSAYAN CORRUGATED: KWATOKO
VARIETY
Des. *Gifford and Smith, 1978.

TUSAYAN CORRUGATED: STAR
MOUNTAIN VARIETY
Des. *Gifford and Smith, 1978.

TUSAYAN CORRUGATED: TUSAYAN
VARIETY
Des. *Gifford and Smith, 1978.

TUSAYAN GRAY WARE
Ca. AD 600-1300
Syn. Gray Ware, Hough, 1903.
Des. Colton and Hargrave, 1937;
Colton, 1956.
Illus. Smith, 1952; Hobler, 1974;
Jennings, 1978.

TUSAYAN PINCHED
AD 1050-1100
Syn. Tusayan Applique, Colton,
1955.
Des. *Colton, 1955.

TUSAYAN POLYCHROME
AD 1150-1300

Des. *Kidder and Guernsey, 1919;
*Hargrave, 1932; Hawley, 1936;
*Colton and Hargrave, 1937;
*Colton, 1956, 5B-9; Smith,
1971; Dittert and Plog, 1980.
Illus. Clarke, 1935; Colton et al.,
1950; Martin and Willis, 1940;
Beals, Brainerd and Smith,
1945; O'Bryan, 1950; Ambler et
al., 1964; Willey, 1966; Anderson, 1969; Gumerman, 1970;
Hobler, 1974; Bice, 1975; Bradley, 1975; Ambler, 1977.

TUSAYAN WHITE WARE
AD 700-1350
Syn. White Ware, Holmes, 1886;
Black and White Ware, Fewkes,
1904.
Des. Colton and Hargrave, 1937;
Colton, 1955, 8B.
Illus. McGregor, 1965.

TUWEEP BROWN
Des. Thompson, 1971.

TUWEEP CORRUGATED
Des. Thompson, 1971.

TUWEEP GRAY
Des. Thompson, 1971.

TUWIUCA BLACK-ON-ORANGE
Ca. AD 1250-1300
Des. Colton and Hargrave, 1937;
*Colton, 1956, 6B-2; Dittert and
Plog, 1980.

TUWIUCA ORANGE
AD 1250-1300
Des. Colton and Hargrave, 1937;
Colton, 1956, 6B-1; Dittert and
Plog, 1980.

TUWIUCA POLYCHROME
AD 1300-1400
Syn. Homolovi Polychrome, Colton,
1956; Winslow Polychrome, Col-
ton, 1956.
Des. Colton and Hargrave, 1937;
*Colton, 1956, 6B-3.

TUZIGOOT BLACK-ON-GRAY
Ca. AD 1150-1425
Des. *Caywood and Spicer, 1935;
Hawley, 1936; Colton and Har-
grave, 1937; *Barnett, 1974.

TUZIGOOT BLACK-ON-RED
Ca. AD 1300-1425
Des. Caywood and Spicer, 1935;
Colton and Hargrave, 1937.

TUZIGOOT BROWN
AD 1150-1400
Syn. Tuzigoot Plain, Colton,
1958.
Des. Colton, 1958, 14-19; Schroe-
der, unpublished manuscript.
Illus. Barnett, 1973.

TUZIGOOT PLAIN
AD 1150-1400
Syn. Tuzigoot Brown, Colton,
1958.
Des. Colton, 1958, 14-19; Schroe-
der, 1960.

TUZIGOOT RED
Ca. AD 1150-1400
Des. *Caywood and Spicer, 1935;
Hawley, 1936; Colton and Har-
grave, 1937; *Colton, 1958,
14-20; Schroeder, 1960.

TUZIGOOT RED-ON-BLACK
Ca. AD 1300-1425
Des. Caywood and Spicer, 1935;
Colton and Hargrave, 1937.

TUZIGOOT SMUDGED
Des. Colton, n.d., manuscript
at MNA.

TUZIGOOT WHITE-ON-RED
Ca. AD 1300-1425
Syn. Prescott White-on-red.
Des. Caywood and Spicer, 1935;
Hawley, 1936; Colton and
Hargrave, 1937; Colton, 1958;
14-21.

TWIN TREES BLACK-ON-WHITE
Ca. AD 800s
Des. *O'Bryan, 1950; *Abel,
1955, 12A-2.
(This type name was dropped at
the Fifth SW Ceramic Conf.,
1963.)

TWIN TREES BLACK-ON-WHITE:
DURANGO VARIETY
Des. *Ellwood in Gooding, 1980.

TWIN TREES PLAIN
AD 575-900

Syn. Chapin Gray, Rohn, 1977.
Des. Morris, 1936; *O'Bryan, 1950;
    *Abel, 1955, 10A-2; Rohn, 1959.

TWIN TREES PLAIN: DURANGO
    VARIETY
Des. *Ellwood in Gooding, 1980.

UINTA GRAY
Ca. AD 650-950
Syn. Uinta Plain, Wormington, 1955;
    Turner Gray: Variety I, Worm-
    ington, 1955; Turner Gray:
    Cisco Variety, Lister, 1960.
Des. Stewart, 1936; Hawley, 1936;
    Wormington, 1955; Marwitt, 1970;
    Madsen, 1970; Madsen, 1972;
    *Madsen, 1977.

UINTA PLAIN
Ca. AD 650-950
Syn. Turner Gray: Variety II,
    Wormington, 1955; Uinta Gray,
    Madsen, 1977; Turner Gray:
    Cisco Variety, Lister et al.,
    1960.
Des. Wormington, 1955.

UNCOMPAHGRE SMEARED: VARIETY
1
Des. *Forsyth, 1972.
(Differs from Mancos Corrugated:
    Variety 1 only with respect to
    surface manipulation.)

UNCOMPAHGRE SMEARED: VARIETY
2
Des. *Forsyth, 1972.
(Differs from Mancos Corrugated:
    Variety 2 only with respect to
    surface manipulation.)

UNCOMPAHGRE SMEARED: VARIETY
3
Des. *Forsyth, 1972.
(Differs from Mancos Corrugated:
    Variety 3 only with respect to
    surface manipulation.)

UPPER GILA CORRUGATED
Syn. Reserve Indented Corrugated,
    Rinaldo and Bluhm, 1956.
Des. Kidder, 1924; Hawley, 1936;
    Nesbitt, 1938; *Martin and Ri-
    naldo, 1950.

UTAH DESERT GRAY
Des. Rudy, 1953.

UTE WARE
Des. Opler, 1939; Gifford, 1940;
    Stewart, 1941; Huscher, 1943.

VADITO BLACK-ON-WHITE
Des. Dick, 1965.

VADITO MICACEOUS
Des. Dick, 1965.

VAHKI PLAIN
Ca. 300-100BC
Des. *Gladwin et al., 1937;
    Haury, 1937; *Haury, 1976.
Illus. DiPeso, 1956; McGregor,
    1965; Willey, 1966.

VAHKI RED
Ca. 300-100BC
Des. *Gladwin et al., 1937;
    Haury, 1937; *Antieau, 1981.
Illus. McGregor, 1965; Haury,
    1976.

VALLECITOS BLACK-ON-WHITE
AD 1250-1300
Des. *Mera, 1935; Hawley, 1936;
    *Bice and Sundt, 1972; Dittert
    and Plog, 1980.
Illus. Bice, 1975.

VALSHNI RED
Des. Withers, 1941; *Withers,
    1973.

VAMORI RED-ON-BROWN
Des. Withers, 1941; Haury, 1950;
    *Withers, 1973.

VERDE BLACK-ON-GRAY
AD 1050-1200
Syn. Verde Black-on-white, Glad-
    win, 1930; Aquarius Black-on-
    gray, Colton, 1958; Verde
    Polychrome, Colton, 1958;
    Prescott Black-on-brown, Col-
    ton, 1958.
Des. *Gladwin and Gladwin, 1930c;
    Caywood and Spicer, 1935;
    *Colton, 1958, 17-1; *Barnett,
    1974.
Illus. Spicer and Caywood, 1936;
    King, 1949; Cummings, 1953;
    Gladwin, 1957; Euler and Dob-
    yns, 1962; McGregor, 1965;
    Barnett, 1970; Weed, 1970;
    Barnett, 1973.

VERDE BLACK-ON-WHITE
AD 1050-1200
Syn. Verde Black-on-gray, Colton,
1958; Verde Polychrome, Colton,
1958; Prescott Black-on-brown,
Colton, 1958.
Des. Gladwin, 1930.
Illus. McGregor, 1965; Weed, 1970.

VERDE BROWN
Ca. AD 1100-1300
Des. *Caywood and Spicer, 1935;
Hawley, 1936; Colton and Har-
grave, 1937; *Colton, 1958; 14-
25; Breternitz, 1960a.
Illus. Barnett, 1974.

VERDE BROWN
Pre AD 750-1400
Des. Schroeder, 1960.

Verde Polychrome
AD 1050-1200
Syn. Verde Black-on-gray, Colton,
1958; Verde Black-on-white, Gladwin, 1930; Prescott Black-on-
white.
Des. Caywood and Spicer, 1935; Colton and Hargrave, 1937; *Colton,
1958, 17-1; Barnett, 1974.

VERDE RED
AD 1100-1300
Des. Colton, 1958, 14-16; Schroe-
der, 1960.

VERDE RED-ON-BUFF
Ca. AD 1150-1425
Des. Caywood and Spicer, 1935;
Hawley, 1936; Colton and Har-
grave, 1937; *Barnett, 1974.

VERDE SMUDGED
AD 1100-1300
Des. Colton, 1958, 14-27.

VICTORIA RED-ON-BROWN TEXTURED
Des. DiPeso, 1969; *DiPeso, 1974.

VILLA AHUMADA POLYCHROME
AD 1350-1450
Syn. Red and Black on white slip,
Carey, 1931; Galeana Polychrome,
Gladwin, 1934; Sayles, 1936.
Des. Carey, 1931; Brand, 1935; Haw-
ley, 1936; *Sayles, 1936; Kidder
et al., 1949; DiPeso, 1969; Hu-
man Systems Research, 1973;

*DiPeso, 1974; DiPeso et al.,
1976.
Illus. Chapman, 1931; Gladwin,
1957; Lister, 1958; DiPeso, 1977.

VIRGIN BLACK-ON-WHITE (GRAY)
Des. *Spencer, 1934; Colton, 1952;
*Schwartz et al., 1979.
Illus. Pendergast, 1960; Shutler,
1961.

VIRGIN CORRUGATED
Des. Spencer, 1934.

VIRGIN TOOLED
Des. Spencer, 1934.'

VOSBERG CORRUGATED
Des. Doerschlag, n.d., manuscript
at Dept. of Anthropology,
Arizona State Univ.

VOSBERG PLAIN
Des. Dittert, N.D., manuscript
at Dept. of Anthropology at
Arizona State Univ.

WALAPAI WARE
Des. Gifford, 1940; Dobyns and
Euler, 1956; Dobyns and Euler,
1958.

WALHALLA BLACK-ON-WHITE
Ca. AD 950-1150
Des. *Marshall in Schwartz, 1979.
(This type includes Black Mesa,
Sosi, and Dogoszhi decorative
styles and a variant with cor-
rugated ext.)

WALHALLA CORRUGATED
Ca. AD 950-1150
Des. *Marshall in Schwartz, 1979.

WALHALLA GRAY WARE
Ca. AD 950-1150
Des. *Marshall in Schwartz, 1979.

WALHALLA PLAIN
Ca. AD 950-1150
Des. Marshall in Schwartz, 1979.

WALHALLA WHITE WARE
Ca. AD 950-1150
Des. *Marshall in Schwartz, 1979.

WALLACE POLYCHROME
Ca. AD 1285-1300

Syn. Kwakina Polychrome, Reed,
1955.
Des. Hodge, 1923; Colton and
Hargrave, 1937.
Illus. Martin and Willis, 1940.

WALNUT BLACK-ON-WHITE
AD 1100-1250
Syn. Leupp Black-on-white, Col-
ton, 1955, 9B-6.
Des. *Hargrave, 1932; Hawley, 1936;
Colton and Hargrave, 1937; *Col-
ton, 1955, 9B-5; *Smith, 1971;
*Dittert and Plog, 1980.
Illus. King, 1949; Smith, 1952; Dixon,
1956; Gumerman, 1969; Euler,
1971; Arizona Highways, Feb.
1974; Ambler, 1977.

WALNUT CORRUGATED
AD 1130-1150?
Des. Colton and Hargrave, 1937.

WALNUT WIPED
Ca. AD 1050-1150
Des. *Colton and Hargrave, 1937.

WALPI BLACK-ON-YELLOW
AD 1800-present
Des. *Colton, 1956, 7B-19a.

WALPI ORANGE WARE
AD 1690-early 1900s.
Des. Adams, 1979.

WALPI PLAIN
AD 1690-early 1900s.
Des. Adams, 1979.

WALPI POLYCHROME
AD 1800-present
Syn. Zuni Tradition, *Colton,
1956, 7B-18.
Des. Kidder, 1936; *Frank and Har-
low, 1974; *Dittert and Plog, 1980.
Illus. Barry, 1981.

WALPI YELLOW
AD 1800-present
Des. Colton, 1956, 7B-19b.

WASHINGTON BLACK-ON-CREAM
Des. Spencer, 1934.

WASHINGTON BLACK-ON-GRAY
Des. Colton, 1952; Schroeder, 1955.
Illus. Shutler, 1961.

WASHINGTON CORRUGATED
Des. Colton et al., 1952.
Illus. Shutler, 1961.

WASHINGTON GRAY
(No known description)
Illus. Shutler, 1961.

WEPO BLACK-ON-PLAIN
AD 1690-early 1900s
Des. Adams, 1979.

WEPO BLACK-ON-WHITE
Des. Gumerman, 1972.

WEPO PLAIN
AD 1690-early 1900s
Des. Adams, 1979.

WEPO POLYCHROME
Des. Colton, 1956.
Illus. Harlow, 1970.
(A variety of Polacca Polychrome.)

WETHERILL BLACK-ON-WHITE
Ca. AD 1050-1125
Des. *Hayes, 1964.

WHETSTONE PLAIN
Des. *DiPeso, 1953.

WHETSTONE PLAIN: BELFORD
VARIETY
Des. DiPeso, 1958.

WHIPPLE BLACK-ON-WHITE
AD 940-1100
Syn. Reserve Black-on-white,
*Martin and Rinaldo, 1950.
Des. *Colton, 1941a.

WHITE MOUND BLACK-ON-WHITE
AD 675-900
Des. Haury, 1936; Hawley, 1936;
*Gladwin, 1945; Cibola White
Ware Conf., 1958; Dittert and
Plog, 1980.
Illus. Adams, 1949; O'Bryan,
1950; Gladwin, 1957; Martin
and Rinaldo, 1960a; Gumer-
man, 1969; Olson, 1971.

WHITE MOUNTAIN BROWN WARE
(No published description.)

WHITE MOUNTAIN RED WARE
AD 1000-1500
Des. Schmidt, 1928; Hargrave,

1935; Colton and Hargrave,
1937; *Carlson, 1970.
Illus. Schaeffer, 1956.

WHITMORE BLACK-ON-WHITE
Ca. AD 1080-1125
Syn. Shato Black-on-white, Sosi
Style.
Des. Thompson, 1986.

WIDE RUIN BLACK-ON-WHITE
AD 1250-1300
Des. Colton and Hargrave, 1937;
Smith, 1958; Dittert and Plog,
1980; Hudson, 1980.

WINGATE BLACK-ON-RED
AD 1047-1200
Des. *Gladwin, 1931; Hawley, 1936;
*Colton and Hargrave, 1937;
Smiley, Stubbs and Bannister,
1953; Second SW Ceramic Conf.,
1959; *Carlson, 1970; Human
Systems Research, 1973; Dittert
and Plog, 1980.
Illus. Martin and Willis, 1940;
O'Bryan, 1950; Wendorf et al.,
1956; Wormington, 1956; Breter-
nitz, 1959; Vivian, 1959; Lister
and Lister, 1969; McNutt, 1969;
Barnett, 1974a; Washburn, 1977.

WINGATE BLACK-ON-WHITE
Syn. Chaco Black-on-white, Wingate
Phase. Mentioned in Martin,
1936, as a Chaco type from
Lowry Ruin.
Illus. Martin and Willis, 1940.

WINGATE CORRUGATED
Ca. AD 1050
Des. Mera, 1934; Hawley, 1936;
Colton and Hargrave, 1937.

WINGATE POLYCHROME
AD 1125-1200
Syn. Querino Polychrome, Colton
and Hargrave, 1937; Houck Polychrome, Carlson, 1970.
Des. Mera, 1934; Carlson, 1962;
*Carlson, 1970.
Illus. Martin and Willis, 1940; Rinaldo, 1959; Martin, 1967; Lister
and Lister, 1969; Bice and Sundt,
1972; Arizona Highways, Feb.
1974; Barnett, 1974a; Bice, 1975.

WINGFIELD PLAIN

(A variety of Gila Plain.)
Des. Colton, 1941; Breternitz,
1960b; *Antieau, 1981.
Illus. Ezell, 1954; DiPeso, 1956;
Smith, 1977.

WINGFIELD RED
Des. *DiPeso, 1956.

WINONA BLACK-ON-RED
Des. Colton and Hargrave, 1937.

WINONA BROWN
AD 1075-1200
Des. *Colton and Hargrave, 1937;
*Colton, 1958; 14-4.
Illus. Smith, 1952; McGregor, 1965.

WINONA CORRUGATED
AD 1080-1120
Des. *Colton and Hargrave, 1937.

WINONA RED
AD 1080-1120
Des. Colton and Hargrave, 1937.

WINONA RED-ON-BUFF
Ca. AD 1050-1150
Des. Colton and Hargrave, 1937.

WINONA RED-ON-TAN
AD 964-?
Syn. San Lorenzo Red-on-brown,
Haury, 1936.
Des. Colton and Hargrave, 1937.

WINONA SMUDGED
AD 1080-1120
Des. Colton and Hargrave, 1937.

WINSLOW ORANGE WARE
AD 1300-1400
Syn. Homolovi Polychrome, *Colton and Hargrave, 1937.
Des. Mera, 1934; Colton and Hargrave, 1937; *Colton, 1956,
6B-3.

WIYO BLACK-ON-WHITE
AD 1300-1400
Des. *Mera, 1935; Hawley, 1936;
Kidder and Shepard, 1936;
Stubbs and Stallings, 1953;
Sudar-Murphy and Laumbach,
1977; Warren, 1977c; Dittert
and Plog, 1980.

WIYO BLACK-ON-WHITE: SEGURO
VARIETY
Des. Lange, 1968.

WOODRUFF BROWN
Pre AD 800
Syn. Forestdale Plain, Haury, 1940.
Des. Mera, 1934b; Hawley, 1936;
Colton and Hargrave, 1937.

WOODRUFF INCISED
Pre AD 800
Des. Mera, 1934b; Colton and
Hargrave, 1937.

WOODRUFF RED
Pre AD 800
Syn. Forestdale Red, Haury, 1940.
Des. Mera, 1934b; Hawley, 1936;
Colton and Hargrave, 1937.

WOODRUFF SMUDGED
Ca. AD 300-700
Syn. Forestdale Smudged, Haury,
1940a.
Des. Mera, 1934b; Hawley, 1936;
Colton and Hargrave, 1937.
Illus. Dittert and Ruppe, 1951;
Wendorf et al., 1956.

WUPATKI BLACK-ON-WHITE
AD 1125-1300
Des. *Hargrave, 1932; Hawley,
1936; *Colton and Hargrave,
1937; *Colton, 1955, 8B-7; Dittert and Plog, 1980.
Illus. Colton, 1946; Colton, 1953.

WUPATKI POLYCHROME
Des. Reed, 1938a.

YAVAPAI PLAIN
Syn. Kirkland Gray, Colton, 1958,
18-6.
Des. Gladwin, 1934.

YAVAPAI (NORTHEASTERN AND
WESTERN) WARE
Des. Gifford, 1936; Dobyns and
Euler, 1958.

YAVAPAI (SOUTHEASTERN) WARE
Des. Gifford, 1932; Breternitz,
1959.

YOUNGS BROWN
AD 1075-1150

Des. *Colton, 1941; *Colton, 1958,
14-6.

YUMA WARE
Des. Forde, 1931; *Spier, 1933;
*Rogers, 1936.
Illus. Museum of Arizona, 1959
(cover); Arizona Highways,
May 1974.

YUNQUE GLAZE-ON-RED
Des. Honea, 1966.

ZIA (TSIA) POLYCHROME
AD 1875-present
Des. Mera, 1932; Kidder and Shep-
ard, 1936; *Chapman, 1938;
Stubbs, 1950; *Harlow, 1970;
*Harlow, 1973; *Frank and Har-
low, 1974; *Dittert and Plog,
1980.
Illus. Underhill, 1944; Wormington,
1951; Bahti, 1964; Feder, 1965;
Tanner, 1968; Arizona Highways,
May 1974; Maxwell Museum, 1974;
Barry, 1981; Trimble, 1987.

ZUNI POLYCHROME
AD 1850-1920
Des. *Bunzel, 1929; Chapman,
1933; *Kidder and Shepard,
1936; *Chapman, 1938; Mera,
1939; *Harlow, 1973; *Frank
and Harlow, 1974; *Dittert
and Plog, 1980.
Illus. Underhill, 1941; Wormington,
1951; Bahti, 1964; Feder, 1965;
Tanner, 1968; Arizona Highways,
May 1974; Bice, 1975; Dillingham,
1977; Barry, 1981.

ZUNI TRADITION
AD 1800-present
Syn. Walpi Polychrome, Colton,
1956.
Des. *Colton, 1956, 7B-18.

ZUNI WHITE-ON-RED
Syn. "Unnamed" White-on-red,
Smith, Woodbury and Wood-
bury, 1966.
Des. Colton, manuscript at Mu-
seum of northern Arizona.
Illus. Toulouse, 1977.

INDEX
(Numbers refer to entries, not pages.)

Abo, Mission of San Gregorio de, New Mexico, 862
Ackmen-Lowry area, 595
Acoma Pueblo, 227, 472, 933; contemporary pottery, 209, 673; ar-
    chaeology, 747; compared with Laguna pottery, 257; and Zuni
    types, 777
Advent of pottery, in Southwest, 551; in San Juan area, 646
Alameda Brown Ware, 173
Alameda Pueblo, New Mexico, 46
Alfred Herrera site, New Mexico, 464, 889
Alkali Ridge sites, Utah, 97
Alma Neckbanded, temporal placement, 906
Analogous types, 166
Analysis, pottery (see Pottery, Southwestern)
Anasazi pottery (see Pottery, Southwestern)
Anglo influences, on Pueblo pottery, 861
Antelope House, Canyon de Chelly, 643
Apache pottery, 113, 338; archaeology, 378, 474; chemical analysis, 808
Archaeology textbooks; pottery illustrations, 187, 345, 522, 619,
    939, 956; Arizona, 597
Arizona: Central, 774; Eastern, 576; East-central, 179, 184, 192,
    243, 244, 560, 601; Northeastern, 372, 466, 526; Northern,
    175; Northwestern, 60, 234, 618; prehistoric pottery, 691;
    Southeastern, 213, 214, 241, 637, 750; West-central, 815.
Arizona Public Service, 345 KV line survey, 674
Arizona strip, 168, 855
Artifacts: ceramic, 52; clay, 523
Artificial Leg site, New Mexico, 313
Atitlan-Las Cuevas Citadel, Mexico, 919
Avanyu, relation to hand sign, 941
Awatovi (Awatobi), Arizona, 96, 120, 279, 280, 342, 800, 886
Aztec Ruin, New Mexico, 309, 645, 718, 877

Babocomari Village, Arizona, 213
Backhoe Village, Utah, 587
Badger House community, Mesa Verde, 444
Bagley Ranch Ruin, New Mexico, 497
Bandelier National Monument, 138, 473, 864; Mesa Verde influence
    on, 806

Color, dictionary, 589; chart (Munsell), 800
Colorado: prehistoric pottery trails, 664; pueblo sherds in northern, 486; southwestern, 3, 379, 725
Colorado River, lower, survey of, 762
Compressive strength of pottery, 104
Computers, use in pottery analysis, 63, 107, 537
Consumer's guide to Hopi pottery, 457
Contemporary pottery (see also Pottery, Southwestern), overview, 32
Cooking pots, North American, 563
Coombs Site, Utah, 564, 571, 572
Cordera, Helen (Cochiti), 642
Cordova Cave, New Mexico, 596
Coronado Project, St. Johns, Arizona, 849
Corrugated pottery, 664, 918; age of, 644; analysis of surface characteristics, 684; buff, 530; cleaning of, 918; gray, 342; indicator of interaction spheres, 114; Mesa Verde area, 684
Cortez Black-on-white, dating, 518
Cottonwood Creek, Colorado, 479
Craft specialization in prehistoric pottery, 382
Crooked River Village, Arizona, 929
Cross Canyon Group, Arizona, 675
Cultural resource management, analytical approach, 694
Cultural succession, 943
Cummings Mesa, Utah and Arizona, 15
Curvature measurement of pot sherds, 383

Dates: pottery types, 90, 91; late Zuni sites, 530
Dating (see also Pottery, Southwestern), 647; methods of, 617; Rio Grande sites, 795
Datura seeds, vessels shaped like, 575
Dead Valley, Arizona, 243, 244, 744
Decoration, pottery: compare Hohokam with Anasazi, 545; life forms in, 142; styles of, 307
Deep Creek, Utah, 590
Denison Site, New Mexico, 882
Depository, ceramic, MNA, 171, 357
Design analysis, pottery, 119, 697, 903; abstract geometric, 26; archaeological data and ethnological observations, 911; chronological seriation, 396; comparison of three types, 182; Hohokam, 19, 661; non hierarchial, 503; Santa Fe Black-on-white, 846; symmetry, 82, 901, 902, 904, 962, 963
Designs, painted pottery, 30, 155; Elden Pueblo, 469; formal, 775; Hopi, 286; Mesa Verde, 723; Mimbres, 501; rotational, 834; structural, 835; terminology, 238; variability, 695; variation, multivariate approach, 696
Design styles, pottery, 169; analysis of, 362, 695, 699; Cibola white ware, 843; evolution, 411; temporal variation, 363
Dinwiddie Site, New Mexico, 638
Do Bell Site, Arizona, 418